# PROCEEDINGS

OF THE

# 1996 INTERNATIONAL CONFERENCE

ON

# PARALLEL PROCESSING

August 12 - 16, 1996

Vol. III  Software
K. Pingali, Editor
Cornell  University

Sponsored by
INTERNATIONAL ASSOCIATION FOR COMPUTERS
AND COMMUNICATIONS
THE PENNSYLVANIA STATE UNIVERSITY

IEEE Computer Society Press
Los Alamitos, California

Washington ● Brussels ● Tokyo

IEEE Computer Society Press
10662 Los Vaqueros Circle
P.O. Box 3014
Los Alamitos, CA 90720-1314

IEEE Computer Society Press Order Number PR07623
ISBN 0-8186-7623-X
ISSN 0190-3918

*Additional copies may be ordered from*:

IEEE Computer Society Press
Customer Service Center
10662 Los Vaqueros Circle
P.O. Box 3014
Los Alamitos, CA 90720-1314
Tel: + 1-714-821-8380
Fax: + 1-714-821-4641
E-mail: cs.books@computer.org

IEEE Computer Society
13, Avenue de l'Aquilon
B-1200 Brussels
BELGIUM
Tel: + 32-2-770-2198
Fax: + 32-2-770-8505
euro.ofc@computer.org

IEEE Computer Society
Ooshima Building
2-19-1 Minami-Aoyama
Minato-ku, Tokyo 107
JAPAN
Tel: + 81-3-3408-3118
Fax: + 81-3-3408-3553
tokyo.ofc@computer.org

Printed in the United States of America

 The Institute of Electrical and Electronics Engineers, Inc.

# PREFACE

With great pleasure, we present the proceedings of the 25th International Conference on Parallel Processing, a premier forum for computer professionals.

We have received 270 papers. After intensive review, the Program Committee accepted 90; the details are tabulated below:

| Track | Submissions | Accepted Papers (R) | (C) | (Total) |
|-------|-------------|---------------------|-----|---------|
| I     | 112         | 28                  | 10  | 38 (33.9%) |
| II    | 77          | 16                  | 9   | 25 (32.4%) |
| III   | 81          | 27                  | 0   | 27 (33.3%) |

Track I covers architectures and networks; track II algorithms and applications; and track III software. There is one submission from Cornell and it was handled by committee member Dr. C. Das of Penn State University.

Your attention is called to an excellent workshop organized by Dr. H. J. Siegel. What is new this year is that H. J. and the co-chairs of the workshop form a panel to summarize and extend the workshop presentation in the evening of August 12, Monday.

The first keynote will be presented by Dr. C. J. Tan on Deep-Blue, the IBM chess playing parallel processor. Dr. Tan and three of his colleagues will provide further elaboration of their project in a panel discussion.

We have arranged two other keynote addresses on the applications of parallel computing and parallel systems. Dr. Thomas Hughes will present one on "Parallel Computing in the Real World." Dr. Richard Linderman will discuss "Moving Real-Time Signal and Image Processing Toward Parallel High-Performance Computers." On August 14, Wednesday, Dr. G. Bilardi will moderate a distinguished panel on a pressing topic: "Communications Issues in Parallel Systems."

We would like to thank the program committee members and the referees for their contribution. We appreciate the support of the Departments of Electrical Engineering and Computer Science at Cornell University. Shelley Weight provided indispensable services throughout the process; Helene Croft helped operations of the software track. Finally, we would like to thank Dr. T. Feng and Dr. M. Liu for their ever-ready help and support.

A. Bojanczyk, Program Co-chair
K. Pingali, Program Co-chair
A. Reeves, Program Co-chair
H. C. Torng, Program Chair

Cornell University
Ithaca, NY 14853

# Keynote Speakers

Speaker: **C. J. Tan, IBM T. J. Watson Research Center**

Topic: Deep-Blue -- the IBM chess playing parallel processor

Speaker: **Thomas J. R. Hughes, Stanford University and Centric Engineering Systems, Inc.**

Topic: Parallel Computing in the Real World

Speaker: **R. Linderman, Rome Research and Development Center**

Topic: Moving Real-Time Signal and Image Processing Toward Parallel High-Performance Computers

# Panel Sessions

**Panel I:**     **Summary of Workshop on Challenges for Parallel Processing: Are the Proposed Solutions Reasonable?**

Moderator:     **H. J. Siegel** (Workshop chair), **Purdue University**

Panelists:     Seth Abraham - Purdue University (ECE)
Rudolf Eigenmann - Purdue University (ECE)
Susanne Hambrusch - Purdue University (CS)
John R. Rice - Purdue University (CS)
          (Workshop Vice-Chairs)


**Panel II:**     **Deep Blue -- the IBM chess playing parallel processor**

Moderator:     **C. J. Tan, IBM T. J. Watson Research Center**

Panelists:     M. Campbell, IBM T. J. Watson Research Center
A. J. Hoane, Jr., IBM T. J. Watson Research Center
Feng-Hsiung Hsu, IBM T. J. Watson Research Center


**Panel III:**     **Communications Issues in Parallel Systems**

Moderator:     **Gianfranco Bilardi, University of Illinois at Chicago Circle**

Panelists:     To be announced.


# Conference Awards

## Outstanding Paper Awards

S. B. Hambrusch (Purdue), A. A. Khokhar (Delaware), and Y. Liu (Purdue): "Scalable S-to-P Broadcasting on Message-Passing MPPs."

J. Y. L. Park, H. -A. Choi (George Washington), L. Ni and N. Nupairoj (Michigan State): "Construction of Optimal Multicast Trees Based on Parameterized Communication Model."

G. Knittel (U. of Tubingen): "A Parallel Algorithm for Scientific Visualization."

# List of Referees -- Full Proceedings

Abandah, G. A.
Abdelguerfi, M.
Aboelaze, M
Abram, G.
Acharya, A.
Adams, G. B.
Adve, V.
Aggarwal, A.
Aggarwal, R.
Agrawal. G.
Ailamaki, A.
Akl, S.G.
Allen, J.
Almasi, G.
Alonso, G.
Alpern, B.
Alpern, B.
Alpert, R. D.
Amin, M.
Ammar, H. H.
Anderson, C.
Anderson, J.
Andesland, M.

Bagherzadeh, N.
Baker, J. W.
Banerjee, P.
Banicescu, I.
Bapty, T. A.
Bartos, R.
Basak, D.
Batcher, K. E.
Beguelin, A.
Bennett, J.
Bennett, R.
Berenbaum, A.
Beynon, M.
Bhandarkar, S.
Bhuyan, L. N.
Blumofe, R.
Bojanczyk, A.
Brady, R.
Braun, T. A.

Carrig, J. J.
Carter, L.
Casavant, T.
Castenada, R.
Chandra, R.
Chang, C.

Charney, M.
Chase, C.
Chaudhary, V.
Chen, L-C.
Cheng, A.
Cheng, C-T.
Chlebus, B.
Cho, S.
Choi, L.
Choi, Y.
Chrisochoides, N.
Cierniak, M.
Cleary, A. J.
Coleman, D.
Coletti, N.
Concepcion, A.
Conroy, J.
Cormen, T. H.
Coyle, M.
Crockett, T. W.

Dai, D.
Darema, F.
Das, C.
Dasgupta, S.
de Azevedo, M.
Dehnert, J.
del Rosario, J.
Delp, E.
Demmel, J.
Deshmukh, R.
Dietz, H.
Dietz, R.
Diks, K.
Dimopoulos, N.
DiNucci, D. C.
Donaldson, V.
Dwyer, H.

Edelman, A.
Edwards, C.
El-Abbadi, A.
El-Amawy, A.
El-Ghazawi, T.
Ercal, F.

Feo, J.
Fine, T.
Flynn, M.
Fortes, J. A. B.

Franklin, M.
Fu, C.
Fuchs, K.

Ghosh, S.
Ghozati, S-A.
Grama, A.
Greenberg, R.
Gross, T.
Grout, J.
Gunnels, J. A.
Gupta, M.
Gupta, R.

Ha, J-H.
Haas, Z.
Haines, M.
Hambrusch, S.
Han, E. H.
Hansen, G.
Haupt, T.
Havlak, P.
Heath, M.
Helman, D.
Hendrickson, B.
Henry, G.
Herman, T.
Hiranandani, S.
Hoare, R.
Hoeflinger, J.
Hoisie, A.
Holzrichter, M.
Hotovy, S.
Huang, S. H.
Huang, Y.
Huelsbergen, L.
Hummel, S. F.
Huss-Lederman, S.

Irigoin, F.
Ito, M. R.
Iyengar, V.
Iyer, R.

Ja'Ja', J.
Jacob, J.
Jeremiassen, T.
John, L. K.
Johnsson, L.
Johnsten, T.
Joshi, M.

Kaklamanis, C.
Kale, L. V.

Gallopoulos, E.
Gallopoulos, S.
Gessesse, G. A.
Ghosh, J.
Kannan, R.
Keefe, T.
Kesavan, R.
Kesselman, C.
Khokhar, A.
Khuller, S.
Kiemelman, D.
Kim, S.
Klimkowski, K.
Koc, C. K.
Kodukula, I.
Koelbel, C.
Kong, J.
Kontothanassis, L.
Kotlyar, V.
Koufaty, D. A.
Kraemer, E.
Kuhl, J.
Kumar, A.
Kumar, V.
Kwai, D-M.

Lai, T. S.
Lai, T. H.
Larus, J.
Lawrence, T.
Leathrum, J. F.
Ledeczi, A.
Lee, G.
Lee, J.
Lee, K.
Lee, S. Y.
Leinberger, W.
Li, J.
Li, W.
Li, Y.
Liao, A.
Lifka, D.
Lin, R.
Lin, W-Y.
Lin, W. M.
Liszka, K. J.
Liu, G.
Lo, V.
Lopez, M.
Loveman, D.
Lu, C. C.
Lucas, M. T.
Lyon, L.
Lytle, W.

Maffeis, S.
Mahapatra, N.
Mahgoub, I.
Makki, K.
Makki, S.
Malaiya, Y. K.
Malinowski, A.
Marsolf, B.
Martinez, J. F.
Martonosi, M.
McIntosh, N.
McKinley, K. S.
McKinley, P.
McLellan, R.
Mehrotra, P.
Michael, M.
Miller, J.
Mircevski, D.
Moga, A.
Mohapatra, P.
Moon, B.
Morrow, G.
Moustakidis, G.

Natarajan, R.
Navarra, A.
Neves, N.
Ni, L.
Nikhil, R.

O'Hallarn, D.
Oh, Y.
Olariu, S.
Oner, K.

Padua, D.
Paek, Y.
Paleczny, M.
Palem, K.
Panda, D.
Parashar, M.
Parhami, B.
Parks, T.
Patel, M. I.
Patra, A. K.
Periaux, J.
Pingali, K.
Pinkston, T. M.
Pissinou, N.
Plevyak, J.
Pottenger, W.
Poulos, A.
Prakash, R.

Pugh, B.

Qiao, W.
Qiu, K.

Rai, S.
Ramkumar, B.
Ramos, M.G.
Ranganathan, M.
Ranganathan, N.
Ranka, S.
Rauchwerger, L.
Ravada, S.
Ravikumar, B.
Reeves, A.
Reimann, D. A.
Rigoutsos, I.
Rivers, J. A.
Rogers, A.
Rosser, E.
Roth, J.
Rubinfeld, R.
Rudd, K. W.
Ruttenberg, J.
Rytter, W.

Saad, Y.
Saltz, J.
Samsudin, A.
Sansano, A.
Sarkar, V.
Scheetz, T. E.
Schieber, B.
Schneider, F.
Scott, M. L.
Sengupta, A.
Seo, S-W.
Serrano, M.
Sethi, A.
Shah, H. V.
Shah, J.
Shang, W.
Sharma, S. D.
Sharma, V.
Shpeisman, T.
Siegel, H. J.
Singh, A. D.
Sinha, A.
Sivaram, R.
Sivasubramaniam, A.
Snir, M.
So, J. J. E.
Somani, A.
Spezialetti, M.

Srimani, P.
Srivastava, A.
Stodghill, P.
Strumpen, V.
Sundaresan, N.
Swartz, W.

Talmor, D.
ten Bruggencate, M.
Thakur, R.
Thekkath, R.
Toledo, S. A.
Torng, H. C.
Towle, R.
Trefethen, A.
Tsanakas, P.
Tuecke, S.
Tzeng, N-F.
Uysal, M.

Vaidya, A.
van de Geijn, R.
Vanapipot, K.
VanderWiel, S.
Varavithya, V.
Vavasis, S.
Vinnakota, B.
Vitter, J. S.
von Laszewski, G.

Wallace, S.
Wang, X.
Watson, D. W.
Welling, J.
Whitley, L. D.
Wisniweski, R.
Wu, J.

Yan, Y.
Yang, T.
Yeh, C-H.
Yener, B.
Yoo, B. S.
Youn, H. Y.
Yousif, M.

Zahorjan, J.
Zaki, M. J.
Zhang, C. N.
Zhang, X.
Zhang, Y.
Zheng, S. Q.
Zhong, P.
Ziavras, S.

Zimmerman, A.
Zollweg, J.A.
Zucker, D. F.

# Author Index -- Full Proceedings

# TABLE OF CONTENTS
## VOLUME III - SOFTWARE

(R): Regular Papers
(C): Concise Papers

### Session 1C. Compiler Optimizations
Chair: Rishiyur Nikhil

### Session 2C. Loop Partitioning
Chair: David Padua

### Session 3C. Performance Analysis
Chair: Prith Banerjee

## Session 8C. Load Balancing II
Chair: S. Y. Lee

## Session 9C. Systems Issues
Chair: Bal Ramkumar

# Array Operation Synthesis to Optimize HPF Programs*

Gwan-Hwan Hwang    Jenq Kuen Lee

Department of Computer Science, National Tsing-Hua University, Hsinchu, Taiwan

ghhwang@cs.nthu.edu.tw    jklee@cs.nthu.edu.tw

Dz-Ching R. Ju

Hewlett-Packard Company, Cupertino, CA 95014, USA

royju@hpclapd.cup.hp.com

## Abstract

*The synthesis of consecutive array operations or array expressions into a composite access function of the source arrays at compile time has been shown[2] that it can reduce the redundant data movement, temporary storage usage, and loop synchronization overhead on flat shared memory parallel machines with uniform memory accesses. However, it remains open how the synthesis scheme can be incorporated into optimizing HPF programs on distributed memory machines by taking into account communication costs. In this paper, we propose solutions to address this open problem. We first apply the array operation synthesis (developed earlier by us for Fortran 90 programs) to HPF programs and demonstrate its performance benefits on distributed memory machines. In addition, to prevent a situation we call "synthesis performance anomaly", we derive a cost model and present an optimal solution based on the cost model to guide the array synthesis process on distributed memory machines. We also show that the optimal problem is NP-hard. Therefore, we develop a practical heuristic algorithm for compilers to devise synthesis strategy on distributed memory machines with HPF programs. Experimental results show significant performance improvement over the base codes for HPF code fragments from real applications on a DEC alpha Farm by incorporating our proposed optimizations.*

## 1 Introduction

An increasing number of programming languages, such as Fortran 90[5], HPF (High Performance Fortran)[1], APL, provide a rich set of intrinsic array functions and array constructs. These intrinsic array functions and array expressions operate on the elements of a multi-dimensional array object concurrently without requiring iterative statements. These array operations provide a rich source of data parallelism. Multiple consecutive array operations specify a particular mapping relationship between the source arrays and final target array. A straightforward compilation for these consecutive array functions or array expressions may translate each array operation into a (parallel) nested loop and use a temporary array to pass intermediate results to subsequent array functions. Synthesis of multiple consecutive array functions or array expressions can compose several data access functions into an equivalent composite reference pattern. Thus, the synthesis can improve performance by reducing redundant data movement, temporary storage usage, and parallel loop synchronization overhead.

Recently, we develop a functional approach to perform array operation synthesis for Fortran 90 programs on flat shared memory machines with uniform memory accesses[2]. Our scheme is based on the composition of mathematic functions. It starts with deriving a mathematic access function for each intrinsic array function. We then use a function composition approach to compose those access functions. This composition is semantically equivalent to the synthesis of array functions. Our scheme can handle compositions of extensive Fortran 90 array constructs, such as RESHAPE, SPREAD, EOSHIFT, TRANSPOSE, CSHIFT, and MERGE, array section move, array reduction functions, WHERE and ELSE-WHERE constructs. None of existing methods can synthesize such an extensive set of array operations. Details of previous work on array operation synthesis can be found in [3].

In spite of the success of the synthesis scheme for Fortran 90 programs on flat shared memory machines, it remains open how the synthesis scheme can be incorporated into optimizing HPF programs on distributed memory machines by taking into account communication costs. In this paper, we propose solutions to address this open issue. Currently, in the process of compiling HPF programs, a compiler partitions the program using the owner-computes rule[15]. An explicit communication is necessary for a remote memory access. Array operation synthesis is able to reduce the number of memory references including loads and stores[3]. However, in distributed memory machine, the memory references include both local references and remote references (communication). A remote memory access usually takes far longer than a local memory access. Although the array operation synthesis can reduce the total number of memory references, a naive application of the synthesis process adopted from flat shared memory parallel machines may actually increase the amount of remote memory loads for programs running on distributed memory machines, which may result in an adverse effect on execution time performance. We call such a behav-

---
*G.H. Hwang and J.K. Lee's work was supported in part by NSC of Taiwan under grant No. NSC85-2213-E-007-050 and NSC85-2221-E-007-031.

ior "synthesis anomaly". In this paper, we first apply the array synthesis scheme (developed earlier by us for Fortran 90 programs) to HPF programs and demonstrate its potential performance benefits on distributed memory machines. To prevent the synthesis anomaly, we derive a cost model and present an optimal solution based on the cost model to guide the array synthesis process on distributed memory machines. In addition, we also show that the optimal problem is NP-hard. Therefore, we develop a practical heuristic algorithm for compilers to devise synthesis strategy on distributed memory machines with HPF programs. To demonstrate the effects of our proposed algorithms, we have conducted experiments on an 8-node DEC alpha Farm with an HPF compiler. Experimental results show speedups from 1.60 to 8.0 for HPF code fragments from real applications on a DEC alpha Farm by incorporating our proposed optimizations.

## 2 Motivating Examples

In this section, we use examples to motivate the need of our optimization mechanism for HPF programs. Our work deals with the array operation synthesis with HPF programs on distributed memory machines. Let us first consider the HPF code fragment below.

**HPF Code Fragment 1**
```
        REAL A(N,2*N), B(2*N) , C(2*N,2*N)
        REAL D(2*N,N), E(N), F(N), G(N)
!HPF$   TEMPLATE TEMP(N*N*4,N*N*4)
!HPF$   ALIGN A(i,j) WITH TEMP(4*i-3,4*j-3)
!HPF$   ALIGN B(i) WITH TEMP(*,4*i-3)
!HPF$   ALIGN C(i,j) WITH TEMP(4*j-3,i)
!HPF$   ALIGN D(i,j) WITH TEMP(4*j-3,4*i-3)
!HPF$   ALIGN G(i) WITH TEMP(4*i-3,*)
        D=C(:,1:4*N:4)
        E=SUM(A+TRANSPOSE(D),DIM=2)
        F=SUM(SPREAD(B,DIM=2,NCOPIES=N)+D,DIM=1)
        G=B(1:2*N:2)+E+F
```

The code example above is a revised version of the Fortran 90 program first used by Chatterjee et. al[13]. The current technique for compilers to optimize the above code is to first produce a temporary array for each intrinsic array operation and use a temporary array to pass the intermediate result to following array functions. It then tries to find an alignment and a distribution for each array to optimize the completion time. The related work in solving this problem by the above technique can be seen in [6, 9, 10, 11, 12, 13]. Following Chatterjee's scheme (known as one of the best schemes for this type of optimization), we get the optimized code below[13].

**HPF Code Fragment 2**
```
        REAL A(N,2*N), B(2*N) , C(2*N,2*N)
        REAL D(2*N,N),E(N),F(N),G(N)
        REAL T1(N,2*N),T2(N,2*N),T3(2*N,N),T4(2*N,N)
        REAL T5(N),T6(N)
!HPF$   TEMPLATE TEMP(N*N*4,N*N*4)
!HPF$   ALIGN A(i,j),T1(i,j),T2(i,j) WITH TEMP(4*i-3,4*j-3)
!HPF$   ALIGN B(i) WITH TEMP(*,4*i-3)
!HPF$   ALIGN C(i,j) WITH TEMP(4*j-3,i)
!HPF$   ALIGN D(i,j),T3(i,j),T4(i,j) WITH TEMP(4*j-3,4*i-3)
!HPF$   ALIGN E(i),F(i),T5(i),T6(i),G(i) WITH TEMP(4*i-3,*)
        D=C(:,1:4*N:4)
        T1=TRANSPOSE(D)
        T2=A+T1
        E=SUM(T2,DIM=2)
        T3=SPREAD(B,DIM=2,NCOPIES=N)
        T4=T3+D
        F=SUM(T4,DIM=1)
        T5=B(1:2*N:2)
        T6=T5+E
        G=T6+F
```

However, the scheme above has not considered the optimization opportunities for array operation synthesis. If we apply our synthesis scheme in [2] originally aimed at Fortran 90 programs directly with Code Fragment 1, we get an optimized code in the following pseudo code format.

**HPF Code Fragment 3**
```
        REAL A(N,2*N), B(2*N) , C(2*N,2*N)
        REAL D(2*N,N),E(N),F(N),G(N)
!HPF$   TEMPLATE TEMP(N*N*4,N*N*4)
!HPF$   ALIGN A(i,j) WITH TEMP(4*i-3,4*j-3)
!HPF$   ALIGN B(i) WITH TEMP(*,4*i-3)
!HPF$   ALIGN C(i,j) WITH TEMP(4*j-3,i)
!HPF$   ALIGN D(i,j) WITH TEMP(4*j-3,4*i-3)
!HPF$   ALIGN G(i) WITH TEMP(4*i-3,*)
        FORALL (I=1:N)
```
$$G(I)=B(2*I)+SUM_{J=1:2*N:1}(A(I,J)+C(J,4*I))+$$
$$SUM_{J=1:2*N:1}(B(J)+D(J,4*I))$$
```
        END FORALL
```

To compare the Code Fragments 3 with 2, we execute the codes by DEC HPF compiler [17] on an 8-node DEC alpha Farm with an FDDI network. We run the two code fragments 100 times. Also, the problem size, N, is set to be 128. The code optimized by our synthesis scheme is almost 5.5 times faster than the code generated by solely using automatic selections of alignments and distributions for arrays. We list the number of loads and stores, and the time for these two codes in the table below.

|  | number of loads | number of stores | execution time (sec) |
|---|---|---|---|
| Code fragment 2 | $16N^2 + 5N$ | $10N^2 + 5N$ | 6.110 |
| Code fragment 3 | $8N^2 + 4N$ | $N$ | 1.103 |

From the above observation, one may be inclined to conclude that the earlier proposed array operation synthesis is sufficiently applicable to optimizing the array operations for distributed memory machines without any modification. However, if we consider the Code Fragment 4, the communication cost may be increased due to the array operation synthesis.

**HPF Code Fragment 4**
```
!HPF$ TEMPLATE TEMP(N,N)
      REAL A(N,N), B(N,N) , C(N,N)
!HPF$ ALIGN A(i,j),B(i,j),C(i,j) with TEMP(i,j)
      C=TRANSPOSE( A+B , 1)
```

A compilation without array operation synthesis produces the following code:

**HPF Code Fragment 5**
```
1 !HPF$ TEMPLATE TEMP(N,N)
2       REAL A(N,N), B(N,N), C(N,N), T1(N,N)
3 !HPF$ ALIGN A(i,j),B(i,j),C(i,j) with TEMP(i,j)
6 !HPF$ ALIGN T1(i,j) with A(i,j)
7       T1=A+B
8       C=TRANSPOSE(T1)
```

Using the array operation synthesis scheme, the resulted code is as follows:

**HPF Code Fragment 6**
```
!HPF$ TEMPLATE TEMP(N,N)
      REAL A(N,N), B(N,N), C(N,N)
!HPF$ ALIGN A(i,j),B(i,j),C(i,j) with TEMP(i,j)
      FORALL (i=1:N , j=1:N)
          C(i,j)=A(j,i)+B(j,i)
      END FORALL
```

In the Code Fragment 5, due to the fact that arrays A, B, and T1 are all aligned, the only communication is from T1 to C. In the Code Fragment 6, however, elements of arrays A and B will both be sent to the processors which own the corresponding target elements of array C according to the owner-computes rule. The amount of communication of the code after array operation synthesis is two times greater than the code without array operation synthesis. As a result, when we actually execute the programs with the HPF compiler on an 8 node DEC alpha Farm. We run the two code fragments 100 times, and N is set to be 512. The execution time of Code Fragment 6 (with array synthesis) is 3.822 seconds, whereas Code Fragment 5 (without array synthesis) is 3.776 seconds. The synthesis optimization may actually increase the execution time. We call such a behavior, *synthesis anomaly*. In this paper, we will try to solve this problem by deriving a cost model and using the cost model to decide if a temporary array in the target array expression should be eliminated or not.

## 3  Array Operation Synthesis

Our previously proposed array operations optimization is to synthesize consecutive array operations or array expression into a single composite mathematical function[2, 3]. For the sake of completeness, we present an overview of the array operation synthesis scheme in this section.

### 3.1  Data Access Functions of Array Operations

We use a *data access function* to specify the mapping between the elements of the source and target arrays of an array operation. For certain array operations, the data accesses can not be represented in a single data access pattern, but instead they can be represented in multiple data access patterns, each with its own array index range. We use a segmentation descriptor to represent an array index range of a data access pattern. Following are several examples of data access functions:

**Example 1** Assume A and B are two-dimensional arrays. The data access function of B=TRANSPOSE(A) is B[i,j]=A[j,i]. It is only with one data access pattern.

**Example 2** Assuming that A and B are 4 by 4 matrices, the data access function of B=CSHIFT(A,1,1) is

$$B[i,j] = \begin{cases} A[i-3,j] & \phi(/i,j/,/4{:}4,1{:}4/) \\ A[i+1,j] & \phi(/i,j/,/1{:}3,1{:}4/) \end{cases}$$

This data access function is with two data access patterns. Each data access pattern applies to different index domain which is delimited by the corresponding segmentation descriptor. For instance, when $4 \le i \le 4$ and $1 \le j \le 4$, B[i,j]=A[i-3,j]. Similarly, when $1 \le i \le 3$ and $1 \le j \le 4$, B[i,j]=A[i+1,j].

### 3.2  Synthesis of Array Operations

We use the following example as the running example in this subsection.
```
B=CSHIFT(( TRANSPOSE(EOSHIFT(A,1,"0",1)) +
     RESHAPE(C,/4,4/) ),1,1)
```
The first step of array operation synthesis is to prepare the data access function for each array operation. For the EOSHIFT function, the data access function is:

$$T1[i,j] = \begin{cases} A[i+1,j] & \phi(/i,j/,/1{:}3,1{:}4/) \\ 0 & \phi(/i,j/,/4{:}4,1{:}4/). \end{cases}$$

The access function for the TRANSPOSE function is T2[i,j]= T1[j,i], for the RESHAPE function is T3[i,j]=C[i+j*4-4], for the "+" operation is T4[i,j]=$\mathcal{F}1$(T2[i,j],T3[i,j]), where $\mathcal{F}1$(x,y)=x+y, and for "*" operation is T5[i,j]=$\mathcal{F}2$(T4[i,j], D[i,j]), where $\mathcal{F}2$(x,y)=x*y. The access function for the CSHIFT function is

$$B[i,j] = \begin{cases} T5[i+1,j] & \phi(/i,j/,/1{:}3,1{:}4/) \\ T5[i-3,j] & \phi(/i,j/,/4{:}4,1{:}4/). \end{cases}$$

After array operation synthesis, we can derive a sole synthesized data access function as follows:

$$B[i,j] = \begin{cases} (A[j+1,i+1] + C[i+4*j-3])*D[i+1,j] \\ \quad \phi(/i,j/,/1{:}3,1{:}4/) \wedge \phi(/j,i+1/,/1{:}3,1{:}4/) \\ (0 + C[i+4*j-3])*D[i+1,j] \\ \quad \phi(/i,j/,/1{:}3,1{:}4/) \wedge \phi(/j,i+1/,/4{:}4,1{:}4/) \\ (A[j+1,i-3] + C[i+4*j-7])*D[i+1,j] \\ \quad \phi(/i,j/,/4{:}4,1{:}4/) \wedge \phi(/j,i-3/,/1{:}3,1{:}4/) \\ (0 + C[i+4*j-3])*D[i+1,j] \\ \quad \phi(/i,j/,/4{:}4,1{:}4/) \wedge \phi(/j,i-3/,/4{:}4,1{:}4/) \end{cases}$$

We can use it to generate a parallel nested loop.

```
FORALL i=1 to 4, j=1 to 4
  IF (i,j)∈(φ(/i,j/,/1:3,1:4/) ∧ φ(/j,i+1/,/1:3,1:4/)) THEN
    B[i,j]=(A[j+1,i+1]+C[i+4*j-3])*D[i+1,j]
  IF (i,j)∈(φ(/i,j/,/1:3,1:4/) ∧ φ(/j,i+1/,/4:4,1:4/)) THEN
    B[i,j]=C[i+4*j-3]*D[i+1,j]
  IF (i,j)∈(φ(/i,j/,/4:4,1:4/) ∧ φ(/j,i-3/,/1:3,1:4/)) THEN
    B[i,j]=(A[j+1,i-3]+C[i+4*j-7])*D[i+1,j]
  IF (i,j)∈(φ(/i,j/,/4:4,1:4/) ∧ φ(/j,i-3/,/4:4,1:4/)) THEN
    B[i,j]=C[i+4*j-7]*D[i+1,j]
```

We have also developed a systematic method to combine predicates of testing index ranges and loop bounds. The optimized code is as follows:

```
FORALL i=1 to 3, j=1 to 3
    B[i,j]=(A[j+1,i+1]+C[i+4*j-3])*D[i+1,j]
FORALL i=1 to 3, j=4 to 4
    B[i,j]=C[i+4*j-3]*D[i+1,j]
FORALL i=4 to 4, j=1 to 3
    B[i,j]=(A[j+1,i-3]+C[i+4*j-7])*D[i+1,j]
FORALL i=4 to 4, j=4 to 4
    B[i,j]=C[i+4*j-7]*D[i+1,j]
```

The details of array operation synthesis can be found in [2, 3].

## 4  Synthesis of HPF Programs on Distributed Memory Machines

As mentioned in Section 2, a naive application of the synthesis scheme to HPF programs may actually increase the execution time of HPF programs due to increased remote memory accesses. In the following discussions, we will first introduce a cost model, and based on this model, we will develop an optimal algorithm to guide the synthesis process to avoid performance anomaly. Note that our work here will focus on the synthesis anomaly due to the execution on distributed memory machines. Previously, in the sequential programs or flat shared memory parallel programs, the synthesis may increase the execution time of programs due to the replication of computation while intermediate arrays are eliminated. This occurs when the array considered to be eliminated is replicated by a *one-to-many array operation*, such as spread, or when eliminating temporaries which will be used multiple times. The prevention strategies for the problem of replication is documented in [2]. Throughout this paper, we will assume the replication problem has been taken care of, and will focus only on the issues due to the remote communication costs. In addition, we assume the HPF semantics that all data placement of named arrays are specified by users. The data placement includes alignments and distributions of arrays. We do not consider the case that alignments and distributions of the source and target arrays are not specified, though in such cases, we can always first perform Chatterjee's algorithm[13] before doing synthesis to get approximate alignments and distributions of the source and target arrays.

## 4.1 Communication Cost Model for Alignment Analysis

An often-used communication cost model for alignment analysis is to model the communication cost to be the amount of the data moved if the target array and the source array are misaligned. In [7], it defines the abstract machine to be of the same shape as the spatial index domain of the program, that is, each processor owns a element of arrays. Chatterjee et al. modelled the communication cost to be the amount of the misaligned data multiplied by a distance function [13]. Our cost model is also developed based on modelling the communication cost to be the amount of the misaligned data multiplied by a distance function. The cost model is defined below.

**Definition 1** Suppose we want to move array $B[\,g_1(i_1, \cdots, i_k), \cdots, g_m(i_1, \cdots, i_k)\,]$ to $A[\,f_1(i_1, \cdots, i_k), \cdots, f_n(i_1, \cdots, i_k)\,]$ within the index domain defined by the segmentation descriptor $\gamma = \phi(/i_1, \cdots, i_k/, /l_1 : u_1 : s_1, \cdots, l_k : u_k : s_k /)$. That is, we want to execute the following section movement.

$$\forall (i_1, \cdots, i_k) \in \gamma, \quad A[f_1(i_1, \cdots, i_k), \cdots, f_n(i_1, \cdots, i_k)] = B[g_1(i_1, \cdots, i_k), \cdots, g_m(i_1, \cdots, i_k)].$$

We define the communication cost of the above section movement as

$$\sum_{(i_1, \cdots, i_k) \in \gamma} \mathcal{D}(\, A[f_1(i_1, \cdots, i_k), \cdots, f_n(i_1, \cdots, i_k)]\,, \; B[g_1(i_1, \cdots, i_k), \cdots, g_m(i_1, \cdots, i_k)]\,)$$

where $\mathcal{D}$ is called *distance function*.

The distance function corresponds to the cost per unit data of moving from the source array to the target array. To more precisely estimate the communication cost of data movement between arrays, one should consider both the alignment and the distribution of the source and target arrays to decide the distance function $\mathcal{D}$. For simplicity, we define the distance function in the Definition 3 below. Although the model simplifies real systems, our framework to be presented in Section 4.2, 4.3, and 5 are completely extensible with a more accurate definition of the distance function $\mathcal{D}$.

Without loss of generality, we assume all the named arrays are aligned to an auxiliary cartesian grid called a template[1]. A template may be used as an abstract align-target that may then be distributed onto the parallel machine. Even if users do not specify a global template array, a simple transformation can derive a global template array in a program. The general form of the alignment relation in HPF is:

!HPF$ ALIGN $A(i_1, i_2, \cdots, i_p)$ with $T(f_1(i_1, i_2, \cdots, i_p)$,
$\quad\quad f_2(i_1, i_2, \cdots, i_p), \cdots, f_q(i_1, i_2, \cdots, i_p))$

where $f_k(i_1, i_2, \cdots, i_p)$, k=1 to q, is either a "*" (broadcasting to the whole dimension) or $C_0 * i_r + C_1$, and $1 \leq$ r $\leq$ p, $C_0$ and $C_1$ are integers.

If an array A is aligned with a template T in the preceding manner, then we use the following definition to describe each reference of array A.

**Definition 2** If A is aligned with T according to the above alignment relation, a **reference location** of $A(g_1(i_1, i_2, \cdots, i_p), \cdots, g_p(i_1, i_2, \cdots, i_p))$ with respect to template T is:

$$T(\, f_1(g_1(i_1, i_2, \cdots, i_p), g_2(i_1, i_2, \cdots, i_p), \cdots, g_p(i_1, i_2, \cdots, i_p)),$$
$$f_2(g_1(i_1, i_2, \cdots, i_p), g_2(i_1, i_2, \cdots, i_p), \cdots, g_p(i_1, i_2, \cdots, i_p)),$$
$$\cdots,$$
$$f_q(g_1(i_1, i_2, \cdots, i_p), g_2(i_1, i_2, \cdots, i_p), \cdots, g_p(i_1, i_2, \cdots, i_p))\,)$$

For example, arrays A and B are aligned with template T in the following relations:
!HPF$ ALIGN A(i,j) WITH T$(2 * i - 5, *, 3 * j)$
!HPF$ ALIGN B(i,j) WITH T$(i + 3, *, 2 * j)$
The reference location of $A(2 * i, 2 * j)$ with respect to template T is $T(2 * (2 * i) - 5, *, 3 * (2 * j)) = T(4 * i - 5, *, 6 * j)$. Similarly, the reference location of $B(4 * i - 8, 3 * j)$ with respect to T is $T((4 * i - 8) + 3, *, 2 * (3 * j)) = T(4 * i - 5, *, 6 * j)$. The reference locations of $A(2 * i, 2 * j)$ and $B(4 * i - 8, 3 * j)$ with respect to T are identical.

**Definition 3** We define the distance function as follows: $\mathcal{D}(A[f_1(i_1, \cdots, i_k), \cdots, f_n(i_1, \cdots, i_k)], B[g_1(i_1, \cdots, i_k), \cdots, g_m(i_1, \cdots, i_k)]) = 1$ if the reference location of $A[f_1(i_1, \cdots, i_k), \cdots, f_n(i_1, \cdots, i_k)]$ and $B[g_1(i_1, \cdots, i_k), \cdots, g_m(i_1, \cdots, i_k)]$ are not identical with repect to the global template; $\mathcal{D}(A[f_1(i_1, \cdots, i_k), \cdots, f_n(i_1, \cdots, i_k)], B[g_1(i_1, \cdots, i_k), \cdots, g_m(i_1, \cdots, i_k)]) = 0$ otherwise.

We present an example here to demonstrate how the cost model can be used. Let us consider again Code Fragment 4, 5, and 6 in Section 2. Be reminded that code fragment 5 is the compiled version without array synthesis. The data access function of T1=A+B in statement 7 is T1[i,j]=A[i,j]+B[i,j]. Since A[i,j], B[i,j], and T1[i,j] are all with the same reference location, there are $2 * N^2$ real numbers local memory loads without any remote memory references. In statement 8, the data access function is C[i,j]=T1[j,i], but C[i,j] and T1[j,i] are with different reference locations. The communication cost is $\sum_{(i,j) \in \phi(/i,j/, /1:N, 1:N/)} \mathcal{D}(C[i,j], T1[j,i]) = N^2 * 1 = N^2$. Hence, the execution of the entire array expression has a communication cost of $N^2$. In contrast to the above result, consider the cost in the synthesized version in the code fragment 6. Using the array operation synthesis scheme, the resulted data access function of C=TRANSPOSE(A+B, 1) is C[i,j]=A[j,i]+B[j,i]. Since C[i,j] is not aligned with A[j,i] and B[j,i], the communication cost for executing the entire array expression is $\sum_{(i,j) \in \phi(/i,j/, /1:N, 1:N/)} \mathcal{D}(C[i,j], A[j,i]) + \sum_{(i,j) \in \phi(/i,j/, /1:N, 1:N/)} \mathcal{D}(C[i,j], B[j,i]) = 2 * N^2$. In the above example, we find that array operation synthesis reduces the amount of memory loads from $3 * N^2$ to $2 * N^2$. However, it increases the communication cost from $N^2$ to $2 * N^2$ under our cost function.

## 4.2 Optimal Solution for Executing Array Expression on Distributed Memory Machines

To obtain the optimal solution for executing array expressions under the owner-computes rule model, one may have to synthesize only part of the array operations in the target array expressions. Since each synthesis of two array operations will eliminate one temporary array, the problem turns out to be the decision problem to decide if a temporary array in the target array expression should be eliminated. Furthermore, we must find the alignment

F=CSHIFT(MERGE((A+B)*C,D,E),1,1)

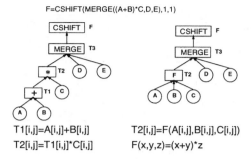

T1[i,j]=A[i,j]+B[i,j]        T2[i,j]=F(A[i,j],B[i,j],C[i,j])

T2[i,j]=T1[i,j]*C[i,j]       F(x,y,z)=(x+y)*z

Figure 1: Parse tree for C($\{T_2, T_3\}$,AE)

and distribution for those temporary arrays which are not eliminated. Assume that a straightforward compilation produces N temporary arrays. The possible cases which we have to consider are $2^N$, as we will decide whether each temporary array should be eliminated by the synthesis process or not. The following definition describes the minimum cost in one of the $2^N$ cases.

**Definition 4** The cost function $\mathcal{C}$(U,AE) denoting the minimum cost of executing the parse tree under the encoding set U is defined as follows:

(1)AE is an array expression. The array expression parse tree constructed from AE is $\mathcal{P}$ which consists of N temporary arrays, $T_1, T_2, \cdots, T_N$.

(2) U $\in 2^{\{T_1, T_2, \cdots, T_N\}}$. U is a set which encodes the existence of the temporary arrays from $T_1$ to $T_N$. If $T_i \notin$ U, then the temporary array $T_i$ will be eliminated by the array operation synthesis. Otherwise, $T_i$ will be kept.

(3) We use U and $\mathcal{P}$ to construct another parse tree $\mathcal{P}'$. $\mathcal{P}'$ is obtained by using array operation synthesis scheme to eliminate the temporary arrays which are not in U.

(4) The $\mathcal{C}$(U,AE) is defined as the minimum cost of executing $\mathcal{P}'$ among those possible alignments of the kept temporary arrays.

We use U and $\mathcal{P}$ to construct another parse tree $\mathcal{P}'$. For example, in Figure 1, AE is F = CSHIFT( MERGE( (A+B)*C,D,E),1,1), and the parse tree in the left-hand-side of the figure is $\mathcal{P}$. In order to compute the C($\{T_2, T_3\}$,AE), we have to construct $\mathcal{P}'$ according to $\{T_2, T_3\}$. Because only $T_1$ is not in $\{T_2, T_3\}$, the temporary array T1 is eliminated by the array operation synthesis and the other temporary arrays are kept. By eliminating T1 in the synthesis scheme, we get the parse tree $\mathcal{P}'$ in the right-hand-side of Figure 1. Note that the cost of executing $\mathcal{P}'$ depends on the alignment and distribution of the temporary arrays left in $\mathcal{P}'$. Each different kind of alignment and distribution of temporary arrays will result in different running time in executing $\mathcal{P}'$. Within all the possible cases for aligning the temporary arrays in $\mathcal{P}'$, the $\mathcal{C}$(U,AE) is defined as the minimum cost of executing $\mathcal{P}'$ among those possible alignments of the kept temporary arrays. Then, the minimum cost for evaluating the target array expression AE can be derived as follows:

$$\Omega = \mathbf{MIN}\{\mathcal{C}(U, AE) \mid U \in 2^{\{T_1, T_2, \cdots, T_N\}}\}$$

**Theorem 1** *The complexity of calculating $\Omega$ is NP-hard.*

*Proof:* The function C(U,AE) in calculating $\Omega$ can be easily reduced from the data alignment problem which has been proven to be NP-complete[6, 14]. Let AE be an array expression and the parse tree constructed from AE is with N temporary arrays, the data alignment problem is the same problem of calculating C(U,AE), where U=$\{T_1, T_2, \cdots, T_N\}$. Since the complexity of choosing alignment of temporary arrays is NP-complete, the calculating of $\Omega$ is NP-hard. *Q.E.D*

We also devise an algorithm by employing dynamic programming techniques to find the optimal solution. Due to the space limitation, it is presented in technical report [4].

## 5 Heuristic Algorithm to Reduce Synthesis Anomaly

Due to the fact that the optimal algorithm presented in Section 4 is NP-hard, we present a practical and efficient heuristic algorithm in this section to guide the synthesis process to reduce synthesis anomaly on distributed memory machines.

For a HPF program with consecutive array operations, our optimization strategy is to synthesize continuous array operations whenever possible. We then use our heuristic algorithm to guide the process of code generation. It may rolls back a temporary array if a particular synthesis significantly increases communication costs. Consider the following code fragment.

**HPF Code Fragment 7**
```
!HPF$   TEMPLATE TEMP(300,300)
        REAL A(100,100),B(100,100),C(100,100)
        REAL D(100,100),E(100,100),F(200,100), G(300,100)
!HPF$   ALIGN A(i,j),B(i,j),C(i,j),D(i,j),E(i,j) with TEMP(i,j)
!HPF$   ALIGN F(i,j) with TEMP(3*i−1,j)
!HPF$   ALIGN G(i,j) with TEMP(2*i,j)
        C(1:100,:)=F(1:200:2,:)
        D(1:100,:)=G(1:300:3,:)
        E=CSHIFT( TRANSPOSE(A+B),1,1 ) *
                 (TRANSPOSE(C)-TRANSPOSE(D) )
```

It yields the following data access function to use array operation synthesis scheme to synthesize the last three statements.

$$E[i, j] = \begin{cases} (A[j, i+1] + B[j, i+1]) * (F[2*j-1, i] - G[3*j-2, i]) \mid \\ \phi(/i, j/, /1:99, 1:100/) \\ (A[j, i-99] + B[j, i-99]) * (F[2*j-1, i] - G[3*j-2, i]) \mid \\ \phi(/i, j/, /99:99, 1:100//) \end{cases}$$

A straightforward code generation would simply use the target data access pattern to generate the loop body of the parallel loop for a synthesized data access function. For example, for the first data access pattern, E[i,j] = (A[j,i+1]+B[j,i+1])*(F[2*j-1,i] - G[3*j-2,i]), a straightforward method would produce a parallel loop nest as follows:

```
FORALL (i=1:99)
    FORALL (j=1:100)
        E(i,j)=(A(j,i+1)+B(j,i+1))*(F(2*j-1,i)-G(3*j-2,i))
    END FORALL
END FORALL
```

However, this code increases the communication cost and causes a synthesis anomaly. Figure 2 shows the expression tree of the data access pattern. The expression A(j, i+1) is actually aligned with B(j,i+1), as they both have the same *reference location* (see Definition 2), T(j,i+1). Similarly, F(2*j-1,i) is aligned with G(3*j-2,i), as both of them have the same reference location T(6*j-4,i). Assuming the owner-computes rule is used, we will be

$E(i,j)=(A(j,i+1)+B(j,i+1))*(F(2*j-1,i)-G(3*j-2,i))$

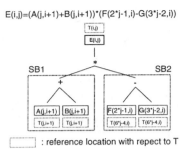

Figure 2: Expression tree of the target data access pattern

| Time (seconds) | p=1 | p=2 | p=4 | p=8 |
|---|---|---|---|---|
| (1) (PURDUE-Set Prob9) | 8.901 | 8.239 | 7.293 | 3.682 |
| (1) Synthesized code | 2.930 | 1.427 | 0.981 | 0.526 |
| (1) Improvement | 3.038 | 5.774 | 7.434 | 7.000 |
| (2) (Magnetic E.) base code | 13.988 | 7.007 | 3.511 | 1.787 |
| (2) Synthesized code | 8.472 | 4.246 | 2.127 | 1.075 |
| (2) Improvement | 1.651 | 1.650 | 1.651 | 1.662 |
| (3) (Sandia Wave) | 4.696 | 6.636 | 4.515 | 2.355 |
| (3) Synthesized code | 1.963 | 0.822 | 0.594 | 0.393 |
| (3) Improvement | 2.232 | 8.073 | 7.601 | 5.992 |

Table 1: Performance of the first 3 suites on Digital Alpha Farm with 8 workstations .

sending elements of arrays A and B (as well as F and G) to the owners of corresponding elements of E. This results in more communication traffics than the code without synthesis, in which only the summation of A and B (as well as the subtraction of C and D) is sent to the corresponding owners of E elements. Therefore, the code causes a synthesis anomaly. In the following, we propose a heuristic algorithm to guide the process of code generation. The heuristic algorithm may decide to roll back certain temporary arrays to reduce synthesis anomaly behaviors.

**Algorithm 1 : A Heuristic Algorithm to Reduce Synthesis Anomaly**
**Input:**
A *data access pattern* with its corresponding index range. The alignment of all source arrays which appear in this data access pattern. Assume the global template array is $T$.
**Begin_of_Algorithm**
*Step 1.* Construct the expression tree of the target data access pattern. (Note that the leaf nodes in the expression tree represent the usage of source arrays, root node is the target array location, and internal nodes are operators of array elements.)
*Step 2.* Derive the reference location with respect to template $T$ of all of the source arrays and target array in the expression tree.
*Step 3.* Traverse the expression tree to find the maximal subtrees which the number of their leaf nodes is greater than 1 and all their leaf nodes have the same reference location with respect to template $T$, but this reference location is different from the root node's reference location.
*Step 4.* For each subtree which is found in previous step, we use a separate parallel loop to execute its corresponding subexpression and roll back the synthesis method here to re-generate a temporary array to save the intermediate results of the computation of the subtree.
*Step 5.* The newly generated temporary array is assigned to align with the subtree which it represents. The generated temporary array is then inserted into the original expression tree to pass the intermediate results.
**End_of_Algorithm**

We use the following example to illustrate Algorithm 1:

**Example 3** We will use the example in Figure 2 as a running example to illustrate the heuristic algorithm.

*Step 1.* Figure 2 shows the expression tree of the target data access pattern.
*Step 2.* In Figure 2, we also show the derived reference location of each named array with respect to the template array $T$. In this case, A(j, i+1) and B(j,i+1) have the same reference location, $T(j,i+1)$. Similarly, F(2*j-1,i) and G(3*j-2,i), have the same reference location $T(6*j-4,i)$.
*Step 3.* We find two such subtrees, SB1 and SB2. See Figure 2.
*Step 4. & Step 5.* The algorithm generates code for the target data access pattern as follows. The temporary array got rolled back is assigned to align with the reference location of the subtree selected.

```
!HPF$ ALIGN TA1(i,j) WITH TEMP(j,i+1)
!HPF$ ALIGN TA2(i,j) WITH TEMP(6*j-4,i)
    . . .
    FORALL (i=1:99)
        FORALL (j=1:100)
            TA1(i,j)=A(j,i+1)+B(j,i+1)
        END FORALL
    END FORALL
    FORALL (i=1:99)
        FORALL (j=1:100)
            TA2(i,j)=F(2*j-1,i)-G(3*j-2,i)
        END FORALL
    END FORALL
    FORALL (i=1:99)
        FORALL (j=1:100)
            E(i,j)=TA1(i,j)*TA2(i,j)
        END FORALL
    END FORALL
```

In our heuristic algorithm above, we do not roll back a single-source-node tree, as it will not produce anomaly under normal circumstances. In addition, the communication cost of codes generated from our heuristic algorithm is always better or as good as the straightforward code generation of synthesis. We show the result below.

**Theorem 2** *The communication cost of the code generated from algorithm 1 is less than or equal to the communication cost of straightforward code generation.*

*Proof:* See the technical report [4].

# 6   Experiments and Implementation

Three HPF programs with array operations shown in the Appendix A are used to evaluate the effectiveness of our proposed scheme. They are program fragments extracted from real applications. The execution time shown in Table 1 is obtained by running each program fragment on an 8-node DEC alpha Farm with the DEC HPF compiler [17].

Our DEC alpha Farm is a workstation cluster (8 alpha 3000/900) connected via FDDI (ring) networks. The base code is a straightforward compilation by using the DEC Fortran 90 compiler with HPF extensions. The synthesized codes are obtained by using our synthesis mechanism and incorporating our heuristic algorithm to reduce performance anomaly. The dimension size of the data grid in our test case is 128. The execution times are measured by running the program fragments 100 times. The first test suite is the innermost loop in the Problem 9 of Purdue Set[8]. Most of the programs in the Purdue Set were extracted from large real applications. Problem 9 is to perform a logarithmic transformation $d_i = log(1+d_i)$ for a set of data $d_i, i = 1, \cdots, N$ and compute first four Fourier moments $F_j = \Sigma_{i=1}^{N} d_i * cos(Pi*j/(N+1))$. Our optimizations improve performance by 7 times on 8 processor nodes, as it significantly cut down the amount of remote communications. The speedup is measured by the execution time of the base version over the execution time of the optimized version on the same number of processors. The code fragment in the second suite is from the APULSE routine in the electromagnetic scattering problem[16]. The performance is improved by more than 60 percent regardless of the number of processors. The code fragment in the third suite is extracted from the Sandia Wave application. The performance is improved by nearly six times on eight processors.

For further observing the effect on reducing communication costs, we then focus on Table 2, where simple code fragments are used to explicitly compare the performance effects with or without our heuristic algorithm in reducing synthesis anomaly. We amplify these effects by constructing examples which can actually produce synthesis anomaly behaviors. The experiment is done in nCUBE/2 with 16 nodes. In this experiment, we no longer use an HPF compiler, but to generate explicit message passing codes by calculating the sending set and receiving set. In the base code part, the alignments of the temporary arrays are carefully chosen according to Chatterjee's scheme[13] so as to reduce communication costs. There is no synthesis optimization in the base version. In addition, the experiment is conducted in a way that all the factors can be under control, as the DEC HPF compiler is usually like a black box to us. Without our heuristic, a naive application of synthesis scheme results in performance anomaly in the Test Suite 5 and 8. In the Test Suite 6 and 7, the application of our heuristic algorithm can further improves the performance of the synthesized code.

Currently, we have a preliminary implementation of our proposed scheme, called SYNTOOL. It provides a prototype for the experiments in this section. The SYNTOOL takes data access functions as inputs and performs an automatic array operation synthesis to obtain a synthesized data access function as discussed in this paper.

## 7 Conclusion

An increasing number of programming languages, such as Fortran 90, HPF, and APL, are providing a rich set of intrinsic array functions and array expressions. These constructs which constitute an important part of data parallel languages provide excellent opportunities for compiler optimizations. Previously, we proposed an array operation synthesis scheme to synthesize multiple consecutive array functions or array expressions by composing several data access functions into an equivalent composite reference pattern. Thus, the synthesis can improve performance by reducing redundant data movement, temporary storage usage, and parallel loop synchronization overhead. Performance benefits had been demonstrated for programs running on shared memory multiprocessor machines with uniform memory accesses in earlier work.

In this paper, we propose solutions to an open problem how the synthesis scheme can be incorporated into optimizing HPF programs on distributed memory machines by taking into account communication costs. We first propose an optimal solution for array synthesis on distributed memory machines and show that the optimal problem is NP-hard. Therefore, we develop a practical heuristic algorithm for compilers to devise synthesis strategy on distributed memory machines with HPF programs. Experimental results show speedups from 1.60 to 8.0 for HPF code fragments from real applications on a DEC alpha Farm by incorporating our proposed optimizations. We have demonstrated that it is also profitable in applying the array synthesis optimization to programs running on distributed memory machines.

## References

[1] C. Koelbel, D. Loveman, R. Schreiber, G. Steele and M. Zosel. *The High Performance Fortran Handbook*, MIT-press, Cambridge, 1994.

[2] Gwan-Hwan Hwang, Jenq Kuen Lee, and Dz-ching Ju. *An Array Operation Synthesis Scheme to Optimize Fortran 90 Programs*, Proceedings of ACM SIGPLAN Conference on Principles and Practice of Parallel Programming, pp. 112-122, July 1995.

[3] Gwan-Hwan Hwang, Jenq Kuen Lee, and Dz-ching Ju. *A Functional Approach to Synthesize Fortran 90 Array Operations*, in submission to Journal of Parallel and Distributed Computing. Available on WWW at http://falcon.cs.nthu.edu.tw/~ghhwang/papers.html.

[4] Gwan-Hwan Hwang, Jenq Kuen Lee, and Dz-ching Ju. *Array Operation Synthesis to Optimize HPF programs*, Technical Report, Department of computer science, National Tsing-Hua University, 1996. Available on WWW at http://falcon.cs.nthu.edu.tw/~ghhwang/papers.html.

[5] Jeanne C. Adams, Walter S. Brainerd, Jeanne T. Martin, Brian T. Smith, and Jerrold L. Wagener. *Fortran 90 Handbook complete ANSI/ISO reference*, Intertext Publications McGraw-Hill Book Company, 1992.

[6] J. Li and M. Chen. *The data alignment phase in compiling programs for distributed-memory machines*, Journal of parallel and Distributed Computing, Vol. 13, pp. 213-221, Oct. 1991.

[7] J. Li and M. Chen. *Compiling Communication-Efficient Programs for Massively Parallel Machines*, IEEE Tran. On Parallel and Distributed Systems, Vol. 2, No. 3, July 1991.

[8] J.R. Rice, J. Jing. *Problems to Test Parallel and Vector Languages*, Purdue University Tech. Rep. CSD-TR-1016, 1990.

[9] J.M. Anderson and M.S. Lam. *Global optimizations for parallelism and locality on scalable parallel machines*, in Proceedings of the ACM SIGPLAN'93 Conference on Programming Language Design and Implementation, pp. 112-125, June 1993.

[10] J.R. Gilbert and R. Schreiber. *Optimal expression evaluation for data parallel architectures*, Journal of Parallel and Distributed Computing, Vol.13, pp. 58-64, Sept. 1991.

[11] K. Knob, J.D. Lukas, and G.L. Steele. *Data optimization: allocation of arrays to reduce communication on SIMD Machines*, Journal of parallel and Distributed Computing, Vol.2, pp. 102-118, Feb. 1990.

[12] M. Gupta and P. Banerjee. *Demonstration of automatic data partitioning techniques for parallelizing compilers on multicomputers*, IEEE Transactions on Parallel and Distributed Systems, Vol. 3, pp. 179-193, Mar. 1992.

| | Number of stores | Number of loads | Communication costs | Execution time (microseconds) |
|---|---|---|---|---|
| The 4-th suite base code | $3*N^2$ | $4*N^2$ | $2*N^2$ | 2901 |
| Synthesized code without Algorithm 1 | $N^2$ | $2*N^2$ | $N^2$ | 1251 |
| Synthesized code with Algorithm 1 | $N^2$ | $2*N^2$ | $N^2$ | 1251 |
| Improvement | 3 | 2 | ? | 2.318 |
| The 5-th suite base code | $2*N^2$ | $3*N^2$ | $N^2$ | 1453 |
| Synthesized code without Algorithm 1 | $N^2$ | $2*N^2$ | $2*N^2$ | 1824 |
| Synthesized code with Algorithm 1 | $2*N^2$ | $3*N^2$ | $N^2$ | 1452 |
| Improvement | 1 | 1 | | 1 |
| The 6-th suite base code | $7*N^2$ | $11*N^2$ | $3*N^2$ | 17457 |
| Synthesized code without Algorithm 1 | $N^2$ | $5*N^2$ | $3*N^2$ | 13382 |
| Synthesized code with Algorithm 1 | $2*N^2$ | $6*N^2$ | $N^2$ | 10267 |
| Improvement | 3.5 | 1.833 | 3 | 1.700 |
| The 7-th suite base code | $8*N^2$ | $13*N^2$ | $6*N^2$ | 19178 |
| Synthesized code without Algorithm 1 | $N^2$ | $6*N^2$ | $5*N^2$ | 12006 |
| Synthesized code with Algorithm 1 | $3*N^2$ | $8*N^2$ | $2*N^2$ | 7858 |
| Improvement | 2.667 | 1.625 | 3 | 2.441 |
| The 8-th suite base code | $4*N^2$ | $9*N^2$ | $N^2$ | 5361 |
| Synthesized code without Algorithm 1 | $N^2$ | $6*N^2$ | $6*N^2$ | 5505 |
| Synthesized code with Algorithm 1 | $2*N^2$ | $7*N^2$ | $N^2$ | 3994 |
| Improvement | 2 | 1.286 | 1 | 1.342 |

Table 2: Performance of five suites on nCUBE/2.

[13] S. Chatterjee, J.R. Gilbert, R.Schreiber, and S.-H. Teng. *Automatic Array Alignment in Data-Parallel Programs*, Proceedings of the Twentieth Annual SIGPLAN-SIGACT Symposium on Principles of Programming Languages, Charleston, SC, January 1993, pp. 16-28.

[14] T. J. Sheffler, R. Schreiber, J.R. Gilbert, and S. Chatterjee. *Aligning Parallel Arrays to Reduce Communication*, Proceedings of Frontiers '95, McLean, VA, February 1995, pp. 324-331.

[15] Zima, H., and Chapman, B. *Compiling for distributed-memory systems*. Proceeding IEEE 81, 2 (Feb.1993), 264-287.

[16] A. Mohamer, G. Fox, G. Laszewski, M. Parashar, T. Haupt, K. Mills, Y. Lu, N. Lin, N. and Yeh. *Applications Benchmark Set for Fortran-D and High Performance Fortran*, Technical Report SCCS327, NPAC, Syracuse University.

[17] Jonathan Harris *et al. Compiling High Performance Fortran for Distributed-memory Systems*, Digital Technical Journal Volume 7, Number 3.

## A  Code Fragments for Experiments

```
1. !HPF$ TEMPLATE TEMP(N,N)
   !HPF$ DISTRIBUTE TEMP(BLOCK,BLOCK)
         REAL    T(N,N), U(N,N),RIP(N,N),RIN(N,N)
         REAL    B(N,N),PATTERN(N,N),ERRM(N,N)
   !HPF$ ALIGN T(i,j),U(i,j),RIP(i,j),RIN(i,j) WITH TEMP(i,j)
   !HPF$ ALIGN B(i,j),PATTERN(i,j),ERRM(i,j) WITH TEMP(i,j)
         RIP=EOSHIFT(U,DIM=1,SHIFT=1)
         RIN=EOSHIFT(U,DIM=1,SHIFT=-1)
         T=U+RIP+RIN+EOSHIFT(U,DIM=2,SHIFT=1)+
   *        EOSHIFT(U,DIM=2,SHIFT=-1)+
   *        EOSHIFT(RIP,DIM=2,SHIFT=1)+
   *        EOSHIFT(RIP,DIM=2,SHIFT=-1)+
   *        EOSHIFT(RIN,DIM=2,SHIFT=1)+
   *        EOSHIFT(RIN,DIM=2,SHIFT=-1)
         T=T/PATTERN
         WHERE (ABS(U).GT.0.001)
            ERRM=ABS((U-T)/U)
         ELSEWHERE
            ERRM=ABS((U-T)/0.001)
         ENDWHERE
2. !HPF$ TEMPLATE TEMP(N*N,N*N)
   !HPF$ DISTRIBUTE TEMP(CYCLIC,CYCLIC)
         REAL    KIA(N,N),XMA(N,N),YI(N,N),KMM(N),XM(N)
         INTEGER KM,KI,KII(N)
   !HPF$ ALIGN KIA(i,j),XMA(i,j),YI(i,j) WITH TEMP(i,j)
   !HPF$ ALIGN KII(i),XM(j) WITH YI(i,*)
   !HPF$ ALIGN KMM(i) WITH XM(i)
         KIA=SPREAD(KII,DIM=2,NCOPIES=KM)
         KJA=SPREAD(KJJ,DIM=1,NCOPIES=KN)
         XM=(KMM+0.5)*HW1/KM*SGN(START1)
         XN=(KNN+0.5)*HW2/KN*SGN(START2)
         XMA=SPREAD(XM,DIM=1,NCOPIES=KI)
         XNA=SPREAD(XN,DIM=2,NCOPIES=KJ)
```

```
         WHERE(KIA.EQ.1)
         YI=1./SQRT(HW1)
         ELSEWHERE
         YI=SQRT(2./HW1)*COS(3.141592654*(KIA-1)*XMA/HW1)
         END WHERE
         WHERE(KJA.EQ.1)
         YJ=1 /SQRT(HW2)
         ELSEWHERE
         YJ=SQRT(2./HW2)*COS(3.141592654*(KJA-1)*XNA/HW2)
         END WHERE
3. !HPF$ TEMPLATE TEMP(N,N)
   !HPF$ DISTRIBUTE TEMP(BLOCK,BLOCK)
         REAL    f1(N,N), zxp(N,N), zxm(N,N)
         REAL    zyp(N,N), zym(N,N), fderiv(N,N)
         REAL    fxp(N,N), fxm(N,N), fyp(N,N), fym(N,N)
   !HPF$ ALIGN f1(i,j),zxp(i,j),zyp(i,j),zym(i,j),fxp(i,j) WITH TEMP(i,j)
   !HPF$ ALIGN fderiv(i,j),fxm(i,j),fyp(i,j),fym(i,j) WITH TEMP(i,j)
         FXP = CSHIFT(F1,1,+1)
         FXM = CSHIFT(F1,1,-1)
         FYP = CSHIFT(F1,2,+1)
         FYM = CSHIFT(F1,2,-1)
         FDERIV = ZXP * (FXP - F1) + ZXM * (FXM - F1) +
                  ZYP * (FYP - F1) + ZYM * (FYM - F1)
4. !HPF$ TEMPLATE TEMP(N,N)
   !HPF$ DISTRIBUTE TEMP(BLOCK,BLOCK)
         REAL    A(N,N), B(N,N), C(N,N)
   !HPF$ ALIGN A(i,j),B(i,j),C(i,j) WITH TEMP(i,j)
         C=TRANSPOSE(TRANSPOSE(A,1)+B)
5. !HPF$ TEMPLATE TEMP(N,N)
   !HPF$ DISTRIBUTE TEMP(BLOCK,BLOCK)
         REAL    A(N,N), B(N,N), C(N,N)
   !HPF$ ALIGN A(i,j),B(i,j),C(i,j) WITH TEMP(i,j)
         C=TRANSPOSE( A+B , 1)
6. !HPF$ TEMPLATE TEMP(N,N)
   !HPF$ DISTRIBUTE TEMP(BLOCK,BLOCK)
         REAL    A(N,N), B(N,N), C(N,N), D(N,N), E(N,N), F(N,N)
   !HPF$ ALIGN A(i,j),B(i,j),C(i,j),D(i,j),E(i,j),F(i,j) WITH TEMP(i,j)
         F=TRANSPOSE( SIN(TRANSPOSE(A)+TRANSPOSE(B)+C*D-E))
7. !HPF$ TEMPLATE TEMP(N,N)
   !HPF$ DISTRIBUTE TEMP(BLOCK,BLOCK)
         REAL    A(N,N), B(N,N), C(N,N), D(N,N), E(N,N), F(N,N)
         REAL    G(N,N), H(N,N), I(N,N), J(N,N), K(N,N)
         LOGICAL LA(N,N)
   !HPF$ ALIGN A(i,j),B(i,j),C(i,j),D(i,j),E(i,j),F(i,j) WITH TEMP(i,j)
   !HPF$ ALIGN G(i,j),H(i,j),IA(i,j),JA(i,j),KA(i,j),LA(i,j) WITH TEMP(i,j)
         FORALL (i=1:N,j=1:N)
            A(i,j)=B(N-i+1,j)
         END FORALL
         FORALL (i=1:N,j=1:N)
            C(i,j)=D(N-i+1,j)
         END FORALL
         FORALL (i=1:N,j=1:N)
            E(i,j)=F(N-i+1,j)
         END FORALL
         G=TRANSPOSE(H)
         IA=TRANSPOSE(JA)
         KA=MERGE(A+C+E,G+IA,LA)
8. !HPF$ TEMPLATE TEMP(N,N)
   !HPF$ DISTRIBUTE TEMP(BLOCK,BLOCK)
         REAL    A(N,N), B(N,N), C(N,N), D(N,N), E(N,N), F(N,N), G(N,N)
   !HPF$ ALIGN A(i,j),B(i,j),C(i,j),D(i,j),E(i,j),F(i,j),G(i,j) WITH TEMP(i,j)
         G=CSHIFT( (A+B+C+D)*E-F),1,3)
```

# POLYNOMIAL-TIME NESTED LOOP FUSION WITH FULL PARALLELISM*

Edwin H.-M. Sha and Chenhua Lang
Dept. of Computer Science & Eng.
University of Notre Dame
Notre Dame, IN 46556

Nelson L. Passos
Dept. of Computer Science
Midwestern State University
Wichita Falls, Texas 76308

Abstract-- *Data locality and synchronization overhead are two important factors that affect the performance of applications on multiprocessors. Loop fusion is an effective way for reducing synchronization and improving data locality. Traditional fusion techniques, however, either can not address the case when fusion-preventing dependences exist in nested loops, or can not achieve good parallelism after fusion. This paper gives a significant improvement by presenting several efficient polynomial-time algorithms to solve these problems. These algorithms combined with the retiming technique allow nested loop fusion in the existence of outmost loop-carried dependences as also in the presence of fusion-preventing dependences. Furthermore, our technique is proved to achieve fully parallel execution of the fused loops.*

## INTRODUCTION

Multi-dimensional applications such as image processing, fluid mechanics and weather forecasting, may deal with billions of data values, requiring high performance computers. Loop transformations offer effective ways to improve parallelism and achieve efficient use of the memory [8, 11, 12]. Consecutive loops in a program are responsible for computational overhead due to repetitive access to data elements residing in non-local memories, and also for synchronization between processors in a parallel environment. Loop fusion is a loop-reordering transformation that merges multiple loops into a single one [1, 2, 3, 4]. By increasing the granule size of the loops, it is possible to improve data locality and to reduce synchronization. However, the existing techniques do not consider the implementation of loop fusion with multi-dimensional dependences. In this paper, we develop a new technique based on multi-dimensional retiming in order to perform the loop fusion and to achieve a fully parallel execution of the innermost fused loop.

Researchers in this area are focusing on solutions to two problems: first, fusion is not always legal because of the existence of fusion-preventing dependences between

```
DO k1 i = 0, n

    DOALL k2 j = 0,m
    ....
k2   CONTINUE

    DOALL k3 j = 0,m
    ....
k3   CONTINUE
      .
      .
K1 CONTINUE
```

Fig. 1: Program Model

loops being fused. Second, fusion may introduce loop-carried dependences and thus reduce loop parallelism [2, 11]. Kennedy and McKinley [4] perform loop fusion to combine a collection of loops and use loop distribution to improve parallelism. However they do not address the case when fusion-preventing dependences exist and when the iteration spaces of candidate loops are not identical. Naraig and Tarek [6] suggest a "shift-and-peel" loop transformation to fuse loops and allow parallel execution. The shifting part of the transformation may fuse loops in the presence of fusion-preventing dependences. However, when the number of peeled iterations exceeds the number of iterations per processor, this method is not efficient. Our nested loop technique can do legal loop fusion even in the case of fusion-preventing dependences, guaranteeing to achieve full parallelism of the innermost loop.

A simple example of our target problem is shown in Figure 1. The innermost loops are assumed to be fully parallel loops, and the original program contains only constant distance data dependences. We model the problem by a *multi-dimensional loop dependence graph (MLDG)*, where each innermost loop is represented as a node. Since outmost loop-carried dependences are permitted in the model, cycles are natural in the graph. Instead of simply fusing the candidate loop nests directly, we reschedule the loops by applying multi-dimensional retiming to the MLDG. A new MLDG is constructed through the retiming function, such that after retiming no fusion-preventing dependences exist and the loop fusion is legal.

*This work was supported in part by the NSF CAREER GRANT MIP-95-01006, and by the William D. Mensch, Jr. Fellowship.

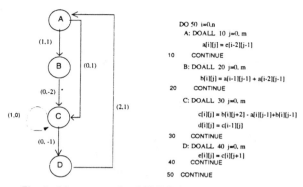

Fig. 2: (a) an example of 2LDG (b) equivalent code

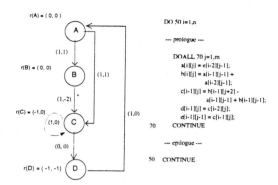

Fig. 3: (a) 2LDG after retiming (b) equivalent code

Three cases and their corresponding polynomial-time algorithms are discussed in this paper. When no cycle exists, after applying our fusion technique the innermost loop becomes parallel; when cycle exists, however, it is necessary to satisfy certain restrictions in order to obtain the full parallelism after applying our fusion technique. The third case consists of a general solution where, after retiming and loop fusion, a hyperplane is computed such that all iterations comprising the innermost loop can be done in parallel [7]. For simplicity, we discuss two-dimensional cases only. The multi-dimensional case is a straight forward extension of the concepts presented. Figure 2(a) shows an example of a two-dimensional loop dependence graph ($2LDG$) consisting of 4 nodes, equivalent to the 4 innermost loops of the code of figure 2(b). The nodes in the graph represent each of the DO ALL loops according to the labels A, B, C, D. The edges between the nodes show that there exists a data dependence between them. For example, data produced in loop A will be consumed by loop B. The edge weight shows a multi-dimensional offset between the data production and consumption. Applying our new technique we obtain the retimed graph presented in figure 3(a). Figure 3(b) shows the pseudo code after retiming and loop fusion. It is easy to notice that the resulting innermost loop is fully parallel. A prologue sequence, and respective epilogue, are created in order to provide the correct computation sequence. Such additional code usually requires a small computation time when compared to the total execution of the innermost loop and can be considered negligible. The resulting fused loop has a lower number of synchronization requests than the initial group of four loops, reducing the synchronization overhead.

## BASIC CONCEPTS

### Data Dependences

Data dependence is the most important factor to be considered in the loop fusion. There are three kinds of dependences between two statements in a program, commonly mentioned in the literature: *true dependence, antidependence* and *output dependence* [1, 4]. In this paper we consider some new terms such as *outmost loop-carried dependence* and *self-dependence*.

An *outmost loop-carried dependence* occurs when one statement stores a data value on one iteration, and that value is fetched on a later iteration of the outmost loop. *Self-dependence* is a special case of outmost loop-carried dependence where the data is produced and consumed by the same innermost loop. Later it will be shown that the fusion in the presence of outmost loop-carried dependences is always legal. When one statement stores a data value and in the same iteration of the outmost loop, another statement uses that value, the fusion may not always be legal. This is *fusion-preventing dependences*. Fusion-preventing dependences are dependences that after fusion become reverse to the control flow, making the fusion illegal.

An *iteration space* is a Cartesian space, where each iteration is represented by a point $(i,j)$ such that $i$ represents the index of the outmost loop and $j$ represents the index of the innermost loop. In our model, there are different iteration spaces for each innermost loop. For example, in figure 2 (b) there are four iteration spaces. Loop fusion combines the iteration spaces into one single space. Because of array reuse, data dependences may exist between the different iteration spaces. Considering the overlap of the iteration spaces, if a computation in iteration $(i_1, j_1)$ of a loop B depends on data produced in iteration $(i_2, j_2)$ of a loop A, then we say that there is a *loop dependence vector* $d_L = (k_1, k_2) = (i_1 - i_2, j_1 - j_2)$ that represents the data dependence between those loops. In figure 2(b), there is a loop dependence vector (0,-2) between loops B and C, and there are loop dependence vectors (1,1) and (2,1) between loops A and B. These loop dependence vectors are important information for legal loop fusion.

## Problem Model

We model the loop fusion problem as a graph in which each innermost loop is represented by a node and the data dependences between loops are represented as directed edges between the nodes. Recall that in figure 2(b) there are two loop dependence vectors $(1,1)$ and $(2,1)$ between nodes A and B. These two vectors are represented by a function called $D_L$. Our algorithm will only use the minimal loop dependence vector denoted by a function designated $\delta_L$. The weight of each edge is the minimal loop dependence vector between its end nodes. Such a graph is called a *multi-dimensional loop dependence graph* as defined below:

**Definition 1** A *multi-dimensional loop dependence graph (MLDG)* $G = (V, E, \delta_L, D_L)$ is a node-weighted and edge-weighted directed graph, where $V$ is the set of innermost loop nests, $E \subseteq V \times V$ is the set of dependence edges between the loops, $\delta_L$ is a function from $E$ to $Z^n$, representing the minimal loop dependency vector in lexicographic order associated with an edge, and $D_L$ is a function from $E$ to $2^{Z^n}$, representing the set of loop dependency vectors between two nodes, where $n$ is the number of dimensions.

Figure 2 is an example of an MLDG . In this example, $V = \{A, B, C, D\}$ and $E = \{e_1 : (A, B), e_2 : (B, C), e_3 : (C, D), e_4 : (A, C), e_5 : (D, A), e_6 : (C, C)\}$ where, $\delta_L(e_1) = (1,1)$, $\delta_L(e_2) = (0,-2)$, $\delta_L(e_3) = (0,-1)$, $\delta_L(e_4) = (0,1)$, $\delta_L(e_5) = (2,1)$, $\delta_L(e_6) = (1,0)$, and $D_L(e_1) = \{(1,1),(2,1)\}$, $D_L(e_2) = \{(0,-2),(0,1)\}$, $D_L(e_3) = \{(0,-1)\}$, $D_L(e_4) = \{(0,1)\}$, $D_L(e_5) = \{(2,1)\}$, $D_L(e_6) = \{(1,0)\}$.

The particular case when there are two or more different loop dependence vectors between two nodes, which are less than $(1, -\infty)$, is very important to our new technique. Such case will introduce some problems in achieving a fully parallel solution after fusion. In order to handle such constraints, we say that such edges are called *parallelism hard edges, hard-edges* for short.

We use $\xrightarrow{*}$ to represent a hard-edge in our graph. In figure 2(a), edge $(B, C)$ is a hard-edge because there are two loop dependence vectors $(0, -2) < (1, -\infty)$ and $(0, 1) < (1, -\infty)$ between B and C. Edge $(A, B)$ is not a hard-edge because none of the loop dependence vectors for that edge is less than $(1, -\infty)$. From now on, we will represent two dimensional vectors $r$ by $(r[1], r[2])$. For any cycle $c$ in an $MLDG$, $\delta_L(c)$ is defined as $\sum_{e_i \in c} \delta_L(e_i)$.

We say that an MLDG is *legal* if there is no dependence vector reverse to the computational flow, i.e., the nested loop is executable. It is obvious that the cycles in a legal MLDG are characterized as stated in the lemma below.

**Lemma 1** *Given a 2LDG=$(V, E, \delta_L, D_L)$, if the 2LDG is legal, then each cycle $c$ in $G$ satisfies $\delta_L(c) \geq (1, -\infty)$.*

In figure 2(a), cycle $c_1 = A \to B \to C \to D \to A$ has $\delta_L(c_1) = (3,-1)$, and cycle $c_2 = A \to C \to D \to A$ has $\delta_L(c_2) = (2,1)$, showing that the 2LDG is legal.

## Multi-Dimensional Retiming

Passos and Sha proposed multi-dimensional retiming techniques to obtain full parallelism in nested loops [7]. The multi-dimensional retiming concept is helpful in solving loop fusion problem, so we will review some of these concepts below.

A *two-dimensional retiming* $r$ of an MLDG $G = (V, E, \delta_L, D_L)$ is a function that transforms the iteration spaces of the innermost loops. A new 2LDG $G_r = (V, E, \delta_{Lr}, D_{Lr})$ is created, such that each outmost iteration still has one execution of each node in $V$. The retiming vector $r(u)$ of a node $u \in V$ represents the offset between the original iteration space representing $u$, and the one after retiming. The loop dependence vectors change accordingly to preserve dependences, i.e., $r(u)$ represents $\delta_L$ components pushed into the edges $u \longrightarrow v$, and subtracted from the edges $w \longrightarrow u$, where $u, v, w \in V$. Therefore, we have $\delta_{Lr}(u, v) = \delta_L(u, v) + r(u) - r(v)$ and $D_{Lr}(u, v) = \{d_L(u, v) + r(u) - r(v)\}$ for each edge $u \longrightarrow v$ and $d_L(u, v) \in D_L(u, v)$. Also, $\delta_{Lr}(c) = \delta_L(c)$ for each cycle $c \in G$.

For example in figure 3(a), the retiming function for the four nodes is $r(A) = (0,0)$, $r(B) = (0,0)$, $r(C) = (-1, 0)$ and $r(D) = (-1, -1)$. After retiming, the weight of edge $D \to A$ becomes $\delta_{Lr}(D, A) = \delta_L(D, A) + r(D) - r(A) = (2, 1) + (-1, -1) - (0, 0) = (1, 0)$, and the set of loop dependence vectors of edge $D \to A$ becomes $D_{Lr} = \{(1, 0)\}$. The weight of the cycles remain unchanged, $\delta_{Lr}(c_1) = (3, -1) = \delta_L(c_1)$ for $c_1 = A \to B \to C \to D \to A$, and $\delta_{Lr}(c_2) = (2, 1) = \delta_L(c_2)$ for $c_2 = A \to C \to D \to A$.

Sometimes, a multi-dimensional retiming may require a change in the schedule vector. A *schedule vector $s$* is the normal vector for a set of parallel equitemporal hyperplanes that define a sequence of execution of the iterations. We say that a schedule vector $s$ is a *strict schedule vector* for an MLDG $G = (V, E, \delta_L, D_L)$ if for each $d_L(e) \neq (0, 0, \cdots, 0)$, $d_L(e) \in D_L(e)$, $d_L(e) \cdot s > 0$. For example, $s = (1, 0)$ is a strict schedule vector for the example of figure 3(a).

## 2-D Linear Inequality System

We will use a special ILP model, which can be efficiently solved in polynomial-time, to find our retiming function. Therefore, we present a brief review of this problem.

**Problem ILP** Given a set of m linear inequalities of the form $x_j - x_i \leq a_{ij}$ on the unknown integer $x_1, x_2, \cdots, x_n$, where $a_{ij}$ are given integer constants. Determine feasible values for the unknown $x_i$, or determine that no such values exist [9]. This is equivalent to a constraint graph $G = (V, E, w)$, with each vertex $v_i$ corresponding to one of the n unknown variables $x_i, i = 1, 2, \cdots, n$ and one extra vertex $v_0$. $V = \{v_0, v_1, \cdots, v_n\}$ and $E = \{(v_i, v_j) : x_j - x_i \leq a_{ij}$ is a constraint$\} \cup \{(v_0, v_1), (v_0, v_2), \cdots, (v_0, v_n)\}$, with $w(v_i, v_j) = a_{ij}$, and $w(v_0, v_i) = 0$.

**Theorem 2** *The inequality system has a feasible solution if and only if the corresponding constraint graph has no cycle with negative weight.*

Using Bellman-Ford Algorithm, the shortest path from $v_0$ to $v_i$ is a feasible solution $x_i$ of this inequality system. Now, we can extend this method to two dimensions.

**Problem 2-ILP** Given a set of m linear inequalities of the form $r_j - r_i \leq w_{ij}$ on the unknown two-dimensional vectors $r_1, r_2, \cdots, r_n$, where $w_{ij}$ are given two-dimensional vectors. Determine feasible values for the unknown $r_i$, or determine that no such values exist. This is equivalent to the constraint graph $G = (V, E, w)$, with each vertex $v_i$ corresponding to one of the n unknown variables $r_i, i = 1, 2, \cdots, n$. $V = \{v_0, v_1, \cdots, v_n\}$ and $E = \{(r_i, r_j) : r_j - r_i \leq w_{ij}$ is a constraint$\} \cup \{(v_0, v_1), (v_0, v_2), \cdots, (v_0, v_n)\}$, with $w(v_i, v_j) = w_{ij}$, and $w(v_0, v_i) = (0, 0)$.

**Theorem 3** *The inequality system has feasible solution if and only if each cycle of the corresponding constraint graph has the weight $w(c) \geq (0, 0)$.*

Using Bellman-Ford Algorithm, the shortest path from $v_0$ to $v_i$, using a lexicographical ordering is a feasible solution $r_i$ of this inequality system.

## LEGAL LOOP FUSION

### Loop Fusion by Retiming

Loop fusion combines adjacent loop bodies into a single body. However fusion is not always legal. Assuming two statements $S_1$ and $S_2$ in two different candidate loops, if the calculation of $S_2$ depends on the result from $S_1$, but after loop fusion, the execution of $S_2$ becomes earlier than $S_1$, this kind of loop fusion is illegal [6, 11]. Figure 4(b) shows the code after an illegal loop fusion. In this example, c[i][j] depends on b[i][j+2], but b[i][j+2] has not been calculated yet. In figure 5 it is shown the iteration space after the illegal fusion: iteration (0,0) depends on the results from iterations (0,1) and (0,2), however these iterations have not been executed.

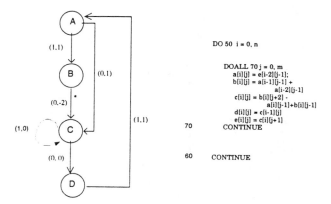

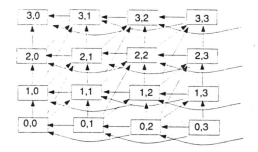

Fig. 4: (a) 2LDG (b) illegal loop fusion

Fig. 5: iteration space after illegal loop fusion

In order to predict if a loop fusion is legal let us examine a general form of loop dependence vector: $d_L = (d_L[1], d_L[2])$, Three cases may occur:

(1) $d_L[1] > 0$: it means that the dependence is carried by the outmost loop. In this case, after loop fusion, the dependence direction is preserved and loop fusion is safe.

(2) $d_L[1] = 0, d_L[2] \geq 0$: this is the case of a data dependence in the same iteration of the outmost loop, and after fusion, the dependence becomes forward loop-carried by the innermost loop or loop-independent. Therefore, the dependence direction is preserved, and the loop fusion is also safe.

(3) $d_L[1] = 0, d_L[2] < 0$: this is also a case of dependence in the same iteration of the outmost loop, and after fusion, the dependence becomes antidependent. The dependence direction is reversed and the straightforward loop fusion is then illegal.

So, if all the vectors $d_L$ satisfy $d_L \geq (0, 0)$, loop fusion is legal, as expressed in the following theorem:

**Theorem 4** *Given a 2LDG $G = (V, E, \delta_L, D_L)$, if $\delta_L(e) \geq (0, 0)$ $\forall e \in E$, then the loop fusion is legal.*

But, is it possible to find a retiming function for a legal 2LDG $G$ such that after retiming the weight of each edge in $G_r = (V, E, \delta_{Lr}, D_{Lr})$ satisfies $\delta_{Lr}(e) \geq (0, 0)$? In the following, we will prove that such a retiming function can always be found for a legal 2LDG. We solve this problem by using a 2-D Linear Inequality System. First we find the relationship between our 2LDG and the constraint graph of our specified inequality system. It is obvious from the definition of constraint graph that the following lemma is true.

**Lemma 5** *Given a 2LDG $G = (V, E, \delta_L, D_L)$ and the inequality system $r(v_j) - r(v_i) \leq \delta_L(e)$ $\forall e : v_i \rightarrow v_j \in E$, a constraint graph of the inequality system can be defined by $G' = (V', E', w')$ such that $V' = V \cup \{v_0 : v_0 \notin V\}$, $E' = E \cup \{(v_0, v_i) : v_i \in V\}$, $w'(v_i, v_j) = \delta_L(e)$ $\forall e : v_i \rightarrow v_j \in E$ and $w'(v_0, v_i) = (0, 0)$ for all $v_i \in V$.*

Using the lemma above we show how to find a legal retiming to satisfy the requirements for a loop fusion.

**Theorem 6** *Given a legal 2LDG $G = (V, E, \delta_L, D_L)$, there exists a legal retiming r, such that, after retiming, loop fusion is always legal.*

### The Algorithm

In our technique we use a modified version of the Bellman-Ford algorithm to compute the retiming function, which is the shortest path from $v_0$ to each other node, as shown in the procedure BF below.

**Procedure BF**
**Input:** a constraint graph $G' = (V', E', w')$.
**Output:** retiming function $r$.
**Begin**
/* Using Belman-Ford algorithm to compute the retiming function */
   $r(v_0) = (0, 0)$
   **for** each node $v \in V' - \{v_0\}$ **do begin**
      $r(v) = (\infty, \infty)$
   **endfor**
   **for** $k \rightarrow 1$ to $|V'| - 1$ **do begin**
      **for** each edge $(v_i, v_j) \in E'$ **do begin**
         **if** $r(v_j) > r(v_i) + w'(v_i, v_j)$
         **then** $r(v_j) = r(v_i) + w'(v_i, v_j)$
         **endif**
      **endfor**
   **endfor**
   **return**
**End**

The ability to predict a retiming function for a legal fusion of any 2LDG allows us to define a new algorithm as follows.

**Legal Loop Fusion Retiming Algorithm(LLOFRA)**
**Input:** a 2LDG $G = (V, E, \delta_L, D_L)$.
**Output:** retiming function $r$ of the 2LDG.
**Begin**
/*Construct the constraint graph $G' = (V', E', w')$ from G */
   $V' \longleftarrow V \cup \{v_0\}$
   $E' \longleftarrow E \cup \{v_0 \rightarrow v_i : v_i \in V\}$
   **for** each edge $e \in E$ **do begin**
      $w'(e) = \delta_L(e)$
   **endfor**

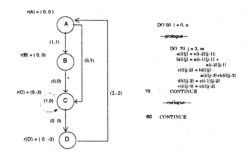

Fig. 6: (a) 2LDG after retiming (b) legal fusion after retiming

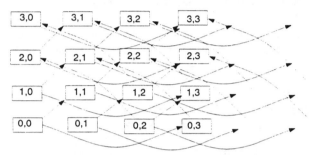

Fig. 7: iteration space after retiming and loop fusion

   **for** each $e' \in E' - E$ **do begin**
      $w'(e') = (0, 0)$
   **endfor**
/* Using Belman-Ford algorithm to compute the retiming function */
   $r = BF(G')$
**End**

For the example of figure 2(a) the retiming function computed by the algorithm above is $r(A) = (0, 0), r(B) = (0, 0), r(C) = (0, -2)$, and $r(D) = (0, -3)$. Using such a function, we obtain the new 2LDG shown in figure 6(a). Figure 6(b) shows the code for the innermost loop after fusion and retiming.

However, after loop fusion the innermost loop may not be executed with full parallelism because of new innermost loop-carried dependences. For example, figure 7 shows the iteration space for the example in figure 6. It is obvious that it contains data dependences between the iterations of the innermost loop (a row in the iteration space). Hence, the execution of the innermost loop becomes serial and not fully parallel as desired. However, before loop fusion, the iterations of each candidate loop could be executed in parallel, and synchronization was only required to ensure that all iterations of one candidate loop would be executed before any iteration of another candidate loop.

## PARALLEL LOOP FUSION

### Fully Parallel Loop Fusion

We know that fusion is safe if all the dependence vectors are greater than or equal to $(0,0)$. But, how about the parallelism after fusion? In this subsection, we discuss in which cases we can find a retiming function such that after retiming and loop fusion the innermost loop can be executed in parallel, which we define as a DO ALL loop as follows:

**Definition 2** An innermost loop is said *DO ALL* if and only if all iteration $(i, 0), (i, 1), \cdots$ can be done in parallel.

An innermost loop DO ALL means that, for any two iterations $(i, j_1)$ and $(i, j_2)$, there is no data dependence between them, i.e., no dependence vector $(0, k), k \neq 0$, exists. We know that fusion is safe if all dependence vectors do satisfy $d_L(e) \geq (0, 0)$. The following concepts discuss the problem of the parallelism after fusion. We begin by identifying the conditions for the innermost loop to be DO ALL.

**Theorem 7** *Given a 2LDG* $G = (V, E, \delta_L, D_L)$, *if after loop fusion it can be executed according to a strict schedule vector* $s = (1, 0)$, *then the innermost loop nest is DO ALL.*

The above theorem has an immediate corollary:

**Corollary 8** *Given a 2LDG* $G = (V, E, \delta_L, D_L)$, *transformed in* $G_r = (V, E, \delta_{Lr}, D_{Lr})$ *after retiming and loop fusion, the innermost loop nest is DO ALL if and only if all dependence vectors satisfy the condition* $d_{Lr}(e) \geq (1, -\infty)$ *or* $d_{Lr}(e) = (0, 0), e \in E, d_{Lr}(e) \in D_{Lr}(e)$.

The following theorems will predict if we can find a legal retiming function to achieve loop fusion and full parallelism. We solve this problem by using the model of integer linear problem and the Bellman-Ford algorithm as described in the previous section.

**Acyclic MLDGs**

**Theorem 9** *Given a 2LDG* $G$, *if* $G$ *is acyclic, then there exists a legal retiming* $r$, *such that after retiming and loop fusion the innermost loop nest is DO ALL.*

Now we modify the algorithm LLOFRA in order to obtain a retiming function for legal fusion and full parallelism.

**Legal Loop Fusion and Full Parallelism for Acyclic MLDGs (Acyc-Fusion-PAR)**
**Input:** a 2LDG $G = (V, E, \delta_L, D_L)$.
**Output:** retiming function $r$ of the 2LDG.
**Begin**
/* Construct the constraint graph $G' = (V', E', w')$ from $G$ */
  $V' \longleftarrow V \cup \{v_0\}$
  $E' \longleftarrow E \cup \{v_0 \rightarrow v_i : v_i \in V\}$
  **for** each edge $e \in E$ **do begin**
    $w'(e') = \delta_L(e) - (1, -\infty)$
  **endfor**
  **for** each $e' \in E' - E$ **do begin**
    $w'(e') = (0, 0)$
  **endfor**
/* Using Belman-Ford Algorithm to compute the retiming function */

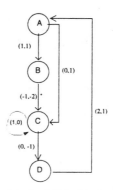

Fig. 8: $G - (1, 0)$ of 2LDG in figure 2

  $r = BF(G')$
/* Set the second component of $r$ */
  **for** each node $v \in V$ **do begin**
    $r(v)[2] = 0$
  **endfor**
**End**

**Cyclic MLDGs**

In the case of cyclic MLDGs, we begin with a case with the innermost loop can be DO ALL by satisfying the constraints described in theorem below. The graph in figure 2 falls into this category. Later we will discuss the general cyclic MLDG. We first define a new reduced graph $G - h$.

**Definition 3** Given a 2LDG $G = (V, E, \delta_L, D_L)$ and a two dimensional vector $h$, $G - h = (V, E, w'')$ where $w''(e) = \delta_L(e) - h$ for each hard-edge and $w''(e) = \delta_L(e)$ for any other edges.

Figure 8 shows an example based on the 2LDG in figure 2. Now, we extended the solution for acyclic graph to the cyclic graph.

**Theorem 10** *Given a 2LDG* $G = (V, E, \delta_L, D_L)$, *then there is a legal retiming* $r$ *such that, after retiming and loop fusion, the innermost loop nest is DO ALL iff each cycle in* $G - (1, 0) = (V, E, w'')$ *satisfies* $w''(c) \geq (0, -\infty)$.

The algorithm for finding the retiming function for these loops that can be fused with full parallelism according to the theorem above is given as follows. In order to achieve full parallelism of the innermost fused loop, we need to retime the graph such that the weight of the hard-edges become larger than $(1, -\infty)$ and the weight of the remaining edges are transformed to be bigger than $(1, -\infty)$ or equal to $(0,0)$.

**Legal Loop Fusion and Full Parallelism for Cyclic MLDGs (Cyc-Fusion-PAR)**
**Input:** a 2LDG $G$ and $G - (1, 0) = (V, E, w'')$
**Output:** retiming function $r$ of the 2LDG.
**Begin**

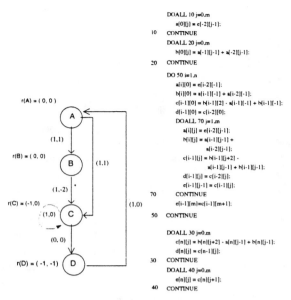

```
        DOALL 10 j=0,m
            a[0][j] = c[-2][j-1];
    10  CONTINUE
        DOALL 20 j=0,m
            b[0][j] = a[-1][j-1] + a[-2][j-1];
    20  CONTINUE

        DO 50 i=1,n
            a[i][0] = c[i-2][-1];
            b[i][0] = a[i-1][-1] + a[i-2][-1];
            c[i-1][0] = b[i-1][2] - a[i-1][-1] + b[i-1][-1];
            d[i-1][0] = c[i-2][0];
            DOALL 70 j=1,m
                a[i][j] = c[i-2][j-1];
                b[i][j] = a[i-1][j-1] +
                    a[i-2][j-1];
                c[i-1][j] = b[i-1][j+2] -
                    a[i-1][j-1] + b[i-1][j-1];
                d[i-1][j] = c[i-2][j];
                e[i-1][j-1] = c[i-1][j];
    70      CONTINUE
            e[i-1][m]=c[i-1][m+1];
    50  CONTINUE

        DOALL 30 j=0,m
            c[n][j] = b[n][j+2] - a[n][j-1] + b[n][j-1];
            d[n][j] = c[n-1][j];
    30  CONTINUE
        DOALL 40 j=0,m
            e[n][j] = c[n][j+1];
    40  CONTINUE
```

Fig. 9: (a)2LDG after retiming (b) pseudo code

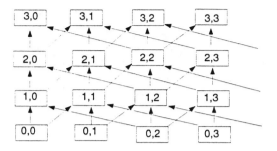

Fig. 10: iteration space after retiming and fusion

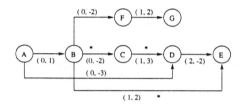

Fig. 11: Acyclic 2LDG before retiming

```
/* Construct constraint graph G' = (V', E', w') from G − (1, 0) */
V' ⟵ V ∪ {v₀}
E' ⟵ E ∪ {v₀ → vᵢ : vᵢ ∈ V}
for each edge e ∈ E do begin
    w'(e')[1] = w''(e)[1]
    w'(e')[2] = 0
endfor
for each edge e ∈ E do begin
    w'(e') = (0, 0)
end
/* Using Belman-Ford algorithm to compute the first component of
        retiming function */
r = BF(G')
/* Compute the second component of retiming function */
    for  each non-hard-edge e(vⱼ, vᵢ) ∈ E and δ_Lr(e)[1] = 0 do begin
        construct the system r(vⱼ)[2] − r(vᵢ)[2] = δ_L(e)[2]
    endfor
    r(v)[2] = solution to the equation system
End
```

When applying this algorithm to the example in figure 2, we compute $G - (1, 0)$ and create a pseudo-one-dimensional constraint graph where the second component of the weights is always zero. Using Bellman-Ford algorithm we can get the first component of retiming function: $r(A)[1] = 0, r(B)[1] = 0, r(C)[1] = -1, r(D)[1] = -1$. Then we derive the equation system $r(D)[2] - r(C)[2] = -1$. Solving this equation system we can get $r(D)[2] = -1, r(C)[2] = 0$. For the others we define $r(A)[2] = 0, r(B)[2] = 0$. Figure 9 shows the resulting retiming function and the 2LDG after retiming. In figure 10, we show the iteration space after retiming and fusion. It is obvious that the innermost loop can be done in parallel.

### Fully Parallel in a Hyperplane

In the case when the constraints established in theorem 10 are not satisfied, the full parallelism of the innermost loop is achieved by using a wavefront approach. We begin showing how to solve this problem by defining a DO ALL hyperplane as follows.

**Definition 4** A hyperplane is said *DO ALL with respect to a schedule vector s* if it is perpendicular to $s$ and all the iterations in the hyperplane can be done in parallel.

The conditions required to obtain a DO ALL hyperplane via retiming are expressed in the lemma below:

**Lemma 11** *Given a 2LDG G, transformed by retiming in* $G' = (V, E, \delta_{Lr}, D_{Lr})$, *if all the dependence vectors satisfy* $d_{Lr}(e) \geq (0, 0), d_{Lr}(e) \in D_{Lr}, e \in E$, *then there exists a hyperplane h such that h is DO ALL.*

The theorem below shows that a retiming function always exist such that a DO ALL hyperplane can be found.

**Theorem 12** *Given a 2LDG G = (V, E, \delta_L, D_L), if all the cycles* $c \in G$ *satisfy* $\delta_L(c) > (0, 0)$, *then we can find a legal retiming r, such that after retiming and loop fusion, there is a hyperplane where all iterations are parallel.*

### EXAMPLES

A first example is an acyclic case, represented by figure 11, which shows the MLDG before loop fusion. This MLDG needs 7 synchronizations for each outmost loop iteration. Assuming $n$ as the number of iterations of the outmost loop, we need $7 * n$ synchronizations. Because of

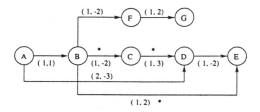

r(A)=(0,0)    r(B)=(-1,0)    r(C)=(-2,0)    r(D)=(-2,0)    r(E)=(-1,0)

r(F)=(-2,0)    r(G)=(-2,0)

Fig. 12: Acyclic 2LDG after retiming

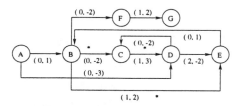

Fig. 13: Cyclic 2LDG before retiming

fusion-preventing dependences such as $(0,-2)$, $(0,-3)$ exist, we cannot fuse loops directly. Applying our technique, after retiming we remove the fusion-preventing dependences and can do loop fusion legally. The fused loop requires only one synchronization for each outmost loop iteration, for a total of $(n-2)$ synchronizations. The resulting innermost loop can be executed as a DO ALL loop.

Our second example, is a variation of the previous example, and it corresponds to the MLDG shown in figure 13. It contains loop-carried dependences making the problem more complex. In this case, we can notice that the initial fusion can not be done by the algorithm that deals with acyclic graphs because the constraints imposed by the existing cycles in the graph. The algorithm Cyc-Fusion-PAR is used after we verified that the MLDG satisfies the condition of theorem 10. The resulting retimed MLDG ready for fusion with fully parallel nested loop is shown in figure 14.

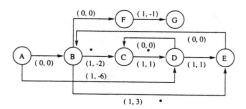

r(A)=(0,-1)    r(B)=(0,0)    r(C)=(-1,0)    r(D)=(-1,2)

r(E)=(0,-1)    r(F)=(0,-2)    r(G)=(0,1)

Fig. 14: Cyclic 2LDG after retiming

## CONCLUSION

Loop fusion is an effective way to reduce synchronization and improve data locality. Existing loop fusion techniques may not be able to deal with fusion-preventing dependences in nested loops, while obtaining a fully parallel fused loop. This paper has introduced a new technique, based on multi-dimensional retiming concepts, able to achieve a fully parallel fused loop. Loops are modeled by *loop dependence graphs*, where nodes represent the innermost loops and edges represent data dependences. New algorithms have been presented, covering three distinct situations, going from a trivial acyclic graph to complex cyclic ones with fusion-preventing dependences. The theory presented, and preliminary results, show the efficiency of the algorithms and that it is always possible to obtain a parallel fused loop by applying this methodology to nested loops.

## REFERENCES

[1] J. R. Allen and K. Kennedy, " Automatic Translation of Fortran Programs to Vector Form", in *ACM Transactions on Programming Languages and Systems*, Oct. 1987, pp. 491-542.

[2] U. Banerjee, "Loop Parallelization", Kluwer Academic Publishers, Norwell, MA, 1994.

[3] F. H. M. Franssen, F. Balasa, " Modeling Multidimensional Data and Control Flow", *IEEE Transactions on Very Large Scale Integration Systems*, Vol. 1, No. 3, Sep. 1993, pp. 319-326.

[4] K. Kennedy and K. S. McKinley, " Maximizing Loop Parallelism and Improving Data Locality via Loop Fusion and Distribution", in *Languages and Compilers for Parallel Computing-Sixth International Workshop*, ed. U. Banerjee et al., Springer-Verlag, Berlin, 1994, pp. 301-320.

[5] C. E. Leiserson and J. B. Saxe, " Retiming Synchronous Circuitry", *Algorithmica*, 6, 1991, pp. 5-35.

[6] N. Manjikian and T. S. Abdelrahman, " Fusion of Loops for Parallelism and Locality", in *1995 International Conference on Parallel Processing*, 1995, pp. II-19-II-28.

[7] N. L. Passos and E. H.-M. Sha, " Full Parallelism in Uniform Nested Loops Using Multi-Dimensional Retiming", *Proc. of 23rd International Conference on Parallel Processing*, 1994, Vol.II, pp. 130-133.

[8] A. K. Porterfield, " Software Methods for Improvement of Cache Performance on Supercomputer Applications", *PhD thesis, Dept. of Computer Science, Rice University*, April 1989.

[9] H. C. Thomas, E.L. Charles and L.R. Ronald, *Introduction to Algorithm*, the MIT Press.

[10] J. Warren, " A Hierachical Basis for Reordering Transformations", in *Proc. 11th ACM Symposium on the Principles of Programming Languages*, June 1984, pp. 272-282.

[11] M. Wolfe, "Optimizing Supercompilers for Supercomputers", MIT Press, Cambridge, MA, 1989.

[12] M. Wolf and M. Lam, " An Algorithmic Approach to Compound Loop Transformations", in *Advances in Languages and Compilers for Parallel Computing*, eds. A. Nicolau, D. Gelernter, T. Gross and D. Padua, The MIT Press, Cambridge, MA, 1991, pp. 243-259.

# COMPILER SUPPORT FOR PRIVATIZATION ON DISTRIBUTED-MEMORY MACHINES

Daniel J. Palermo, Ernesto Su, Eugene W. Hodges IV, and Prithviraj Banerjee
Center for Reliable and High-Performance Computing
University of Illinois at Urbana-Champaign
Urbana, IL 61801
{palermo, ernesto, ewhodges, banerjee}@crhc.uiuc.edu

## ABSTRACT

*The practice of using temporary scalar or array variables to store the results of common subexpressions presents several challenges to a parallelizing compiler. Not only does dependence analysis and, as a result, parallelization suffer, but existing techniques used for partitioning programs and generating communication for parallel execution on distributed-memory multicomputers also tend to break down. Techniques that have been developed over the years to compensate for this programming practice include scalar expansion, global forward substitution, and privatization, each of which has its own strengths and weaknesses. Compared to scalar expansion and global forward substitution, privatization has the advantage of not causing an increase in memory requirements or operation counts, but when compiling for distributed-memory machines it causes several new problems to arise. In this paper, we present a simple extension to a uniform array-region analysis framework that utilizes privatization information to partition loops and generate efficient communication, using the owner-computes rule, in the presence of temporary variables.*

## 1. INTRODUCTION

Programmers often reduce the complexity of computations by using temporary scalar or array variables to store the values of common subexpressions. Not only does dependence analysis and, as a result, parallelization suffer, but existing techniques used for partitioning programs and generating communication for parallel execution on distributed-memory multicomputers also tend to break down. In order to improve the parallelization of programs which are written using this practice, several techniques have been developed over the years to help cope with these problems. These techniques include global forward substitution [2, 3], scalar expansion [2, 3, 4], and scalar [5] or array [6, 7] privatization.

Both scalar expansion and forward substitution have several drawbacks in terms of memory requirements as well as operation count while privatization suffers from none of these problems. When compiling for distributed-memory machines scalar expansion and forward substitution can be easily handled by existing techniques for partitioning programs and generating communication, but privatization causes several new problems to arise. The main difference between privatization and the other techniques is that privatization is implicit (in the sense that the privatizable variables are merely indicated as such) whereas scalar expansion and forward substitution are explicit. Scalar expansion replaces temporary variables with expanded temporary arrays (and can be viewed as a form of explicit privatization) while forward substitution completely removes the references to the temporary variables.

For distributed-memory environments, knowledge of which iterations each processor will execute a given statement is necessary in order to partition loops and statically generate any required communication. Since a reference to an implicitly privatized scalar or array variable will not contain subscripts corresponding to the loops over which it is privatized, this ownership information is absent and the variable would normally be considered to be replicated across the processors if any of these loops were partitioned.

If a loop is partitioned by directly distributing iterations across the available processors without regards to the data distribution of the references contained within it, communication is determined by comparing the ownership of a reference directly against the ownership of the iterations of the partitioned loop bounds. Even though private variables can normally be handled in this case by just ignoring them during communication analysis for the loops over which they are privatized, this form of computation partitioning can potentially result in both a pre- and post-loop communication phase (to obtain non-local data required for the computation and then to write back non-local results that were computed locally).

The alternative is to partition a loop by distributing the iterations such that the processor which performs a given iteration actually owns the data items computed within that iteration. This approach has become known as the *owner-computes* rule. The advantage of the owner-computes rule is that it allows all required communication to be performed once (to only obtain non-local data required for the computation), before a parallel computation begins. Communication is now determined by comparing the iteration ownership of references read against the references that are written for a given statement. Unfortunately, private variables can no longer be just ignored as the iterations for which they are owned by a processor must be known in order to determine the communication.

In this paper, we present a simple extension to a uniform array-region analysis framework that utilizes privatization information to partition loops and generate efficient communication, using the owner-computes rule, in the presence of temporary variables. This framework has been developed as part of the PARADIGM compiler project [1] at the University of Illinois.

The remainder of this paper is organized as follows: Section 2 describes the different approaches that are available for handling temporary variables which are used to store the values of common subexpressions. The techniques we have developed to support privatization using the owner-computes rule are described in Section 3. Experimental results obtained using an Intel Paragon to compare the different techniques are presented and evaluated in

This research was supported in part by the National Aeronautics and Space Administration under Contract NASA NAG 1-613, in part by an Office of Naval Research Graduate Fellowship, and in part by the Advanced Research Projects Agency under contract DAA-H04-94-G-0273 administered by the Army Research office.

```
DO I = 2, IL
   XX          = X(I,1,1) - X(I-1,1,1)
   YX          = X(I,1,2) - X(I-1,1,2)
   PA          = P(I,2) + P(I,1)
   FS(I,1,1) = 0.
   FS(I,1,2) = - YX * PA
   FS(I,1,3) =   XX * PA
   FS(I,1,4) = 0.
ENDDO
```

Figure 1: Example Loop Utilizing Temporaries

Section 4. Related work in this area is then discussed in Section 5 and our conclusions are presented in Section 6.

# 2. APPROACHES

To illustrate each of the different approaches, each will be applied to an example loop which uses temporary variables to store intermediate computations. In Figure 1 such a loop, which appears in the EFLUX subroutine in FLO52 from the Perfect Club [8] suite, is shown. In this example, all three scalars (XX, YX, and PA) are temporary variables used only to store partial subexpressions that are immediately used in the computation.

## 2.1 Direct Application of the Owner-Computes Rule

It is possible to perform a direct application of the owner-computes rule to the code shown in Figure 1 (with the first dimension of the arrays partitioned across a linear array of processors). Due to the fact that the scalar variables create a single convergence point for the values of the computation, several problems will arise.

The first, and most significant, problem is that it is not possible to partition the loop across the processors. Since scalars are normally replicated on all processors, every processor must execute every iteration of the loop in order to satisfy the owner-computes rule. If the ownership of the scalars were assigned to a specific processor, the situation would actually become worse as this would only serve to serialize the computation on that processor resulting in every other processor waiting to receive the scalar values as they are computed (for this reason, single ownership of scalars will not be considered any further).

The second, less significant, problem which arises with replicated scalars is that to compute their values all processors must broadcast their portions of the partitioned arrays in order make the required data available on all processors. If the owner-computes rule were instead relaxed to an owner-stores rule, the communication is reduced somewhat as the actual computation could be carried out where the data existed and only the result of the computation would be broadcast to all processors. Either way, there will be a lot of communication occurring simultaneously among the processors, which can potentially degrade performance due to network contention.

## 2.2 Global Forward Substitution

In cases where there is only one control path between the last write of a temporary variable and its use, it is also possible to perform global forward substitution [2, 3] to replace all uses with the actual expression used to compute the temporary. Since each use of a temporary is replaced with the temporary's expression, the major drawback of forward substitution is the potential for increasing

```
DO I = 2, IL
   FS(I,1,1) = 0.
   FS(I,1,2) = - (X(I,1,2) - X(I-1,1,2))
&                    * (P(I,2) + P(I,1))
   FS(I,1,3) =   (X(I,1,1) - X(I-1,1,1))
&                    * (P(I,2) + P(I,1))
   FS(I,1,4) = 0.
ENDDO
```

Figure 2: After Performing Global Forward Substitution

the operation count and degrading the performance of a program through redundant computation. This will occur whenever a temporary is used in multiple references.

The code in Figure 2 is the result of performing global forward substitution on the example in Figure 1. As the temporary PA was used twice in the original code, after the transformation the operation count of the loop body has been increased by one which, overall, has added $IL - 2$ operations to the loop. In general the reuse of temporaries that were computed from complex expressions can have a large impact on the overall operation count of a program.

The resulting code in Figure 2 can now be easily analyzed to statically partition the loop and generate communication according to the owner-computes rule. Once the code has been partitioned, it is possible that the adverse effects of forward substitution could be reduced or eliminated if the target machine's node compiler was able to optimize the computation through common subexpression elimination (which is the inverse of global forward substitution). It is debatable, however, to what extent most commercial optimizing compilers would actually perform common subexpression elimination for floating point expressions (this question will be examined in more detail in Section 4).

```
DO I = 2, IL
   XX(I)       = X(I,1,1) - X(I-1,1,1)
   YX(I)       = X(I,1,2) - X(I-1,1,2)
   PA(I)       = P(I,2) + P(I,1)
   FS(I,1,1) = 0.
   FS(I,1,2) = - YX(I) * PA(I)
   FS(I,1,3) =   XX(I) * PA(I)
   FS(I,1,4) = 0.
ENDDO
```

Figure 3: After Performing Scalar Expansion

## 2.3 Scalar Expansion

Scalar expansion is a technique that can be used to promote scalar temporaries into arrays of temporary values [2, 3, 4]. Since a scalar is replaced with an array (with dimensions related to the extent of the loops bounds in which the scalar was contained), scalar expansion can greatly increase the memory requirements of a program. The benefit, however, is fairly obvious when examining the resulting code in Figure 3. The convergence points due to the scalar temporaries have been effectively eliminated as arrays of temporaries are now used instead. The loops can now be partitioned across the processors and communication requirements have dropped significantly as the broadcast operations are no longer necessary as only a single element shift of data is required to obtain non-local values.

```
!HPF$ INDEPENDENT, NEW(XX, YX, PA)
     DO I = 2, IL
        XX        = X(I,1,1) - X(I-1,1,1)
        YX        = X(I,1,2) - X(I-1,1,2)
        PA        = P(I,2) + P(I,1)
        FS(I,1,1) = 0.
        FS(I,1,2) = - YX * PA
        FS(I,1,3) =   XX * PA
        FS(I,1,4) = 0.
     ENDDO
```

Figure 4: Specification of Privatization

## 2.4 Privatization

Other research in the area has resulted in several techniques which can be used to determine when variables appearing within are loop are simply used as scratch space for the current iteration and can therefore be treated as a private reference for each iteration of the loop. A privatizable reference can be either a scalar variable [5] or an array [6, 7].

In Figure 4, the example is shown along with the High Performance Fortran (HPF) [9] NEW directive which is provided for specifying that a variable can be privatized with respect to the associated loop. This allows privatization to be specified either manually by a programmer or automatically through a separate compiler pass.

Privatization is similar to defining variables which are local to a loop nest, as is possible in Cedar Fortran [10]. Since the privatized variables will only be used within a single iteration before being overwritten, only one copy of each variable need be maintained for each processor as opposed to actually maintaining one for each iteration. For this reason, an efficient implementation of privatization will require the same amount of memory and perform the same number of operations as the original program.

## 2.5 Summary of the Approaches

The advantages of each of the different approaches for handling variables which are used to compute common subexpressions are summarized in Table 1. For a given technique, each category indicates: memory utilization is maintained, performance is maintained, or compilation for distributed memory is simplified.

Even though privatization is the most attractive of these techniques in terms of memory use and potential performance, it causes several new problems to arise when compiling for distributed-memory machines using the owner-computes rule. These problems along with the technique that we have developed to handle privatized variables within the PARADIGM compilation framework will be discussed in the next section.

Table 1: Advantages of Each of the Available Approaches

| | Memory | Performance | Compilation |
|---|---|---|---|
| Direct partitioning | √ | | |
| Scalar expansion | | √ | √ |
| Fwd. substitution | √ | | √ |
| Privatization | √ | √ | |

## 3. SUPPORT FOR PRIVATIZATION

In this section, we will first briefly describe PARADIGM's approach to parallelization, which involves the tasks of static loop partitioning and communication generation. We will then discuss how privatization is handled in the compilation framework.

### 3.1 Basic Compilation Strategy

PARADIGM applies the owner-computes rule to distribute computation across processors through loop partitioning. Given a program's data distribution information, which can be either manually specified with HPF directives or automatically generated by PARADIGM [11], the compiler first computes the ACCESS sets of all references enclosed in loops. The ACCESS set of a reference with respect to a particular processor is the set of loop iterations for which the reference is local to the processor. According to the owner-computes rule, a processor only executes loop iterations for which some reference on the left-hand side (*lhs*) of an assignment statement in the loop is local to that processor. In other words, the loop can be partitioned by having each processor execute only the loop iterations that are in the union of the *lhs* ACCESS sets in the loop. This union forms the *reduced iteration set* (RIS) of the loop [12]. For example, the loop:

$$\text{DO } i = L, U$$
$$A(i) = \cdots$$

after loop partitioning becomes:

$$\text{DO } i \in \{i \mid A(i) \text{ is stored locally}\}$$
$$A(i) = \cdots$$

In addition, if the RIS causes an access to a non-local right-hand side (*rhs*) reference in the loop, it must be received from the processor that owns it. To determine which iterations require interprocessor communication, PARADIGM computes the set difference between the *lhs* and *rhs* ACCESS sets [13, 14].

It is worth mentioning that PARADIGM also supports the FORALL construct, providing a pass that rewrites FORALL into DOALL loops while maintaining the original semantics [15]. This process occurs before the computation of ACCESS sets.

Since scalar variables are normally replicated on all processors (as discussed in Section 2.1), partitioning a loop containing scalars by directly applying the owner-computes rule will result in code with very poor performance. If, for example in Figure 1, XX is replicated, its ACCESS set is the entire iteration space. Since the RIS is the union of the ACCESS sets of the enclosed *lhs* references, the I loop must therefore also traverse the entire iteration space regardless of the distribution of the other *lhs* references in the loop. In other words, this loop is not partitioned, and hence no useful speedup can be expected. Worse yet, because the *lhs* is replicated, any *rhs* array that is partitioned will cause an all-to-all broadcast which effectively replicates the *rhs* arrays on all processors as well, tremendously wasting both time and memory. As discussed in Section 2.4, these problems can be overcome by privatizing the temporary variables.

### 3.2 Privatization Techniques in PARADIGM

In PARADIGM, privatization information is assumed to be either provided by a separate pass or specified through the use of the HPF INDEPENDENT directive with a NEW clause, as shown in Figure 4. Given a variable in the NEW clause, a reference appearing inside the associated loop is considered private. This implies that a private copy "exists" for each iteration of that loop (as well as the iterations of any outer loops). References appearing outside of the loop are not private.

```
PARTITION(loop_nest)
 1   for each ref in loop_nest
 2   do Compute ACCESS set for ref
 3   for each loop in loop_nest
 4   do Compute new loop bounds for loop,
 5        UNION of lhs ACCESS sets
 6
 7   ▷ Extension to update ACCESS sets
 8   ▷ for privatized references
 9   for each priv_ref in loop_nest
10   do if priv_ref = LHS(STMT(priv_ref))
11        then add set dimensions collected from
12              outer loops to ACCESS(priv_ref)
13        else  add private portion of
14              ACCESS(LHS(STMT(priv_ref)))
15              to ACCESS(priv_ref)
16
17   for each stmt in loop_nest
18   do Compute communication sets for stmt
```

Figure 5: Loop Partitioning Algorithm
Macros accessing fields in structures are shown in CAPS
Functions are indicated by SMALLCAPS

In order to deal with privatized references, the loop partitioning and communication generation algorithm is performed with the following extension. Let $T$ be a reference to a temporary variable that has been declared as private. During the computation of the RIS all lhs references that have been specified to be private for the loop are ignored. After all of the loops have been partitioned according to their RIS, the ACCESS set of all private references, $T$, appearing on the lhs are augmented with the set collected from the enclosing loops for which $T$ is private.[a]

This means that the value of $T$ will be computed for only those iterations of the (partitioned) loop nest executed by a specific processor to carry out the computation of the non-privatized references. For a privatized reference that is on the rhs, its ACCESS is augmented with the portion of the lhs ACCESS set of the statement in which it is contained, thus encompassing iterations over which it is private.

This technique applies to both privatized scalars and arrays in a straightforward manner. The only difference is that privatized arrays also have their own ACCESS set dimensions (corresponding to their array dimensions) which must be included in addition to the privatized set dimensions obtained as described previously.

Once all of the ACCESS sets have been computed, communication generation is performed without modification [13, 14]. Communication may be generated for a statement that computes a privatized temporary $T$, but it will be limited to only those iterations that each processor will be executing according to the partitioned RIS for the loop nest. For the uses of privatized tempo-

---

[a] ACCESS sets of lhs private references could also be obtained from the union of the ACCESS sets from the lhs of the assignments containing their uses. This requires tracing the flow for each private reference and will only show a benefit when the private variables are used in statements in which the union of their lhs is much smaller than the union of all the lhs within the loop nest.

```
      PROGRAM STENCIL
      INTEGER I, J
      REAL T1, T2
      REAL A(1000,1000), B(1000,1000)
      REAL C(1000,1000), D(1000,1000)
!HPF$ INDEPENDENT
      DO 10 J = 2, 999
!HPF$ INDEPENDENT, NEW(T1, T2)
      DO 10 I = 2, 999
         T1 = (A(I,J) + A(I-1,J-1) + A(I,J-1) +
     &     A(I+1,J-1) + A(I-1,J) + A(I+1,J+1) +
     &     A(I-1,J+1) + A(I,J+1) + A(I+1,J)) / 9.
         T2 = (B(I,J) + B(I-1,J-1) + B(I,J-1) +
     &     B(I+1,J-1) + B(I-1,J) + B(I+1,J+1) +
     &     B(I-1,J+1) + B(I,J+1) + B(I+1,J)) / 9.
         C(I,J) = T1 + T2
         D(I,J) = T1 - T2
   10 CONTINUE
      END
```

Figure 6: Serial Code of STENCIL

raries, the values of the private references will be available for every iteration of the loops over which they have been privatized. By assigning private rhs ACCESS sets in the manner described previously, their set differences with the corresponding lhs will be empty, and therefore no communication will be generated for these references over loops for which they are private.

The overall partitioning technique with support for privatization (summarized in Figure 5), can now be applied to the example in Figure 4. The RIS of the I loop will be computed as the union of the ACCESS sets of FS(I,1,1), FS(I,1,2), FS(I,1,3), and FS(I,1,4). The ACCESS sets of XX, YX and PA in the first three assignments are then collected from the enclosing loops for which they are private. For this example, this is just RIS of the I loop. Communication would be generated for X for the first two statements based on the ACCESS sets of XX, YX, and X. No communication is generated for the last four statements, since all of their rhs references are privatized (or constant).

## 4. EVALUATION

Two benchmarks, STENCIL and EFLUX, are used to evaluate the effectiveness of the different approaches. STENCIL, shown in Figure 6, is a synthetic example involving 9-point stencil computations on several $1000 \times 1000$ arrays. EFLUX is a subroutine from the Perfect Club Benchmark FLO52 [8], with the first dimension of each array increased to 5000 (was originally 194). Its code, listed in Figure 7, also includes additional HPF directives that help the compiler identify privatizable variables. For clarity, initialization loops were excluded from both of these listings. The arrays in STENCIL were 2-D BLOCK distributed, whereas those in EFLUX were distributed by BLOCK along the first dimension. Both of these data distribution schemes were automatically selected by PARADIGM.

The parallel versions of these benchmarks using privatization are generated directly by the compiler from the sequential code plus HPF directives. Figure 8 shows the output of PARADIGM for EFLUX using privatization support. To test a direct application

```
            PROGRAM EFLUX                                    YX        = X(I,1,2) - X(I-1,1,2)
            INTEGER IL, JL, I2, J2                           PA        = P(I,2)   + P(I,1)
            PARAMETER(I2=5000, J2=34, IL=I2-1, JL=J2-1)      FS(I,1,1) = 0.
   C        EULER FLUXES                                     FS(I,1,2) = -YX*PA
            DIMENSION DW(I2,J2,4), FS(I2,J2,4)               FS(I,1,3) =  XX*PA
            DIMENSION W(I2,J2,4), P(I2,J2), X(I2,J2,2)       FS(I,1,4) = 0.
   !HPF$ INDEPENDENT                                    25 CONTINUE
            DO 10 J = 2, JL                            !HPF$ INDEPENDENT
   !HPF$ INDEPENDENT, NEW(XY, YY, PA, QSP, QSM)              DO 30 J = 2, JL
            DO 10 I = 1, IL                            !HPF$ INDEPENDENT, NEW(XX, YX, PA, QSP, QSM)
            XY        = X(I,J,1) - X(I,J-1,1)                DO 30 I = 2, IL
            YY        = X(I,J,2) - X(I,J-1,2)                XX        = X(I,J,1)  -X(I-1,J,1)
            PA        = P(I+1,J) + P(I,J)                    YX        = X(I,J,2)  -X(I-1,J,2)
            QSP       = (YY*W(I+1,J,2)                       PA        = P(I,J+1)  +P(I,J)
          &             - XY*W(I+1,J,3))/W(I+1,J,1)          QSP       = (XX*W(I,J+1,3)
            QSM       = (YY*W(I,J,2) - XY*W(I,J,3))/W(I,J,1) &             - YX*W(I,J+1,2))/W(I,J+1,1)
            FS(I,J,1) = QSP*W(I+1,J,1) + QSM*W(I,J,1)        QSM       = (XX*W(I,J,3) - YX*W(I,J,2))/W(I,J,1)
            FS(I,J,2) = QSP*W(I+1,J,2) + QSM*W(I,J,2) + YY*PA FS(I,J,1) = QSP*W(I,J+1,1) + QSM*W(I,J,1)
            FS(I,J,3) = QSP*W(I+1,J,3) + QSM*W(I,J,3) - XY*PA FS(I,J,2) = QSP*W(I,J+1,2) + QSM*W(I,J,2) - YX*PA
            FS(I,J,4) = QSP*(W(I+1,J,4) + P(I+1,J))          FS(I,J,3) = QSP*W(I,J+1,3) + QSM*W(I,J,3) + XX*PA
          &             + QSM*(W(I,J,4) + P(I,J))            FS(I,J,4) = QSP*(W(I,J+1,4) + P(I,J+1))
      10 CONTINUE                                         &             + QSM*(W(I,J,4)  +P(I,J))
            DO 20 N = 1, 4                             30 CONTINUE
            DO 20 J = 2, JL                                  DO 40 N = 1, 4
            DO 20 I = 2, IL                                  DO 40 J = 2, JL
            DW(I,J,N) = FS(I,J,N) - FS(I-1,J,N)              DO 40 I = 2, IL
      20 CONTINUE                                           DW(I,J,N) = DW(I,J,N) + FS(I,J,N) - FS(I,J-1,N)
   !HPF$ INDEPENDENT, NEW(XX, YX, PA)                    40 CONTINUE
            DO 25 I = 2, IL                                  END
            XX        = X(I,1,1) - X(I-1,1,1)
```

Figure 7: EFLUX Taken from the Perfect Club Benchmark FLO52 [8] Augmented with HPF Directives

---

of the owner-computes rule without privatization, the HPF NEW() clauses are removed before compiling with PARADIGM. Without these clauses, previously privatized variables are treated as regular scalars that are replicated on all processors. For scalar expansion and forward substitution, the corresponding code transformations were first performed manually to the sequential code, and were then compiled by PARADIGM to obtain the parallel version.

For timing purposes, both benchmarks were iterated 100 times on an Intel Paragon for each approach. Table 2 shows EFLUX's execution times and speedups, for up to 16 processors, for the four approaches. Similarly, Table 3 shows the results for STENCIL. Notice that the serial times for privatization and the direct application of the owner-computes rule are the same, since they do not restructure the original sequential program as do scalar expansion and forward substitution. This sequential time is used as the baseline to compute speedup for all four approaches.

As expected, a direct application of the owner-computes rule does not provide any significant speedup regardless of the number of processors involved, because loops containing private variables are not partitioned. For EFLUX, only two small loop nests (20 and 40) are parallelizable under this approach, while none of the loops in STENCIL are parallelizable. The failure to partition such loops leads to redundant computations as well as increased network traffic to replicate arrays on all processors. In contrast, privatization shows the best results, especially in STENCIL, with near-ideal speedups.

Although scalar expansion comes close in terms of speedup, it has the disadvantage of using significantly more memory than the other three approaches. Table 4 lists the memory usage of uniprocessor runs, and shows that scalar expansion requires 47% more memory in EFLUX and 50% more in STENCIL. This not only

limits the problem size allowed, but also can give rise to adverse cache effects due to a larger working set.

Forward substitution performed two to three times slower than privatization because the expressions after substitution resulted in a substantially increased operation count, and the increased complexity of these expressions made it difficult for the sequential compiler to perform any significant common subexpression elimination.

## 5. RELATED WORK

Both scalar [5] and array [6, 7] privatization techniques have been the focus of much research over the past several years. As most of these techniques have been used in relation to shared-memory multiprocessors to enable parallelization, not much work has been done to also allow distributed-memory compilation to benefit from these efforts .

Privatization was not supported in either the Fortran D [12] or Vienna Fortran [16] but has since been added to the HPF language definition [9]. Whenever situations arose that could have been handled by privatization, techniques such as global forward substitution [17] were commonly applied instead.

More recently, a prototype HPF compiler being developed as part of the SP2 project [18] has addressed this issue in a different manner. In this project, scalars are assumed to be replicated by default, but for each definition of the scalar that can be privatized, decision to use the privatization are determined in a separate pass by examining different alignments for each use of the private variable. Privatization is used if there is a lower estimated cost resulting from communication being moved outside of the loop. As mentioned earlier in Section 3, this requires tracing the flow for

```
      PROGRAM eflux
      include 'fnx.h'
      CHARACTER m$buf(680)
      INTEGER my$proc, m$numproc, m$status
      INTEGER my$pid, my$p(2), m$num(2), m$numdim
      INTEGER m$to(-1:1,-1:1)
      INTEGER m$bx1, m$bp1, m$bw1, m$bfs1, m$bdw1
      INTEGER f$pack2, f$unpack2, f$pack3, f$unpack3
      INTEGER m$inc, m$off
      INTEGER i1, j1, i2, j2
      PARAMETER(i2 = 5000, j2 = 34, i1 = 4999, j1 = 33)
      REAL dw(313,34,4), fs(0:313,34,4), w(314,34,4)
      REAL p(314,34), x(0:313,34,2)
      INTEGER j, i

      my$proc = mynode()
      my$pid = mypid()
      m$numproc = numnodes()
      CALL gsync()
c     *** Minimum mesh configuration
      m$numdim = 2
      m$num(1) = 16
      m$num(2) = 1
c     *** Reconfigure for available processors
      CALL m$gridinit(m$numdim, m$num, m$numproc)

      my$p(1) = mod(my$proc,m$num(1))
      my$p(2) = my$proc / m$num(1)
      m$to( -1,0) = m$num(1) * my$p(2) + my$p(1) - 1
      m$to(1,0) = m$num(1) * my$p(2) + my$p(1) + 1

      m$bdw1 = ceil(float(5000) / m$num(1))
      m$bfs1 = ceil(float(5000) / m$num(1))
      m$bw1 = ceil(float(5000) / m$num(1))
      m$bp1 = ceil(float(5000) / m$num(1))
      m$bx1 = ceil(float(5000) / m$num(1))
!HPF$ INDEPENDENT
      IF (my$p(1) .GE. 1) THEN
        m$off = 1
        m$inc = f$pack3(w,4,1,314,1,34,1,4,1,1,1,1,
     1  34,1,1,4,1,m$buf)
        m$off = m$off + m$inc
        m$inc = f$pack2(p,4,1,314,1,34,1,1,1,1,34,1,
     1  m$buf(m$off))
        m$off = m$off + m$inc
        CALL csend(0,m$buf,m$off - 1,m$to( -1,0),my$pid)
      END IF
      IF (my$p(1) .LE. (m$num(1) - 2)) THEN
        CALL crecv(0,m$buf,680)
        m$off = 1
        m$inc = f$unpack3(w,4,1,314,1,34,1,4,m$bw1
     1  + 1,m$bfs1 + 1,1,1,34,1,1,4,1,m$buf)
        m$off = m$off + m$inc
        m$inc = f$unpack2(p,4,1,314,1,34,m$bp1
     1  + 1,m$bfs1 + 1,1,1,34,1,m$buf(m$off))
        m$off = m$off + m$inc
      END IF
      DO 10 j = 2,33
!HPF$ INDEPENDENT, NEW (xy, yy, pa, qsp, qsm)
      DO 10 i = 1,MIN(-m$bfs1 * my$p(1) + 4999,m$bfs1)
        xy = x(i,j,1) - x(i,j - 1,1)
        yy = x(i,j,2) - x(i,j - 1,2)
        pa = p(i + 1,j) + p(i,j)
        qsp = (yy * w(i + 1,j,2) - xy * w(i + 1,j,3))
     1  / w(i + 1,j,1)
        qsm = (yy * w(i,j,2) - xy * w(i,j,3)) / w(i,j,1)
        fs(i,j,1) = qsp * w(i + 1,j,1) + qsm * w(i,j,1)
        fs(i,j,2) = qsp * w(i + 1,j,2) + qsm * w(i,j,2)
     1  + yy * pa
        fs(i,j,3) = qsp * w(i + 1,j,3) + qsm * w(i,j,3)
     1  - xy * pa
        fs(i,j,4) = qsp * (w(i + 1,j,4) + p(i + 1,j))
     1  + qsm * (w(i,j,4) + p(i,j))
10    CONTINUE
```

```
      IF (my$p(1) .LE. (m$num(1) - 2)) THEN
        m$inc = f$pack3(fs,4,0,313,1,34,1,4,m$bdw1,
     1  m$bfs1,1,1,34,1,1,4,1,m$buf)
        CALL csend(1,m$buf,m$inc,m$to(1,0),my$pid)
      END IF
      IF (my$p(1) .GE. 1) THEN
        CALL crecv(1,m$buf,544)
        m$inc = f$unpack3(fs,4,0,313,1,34,1,4,0,0,
     1  1,1,34,1,1,4,1,m$buf)
      END IF
      DO 20 n = 1,4
        DO 20 j = 2,33
          DO 20 i = MAX(-m$bdw1 * my$p(1) + 2,1),
     1    MIN(-m$bdw1 * my$p(1) + 4999,m$bdw1)
            dw(i,j,n) = fs(i,j,n) - fs(i - 1,j,n)
20    CONTINUE
!HPF$ INDEPENDENT, NEW (xx, yx, pa)
      IF (my$p(1) .LE. (m$num(1) - 2)) THEN
        m$inc = f$pack3(x,4,0,313,1,34,1,2,m$bfs1,
     1  m$bx1,1,1,34,1,1,2,1,m$buf)
        CALL csend(2,m$buf,m$inc,m$to(1,0),my$pid)
      END IF
      IF (my$p(1) .GE. 1) THEN
        CALL crecv(2,m$buf,272)
        m$inc = f$unpack3(x,4,0,313,1,34,1,2,0,0,
     1  1,1,34,1,1,2,1,m$buf)
      END IF
      DO 25 i = MAX(-m$bfs1 * my$p(1) + 2,1),
     1 MIN(-m$bfs1 * my$p(1) + 4999,m$bfs1)
        xx = x(i,1,1) - x(i - 1,1,1)
        yx = x(i,1,2) - x(i - 1,1,2)
        pa = p(i,2) + p(i,1)
        fs(i,1,1) = 0.
        fs(i,1,2) =  -yx * pa
        fs(i,1,3) = xx * pa
        fs(i,1,4) = 0.
25    CONTINUE
!HPF$ INDEPENDENT
      IF (my$p(1) .LE. (m$num(1) - 2)) THEN
        m$inc = f$pack3(x,4,0,313,1,34,1,2,m$bfs1,
     1  m$bx1,1,1,34,1,1,2,1,m$buf)
        CALL csend(3,m$buf,m$inc,m$to(1,0),my$pid)
      END IF
      IF (my$p(1) .GE. 1) THEN
        CALL crecv(3,m$buf,272)
        m$inc = f$unpack3(x,4,0,313,1,34,1,2,0,0,
     1  1,1,34,1,1,2,1,m$buf)
      END IF
      DO 30 j = 2,33
!HPF$ INDEPENDENT, NEW (xx, yx, pa, pa, qsp, qsm)
      DO 30 i = MAX(-m$bfs1 * my$p(1) + 2,1),
     1  MIN(-m$bfs1 * my$p(1) + 4999,m$bfs1)
        xx = x(i,j,1) - x(i - 1,j,1)
        yx = x(i,j,2) - x(i - 1,j,2)
        pa = p(i,j + 1) + p(i,j)
        qsp = (xx * w(i,j + 1,3) - yx * w(i,j + 1,2))
     1  / w(i,j + 1,1)
        qsm = (xx * w(i,j,3) - yx * w(i,j,2)) / w(i,j,1)
        fs(i,j,1) = qsp * w(i,j + 1,1) + qsm * w(i,j,1)
        fs(i,j,2) = qsp * w(i,j + 1,2) + qsm * w(i,j,2)
     1  - yx * pa
        fs(i,j,3) = qsp * w(i,j + 1,3) + qsm * w(i,j,3)
     1  + xx * pa
        fs(i,j,4) = qsp * (w(i,j + 1,4) + p(i,j + 1))
     1  + qsm * (w(i,j,4) + p(i,j))
30    CONTINUE
      DO 40 n = 1,4
        DO 40 j = 2,33
          DO 40 i = MAX(-m$bdw1 * my$p(1) + 2,1),
     1    MIN(-m$bdw1 * my$p(1) + 4999,m$bdw1)
            dw(i,j,n) = dw(i,j,n) + fs(i,j,n)
     1    - fs(i,j - 1,n)
40    CONTINUE
      END
```

Figure 8: EFLUX Compiled Using Privatization (with a Minimum 16 × 1 Processor Configuration)

Table 2: Performance of EFLUX (100 Iterations)

| Approach | Number of Processors | | | | |
|---|---|---|---|---|---|
| | 1 | 2 | 4 | 8 | 16 |
| | Time (sec.) | | | | |
| Direct partitioning | 236 | 243 | 211 | 200 | 194 |
| Forward substitution | 626 | 315 | 165 | 84 | 45 |
| Scalar expansion | 305 | 162 | 90 | 48 | 28 |
| Privatization | 236 | 116 | 65 | 34 | 24 |
| | Speedup | | | | |
| Direct partitioning | 1.00 | 0.97 | 1.12 | 1.18 | 1.22 |
| Forward substitution | 0.38 | 0.75 | 1.43 | 2.80 | 5.19 |
| Scalar expansion | 0.77 | 1.46 | 2.62 | 4.93 | 8.51 |
| Privatization | 1.00 | 2.03 | 3.65 | 6.83 | 9.84 |

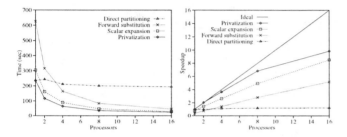

Table 3: Performance of STENCIL (100 Iterations)

| Approach | Number of Processors | | | | |
|---|---|---|---|---|---|
| | 1 | 2 | 4 | 8 | 16 |
| | Time (sec.) | | | | |
| Direct partitioning | 1010 | 1086 | 1070 | 1063 | 1067 |
| Forward substitution | 1832 | 913 | 469 | 229 | 116 |
| Scalar expansion | 1318 | 534 | 274 | 152 | 79 |
| Privatization | 1010 | 501 | 246 | 130 | 69 |
| | Speedup | | | | |
| Direct partitioning | 1.00 | 0.93 | 0.94 | 0.95 | 0.95 |
| Forward substitution | 0.55 | 1.11 | 2.15 | 4.40 | 8.70 |
| Scalar expansion | 0.77 | 1.89 | 3.68 | 6.64 | 12.83 |
| Privatization | 1.00 | 2.01 | 4.11 | 7.73 | 14.70 |

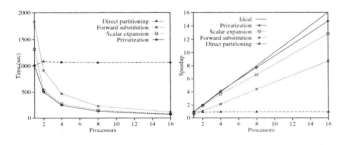

Table 4: Memory Usage

| Approach | Application | |
|---|---|---|
| | EFLUX | STENCIL |
| Scalar expansion | 14.2 MB | 22.9 MB |
| All others | 9.7 MB | 15.3 MB |

each private reference and will only show a benefit when the private variables are used in statements in which the union of their *lhs* is much smaller than the union of all of the *lhs* within the loop nest. In our compiler, privatization is always used when provided since we assume that it is always beneficial.

Currently, commercial HPF compilers are available from Applied Parallel Research (APR), Digital Equipment Corporation (DEC), and The Portland Group (PGI), among others. APR's xHPF [19] has its own DO PAR directive instead of the standard INDEPENDENT directive. It was not clear from the documentation whether it supports private variables and, if so, how they are specified. On the other hand, HPF compilers from DEC [?] and PGI [21] do support the INDEPENDENT directive, but they do not elaborate on how they handle private variables.

## 6. CONCLUSIONS

In this paper, we examined several approaches to compile loops that use temporary variables to store intermediate data, presented a uniform approach for handling privatized variables during loop partitioning and communication generation for distributed-memory multicomputers, and experimentally obtained performance results for the different approaches for two benchmarks. For these benchmarks, the results have shown that:

- A direct application of the owner-computes rule results in little or no performance improvements when using privatized variables.

- Forward substitution provides modest speedups with no increase in memory requirements.

- Scalar expansion yields good speedups at the expense of substantial memory overhead.

- Privatization exhibits the best speedups, with no increase in memory usage, and does not require code restructuring.

As these privatization techniques are based only on how the ACCESS sets are assigned to the private references, they will also apply to CYCLIC and BLOCK-CYCLIC distributions [13].

## REFERENCES

[1] D. Padua and M. Wolfe, "Advanced Compiler Optimizations for Supercomputers," *Communications of the ACM*, vol. 29, pp. 1184–1201, Dec. 1986.

[2] M. J. Wolfe, *Optimizing Supercompilers for Supercomputers*. PhD thesis, Center for Supercomputing Research and Development, University of Illinois, Urbana, IL, Oct. 1982. CSRD-329.

[3] H. Zima and B. Chapman, *Supercompilers for Parallel and Vector Computers*, pp. 266–320. New York: ACM Press, 1990.

[4] M. Burke, R. Cytron, J. Ferrante, and W. Hsieh, "Automatic Generation of Nested, Fork-Join Parallelism," *The Journal of Supercomputing*, vol. 3, pp. 71–88, July 1989.

[5] D. E. Maydan, S. P. Amarasinghe, and M. S. Lam, "Array Data Flow Analysis and its Use in Array Privatization," in *Proceedings of the 20th ACM SIGPLAN Symposium on Principles of Programming Languages*, (Charleston, SC), pp. 2–15, Jan. 1993.

[6] P. Tu and D. Padua, "Automatic Array Privatization," in *Proceedings of the Sixth Workshop on Languages and Compilers for Parallel Computing*, vol. 768 of *Lecture Notes in Computer Science*, (Portland, OR), pp. 500–521, Springer-Verlag, Aug. 1993.

[7] P. Banerjee, J. A. Chandy, M. Gupta, E. W. Hodges IV, J. G. Holm, A. Lain, D. J. Palermo, S. Ramaswamy, and E. Su, "The PARADIGM Compiler for Distributed-Memory Multicomputers," *IEEE Computer*, vol. 28, pp. 37–47, Oct. 1995.

[8] Perfect Club, "The Perfect Club Benchmarks: Effective Performance Evaluation of Supercomputers," *The International Journal of Supercomputing Applications*, vol. 3, pp. 5–40, Fall 1989.

[9] C. Koelbel, D. Loveman, R. Schreiber, G. Steele Jr., and M. Zosel, *The High Performance Fortran Handbook*. Cambridge, MA: The MIT Press, 1994.

[10] J. Hoeflinger, "Cedar Fortran Programmer's Handbook," Tech. Rep. CSRD-1157, Center for Supercomputing Research and Development, University of Illinois, Urbana, IL, Oct. 1991.

[11] M. Gupta and P. Banerjee, "Demonstration of Automatic Data Partitioning Techniques for Parallelizing Compilers on Multicomputers," *IEEE Transactions on Parallel and Distributed Systems*, vol. 3, pp. 179–193, Mar. 1992.

[12] S. Hiranandani, K. Kennedy, and C. Tseng, "Compiling Fortran D for MIMD Distributed Memory Machines," *Communications of the ACM*, vol. 35, pp. 66–80, Aug. 1992.

[13] E. Su, A. Lain, S. Ramaswamy, D. J. Palermo, E. W. Hodges IV, and P. Banerjee, "Advanced Compilation Techniques in the PARADIGM compiler for Distributed Memory Multicomputers," in *Proceedings of the 9th ACM International Conference on Supercomputing*, (Barcelona, Spain), pp. 424–433, July 1995.

[14] E. Su, D. J. Palermo, and P. Banerjee, "Processor Tagged Descriptors: A Data Structure for Compiling for Distributed-Memory Multicomputers," in *Proceedings of the 1994 International Conference on Parallel Architectures and Compilation Techniques*, (Montréal, Canada), pp. 123–132, Aug. 1994.

[15] E. W. Hodges IV, "High Performance Fortran Support for the PARADIGM Compiler," Master's thesis, Department of Electrical and Computer Engineering, University of Illinois, Urbana, IL, Oct. 1995.

[16] B. Chapman, P. Mehrotra, and H. Zima, "Programming in Vienna Fortran," *Scientific Programming*, vol. 1, pp. 31–50, Aug. 1992.

[17] T. Fahringer, *Automatic Performance Prediction for Parallel Programs on Massively Parallel Computers*. PhD thesis, University of Vienna, Vienna, Austria, Sept. 1993. TR93-3.

[18] M. Gupta, S. Midkiff, E. Schonberg, V. Seshadri, D. Shields, K.-Y. Wang, W.-M. Ching, and T. Ngo, "An HPF Compiler for the IBM SP2," in *Proceedings of Supercomputing '95*, (San Diego, CA), Dec. 1995.

[19] Applied Parallel Research, Inc., Placerville, CA, *XHPF User's Guide, version 2.0*, 1995.

[20] D. B. Loveman, "The DEC High Performance Fortran 90 Compiler Front End," in *Frontiers '95: The Fifth Symposium on the Frontiers of Massively Parallel Computation*, (McLean, VA), pp. 46–53, 1995.

[21] The Portland Group, Inc., Wilsonville, OR, *PGHPF User's Guide*, 1995.

# ON OPTIMAL SIZE AND SHAPE OF SUPERNODE TRANSFORMATIONS *

Edin Hodžić [†]
HaL Computer Systems
1315 Dell Ave.
Campbell, CA 95008
dino@hal.com

Weijia Shang
Department of Computer Eng.
Santa Clara University
Santa Clara, CA 95053
wshang@scus19.scu.edu

Abstract — *Supernode transformation has been proposed to reduce the communication startup cost by grouping a number of iterations in a perfectly nested loop with uniform dependencies as a supernode which is assigned to a processor as a single unit. A supernode transformation is specified by $n$ families of hyperplanes which slice the iteration space into parallelepiped supernodes, the grain size of a supernode, and the relative side lengths of the parallelepiped supernode. The total running time is affected by the three factors. In this paper, how to find an optimal grain size and an optimal relative side length vector, with the goal of minimizing total running time, is addressed. Our results show that the optimal grain size is proportional to the ratio of the communication startup cost and the computation speed of the processor, and that the optimal supernode shape is similar to the shape of the index space, in the case of hypercube index spaces and supernodes.*

## 1  INTRODUCTION

Supernode partitioning is a transformation technique that groups a number of iterations in a nested loop in order to reduce the communication startup cost. This paper addresses the problem of finding the optimal grain size and shape of the supernode transformation so that the total running time, which is the sum of communication time and computation time, is minimized.

Algorithms considered in this paper are nested loops with uniform dependences [14]. Such an al-

gorithm can be described by its iteration index space consisting of all iteration index vectors of the loop nest and a dependence matrix consisting of all uniform dependence vectors as its columns.

A problem in distributed memory parallel systems is the communication startup cost, the time it takes a message to reach transmission media from the moment of its initiation. The communication startup cost is usually orders of magnitude greater than the time to transmit a message across transmission media or to compute data in a message. Supernode transformation has been proposed [3, 4, 5, 10, 11, 12, 17] to reduce the number of messages sent between processors by grouping multiple iterations into supernodes. [1] After the supernode transformation, several iterations are grouped into one supernode and this supernode is assigned to a processor as a unit for execution. The data of the iterations in the same supernode, which need to be sent to another processor, are grouped as a single message so that the number of communication startups is reduced from the number of iterations in a supernode to one. A supernode transformation is characterized by the hyperplanes which slice the iteration index space into parallelepiped supernodes, the grain size of the supernode and the relative lengths of the sides of a supernode. All the three factors mentioned above affect the total running time. A larger grain size reduces communication startup cost more, but may delay the computation of other processors waiting for the message. Also, a square supernode may not be as good as a rectangular supernode with the same grain size. In this paper, how to find an optimal grain size and an optimal relative side length

*This research was supported in part by the National Science Foundation under Grant CCR-9502889 and by the Clare Boothe Luce Assistant Professorship from Henry Luce Foundation.

[†]Supported by HaL Computer Systems, 1315 Dell Ave., Campbell, CA 95008.

[1]Supernode transformation is conceptually similar to LSGP (Locally Sequential Globally Parallel) partitioning [3, 7, 10, 12], where a group of iterations is assigned to a single processing element for sequential execution while different processing elements execute respectively assigned computations in parallel.

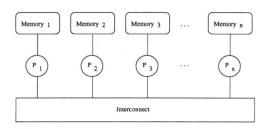

Figure 1: Distributed memory parallel computer model

vector, or an optimal shape of a supernode is addressed.

The approach in this paper is as follows. Unlike other related work where a supernode transformation is specified by $n$ side lengths of the parallelepiped supernode, and the $n$ partitioning hyperplanes, a supernode transformation in this paper is specified by a grain size $g$ of a supernode, the relative side length vector $\mathbf{R}$ which describes the side lengths of a supernode relative to the supernode size, and $n$ partitioning hyperplanes described by matrix $H$ which contains the normal vectors of the $n$ independent hyperplanes as rows. This allows us, for given partitioning hyperplanes, to find the optimal grain size and the optimal shape separately because they are independent in our formulation. Our results show that the optimal grain size is proportional to the ratio of the communication startup cost and the computation speed of the processor and the optimal supernode shape is proportional to the iteration index space, for algorithms with hypercube index sets and supernodes. The problem of choosing partitioning hyperplanes which enable a shortest total running time is still open.

The rest of the paper is organized as follows. Section 2 presents necessary definitions, assumptions, terminology, and models. Section 3 discusses how to find the optimal grain size of a supernode transformation. Section 4 shows how to find an optimal relative side length vector. Section 5 briefly describes related work and the contribution of this work compared to previous work. Section 6 concludes this paper.

## 2   BASIC DEFINITIONS, MODELS AND ASSUMPTIONS

Figure 1 shows a model of distributed memory parallel computer. Each processor has access to its local memory and is capable of communicating with other processors by passing messages. The cost of sending a message can be modeled by $t_s + bt_t$, where $t_s$ is the startup time, $b$ is the amount of data to be transmitted, and $t_t$ is the transmission rate, i.e., the transmission time per unit data. In most distributed memory parallel systems, startup cost, $t_s$, is usually orders of magnitude greater than the transmission time, $bt_t$. Transmission time can also be overlapped with other computations (or another message startup). For these two reasons, in this paper we assume that the cost of sending a message consists of startup cost only. The transmission time is ignored. The computation speed of a single processor in a distributed memory parallel computer is characterized by the time it takes to compute a single iteration of a nested loop. This parameter is denoted by $t_c$.

We consider algorithms which consist of a single nested loop with uniform dependences [14]. Such algorithms can be described by a pair $(J, D)$, where $J$ is an iteration index space and $D$ is an $n \times m$ dependence matrix. Each column in the dependence matrix represents a dependence vector. We assume that $m \geq n$, matrix $D$ has full rank (which is equal to the number of loop nests $n$), and the determinant of the Smith normal form of $D$ is equal to one. As discussed in [15], if the above assumptions are not satisfied, then the iteration index space $J$ contains independent components and can be partitioned into several independent sub-algorithms with the above assumptions satisfied. Furthermore, we assume that only true loop carried dependences [16] are included in matrix $D$ since only those dependences cause communication, while other types of dependences can be eliminated using known transformation techniques (e.g. variable renaming).

Supernode partitioning [3, 5, 10, 12, 17] is a loop transformation technique that groups multiple iterations (nodes) into a *supernode* (super iteration). A supernode is assigned as a single unit to a processor for execution. As shown in the next example, if we group iterations into supernodes, we incur fewer startup costs because fewer messages are transmitted. Hence the communication cost and therefore, the total running time can be reduced. The iteration space is sliced by $n$ independent families of parallel equidistant hyperplanes. These hyperplanes partition the iteration index space into $n$-dimensional parallelepiped supernodes. Hyperplanes can be defined by the normal vectors orthogonal to each of the hyperplanes. The $n \times n$ matrix containing the $n$ normal vectors as rows is denoted by $H$ which is of full rank because these hyperplanes are independent. Supernodes can be defined by matrix $H$ and distances between adjacent parallel hyperplanes. Let $l_i$ be the distance of two adjacent hyperplanes with normal vector $\mathbf{H_i}$ and *the supernode side length vector* $\mathbf{L} = (l_1, l_2, ..., l_n)$. The *grain size, or supernode volume*, denoted by $g$, is defined as the number of iterations in one supernode. The supernode volume and the length $l_i$ are related as follows:

$$g = k \prod_{i=1}^{n} l_i$$

where $0 < k \leq 1$ depends on the angles between hyperplanes. For example, when supernodes are hypercubes, $k = 1$. We also define the *supernode relative side length vector*, $\mathbf{R} = (r_1, r_2, ..., r_n)$, where $r_i$ is given as

$$r_i = l_i \sqrt[n]{\frac{k}{g}}$$

and clearly

$$\prod_{i=1}^{n} r_i = 1.$$

Vector $\mathbf{R}$ describes side lengths of a supernode relative to the supernode size. For example, if $n = 2$, $\mathbf{R} = (1, 1)$, then the supernode is a 2-dimensional equal side diamond. A supernode transformation is completely specified by $H$, $\mathbf{R}$, and $g$, and denoted by $(H, \mathbf{R}, g)$.

After the supernode transformation, we obtain a new dependence structure $(J_s, D_s)$ where each node in the *supernode index space* $J_s$ is a supernode. The *supernode dependence matrix* $D_s$ in general is different from $D$. As discussed in [5], partitioning hyperplanes defined by matrix $H$ have to satisfy $HD \geq 0$, i.e., each entry in the product matrix is greater than or equal to zero, in order to have $(J_s, D_s)$ computable. That is, all dependence vectors in $D_s$ are contained in a convex cone. Matrix $E = H^{-1}$ is a matrix of extreme vectors of dependence vectors. In other words, each dependence vector $\mathbf{d_i}$ in $D_s$ can be expressed as a non-negative linear combination of columns in $E$. Also, the $n$ columns of $E$ are the $n$ vectors collinear with the $n$ sides of the parallelepiped supernode.

For an algorithm $A = (J, D)$, a linear schedule [14] is defined as $\sigma_\pi : J \to N$, such that

$$\sigma_\pi(\mathbf{j}) = \left\lfloor \frac{\pi \mathbf{j} + f}{disp(\pi)} \right\rfloor, \forall \mathbf{j} \in J,$$

where $\pi \in Z^{1 \times n}$, $disp(\pi) = \min\{\pi \mathbf{d_i} : \mathbf{d_i} \in D\} > 0$, $\gcd(\pi_1, ..., \pi_n) = 1$, and $f = -\min\{\pi \mathbf{j} : \mathbf{j} \in J\}$. A linear schedule assigns each node $\mathbf{j} \in J$ an execution step with dependence relations respected. The length of a linear schedule is defined as

$$P(\pi) = \max\{\sigma_\pi(\mathbf{j}) : \mathbf{j} \in J\} - \min\{\sigma_\pi(\mathbf{j}) : \mathbf{j} \in J\}$$
$$= \frac{\max\{\pi(\mathbf{j_1} - \mathbf{j_2}) : \mathbf{j_1}, \mathbf{j_2} \in J\}}{\min\{\pi \mathbf{d_i} : \mathbf{d_i} \in D\}}.$$

Note that $\mathbf{j_1}$ and $\mathbf{j_2}$ for which $\sigma_\pi(\mathbf{j_1}) - \sigma_\pi(\mathbf{j_2})$ is maximum are always extreme points in the iteration index space.

The execution of an algorithm $(J, D)$ is as follows. We apply a supernode transformation with $(H, \mathbf{R}, g)$ and obtain $(J_s, D_s)$. An optimal linear schedule $\pi$ can be found for $(J_s, D_s)$. The processing based on the linear schedule alternates between computation phases and communication phases. That is, in step $i$, we assign supernodes $\mathbf{j} \in J_s$ with the same $\sigma_\pi(\mathbf{j}) = i$ to available processors. After each processor finishes all the computations of a supernode, processors communicate to pass messages. After the communication is done, we go to step $i + 1$. Hence, the total running time of an algorithm depends on all of the following: $(J, D)$, $H$, $g$, $\mathbf{R}$, $\pi$, $t_c$ and $t_s$. Let $T$ be the total running time. The problem of finding an optimal supernode transformation is an optimization problem of finding parameters $H$, $g$, $\mathbf{R}$, and $\pi$, such that the total running time, $T((J, D), H, g, \mathbf{R}, \pi, t_c, t_s)$ is minimized. This paper addresses the problems of how to find an optimal grain size $g$ and optimal supernode relative length vector $\mathbf{R}$. How to find an optimal linear schedule for $(J_s, D_s)$ can be found in [1, 14]. How to find an optimal $H$ in general remains open, although discussed in [5, 10].

Once the supernode partitioning parameters are chosen, the optimal number of processors in a system can be determined as the maximum number of independent supernodes in a computation phase, which is the maximum number of supernodes to which the linear schedule $\sigma_\pi$ assigns the same value:

$$p = \max\{|X_i| : X_i = \{\mathbf{x} : \mathbf{x} \in J_s,$$
$$\sigma_\pi(\mathbf{x}) = i, i \in N\}\},$$

where $i$ is the constant assigned by the linear schedule $\sigma_\pi$ to all supernodes in the same phase, and $J_s$ is the supernode index space.

Example 2.1 To illustrate the notions introduced above, we show an example of supernode transformation applied to an algorithm and how it affects algorithm's total running time. Let's assume $t_c = 10\mu s$ and $t_s = 300\mu s$. Consider algorithm $(J, D)$ where $J = \{(i, j) : 1 \leq i \leq 100, 1 \leq j \leq 200\}$ and

$$D = \begin{pmatrix} 0 & 1 & 1 \\ 1 & 0 & 1 \end{pmatrix}.$$

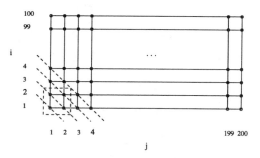

Figure 2: The iteration index space before supernode transformations.

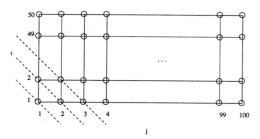

Figure 3: The supernode index space where each supernode is a square containing four iterations.

The algorithm consists of two loops with three dependence vectors: $\begin{pmatrix} 0 \\ 1 \end{pmatrix}$, $\begin{pmatrix} 1 \\ 0 \end{pmatrix}$ and $\begin{pmatrix} 1 \\ 1 \end{pmatrix}$. The optimal linear schedule vector for this algorithm is $\pi = (1, 1)$ [14]. The length of the schedule is $\pi \begin{pmatrix} 100 \\ 200 \end{pmatrix} - \pi \begin{pmatrix} 1 \\ 1 \end{pmatrix} = 298$. Figure 2 shows the iteration index space with linear schedule wave fronts. If a supernode consists of only one iteration, then, in the execution of the algorithm, there are 299 computation phases and 298 communication phases. One computation phase takes $t_c = 10\mu s$, and every communication phase takes $t_s = 300\mu s$. Total running time is: $T_1 = 299t_c + 298t_s = 92.4ms$, with 100 processors. The sequential running time is $T_s = 200 \times 100 \times t_c = 200ms$.

Consider now a supernode transformation applied to the algorithm. Let the hyperplane matrix

$$H = \begin{pmatrix} 1 & 0 \\ 0 & 1 \end{pmatrix}. \qquad (1)$$

Matrix $H$ defines two families of lines parallel to the two axes. For this matrix $H$, constant $k = 1$ because the two lines are orthogonal. Let $g = 4$ and $\mathbf{R} = (1, 1)$. Then the length vector $\mathbf{L} = (2, 2)$

and each supernode is a 2-dimensional square containing four iterations. Figure 2 shows one supernode outlined with a dashed square. The supernode index space and dependence matrix are then $J_s = \{(i, j) : 1 \le i \le 50, 1 \le j \le 100\}$ which is shown in Figure 3 and $D_s = D$. The optimal linear schedule vector for this $(J_s, D_s)$ is $\pi = (1, 1)$ [14] and the schedule length is $\pi \begin{pmatrix} 50 \\ 100 \end{pmatrix} - \pi \begin{pmatrix} 1 \\ 1 \end{pmatrix} = 148$. Figure 3 shows supernode index space with the linear schedule wave fronts. The computations of one supernode take $gt_c = 40\mu s$, and the total running time is $T_2 = 149gt_c + 148t_s = 50.36ms$, with 50 processors. In this simple example speedup between $T_1$ and $T_2$ is close to 2. Note that supernode transformation parameters are chosen arbitrarily and are not optimal. Later, it is shown that the total running time can be improved further by an optimal solution.

## 3 OPTIMAL SUPERNODE SIZE

In this section we derive an expression for the optimal supernode size $g$. The basic idea is to consider the partial derivation of the total running time with respect to the supernode size $g$ since the total running time is a convex function of $g$. An example is used to show how to improve the total running time by using the optimal supernode size.

Consider algorithm $A_s = (J_s, D_s)$, with supernode index space $J_s$ and dependence matrix $D_s$ obtained by applying a supernode transformation $(H, \mathbf{R}, g)$ to algorithm $A = (J, D)$. According to [5], in a valid supernode transformation with hyperplanes $H$, all dependence vectors $\mathbf{d} \in D$ should be contained in the convex cone of the $n$ extreme directions forming the parallelepiped supernode. Hence, if the supernode grain size is reasonably large, and the components of $\mathbf{d} \in D$ are reasonably small, then all dependence vectors $\mathbf{d} \in D$, if originating at the extreme point of the convex cone of the parallelepiped supernode, should be contained inside the parallelepiped supernode. Therefore, it is reasonable to assume in this paper that the components of the dependence matrix $D_s$ are $0, 1$, or $-1$. The following lemma gives sufficient conditions for this assumption to be true:

<u>Lemma 3.1</u> *Components of dependence matrix $D_s$, in the transformed algorithm, $(J_s, D_s)$, take values $0, 1$, or $-1$ if $(H\mathbf{d})_j \le L_j$, $\mathbf{d} \in D$, $1 \le i \le m$, $1 \le j \le n$, where $(H\mathbf{d})_j$ is the $j$-th component of vector $H\mathbf{d}$.*

Proof: Consider dependence vector $\mathbf{d} \in D$. According to [5], $\mathbf{d}$ can be expressed as a nonnegative linear combination of column vectors in $E$, i.e., $\mathbf{d} = E\mathbf{x}$. Hence, the $i$-th entry of $\mathbf{x}$, $x_i$, is the $i$-th coordinate of $\mathbf{d}$ expressed in basis $E$ or the projection of $\mathbf{d}$ on the $i$-th column vector $\mathbf{e_i} \in E$. Because $E^{-1} = H$, we have $\mathbf{x} = H\mathbf{d}$. Thus, if $(H\mathbf{d})_j = x_i \leq L_i$, $i = 1, ..., n$, vector $\mathbf{x}$ originating in one supernode must sink either in the same supernode or in a neighboring supernode which implies that $d_{ij}$, an entry in matrix $D_s$, takes value 0, 1, or -1. $\square$

The linear schedule length, as defined in the previous section, usually corresponds to the number of communication phases in execution of an algorithm. The number of computation phases is one more than the number of communication phases. Supernode transformations often generate incomplete supernodes at the boundary of index space. For example, for the iteration index space in Figure 2, if the $j$ axis is from 1 to 2001 and the same supernode transformation as in Example 2.1 is applied, then the supernodes in the rightmost column contain only two iterations and are incomplete. Thus, the first and/or the last computation phases are often shorter than other computation phases. For this reason, we will assume that the number of computation phases and the number of communication phases are equal, and are equal to the linear schedule length, denoted by $P$.

For algorithm $(J_s, D_s)$, we can find an optimal linear schedule vector $\pi_\mathbf{s}$ by the method in [1, 14]. Let $P_s = length(\pi_s)$. Then, the total running time of algorithm $(J_s, D_s)$ is given by:

$$T_s = P_s(gt_c + ct_s), \qquad (2)$$

where $c$ is the number of messages sent by one processor in one communication phase.

Consider two supernode transformations, $(H, \mathbf{R}, g_1)$ and $(H, \mathbf{R}, g)$, with the same $H$ and $\mathbf{R}$, and different supernode sizes, $g_1$ and $g$. Let $J_{s_1}$ and $J_s$ be the corresponding supernode index spaces. Lemma 3.2 shows how an index space changes as the supernode size changes.

**Lemma 3.2** *Let $J_{s_1} = \{\mathbf{j} : A\mathbf{j} \leq \mathbf{b}\}$ be the supernode index set with $g_1$ and $J_s$ be the supernode index set with $g$. Then*

$$J_s = \left\{ \mathbf{j} : A \sqrt[n]{\frac{g}{g_1}} \mathbf{j} \leq \mathbf{b} \right\}, \qquad (3)$$

*where $n$ is the number of loop nests in the original algorithm.*

Proof: Let $\mathbf{y}$ be a point in the convex hull of the original index set $J$ before the supernode transformation, $\mathbf{y_1}$ be the image of $\mathbf{y}$ in the convex hull of $J_{s_1}$, and $\mathbf{y}'$ be the image of $\mathbf{y}$ in the convex hull of $J_s$. First, we prove that $\mathbf{y}' = \sqrt[n]{\frac{g_1}{g}} \mathbf{y_1}$ as the grain size changes from $g_1$ to $g$. Without loss of generality, we assume $\mathbf{e_i} \in E$, $i = 1, ..., n$, to be of unit length. Let $\mathbf{v}_{i,1} = l_{i,1}\mathbf{e_i}$, $i = 1, ..., n$, where $l_{i,1}$, $i = 1, ..., n$, are side lengths of parallelepiped supernodes with supernode grain size $g_1$. Vector $\mathbf{v}_{i,1}$ is the $i$-th side of the parallelepiped supernode. Because $E$ is of full rank, vectors $\mathbf{v}_{i,1}$, $i = 1, ..., n$ form a base in the $n$ dimensional vector space. Hence, point $\mathbf{y}$ can be represented as a linear combination of vectors $\mathbf{v}_{i,1}$. Let $\mathbf{y} = \sum_1^n a_{i,1} \mathbf{v}_{i,1}$, where $a_{i,1}$ $i = 1, ..., n$, are coordinates of point $\mathbf{y}$ in base $\{\mathbf{v}_{i,1}, i = 1, ..., n\}$. Also $\mathbf{y}$ is a linear combination of vectors $\mathbf{v_i} = l_i \mathbf{e_i}$, where $l_i$, $i = 1, ..., n$, are the side lengths of the parallelepiped supernodes with grain size $g$. Let $\mathbf{y} = \sum_1^n a_i \mathbf{v_i}$, where $a_i$ are coordinates of point $\mathbf{y}$ in base $\{\mathbf{v_i}, i = 1, ..., n\}$. Since $l_i = r_i \sqrt[n]{\frac{g}{k}}$ and $l_{i,1} = r_i \sqrt[n]{\frac{g_1}{k}}$, we have $l_i = r_i \sqrt[n]{\frac{g}{g_1}} \sqrt[n]{\frac{g_1}{k}} = \sqrt[n]{\frac{g}{g_1}} l_{i,1}$. Therefore, it follows that $\mathbf{v_i} = \sqrt[n]{\frac{g}{g_1}} \mathbf{v}_{i,1}$. Hence, we have $\sum_1^n a_i \mathbf{v_i} = \sum_1^n a_{i,1} \mathbf{v}_{i,1} = \sum_1^n a_{i,1} \sqrt[n]{\frac{g_1}{g}} \mathbf{v_i}$, i.e., $a_i = a_{i,1} \sqrt[n]{\frac{g_1}{g}}$, $i = 1, ..., n$. This implies that for a given point $\mathbf{y}$, its coordinate vector $\mathbf{a}$ in base $\{\mathbf{v_i}, i = 1, ..., n\}$, and coordinate vector $\mathbf{a_1}$ in base $\{\mathbf{v_{i,1}}, i = 1, ..., n\}$, are related as $\mathbf{a} = \sqrt[n]{\frac{g_1}{g}} \mathbf{a_1}$. Euclidean coordinates of $\mathbf{y_1}$ in $J_{s_1}$ and $\mathbf{y}'$ in $J_s$ are $\mathbf{y_1} = E a_1$ and $\mathbf{y}' = E a$. Thus, $\mathbf{y}$'s images in $J_s$ and $J_{s_1}$ are related as $\mathbf{y}' = \sqrt[n]{\frac{g_1}{g}} \mathbf{y_1}$, or $\mathbf{y_1} = \sqrt[n]{\frac{g}{g_1}} \mathbf{y}'$. Therefore, the index space $J_{s_1} = \{\mathbf{j} : A\mathbf{j} \leq \mathbf{b}\}$ transforms to (3) as the grain size changes from $g_1$ to $g$ since for each point, $\mathbf{j}$, in convex hull of $J_s$, its image, $\sqrt[n]{\frac{g}{g_1}} \mathbf{j}$, belongs to the convex hull of $J_{s_1}$. $\square$

The dependence matrix does not change as supernode size changes from $g_1$ to $g$. This follows from the assumption that components of dependence vectors in transformed algorithm take values from $\{0, 1, -1\}$ and from the fact that supernode shape defined by $H$ and $\mathbf{R}$ does not change. The following lemma shows that an optimal linear schedule does not change as supernode size $g$ changes.

**Lemma 3.3** *Optimal linear schedule vectors for two supernode transformations $(H, \mathbf{R}, g_1)$ and $(H, \mathbf{R}, g)$, which differ only in supernode size, are identical.*

Proof: An optimal linear schedule of the transformed algorithm $(J_{s_1}, D_s)$ with supernode size $g_1$ is given by a solution to the following linear program [1]:

$$\min_{\pi D_s \geq 1} \left( \max_{\substack{A\mathbf{p} \leq \mathbf{b} \\ A\mathbf{q} \leq \mathbf{b}}} \pi(\mathbf{p} - \mathbf{q}) \right), \qquad (4)$$

where $A$ and $\mathbf{b}$ correspond to constraint matrix and size vector of $J_{s_1}$. As we change supernode size to $g$, index space transforms to (3). Thus the linear program (4) becomes:

$$\min_{\pi D_s \geq 1} \left( \max_{\substack{A \sqrt[n]{\frac{g}{g_1}}\mathbf{p} \leq \mathbf{b} \\ A \sqrt[n]{\frac{g}{g_1}}\mathbf{q} \leq \mathbf{b}}} \pi(\mathbf{p} - \mathbf{q}) \right) \qquad (5)$$

Substituting variables $\mathbf{p}$ and $\mathbf{q}$ in (5) with $\sqrt[n]{\frac{g_1}{g}}\mathbf{p}'$ and $\sqrt[n]{\frac{g_1}{g}}\mathbf{q}'$ respectively, we get a program which has the same solution point as (4) (although different optimal value):

$$\min_{\pi D_s \geq 1} \left( \max_{\substack{A\mathbf{p}' \leq \mathbf{b} \\ A\mathbf{q}' \leq \mathbf{b}}} \sqrt[n]{\frac{g_1}{g}} \pi(\mathbf{p}' - \mathbf{q}') \right).$$

Therefore, optimal linear schedule vector does not change as supernode size changes. □

According to Lemmas 3.1, 3.2 and 3.3, the linear schedule length changes with a factor $\sqrt[n]{\frac{g_1}{g}}$ as the supernode size changes from $g_1$ to $g$, i.e. $P_g = \sqrt[n]{\frac{g_1}{g}} P_{g_1}$. This relation between linear schedule lengths $P_{g_1}$ and $P_g$ for transformations with different supernode sizes is established in the continuous space. The relation is acceptable for large supernode index spaces, however it may not hold for small supernode index spaces because of discrete nature of iteration index spaces. Thus we have to assume here, that the problem size of the algorithm $(J, D)$ is reasonably large.

From the previous discussion, the total running time can be written as

$$\begin{aligned} T(g) &= P_g(gt_c + ct_s) \\ &= \sqrt[n]{\frac{g_1}{g}} P_{g_1}(gt_c + ct_s) \\ &= \sqrt[n]{g_1} P_{g_1}(t_c g^{\frac{n-1}{n}} + ct_s g^{-\frac{1}{n}}). \end{aligned} \qquad (6)$$

In the above expression, $g_1$ and $P_{g_1}$ are constants, and the total running time depends only on supernode size $g$, the number of messages sent by one

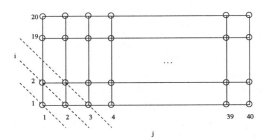

Figure 4: The supernode index space with an optimal supernode size.

processor in a communication phase, $c$, and architectural parameters: the computation cost for a single iteration $t_c$, and the communication startup cost for a single message $t_s$. We are now ready to derive the optimal supernode size.

<u>Theorem 3.4</u>  *For an algorithm $(J, D)$ and supernode transformation with $H$ and $\mathbf{R}$, the optimal supernode size is:*

$$g_o = \frac{ct_s}{(n-1)t_c}. \qquad (7)$$

<u>Proof:</u>  The function $T(g)$ given by (6) is convex and reaches minimum when $T'(g) = 0$. Solving this equation for $g$, we get:

$$\begin{aligned} 0 &= T'(g_o) \\ 0 &= \sqrt[n]{g_1} P_{g_1}(t_c \frac{n-1}{n} g_o^{-\frac{1}{n}} + ct_s \frac{-1}{n} g_o^{-\frac{n+1}{n}}) \\ 0 &= (n-1)t_c g_o^{-\frac{1}{n}} - ct_s g_o^{-\frac{n+1}{n}} \\ 0 &= (n-1)t_c g_o - ct_s \\ g_o &= \frac{ct_s}{(n-1)t_c}. \end{aligned}$$

□

Example 3.1  Consider the algorithm in Example 2.1. The number of nested loops is, $n = 2$. Assuming that all iterations of one column are assigned to the same processor, each processor will send one message to its right neighbor in a single communication phase. Thus, $c = 1$. According to Theorem 3.4, the optimal supernode size is $g_o = \frac{300}{10} = 30$. If the same $H$ given by (1), and relative length vector $\mathbf{R} = (1, 1)$ is used, then the length of each side of the square supernode is $l = 5.48$. Let's consider the closest integer as the value for $\mathbf{L}$, i.e., $\mathbf{L} = (5, 5)$. Then, $g = 25$, and $J_s = \{(i, j) : 1 \leq i \leq 20, 1 \leq j \leq 40\}$. The optimal linear schedule vector for this algorithm is $\pi = (1, 1)$ and the schedule length is $\pi \begin{pmatrix} 20 \\ 40 \end{pmatrix} - \pi \begin{pmatrix} 1 \\ 1 \end{pmatrix} = 58$. Figure 4 shows the supernode index space with the linear schedule wave fronts. The total running time is then $T_3 = 59gt_c + 58t_s = 32.15ms$, with 20 processors. Compared to the supernode transformation in Example 2.1 with $g = 4$, the total running time is improved from $T_2 = 50.36ms$ with 50 processors to $T_3 = 32.15ms$ with only 20 processors. Further improvement in total running time is achieved when an optimal supernode relative side length vector is used, as discussed in the next section.

## 4 OPTIMAL SUPERNODE SHAPE

The shape of supernodes is defined by two supernode transformation parameters: $H$ and $\mathbf{R}$. In this section, for a given $H$ and an optimal grain size $g_o$, how to find an optimal supernode relative length vector $\mathbf{R}$ is addressed. In the first subsection, a special case where index set $J$ and supernodes are hypercubes (the $n$ sides may not be equal) is discussed and an optimal linear schedule vector and optimal $\mathbf{R}$ are derived. In the second subsection, the general case is discussed and the problem of finding an optimal $\mathbf{R}$ is formulated as a nonlinear programming problem.

### 4.1 The Hypercube Index Space Case

In this subsection we consider the special case where index space $J$ is an $n$-dimensional hypercube and the partitioning hyperplane matrix $H = E = I$. That is, both the index space and the supernodes are hypercubes. The following theorem gives an optimal supernode relative length vector $\mathbf{R}$ and an optimal linear schedule vector for this special case. Also, let $\mathbf{1}$ be a vector whose components are all one.

Theorem 4.1   Consider algorithm $(J, D)$ where $J = \{j : 0 \leq j_i \leq N_i, 1 \leq i \leq n\}$, supernode transformation $(H, \mathbf{R}, g)$ and transformed algorithm $(J_s, D_s)$. If $H = E = I$, the identity matrix, and $I \subseteq D_s$, then an optimal linear schedule vector, $\pi$, and supernode relative length vector, $\mathbf{R} = (r_1, r_2, \ldots, r_n)$, are given by:

$$\pi = \mathbf{1} \tag{8}$$

$$r_i = \frac{N_i}{\sqrt[n]{\prod_{j=1}^n N_j}} \tag{9}$$

or

$$\frac{r_1}{N_1} = \frac{r_2}{N_2} = \ldots = \frac{r_n}{N_n} = \frac{1}{\sqrt[n]{\prod_{j=1}^n N_j}}. \tag{10}$$

Proof: The schedule length of the linear schedule with linear schedule vector $\pi$ and supernode side lengths $l_i$ is:

$$P(\pi) = \frac{\pi \begin{pmatrix} N_1/l_1 \\ N_2/l_2 \\ \ldots \\ N_n/l_n \end{pmatrix}}{\min_{\mathbf{d_i} \in D_s} \{\pi \mathbf{d_i}\}} = \frac{\sqrt[n]{\frac{k}{g}} \pi \begin{pmatrix} N_1/r_1 \\ N_2/r_2 \\ \ldots \\ N_n/r_n \end{pmatrix}}{\min_{\mathbf{d_i} \in D_s} \{\pi \mathbf{d_i}\}}$$

$$= \frac{\sqrt[n]{\frac{k}{g}} \pi \begin{pmatrix} N_1/r_1 \\ N_2/r_2 \\ \ldots \\ N_n \prod_{j=1}^{n-1} r_j \end{pmatrix}}{\min_{\mathbf{d_i} \in D_s} \{\pi \mathbf{d_i}\}}. \tag{11}$$

For any $i \in \{1, \ldots, n-1\}$, we can obtain an expression for optimal $r_i$ by bringing $P(\pi)$ in (11) to (2) and solving equation $\frac{\partial T}{\partial r_i} = 0$:

$$0 = \frac{\partial T}{\partial r_i} = \frac{\partial P}{\partial r_i}(gt_c + ct_s)$$

$$0 = \sqrt[n]{\frac{k}{g}} \left( \frac{-N_i \pi_i}{r_i^2} + \frac{N_n \pi_n \prod_{j=1}^{n-1} r_j}{r_i} \right)(gt_c + ct_s)$$

$$\frac{N_i \pi_i}{r_i^2} = \frac{N_n \pi_n \prod_{j=1}^{n-1} r_j}{r_i}$$

$$\frac{N_i \pi_i}{r_i} = \frac{N_n \pi_n}{r_n} = s.$$

Then, $\prod_1^n N_j \pi_j = s^n$, and $r_i = \frac{N_i \pi_i}{\sqrt[n]{\prod_1^n N_j \pi_j}}$. Replacing $r_i$ in (11) by $r_i = \frac{N_i \pi_i}{\sqrt[n]{\prod_1^n N_j \pi_j}}$, we get

$$P(\pi) = \frac{\sqrt[n]{\frac{k}{g}} \sqrt[n]{\prod_1^n N_j \pi_j} n}{\min_{\mathbf{d_i} \in D_s} \{\pi \mathbf{d_i}\}}$$

$$= \frac{\sqrt[n]{\frac{k}{g}} \sqrt[n]{\prod_1^n N_j \pi_j} n}{\min_{1 \leq i \leq n} \pi_i}. \tag{12}$$

The expression (12) is minimized when $\pi = \mathbf{1}$. Then, $r_i = \frac{N_i}{\sqrt[n]{\prod_1^n N_j}}$. $\square$

The above theorem implies that the optimal supernode shape is similar to the shape of the original index set $J$ so that the resulting supernode index set $J_s$ is a hypercube with equal sides. The following example shows how to find the optimal shape according to Theorem 4.1.

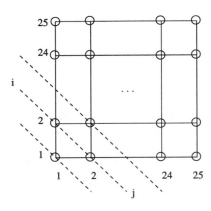

Figure 5: The supernode index space with an optimal grain size and shape.

**Example 4.1** Consider the algorithm in Example 2.1. According to Theorem 4.1, the optimal $\mathbf{R} = (\frac{\sqrt{2}}{2}, \sqrt{2})$ and the optimal linear schedule vector $\pi = (1, 1)$. With optimal $g_o = 30$, we can use $\mathbf{L} = (4, 8)$, yielding approximate $g = 32$. Figure 5 shows the algorithm supernode index space after the supernode transformation with $H$ defined in (1), $g = 32$ and the optimal supernode relative length vector $\mathbf{R} = (\frac{\sqrt{2}}{2}, \sqrt{2})$. The schedule length is then $\pi \begin{pmatrix} 25 \\ 25 \end{pmatrix} - \pi \begin{pmatrix} 1 \\ 1 \end{pmatrix} = 48$ and the total running time is $T_4 = 49gt_c + 48t_s = 30.1ms$, with 25 processors. This improves the total running in Example 3.1 with $\mathbf{R} = (1, 1)$.

Note that the values for supernode size and lengths of supernode sides computed based on Theorems 3.4 and 4.1 may not be integral. We should choose approximate integral values for supernode side lengths, $L$, which are close to the optimal ones and for which the volume of the resulting supernode is close to the optimal grain size, $g_o$. A simple heuristic is to use approximate values for $L$ such that the volume of the resulting supernode is greater or equal $g_o$, because the total running time function increases faster for values of $g < g_o$ and slower for values $g > g_o$. Alternatively, the total running time can be evaluated for different approximate values and the best approximation can be used.

### 4.2 The General Case

The basic idea for the general case is as follows. We assume the optimal $g$ has been found and $H$ is given, and start from a feasible $\mathbf{R}$ with $r_i = 1$, i.e., a supernode transformation with equal side parallelepiped

supernodes. Then we change the feasible $\mathbf{R}$ to different values. When $\mathbf{R}$ changes, the dependence matrix $D_s$ does not change but the shape of the supernode index set may change. The following lemma shows how the supernode index space changes as the relative side length vector $\mathbf{R}$ changes.

<u>Lemma 4.2</u>  *Let $(J_s', D_s)$ be the algorithm from a supernode transformation $(H, \mathbf{R}', g_o)$ where $J_s' = \{\mathbf{j} : A\mathbf{j} \leq \mathbf{b}, A \in R^{a \times n}, \mathbf{b} \in R^a, \mathbf{j} \in Z^n, a, n \in Z\}$, $g_o$ is the optimal grain size and $\mathbf{R}' = (1, ..., 1)$. Consider another supernode transformation $(H, \mathbf{R}, g_o)$ where $\mathbf{R} = (r_1, ..., r_i, ..., r_n)$ and let $Q$ be a diagonal matrix with diagonal elements $Q_{ii} = \frac{1}{r_i}$, $i = 1, ..., n$. Then, the algorithm obtained from the supernode transformation $(H, \mathbf{R}, g_o)$ is $(J_s, D_s)$ where $J_s = \{\mathbf{j} : AEQ^{-1}H\mathbf{j} \leq \mathbf{b}\}$.*

<u>Proof:</u>  Consider a vector $\mathbf{v}'$ in the convex hull of $J_s'$. It can be expressed in terms of extreme vectors of the parallelepiped supernode, i.e., $\mathbf{v}' = E\mathbf{v}_\mathbf{e}'$. Then, from $E = H^{-1}$, $\mathbf{v}_\mathbf{e}' = H\mathbf{v}'$. Let $\mathbf{v} \in J_s$ be the image of $\mathbf{v}'$ as $\mathbf{R}'$ changes to $\mathbf{R}$ and $\mathbf{v} = E\mathbf{v}_\mathbf{e}$. According to the definition of $r_i$'s (they are proportional to supernode side lengths), $\mathbf{v}_\mathbf{e} = Q\mathbf{v}_\mathbf{e}'$. Then

$$
\begin{aligned}
\mathbf{v} &= E\mathbf{v}_\mathbf{e} \\
&= EQ\mathbf{v}_\mathbf{e}' \\
&= EQH\mathbf{v}'
\end{aligned}
$$

Therefore, $\mathbf{v}'$ in $J_s'$ and its image $\mathbf{v}$ in $J_s$ are related by the above equation.

Consider a normal row vector $\mathbf{u}'$ orthogonal to an $n - 1$ dimensional boundary face of the supernode index set $J_s'$. This normal vector may change as the relative side length vector $\mathbf{R}$ changes. We want to find out the normal vector $\mathbf{u}$ of the corresponding boundary face in $J_s$. Let $\mathbf{v}'$ and $\mathbf{v}$ be vectors in the corresponding boundary face of $J_s'$ and $J_s$, respectively. Then,

$$
\begin{aligned}
\mathbf{u}'\mathbf{v}' &= 0 \\
\mathbf{u}\mathbf{v} &= 0 \\
\mathbf{u}EQH\mathbf{v}' &= 0,
\end{aligned}
$$

and from

$$\mathbf{u}'(EQH)^{-1}EQH\mathbf{v}' = 0,$$

we have

$$\mathbf{u} = \mathbf{u}'(EQH)^{-1} = \mathbf{u}'EQ^{-1}H.$$

Note that for every vector $\mathbf{v}'$, for which $\mathbf{u}'\mathbf{v}' = a$, $a$ is a constant, $\mathbf{u}\mathbf{v} = \mathbf{u}'\mathbf{v}' = a$. Therefore, a boundary face with normal vector $\mathbf{u}'$ in $J_s'$ is changed to the boundary face with normal vector $\mathbf{u} = \mathbf{u}' EQ^{-1}H$ in $J_s$.

We assume, no matter how the relative side length vector $\mathbf{R}$ changes, the resulting supernode transformation still satisfy the assumption we made in section 3. That is, all dependence vectors in $D$ are contained in the parallelepiped supernode. Therefore, the dependence matrix of the supernode transformation with $(H, \mathbf{R}, g_0)$ is still $D_s$. $\square$

An optimal linear schedule for algorithm $(J_s', D_s)$ can be found by solving the following linear optimization problem [1]:

$$\min_{\pi D_s \geq 1} \left( \max_{\substack{A\mathbf{p} \leq \mathbf{b} \\ A\mathbf{q} \leq \mathbf{b}}} \pi(\mathbf{p} - \mathbf{q}) \right).$$

The optimal linear schedule for algorithm $(J_s, D_s)$ may be different from the optimal linear schedule of $(J_s', D_s)$ because the supernode index set changes. There are $n$ additional variables $r_i$, $i = 1, \ldots n$ in finding the optimal linear schedule for algorithm $(J_s, D_s)$ and the problem becomes a non-linear optimization problem [1]:

$$\min_{\substack{\pi D_s \geq 1 \\ \prod_{i=1}^{n} r_i = 1 \\ r_i \geq \sqrt[n]{\frac{k}{g}}}} \left( \max_{\substack{AEQ^{-1}H\mathbf{p} \leq \mathbf{b} \\ AEQ^{-1}H\mathbf{q} \leq \mathbf{b}}} \pi(\mathbf{p} - \mathbf{q}) \right).$$

The maximization portion of this problem is a dual to the following minimization problem [1]:

$$\min(\mathbf{X_1} + \mathbf{X_2})\mathbf{b}$$

$$\begin{aligned}
\mathbf{X_1} AEQ^{-1}H &= \pi \\
\mathbf{X_2} AEQ^{-1}H &= -\pi \\
\mathbf{X_1} &\geq 0 \\
\mathbf{X_2} &\geq 0.
\end{aligned}$$

Therefore, to find the optimal $\mathbf{R}$ and optimal linear schedule is formulated as the following non-linear minimization problem whose solution gives an optimal linear schedule vector, $\pi$, and optimal relative supernode side lengths, $r_i$, $i = 1, \ldots, n$:

$$\min(\mathbf{X_1} + \mathbf{X_2})\mathbf{b}$$

$$\begin{aligned}
\pi D_s &\geq 1 \\
\prod_{i=1}^{n} r_i &= 1
\end{aligned}$$

$$\begin{aligned}
r_i &\geq \sqrt[n]{\frac{k}{g}} \\
\mathbf{X_1} AEQ^{-1}H &= \pi \\
\mathbf{X_2} AEQ^{-1}H &= -\pi \\
\mathbf{X_1} &\geq 0 \\
\mathbf{X_2} &\geq 0.
\end{aligned}$$

## 5  RELATED WORK

In this section we give a brief overview of previous related work. Lamport [6] proposed hyperplane scheduling technique in 1974. All iterations on the same hyperplane can execute simultaneously with dependences respected. Irigoin and Triolet [3] proposed the supernode partitioning technique for multiprocessors in 1988. The idea was to combine multiple loop iterations in order to provide vector statements, parallel tasks and data reference locality. Ramanujam and Sadayappan [5] studied tiling multidimensional iteration spaces for multiprocessors. They showed the equivalence between the problem of finding a partitioning hyperplane matrix $H$, and the problem of finding a cone for a given set of dependence vectors, i.e., finding a matrix of extreme vectors $E$. They presented an approach to determining partitioning hyperplanes to minimize communication volume. They also discussed a method for finding an optimal supernode size. Their result for optimal supernode size applies to a less general class of algorithms than this paper (unit computation cost $t_c$, and supernode with equal side lengths). Reference [10] discusses the choice of cutting hyperplanes and supernode shape with the goal of minimizing the communication volume in a scalable environment. It includes a very good description of the tiling technique. Unlike [10], we study the problem of supernode (tile) size and shape separately from the problem of choosing families of cutting hyperplanes and our goal is to minimize the total running time. In [15], it is shown how to partition algorithms with uniform dependencies into multiple independent sub-algorithms. In [4], the optimal tile size is studied under different model and assumptions. It is assumed that an $N_1 \times \ldots \times N_n$ hypercube index space is mapped to a $P_1 \times \ldots \times P_{n-1}$ processor space and the optimal side lengths of the hypercube tile are given as $\frac{N_i}{P_i}$ for certain kind of dependence structure.

Compared to the related work, our optimization criterion is to minimize the total running time, rather than communication volume or ratio between communication and computation volume, further we used a different approach where we specify a supernode transformation by a grain size of supernodes, the relative side length vector **R** and $n$ partitioning hyperplanes so that we can model the grain size of supernodes as a variable independent of other factors such as the dependence structure, the partitioning hyperplanes, the shape or the relative side lengths of the supernodes. Hence our method can be applied to find the optimal grain size for any uniform dependence algorithm with any partitioning hyperplanes. After we have the optimal grain size, we can determine the optimal shape and the partitioning hyperplanes.

## 6  CONCLUSION

In this paper we derived the optimal supernode size, which is a simple expression of the communication startup cost and computation speed, and the optimal shape for constant bounded loop nests, described by a relative side length vector, for supernode transformations, with the goal of minimizing the total running time. The results could be used by a parallelizing compiler for a distributed computer system to decide the grain size when breaking a task into subtasks. We also give a non-linear optimization model for determining a supernode shape and linear schedule which minimizes the total running time for general cases.

The problem of finding an optimal set of hyperplanes which partitions iteration index space into supernodes, in the framework we used in this paper, remains open.

## REFERENCES

[1] A. Darte, L. Khachiyan, and Y. Robert, "Linear Scheduling is Close to Optimality," *Proc. of 1992 Application Specific Array Processors*, edited by J. Fortes, E. Lee, T. Meng.

[2] E. Montagne, M. Rukoz, R. Suros, and F. Breant, "Modeling Optimal Granularity When Adapting Systolic Algorithms to Transputer Based Supercomputers," *Parallel Computing*, Vol. 20, 1994, pp. 807–814.

[3] F. Irigoin and R. Triolet, "Supernode Partitioning," *Proceedings of the Fifteenth Annual ACM SIGACT–SIGPLAN Symposium on Principles of Programming Languages*, San Diego, California, January 1988, pp. 319–329.

[4] H. Ohta, Y. Saito, M. Kainaga, and H. Ono, "Optimal Tile Size Adjustment in Compiling General DOACROSS Loop Nests," *Proc. 1995, Int. Conf. on Supercomputing.*

[5] J. Ramanujam and P. Sadayappan, "Tiling Multidimensional Iteration Spaces for Multicomputers," *J. of Parallel and Dist. Comp.* 1992, 16, pp. 108–120.

[6] L. Lamport, "The Parallel Execution of DO Loops," *Comm. ACM*, Vol. 17, No. 2, Feb. 1974, pp. 83–93.

[7] S. Y. Kung, *VLSI Array Processors*, Prentice Hall, Englewood Cliffs, New Jersey, 1988.

[8] M. S. Bazarra, H. D. Sherali, and C. M. Shetty, *Nonlinear Programming — Theory and Algorithms*, John Wiley & Sons, Inc., New York, Second Edition, 1993.

[9] O. Hellwig, "Estimating an Optimal Number of Processors in a Parallel Distributed System," M.S. thesis, Santa Clara University, January 1995.

[10] P. Boulet, A. Darte, T. Risset and Y. Robert, "(Pen)–Ultimate Tiling", Laboratoire LIP-IMAG, CNRS URA 1398, Ecole Normale Supérieure de Lyon, 69364 LYON Cedex 07, November 9, 1993.

[11] R. Andonov and S. Rajopadhye, "Optimal Tiling," *Tech. Rep. PI-792.*, IRISA, Campus de Beaulieu, Rennes, France, January 1994.

[12] R. Schreiber and J. J. Dongarra, "Automatic Blocking of Nested Loops", Technical Report 90.38, RIACS, August 1990.

[13] S. Hiranandani, K. Kennedy, and C.-W. Tseng, "Evaluating Compiler Optimizations for Fortran D," *J. of Parallel and Dist. Comp.*, Vol 21, 1992, pp. 27–45.

[14] W. Shang and J. A. B. Fortes, "Time Optimal Linear Schedules for Algorithms with Uniform Dependencies," *IEEE Trans. on Comp.*, Vol. 40, No. 6, June 1991.

[15] W. Shang and J. A. B. Fortes, "Independent Partitioning of Algorithms with Uniform Dependencies," *IEEE Trans. on Comp.*, Vol. 41, No. 2, February, 1992, pp. 190–206.

[16] H. Zima and B. Chapman, *Supercompilers for Parallel and Vector Computers*, Addison-Wesley Publishing Company, New York.

[17] M. Wolfe, "More Iteration Space Tiling," *Supercomp. '89*, pp. 655–664.

# A Compile Time Partitioning Method for DOALL Loops on Distributed Memory Systems*

Santosh Pande
Department of ECECS
PO Box 210030
University of Cincinnati
Cincinnati, Ohio 45221–0030
E-mail : santosh.pande@uc.edu

## Abstract

The loop partitioning problem on modern distributed memory systems is no longer *fully communication bound* primarily due to a significantly lower ratio of communication/computation speeds. The useful parallelism may be exploited on these systems to an extent that the communication balances the parallelism and does not produce a very high overhead to nullify all the gains due to the parallelism.

In this work, we describe a compile time partitioning and scheduling approach based on the above motivation for DOALL loops where communication without data replication is inevitable. First, the *code partitioning phase* analyzes the references in the body of the DOALL loop nest and determines a set of directions for reducing a larger degree of communication by trading a lesser degree of parallelism. Next, the *data distribution phase* uses a new *larger partition owns* rule to achieve computation+communication load balance. The *granularity adjustment phase* attempts to further eliminate communication through merging partitions to reduce the completion time. Finally, the *load balancing phase* attempts to reduce the number of processors without degrading the completion time and the *mapping phase* schedules the partitions on available processors. Relevant theory and algorithms are developed along with a performance evaluation on Cray T3D.

## 1  Introduction

Compiling for distributed memory systems continues to pose complex, challenging problems to the researchers. Some of the important research directions include, data parallel languages such as *HPF/Fortran 90D* [6, 8], *communication free partitioning*[12, 4, 5], *communication minimization* [2], *data alignment* [14, 3, 13, 1, 9], *mapping functional parallelism* [11] and *optimizing data redistributions* [7].

Most of the current methods for loop partitioning on distributed memory systems are data driven in which the data distribution is first determined by the compiler (either automatically or through user specified primitives ) and then the code is distributed by examining the underlying data and using the 'owner computes' rule. This approach is adopted by almost all data parallel languages and their compilers. The main motivation behind this approach is to minimize the communication through a simple yet effective technique. We feel that, with the availability of massively parallel systems with very low communication latencies, one should attempt to minimize the completion time without being limited by the communication latencies alone. In order to achieve this, since parallelism is an inherent characteristic of the code, one should take an orthogonal approach of first partitioning the code to maximize parallelism and then allocate the data appropriately. In this work, we describe such a approach through a compile time, partitioning and scheduling method for DOALL loops.

Section 2 describes the previous work on DOALL partitioning on distributed memory systems and discusses our approach. Section 3 introduces necessary terms and definitions. Section 4 develops the theory and section 5 discusses the algorithms for DOALL iteration and data space partitioning. Section 6 discusses the algorithms for granularity adjustment, load balancing and mapping. Section 7 deals with the performance results on Cray T3D and conclusions.

## 2  DOALL Partitioning

The DOALL loops offer the highest amount of parallelism to be exploited in many important applications. The primary motivation in DOALL partitioning on distributed memory systems is reducing data communication overhead. The previous work on this topic has focused on *completely eliminating* communication to achieve a *communication free* iteration and data space partition [12, 4, 5, 1]. The main motivation behind this approach was the extremely high costs of inter-processor communication in older systems. But in many practical DOALL loops, *communication free partitioning* may not be possible due to the incompatible reference instances of a given variable encountered in the loop body or due to incompatible variables [12, 5]. The parallelization of such DOALL

*This work is supported by the National Science Foundation grant no. CCR-9412407

loops was therefore hampered on older systems. In this work, our motivation is to develop an iteration and data space partitioning method for these DOALL loops where the reference patterns do not permit a communication free partition without replicating the data. The focus, thus, is on *communication minimization* as against *communication elimination* in previous approaches. We choose not to replicate the data since it involves a point-point or broadcast type communication and poses an initial data distribution overhead on every loop slice.

## 2.1 Our approach

Figure 1 shows the structure of our compile time DOALL partitioner and scheduler. It consists of five phases:

- Code Partitioner : This phase is responsible for analyzing the references in the body of the DOALL loop nest and determine a set of directions to partition the iteration space to minimize the communication by minimally trading the parallelism.

- Data Partitioner : This phase visits the iteration partitions generated above in the order of decreasing sizes and uses a *larger partition owns* rule to generate the underlying data distribution so that larger compute intensive partitions incur lesser communication overhead and vice-versa. The *larger partition owns* rule says that if the same data item is referenced by two or more partitions, the largest partition owns the data item. The goal is to generate computation+communication load balanced partitions.

- Granularity Adjustment : This phase analyzes whether the granularity of the partitions generated above is optimal or not. It attempts to combine two partitions which have a data communication and determines if the resulting partition is better in terms of completion time. It continues this process until the resulting partition has a worse completion time than any of the partitions from which it is formed. In this manner, a significant amount of communication is eliminated by this phase to improve the completion time.

- Load Balancing : This phase attempts to combine the load of several lightly loaded processors to reduce the number of required processors. Such merging is carried out only to the extent that the overall completion time does not degrade.

- Mapping : This phase is responsible for mapping the partitions from the previous phase to a given number of processors by minimally degrading the overall completion time. The partitions that minimally degrade the completion time on merger are combined and the process is continued till the number of partitions equal the number of available processors.

We first develop the theory behind code and data partitioning phases shown in Figure 1.

## 3 Terms and Definitions

We limit ourselves to the perfectly nested normalized DOALL loops. We define each of the occurrences of a given variable in the loop nest as its *reference instance*. For example, different occurrences of a given variable 'B' are defined as the *reference instances* of 'B' and different instances are denoted as $B_1$, $B_2$, $B_3$, ..., etc. for convenience. The *iteration space* of n-nested loop is defined as $I = \{(i_1, i_2, i_3, ...i_n) | L_j \le i_j \le U_j, 1 \le j \le n\}$, where $i_1, i_2, ..., i_n$ are different index variables of the loop nest. In the loop body, an instance of a variable 'B' references a subset of the data space of variable 'B'. For example, the instance $B_1 \equiv B[i_1 + \sigma_1^1, i_2 + \sigma_2^1, i_3 + \sigma_3^1 ...]$, references the data space of matrix B decided by the iteration space as defined above and the the the offsets $\sigma_1^1, \sigma_2^1, \sigma_3^1, ....$. Each partition of the iteration space is called the *iteration block*. In order to generate communication free data and iteration partition, we determine partitioning directions in the iteration and data spaces such that the references generated in each iteration block can be disjointly partitioned and allocated on local memory of a processor to avoid communication. Although most of the discussion in this paper uses constant offsets for the variable references in each dimension, in general, the references can be *uniformly generated* [4] so that it is possible to perform *communication free partitioning analysis*. Please note that our approach uses *communication free partitioning analysis* as the underlying method (as described in later sections); thus, the underlying assumptions and restrictions are the same as any of those methods described in literature [12, 5, 4, 1].

A set of reference instances of a variable is called the *instance set* of that variable. A set of *reference instances* of a variable for which communication free data and iteration partition can be determined is defined as a set of *compatible instances* of a variable. If a communication free partition can not be found, such a set of reference instances is called a set of *incompatible instances*. If a communication free partition can be determined for a set of *variables* considering all their instances, it is called as a set of *compatible variables*; otherwise it is called as a set of *incompatible variables*. In this paper, we focus on minimizing the communication when we have a set of *incompatible instances* of a variable so that a communication free partition can not be found. Minimizing communication for a set of *incompatible variables* is even more hard and is not attempted here.

### 3.1 Example

Consider the following code:

```
for i := 1 to N
  for j := 1 to N
    a[i,j] := (b[i,j] + b[i-1,j-1]+ b[i-1,j]
            + b[i-1,j+1] + b[i,j-1]
            + b[i,j+1] + b[i+1,j-1]
            + b[i+1,j] + b[i+1,j+1])/9
  endfor
endfor
```

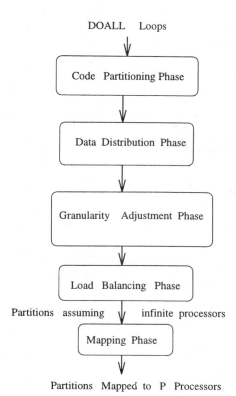

Figure 1: DOALL Partitioner and Scheduler

For this code, it is not possible to determine a communication free iteration and data partitioning direction. Let $b_1 \equiv b[i,j]$, $b_2 \equiv b[i-1, j-1]$, $b_3 \equiv b[i-1, j]$, $b_4 \equiv b[i-1, j+1]$, $b_5 \equiv b[i, j-1]$, $b_6 \equiv b[i, j+1]$, $b_7 \equiv b[i+1, j-1]$, $b_8 \equiv b[i+1, j]$, $b_9 \equiv b[i+1, j+1]$. Thus, the instance set for the variable b is given by $\{b_1, b_2, ..., b_9\}$ for the nine occurrences of b. All these reference instances are, therefore, *incompatible*.

## 4 Problem

We begin by stating the problem of communication minimization for *incompatible instances* of a variable as follows:

Given an *instance set* of a variable B, denoted by $S_B = \{B_1, B_2, B_3, ..., B_m\}$ which may comprise of *incompatible instances* occurring within a loop nest as described before, determine a set of communication minimizing directions so that the volume of communication reduced is at least equal to or more than the parallelism reduced. We measure the volume of communication by the number of non-local references (the references which which fall outside the underlying data partition) corresponding to an iteration block. In our formulation of the problem, no data replication is allowed. There is only one copy of the each array element kept at one of the processors and whenever any other processor references it, there is a communication : one send at the owner processor and one receive at the one which needs it. The justification for reducing the above volume of communication is that the data

communication latency in most distributed memory systems consists of a fixed start-up overhead to initiate communication and a variable part proportional to the length of (or to the number of data items) the message. Thus, reducing the number of non-local data values, reduces this part of communication latency. Of course, one may perform message vectorization following our partitioning phase to group the values together to be sent in a single message to amortize on start-up costs. Such techniques are presented elsewhere [10] and do not form a part of this paper.

We measure the amount of parallelism reduced by the number of additional iterations being introduced in an iteration block to eliminate the communication.

### 4.1 Compatibility Subsets

We begin by outlining a solution which may attain the above objective. We first partition the *instance set* of a variable, $S_B$, into $\rho$ subsets $S_B^1, S_B^2, ..., S_B^\rho$ which satisfy the relation:

- All the reference instances of the variable belonging to a given subset are compatible so that one can determine a direction for communication free partitioning. Formally, $\forall B_i \in S_B^j$, $\exists (d_1^j, d_2^j, ..., d_r^j)$ such that partitioning along direction vector $(d_1^j, d_2^j, ..., d_r^j)$ achieves communication free partition, where, $1 \leq j \leq \rho$.

- At least one reference instance belonging to a given subset is incompatible with all the reference instances belonging to any other subset. Formally, $\exists B_l \in S_B^k$ so that it is incompatible with all $B_i \in S_B^j$, where, $j \neq k$, $1 \leq j, k \leq \rho$. In other words, one can not find a communication free partition for $S_B^j \cup \{B_l\}$, for some $B_l \in S_B^k$.

It is easy to see that the above relation is a *compatibility* relation. It is well known that the *compatibility* relation only defines a *covering* of the set and does not define mutually disjoint partitions. We, therefore, first determine $\rho$ *maximal compatibility subsets* : $S_B^1, S_B^2, ..., S_B^\rho$ from the above relation. For each of the maximal compatibility subsets, there exists a direction for communication free partitioning. The algorithm to compute *maximal compatibility subsets* is described in the next section. Following Lemma [1] summarizes the maximum and minimum number of *maximal compatibility subsets* that can result from the above relation.

<u>Lemma 1</u> : If $m \equiv |S_B|$ and if $\rho$ *maximal compatibility subsets* result from the above relation on $S_B$, then $2 \leq \rho \leq C_2^m$.

The bounds derived in the above lemma allow us to prove the overall complexity of our *Communication Minimizing Algorithms* discussed in the section 5.

The next step is to determine a set of cyclically alternating directions from the compatibility subsets found above to maximally cover the communication.

### 4.2 Cyclic Directions

Let the instance set $S_B$ for a variable B be partitioned into $S_B^1, S_B^2, ..., S_B^\rho$ which are maximal compatibility subsets under the relation of communication free partitioning. Let Comp(B) be the set of communication free partitioning directions corresponding to these compatibility subsets. Thus, Comp(B) = $\{D^1, D^2, ..., D^\rho\}$, where, $D^j = (d_1^j, d_2^j, ..., d_r^j)$ is the direction of communication free partitioning for the subset $S_B^j$. The problem now is to determine a subset of Comp(B) which maximally *covers* the directions in Comp(B) ( a given direction is said to be *covered* by an ordered set of other directions, if the partitioning along the directions in the ordered set obviates the need for communication along the given direction).

Let such a subset of Comp(B) be denoted by Cyclic(B). Let, Cyclic(B) = $\{D^{\pi^{-1}(1)}, D^{\pi^{-1}(2)}, ..., D^{\pi^{-1}(t)}\}$, where $D^{\pi^{-1}(i)} = D^j$ or $i \equiv \pi(j)$ defines a permutation which maps jth element of Comp(B) at ith position in Cyclic(B) where $|Cyclic(B)| \equiv t$. We now state the property which allows us determining such a maximal, ordered subset Cyclic(B) of Comp(B):

**Property 1** : The subset Cyclic(B) must satisfy all of the following:

1. $D^{\pi^{-1}(j)} = D^{\pi^{-1}(j-1)} + D^{\pi^{-1}(j-2)}$, where, $3 \leq j \leq t$. Each of the directions $D^{\pi^{-1}(j)}$ direction is then said to be *covered* by directions $D^{\pi^{-1}(j-1)}$ and $D^{\pi^{-1}(j-2)}$. Thus, each of the elements of the ordered set Cyclic(B) must be *covered* by the previous two elements, the exception being the first two elements of Cyclic(A).

2. Consider Comp(B) - Cyclic(B), and let some $D^k$ belong to this set. If $D^k = c_1 * D^{\pi^{-1}(t)} + \sum_{i=1}^j D^{\pi^{-1}(i)}$, where, $1 \leq j \leq (t-1)$, $c_1 \in I^+$ (in other words, if the direction $D^k$ can be expressed as a linear combination of multiple of $D^{\pi^{-1}(t)}$ and a summation of a subset of ordered directions as above), then it is *covered* and there is no communication along it. Let Uncov(B) be the subset of Comp(B) - Cyclic(B) such that $\forall D^k \in Uncov(B)$, $D^k \neq c_1 * D^{\pi^{-1}(t)} + \sum_{i=1}^j D^{\pi^{-1}(i)}$, i.e., none of its elements is covered and let $s \equiv |Uncov(B)|$.

3. Cyclic(B) is that subset of Comp(B) which satisfying the properties stated in 1 and 2 as above leads to minimum s.

Stated more simply, Cyclic(B) is an ordered subset of Comp(B) which leaves minimum number of uncovered direction in Comp(B). If we determine Cyclic(B) and follow the corresponding communication free directions cyclically from $D^{\pi^{-1}(1)}$ to $D^{\pi^{-1}(t-1)}$ (such as $D^{\pi^{-1}(1)}, D^{\pi^{-1}(2)}, ..., D^{\pi^{-1}(t-1)}, D^{\pi^{-1}(1)}, D^{\pi^{-1}(2)}, ..$), communication is reduced by a larger degree than loss of parallelism which is beneficial. The following Lemma formally states the result:

<u>Lemma 2</u>: If we follow iteration partitioning cyclically along the directions corresponding to Cyclic(B) as above, for each basic iteration block (basic iteration block is achieved by starting at a point in iteration space and by traversing once along the directions corresponding to Cyclic(B) from there), parallelism is reduced by (t-1) (due to sequentialization of (t-1) iterations) and the communication is reduced by $(\rho+t)$-(s+3), where $\rho \equiv |Comp(B)|$, $t \equiv |Cyclic(B)|$ and $s \equiv |Uncov(B)|$.

<u>Corollary 1</u> : According to the above lemma, we must find at least one pair of directions which covers at least one other direction in Comp(B) to reduce more communication than parallelism.

Thus, in order to maximally reduce communication, we must find Cyclic(B) from Comp(B) so that it satisfies Property 1. As one can see, the directions in Cyclic(B) form a Fibonacci Sequence as per Property 1 maximally covering the remaining directions in Comp(B). Our problem is, thus, to find a maximal Fibonacci Sequence as a subset of Comp(B). The algorithm to determine such a sequence is discussed in the next section.

## 5 Communication Minimizing Algorithms

In order to minimize the communication, the first step is to determine the maximal compatibility subsets from the instance set of a variable. The second step is to determine a Fibonacci sequence which maximally covers the communication.

---

[1] All proofs omitted due to lack of space

In this section, we discuss the two algorithms based on the theory developed in last section. The first algorithm determines the *maximal compatibility subsets* of the instance set of a given variable and the second one determines a maximal Fibonacci Sequence as discussed in the last section. We also analyze the complexity of these algorithms.

## 5.1 Algorithm : Maximal Compatibility Subsets

This algorithm finds the *maximal compatibility subsets*, Comp(B) of a variable B, given the instance set $S_B$ as an input.

As one can see that the *compatibility* relation of communication free partitioning for a set of a references (defined before) is reflexive and symmetric but not necessarily transitive. If a and b are *compatible*, we denote this relation as $a \approx b$.

1. Initialize Comp(B) := $\phi$, k := 1.

2. for every reference instance $B_i \in S_B$ do

   (a) Find $B_j \in S_B$ such that $B_i \approx B_j$ but both $B_i, B_j \notin S_B^p$, for $1 \leq p < k$. In other words, find a pair of references such that it has not been put into some compatibility subset already constructed so far (k is the number of compatibility subsets constructed so far).

   (b) Initialize $S_B^k := \{B_i, B_j\}$ (put the pair satisfying above property into a new subset $S_B^k$ being constructed).

   (c) For every $B_l \in (S_B - S_B^k)$, do
   - if $\forall B_m \in S_B^k$, $B_l \approx B_m$, $S_B^k := S_B^k \cup \{B_l\}$.
   - Add the constructed subset $S_B^k$ to Comp(B), $Comp(B) := Comp(B) \cup S_B^k$, k := k+1.

   (d) Repeat steps (a) through (c) above till no $B_j$ can be found satisfying condition in (a).

3. After all the subsets are constructed, replace each of them by the corresponding communication free partitioning directions. That is, for Comp(B) constructed above, replace each $S_B^i$ by $D^i$, where, $D^i$ is the corresponding communication free direction for $S_B^i$.

As one can see that the above algorithm checks for compatibility relation from an element of $S_B$ to all the other elements of $S_B$ and therefore, its worst case complexity $O(|S_B|^2)$.

Consider the example in section 3.1. By following the above algorithm, the maximal compatibility subsets found are (directions for communication free partitions are shown next to each of them):

- $b_1$ : $\{b_1, b_2, b_9\}$ (1,1), $\{b_1, b_3, b_8\}$ (1,0), $\{b_1, b_4, b_7\}$ (1,-1), $\{b_1, b_5, b_6\}$ (0,1).

- $b_2$ : $\{b_2, b_3, b_4\}$ (0,1), $\{b_2, b_5, b_7\}$ (1,0), $\{b_2, b_6\}$ (1,2), $\{b_2, b_8\}$ (2,1).

- $b_3$ : $\{b_3, b_5\}$ (1,-1), $\{b_3, b_6\}$ (1,1), $\{b_3, b_7\}$(2,-1), $\{b_3, b_9\}$ (2,1).

- $b_4$ : $\{b_4, b_5\}$ (1,-2), $\{b_4, b_6, b_9\}$(1,0), $\{b_4, b_8\}$ (2,-1).

- $b_5$ : $\{b_5, b_8\}$(1,1), $\{b_5, b_9\}$ (1,2).

- $b_6$ : $\{b_6, b_7\}$(1,-2), $\{b_6, b_8\}$ (1,-1).

- $b_7$ : $\{b_7, b_8, b_9\}$ (0,1).

## 5.2 Algorithm : Maximal Fibonacci Sequence

Following algorithm determines the set Cyclic(B) using Comp(B) as an input.

1. Sort the set Comp(B). If $\{D^1, D^2, ..., D^\rho\}$ is the sorted set, it must satisfy the following order:

   - $D_1^i < D_1^{i+1}$, or
   - if $D_j^i := D_j^{i+1}$ for all j such that $1 \leq j \leq k$ and $D_{k+1}^i < D_{k+1}^{i+1}$ for some k, such that $1 \leq k \leq r - 1$.

   The elements $D^1, D^2, ..., D^\rho$ are then said to be sorted in non-decreasing order $<$ such that $D^1 < D^2 < D^3 ....$

2. Initialize set MaxFib := $\phi$, max := 0.

3. for i :=1 to n
   for j := i+1 to n

   (a) Let $D := D^i + D^j$. Initialize last := j, Fib := $\phi$, k := j+1.

   (b) while $(D^k < D)$
   k := k+1

   (c) if $(D^k = D)$, $Fib := Fib \cup D^k$, $D := D^k + D^{last}$, last := k, k:=k+1.

   (d) Repeat steps (b) and (c) above till $k > n$.

   (e) Let q be the number of additional directions covered in Comp(B) by Fib as per Property 1. In other words, let $D \in Comp(B) - Fib$. If $D = c_1 * D^{last} + \sum_{l=1}^{v} D^l$, where, $1 \leq v \leq |Fib|$, $c_1 \in I^+$, D is already covered by Cyclic(B). Determine q, the number of such covered directions in Comp(B) - Fib.

   (f) if $max < |Fib| + q$, MaxFib := Fib, max := $|Fib| + q$.

4. Cyclic(B) := MaxFib.

As one can see, the sorting step for the above algorithm would require $O(\rho \log \rho)$ and the step of finding the maximal cover would require $O(\rho^3)$. Thus, the total complexity of the algorithm is $O(\rho \log \rho + \rho^3)$. From Lemma 1, since $\rho \leq |S_B|^2$, the overall complexity of the algorithm is $O(|S_B|^2 \log|S_B| + |S_B|^6)$.

For the example in section 3.1, the above algorithm would compute Cyclic(b) = $\{(0,1),(1,-2),(1,-1)\}$ since it results in maximally reducing the communication. These directions also cover communication along $(1,0)$ and $(2,-1)$. Thus, by cyclically following $(0,1)/(1,-2)$ directions, one could reduce communication by 5 losing parallelism by 2 per basic iteration block.

### 5.3 Iteration and Data Partitioning

Once the set of cyclic directions (Cyclic(B)) is found as above, the next step is to carry out the iteration and data partitioning. The basic idea is to follow directions $D^{\pi^{-1}(1)}, D^{\pi^{-1}(2)}, ..., D^{\pi^{-1}(t-1)}$ cyclically to perform iteration partitioning from a given base point in the iteration space.

In order to determine the data partition, we apply the following simple algorithm which uses *larger partition owns* rule:

- Sort the partitions in the decreasing order of their sizes in terms of the number of iterations.

- Find out all the data references generated in a given partition and allocate that data to the respective processor. If the generated reference is already owned by a larger partition generated previously, add it to the set of non-local references.

- Generate communication primitives to obtain the non-local references for the given partition.

## 6 Loop Scheduling

For scheduling the partitions generated above on actual physical processors, first a task graph is constructed on which granularity adjustment and load balancing is carried out. Then the partitions are scheduled (mapped) on a given number of available processors.

Each node of the task graph denotes one loop partition and the weight of the node is equal to the number of iterations in that loop partition. There is a directed edge from one node to another which represents the direction of data communication. The weight of the edge is equal to the number of data values being communicated. Let G(V, E) denote such a task graph where V is the set of nodes and E is the set of edges as described above. Let $t(v_i)$ denote the weight of node $t_i \in V$ and $c(v_j, v_i)$ denote the weight of edge $(v_j, v_i) \in E$.

Each of the nodes (which denotes a loop partition) starts execution in the following order:

- Send : The partition first sends the data needed by other partitions.

- Receive : After sending the data, the partition receives the data it needs sent by other partitions.

- Compute : After receiving the data in the above step, the partition executes the assigned loop iterations.

The total time required for the execution of each partition is, thus, equal to Send time + Receive time + Compute time. The Send time is proportional to the total number of data values sent out (total weight ) on all outgoing edges and the receive time is proportional to the total number of data values received (total weight) on all incoming edges. The compute time is proportional to the number of iterations (node weight).

We now describe three scheduling phases as outlined before. All of these heuristics traverse the task graph in reverse topological order by following simple breadth first rule as follows:

- Visit the leaf nodes of the graph.

- Visit the predecessor of a given node such that all of its successors are already visited.

- Follow this procedure to visit backwards from leaf nodes till all the nodes including root node are visited.

### 6.1 Granularity Adjustment

Refer to Figure 2.

- Calculate the completion time of each node $v_j$ given by $tcom(v_j) = k_1 * \sum_{(v_j,v_i) \in E} c(v_j, v_i) + k_2 * \sum_{(v_k,v_j) \in E} c(v_k, v_j) + t(v_j)$, where the cost of one iteration is assumed to be 1 and the cost of one send is assumed to be $k_1$ and that of one receive to be $k_2$.

- Visit the nodes of the graph in the reverse topological order described as above. Suppose we choose a predecessor $v_k$ of node $v_j$ for merging to adjust granularity.

- Determine the completion time of merged node $v_{jk}$ given by $tcom(v_{jk}) = tcom(v_j) + tcom(v_k) - c(v_j, v_k) * (k_1 + k_2)$.

- Compare it with each of $tcom(v_j)$ and $tcom(v_k)$ and if $tcom(v_{jk})$ is lesser than both, merge $v_j$ and $v_k$.

- Continue the process by attempting to expand the partition by considering $v_{jk}$ and a predecessor of $v_k$ next and so on.

- If $tcom(v_{jk})$ is greater than either of $tcom(v_j)$ or $tcom(v_k)$, reject the merger of $v_j$ and $v_k$. Next, attempt merger of $v_k$ and one of predecessors and so on.

- Repeat all the steps again on the new graph resulting from the above procedure and iterate the procedure until no new partitions are merged together (condition of graph invariance).

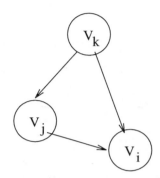

Figure 2: Portion of Task Graph

## 6.2 Load Balancing

Refer to Figure 2.

- Let T be the overall loop completion time generated by the above phase.

- Visit the nodes of the graph in the reverse topological order described as above. Suppose we choose a predecessor $v_k$ of node $v_j$ to merge the partitions.

- Determine the completion time of merged node $v_{jk} = tcom(v_j) + tcom(v_k) - c(v_j, v_k) * (k_1 + k_2)$. Obviously, $tcom(v_{jk})$ will be higher than that of either of $tcom(v_k)$ or $tcom(v_j)$ since if it were not the case, the two partitions would have been merged by the granularity adjustment algorithm.

- Compare $tcom(v_{jk})$ with T and if $tcom(v_{jk})$ is lesser than T, merge $v_j$ and $v_k$.

- Continue the process by attempting to expand the partition by considering $v_{jk}$ and predecessor of $v_k$ next and so on.

- If $v_{jk}$ is greater than T, reject the merger of $v_j$ and $v_k$. Next, attempt merger of $v_k$ and one of its predecessor and so on.

- Keep repeating this process and if at any stage the completion time of the merged node is worse than the overall completion time T, reject it and attempt a new one by considering predecessor and its predecessor and so on.

## 6.3 Mapping

Refer to Figure 2.

- Let there be P available processors on which the partitions resulting from previous phase are to be mapped, where # partitions > P.

- Traverse the task graph in the reverse topological order as described earlier. Suppose we choose a predecessor $v_k$ or a node $v_j$ for a possible merge to reduce the number of processors.

- Determine the completion time of merged node $v_{jk}$: $tcom(v_{jk}) = tcom(v_j) + tcom(v_k) - c(v_j, v_k) * (k_1 + k_2)$. Obviously, $tcom(v_{jk})$ will be higher than the loop completion time T. Store the $tcom(v_{jk})$ in a table.

- Attempt the merger of another node and its predecessor and store it in a table. Repeat this process for all the nodes and chosse the pair which results in minimum completion time when merged and combine them. This reduces the number of partitions by 1.

- Continue the above process till the number of partitions is reduced to P.

## 7 Performance on Cray T3D

The following example codes are used to test the method on a Cray T3D system with 32 processors:

```
Example I:
---------
for i = 2 to N
  for j = 2 to N
    for k = 1 to Upper
      A[i,j,k] = B[i-2,j-1,k]
              +B[i-1,j-1,k]
              +B[i-1,j-2,k]
    endfor
  endfor
endfor

Example II:
----------
for i := 1 to N
  for j := 1 to N
    for k := 1 to Upper
    a[i,j,k] := (b[i,j,k] + b[i-1,j-1,k]
            + b[i-1,j,k] + b[i-1,j+1,k]
            + b[i,j-1,k] + b[i,j+1,k]
            + b[i+1,j-1,k] + b[i+1,j,k]
            + b[i+1,j+1,k])/9
    endfor
  endfor
endfor
```

In the above examples, there is an inner loop in k dimension. The number of iterations in this loop, Upper,

Table 1: Example I : Performance on Cray T3D

| Problem Size | Processors | Direction | Sequential Time (sec) | Parallel Time (sec) | Speedup |
|---|---|---|---|---|---|
| 4x4 | 4 | Cyclic | 15.8 | 7.6 | 2.08 |
| 4x4 | 4 | (0,1) | 15.8 | 15.1 | 1.05 |
| 4x4 | 4 | (-1,0) | 15.8 | 15.52 | 1.02 |
| 8x8 | 8 | Cyclic | 52.73 | 16.3 | 3.23 |
| 8x8 | 8 | (0,1) | 52.73 | 29.07 | 1.81 |
| 8x8 | 8 | (-1,0) | 52.73 | 30.09 | 1.75 |
| 16x16 | 16 | Cyclic | 213.9 | 33.66 | 6.35 |
| 16x16 | 16 | (0,1) | 213.9 | 61.5 | 3.47 |
| 16x16 | 16 | (-1,0) | 213.9 | 63.3 | 3.38 |
| 32x32 | 32 | Cyclic | 919.7 | 68.42 | 13.44 |
| 32x32 | 32 | (0,1) | 919.7 | 113.44 | 8.1 |
| 32x32 | 32 | (-1,0) | 919.7 | 117.6 | 7.82 |

are chosen as 10 million in case of Example I and 1 million in case of Example II to make computation in loop body comparable to communication. As one can see, there is no problem in terms of communication free partitioning in k dimension. However, in i and j dimensions, due to reference patterns, no communication free partition exists and thus, the outer two loops (in i and j dimension) and the underlying data are distributed by applying the techniques described in sections 5 and 6. For Example I, the cyclical direction of partitioning are $(0,1,0)/(-1,0,0)$ and for Example II, the cyclical directions are $(0,1,0)/(1,-2,0)$ as explained earlier. The number partitions found by the method for each of these examples is equal to N , the size of the problem. Thus, the size of the problem N is appropriately chosen to match the number of processors.

The method is tested for N=4 (4 processors), N=8 (8 processors), N=16 (16 processors) and N=32 (32 processors). The timings are obtained using clock() system call on Cray T3D which allows measuring timings in micro-seconds. The sequential (as shown above) and the parallel versions are implemented and speedup is calculated as the ratio of time required for each. Refer to Table 1 and 2 for the results for each example. It can be clearly seen that it is possible to effectively parallelize both of these examples which are quite demanding in terms of communication by employing our method. The speedup values are quite promising in spite of heavy inherent communication in these applications.

We also implemented Example I using (0,1) (column-wise) and (-1,0) (row-wise) as directions of partitioning using owner computes rule. The speedups obtained by using these directions are also shown in Table 1. It can be clearly seen that our method outperforms these partitioning by almost a factor of 2 in terms of speedups. For Example II, after performing load balancing, the number of partitions reduced from 16 to 8. Figure 3 gives the completion times of the respective processors. One can see that these processors are quite well load balanced. Finally, the mapping

phase attempts to map these 8 partitions onto 8 or fewer processors. The completion times of these mappings for # processors = 8 through 1 are shown in Figure 4. One can see that the method has a good scalability.

## 7.1 Conclusions

In this paper, we have presented a framework for partitioning and scheduling (mapping) the DOALL loops in a communication efficient manner and shown that the method performs better than data driven code generation such as 'owner computes' rule. We have demonstrated that it is possible to efficiently parallelize such loops (which may be quite demanding in terms of communication requirements) on modern distributed memory systems with low ratios of communication/computation speeds. Many practical loops encountered in important codes such as image processing, weather modeling etc. exhibit the above characteristic. The method, thus, allows effective partitioning of such important codes on distributed memory systems and is likely to be of significant value in exploiting the useful parallelism in them.

## References

[1] D. Bau, I. Kodukula, V. Kotlyar, K. Pingali and P. Stodghill, "Solving Alignment Using Elementary Linear Algebra", *Proceedings of 7th International Workshop on Languages and Compilers for Parallel Computing*, LNCS 892, 1994, pp. 46–60.

[2] J. Anderson and M. Lam, "Global Optimizations for Parallelism and Locality on Scalable Parallel Machines", *Proceedings of SIGPLAN '93 conference on Programming Language Design and Implementation*, June 1993, pp. 112–125.

[3] S. Chatterjee, J. Gilbert, R. Schreiber and S. - H. Teng, "Automatic Array Alignment in Data Parallel Programs", *20th ACM Symposium on Principles of Programming Languages*, pp. 16–28, 1993.

Table 2: Example II : Performance on Cray T3D

| Problem Size | Processors | Sequential Time (sec) | Parallel Time (sec) | Speedup |
|---|---|---|---|---|
| 4x4 | 4 | 9.7 | 2.57 | 3.77 |
| 8x8 | 8 | 35.1 | 9.78 | 3.59 |
| 16x16 | 16 | 130.92 | 19.12 | 6.8 |
| 32x32 | 32 | 543.3 | 43.24 | 12.56 |

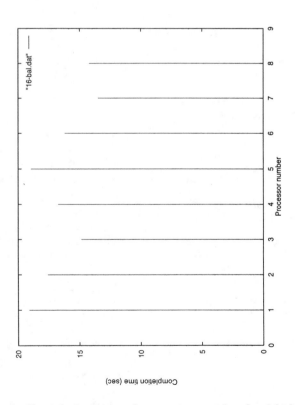

Figure 3: Completion times for processors after load balancing

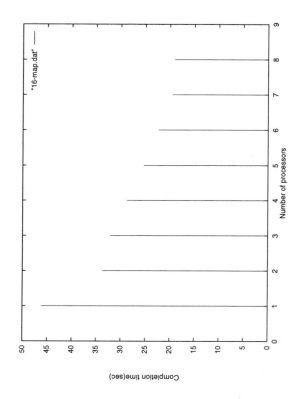

Figure 4: Completion times for variable number of available processors : P = 1 to P = 8

[4] T. Chen and J. Sheu, "Communication-Free Data Allocation Techniques for Parallelizing Compilers on Multicomputers", *IEEE Transactions on Parallel and Distributed Systems*, Vol. 5, No.9, September 1994, pp. 924–938.

[5] C. -H. Huang and P. Sadayappan, "Communication free Hyperplane Partitioning of Nested Loops", *Journal of Parallel and Distributed Computing*, Vol. 19, No. 2, October '93, pp. 90-102.

[6] S. Hiranandani, K. Kennedy and C. -W. Tseng, "Compiling Fortran for MIMD Distributed-Memory Machines", *Communications of ACM*, August 1992, Vol. 35, No. 8, pp. 66-80.

[7] S. D. Kaushik, C. -H. Huang, R. W. Johnson and P. Sadayappan, "An Approach to Communication-Efficient Data Redistribution", *Proceedings of 1994 ACM International Conference on Supercomputing*, pp. 364–373, June 1994.

[8] C. Koelbel and P. Mehrotra, "Compiling Global Name-Space Parallel Loops for Distributed Execution", *IEEE Transactions on Parallel and Distributed Systems*, October 1991, Vol. 2, No. 4, pp. 440-451.

[9] A. Lim and M. Lam, "Communication-free Parallelization via Affine Transformations", *Proceedings of 7th International Workshop on Languages and Compilers for Parallel Computing*, LNCS 892, 1994, pp. 92–106.

[10] D. J. Palermo, E. Su, J. Chandy and P. Banerjee, "Communication Optimizations Used in the PARADIGM Compiler", *Proceedings of the 1994 International Conference on Parallel Processing*, Vol. II (Software), pp. II-1 – II-10.

[11] S. S. Pande, D. P. Agrawal and J. Mauney, "A Scalable Scheduling Method for Functional Parallelism on Distributed Memory Multiprocessors", *IEEE Transactions on Parallel and Distributed Systems* Vol. 6, No. 4, April 1995, pp. 388–399

[12] J. Ramanujam and P. Sadayappan, "Compile-Time Techniques for Data Distribution in Distributed Memory Machines", *IEEE Transactions on Parallel and Distributed Systems*, Vol. 2, No. 4, October 1991, pp. 472–482.

[13] B. Sinharoy and B. Szymanski, "Data and Task Alignment in Distributed Memory Architectures", *Journal of Parallel and Distributed Computing*, 21, 1994, pp. 61–74.

[14] H. Xu and L. Ni, "Optimizing Data Decomposition for Data Parallel Programs", *Proceedings of International Conference on Parallel Processing*, August 1994, Vol. II, pp. 225-232.

# Unique Sets Oriented Partitioning of Nested Loops with Non-uniform Dependences*

Jialin Ju and Vipin Chaudhary
Parallel and Distributed Computing Laboratory
Wayne State University, Detroit, MI
Phone: (313) 577-0605
Email: *vipin@eng.wayne.edu*

## ABSTRACT

*Although many methods exist for nested loop partitioning, most of them perform poorly when parallelizing loops with non-uniform dependences. This paper addresses the issue of parallelizing nested loops with non-uniform dependences. Our approach is based on convex hull theory, which has adequate information to handle non-uniform dependences. We introduce the concept of Complete Dependence Convex Hull, unique head and tail sets and abstract the dependence information into these sets. These sets form the basis of the iteration space partitions. The properties of the unique head and tail sets are derived using Convex Hull theory. Depending on the relative placement of these unique sets, the partitioning problem is grouped in to several cases. Several partitioning schemes are also suggested for implementing our technique. Preliminary implementation results of our scheme on the Cray J916 and comparison with other schemes show a dramatic improvement in performance.*

## INTRODUCTION

Loops with cross-iteration dependences can be roughly divided into two groups. The first group is loops with static regular dependences, which can be analyzed during compile time. Example 1 belongs to this group. The other group consists of loops with dynamic irregular dependences, which have indirect access patterns eg. loops used for edge-oriented representation of sparse matrices. These kind of loops cannot be parallelized at compile time, for lack of sufficient information.

[1] This work was supported in part by NSF MIP-9309489, US Army Contract DAEA-32-93-D-004 and Ford Motor Company Grant #0000952185

**Example 1:**

```
do i = 1, 12
    do j = 1, 12
        A(2 * i + 3, j + 1) = · · ·
        · · · = A(2 * j + i + 1, i + j + 3)
    enddo
enddo
```

Static regular loops can be further divided into two sub groups; the ones with uniform dependences and the other with non-uniform dependences. The dependences are uniform only when the pattern of dependence vectors is uniform ie. the dependence vectors can be expressed by some constants which are *distance vectors*. Similarly we call dependences non-uniform when the dependence vectors are in some irregular pattern which cannot be expressed with *distance vectors*. Figure 1 shows the non-uniform dependence pattern of Example 1, which has a non-uniform dependence, in the iteration space,

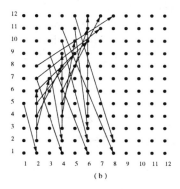

(b)

Figure 1: *Iteration space of Example 1*

In an empirical study, Shen *et al.* [1] observed that nearly 45% of two dimensional array references are coupled and most of these lead to non-uniform dependences. This paper focuses on parallelizing loops

III-45

with such dependences. Our approach is based on *Convex Hull* theory which has been proven [2] to have enough information to handle non-uniform dependences. Based on our Unique Set technique, we will divide the iteration space into several parallel regions, such that all the iterations in each region can be executed in parallel in most cases. In the worst case only the last region has to be run sequentially.

Research in parallelizing non-uniform nested loops has been limited. Tzen and Ni[3] proposed the Dependence Uniformization technique. This technique computes a set of basic dependence vectors using Dependence Slope theory and adds them to every iteration in the iteration space. This uniformization helps in applying existing partitioning and scheduling techniques, but imposes too many additional dependences to the iteration space. Our approach provides more accurate information about the iteration space and finds more parallelism. Two other techniques based on Convex Hull theory have been proposed recently. Zaafrani and Ito [4] proposed a three region approach which divides the iteration space into two parallel regions and one serial region. Punyamurtula and Chaudhary [5] use a Minimum Dependence Distance Technique to partition the iteration space into regular tiles. Our technique subsumes both the above techniques.

The rest of this paper is organized as follows. Section two describes our program model, reviews some fundamental concepts and introduces the concept of a Complete Dependence Convex Hull. Section three gives the definition of Unique Sets and methods to find them. Section four presents our Unique Set oriented partitioning technique. Section five confirms our claims with results comparing our technique with previously proposed techniques. Finally, we conclude in section six. Due to the space restrictions all the proofs of the theorems and corollaries have been omitted. Please refer to the technical report[6] for further details.

## PROGRAM MODEL AND DEPENDENCE REPRESENTATION

Studies [7, 1] show that most of the loops with complex array subscripts are two dimensional loops. In order to simplify explaining our techniques, our Program Model has a normalized, doubly nested loops with coupled subscripts (*i.e.*, subscripts are linear functions of loop indices). Both lower and upper bounds for indices should be known at compile time. Our general program model is:

$$\text{do } i = L_1, U_1$$
$$\quad \text{do } j = L_2, U_2$$
$$\quad\quad A(a_{11}i + b_{11}j + c_{11}, a_{12}i + b_{12}j + c_{12}) = \cdots$$
$$\quad\quad \cdots = A(a_{21}i + b_{21}j + c_{21}, a_{22}i + b_{22}j + c_{22})$$
$$\quad \text{enddo}$$
$$\text{enddo}$$

The most common method to compute data dependences involves solving a set of linear Diophantine equations with a set of constraints formed by the iteration boundaries. Given the program model above, we want to find a set of integer solutions $(i_1, j_1, i_2, j_2)$ that satisfy the system of Diophantine equations (1) and the system of linear inequalities (2) .

$$a_{11}i_1 + b_{11}j_1 + c_{11} = a_{21}i_2 + b_{21}j_2 + c_{21}$$
$$a_{12}i_1 + b_{12}j_1 + c_{12} = a_{22}i_2 + b_{22}j_2 + c_{22} \qquad (1)$$

$$\begin{cases} L_1 \le i_1 \le U_1 \\ L_2 \le j_1 \le U_2 \\ L_1 \le i_2 \le U_1 \\ L_2 \le j_2 \le U_2 \end{cases} \qquad (2)$$

The Dependence Convex Hull(DCH) is a convex polyhedron and is a subspace of the solution space. Please refer to [3] for the definition.

There are two approaches to solving the system of Diophantine equations in (1). One way is to set $i_1$ to $x_1$ and $j_1$ to $y_1$ and solve for $i_2$ and $j_2$.

$$\begin{cases} i_2 = \alpha_{11}x_1 + \beta_{11}y_1 + \gamma_{11} \\ j_2 = \alpha_{12}x_1 + \beta_{12}y_1 + \gamma_{12} \end{cases}$$

where $\alpha_{11} = (a_{11}b_{22} - a_{12}b_{21})/(a_{21}b_{22} - a_{22}b_{21})$, $\beta_{11} = (b_{11}b_{22} - b_{12}b_{21})/(a_{21}b_{22} - a_{22}b_{21})$, $\gamma_{11} = (b_{22}c_{11} + b_{21}c_{22} - b_{22}c_{21} - b_{21}c_{12})/(a_{21}b_{22} - a_{22}b_{21})$, $\alpha_{12} = (a_{21}a_{12} - a_{11}b_{22})/(a_{21}b_{22} - a_{22}b_{21})$, $\beta_{12} = (a_{21}b_{12} - a_{22}b_{11})/(a_{21}b_{22} - a_{22}b_{21})$, $\gamma_{12} = (a_{21}c_{12} + a_{22}c_{21} - a_{21}c_{22} - a_{22}c_{11})/(a_{21}b_{22} - a_{22}b_{21})$

The solution space **S** is the set of points $(x, y)$ satisfying the equations given above. The set of inequalities can be written as

$$\begin{cases} L_1 \le & x_1 & \le U_1 \\ L_2 \le & y_1 & \le U_2 \\ L_1 \le & \alpha_{11}x_1 + \beta_{11}y_1 + \gamma_{11} & \le U_1 \\ L_2 \le & \alpha_{12}x_1 + \beta_{12}y_1 + \gamma_{12} & \le U_2 \end{cases} \qquad (3)$$

where (3) defines a DCH denoted by **DCH1**.

Another approach is to set $i_2$ to $x_2$ and $j_2$ to $y_2$ and solve for $i_1$ and $j_1$.

$$\begin{cases} i_1 = \alpha_{21}x_2 + \beta_{21}y_2 + \gamma_{21} \\ j_1 = \alpha_{22}x_2 + \beta_{22}y_2 + \gamma_{22} \end{cases}$$

where $\alpha_{21} = (a_{21}b_{12} - a_{22}b_{11})/(a_{11}b_{12} - a_{12}b_{11})$, $\beta_{21} = (b_{12}b_{21} - b_{11}b_{22})/(a_{11}b_{12} - a_{12}b_{11})$, $\gamma_{21} =$

$(b_{12}c_{21} + b_{11}c_{12} - b_{12}c_{11} - b_{11}c_{22})/(a_{11}b_{12} - a_{12}b_{11})$, $\alpha_{22} = (a_{11}a_{22} - a_{12}b_{21})/(a_{11}b_{12} - a_{12}b_{11})$, $\beta_{22} = (a_{11}b_{22} - a_{12}b_{21})/(a_{11}b_{12} - a_{12}b_{11})$, $\gamma_{22} = (a_{11}c_{22} + a_{12}c_{11} - a_{11}c_{12} - a_{12}c_{21})/(a_{11}b_{12} - a_{12}b_{11})$

The solution space **S** is the set of points $(x, y)$ satisfying the solution given above. In this case the set of inequalities can be written as

$$\begin{cases} L_1 \leq & \alpha_{21}x_2 + \beta_{21}y_2 + \gamma_{21} & \leq U_1 \\ L_2 \leq & \alpha_{22}x_2 + \beta_{22}y_2 + \gamma_{22} & \leq U_2 \\ L_1 \leq & x_2 & \leq U_1 \\ L_2 \leq & y_2 & \leq U_2 \end{cases} \quad (4)$$

where (4) defines another DCH, denoted by **DCH2**.

We introduce a new term *Complete DCH* to represent the union of DCH1 and DCH2 (which were constructed by (3) and (4)) and we shall demonstrate that the Complete DCH contains all the information we need to parallelize the loop.

### Definition 1 (Complete DCH (CDCH))

*The Complete DCH is the union of two closed sets of integer points in the iteration space, which satisfy (3) or (4).*

We use an arrow to represent a dependence in the iteration space. We call the arrow's head *the dependence head* and the arrow's tail *the dependence tail*. Figure 2 shows the CDCH of Example 1.

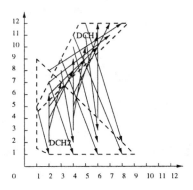

Figure 2: *CDCH of Example 1*

**Theorem 1** *All the dependence heads and tails lie within the CDCH. The head and tail of any particular dependence lie separately in the two DCHs of the CDCH.*

If iteration $(i_2, j_2)$ is dependent on iteration $(i_1, j_1)$, then we have a dependence vector D(x, y) with $d_i(x,y) = i_2 - i_1$, $d_j(x,y) = j_2 - j_1$. So, for DCH1, we have

$$d_i(x_1, y_1) = (\alpha_{11} - 1)x_1 + \beta_{11}y_1 + \gamma_{11}$$
$$d_j(x_1, y_1) = \alpha_{12}x_1 + (\beta_{12} - 1)y_1 + \gamma_{12} \quad (5)$$

For DCH2, we have

$$d_i(x_2, y_2) == (1 - \alpha_{21})x_2 - \beta_{21}y_2 - \gamma_{21}$$
$$d_j(x_2, y_2) = -\alpha_{22}x_2 + (1 - \beta_{22})y_2 - \gamma_{22} \quad (6)$$

Clearly, if we have a solution $(x_1, y_1)$ in DCH1, we must have a solution $(x_2, y_2)$ in DCH2, because they are derived from the same set of linear Diophantine equations (1).

## UNIQUE SETS IN THE ITERATION SPACE

As we have shown, all dependences lie within the CDCH. In other words, the iterations lying outside the CDCH are independent and can be executed in parallel. Hence we only have to worry about the iterations inside CDCH.

### UNIQUE HEAD AND UNIQUE TAIL SETS

DCH1 and DCH2 are our primitive sets. For a particular set it is possible that it contains both, dependence heads and tails.

**Definition 2 (Unique Head(Tail) Set)** *Unique head(tail) set is a set of integer points in the iteration space that satisfies the following conditions:*

1. *it is subset of one of the DCHs (or is the DCH itself).*

2. *it contains all the dependence arrow's heads(tails), but does not contain any other dependence arrow's tails(heads).*

Obviously the DCHs in Figure 2 are not the unique sets we are trying to find, because each DCH contains all the dependence heads of one kind and at the same time contains all the dependence tails of the other kind. Therefore, these DCHs must be further partitioned into smaller unique sets.

### FINDING UNIQUE HEAD AND UNIQUE TAIL SETS

We first examine the properties of DCH1 and DCH2.

**Theorem 2** *DCH1 contains all flow dependence tails and all anti dependence heads (if they exist) and DCH2 contains all anti dependence tails and all flow dependence heads (if they exist).*

The above theorem tells us that DCH1 and DCH2 are not unique head or unique tail sets. If there exist only flow or anti dependence, DCH1 either contains all the flow dependence tails or anti dependence heads, and DCH2 either contains all the flow dependence heads or anti dependence tails. Under these conditions, both DCH1 and DCH2 are unique sets. The following theorem states the condition for DCH1 and DCH2 to be unique sets.

**Theorem 3** *If $d_i(x,y) = 0$ does not pass through any DCH, then there is only one kind of dependence, either flow or anti dependence, and the DCH itself is the Unique Head set or the Unique Tail set.*

DCH1 and DCH2 are constructed from the same system of linear Diophantine equations and inequalities. The following two theorems highlight their common attributes.

**Theorem 4** *If $d_i(x_1,y_1) = 0$ does not pass through DCH1, then $d_i(x_2,y_2) = 0$ does not pass through DCH2.*

**Corollary 1** *When $d_i(x_1,y_1) = 0$ does not pass through DCH1,*

1. *if DCH1 is on the side of $d_i(x_1,y_1) > 0$, then*

   (a) *DCH1 is the flow dependence Unique Tail set, and*

   (b) *DCH2 is the flow dependence Unique Head set.*

2. *if DCH1 is on the side of $d_i(x_1,y_1) < 0$, then*

   (a) *DCH1 is the anti dependence Unique Head set, and*

   (b) *DCH2 is the anti dependence Unique Tail set.*

**Corollary 2** *When $d_i(x_1,y_1) = 0$ does not pass through DCH1,*

1. *if DCH1 is on the side of $d_i(x_1,y_1) > 0$, then DCH2 is on the side of $d_i(x_2,y_2) > 0$.*

2. *if DCH1 is on the side of $d_i(x_1,y_1) < 0$, then DCH2 is on the side of $d_i(x_2,y_2) < 0$.*

We have now established that if $d_i(x_1,y_1) = 0$ does not pass through DCH1, then both DCH1 and DCH2 are Unique Sets.

When $d_i(x,y) = 0$ passes through the CDCH, a DCH might contain both dependence heads and tails (even if DCH1 and DCH2 do not overlap). This makes it harder to find the unique head and tail sets. The next theorem looks at some common attributes when $d_i(x,y) = 0$ passes through the CDCH.

**Theorem 5** *If $d_i(x_1,y_1) = 0$ passes through DCH1, then $d_i(x_2,y_2) = 0$ must pass through DCH2.*

Using the above theorem we can now deal with the case where a DCH contains all the dependence tails of one kind and all the dependence heads of another kind.

**Theorem 6** *If $d_i(x,y) = 0$ passes through a DCH, then it will divide that DCH into a unique tail set and a unique head set. Furthermore, $d_j(x,y) = 0$ decides on the inclusion of $d_i(x,y) = 0$ in one of the sets.*

Note that if $d_j(x_1,y_1) > 0$, then the line segment corresponding to $d_i(x_1,y_1) = 0$ belongs to the flow dependence Unique Tail set and if $d_j(x_1,y_1) < 0$, then the line segment corresponding to $d_i(x_1,y_1) = 0$ belongs to the anti dependence Unique Head set. The iteration corresponding to the intersection of $d_i(x_1,y_1) = 0$ and $d_j(x_1,y_1) = 0$ has no cross-iteration dependence. If the intersection point of $d_i(x_1,y_1) = 0$ and $d_j(x_1,y_1) = 0$ lies in DCH1, then one segment of the line $d_i(x_1,y_1) = 0$ inside DCH1 is a subset of the flow dependence unique tail set and the other segment of the line $d_i(x_1,y_1) = 0$ inside DCH1 is a subset of the anti dependence unique head set.

For DCH2, we have similar results as above.

**Corollary 3** *When $d_i(x_1,y_1) = 0$ passes through DCH1, then*

1. *DCH1 is the union of the flow dependence Unique Tail set and the anti dependence Unique Head set, and*

2. *DCH2 is the union of the flow dependence Unique Head set and the anti dependence Unique Tail set.*

Figure 3 illustrates the application of our results to example 1. Clearly $d_i(x_1,y_1) = 0$ divides DCH1 into two parts. The area on the left side of $d_i(x_1,y_1) = 0$ is the Unique Tail set for flow dependence and the area on the right side of $d_i(x_1,y_1) = 0$ is the Unique Head set for anti dependence. $d_i(x_2,y_2) = 0$ divides DCH2 into two parts too. The area below $d_i(x_2,y_2) = 0$ is the Unique Head set for flow dependence and the area above $d_i(x_2,y_2) = 0$ is the Unique Tail set for anti dependence.

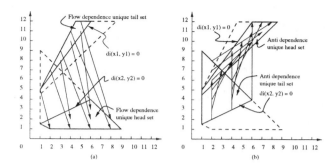

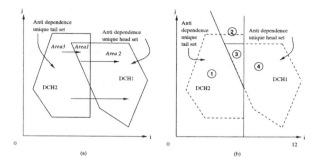

Figure 3: *Unique Head sets and Unique Tail sets of (a) Flow dependence, (b) Anti dependence*

## UNIQUE SETS ORIENTED PARTITIONING

Based on the Unique Head and Tail Sets that we identify, there exist various combinations of overlaps (and/or disjointness) of these Unique Head and Tail sets. We categorize these combinations as various cases starting from simpler cases and leading up to the more complicated ones. Because of lack of space we will not discuss all combinations. However, these combinations are not too many and can be generated systematically.

**Case 1** *There is only one kind of dependence and DCH1 does not overlap with DCH2.*

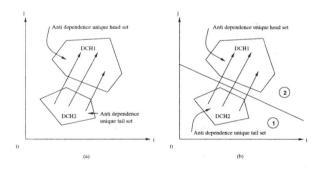

Figure 4: *One kind of dependence and DCH1 does not overlap with DCH2*

Figure 4(a) illustrates this case. Any line drawn between DCH1 and DCH2 divides the iteration space into two areas. The iterations within each area can be executed concurrently. However, the area containing DCH2 needs to execute before the area containing DCH1 (as shown by the partitioning in Figure 4(b)). The execution order is given by $1 \rightarrow 2$.

**Case 2** *There is only one kind of dependence and DCH1 overlaps with DCH2.*

Figure 5: *One kind of dependence and DCH1 overlaps with DCH2*

Figure 5(a) illustrates this case. DCH1 and DCH2 overlap to produce three distinct areas denoted by *Area*1, *Area*2 and *Area*3, respectively. *Area*2 and *Area*3 are either Unique Tail or Unique Head sets and thus iterations within each set can execute concurrently. *Area*1 contains both tail and heads of dependences. One can apply the *Minimum Dependence Distance Tiling* technique proposed by Punyamurtula and Chaudhary [5] to *Area*1. Depending on the type of dependence there are two distinct execution orders possible. If DCH1 is a Unique Tail set, then the execution order is $Area2 \rightarrow Area1 \rightarrow Area3$. Otherwise, the execution order is $Area3 \rightarrow Area1 \rightarrow Area2$. Figure 5(b) shows one possible partitioning.

**Case 3** *There are two kinds of dependences and DCH1 does not overlap with DCH2.*

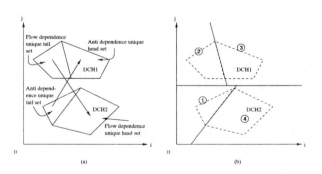

Figure 6: *Two kinds of dependences and DCH1 does not overlap with DCH2*

Figure 6(a) illustrates this case. Since DCH1 and DCH2 are disjoint we can partition the iteration space into two with DCH1 and DCH2 belonging to distinct partitions. From theorem 6 we know that $d_i(x, y) = 0$ will divide the DCHs into Unique Tail and Unique Head sets. We next partition the area with DCH1 by the line $d_i(x_1, y_1) = 0$, and the area with DCH2 by the line $d_i(x_2, y_2) = 0$. So, we have four partitions, each of which is totally parallelizable. Figure 6(b) gives one possible partition with execution order as $1 \rightarrow 2 \rightarrow 3 \rightarrow 4$. Note that the Unique Head sets must execute after the Unique Tail sets.

**Case 4** *There are two kinds of dependences and DCH1 overlaps with DCH2, and there is at least one isolated unique set.*

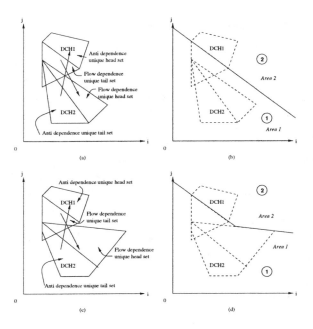

Figure 7: *Two kinds of dependences and one isolated unique set*

Figures 7(a) and 7(c) illustrate this case. What we want to do is to separate this isolated unique set from the others. The line $d_i(x, y) = 0$ is the best candidate to do this. If $d_i(x, y) = 0$ does not intersect with any other unique set or another DCH, then it will divide the iteration space into two parts as shown Figure 7(b). If $d_i(x, y) = 0$ does intersect with other unique sets or another DCH, we can add one edge of the other DCH as our boundary to partition the iteration space into two as shown in Figure 7(d). Let us denote the partition containing the isolated unique set by *Area*2. The other partition is denoted by *Area*1. If *Area*2 contains a unique tail set, then *Area*2 must execute before *Area*1, otherwise *Area*2 must execute after *Area*1. The next step is to partition *Area*1. Since *Area*1 has only one kind of dependence (as long as we maintain the execution order defined above) and DCH1 overlaps with DCH2, it falls under the category of case 2 and can be further partitioned as earlier.

**Case 5** *There are two kinds of dependence and all unique sets are overlapping with each other.*

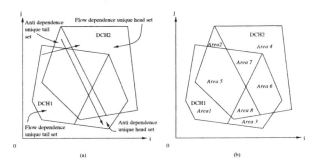

Figure 8: *Two kinds of dependence and all unique sets overlapped each other*

Figure 8(a) illustrates this case. The CDCH can be partitioned into at most eight parts as shown in Figure 8(b). *Area*1 contains only flow dependence tails. *Area*2 contains only anti dependence tails. *Area*3 contains only anti dependence heads. *Area*4 contains only flow dependence heads. *Area*5 contains flow dependence tails and anti dependence tails. *Area*6 contains flow dependence heads and anti dependence heads. *Area*7 contains flow dependence tails and flow dependence heads. *Area*8 contains anti dependence tails and anti dependence heads.

*Area*1, *Area*2, and *Area*5 can be combined together into a larger area, because they contain only the dependence tails. Let us denote this combined area by *AreaI*. In the same way, *Area*3, *Area*4, and *Area*6 can also be combined together, because they contain only the dependence heads. Let us denote this combined area by *AreaII*. *AreaI* and *AreaII* are fully parallelizable. The execution order becomes *AreaI* $\rightarrow$ *Area*7 $\rightarrow$ *Area*8 $\rightarrow$ *AreaII*. Since *Area*7 and *Area*8 contain both dependence heads and tails, we can apply *Minimum Dependence Distance Tiling* technique to parallelize this area.

## PRELIMINARY EXPERIMENTAL RESULTS

We executed Example 1 on a Cray J916 with 16 processors and 4 GBytes of RAM with different partitioning schemes. We analyzed the program using the *Autotasking Expert System* (atexpert), which is a tool developed by CRI for accurately measuring and graphically displaying tasking performance from a job run on an arbitrarily loaded CRI system. It can predict speedups on a dedicated system from data collected from a single run on a non-dedicated system.

We used *User-directed tasking* directives to construct our fully parallelizable area in the iteration space. We set the upper bounds of the loop to 1000.

The iteration space for Example1 is shown in Figure 9. In Figure 9(a), *Area*1 contains the flow dependence

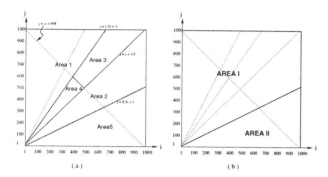

Figure 9: *Iteration space of Example 2*

tail set and part of the anti dependence tail set. *Area*2 contains only anti dependence tails. *Area*3 contains only anti dependence heads. *Area*4 contains both anti dependence heads and tails. *Area*5 contains the flow dependence head set. In figure 9(b), *AREA I* is the combination of *Area*1, *Area*2, *Area*3 and *Area*4, and *AREA II* is the same as *Area*5.

Obviously this example falls into the category of case 4. Based on unique sets, we can first isolate a parallel area which contains the flow dependence Unique Head set. That area is *Area*5 and it should execute last. The iteration space beyond this area, which is *AREA II*, falls into case 2. Now we need only consider one kind of dependence, anti dependence. At this point, we can either continue our partitioning according to the anti dependence Unique Head set and Tail set, or apply *minimum dependence distance tiling* technique to *AREA I*. We show these two approaches in the following schemes. In addition, we add the case where the last region of the first approach is run sequentially for comparison purposes (corresponding to scheme 2).

1. **Scheme 1:** executing in the order of *AREA I* → *AREA II*, where *AREA II* is fully parallel. In *AREA I* apply the *minimum dependence distance tiling* technique. Here minimum distance is 4 in the $j$ direction(*i.e.*, tiling size is 4 in the $j$ direction).

2. **Scheme 2:** executing in the order of *Area*1 → *Area*2 → *Area*3 → *Area*4 → *Area*5, where *Area*1, *Area*2, *Area*3 and *Area*5 execute in parallel and *Area*4 executes in serial order.

3. **Scheme 3:** executing in the order of *Area*1 → *Area*2 → *Area*3 → *Area*4 → *Area*5, where *Area*1, *Area*2, *Area*3 and *Area*5 execute fully in parallel. We apply the *minimum dependence distance tiling* technique to *Area*4(Here minimum distance is 4 too).

The results for the above schemes are shown in Figure 10, 11, and 12, respectively. The solid line is the

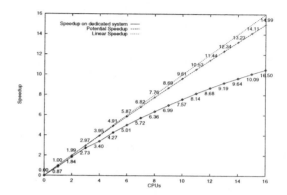

Figure 10: *Speedup for Scheme 1*

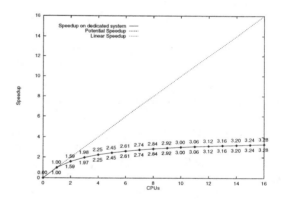

Figure 11: *Speedup for Scheme 2*

speedup on a dedicated system. The dashed line is the potential speedup which is the maximum speedup under ideal conditions for this program. The dotted line shows linear speedup, the boundary for all speedups.

Zaafrani and Ito's three-region region method[4] was also implemented and the result is shown in Figure 13. Clearly all three partitioning schemes we proposed show better results than the three-region method. The sequential region in our scheme is much smaller than in theirs.

Among our three schemes, Scheme 2 is the worst, showing 74.1% parallel and 25.9% serial parts. Scheme 1 comes in second, with 99.6% parallel and 0.4% serial

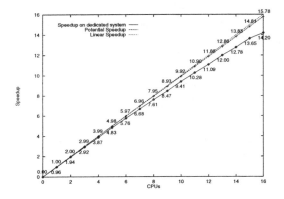

Figure 12: *Speedup for Scheme 3*

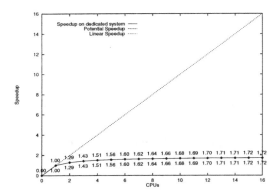

Figure 13: *Speedup for Zaafrani and Ito's three-region method*

parts. Scheme 3 is the best, it shows 99.9% parallel and 0.1% serial parts. The reason that Scheme 2 is worst is that it has a sequential region in the iteration space, which becomes a bottleneck. Scheme 3 is far better than Scheme 2, leaving nothing in the iteration space that would run sequentially. Scheme 1 uses tiling technique in *AREA I*, which divides *AREA I* into many small, fully parallel regions. These tiles would run sequentially. Scheme 3 shows almost linear speedup, since there are no sequential regions.

From our preliminary results, it appears that the iteration space should be partitioned into parallel regions based on unique sets and the non-parallelizable region should be partitioned using the minimum dependence distance tiling technique.

## CONCLUSION

In this paper, we systematically analyzed the characteristics of the dependences in the iteration space with the concepts of Complete Dependence Convex Hull, Unique Head sets and Unique Tail sets, which iso-

lated the dependence information and showed the relationship among the dependences. We also proposed the Unique sets oriented partitioning of the iteration space. The suggested scheme was implemented on a Cray J916 and compared with the three-region technique. Preliminary results exhibit marked improvement in speedups.

## ACKNOWLEDGMENTS

We would like to thank Sumit Roy and Chengzhong Xu for their constructive comments on the contents of this paper.

# References

[1] Z. Shen, Z. Li, and P. C. Yew, "An empirical study on array subscripts and data dependencies," in *Proceedings of the International Conference on Parallel Processing*, pp. II–145 to II–152, 1989.

[2] Y. Q. Yang, C. Ancourt, and F. Irigoin, "Minimal data dependence abstractions for loop transformations: Extended version," *International Journal of Parallel Programming*, vol. 23, no. 4, pp. 359–388, 1995.

[3] T. H. Tzen and L. M. Ni, "Dependence uniformization: A loop parallelization tehnique," *IEEE transactions on Parallel and Distributed Systems*, vol. 4, pp. 547–558, May 1993.

[4] A. Zaafrani and M. Ito, "Parallel region execution of loops with irregular dependences," in *Proceedings of the International Conference on Parallel Processing*, pp. II–11 to II–19, 1994.

[5] S. Punyamurtula and V. Chaudhary, "Minimum dependence distance tiling of nested loops with non-uniform dependences," *Symp. on Parallel and Distributed Processing*, pp. 74–81, 1994.

[6] J. Ju and V. Chaudhary, "Unique sets oriented partitioning of nested loops with non-uniform dependences," *Technical Report PDCL 96-03-39*, Parallel and Distributed Computing Laboratory, Wayne State University, 1996.

[7] Z. Li, P. Yew, and C. Zhu, "An efficient data dependence analysis for parallelizing compilers," *IEEE transactions on Parallel and Distributed Systems*, pp. 26–34, Jan. 1990.

# Towards automatic performance analysis*

Amitabh B. Sinha
Informix Software
Menlo Park, CA 94025
email: amitabh@informix.com

Laxmikant V. Kalé
Department of Computer Science
University of Illinois
Urbana, IL 61801
email: kale@cs.uiuc.edu

**Abstract** – *Most existing performance tools provide generic measurements and visual displays. It is then the responsibility of the users to analyze the performance of their programs using the displayed information. This can be a non-trivial task, because one needs to identify specific pieces of information needed for such analysis. A good performance analysis tool should be able to provide intelligent analysis, and not just feedback, about the performance of a parallel program. Such automatic performance analysis is feasible for programming paradigms that expose sufficient information about program behavior. Charm, a portable, object-based, and message-driven parallel programming language is one such paradigm. In this paper, we describe the design and implementation of Projections:Expert, a framework for automatic performance analysis for Charm programs.*

## 1 Introduction

In order to improve the performance of a particular parallel algorithm, one must identify the critical factor that is affecting the performance of the program negatively in the most significant way *and* the component of the algorithm that is responsible for this factor. Performance feedback and analysis tools which provide such information are crucial towards improving the performance of parallel programs. One widely used technique for performance feedback is visualization. Tools, such as ParaGraph [3], Pablo [9], etc., provide visual feedback about the utilization of processors, message traffic, etc. It is the responsibility of the users to use the displayed information to analyze the performance of their programs. This by itself can be a non-trivial task and is made even more difficult for long-running programs, because the amount of performance information can be staggering. One way to make performance analysis of long-running programs simpler is to *automatically provide the user with feedback about the components of a parallel program responsible for poor performance*, along with information about the performance loss due to each such component.

Automatic performance analysis at first seems to be an intractable problem: there are a myriad different possible performance problems and analysis techniques. However,

experience [11] with the performance of many real parallel applications suggests that poor performance is often due to well-recognized categories of problems, such as load imbalance, time taken for synchronization, etc. Thus, automatic analysis is feasible if information about program behavior needed to detect such problems is available. A system can acquire information about a user's program in the following two broad ways:

(i) **Compiler support**: Compilers can be used to determine information about user program behavior. The information may be readily available through language constructs or user annotation, e.g., if the user declares a variable as readonly. The information may not be readily available, in which case, the compiler needs to infer such information from the program, e.g., parallelizing compilers [8], expose information about parallelism in the program.

(ii) **System libraries**: The system can also acquire information about a program's behavior if known system libraries are used, e.g., the use of the *barrier* construct provided by most message passing SPMD languages indicates a global synchronization in the program.

In this paper, we describe Projections:Expert, a framework for automatic performance analysis for programs written in an object-based, message-driven, and portable parallel language called Charm [4][1]. The language features, execution model, and system libraries of Charm allow us to readily acquire information about program behavior. We describe them in Section 2. In Section 3, we present the top-level algorithm and techniques for automatic analysis. In Section 4, we present a case study to illustrate the use of the tool. The interested reader is referred to other case studies presented in [10]. In Section 5, we discuss the applicability of our methodology to other programming paradigms, such as MPI. In Section 6, we review some related work in automatic performance analysis. Finally, in Section 7, we present our conclusions.

## 2 Charm

In this section, we show how information about a Charm program's behavior is acquired through language

*This research was supported in part by the National Science Foundation grants CCR-90-07195 and CCR-91-06608.

[1]Charm programs ran portably across shared memory machines, including Sequent Symmetry, distributed memory machines, including networks of UNIX workstations, IBM SP-2, Intel Paragon, and CM-5. The discussion in this paper is also applicable to the C++ extension of Charm called Charm++ [5].

constructs and system libraries.

## 2.1 Language constructs

The basic unit of computation in a Charm program is an entity called *chare*. The syntax of a *chare* is shown in Figure 1. A *chare* has its own data area, which is accessible to its *entry functions*, *private* functions, and *public* functions. *Entry functions* are functions, which are sequentially executed when a message addressed to that entry function is delivered. The syntax of a message declaration is the same as that of a *struct* declaration in C.

Chares are medium grained processes, and can be dynamically created using the *CreateChare* system call. The execution model of Charm is message-driven: a message is addressed to an *entry function* of a chare; when the message is picked up for execution at its destination processor, it results in the invocation of the specified *entry function*. Further the execution model of Charm ensures that the code-block associated with a message is executed in a non-preemptive fashion. In this programming model, the system can easily decompose the program into sub-tasks — the code-block associated with a message constitutes a sub-task. At the lowest level, a Charm program consists of messages and the execution of entry functions. Because the execution model of Charm is message driven there is a clear association between sub-tasks and the type of message that caused it. Further, the different types of sub-tasks and messages are all statically determined, because: (i) a message must correspond to one of the defined message types, and (ii) a sub-task must correspond to one of the defined entry functions.

*Private* functions are blocks of C-code, which are accessible only from within the chare. *Public* functions are blocks of C-code, which are synchronously accessible from other chares on the same processor.

Charm also provides another kind of process called a branch office chare (BOC). The syntax of a BOC is the same as that of a chare. A BOC is a replicated chare: there exists a branch or copy of the chare on each processor. All the branches of a BOC are referred to by a unique identifier. This identifier is assigned when a BOC instance is created using the *CreateBoc* call. Figure 1 shows a simple ring program written using a BOC.

The programming model of Charm we have presented so far allows chares to share information with other chares only through messages. Charm supports multiple specific modes of information sharing [6]. Each mode is an abstract data type (ADT), and can be accessed and mutated only via the defined functions of the corresponding ADT. The specific modes of information sharing are:

**(1) Readonly**: A readonly variable is initialized once and is not altered thereafter.

**(2) Distributed table**: A distributed table is a set of entries, where each entry is a "record" with an integer key, and an untyped data field. Distributed tables are accessed and modified only via the three calls: **Insert**, **Delete**, and **Find**.

**(3) Accumulator**: An accumulator is a counter-like variable, with a commutative associative update function.

```
chare main {
    entry CharmInit: {
        MSG1 *msg; ChareNumType boc;
        msg = (MSG *) CkAllocMsg(MSG);
        boc = CreateBoc(Ring, Ring@Start, msg); }
}


BranchOffice Ring {
    int right;
    entry Start: (message MSG *msg) {
        right = (CkMyPeNum()+1) % CkMaxPeNum();
        if (CkMyPeNum()==0)
            SendMsgBranch(msg, Ring@Pass, right); }

    entry Pass: (message MSG *msg) {
        if (CkMyPeNum()==0) CkExit();
        else {
            PrivateCall(print());
            SendMsgBranch(msg, Ring@Pass, right); }
    }

    private print() {
        CkPrintf("Sent message to neighbor %d", right); }}
}
```

Figure 1: A ring program.

Its value can be read only once, destructively.

**(4) Monotonic**: A monotonic variable has a monotonically changing value, and is frequently updated and read. The requirements on reads are relaxed so that the most up-to date value may not be provided; the system ensures that new values are propagated as quickly as possible. Such a variable is useful in storing the cost of best solution in branch-and-bound computations, where every chare needs to know the current best bound which can be updated whenever a better bound is found.

The usage of one of these modes in a Charm program provides us with more information about the nature of information sharing in the program.

## 2.2 System libraries

The Charm system includes several standard system libraries which implement message queues, load balancing, and quiescence detection. Knowledge of the behavior of these libraries provide information about program behavior, which is useful for automatic performance analysis.

In the runtime execution model of Charm, messages arriving at a processor are queued. Charm provides the user with the ability to link a library, which decides how the runtime selects from amongst the enqueued messages. The choices include libraries which implement lifo, fifo, fifolifo, and prioritized queueing. From the perspective of performance analysis, queuing strategies provide information about the times at which messages were queued and dequeued, and the order in which messages were executed by the runtime system.

Quiescence is the state of execution, when there are no messages left in the system. The absence of messages in the system signals that there is no activity. Further, since no spontaneous activity is permitted in Charm, the absence of messages also indicates that no activity can occur in the future. One of the characteristics of program behavior that is important in performance analysis are the periods of global synchronization, where no user computation occurs. The quiescence detection library provides such information for Charm programs.

In the Charm execution model, all messages are deposited in a message-pool from where messages are picked up by processors whenever they become free. In the shared memory implementation of Charm, the pool of messages is shared by all processors; in the nonshared memory implementation, the message-pool is implemented in a distributed fashion with each processor having its own local message-pool, which are automatically load balanced. An automatic and dynamic load balancing strategy provides the performance system with information about the mapping of tasks and their computational requirements.

## 3 Integrated Automatic Performance Analysis

A trace of a Charm program's execution is obtained by linking the program with a set of "tracing" libraries. There is no need to instrument the user code, because all the calls to the tracing libraries are made by the runtime system. A *sub-task* in the trace is the execution of an entry function. Let $V$ denote the set of all *user* sub-tasks in the execution of the program, and let $V_p$ denote the set of user sub-tasks on processor $p$. A sub-task $v \in V$ has a time $v_c$ at which the call to create it was made, a time $v_s$ at which the system picked up the message for execution, and a time $v_f$ at which the system finished executing it. A sub-task $y \in V$ is said to be created by a sub-task $x \in V$, if the message that triggered the entry function corresponding to $y$ was created in the entry function corresponding to $x$. Let $x \to y$ denote the fact that $x$ created $y$. Let $E = \{(x,y) \mid x \to y\}$ be the set of edges on the vertices defined by the set $V$. Now $(V, E)$ defines a graph of the sub-tasks in the execution of a Charm program. We denote $(V, E)$ as the *task graph*.

There are two important issues (perturbation and global time) in any trace-based analysis in a distributed system. Both issues are discussed at length in [10], and we will mention them only briefly here because of space considerations. (i) Perturbation due to tracing is typically about 5% of the execution time. We have developed a novel technique using program replay to further reduce perturbation due to tracing. (ii) Our traces are recorded using local time information, and are collectively adjusted after traces have been collected to provide approximate (but, logically consistent [2]) global time. This global time works well for us because our analysis looks mostly at logical collections of sub-tasks.

---

[2] An event does not occur before its creating event.

```
Expert() {
    float threshold = 0.75;
    TASK_LIST *point_list;

    /* determine logically independent phases */
    DetermineLogicalSeparationPoints(&point_list);

    /* for each logical phase */
    for (current=point_list; current; current=next) {
        next = current→next;
        utilization = ComputeTaskCounts();
        if (utilization < threshold)
            PhaseByPhaseAnalysis(current, next);
        PrintPhaseReport();
    }
    DetermineCriticalPath();
    WastefulWorkAnalysis();
    EvaluateLoadBalancing();
    SharedVariableAnalysis();
    CriticalPathAnalysis();
    PrintSummaryReport();
}
```

Figure 2: The performance analysis expert

The top-level algorithm for our performance analysis system appears in Figure 2. The function **DetermineLogicalSeparationPoints** determines sub-tasks, which allow the execution of the program to be partitioned into logically independent phases. The performance of sub-tasks within each logically independent phase is analyzed separately. In Section 3.1, we define logical separation points and show how they can be computed.

Once logically independent phases are determined, each phase is analyzed independently. The function, **ComputeTaskCounts**, is called to compute the the processor utilization[3] and the following quantities for the current logically independent phase:

$N_e^p$: the number of instances of execution of the entry function $e$ on processor $p$,

$G_e^p$: the average granularity (i.e., execution time per invocation) for the entry function $e$ on processor $p$,

$N_e$: the number of instances of execution of the entry function $e$ on all processors ($\sum_p N_e^p$),

$T_e$: the total time spent executing entry function $e$ across all processors ($\sum_p (N_e^p G_e^p)$), and

$G_e$: the average granularity for the entry function $e$ on all processors ($T_e/N_e$).

Analysis techniques are invoked for a phase if the processor utilization during that phase falls below a threshold, which

---

[3] We define *processor utilization* to be the average percent of time spent by each processor in executing user code inside program entry functions. System overhead is counted separately.

is 75%[4] by default. We discuss the analysis carried out for each logically independent phase in Section 3.2.

Some analysis techniques are invoked on the entire execution. These include examination of the degree of speculative computation (*WastefulWorkAnalysis*), evaluation of the efficacy of the system load balancing libraries (*EvaluateLoadBalancing*), evaluation of the performance of shared variables (*SharedVariableAnalysis*), and critical path analysis (*CriticalPathAnalysis*) to determine those entry functions which contribute the most to the execution time. A description of these techniques is beyond the scope of this paper because of space limitations. The interested reader is referred to [10] for details.

## 3.1 Logical separation points

One critical issue that needs to be examined is the range of time over which a program's trace should be analyzed. For example, in order to compare the loads on many processors, one would need to identify the time from which to start counting sub-tasks and the time at which to finish counting sub-tasks on all the processors. There are many possibilities. The analysis could be carried over the duration of the entire program or over fixed periodic intervals of time (the interval can be user-specified or can be some heuristically chosen value). However, a program often goes through different natural phases in its execution, each one different from the other. For example, in an iterative solver each iteration can be thought of as a phase. In such a situation, the impact of different performance criterion may be different on different iterations, and hence the analysis could be different for each iteration. Therefore an analysis carried out over the entire program or any pre-defined interval may provide incorrect feedback, because they may not coincide with the phases in execution. The best ranges of time would be those which correspond naturally to different phases of computation in the user program. We define the sub-tasks which separate a program into such natural phases as *logical separation points*. Since logical separation points demarcate the execution of the program into phases which are logically independent, performance analysis of each logically independent phase can be done independent of any other phase.

One key factor seems to be the separation of phases in time, so we provide temporal conditions for an event to be a logical separation event. From the intuitive notion of logical separation points as global synchronization sub-tasks, a sub-task $x$ can be a logical separation point if there are no sub-tasks (excluding ones created by $x$) (i) which occur concurrently with $x$, and (ii) which are created before the completion of $x$, and are processed after $x$. We have designed and implemented an $O(n * log(p))$ algorithm [10] to determine logical separation points, where $n$ is the number of sub-tasks and $p$ the number of processors.

Once the logical separation points of an execution are determined, the program's execution can be partitioned into *logically independent* phases: each phase is the set

of sub-tasks that occurs between consecutive logical separation points. In an iterative solver, for example, each iteration would be a logically independent phase.

## 3.2 Phase by phase analysis

Phase by phase analysis is invoked when the utilization falls below 75%. The broad goal of **PhaseByPhaseAnalysis**, shown in Figure 3, is to provide feedback to increase the utilization of processors [5].

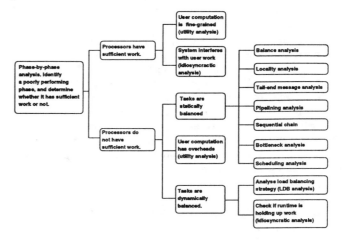

Figure 3: Phase-by-phase analysis.

If processor utilization is poor even though there is work in the processor's queues, then one possibility is that the overheads of task creation dominate useful computation. Utility analysis can be carried out to determine the parts of code that are responsible for such performance loss. Processor utilization may be poor because there is no work in the processor's queue, i.e., the processor idles. Then other techniques, such as the following, become relevant. If the tasks involved are those which are dynamically mappable under the control of a load balancing strategy, then it becomes necessary to analyze the performance of the strategy itself. However, if the tasks involved are statically mapped, then a processor could idle (i) if the load on that processor was less than the load on other processors (balance analysis), or (ii) if the degree of parallelism was insufficient, so that there wasn't enough work to give to every processor (degree of parallelism analysis), or (iii) if the next message the processor was supposed to receive was a large message (pipelining analysis).

The application of multiple performance analysis techniques in the automatic performance analysis framework will often result in a large number of performance problems. In most cases, there are only a few severe performance problems to which it is worth paying attention. In order

---

[4] The choice of 75% as good processor utilization is a heuristic.

[5] Caveat: In *speculative* computations, the total amount of work that all processors do depends on the order in which the execution of sub-tasks in the computation is scheduled. If a poor schedule is chosen, processors can end up doing a large amount of wasteful work. Though this will keep the processors busy, the turnaround time of the program will increase (speculative work is examined in wasteful work analysis).

to make performance analysis worthwhile, one should be able to identify the worst offenders so that users can then concentrate their efforts on solving the most contentious problems first. In order to do this, an automatic performance analysis system must estimate the severity of each performance problem it has identified and rank them accordingly. We define the **severity** of a performance problem informally as the amount of reduction in the program's execution time if the problem is corrected (note that by time we mean something similar to wall-clock time for a dedicated system) [6].

Often the reduction in one part of the computation on a subset of processors may not result in a corresponding reduction in the overall execution time because of overlapping work on other processors. In order to deal with this, we define the function **overlap** as the maximum time spent in user computation on any processor between time $t_1$ and $t_2$. Why is the overlap function useful? Suppose there is a performance problem, that if solved could eliminate the time interval $(t_1, t_2)$ from the program's execution time on one of the processors. Because at least one processor has computation equal to $overlap(t_1, t_2)$ in that same interval of time, so the best case improvement in the program's performance could only be $t_1 - t_2 - overlap(t_1, t_2)$.

We have briefly motivated some techniques for performance analysis. We describe some of these techniques in more detail later in this section.

## Task utility analysis

An activity, such as the creation of a task has an associated cost and utility. Utility analysis attempts to measure the cost/utility ratio of an activity to decide whether the activity is really useful. How can one determine whether it is useful to create a task? The utility or *granularity* of a task in a program is the average computational time needed by the task. The cost of creating a task $e$ is the cost of creating the associated message $m^e$. This includes the cost of allocating the message, the latency involved in sending it to a remote processor[7], and the cost of scheduling the message on that processor. The utility of a task can be determined by comparing the granularity of the task and the cost of creating the associated message.

The granularity of tasks in an application is an important factor in the performance of an application. If the tasks are too fine grained, then the system overheads (communication latency time, message processing time, shared memory access time, context switch time, scheduling, etc.) can adversely dominate the execution of the program. Conversely, if the tasks are too large-grained, then there would be too few tasks to effectively parallelize. Therefore it is necessary to carefully choose an appropriate granularity for tasks in a parallel program. Note that the choice of

---

[6] Our severity estimates are approximate, but work well in most cases to allow us to reason effectively about the relative importance of two different problems.

[7] Communication latency needs to be taken into account as an overhead in situations, where processor idling occurs due to an empty queue, while it should be ignored if transmission delays of message are overlapped with computation.

granularity will need to be machine-dependent.

We illustrate how severity is computed for an entry function known to have small granularity. Assume that $T_x$, the total computational time for entry function $x$ cannot be altered. Since the entry function has poor granularity, performance can be improved if the overheads of executing the entry function is reduced. This is possible if the entry function is executed fewer times with larger granularity; the easiest choice for granularity is the smallest acceptable granularity $I_x$. The current overall overheads are $O_x \sum_p N_x^p$, where $O_x$ is the overhead for entry function $x$. If each execution of the entry function has at least $I_x$, the smallest acceptable granularity, then the entry function $x$ will be executed $T_x/I_x$ times, and the total overheads will therefore be $(T_x/I_x)O_x$. Therefore, the decrease in total overheads will be $(O_x \sum_p N_x^p - T_x * O_x/I_x)$, and so each processor's execution time can potentially be reduced by $O_x(\sum_p N_x^p - T_x/I_x)/P$, where $P$ is the number of processors. □

## Pipelining analysis

Sometimes, in a computation large messages be sent to a remote processor for processing. Since the latency involved in sending a large message is considerably longer if the transmission time of the communication is not overlapped with other work, the receiving processor can be idle for some time before the message arrives. Figure 4(a) shows the case of a large message that arrives at an idle processor.

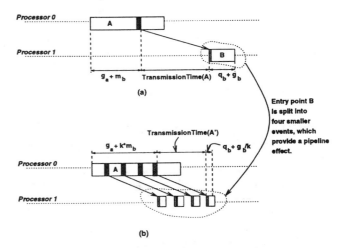

Figure 4: Pipelining when $g_a > g_b$.

The severity of the problem can be reduced if the message is pipelined: the message is broken into smaller fragments, and they are sent out individually. The transmission times of later fragments can then be overlapped with the computation time for the earlier fragments. Figure 4(b) show the effect of pipelining on the same example.

In Figure 4(a), when the large message is sent without pipelining, the duration of time from the beginning of task A to the finish of task B is $(g_a + m_b) + (\alpha + \beta s_b) + (g_b + q_b)$, where the first term is the combined **granularity of A** and the time to allocate the message, the second term is the transmission time for the message to entry function B of size $s_b$, and the third term is the granularity of B and the time to schedule the message for execution, $\alpha$ is the per message, and $\beta$ is the per byte latency to send a message.

In order to compute severity, we make the following assumptions for pipelining: (i) If the large message is split into $k$ smaller ones, then each fractional message would need to be computed by $\frac{1}{k}^{th}$ of the computation associated with entry function A, and (ii) Each of the $k$ small fractions of the large message would result in computation equal to $\frac{1}{k}^{th}$ of the computation associated with entry function B. Thus, in Figure 4(b), a message of size $\frac{s_b}{k}$ is sent at the end of $\frac{g_a}{k}$ computation and causes $\frac{g_b}{k}$ computation at the other end. In addition, each new message requires $m_b$ for allocation. Therefore the new computational time of A is $g_a + m_b k$. The duration of time from the beginning of task A to the finish of the last fraction of task B is $(g_a + m_b k) + (\alpha + \beta(\frac{s_b}{k})) + (q_b + \frac{g_b}{k})$, where the first term is the increased granularity of A, the second term is the transmission time for each fractional message, and the third term is the granularity of $\frac{1}{k}^{th}$ fraction of B and the scheduling time. The reduction in time duration is: $(\beta s_b + g_b)(1 - \frac{1}{k}) + m_b(k - 1)$

Notice that the reduction depends on the degree of pipelining $k$. What is the value of $k$ for the maximum possible reduction? Taking the first derivative of the above equation, we get:

$$-(\beta s_b + g_b)\frac{1}{k^2} + m_b = 0 \Rightarrow k = \sqrt{(\frac{\beta s_b + g_b}{m_b})} \qquad (1)$$

The value of $k$ determined by Equation 1 provides the maximum reduction, because the second derivative is positive. The possible performance improvement is therefore:

$$k_1 = m_b(\sqrt{(\frac{\beta s_b + g_b}{m_b})} - 1) + (\beta s_b + g_b)(1 - \frac{1}{\sqrt{(\frac{\beta s_b + g_b}{m_b})}})$$

Subtracting possible overlap that exists in that period, we determine that the severity of the pipelining problem is: $k_1 - overlap(B_f - k_1, B_f)$.

In some cases, there can be a performance loss because there are a number of small messages going from one processor to another. In such a situation, the exact opposite of pipelining is necessary: performance can be improved if the small messages are combined into one larger message. This is discussed in more detail in [10].

Shared variable analysis

The nature of information sharing and the methods of access of the shared information often affects the performance of the parallel program. The usage of one of the information sharing mechanisms in an application program provides significant insight into the nature of information exchange in the program. This insight can be utilized to provide a more accurate analysis of the performance of programs. Performance concerns that can be addressed when one knows the nature of information sharing (through specifically shared variables) in a Charm program are the utility of creating a shared variable and the nature of its accesses.

An important analysis for a shared variable is to assess whether the cost of it is justified by its use. If some information is represented as a read-only variable, and is not accessed often, the cost of replicating the variable on nonshared memory machines might exceed the savings in access time. In such cases, it might be better to make the variable into an entry in a distributed table, or to replicate it only on the processors that need it. The default implementation of a monotonic variable is the *flooding* implementation. If the updates are very rare, then a better choice would be the *broadcast* implementation. On the other hand, if the updates are very frequent, a better choice would be the *spanning tree* implementation. Details about these various implementation strategies can be found in [6].

Another aspect of locality is to keep accesses to shared variables local as far as possible. In Charm, only the distributed table mechanism is subject to this analysis. The operations on the remaining specific modes of information sharing have been chosen carefully so that most accesses can be implemented with local accesses. If some information is represented as an entry in a distributed table, and it is accessed very frequently by many different processors, analysis could suggest that the data be made read-only. If a large number of entries in the distributed table are accessed only once, it would be most efficient to locate their insertion and access on the same processor, where possible. If an entry of a distributed table is accessed repeatedly on the same processor, then it should be cached.

## 4 Case Study: EGO

In this section, we present an example of performance analysis of a parallel molecular dynamics program (EGO [1]), done with Projections:Expert. At the time the analysis was done, EGO was already in production use. The analysis was done to verify the efficiency of the implementation and to see if Projections:Expert would determine any problems.

In molecular dynamics simulations, a large fraction of the computing time is spent in the evaluation of Coulomb forces, involving $O(N^2)$ floating point operations, where $N$ is the number of atoms in the molecule. The Coulomb forces, which describe the electrostatic interactions in a homogeneous dielectric environment depend on the charges $q_i$ and $q_j$ of pairs $(i,j)$ of atoms and on the corresponding vector $\vec{r}_{ij} = \vec{r}_i - \vec{r}_j$ joining the atoms at positions $\vec{r}_i$ and $\vec{r}_j$. The force between atoms $i$ and $j$ acting on atom $i$ is $\vec{F}_{ij} = \frac{q_i q_j \vec{r}_{ij}}{4\pi \varepsilon r_{ij}^3}$. EGO employs two techniques to reduce the $O(n^2)$ operations needed to compute the electrostatic forces:

(i) Using Newtons's third law, the force between atoms $i$ and $j$ acting on atom $j$ is: $\vec{F}_{ji} = -\vec{F}_{ij}$. Therefore, it is not necessary to compute both $\vec{F}_{ij}$ and $\vec{F}_{ji}$, thus cutting down the computations to about one half.

(ii) In order to gain a substantial speedup, EGO uses a distance classing algorithm to account for long-distance interactions. This algorithm judiciously schedules updates of interactions avoiding unnecessarily frequent computations of interactions between particles which are far apart.

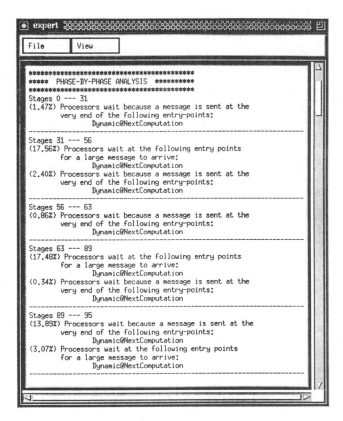

Figure 5: Portion of the phase-by-phase analysis

Figure 6: Analysis report for experimental model of EGO.

We distribute the atoms of a bio-polymer over the available set of processors, each processor computing the interactions corresponding to the set of atoms local to it. An integration begins with each processor computing the electrostatic forces for atoms it owns in the *NextComputation* entry function. Subsequently, it sends out one message containing all its coordinates to the next processor on the ring. The message goes around in a ring, such that each processor computes the pairwise interactions between its atoms and the atoms in the message. When the message returns to the originating processor, an integration is carried out to determine the local energies, followed with a reduction to determine the global energy. Each processor then receives the new energy in a broadcast from processor 0. The next integration step begins after each processor uses the new energy values to compute new positions.

A portion of the phase-by-phase analysis appears in Figure 5. Note the separation of the execution into phases — each phase corresponds to an integration step. The numbers beside the analysis are the severity numbers — they indicate the percentage improvement in execution time for that phase if that problem was solved. The summary analysis given by Projections:Expert for the model appears in Figure 6.

Projection's analysis shows that the biggest performance problem was the large message, containing coordinates and forces, sent out by each processor at the end

of the *NextComputation* entry function. We tried to solve this problem by breaking up the message that arrives at the entry function for Coulomb interactions. The smaller part of the message containing the coordinates is sent out immediately to the neighbor, while the larger packet containing the forces computed in that entry function are sent out only at the end. The performance of the program improved from 660 seconds to 600 seconds, an improvement of about 10%. This may not seem like a large number, but bear in mind that the program we were analyzing was a production quality program, and considerable time had already been spent in examining its efficiency.

The overall size of the trace files for this example were 20K and 50K bytes for the two cases, respectively.

## 5 Applicability

In this section, we discuss the applicability of our methodology in the context of explicitly parallel SPMD based languages. We examine briefly the problems and possible methods of acquiring information about three representative program characteristics: sub-tasks, global synchronization, and modes of information sharing.

In our methodology, message-driven execution allows us to easily identify a sub-task as the execution of an entry function. In the SPMD model, a single process executes continuously on each processor, sending and receiving messages periodically. One possible decomposition of the larger process into smaller sub-tasks is to associate with a message the computation that follows it until the receipt of the next message. However identifying the computation to the user can be cumbersome, because it may not correspond to any natural textual partitions in the code, such as functions. In most cases it is possible to classify messages into types using a combination of tags and line numbers of sends and receives; however this approach can be cumbersome. Further, in the worst case, the system may end up identifying the number of different types of messages in the system to be as large as the number of messages sent in an execution run. This makes it difficult to identify and refer to sub-tasks in a SPMD program. A disciplined approach to writing SPMD programs which allows the compiler to associate sub-tasks with messages — a message driven approach — is therefore needed.

SPMD based programming paradigms can leverage availability of parallel libraries to acquire information. For example, information about global synchronization can be acquired with the usage of known libraries, such as barriers and reduction.

Messages are the sole mechanism of sharing information between sub-tasks on different processors. In the absence of more specific mechanisms for information sharing, it is up to the compiler to determine the specific nature of information sharing being implemented.

These limitations preclude the use of some of our techniques; however others, such as grainsize analysis and pipelining analysis, which depend on knowledge about tasks can still be carried out effectively. Most of the methods described in this paper can be applied to any language based on message driven objects. This is significant as the popularity of parallel object based languages is increasing.

## 6   Related Work

There is a large body of work in performance analysis of parallel programs. The majority of this work has focussed on tools for performance feedback via visualization. In this section, we only discuss related work in automatic performance analysis, namely, ATExpert [7] and $P^3T$ (Parameter based Performance Prediction Tool) [2]. In both these projects, information about the user program is acquired by a parallelizing compiler.

ATExpert is an automatic performance analysis tool based on the Cray Automatic Multitasking compiler. The compiler splits the program into sequential and parallel regions. A parallel region, such as a loop, can be executed in parallel by multiple tasks. In the first step, the ATExpert performance tool identifies the sequential regions in the program, and helps the user reduce their relative contribution to the execution time. In the next step, the tool helps the user make each parallel region more efficient by examining different aspects of the parallelization, such as startup time, convoy effects [7], etc.

Fahringer has developed *Weight Finder* and $P^3T$ to predict the performance of Vienna Fortran programs. In the first step, a sequential profiling run of the program is performed, and the tool collects concrete and characteristic values for sequential program parameters, such as loop iteration counts, true ratios [2], and frequencies. Next, based on the sequential parameters, the tool computes parallel performance parameters, such as work distribution and number of transfers. Finally, the information about the parallel program parameters is used to predict the impact of different data distribution strategies, and the impact of various program transformation strategies, such as loop fusion and interchange. The relative importance of these parameters needs to be identified for each machine by running a set of training programs. Although, in a lot of cases, there is a clear choice of relative importance of parameters, their strategy does not currently include techniques to choose between conflicting results for parameters. Further, they do not provide any information on the optimal order of application of multiple strategies.

## 7   Summary

In this paper, we examined how automatic performance analysis is feasible for a language, such as Charm. We have shown how different performance analysis techniques can be used to evaluate problems. We have also shown how the effectiveness of the analysis can be improved using logical separation points to decompose the program into independent phases. The current system, although effective, does not exploit the full potential of Charm. There is more information available about a Charm program, such as synchronization information. A more sophisticated automatic system can be built by exploiting all available information about Charm programs.

## References

[1] K. Boehncke, H. Heller, H. Grubmüller, and K. Schulten. Molecular dynamics simulations on a systolic ring of transputers. In A. S. Wagner, editor, *NATUG 3:Transputer Research and Applications 3*, pages 83–94, Amsterdam, 1990. North American Transputer Users Group, IOS Press. Pub.# 139.

[2] T. Fahringer. *Automatic performance prediction for parallel programs on massively parallel computers.* PhD thesis, University of Vienna, 1993.

[3] M. T. Heath and J. A. Etheridge. Visualizing the performance of parallel programs. *IEEE Software*, pages 29–39, Sept. 1991.

[4] L. V. Kalé. The Chare kernel parallel programming language and system. In *Proceedings of the 1990 International Conference on Parallel Processing*, volume II, pages 17–25, St. Charles, IL, August 1990.

[5] L. V. Kalé and S, Krishnan. Charm++ : A portable concurrent object oriented system based on C++. In *Proceedings of OOPSLA-93.*, March 1993.

[6] L. V. Kalé and A. B. Sinha. Information sharing in parallel programs. In *IPPS*, April 1994.

[7] J. Kohn and W. Williams. ATExpert. *Journal of Parallel and Distributed Computing*, 18:205–222, 1993.

[8] D. J. Kuck et al. The effects of program restructuring, algorithm change, and archictecture choice on program performance. In *ICPP*, pages 129–138, 1984.

[9] D. A. Reed et al. Scalable performance environments for parallel systems. Technical report, University of Illinois, Urbana, 1991.

[10] A. B. Sinha. *Performance analysis of object-based and message-driven programs.* PhD thesis, Dept. of Computer Science, University of Illinois, Urbana, 1994.

[11] C. B. Stunkel, D. C. Rudolph, W. K. Fuchs, and D. A. Reed. Linear optimization: a case study in performance analysis. In *Proceedings of the Fourth Conference on Hypercube Concurrent Computers and Applications*, March 1989.

# ESTIMATING PARALLEL EXECUTION TIME OF LOOPS WITH LOOP-CARRIED DEPENDENCES[*]

Tsuneo Nakanishi[1], Kazuki Joe[1], Constantine D. Polychronopoulos[2],
Keijiro Araki[3], and Akira Fukuda[1]

[1]Graduate School of Information Science, Nara Institute of Science and Technology
8916–5 Takayama-cho, Ikoma, Nara 630–01, Japan
[2]Center for Supercomputing Research and Development,
University of Illinois at Urbana-Champaign
1308 West Main Street, Urbana, IL 61801–2307, U.S.A.
[3]Department of Computer Science and Communication Engineering,
Graduate School of Information Science and Electorical Engineering, Kyushu University
6–1 Kasuga Koen, Kasuga, Fukuoka 816, Japan
E-mail: nakasu–para@is.aist–nara.ac.jp

**Abstract**—*In this paper, we propose a scheme to estimate exact minimum parallel execution time of the single loop with loop-carried dependences in medium and fine grain parallel execution. The minimum parallel execution time of a loop is given by the critical path length of the dependence graph which represents the code obtained from the fully unrolled loop. However, unrolling loops with large number of iterations requires too much computation time and many storages to be practical. The scheme proposed here provides the minimum parallel execution time without unrolling the loop at all by reducing the problem into an integer linear programming problem and employing the simplex method and a branch-and-bound algorithm to solve it.*

*We also show an experimental implementation of the proposed scheme with Livermore Benchmark Kernels to demonstrate the computation complexity of our scheme is independent of the number of iterations of the given loop unlike the scheme which makes the given loop fully unrolled.*

## INTRODUCTION

Loops are a rich source of parallelism and account for the largest part of program execution time. Parallelizing compilers attempt to exploit parallelism among loop iterations by applying various analyses and restructuring techniques aiming at medium grain parallelism. The order of applying such loop restructuring and optimization techniques has a strong impact on the quality of the resulting parallel code.

Loop parallelization becomes even more challenging when the underlying architecture supports more than one way of exploiting parallelism. This is certainly the case with the majority of modern multiprocessors which support parallelism at

the processor-level (ILP, or instruction-level parallelism) as well as at the system or iteration-level (different groups of iterations of a loop executing on different processors). More alternatives in exploiting parallelism also introduce more trade-offs. For example, given a specific loop, a compiler would have to determine whether to exploit ILP only, iteration-level only, or both ILP and iteration-level parallelism in order to minimize execution time. Several factors come into play including the machine size and the type of code.

However, the central question of interest to our work is designing a methodology which can be used by the compile in order to determine the optimal restructuring for a given loop. In order to determine whether ILP is preferable to parallel loop iterations we need a compile-time metric that would facilitate comparison of projected performance.

In this paper we attempt to use dependence analysis information in order to evaluate the critical path of a given parallel loop, by taking into consideration instruction and iteration-level parallelism. Given that iteration-level parallelism can be estimated in rather straightforward manner, the above would provide a quick and convenient way of estimating the benefit of coupling loop parallelism with ILP.

In the context of this paper we use a more relaxed notion of dependence graphs by assuming that the nodes of such graphs can represent computations (tasks) of any granularity - from the atomic operation to the subroutine level. Dependence graphs, which represent tasks and the constraints on their execution order, are employed by parallelizing compilers for scheduling and restructuring. A node in a dependence graph represents a task, and there is an edge from a node $u$ to a node $v$, denoted by $(u, v)$, iff the task of the node $v$ depends on the task of the node $u$.

There are two types of dependences: data depen-

[*]This work is supported under Research Fellowships of the Japan Society for the Promotion of Science for Young Scientists.

dences and control dependences[4]. In this paper we deal with only data dependences. A node in a data dependence graph has the execution cost (execution time) of the corresponding task as its attribute. On the other hand an edge in a data dependence graph has the communication cost (communication time) of communication caused by the corresponding dependence as its attribute.

The data dependence graph of a basic block is acyclic. The critical path of an acyclic data dependence graph is a path which gives the maximum total cost of the nodes and the edges organizing the path. The critical path cost is equal to the minimum parallel execution time. For that characteristic the critical path cost is often employed for static scheduling and partitioning[6, 7, 12].

The data dependence graph of a loop body is not always acyclic. We cannot detect the critical path of cyclic graphs. On the other hand, when a loop has no branch in its body, the code obtained by completely unrolling the loop is a basic block. In this case we can detect a critical path since its data dependence graph becomes acyclic, and its cost is the minimum parallel execution time of the whole loop. However, it can never be practical to unroll loops completely because of computational cost. In this paper we propose a scheme to evaluate the critical path cost, namely the minimum parallel execution time, of the code obtained by completely unrolling a given loop without unrolling it at all.

Several researchers discuss estimating execution time of doacross loops. Cytron shows execution time of doacross loops when an unlimited number of processors are supplied [2]. Polychronopoulos *et al.* gives the speedup of the doacross loop to its original serial loop with given number of processors in [3]. Since doacross loop is a medium-grain parallel execution model, these works do not consider parallelism inside each loop iteration.

Our scheme reduces the problem into an integer linear programming problem and solves it with the simplex method and a branch-and-bound algorithm. In Section 2 notions on data dependence graphs of loops are introduced. Section 3 shows the way to reduce the problem into an integer linear programming problem and proves its correctness. Section 4 deals with an implementation of the proposed scheme and provides practical evaluation results of its computational complexity. Finally we discuss applications of the proposed scheme to multiply nested loops.

# DATA DEPENDENCE GRAPHS OF LOOPS

In this section we summarize notions on data dependence graphs of a loop. Note that we may use *task* and *node* interchangeably, since tasks and nodes have one-to-one correspondence in data dependence graphs. Likewise for *dependence* and *edge*.

## Loop Task Graph

We refer to the data dependence graph which represents tasks and dependences between the tasks in a loop body as a *loop task graph*. Fig.1(b) shows the loop task graph of the code fragment shown in Fig.1(a). As shown in this example, a loop task graph can be cyclic. Thus we cannot detect the critical path of a loop task graph.

Dependence edges in a loop task graph are classified into the following two classes[9].

- **Loop-Independent Dependence** — dependence such that any pair of tasks concerning the dependence are in the same iteration

- **Loop-Carried Dependence** — dependence such that any pair of tasks concerning the dependence are in different iterations

In the case of a loop-carried dependence, if a task and its dependent task are in the $i$-th iteration and the $(i + d)$-th iteration respectively, we say the *dependence distance* between those tasks is $d$. Remark the dependence distance in the case of a loop-independent dependence is 0. The self-loop edge in a loop task graph is always loop-carried dependence. Dotted edges and the numbers beside them in Fig.1(b) represent loop-carried dependences and their dependence distances respectively.

The graph obtained by removing all the loop-carried dependence edges from a loop task graph is acyclic. The critical path cost of the graph is not the minimum parallel execution time of the whole loop but that of an iteration.

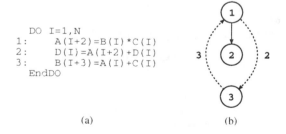

```
    DO I=1,N
1:     A(I+2)=B(I)*C(I)
2:     D(I)=A(I+2)+D(I)
3:     B(I+3)=A(I)+C(I)
    EndDO
```

(a)                    (b)

Fig. 1: Loop Task Graph

## Unrolled Loop Task Graph

The data dependence graph of the code obtained by completely unrolling a loop is acyclic as far as the loop has no branch in its body since the code constructs a basic block. We call this data dependence graph an *unrolled loop task graph*. Fig.2 explains the relation between an unrolled loop task graph and a loop task graph. In Fig.2 we draw the unrolled loop task graph in three dimensions by placing each iteration in the corresponding layer. The nodes corresponding to the same statement in different iterations are placed at the same positions in their own layers. The graph which appears in each layer is equivalent to the graph obtained by removing all the loop-carried dependence edges from the loop task graph. A loop-carried dependence edge goes down across layers and the height difference between the source and the sink of the edge represents its dependence distance. The unrolled task graph is projected on the "ground". The projection is nothing else but the loop task graph.

Let us consider a loop with $N$ iterations. There are $N$ nodes in its unrolled loop task graph whose projections correspond to the same node $v$ in its loop task graph. We refer to those $N$ nodes as *original nodes*[a] of the node $v$. Furthermore, we refer to the node $v$ as a *projected node* of each of those $N$ nodes. We will use similar expressions for edges.

The critical path cost of an unrolled loop task graph is the minimum parallel execution time of the whole loop.

### Projection of Paths

Fig.2 shows how a path (thick line) of an unrolled loop task graph is projected on a loop task graph. We refer to the projected path of a path $p$ of the unrolled loop task graph as a *projection* of the path $p$. Moreover, we refer to the number of times that a projection of a path overlaps on an edge as the *projection overlap degree* of the edge. For example, the projection overlap degrees of edge $a$, $b$, and $c$ in the loop task graph shown in Fig.2 are 2, 0, and 1 respectively.

### Preprocessing the Loop Task Graph

Initially, we apply a number of simplifications to a given loop task graph. At first we append two virtual nodes $START$ and $STOP$ to the loop task graph with cost 0. Next we append loop-independent dependence edges with cost 0 from $START$ to all the nodes which become minimal[b] when all loop-carried dependence edges are removed. Finally we append loop-independent dependence edges with cost 0 from all the nodes, which become maximal[c] when all the loop-carried dependence edges are removed, to $STOP$.

In the normalized graphs it is guaranteed that the critical path of the unrolled loop task graph begins at one of the original nodes of $START$ and ends at one of the original nodes of $STOP$ as we prove later.

---

[a]Term *instances* (of task $v$) are used in common.

[b]We say a node is minimal when the node has no incoming edge.

[c]We say a node is maximal when the node has no outgoing edge.

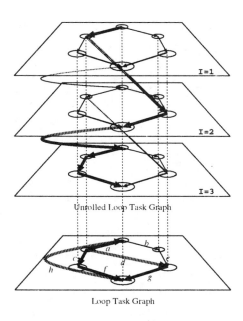

Fig. 2: Unrolled Loop Task Graph

## FORMULATION

The critical path cost of the unrolled loop task graph is the minimum parallel execution time of the whole loop. In this section we describe how to reduce the problem of evaluating a critical path cost of an unrolled loop task graph into an integer linear programming problem.

### Notations and Definitions

We denote a given loop task graph by $G = (V, E)$ and the unrolled loop task graph corresponding to $G$ by $\widetilde{G} = (\widetilde{V}, \widetilde{E})$. $V$ and $E$ are sets of nodes and edges in $G$ respectively. Similarly, $\widetilde{V}$ and $\widetilde{E}$ are sets of nodes and edges in $\widetilde{G}$ respectively. In Table 1 we summarize the other notations we use in this paper and their definitions.

A path of an unrolled loop task graph is defined by a sequence of unique nodes. We define the cost of the path as the sum of costs of nodes and edges that constitute the path. More formally, the cost of a path $p = \langle \widetilde{v_1}, \widetilde{v_2}, ..., \widetilde{v_m} \rangle$[d], say $\Omega(p)$, is defined as expression (1).

---

[d]Notation $\langle a, b, ... \rangle$ means a sequence.

$$\Omega(p) = \omega_{\widetilde{V}}(\widetilde{v_1}) + \sum_{i=1}^{m-1} (\omega_{\widetilde{E}}((\widetilde{v_i}, \widetilde{v_{i+1}})) + \omega_{\widetilde{V}}(\widetilde{v_{i+1}}))$$

$$(1)$$

Table 1: Notations and Definitions

| Notations | Definitions |
|---|---|
| $\omega_V(v)$ | the cost of a node $v$ in $G$ |
| $\omega_E(e)$ | the cost of an edge $e$ in $G$ |
| $sink(e)$ | the end-point of an edge $e$ in $G$ |
| $IN_V(v)$ | the set of edges which enters a node $v$ in $G$ |
| $OUT_V(v)$ | the set of edges which go out from a node $v$ in $G$ |
| $d_E(e)$ | the dependence distance of an edge $e$ in $G$ |
| $\varphi_E(e)$ | the measure of an edge $e$ in $G$ |
| $f_{\widetilde{V}}(\widetilde{v})$ | the projected node of a node $\widetilde{v}$ in $\widetilde{G}$ |
| $f_{\widetilde{E}}(\widetilde{e})$ | the projected edge of an edge $\widetilde{e}$ in $\widetilde{G}$ |
| $\omega_{\widetilde{V}}(\widetilde{v})$ | the cost of a node $\widetilde{v}$ in $\widetilde{G}$ |
| $\omega_{\widetilde{E}}(\widetilde{e})$ | the cost of an edge $\widetilde{e}$ in $\widetilde{G}$ |
| $d_{\widetilde{E}}(\widetilde{e})$ | the dependence distance of an edge $\widetilde{e}$ in $\widetilde{G}$ |
| $F_V(v)$ | the set of the original nodes of a node $v$ in $G$ |
| $F_E(e)$ | the set of the original edges of an edge $e$ in $G$ |
| $\Omega(p)$ | the cost of a path $p$ of $\widetilde{G}$ |

## Target Loops

**Assumption 1** *The loops targeted by this paper are assumed to satisfy the following conditions.*

1. *Single loop*

2. *Constant number of iterations ($N$)*

3. *No branch in a loop body*

4. $\omega_{\widetilde{V}}(\widetilde{v}) = \omega_V(f_{\widetilde{V}}(\widetilde{v}))$ *for any* $\widetilde{v} \in \widetilde{V}$

5. $\omega_{\widetilde{E}}(\widetilde{e}) = \omega_E(f_{\widetilde{E}}(\widetilde{e}))$ *for any* $\widetilde{e} \in \widetilde{E}$

6. $d_{\widetilde{E}}(\widetilde{e}) = d_E(f_{\widetilde{E}}(\widetilde{e}))$ *for any* $\widetilde{e} \in \widetilde{E}$ □

Conditions 4, 5, and 6 mean the cost of a node, the cost of an edge, and the dependence distance of an edge in the unrolled loop task graph are equal to the cost of its original node, the cost of its original edge, and the dependence distance of its original edge respectively. We will discuss a way to remove condition 1 in Section 5.

## Properties of Projections of Paths

The projection of the critical path has the following properties.

**Property 1** *The critical path of $\widetilde{G}$ begins at one of original nodes of $START$ and ends at one of original nodes of $STOP$. (See appendix for the proof.)*□

We consider the problem of evaluating the critical path cost in this paper. According to property 1 we consider only paths which begin at one of original nodes of $START$ and end at one of original nodes of $STOP$. On the other hand the projections of general paths have the following properties under assumption 1.

**Property 2** *A path $p$ of $\widetilde{G}$ begins at one of original nodes of $START$ and ends at one of original nodes of $STOP$. When the measure $\varphi_E(e)$ of an edge $e \in E$ in $G$ is the projection overlap degree of the edge $e$, the cost of the path $p$ is given by expression (2). (The proof is trivial.)*□

$$\Omega(p) = \sum_{e \in E}(\omega_E(e) + \omega_V(sink(e)))\varphi_E(e) \qquad (2)$$

**Property 3** *A path $p$ of $\widetilde{G}$ begins at one of original nodes of $START$ and ends at one of original nodes of $STOP$. When the measure $\varphi_E(e)$ of an edge $e \in E$ in $G$ is the projection overlap degree of the edge $e$, expressions (3) and (4) are satisfied and expression (5) is satisfied for any node $v \in V$ except $START$ and $STOP$ in $G$. (The proof of expression (3) is trivial, and the proofs of expressions (4) and (5) are presented in appendix.)*□

$$\sum_{e \in E} d_E(e)\varphi_E(e) < N \qquad (3)$$

$$\sum_{e \in OUT_V(START)} \varphi_E(e) = \sum_{e \in IN_V(STOP)} \varphi_E(e) = 1 \qquad (4)$$

$$\sum_{e \in OUT_V(v)} \varphi_E(e) - \sum_{e \in IN_V(v)} \varphi_E(e) = 0 \qquad (5)$$

## Formulation

Any edge $e \in E$ in $G$ can have a measure $\varphi_E(e)$. In this paper we refer to the way of assigning measures to all edges in the loop task graph as a *measure definition*. In the previous subsection we draw a path which starts at one of original nodes of $START$ and ends at one of original nodes of $STOP$, and assign each edge to its projection overlap degree as its measure. In this case the measure definition satisfies expressions (3), (4), and (5). Here we consider whether we can draw a path on the unrolled loop task graph such that the projection overlap degree of any edge $e$ is equal to the measure $\varphi_E(e)$ when a measure definition which satisfies expressions (3), (4), and (5) is given in advance.

Let us consider a graph, say $G'$, obtained from $G$ by removing the edges whose measures are 0, deleting isolated nodes, and appending $\varphi_E(e) - 1$ edges such that they are parallel to each remaining edge $e$. The graph $G'$ has the following property.

**Property 4** *There exists a connected component which contains both START and STOP in the graph $G'$. (See appendix for the proof.)* $\square$

Let us consider a connected component which contains both $START$ and $STOP$. According to expression (5) the in-degree and the out-degree of any node in the graph $G'$ except $START$ and $STOP$ are same. Moreover, according to expression (4) the out-degree of $START$ (one) is greater than the in-degree of $START$ (zero) by 1. The in-degree of $STOP$ (one) is greater than the out-degree of $STOP$ (zero) by 1. Therefore, there exists an Eulerian path from $START$ to $STOP$ in the connected component which contains both $START$ and $STOP$[8]. If a measure definition which satisfies expressions (3), (4), and (5) is given and the graph $G'$ consists of only one connected component which contains $START$ and $STOP$, we can define a path $p$ on $\widetilde{G}$ such that the projection overlap degree of any edge $e \in E$ in $G$ is equal to its measure $\varphi_E(e)$ by algorithm 1. The path $p$ starts at one of original nodes of $START$ and ends at one of original nodes of $STOP$.

**Algorithm 1**

1. $i := 1$

2. $\widetilde{cur} :=$ *the node which has the smallest iteration number in $F_V(START)$.*

3. $p := \langle \widetilde{cur} \rangle$

4. $cur :=$ *the $i$-th node of the Eulerian path*

5. *Terminate the algorithm if $cur = STOP$.*

6. $v :=$ *the $(i + 1)$-th node of the Eulerian path, $\widetilde{v} :=$ the node of $\widetilde{G}$ such that $(\widetilde{cur}, \widetilde{v}) \in F_E((cur, v))$*

7. *Append node $\widetilde{v}$ to path $p$.*

8. $cur := v$, $\widetilde{cur} := \widetilde{v}$, $i := i + 1$

9. *Go to 4* $\square$

When we give a measure definition which satisfies expressions (3), (4), and (5) in advance, there are, in general, multiple paths such that the projection overlap degree of any edge $e \in E$ in $G$ is equal to its measure $\varphi_E(e)$. However, it is guaranteed that all the costs of these paths are equal according to expression (2).

When we define the measure of any edge $e \in E$ in $G$ by the projection overlap degree of the edge $e$, let $A$ be a set of measure definitions given by all the paths of $\widetilde{G}$ which starts at one of original nodes of $START$ and ends at one of original nodes of $STOP$. Moreover, let $B$ be a set of measure definitions which satisfy expressions (3), (4), and (5). $A \subseteq B$ is satisfied according to property 3.

According to the above, we can reduce the problem of estimating the critical path cost into the problem of finding a measure definition which satisfies expressions (3), (4), and (5), maximizes the value of expression (2), and has the graph $G'$ be connected. Since the measures of all edges have integral values and expressions (3), (4), and (5) are linear, the problem can be reduced into an integer linear programming problem. We summarize variables, an objective function, and constraints of the integer linear programming problem. Remark that the constraints settle the search space of the problem in $B$ while we must find a measure definition, which gives the critical path cost, out of $A$ included by $B$.

**Variables** measures $\varphi_E(e)$ $(\forall e \in E)$

**Objective Function** expression (2)

**Constraints** expressions (3), (4), and (5)

## EXPERIMENTAL IMPLEMENTATION

To solve the integer linear programming problem described in the previous section, we employ a branch-and-bound algorithm which is combined with the well-known simplex method. One of the most remarkable advantages of our algorithm is that it provides the critical path cost of a given loop without unrolling it at all. In this section we describe the algorithm and show its computational complexity (CPU time) with examples of Livermore Benchmark Kernels.

### Algorithm

The simplex method is a well-known scheme to solve the linear programming problem. In general, a solution obtained by the simplex method is real, thus we employ a branch-and-bound algorithm to search for an integer solution by consulting the real solution. Moreover, we employ the branch-and-bound algorithm to exclude measure definitions which satisfy expressions (3), (4), and (5) but do not define a correct path, that is, do not have the graph $G'$ be connected (see Fig.3 for an example). Algorithm 2 describes the branch-and-bound. As for the simplex method to solve the linear programming problem, see an appropriate literature.

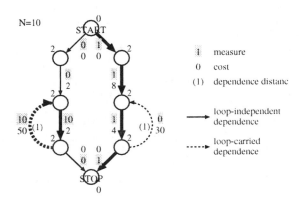

Fig. 3: Incorrect Path Projection

Generally an incumbent is defined in branch-and-bound algorithms. In this paper we define the incumbent as a triplet $(C, \Omega, \varphi)$; $C$ is a set of the constraints, $\Omega$ is the maximum value of the objective function (expression (2)) under the constraints $C$, and $\varphi$ is the measure definition at that time.

**Algorithm 2**

1. *Put an initial solution $(C_0, \Omega_0, \varphi_0)$ into a list lis where $C_0$ is a set of constraints consisting of only expressions (3), (4), and (5).*

2. *Remove the incumbent $(C_{cur}, \Omega_{cur}, \varphi_{cur})$ from the list lis such that $\Omega$ is maximum.*

3. *Terminate the algorithm if all the measures in measure definition $\varphi_{cur}$ are integral and graph $G'$ given by the measure definition $\varphi_{cur}$ is connected. $\Omega_{cur}$ is the critical path cost.*

4. *Choose an edge $e$ which has a non-integral measure val in measure definition $\varphi_{cur}$.*

5. $C_1 := C_{cur} \cup \{Constraint\ \varphi_E(e) \geq \lceil val \rceil\}$

6. *Put an incumbent $(C_1, \Omega_1, \varphi_1)$ into the list lis.*

7. $C_2 := C_{cur} \cup \{Constraint\ \varphi_E(e) \leq \lfloor val \rfloor\}$

8. *Put an incumbent $(C_2, \Omega_2, \varphi_2)$ into the list lis.*

9. *Go to 2.* □

It is well-known that the complexity of the simplex method has an exponential order in the worst case but proportional to the number of constraints, in detail 1.5 to 3 times of the number of constraints, in most cases empirically[1]. The complexity of the branch-and-bound method is also exponential order in the worst case. For avoiding the worst case, our algorithm generates a new incumbent from the

incumbent expected to derive the final incumbent, which gives the critical path length, at each iteration.

Evaluation

We measure the CPU time of a DEC workstation on which our algorithm is applied to obtain the critical path costs of Livermore Benchmark Kernel #10 (21 nodes and 46 edges) and Kernel #13 (19 nodes and 27 edges). For these experiments we assume that each statement constructs one task; the execution cost of each task is the number of lines of assembler codes; the cost of a communication concerning each dependence is the number of transferred variables. CPU times are measured with varying the number of iterations of each loop in Kernel #10 and #13 from 1,000 to 10,000 by 1,000. We perform each measurement 100 times and take the average of these 100 CPU times as the result of the measurement. The result is shown in Fig.4. Remark that the CPU time does not depend on the number of loop iterations at all. Thus the proposed scheme provides a constant computational complexity. Furthermore, measured CPU times (0.93 sec. for Kernel #10 and 0.41 sec. for Kernel #13) are reasonably inexpensive.

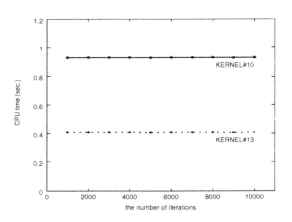

Fig. 4: CPU time

Fig.5 shows the loop task graph of Kernel #10 and its critical path projection (thick line). The number beside each node represents its execution cost. The critical path is $\langle START, 1, 2, 4, 6, 8, 10, 12, 14, 16, 4, 6, 8, ..., 12, 14, 16, 18, 19, STOP \rangle$, and its cost is 69,032 where the number of iterations is 1,000.

## DISCUSSION

We assumed that our algorithm was applied to single loops in previous sections. In this section we

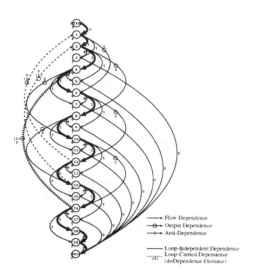

Fig. 5: Livermore Benchmark Kernel #10

discuss two methods to deal with multiply nested loops.

i) In the case of fully nested loops, we can apply the proposed scheme by reducing the nested loops to a single loop with using a loop transformation technique called *loop coalescing*[5].

A node in the data dependence graph after the transformation inherits the cost of the corresponding node in the data dependence graph before the transformation, and it is likewise for edges. We do not have to append the nodes representing codes which calculate previous indices from the index of the new single loop after the transformation.

ii) In the case of partially nested loops, we can take another method. At first we generate a tree which represents a given nest of loops. A node in the tree represents a loop, and an edge $(u, v)$ means the loop $v$ is included in the body of the loop $u$. Let us suppose we have a sequence of the nodes, say $v_1$, $v_2$, ..., and $v_n$, obtained by scanning the tree in the postorder depth-first manner. Node $v_n$ represents the outermost loop.

We apply the proposed scheme to the loops corresponding to nodes $v_1$, $v_2$, ..., and $v_n$ successively. In each application a nested loop is assumed to be a task. The critical path cost of the unrolled loop task graph of the nested loop has already been estimated necessarily since the proposed scheme had been applied in the order defined by postorder depth-first walking of the tree. The critical path cost is used as the cost of the node representing the nested loop. The result of the application to node $v_n$ is the output of this method. However, the result of this method is not the critical path cost of the unrolled loop task graph of the nest of loops but a close upper bound

of the critical path cost.

For example, Fig.6(b) is a tree which represents the nest of loops shown in Fig.6(a). According to postorder depth-first walking, we apply the proposed scheme to loops $L2$ and $L3$ successively. Let us suppose we have minimum parallel execution times: 120 for loop $L2$ and 140 for loop $L3$. Next we construct a loop task graph for loop $L1$ with assuming loop $L2$ as a task with cost 120 and loop $L3$ as a task with cost 140. We apply the proposed scheme to the loop task graph and obtain minimum parallel execution time of loop $L1$.

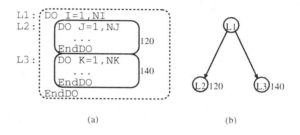

Fig. 6: Application to Partially Nested Loops

## CONCLUSION

In this paper we proposed a scheme for evaluating the cost of the critical path (minimum parallel execution time), of a fully unrolled loop, without actually unrolling the loop. Moreover, the proposed scheme can also detect a critical path[e] of the data dependence graph of an unrolled loop.

The proposed scheme was obtained by reducing the problem into an integer linear programming problem and employing the simplex method and a branch-and-bound algorithm to solve it. The theoretical complexity of our method has an exponential order in the worst case, but our experiments with Livermore Benchmark Kernels demonstrated its practicability. Most importantly, the complexity does not depend on the number of iterations of a loop. This property is quite desirable for implementations.

The critical path cost may be evaluated frequently during compilations. Developing a faster and more optimized algorithm for our integer linear programming problem will be the subject of our future work. The critical path cost is often used for quantitating the quality of scheduling, program partitioning, and data partitioning. Using the proposed scheme to estimate the effectiveness of instruction and iteration-level scheduling, as well as to guide the above optimizations will also be the focus of our

---

[e]Note that there can exist multiple critical paths whose costs are same.

future work. In particular, we plan to extend and apply the proposed scheme to the DPG: Data Partitioning Graph[11] and use it for data partitioning. Actual implementation on an existing parallelizing compiler is underway.

## ACKNOWLEDGEMENTS

We would like to thank the anonymous reviewers for their comments and suggestions.

## REFERENCES

[1] V. Chvátal, *Linear Programming*, W. H. Freeman and Company, (1983).

[2] R. G. Cytron, "Doacross: Beyond Vectorization for Multiprocessors," *Proc. of the 1986 Int'l Conf. on Parallel Processing*, (August, 1986), pp.836–845.

[3] C. D. Polychronopoulos and U. Banerjee, "Processor Allocation for Horizontal and Vertical Parallelism and Related Speedup Bounds," *IEEE Trans. on Computers*, Vol.C-36, No.4, (April, 1987), pp.410–420.

[4] J. Ferrante, K. J. Ottenstein, and J. D. Warren, "The Program Dependence Graph and Its Use in Optimization," *ACM Trans. on Programming Languages and Systems*, Vol.9, No.3, (July, 1987), pp.319–349.

[5] C. D. Polychronopoulos, "Loop Coalescing: A Compiler Transformation for Parallel Machines," *Proc. of the 1987 Int'l Conf. on Parallel Processing*, (1987), pp.235–242.

[6] M. B. Girkar and C. D. Polychronopoulos, "Partitioning Programs for Parallel Execution," *Proc. 1988 Int'l Conf. on Supercomputing*, (1988), pp.216–229.

[7] V. Sarkar, *Partitioning and Scheduling Parallel Programs for Multiprocessors*, The MIT Press, (1988).

[8] R. P. Grimaldi, *Discrete and Combinatorial Mathematics — An Applied Introduction*, 2nd Edition, Addison-Wesley, (1989).

[9] H. Zima and B. Chapman, *Supercompilers for Parallel and Vector Computers*, Addison Wesley, (1990).

[10] D. Lenoski, J. Laudon, K. Gharachorloo, W. D. Weber, A. Gupta, J. Hennessy, M. Horowitz, and M. Lam, "The Stanford Dash Multiprocessor," *IEEE Computer*, Vol.25, No.3, (March, 1992), pp.63–79.

[11] T. Nakanishi, K. Joe, H. Saito, C. D. Polychronopoulos, A. Fukuda, and K. Araki, "The Data Partitioning Graph — Extending Data and Control Dependences for Data Partitioning," *Proc. 7th Annual Workshop on Language and Compilers for Parallel Computing*, (1994), pp.170–185.

[12] T. Nakanishi, K. Joe, H. Saito, A. Fukuda, and K. Araki, "The $CDP^2$ Algorithm — A Combined Data and Program Partitioning Algorithm on the Data Partitioning Graph," *Proc. of the 1995 Int'l Conf. on Parallel Processing*, Vol.2, (1995), pp.177–181.

## APPENDIX

Proof of property 1

Let us suppose the critical path $p$ of $\widetilde{G} = (\widetilde{V}, \widetilde{E})$ begins at one of original nodes, say $\widetilde{v}$, of a node $v \in V$ in $G = (V, E)$ except $START$. According to the definition of $START$, the node $v$ has at least one parent node, say $u \in V$, connected with a loop-independent dependence edge. Therefore, the node $\widetilde{v}$ must have a parent node, say $\widetilde{u} \in \widetilde{V}$, connected with a loop-independent dependence edge. Consider a new path $p'$ obtained by inserting the node $\widetilde{u}$ at the head of the path $p$. Let $\widetilde{e}$ be an edge from the node $\widetilde{u}$ to the head of the path $p$. The cost of the path $p'$ is as below.

$$\Omega(p') = \omega_{\widetilde{V}}(\widetilde{u}) + \omega_{\widetilde{E}}(\widetilde{e}) + \Omega(p)$$

Since $\omega_{\widetilde{V}}(\widetilde{u})$ and $\omega_{\widetilde{E}}(\widetilde{e})$ are non-negative, $\Omega(p') \geq \Omega(p)$ is satisfied. That contradicts the fact that the path $p$ is the critical path. Hence the critical path of an unrolled loop task graph begins at one of original nodes of $START$.

Likewise for the end point of the critical path.□

Proof of property 3

Expression(4) Assume a path $p$ begins at one of original nodes of $START$ and passes through one of original edges of an edge $e$ which goes out of $START$, say $\widetilde{e}$. There exists no edge which enters $START$ according to the definition of $START$. Therefore, the path $p$ never enters other original nodes of $START$, and its projection never passes through the edge $e$ again and the other edges which go out of $START$. Thus $\sum_{e \in OUT(START)} \varphi_E(e) = 1$ is satisfied.

Likewise for $STOP$.□

Expression (5) $\delta_{\widetilde{E}}(\widetilde{e})$ is a function which returns 1 if an edge $\widetilde{e}$ in $\widetilde{G}$ is contained in a path $p$ or

0 otherwise. Note that the following expression is satisfied for any edge $e$ in $G$.

$$\sum_{e \in E} \varphi_E(e) = \sum_{\tilde{e} \in F_E(e)} \delta_{\tilde{E}}(\tilde{e}) \qquad (6)$$

Let a node in $\tilde{G}$, which is not an original node of $START$ nor $STOP$, be $\tilde{v}$. If a path $p$ does not pass through the node $\tilde{v}$,

$$\sum_{\tilde{e} \in IN_{\tilde{V}}(\tilde{v})} \delta_{\tilde{E}}(\tilde{e}) = \sum_{\tilde{e} \in OUT_{\tilde{V}}(\tilde{v})} \delta_{\tilde{E}}(\tilde{e}) = 0.$$

If a path $p$ passes through the node $\tilde{v}$,

$$\sum_{\tilde{e} \in IN_{\tilde{V}}(\tilde{v})} \delta_{\tilde{E}}(\tilde{e}) = \sum_{\tilde{e} \in OUT_{\tilde{V}}(\tilde{v})} \delta_{\tilde{E}}(\tilde{e}) = 1.$$

Therefore, the following expression is satisfied for any node $v$ in $G$.

$$\sum_{e \in IN_V(v)} \sum_{\tilde{e} \in F_E(e)} \delta_{\tilde{E}}(\tilde{e}) = \sum_{e \in OUT_V(v)} \sum_{\tilde{e} \in F_E(e)} \delta_{\tilde{E}}(\tilde{e})$$

We can obtain expression (5) by substituting expression (6).$\square$

Proof of property 4

Let us suppose a matrix $A = (a_{ij})$ whose row and column correspond to a node and an edge in a loop task graph respectively.

$$a_{ij} = \begin{cases} +\varphi(j) & \text{(if edge } j \text{ goes out from node } i) \\ -\varphi(j) & \text{(if edge } j \text{ enters node } i) \\ 0 & \text{(if edge } j \text{ is not adjacent to} \\ & \text{node } i \text{ or edge } j \text{ is a self-loop)} \end{cases}$$

The matrix $A$ can be transformed as below by rearranging rows and columns to gather non-zero elements according to each connected component.

$$\begin{pmatrix} A_{11} & 0 & \cdots & 0 & 0 \\ 0 & A_{22} & \cdots & 0 & 0 \\ \vdots & \vdots & \ddots & \vdots & 0 \\ 0 & 0 & \cdots & A_{nn} & 0 \\ 0 & 0 & \cdots & 0 & 0 \end{pmatrix}$$

Any row which does not correspond to $START$ of each submatrix on the above diagonal elements has non-zero elements, and the sum of those elements is 0 according to expression (5). On the other hand the row which corresponds to $START$ has only one positive non-zero element, and its value is always 1 according to expression (4). We remove the row corresponding to $STOP$, since it is redundant.

Let us suppose $START$ and $STOP$ are not in the same connected component. We pick a submatrix $A_{xx}$ which contains the row corresponding to $START$ and we denote it by $B = (b_{ij})$. A matrix $C = (c_{ij})$ is generated from the matrix $B$ as below.

$$c_{ij} = \begin{cases} +1 & \text{(if } b_{ij} > 0) \\ -1 & \text{(if } b_{ij} < 0) \\ 0 & \text{(if } b_{ij} = 0) \end{cases}$$

When the row corresponding to $START$ is the $i$-th row, expression (7) is satisfied where $\varphi$ is a vector whose $i$-th element is equal to the measure of the edge $i$ and $b$ is a vector such that its $i$-th element is 1 and the other elements are 0.

$$B^t (\ 1 \quad 1 \quad \cdots \quad 1\ ) = C\varphi = b \qquad (7)$$

There does not exist the vector $\varphi$ which satisfies the above expression unless rank $C$ = rank$[C b]$ is satisfied.

Let us denote the $i$-th row vector of the matrix $C$ by $c_i$. Then $c_1 + c_2 + \cdots + c_m = o$ is satisfied where $m$ is the number of rows of the matrix $C$, since each column of the matrix $C$ has two elements whose values are 1 and $-1$. Thus, vectors $c_1$, $c_2$, ..., and $c_m$ are linearly dependent. Hence rank $C$ is less than $m$.

Let us consider the below expression (8) where $c'_i$ is the $i$-th row vector of matrix $[C b]$.

$$a_1 c'_1 + a_2 c'_2 + \cdots + a_m c'_m = o \qquad (8)$$

$c_{i_1}$ is the only vector whose $(n + 1)$-th element is non-zero (1 in this case) among $c'_1$, $c'_2$, ..., and $c'_m$. To satisfy expression (8), the coefficient $a_{i_1}$ must be 0. There is only one edge which goes out of $START$ according to expression (4). Let the column which corresponds to the edge be the $j_1$-th column. In the $j_1$-th column, there is only one element whose absolute value is equal and sign is opposite to the $i_1$-th element. Let the element in the $j_1$-th column be the $i_2$-th element of the $j_1$-th column. To satisfy expression (8), $a_{i_1} - a_{i_2}$ must be 0, namely, $a_{i_2}$ must be 0. Coefficients $a_1$, $a_2$, ..., and $a_m$ can be obtained by iterating the above procedures and their values are all 0, since the matrix $C$ is defined for one connected component. It means vectors $c_1$, $c_2$, ..., and $c_m$ are linearly independent, therefore, rank$[C b]$ = $m$.

There does not exist a vector $\varphi$ which satisfies expression (7), since rank $C$ is not equal to rank$[C b]$. Hence $START$ and $STOP$ must be contained in the same connected component.$\square$

# Performance Analysis and Prediction of Processor Scheduling Strategies in Multiprogrammed Shared-Memory Multiprocessors

Kelvin K. Yue[†] and David J. Lilja[‡]

yue@cs.umn.edu    lilja@ee.umn.edu

†Department of Computer Science, ‡Department of Electrical Engineering
University of Minnesota, Minneapolis, MN 55455

**Abstract** *Small-scale shared-memory multiprocessors are commonly used in a workgroup environment where multiple applications, both parallel and sequential, are executed concurrently while sharing the processors and other system resources. To utilize the processors efficiently, an effective scheduling strategy is required. In this paper, we use performance data obtained from an SGI multiprocessor to evaluate several processor scheduling strategies. We examine gang scheduling (coscheduling), static space sharing (space partitioning), and a dynamic allocation scheme called loop-level process control (LLPC) [12] with three new dynamic allocation heuristics. We use regression analysis to quantify the measured data and thereby explore the relationship between the degree of parallelism of the application, the size of the system, the processor allocation strategy and the resulting performance. We also attempt to predict the performance of an application in a multiprogrammed environment. While the execution time predictions are relatively coarse, the models produce a reasonable rank-ordering of the scheduling strategies for each application. This study also shows that dynamically partitioning the system using LLPC or similar heuristics provides better performance for applications with a high degree of parallelism than either gang scheduling or static space sharing.*

## 1 Introduction

Shared-memory multiprocessor systems have become quite popular for use as high-performance general-purpose machines because of their similarities to traditional uniprocessor systems, both in terms of the system architecture and the programming models. These systems are usually shared by multiple applications that range from completely sequential to highly parallelized. An extension of the traditional Unix time-sharing scheme is often used to schedule the applications on to the processors.

However, time-sharing does not work well in a multiprocessor system due to overhead from context switching, inefficient locking and sychronization, and poor cache utilization. Some alternative solutions, such as *space sharing* (or *space partitioning*) the processors, *gang scheduling* (or *coscheduling*) related tasks [8], dynamically controlling the processor allocation [6, 10, 11], using blocking synchronization [3], and policies that prevent tasks that hold a lock from being swapped out [14], have been proposed and implemented in some existing systems to reduce the performance impact of the above effects. We have also proposed a strategy called *loop-level process control (LLPC)* that works well for loop-level parallelized applications on shared-memory multiprocessors[12].

The goal of this paper is to compare the performance of some of these strategies and propose a model for performance prediction in multiprogrammed systems. We use multiple regression analysis to correlate the parallel characteristics of the applications with the performance data. Based on these regression models, we quantify the differences between the strategies. We also propose three new partitioning heuristics that can be incorporated in the loop-level process control strategy to improve its performance in different conditions.

In the remainder of the paper, Section 2 discusses some of the existing processor allocation strategies while Section 3 presents the three new heuristics for the LLPC strategy. Our methodology and the experimental environment for the performance comparison are described in Section 4. The measured data is evaluated using multiple regression analysis and the results are compared quantitatively in Section 5. Section 6 presents the performance results for several applications from the Perfect Club benchmarks [2] along with the performance predictions based on the regression models. The final section summarizes our observations and concludes the paper.

This work was supported in part by the National Science Foundation under grant no. MIP-9221900 and equipment grant no. CDA-9414015.

## 2  Background and Related Work

One of the most common programming models for shared-memory multiprocessor systems is the *fork-join* model. With this programming model, the parallelism of many existing application programs can be exploited without rewriting the sequential code [5].

If the sequential execution time required by an application on a uniprocessor system is represented as

$$T_s = W_s + W_p, \tag{1}$$

then when this application is parallelized and executed on a system with $P$ processors using this programming model, the total parallel execution time of the application is

$$T_p = W_s + \frac{W_p}{P} + O_p, \tag{2}$$

where $W_s$ is the time required by the portions of the code that have to be executed sequentially, $W_p$ is the time required by the code that can be executed in parallel, and $O_p$ is the extra operation overhead for processes creation, synchronization, and other operations that are not required when the application is executed sequentially.

When this application is executed on a multiprogrammed system where the processors and other resources are shared by several applications, the execution time required will be greater than $T_p$. The magnitude of this performance degradation depends on the system load and the processor allocation strategy used in the system. Simple time-sharing of the processors can significantly degrade the performance primarily due to inefficient locking and synchronization [4, 14].

To improve the locking or synchronization efficiency, some scheduling strategies prohibit active processes from waiting for an inactive process [4], or put waiting processes into a *sleep* state and *yield* their processors to other processes [3, 7]. Another alternative approach is to *gang schedule* or *coschedule* related tasks of an application so that all of the related tasks are allocated processors all at the same time [8]. Another common way to reduce the amount of context switching while improving locking efficiency is to divide the processors into several independent partitions and then allocate each application to its own partition. This type of *space-sharing* or *static partitioning* eliminates the competition between applications for processors. The partitioning can be done in either software or hardware, depending on the machine and the operating system. The main drawback of this strategy is low system utilization.

To improve the system utilization while minimizing context switching overhead, the system can be *dynamically partitioned* [6, 11]. With this strategy, the partition sizes are dynamically adjusted based on the requirements of the

```
allow_p = max[1, min(no_needed,
        total_physical_P - system_load)];
```

Figure 1: LLPC heuristic for determining the number of processes for parallel execution.

different applications. However, using this approach, the scheduler and the applications require precise coordination. This coordination may require a special programming model which is not suitable for the simpler fork-join programming model. Moreover, since some executing processes must be suspended to reassign processors, some critical processes may be suspended, which could affect other dependent processes. Finally, dynamically suspending and reallocating processors can increase the system overhead, which can degrade the performance of the individual applications.

*Loop-Level Process Control (LLPC)* simplifies the dynamic partitioning strategy and adapts it to the fork-join programming model [12]. LLPC reevaluates the processor allocation only at the beginning of each parallel section, such as a parallel loop. By controlling the number of processes an application is allowed to create based on the system load and the application's available parallelism, LLPC allows the application to utilize as many processors as possible without overloading the system. When an application reaches its parallel section, it checks the system load, system_load, to determine the number of processors that are currently in use. Using this value and the number of processes that the parallel section requires to attain maximum parallelism, no_needed, the number of processors that the application is allowed to allocate, allow_p, is calculated using the heuristic shown in Figure 1. The application then creates allow_p processes to execute this parallel section. When all parallel tasks have completed, the application continues the execution of the next sequential portion of the application using only a single processor. When it reaches its next parallel section, it repeats the above allocation procedure.

## 3  New Allocation Heuristics for LLPC

The heuristic used in the original LLPC strategy [12] allocates as many available processors as possible and does not save any processors for the parallel sections of other later-arriving applications. Although other applications will obtain their share of processors eventually, the LLPC approach is too aggressive in favor of the first application at

```
allow_p = max[1, min(no_needed, allocated)];
```

Insurance LLPC:
$$\text{allocated} = \left\lfloor \frac{\text{total\_physical\_P} - \text{system\_load}}{2} \right\rfloor$$

Aggressive insurance LLPC:
$$\text{allocated} = \sum_{i=1}^{\lfloor \log_2 P \rfloor - 1} \left\lfloor \frac{\text{total\_physical\_P} - \text{system\_load}}{\lfloor \text{total\_physical\_P}/2^i \rfloor} \right\rfloor$$

Very aggressive insurance LLPC:
$$\text{allocated} = \sum_{i=0}^{\lfloor \log_2 P \rfloor - 1} \left\lfloor \frac{\text{total\_physical\_P} - \text{system\_load}}{\lfloor \text{total\_physical\_P}/2^i \rfloor} \right\rfloor$$

Figure 2: Proposed LLPC heuristics.

the expense of the others. On a system with a large number of processors, for instance, the applications should be able to share the processors more evenly. To reduce the cases of not having enough processors available for other applications, we extend LLPC with an *insurance allocation policy* [9]. As shown in Figure 2, the *insurance LLPC heuristic (ins-LLPC)* allocates only half of the idle processors to one application while saving half for other late-arriving applications.

While saving half of the idle processors might improve the average performance of all of the applications since processors are more likely to be available when needed, leaving half of the processors idle in a large system will cause low system utilization. If the system is lightly loaded, there is no reason why the current application should not utilize more processors. A more aggressive policy, *aggressive insurance LLPC (aggr-LLPC)*, allocates approximately three-fourths of the available processors at a time, as shown in Figure 2.

Similarly, the *very aggressive insurance LLPC (vaggr-LLPC)*, shown in Figure 2, allocates all but a few of the available processors. Although these heuristics appear quite complicated, they can be implemented very efficiently using simple bitwise shift operations.

On a system with a small number of processors, the differences in the number of processors allocated by these heuristics are negligible, but on a larger system, the differences are more significant [13]. Thus, in large systems, the different heuristics provide a trade-off between the parallelism that can be exploited by a single application, and the overall fairness of the processor allocation policy.

## 4  Performance Evaluation Methodology

To evaluate the proposed algorithms, we measure their performance using an SGI Challenge multiprocessor system. We compare the performance of gang scheduling, space sharing, and loop-level process control, including its three new heuristics, using a synthetic benchmark with variable parallel characteristics on different system configurations (4, 8, and 20 processors). A regression model of the program execution time is developed for each strategy under each system configuration to summarize and compare the performance of the different strategies. Finally, we use the regression models to predict performance when multiprogramming several applications from the Perfect Club benchmarks.

### 4.1  The Synthetic Benchmark

Figure 3 shows the synthetic benchmark application we used for building the regression models. This benchmark allows us to control its parallel characteristics precisely through the parameters i_s, which is the number of iterations in the sequential loop, and i_p, which is the number of iterations in the parallel loop. The parameters i_s and i_p are directly proportional to the amount of serial work, $W_s$, and parallel work, $W_p$, respectively, in Equation 2. For instance, if i_p is much larger than i_s, then the benchmark has a high degree of parallelism and produces a high speedup when executed in parallel. On the other hand, if i_p is much smaller than i_s, the application has a low degree of parallelism and the benefit of executing in parallel will be small. We measure the execution time required by this benchmark using different allocation strategies while varying i_s and i_p to build a regression model for each processor allocation strategy based on these execution time measurements.

### 4.2  Experimental Environment

The benchmark program is executed on an Silicon Graphics Challenge L multiprocessor system running version 5.3 of the IRIX operating system with the XFS file system. This system is a single bus shared-memory architecture and can be configured with four, eight, or twenty MIPS R4400 processors and MIPS R4010 floating point units running at a clock rate of 200MHz. Each processing unit has 16 Kbytes of on-chip data cache and 16 Kbytes of on-chip instruction cache. The secondary cache is a 4 Mbyte unified instruction and data cache. The system has 768 Mbytes of four-way interleaved physical memory when configured with 4 and 8 processors. The 20-processor configuration has 1 Gbyte of interleaved physical memory. All

```
DO M = 1, 100
    /* serial section */
    DO J = 1, i_s
        DO K = 1, size
            4 Read, 3 FP Multiply, and
            1 Store Operations
        ENDDO
    ENDDO

    /* parallel section */
    DOALL J = 1, i_p
        DO K = 1, size
            4 Read, 3 FP Multiply, and
            1 Store Operations
        ENDDO
    ENDDO
ENDDO
```

Figure 3: Synthetic benchmark for the regression models.

measurements for these experiments were performed on a dedicated system.

The benchmark program is parallelized using the SGI Power Fortran Accelerator (PFA). PFA parallelizes a sequential application by detecting sections of the program that can be executed in parallel and marking these parallel sections with compiler directives. The MIPS Fortran 77 compiler generates the executable program using these directives.

Gang scheduling is already implemented in the IRIX operating system [1]. However, the IRIX operating system does not directly implement a space sharing option. Therefore, we emulated space sharing at the user level by creating a fixed number of processes for each application [12]. For instance, on a four-processor system with two applications ready to be executed, each application will be allowed to create two processes for its parallel execution.

Our loop-level process control strategy is implemented as a layer between the application and the operating system [12]. After an application is parallelized by the Power Fortran Accelerator, LLPC calls are inserted manually at the beginning and the end of the parallel loops. The ins-LLPC, aggr-LLPC, and vaggr-LLPC heuristics are implemented using binary shift and add operations [13].

### 4.3 Regression Analysis

After the execution times of the benchmark are measured while varying $i_s$ and $i_p$ with different numbers of processors, multiple regression analysis is used to correlate the execution times to the amount of serial and parallel work within the benchmark. Multiple regression analysis is a statistical technique for relating a dependent variable to two or more independent variables. The regression model allows one to estimate, within the error of the measurements, the dependent variable as a function of the other variables. The regression model also provides a measure of the degree of association or correlation between the variables.

The regression model used in this study is of the following form: $y = b_1 x_1 + b_2 x_2 + e$, where $y$ is the dependent variable, $b_1$ and $b_2$ are the fixed coefficients for the two independent variables, $x_1$ and $x_2$, and $e$ is the error term. In this study, the dependent variable, $y$, corresponds to the execution time of the application, and the independent variables, $x_1$ and $x_2$, correspond to the amount of serial and parallel work, respectively, executed by the application program.

The goodness of fit of the regression model is measured by the coefficient of determination, $R^2$, which is calculated as $R^2 = 1 - $ (Unexplained variation/Total variation). This coefficient of determination represents an estimate of how strongly related the variables are. The higher the value of $R^2$, the better the regression model. An $R^2$ of 1 suggests that the regression model fits perfectly, while an $R^2$ of 0 suggests that there is no correlation between the input variables and the measured output variable.

## 5 Results

### 5.1 Models for a Dedicated System

As a baseline, we first execute one copy of the synthetic benchmark sequentially on a single processor with 64 different combinations of $i_s$ and $i_p$ and develop a regression model for this serial execution time. This analysis gives $T_s = 34.41 i_s + 38.53 i_p$. This model has an $R^2$ of 0.9982 which means that 99.82% of the variation in $T_s$ can be explained by the two variables $i_s$ and $i_p$. The constants 34.41 and 38.53 are the regression parameters for quantifying the *influences* of the sequential code and the parallel code on the application's execution time. Another way to interpret this model is that each iteration in the sequential loop requires about 0.3441 milliseconds (34.41 milliseconds/100 iterations since the outer most loop has 100 iterations) to execute and each iteration in the parallel loop takes about 0.3853 milliseconds. Therefore, given the number of iterations in the sequential section, $i_s$, and the parallel section, $i_p$, we can use this model to predict the sequential execution time. For instance, if we have a benchmark with $i_s = 50$ iterations in the sequential loop and $i_p = 100$ iterations in the parallel loop, the sequential execution time of this benchmark is 5.6 seconds $((0.3441 \times 50 + 0.3853 \times 100) \times 100$ milliseconds). To relate this regression model to the analytical model presented in Section 2, we define $W_s = 34.41 i_s$ and $W_p = 38.53 i_p$.

If the benchmark is executed in parallel on a dedicated 4-processor system (P = 4), the measured regression model for the parallel execution time, $T_p$, is $T_p(P=4) = 51.82\mathrm{i\_s} + 10.28\mathrm{i\_p}$ with an $R^2$ of 0.9792. Normalizing this model in terms of $W_s$ and $W_p$, we have

$$T_p(P=4) = b_1 W_s + b_2 \frac{W_p}{4} = 1.51 W_s + 1.09 \frac{W_p}{4}. \quad (3)$$

We call the parameters $b_1$ and $b_2$ the serial and parallel coefficients, respectively.

Because the parallel work is shared by the four processors, the execution time required by the parallel sections of code is expected to be reduced by a factor of approximately four. The regression model confirms this reduction with the overhead for parallel execution accounting for the 9% increase in the execution time of the parallel section in the model (i.e. $b_2 = 1.09$ instead of the ideal 1.0). On the other hand, the model shows that the time required by the sequential work increased by 51% (i.e. $b_1 = 1.51$, instead of 1.0). This increase is caused mainly by the cache coherence and memory access overhead since the serial and parallel loops of the benchmark access two large arrays. We verify this memory effect by replacing the large arrays with much smaller arrays that fit into the cache memory. In this case, the serial coefficient is reduced from 1.51 to 1.07.

## 5.2 Models for a Multiprogrammed System

This section develops regression models of the execution time of the synthetic benchmark when executing two copies of the benchmark using gang scheduling, space sharing, and LLPC.

### 5.2.1 Gang Scheduling

The execution time required by a parallel application when there are two copies of the application executing simultaneously using gang-scheduling can be approximated as

$$T_{gs} = T_p + O_{gs}, \quad (4)$$

where $T_p$ is the execution time on a dedicated parallel system and $O_{gs}$ is the gang scheduling overhead. This overhead includes the time required for context switching and the time processes are waiting while the processors are allocated to the other application. The context switching overhead is $\frac{T_p}{t_q} O_{cs}$, where $t_q$ is the time slice and $O_{cs}$ is the amount of time required to context switch a process. Notice that $n = T_p/t_q$ is the number of context switches. While the processors are allocated to one application, the second application must wait. This process waiting time is the size of the time slice, $t_q$, multiplied by the number of context switches, $n$, and is equal to $T_p = nt_q$. Therefore, Equation 4 can be refined as

$$T_{gs} = T_p + \frac{T_p}{t_q} O_{cs} + T_p. \quad (5)$$

Substituting $T_p$ from Equation 2 and rewriting the equation in our standard format, we have

$$T_{gs} = (2 + \frac{O_{cs}}{t_q} + O_p')W_s + (2 + \frac{O_{cs}}{t_q} + O_p'')\frac{W_p}{P}, \quad (6)$$

where $O_p'$ and $O_p''$ are factored from $O_p$. Since all of these values are positive, both the serial and parallel coefficients, $b_1$ and $b_2$, must be greater than two. These coefficient values are at least doubled compared to the dedicated execution time since the system is shared by two copies of the application. In fact, the actual regression model for gang scheduling from the measurements of the benchmark on the four-processor (P = 4) SGI system is:

$$T_{gs}(P=4) = 2.45 W_s + 2.46 \frac{W_p}{4} \quad (7)$$

with an $R^2$ of 0.9806.

### 5.2.2 Space Sharing

With space sharing, the two applications share the system evenly so that each can have $P/2$ processors for its execution. The execution time required is then

$$T_{ss} = W_s + \frac{2W_p}{P} + O_p. \quad (8)$$

In the regression model format, we have

$$T_{ss} = (1 + O_p')W_s + (2 + O_p'')\frac{W_p}{P}. \quad (9)$$

The actual regression model derived from the four-processor SGI system measurements is:

$$T_{ss}(P=4) = 1.39 W_s + 2.09 \frac{W_p}{4} \quad (10)$$

with an $R^2$ of 0.9801. As in gang scheduling, the parallel coefficient with space sharing is also doubled, as suggested by Equation 9, since each application can use at most two processors. Moreover, with space spacing, the serial work of the benchmark is not increased by multiprogramming as significantly as when using gang scheduling, as shown by the smaller sequential coefficient in Equation 10 compared to Equation 7.

### 5.2.3 Loop-level Process Control

The loop-level process control strategy adjusts the number of processors allocated to an application dynamically based on the system load so that the allocation is unknown until runtime. As a result, it is very difficult to formulate the exact execution time required by the application. However, we can approximately determine the upper and lower bounds of the execution time required by the application when scheduled with LLPC.

The best scenario for LLPC is that whenever an application reaches its parallel sections, the other application is using only one processor. When this occurs, $P - 1$ processors are available for its parallel execution. In this case, the execution time is

$$T_{llpc}(\text{best}) = W_s + \frac{W_p}{P - 1} + O_p + O_{llpc}. \qquad (11)$$

We define $O_{llpc}$ to be the additional overhead for using LLPC, which is the time required for checking the system load and adjusting the processor allocation. The worst possible case when using LLPC is that only one processor is available throughout the execution and the application is executed sequentially. The execution time for this case is

$$T_{llpc}(\text{worst}) = W_s + W_p + O_{llpc}. \qquad (12)$$

If $r \times 100\%$ of the application's parallel sections are executed with the best case scenario, that is, using all but one processor, and $(1 - r) \times 100\%$ of the parallel code is executed sequentially, then, in our regression model format, we have

$$\begin{aligned} T_{llpc}(\text{overall}) &= (1 + O'_p + O'_{llpc})W_s + [(1 - r)P \\ &+ r\frac{P}{P - 1} + O''_p + O''_{llpc}]\frac{W_p}{P}. \end{aligned} \qquad (13)$$

The actual regression model for LLPC as derived from a four-processor system is

$$T_{llpc}(P = 4) = 1.65W_s + 1.85\frac{W_p}{4} \qquad (14)$$

with an $R^2$ of 0.98. Based on this regression model, we calculate that $r$ is approximately 0.8. Therefore, about 80% of the parallel section is executed under the best allocation of $(P - 1)$ processors.

The analytical model for the insurance LLPC (ins-LLPC) strategy is similar to the one for LLPC except that in the best case, an application can have only $\lceil (P - 1)/2 \rceil$ processors. Therefore the analytical model for ins-LLPC is

$$\begin{aligned} T_{ins-llpc} &= (1 + O'_p + O'_{llpc})W_s + [(1 - r)P \\ &+ r\frac{P}{\lceil (P - 1)/2 \rceil} + O''_p + O''_{llpc}]\frac{W_p}{P}. \end{aligned} \qquad (15)$$

The regression model for ins-LLPC is found to be

$$T_{ins-llpc}(P = 4) = 1.13W_s + 2.50\frac{W_p}{4} \qquad (16)$$

with an $R^2$ of 0.9859. Correlating the regression model with the analytical model, we find $r \approx 0.75$. Therefore,

about 75% of the parallel section is executed using half of the system.

The analytical model for aggr-LLPC is also similar to the one for LLPC. Based on the heuristic shown in Figure 2, the best case for aggr-LLPC is to have $\sum_{i=1}^{\lfloor \log_2 P \rfloor - 1}(P - 1)/(\lfloor P/2^i \rfloor)$ processors executing the application's parallel section and, therefore, its analytical model is

$$\begin{aligned} T_{aggr-llpc} &= (1 + O'_p + O'_{llpc})W_s + [(1 - r)P \\ &+ r\frac{P}{\sum_{i=1}^{\lfloor \log_2 P \rfloor - 1}\lfloor \frac{P-1}{\lfloor P/2^i \rfloor} \rfloor} + O''_p + O''_{llpc}]\frac{W_p}{P}. \end{aligned} \qquad (17)$$

The regression model for aggr-LLPC is

$$T_{aggr-llpc}(P = 4) = 1.14W_s + 2.49\frac{W_p}{4} \qquad (18)$$

and its $R^2$ is 0.9892. This regression model is almost the same as the one for ins-LLPC since with $P = 4$, the partition size for aggr-LLPC is the same as ins-LLPC.

Similarly, the analytical model for the vaggr-LLPC is

$$\begin{aligned} T_{vaggr-llpc} &= (1 + O'_p + O'_{llpc})W_s + [(1 - r)P \\ &+ r\frac{P}{\sum_{i=0}^{\lfloor \log_2 P \rfloor - 1}\lfloor \frac{P-1}{\lfloor P/2^i \rfloor} \rfloor} + O''_p + O''_{llpc}]\frac{W_p}{P} \end{aligned} \qquad (19)$$

and the regression model is

$$T_{vaggr-llpc}(P = 4) = 1.19W_s + 1.87\frac{W_p}{4} \qquad (20)$$

with an $R^2$ of 0.9887.

## 5.3 Performance Comparisons

We summarize all of these regression models, along with the results for the 8-processor and 20-processor systems, in Table 1. Also shown in this table is the model for the parallel execution time on a dedicated system. We observe that gang scheduling always has the largest serial coefficient compared to the other strategies, suggesting that the sequential section of the application is affected by multiprogramming the most when using gang scheduling. On the other hand, space sharing, ins-LLPC, aggr-LLPC, and vaggr-LLPC have the smallest serial coefficients on a four-processor system. Since space spacing forces the application to execute within its partition, the effect from multiprogramming on the application's sequential execution is minimized. The ins-LLPC, aggr-LLPC, and vaggr-LLPC strategies always leave some processors idle so that there are always processors available for the execution of the other application's sequential sections. As a result, the serial coefficients of these heuristics are smaller than the others.

Table 1: Regression models for the different scheduling strategies measured on the SGI Challenge L system ($T = b_1 W_s + b_2 \frac{W_p}{P}$, $b_1$ = serial coefficient, $b_2$ = parallel coefficient).

| Scheduling Strategy | No. of Prcoessors | $R^2$ | $b_1$ | $b_2$ |
|---|---|---|---|---|
| Dedicated | $P = 4$ | 0.9792 | 1.51 | 1.09 |
| | $P = 8$ | 0.9859 | 1.32 | 1.18 |
| | $P = 20$ | 0.9998 | 1.50 | 1.04 |
| Gang Scheduling | $P = 4$ | 0.9806 | 2.45 | 2.46 |
| | $P = 8$ | 0.9806 | 2.44 | 2.99 |
| | $P = 20$ | 0.9996 | 2.92 | 2.72 |
| Space Sparing | $P = 4$ | 0.9801 | 1.39 | 2.09 |
| | $P = 8$ | 0.9898 | 1.26 | 2.11 |
| | $P = 20$ | 0.9959 | 1.48 | 2.27 |
| LLPC | $P = 4$ | 0.980 | 1.65 | 1.85 |
| | $P = 8$ | 0.9813 | 2.02 | 2.11 |
| | $P = 20$ | 0.9968 | 2.49 | 1.96 |
| ins-LLPC | $P = 4$ | 0.9859 | 1.13 | 2.50 |
| | $P = 8$ | 0.9784 | 1.16 | 3.06 |
| | $P = 20$ | 0.9996 | 1.42 | 2.13 |
| aggr-LLPC | $P = 4$ | 0.9892 | 1.14 | 2.49 |
| | $P = 8$ | 0.9847 | 1.49 | 2.96 |
| | $P = 20$ | 0.9953 | 2.29 | 1.81 |
| vaggr-LLPC | $P = 4$ | 0.9887 | 1.19 | 1.87 |
| | $P = 8$ | 0.9850 | 1.52 | 2.66 |
| | $P = 20$ | 0.9978 | 2.35 | 1.86 |

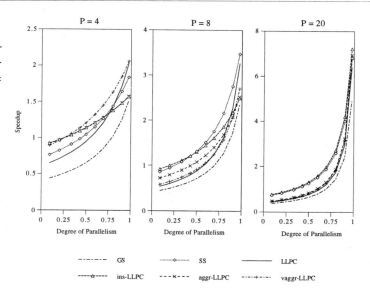

Figure 4: Comparison of the strategies using the regression models while varying the parallel characteristics of the two multiprogrammed applications. *Speedup* $= (W_s + W_p)/(b_1 W_s + b_2 W_p/P)$ and *degree of parallelism* $= W_p/(W_p + W_s)$. Note that the maximum possible parallelism is $P/2$ since two applications are executing.

The serial coefficient for LLPC is higher than most of the other strategies except gang scheduling. Since LLPC does not confine the application within a single partition, nor does it save processors for other applications, it is more affected by the multiprogramming than the other strategies. This effect is not as significant as for gang scheduling, however. On the other hand, the parallel coefficient for LLPC is usually smaller than the other strategies since, unlike space sharing, LLPC does not limit the number of processors allocated to an application and, unlike gang scheduling, applications using LLPC do not directly compete for the processors. Moreover, unlike the three insurance heuristics, LLPC utilizes all of the idle processors when they are available. As a result, the execution of the parallel sections of the code speeds up significantly.

To compare the performance of these strategies under different application characteristics, we calculate the Speedup $((W_s + W_p)/(b_1 W_s + b_2 W_p/P))$ of an application using these regression models while varying the fraction of parallel work (or the degree of parallelism), $W_p/(W_p + W_s)$. In the four-processor case, Figure 4 shows that LLPC performs better than space sharing when the degree of parallelism, $W_p/(W_p + W_s)$, is greater than 0.75. The ins-LLPC and aggr-LLPC strategies are essentially identical when $P = 4$ performing well for applications with a low degree of parallelism. The vaggr-LLPC strategy also saves a small number of processors for other applications, but it is much more aggressive than either ins-LLPC and

aggr-LLPC. Moreover, it does not confine the application within a partition as does space sharing. It combines the characteristics of simple LLPC and the insurance policies to produce the best overall performance in a small system.

In the eight-processor case, space sharing the system by allowing each application to have its own partition with four processors produces the best performance for applications with a degree of parallelism greater than 0.5. The three insurance heuristics perform well when the degree of parallelism is small. When $W_p/(W_p + W_s)$ is greater than 0.75, LLPC can utilize more processors for the parallel work than the insurance heuristics so that the performance of LLPC improves. However, the large sequential coefficient of LLPC in this case causes its performance to be worse than space-sharing. On the twenty-processor system, space sharing and ins-LLPC perform the best when the application's degree of parallelism is less than or equal to 0.8. However, when there is more parallel work within the application, LLPC and the two more aggressive heuristics are more promising. In large systems, such as this configuration, utilizing more processors when they are available while saving only a few for other applications can benefit all of the multiprogrammed applications. In all cases, gang scheduling performs the worst. Also, note that for space sharing to work well, the system must know how many applications will be running so that it can statically partition the processors. If the number of concurrent applications is not known *a priori*, strategies such as LLPC can better adjust to the dynamically varying load [12]

## 6   Performance Prediction of Real Applications

In this section, we use the regression models to *predict* the performance of application programs in a multiprogrammed environment. We then compare these predictions with the actual performance of these applications on the SGI multiprocessor. There are many factors that need to be considered to precisely predict the performance of an application on a dedicated system. For instance, we need to determine the application's memory access patterns, cache coherence overhead, bus traffic, and so on. The prediction becomes even more complicated when the system is multiprogrammed since, not only do we need to determine all of the factors involved in a dedicated system, we also need to consider context switching overhead, interference between applications, cache affinity, etc. Therefore, instead of predicting the exact performance of an application based on these various factors, the goal of our prediction is to provide a rough estimate of the performance when using a given processor allocation strategy executing in a multiprogrammed environment. We make our estimates using the sequential and the dedicated parallel execution times of the application. With this estimate, we can rank-order the processor allocation strategies to determine which performs the best for a particular application.

Three applications from the Perfect Club benchmark suite [2] were selected to represent different parallel characteristics. *Arc2d* solves the Euler equations in generalized curvilinear coordinates using an implicit finite difference algorithm with approximated factorization and a diagonalization of the implicit operators. *Ocean* simulates a two-dimensional fluid flow to study the chaotic behavior of free-slip Rayleigh-Benard convection, and *flo52q* analyzes the transonic flow past an airfoil by solving the unsteady Euler equations. The parallel characteristics of these applications are summarized in Table 2.

Based on the sequential execution times of these benchmark applications, and the parallel execution times on a dedicated 4-processor system, we determine $W_s$ and $W_p$ for these applications using Equations 1 and 3. With $W_s$ and $W_p$, we can predict the execution time of the application when using a particular processor allocation strategy with a given number of processors using the regression models shown in Table 1. As an example, we predict the speedups of the three Perfect Club benchmark applications in a multi-

Table 2: Characteristics of the selected Perfect Club benchmark programs as measured on the SGI Challenge L system.

| Application | Seq. Exec. Time (sec) | No. of Par. Loops Detected by PFA | Speedup (P = 4) |
|---|---|---|---|
| arc2d | 328 | 124 | 3.22 |
| flo52q | 68 | 93 | 2.62 |
| ocean | 194 | 61 | 1.18 |

programmed environment with eight processors. To verify our predictions, we measure the performance of all three combinations of two of the three applications executing concurrently. The predictions and the actual speedups of the applications are summarized in Table 3.

Although the predictions do not exactly match the speedup values of the actual executions, they do demonstrate a close relationship between the applications' characteristics, the processor allocation strategies, and their performance. For instance, our predictions suggest that *arc2d* should have its best performance when using either space sharing or LLPC, which agrees with the actual performance results. Our predictions also suggest that *ocean* has a speedup of less than 1 when using gang scheduling, and, in fact, the measured speedup values for *ocean* using gang scheduling are 0.85 and 1.07.

## 7   Conclusion

We have proposed three new processor allocation heuristics for multiprogrammed multiprocessors based on the idea of dynamically adjusting the processor partitions at the application level. We have evaluated the performance of these heuristics along with gang scheduling, space sharing, and simple loop-level process control on a shared-memory SGI multiprocessor. We used regression analysis to quantify the measured data and thereby explore the relationship between the degree of parallelism of the application, the size of the system, the processor allocation strategy and the resulting performance. We found that gang-scheduling performs significantly worse than the other strategies while space sharing and LLPC have very similar performance in all cases, except that LLPC produces a greater benefit for applications with high degrees of parallelism. In a large system, alternative LLPC strategies that not only dynamically partition the processors but also save a few processors for other late-arriving applications, such as the aggr-LLPC and vaggr-LLPC strategies, perform the best. In these large systems, these strategies allow the applications to allocate enough processors for their execution while simultaneously allowing others to proceed. This type of insurance strategy

Table 3: Predicted and actual speedups of the selected Perfect Club benchmark programs in an 8-processor system. The percentage difference is calculated using (*Actual - Predicted*) / *Predicted* to show how far the actual measurement is from the predicted value.

| Application | GS | SS | LLPC | ins-LLPC | aggr-LLPC | vaggr-LLPC |
|---|---|---|---|---|---|---|
| | | | Predictions | | | |
| arc2d | 2.28 | 3.39 | 3.07 | 2.46 | 2.47 | 2.71 |
| flo52q | 1.79 | 2.84 | 2.34 | 2.21 | 2.13 | 2.28 |
| ocean | 0.75 | 1.38 | 0.93 | 1.34 | 1.13 | 1.13 |
| | | Actual Speedup when multiprogramming 2 applications | | | | |
| arc2d | 2.52 (+11%) | 3.28 (-3%) | 3.12 (+2%) | 2.54 (+3%) | 2.71 (+10%) | 3.07 (+13%) |
| ocean | 0.85 (+13%) | 1.22 (-12%) | 1.04 (+12%) | 1.08 (-4%) | 1.08 (-4%) | 1.08 (-4%) |
| flo52q | 1.62 (-9%) | 2.83 (-0.3%) | 1.74 (-26%) | 1.84 (-20%) | 1.70 (-20%) | 1.84 (-19%) |
| ocean | 1.07 (+43%) | 1.21 (-12%) | 1.11 (+19%) | 1.14 (+0.9%) | 1.14 (+0.9%) | 1.13 (0%) |
| flo52q | 1.48 (-17%) | 2.83 (-0.3%) | 2.72 (+16%) | 2.00 (+7%) | 2.27 (+7%) | 2.34 (+3%) |
| arc2d | 3.90 (+71%) | 3.31 (-2%) | 4.15 (+35%) | 3.04 (+24%) | 3.35 (+36%) | 4.10 (+51%) |

tends to minimize the interference from multiprogramming.

Finally, using the regression models of the allocation strategies developed in this study, we predict the performance of several of the Perfect Club benchmark applications when executed in a multiprogrammed environment. These predictions use only the applications' serial and parallel execution times. While the predictions are not intended to determine the exact performance of an application, they do provide an accurate prediction of which scheduling strategy will perform best under given conditions.

While most of the current research in parallel processing assumes a dedicated system, most of the existing multiprocessors are actually multiprogrammed. This study provides further understanding of the effects of multiprogramming on parallel applications' performance and further supports the benefits of dynamically partitioning the processors based on the applications' characteristics and the dynamically varying system status.

# References

[1] J. Barton and N. Bitar. A scalable multi-discipline, multiple-processor scheduling framework for IRIX. In D. Feitelson and L. Rudolph, editors, *Job Scheduling Strat. for Par. Proc.*, pages 45 – 69. Springer-Verlag, 1995. Lecture Notes in CS V.949.

[2] M. Berry et al. The Perfect Club benchmarks: effective performance evaluation of supercomputers. *Int. J. of Supercomputer App.*, pages 5–40, Fall 1989.

[3] A. Gupta et al. The impact of operating system scheduling polices and synchronization methods on the performance of parallel applications. In *Conf. on Meas. & Model. of Comp. Sys.*, v.19, pp 120-132, 1991.

[4] S. Leutenegger and M. Vernon. The performance of multiprogrammed multiprocessor scheduling policies. In *C. on Meas. & Model. of Comp. Sys.*, 18:226–236, 1990.

[5] D. Lilja. Exploiting the parallelism available in loops. *Computer*, 27(2):13 – 26, February 1994.

[6] V. Naik et al. Performance analysis of job scheduling policies in parallel supercomputing environments. In *Supercomputing*, pages 824–833, 1993.

[7] C. Natarajan, S. Sharma, and R. Iyer. Impact of loop granularity and self-preemption on the performance of loop parallel applications on a multiprogrammed shared-memory multiprocessor. In *1994 International Conference on Parallel Processing*, volume II, pages 174–178, August 1994.

[8] J. Ousterhout. Scheduling techniques for concurrent systems. In *Dist. Comp. Sys. Conf.*, pages 22–30, 1982.

[9] E. Rosti, E. Smirni, L. Dowdy, G. Serazzi, and B. Carlson. Robust partitioning policies of multiprocessor systems. *Performance Evaluation*, 19:141–165, 1994.

[10] C. Severance et al. Automatic self-allocating threads on the Convex Exemplar. In *ICPP*, I:24–31, 1995.

[11] A. Tucker. *Efficient Scheduling on Multiprogrammed Shared-memory Multiprocessors*. PhD thesis, Dept. of CS, Stanford University, 1993.

[12] K. Yue and D. Lilja. Efficient execution of parallel applications in multiprogrammed multiprocessor systems. In *10th International Parallel Processing Symposium*, Apr. 1996.

[13] K. Yue and D. Lilja. Performance analysis and prediction of processor scheduling strategies in multiprogrammed shared-memory multiprocessors. Technical Report HPPC-96-01, HPPC Research Group, U. of MN, 1996. http://www-mount.ee.umn.edu/~lilja/.

[14] J. Zahorjan et al. Spinning versus blocking in parallel systems with uncertainty. In *Int. Sym. on Perf. of Dist. & Par. Sys.*, pages 455–472, 1988.

# The Impact of Speeding up Critical Sections with Data Prefetching and Forwarding[1]

Pedro Trancoso and Josep Torrellas

Center for Supercomputing Research and Development
University of Illinois at Urbana-Champaign, IL 61801
Email: trancoso,torrella@csrd.uiuc.edu

## Abstract

*While shared-memory multiprocessing offers a simple model for process synchronization, actual synchronization may be expensive. Indeed, processors may have to wait for a long time to acquire the lock of a critical section. In addition, a processor may have to stall for a long time waiting for all of its pending accesses to complete before releasing the lock. To address this problem, we target well-known optimization techniques to specifically speed-up accesses to critical sections. We reduce the time taken by critical sections by applying data prefetching and forwarding to minimize the number of misses inside these sections. In addition, we prefetch and forward data in exclusive mode to reduce the stall time before lock release. Our evaluation shows that a simple prefetching algorithm is able to speed-up parallel applications significantly at a very low cost. With this optimization, five Splash applications run 20% faster on average, while one of them runs 52% faster. We also conclude that more complicated, forward-based optimizations are not justified.*

## 1 Introduction

While shared-memory multiprocessing offers a simple model for process synchronization, actual synchronization is often an expensive task. In particular, a common form of synchronization, namely critical sections, is often a source of large overheads in parallel programs. Indeed, to enter the critical section, a processor may have to wait for a long time before it can acquire the lock. In addition, before a processor can release the lock and exit the critical section, it may have to stall for a long time waiting for all of its pending requests to complete. These two overheads often account for a significant fraction of the execution time in parallel programs. Clearly, given that these overheads are concentrated in a very small section of the code, there should be an easy way to determine if they can be optimized away.

One possible approach to speed up critical sections is to provide hardware support to make the acquire and release operations very fast [3]. This approach, however, may not be the most cost-effective one. This is because a large fraction of the execution time of a critical section is often consumed by the ordinary accesses in the section as opposed to the acquire and release accesses.

This occurs, for example, when the ordinary accesses suffer many misses. In fact, misses in the ordinary accesses of the critical section are likely: for instance, 40-85% of the total data read misses in the second-level cache for the five Splash applications [11] considered in this paper occur in critical sections.

A more promising approach to speed up critical sections is to cluster the lock with the data that the lock protects. Then, when a processor acquires the lock, the protected data is made automatically available to the processor. This general approach was used by the KSR-1 designers [5] and by Kagi et al [4]. One difference between these two works is the granularity, which is sub-page (128 bytes) for the KSR-1 and cache line in the second case. Both works, however, have the problem that the variables associated with the lock have to fit in the space available and have to be statically allocated into that same space.

It is better, instead, to speed up critical sections with a technique that is cheaper or that has the flexibility of being useful for other purposes as well. For this reason, we choose data prefetching and forwarding. Data prefetching involves loading the data into the cache ahead of the time of its use [1, 9, 13]. Forwarding involves sending the data to the cache of the future consumer so that by the time the consumer needs the data it can access it locally from its cache [6, 7, 10]. While these techniques have been studied by many researchers, our contribution in this paper is to apply them efficiently and systematically to critical sections. With such a targeted application to key sections of the code, we hope to simplify the compiler analysis required while at the same time provide a multiplicative effect on the rest of the program.

The specific approach that we take is to reduce the time taken by critical sections by using data prefetching and forwarding to minimize the number of misses inside critical sections. In addition, we prefetch and forward data in exclusive mode to reduce the stall time before lock releases. Overall, we conclude that simple prefetching algorithms are enough. With such algorithms, five Splash applications run 20% faster on average, while one of them runs 52% faster. More complicated, forward-based algorithms are not as cost-effective.

The rest of this paper is organized as follows: Section 2 describes the optimizations and the algorithms that implement them; Section 3 presents the experimental setup; Section 4 evaluates the optimizations; finally, Section 5 concludes.

## 2 Optimizing Critical Sections

The goal of the optimizations presented in this paper is to reduce the execution time of critical sections, namely the pieces of code surrounded by a lock acquire and a release. What motivates the interest in this issue is that many

[1]This work was supported in part by the National Science Foundation under grants NSF Young Investigator Award MIP 94-57436 and RIA MIP 93-08098, ARPA Contract No. DABT63-95-C-0097, NASA Contract No. NAG-1-613, Intel Corporation, and the Portuguese government under scholarships JNICT FMRH/BD/1009/94 and JNICT PRAXIS XXI/BD/5877/95.

Splash [11] and other parallel applications have a significant synchronization overhead. For example, for the five Splash applications used in this study, we measured an average synchronization time of 24% of the total execution time (Section 4.4). Speeding up critical sections may therefore have a large performance impact. In addition, since critical sections are fairly small pieces of code, it is conceivable that a detailed analysis may give clues on how to optimize them.

In general, the time taken by critical sections comes from four major sources: (1) instruction execution, (2) processor stall to enforce that only one process is inside the critical section at a time, (3) processor stall waiting for necessary data from memory, and (4) processor stall to enforce the memory consistency model. In this paper, we focus on eliminating the latter two for a release consistency memory system. Indeed, we attempt to decrease the number of accesses to main memory seen by the processor to only one per critical section and eventually to zero. Furthermore, we try to hide stalls required to enforce the memory consistency model.

To do so, we use the well-known techniques of data prefetching and forwarding. Data prefetching involves loading the data into the cache ahead of the time of its use so that by that time the data is already available and no read stall occurs. Forwarding involves the producer processor sending the data to the cache of the future consumer so that by the time the consumer needs the data it can access it locally from its cache. In the following sections, we first describe the optimizations, then present the algorithms, and finally discuss the required architectural support. A more detailed discussion can be found in [12].

## 2.1   Description of the Optimizations

The first optimization attempts to reduce to one the number of accesses to main memory seen by the processor in the critical section. This is done by prefetching right after the acquire all the shared variables that are read in the critical section. Since the prefetches access the memory in a pipelined manner, only one memory access latency will be seen. Even this latency, of course, could be removed if the prefetches were moved outside the critical section. In that case, however, we would run the risk of getting invalidation messages for the prefetched data before acquiring the lock. Finally, we note that some critical sections access data by referencing a pointer. In such cases, it is not possible to overlap the prefetching of the pointer and the prefetching of the data pointed to by the pointer. To minimize stall time, the prefetches must be scheduled carefully. The optimization can be expressed as follows:

**Optimization 1 (Pref)** *Whenever a lock is acquired, prefetch all the shared data that will be read within the critical section.*

The second optimization attempts to hide the single memory access seen by the processor in the first optimization. Indeed, the data to be communicated is forwarded from the first processor to the second right before the first processor releases the lock. These forward statements cost a few cycles to issue. In addition, the issuing processor has to receive an acknowledgement making the completion of each forward before the processor can issue the release. Fortunately, forwards are not blocking and, therefore, can be overlapped with other forwards or with computation.

In the best case, when the second processor acquires the lock, all the data that it needs in its critical section is already in its cache.

There are some problems with this use of data forwarding. The first one is that the processor issuing the forwards needs to know which other processor to send the data to. The most obvious way of doing this is to keep in memory a queue of all the processors waiting for that lock. Then, the releasing processor can read this queue to determine what processor to forward the data to. Reading such queue, of course, involves some overhead. We note in passing that this queue can be used to forward the lock variable itself too.

The second problem is that this optimization works only if, at the time that the lock is about to be released, there is a processor waiting to acquire it. To handle the case where no processor is waiting, we have to combine this optimization with the *Pref* optimization discussed above: before issuing the forwards, the processor has to check if there is any processor waiting. If none is waiting, the forwards are skipped. The consumer processor, after acquiring the locks will first attempt to prefetch data right after the acquire. If the data has already been forwarded to its cache, the prefetch requests will be terminated in the cache in one cycle.

Finally, it is possible that a given lock variable is used in two different critical sections that perform different operations. In this case, the forwards that we suggest may end up sending data that is useless to the acquiring processor. The approach that we follow is to forward the union of variables read by the two critical sections. Overall, this optimization can be expressed as follows:

**Optimization 2 (Forw)** *Whenever a lock is acquired, prefetch all the shared data that will be read within the critical section. Right before executing the release operation, if there is a processor waiting to acquire the lock, forward that same data to the waiting processor.*

The two optimizations presented focus on reads only because we assume that, while read misses stall the processor, writes do not. However, both writes and reads can cause the processor to stall to enforce the memory consistency model. For example, a release may not be issued because the processor is waiting for invalidation acknowledgements resulting from a write. A known way to reduce the effect of this problem is to originally request the data with the intention to write. This means requesting the data in state exclusive at the time of the read. When the data is read in, all sharers are invalidated; when the data is finally written, there is no need to send invalidations. This idea can be combined with prefetching (which is then called exclusive prefetching [9]) or with forwarding (which we call exclusive forwarding). Therefore, we have two more optimizations:

**Optimization 3 (ExPref)** *Whenever a lock is acquired, prefetch in exclusive mode all the shared data that will be written within the critical section, and prefetch all the remaining shared data that will be read within critical section.*

**Optimization 4 (ExForw)** *Whenever a lock is acquired, prefetch in exclusive mode all the shared data that will be written within the critical section, and prefetch all the remaining shared data that will be read within the critical section. Right before executing the release operation, if there is a processor waiting to acquire the lock, forward to* *the processor in exclusive mode all the written shared data and forward to the processor the rest of the read shared data.*

These optimizations perform better for small- to medium-sized critical sections and when locks suffer high contention. For large-sized critical sections, not all the data may be accessed. These characteristics are typical of critical sections that protect control data structures rather than application data. For application data, the critical sections are usually large and their code accesses a large set of data.

## 2.2 Algorithms

Figure 1 shows the pseudo-code for the algorithms that implement the optimizations presented before. We start first with the *Pref* algorithm. We see that the variables that are read in the critical section are grouped in the *READ* list. The union operator that we use is a special operator that performs the union of the memory lines. In particular, for each variable that is read, we try to calculate its memory line. Then, we add the variable to the *READ* list only if no variable already in the *READ* list is mapped to the same line or if the address of the new variable cannot be determined at compile time.

In the algorithm, the variables inserted in the *READ* list depend on how aggressive the algorithm is. Indeed, since the critical section may have several if statements, we have different alternatives. For example, we may choose to insert only the variables that are read no matter what the path taken by the code is. In such case, no useless data will be prefetched. Alternatively, we can insert all variables read in any path. For the experiments in Section 4 we use both schemes. For all applications except *Pthor*, we insert all variables read in any path because the critical sections are very small. For *Pthor*, instead, we insert only variables read no matter what the path is. This is because one critical section in *Pthor* is very large. Finally, we note that, in the algorithm, the order in which the variables are inserted in the *READ* list is the same as the one in which they are taken out and the corresponding prefetches placed in the code. The prefetches are therefore placed in the order of the reads in the code.

The *Forw* algorithm starts by computing the *READ* list for each acquire and inserting the prefetches like in the *Pref* algorithm. Then, it computes the union of the *READ* lists for all the acquires of the same lock. This new list, called *TOTAL_READ*, contains the variables to forward at the end of every critical section protected by that lock. The order of the variables in the list determines the order in which the forward instructions should be inserted. Note that this aggressive approach may have some problems. First, *TOTAL_READ* may include variables that are not present in the cache at the time the forward instruction is issued. This situation can be handled by either transforming the forward into a "no-op" or by requesting the data from the memory system and then forwarding it. We chose to implement the first solution for simplicity reasons. The second problem is that some of the forwarded variables may be useless to the destination processor. We could obviously take the more conservative approach of generating *TOTAL_READ* as the intersection of all the *READ* lists. However, the simple critical sections of our applications do not justify doing so.

The *Forw* algorithm needs the ID of the processor to which the data should be sent. This *Dest* ID is determined by issuing a non-blocking read to the lock queue to find

*Pref* Algorithm:

```
for each critical section C
  READ(C) = ∅
  for each statement s in C from top to bottom
    if (s includes a read to variable v)
      READ(C) = READ(C) ∪ v
  for each variable v in READ(C)
    create ''Prefetch(v)'' statement
    insert it in C right before any non-prefetch
    statement
```

*Forw* Algorithm:

```
perform the Pref algorithm saving READ(C) for
 every critical section C
for each lock variable L
  TOTAL_READ(L) = ∅
  for each C that uses lock variable L
    TOTAL_READ(L) = TOTAL_READ(L) ∪ READ(C)
  for each C that uses lock variable L
    for each variable v in TOTAL_READ(L)
      create a ''Forward(v, Dest)'' statement
      insert it in C right before the releases
```

*ExPref* Algorithm:

```
for each critical section C
  ACCESS(C) = ∅
  for each statement s in C from top to bottom
    if (s includes a read to variable v)
      ACCESS(C) = ACCESS(C) ∪ v
    if (s includes a write to variable v)
      ACCESS(C) = ACCESS(C) ∪ SetExclusive(v)
  for each variable v in ACCESS(C)
    if (IsExclusive(v))
      create a ''Prefetch_ex(v)'' statement
    else
      create a ''Prefetch(v)'' statement
    insert it in C right before any non-prefetch
    statement
```

*ExForw* Algorithm:

```
perform the ExPref algorithm saving ACCESS(C) for
 every critical section C
for each lock variable L
  TOTAL_ACCESS(L) = ∅
  for each C that uses lock variable L
    TOTAL_ACCESS(L) = TOTAL_ACCESS(L) ∪ ACCESS(C)
  for each C that uses lock variable L
    for each variable v in TOTAL_ACCESS(L)
      if (IsExclusive(v))
        create ''Forward_ex(v, Dest)'' statement
      else
        create ''Forward(v, Dest)'' statement
      insert it in C right before the releases
```

Figure 1: *Pref, Forw, ExPref,* and *ExForw* algorithms. *Dest* refers to the processor that is waiting to acquire the lock next. To simplify the forwarding algorithms, we do not show that the releasing processor reads the queue of waiting processors to determine what processor to forward the data to.

```
LOCK(1);        LOCK(1);           LOCK(1);
a = b + c;      Prefetch(b);       Prefetch(b);
d = f—g;        Prefetch_ex(a);    Prefetch_ex(a);
UNLOCK(1);      Prefetch(f);       Prefetch(f);
                Prefetch(f→g);     Prefetch(f→g);
                Prefetch_ex(d);    Prefetch_ex(d);
    (a)         a = b + c;         a = b + c;
                d = f—g;           d = f→g;
                UNLOCK(1);         Forward(b,Dest);
                                   Forward_ex(a,Dest);
        (b)                        Forward(f,Dest);
                                   Forward(f→g,Dest);
                                   Forward_ex(d,Dest);
                                   UNLOCK(1);


                        (c)
```

Figure 2: Example of a critical section (Chart(a)) after applying the *ExPref* (Chart (b)), and *ExForw* (Chart (c)) algorithms. The code after applying *Pref* and *Forw* is exactly the same as shown without the *Prefetch_ex* and *Forward_ex* calls. Variables $b$ and $c$ are allocated in the same cache line.

out which processor is waiting next. This read, which is not shown in the algorithm, is issued right after the acquire. If there is no processor waiting in the lock queue, then the processor can send the forwards to memory or can skip the forwards altogether. In the experiments of Section 4, this case is handled by the processor forwarding to itself, effectively performing "no-op" operations.

The *ExPref* and *ExForw* algorithms are based on the *Pref* and *Forw* algorithms. However, we use the *ACCESS* and *TOTAL_ACCESS* lists instead of the *READ* and *TOTAL_READ* lists respectively. The former two lists contain variables that are read or written, while the latter two contain only variables that are read. In *ACCESS* and *TOTAL_ACCESS*, the variables that are written are marked with the attribute *exclusive*, and the corresponding line is prefetched or forwarded in exclusive mode. Such marking is performed with the *SetExclusive* function and checked with the *IsExclusive* function. The *exclusive* state for a line overwrites the *non-exclusive* state.

A small example of the application of these algorithms is shown in Figure 2. In the figure, variables $b$ and $c$ are allocated in the same cache line. The algorithms presented are very simple and could be refined in many ways. For example, the forwards could be performed at the same time as the last writes to the variables, like it was proposed in [6, 10], thereby saving cycles. Similarly, the prefetch statements could be scheduled better, specially in the context of variables accessed via pointer dereferencing. Finally, our algorithms as they are now prefetch or forward only one iteration of a loop. For all these reasons, the results in Section 4 are conservative.

## 2.3 Architectural Support

The architectural support required by the prefetch operation is modest. A popular implementation of prefetching requires a prefetch instruction that loads data without blocking and takes no exceptions, lock-up free caches to handle multiple outstanding prefetches, and the buffering of some state for each pending prefetch until the prefetch transaction is completed.

The architectural support required by the forwarding operation defined here is a bit more complex. Indeed,

there is the need to implement a per-lock queue where the processors waiting on the lock are inserted in FIFO order. This queue can be implemented in hardware [4] or software [8]. Then, we need to add a forwarding instruction, buffer some state for each pending forward until the forward transaction is completed, modify the cache coherence protocol to support forwarding transactions, and modify the caches to accept lines that have not been requested by the processor. Many optimizations to this base scheme are possible. For example, we could use Poulsen and Yew's [10] and Koufaty *et al*'s [6] combined *write-and-forward* instruction.

## 3  Experimental Setup

In this work we simulate a cache-coherent shared-memory machine (CC-NUMA) with 32 nodes. Each node includes a 4-Kbyte first-level write-through cache and a 64-Kbyte second-level write-back cache. Both caches have 4-word cache lines and are direct-mapped. Each of the nodes contains a part of the global memory and its directory. The processor on each node is a RISC processor with single instruction issue per clock cycle. A hit in the first-level cache is solved without penalty, while a first-level cache line fill takes 14 cycles if the line comes from the secondary cache and 50 cycles if the line comes from the local memory.

The interconnection network is modeled by a fixed latency value of 30 cycles for transmit time and 34 cycles for data transmission (both values for a one-way trip). Contention is modeled in the various resources of the architecture except in the network.

Table 1: Applications used in the experiments.

| Apps. | Description | Problem Size |
|---|---|---|
| *Barnes* | Simulates the evolution of galaxies | 1000 bodies 3 time steps |
| *Cholesky* | Cholesky factorization of a sparse matrix | bcsstk14.O 1806 columns |
| *Mp3d* | Simulates a rarefied hypersonic flow | 10000 particles 10 time steps |
| *Pthor* | Simulates a digital circuit at the logic level | small RISC processor |
| *Water* | Simulates evolution of set of water molecules | 343 molecules 2 time steps |

This architecture is simulated on a simulator based on TangoLite [2], an execution-driven simulator. For this study, the memory simulator was enhanced with some extra functionalities like monitoring all the synchronization variables and introducing prefetching and forwarding directives.

The workloads run are some of the Splash [11] applications. A brief description of the applications and the problem sizes used are presented in Table 1. We run the applications with 32 processors. In these applications, we insert the extra prefetch and forward instructions "by hand".

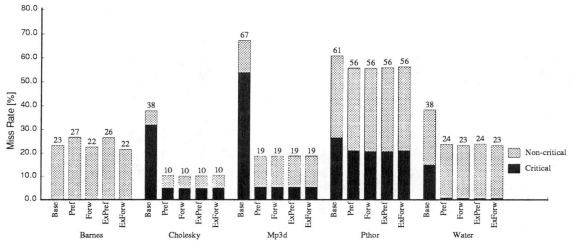

Figure 3: Read miss rate of the second-level cache for different levels of optimization.

## 4 Evaluation

In this section we evaluate the algorithms described in Section 2. Since some of the applications have specific problems that prevented scalability, we start by making some changes to some applications. Then, we present the impact of the proposed optimizations on the read miss rate, synchronization time, and execution time.

### 4.1 Some Problems in Applications

Before we apply the algorithms presented in Section 2, we make changes to some of the applications to reduce the time processors waste waiting in barriers. Much of this time is due to load imbalance in the application. To be fair, this load imbalance needs to be addressed first, before applying the algorithms, since it is the most obvious synchronization problem.

In *Barnes*, the critical sections are very large. For example, some of them include several vector operations implemented using loops. Such large critical sections cause an excessive serialization and, consequently, load imbalance in the application. To fix the problem, we divide the critical sections into smaller critical sections. As a result, more operations can be done in parallel or in pipeline. This modification reduces the execution time by 2%.

*Cholesky* has load imbalance due to the different sizes of the matrix columns. To optimize the execution of the algorithm, the application groups the columns into *supernodes*. Because *supernodes* have different sizes, the work given to each processor is very different. To reduce this problem, we impose a tighter limitation on the *supernodes'* maximum size. As a result, their size ranges are smaller and therefore the work is more balanced. This optimization results in a 10% reduction in the execution time.

### 4.2 Impact of the Optimizations on Read Miss Rates

To determine the effect of our algorithms, we start by examining their impact on the read miss rate. We break down the read miss rate into two distinct categories, the

miss rate due to the read misses within critical sections (*Critical*) and the rest (*Non-critical*). This breakdown allows us to see the weight of the critical sections in terms of the read miss rate. Then, we apply our algorithms and determine the new miss rate breakdown. We can then see how effective our optimizations are.

Figure 3 shows the read miss rate breakdown for the original and optimized codes. The figure shows the miss rate of the 64-Kbyte second-level cache. The miss rates are high because the first-level cache filters many of the references. In this figure, we divide the read miss rate into the *Critical* and *Non-critical* categories. For each application we show five bars which, from left to right, are: *Base* for the original code, *Pref* for the code with the prefetching optimization, *Forw* for the code with the forwarding optimization, *ExPref* for the code with the exclusive prefetching optimization, and *ExForw* for the code with the exclusive forwarding optimization.

From the figure, we can see that, with the exception of *Barnes*, the misses in the critical section contribute significantly to the miss rate of the *Base* version of the applications. Indeed, 40-85% of the miss rate comes from misses in the critical section. This suggests that, by targeting these small, well identified portions of code that are the critical sections, the overall miss rate can be reduced significantly.

If we now consider the other bars, we see that, in most cases, all optimizations have a similar effect. Such effect, however, varies depending upon the application. On the one hand, there are applications like *Cholesky*, *Mp3d*, and *Water* where the miss rate reduction is as large as 40-75%. On the other hand, for *Pthor*, the miss rate reduction is a modest 9%. In all these cases, of course, the miss rate reductions come from reducing the number of misses in the critical section. In *Barnes*, there are very few misses inside critical sections. However, inserting prefetches to eliminate these misses results in an increase in misses outside critical sections.

In these four applications, if we compare the bars corresponding to the different optimizations we observe that, against intuition, *Forw* does not do better than *Pref* and *ExForw* does not do better than *ExPref*. In Section 2, we stressed that forwarding optimizations can potentially

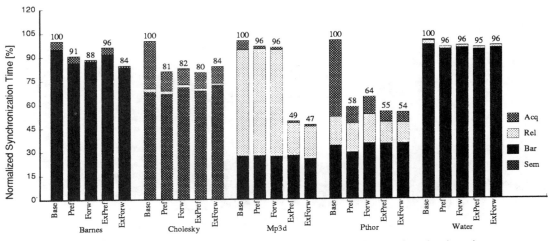

Figure 4: Impact of the optimizations on the synchronization time.

Table 2: Read miss rate coverage.

| Application | Cholesky | Mp3d | Pthor | Water |
|---|---|---|---|---|
| Coverage | 84.6 | 90.3 | 20.5 | 95.3 |

reduce the number of read misses even further than the prefetching optimizations. There are, however, two reasons for not observing much change in the miss rates. The first one is that cache misses that are only partially hidden by prefetching or forwarding are not shown in Figure 3. Consequently, while forwarding may partially hide some misses to a larger degree than prefetching, Figure 3 will not show it. The second reason for not observing much change in the miss rates is that, for some applications, sometimes there are no processors waiting to enter the critical section. In such cases, there is no difference between forwarding and prefetching. Overall, the results in Figure 3 already suggest that forwarding is unlikely to be much more effective than prefetching.

Figure 3 also shows the fraction of the misses in the critical section that have been removed with these optimizations. Such fraction we call the read miss rate *Coverage*. The exact coverage for the *Pref* optimization in the different applications is shown in Table 2. From the table we see that *Cholesky*, *Mp3d*, and *Water* have coverages larger than 80%. Obviously, the algorithms achieve their expected effect. In *Pthor*, instead, the coverage is only 21%. The reason for such a low coverage is that one of the critical sections in *Pthor* is very large. The code for this critical section is spread onto multiple files. As a result, our algorithm inserts many prefetches and forwards. Consequently, as indicated in Section 2.2 we used the conservative versions of the algorithms in Figure 1, which insert variables in the *READ* and *ACCESS* list only if they are read or accessed in all possible paths of execution within the critical section. This reduced the coverage. Finally, we excluded *Barnes* from Table 2 because its coverage does not have much meaning given that there are very few misses in the critical section to start with.

In conclusion, we found that, for the five applications, an average of 50% of the second-level cache read misses occur within critical sections. Our algorithms are able to eliminate on average over 58% of the misses in critical sections, thereby reducing the miss rate by about 35%.

### 4.3 Impact of the Optimizations on Synchronization Time

We now analyze the impact of our algorithms on the synchronization time. The time spent on synchronization can be divided into time waiting in barriers (*Bar*), time spent spinning on a lock before acquiring it (*Acq*), and time spent waiting for the completion of pending requests before releasing a lock (*Rel*). In addition, *Cholesky* has semaphores that arbitrate the assignment of work to threads in a centralized point. Semaphores include additional information like how many resources are available. The time that threads wait in these semaphores we call *Sem*, and is mostly due to load imbalance of the application. Consequently, our optimizations do not address the *Sem* time directly.

Figure 4 shows the breakdown of the synchronization time for the different applications and levels of optimization. For each application, we have five bars that are normalized to the *Base* time and are broken down into *Acq*, *Rel*, *Bar*, and *Sem* time. From the *Base* bars, we can see that there are two types of applications, namely those where *Bar* or *Sem* account for most of the time and those where *Acq* or *Rel* are important. The applications in the first group are *Barnes*, *Cholesky*, and *Water*, while the applications in the second group are *Mp3d* and *Pthor*. This distinction is important because our optimizations cannot target the first group of applications. The first group of applications need changes to balance the load among the processors.

The first two optimizations, namely *Pref* and *Forw*, attempt to reduce the *Acq* time. Indeed, as indicated in Section 2.1, they reduce the misses in critical sections, which speeds up the execution of critical sections and therefore reduces the time that other processors need to wait to get in. Such effect is observed in Figure 4: *Pref* eliminates a large fraction of the *Acq* time in *Cholesky*,

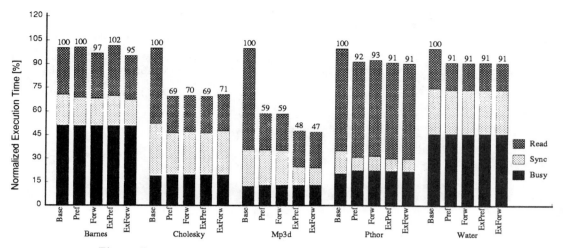

Figure 5: Impact of the optimizations on the execution time of the applications.

*Mp3d*, and *Pthor*, reducing the overall synchronization time significantly in two of these applications. Surprisingly, *Forw* does not do much better than *Pref*. It may be that the contention in the memory subsystem prevents forwarding from hiding the misses to a much larger extent than prefetching. In fact, *Forw* sometimes does worse than *Pref*. The reason is random changes in load balance in the application, which sometimes cause an increase in the *Bar* and *Sem* time. Overall, *Pref* and *Forw* reduce the synchronization time of the five applications by 16% and 15% on average respectively. After applying these optimizations, very little *Acq* time is left in the applications.

The next two optimizations, namely *ExPref* and *Ex-Forw*, attempt to reduce the *Rel* time. This is because, as indicated in Section 2.1, data is prefetched and forwarded in state exclusive and, therefore, there is no need for a later network access that creates invalidations and acknowledgements that delay the release of the lock. These optimizations, therefore, will only have an impact on the applications with *Rel* time, namely *Mp3d* and *Pthor*. The reductions in *Rel* time are large, especially in *Mp3d*. Overall, *ExPref* decreases the synchronization time of *Pref* by 49% and 5% for *Mp3d* and *Pthor* respectively. The reason for the large improvement in *Mp3d* is that this application's critical sections are small and contain many write operations at the end of it. Finally, we note that, possibly for the reason explained before, both *ExPref* and *ExForw* have a similar impact.

The applications with large *Bar* or *Sem* time change relatively less because our optimizations do not target those times. Most of their changes are due to random variation in the *Bar* or *Sem* time due to load balance variations.

Overall, the impact of the algorithms on the synchronization time is a function of the contribution of the *Acq* and *Rel* time to the total synchronization time. For applications with large *Acq* and *Rel* time like *Mp3d* and *Pthor*, we get a large improvement of around 50%. For the other applications, we get more modest results. On average, after applying *ExForw*, the applications reduce their synchronization time by around 25%.

Table 3: Applications characteristics.

|  | Read Miss Reduction? | Sync Time Reduction? | Expected Improvement |
|---|---|---|---|
| *Barnes* | n | n | small |
| *Cholesky* | y | n | medium |
| *Mp3d* | y | y | large |
| *Pthor* | n | y | medium |
| *Water* | y | n | medium |

## 4.4 Impact of the Optimizations on Execution Time

We now assess the impact of the optimizations on the execution time of the applications. Such impact will be a combination of the two effects presented so far: a reduction in read stall time resulting from eliminating some misses in the critical sections (Section 4.2) and a direct reduction in synchronization time (Section 4.3).

To gain insight into what applications may benefit from the optimizations, we summarize in Table 3 the findings in the previous two sections. The first column of the table lists the applications that showed a noticeable reduction in the miss rate (Section 4.2). These applications are *Cholesky*, *Mp3d* and *Water*. These applications, therefore, are likely to show reductions in the read stall time. Similarly, the second column of the table lists the applications that showed a noticeable reduction in the synchronization time (Section 4.3). These applications are *Mp3d* and *Pthor*. As a result, the data in the table suggests that *Barnes* is unlikely to benefit much from the optimizations; *Cholesky*, *Pthor*, and *Water* are likely to benefit to a certain extent; and finally, *Mp3d* is likely to benefit the most.

The actual measurements of the total execution time of the applications are shown in Figure 5. For each application, we show the *Base*, *Pref*, *Forw*, *ExPref*, and *Ex-Forw* environments, all normalized to *Base*'s execution time. For each application, the bars are subdivided into three categories: computation time (*Busy*), synchronization time (*Sync*), and stall time due to read misses (*Read*).

As predicted in Table 3, the figure shows that *Mp3d* has the largest execution time reduction. Such reduction, which reaches 53% in the best case, comes from both a smaller *Read* and a smaller *Sync* time. Again, in agreement with Table 3, *Cholesky*, *Pthor*, and *Water* have medium to large execution time reductions. The reductions are 31%, 9%, and 9% for *Cholesky*, *Pthor*, and *Water* respectively. While the speedups in *Cholesky* and *Water* come from a lower *Read* time, the speedups in *Pthor* come from a lower *Sync* time. Finally, the execution time reduction for *Barnes* is small (5%), as predicted in Table 3.

If we compare the different optimizations, we can observe that, in most cases, *Pref* is enough to obtain most of the speedups. In one case, however, namely *Mp3d*, *Ex-Pref* has a clear advantage over *Pref*. For this reason, we recommend the use of the *ExPref* optimization. We also note that, in general, *Forw* and *ExForw* do not seem to provide any major advantage over *Pref* and *ExPref*. The exception is *Barnes*, where the forward-based optimizations perform better than the prefetch-based ones. This effect, however, is small. Overall, therefore, considering the extra cost of the forward-based optimizations, we conclude that the forward-based optimizations are not worth supporting.

It is well-known that software prefetching has the disadvantage of adding extra instruction overhead to the execution. This does not seem to be a problem for the applications considered. Indeed, it is true that we can observe a small increase in the *Busy* time for *Cholesky*, *Mp3d* and *Pthor*. However, the overall impact of this effect is negligible.

To summarize, we conclude that, with the simple *ExPref* optimization we can obtain nice speedups in the applications considered. On average, these applications run 20% faster. The speedup is larger for applications where the *Read* time is large, many of the read misses occur in the critical section, the *Sync* time is significant, and the *Acq* and *Rel* parts of the *Sync* time are large. When these conditions are met we can obtain large execution time reductions like 52% for *Mp3d*.

## 5   Conclusions

In parallel applications, accesses to critical sections may involve large overheads. Indeed, processors may have to wait for a long time to acquire a lock. In addition, they may have to stall for a long time waiting for all pending requests to complete before releasing it. To address these problems, this paper has proposed and evaluated simple optimizations that speed up accesses in critical sections. Our approach is to reduce the time taken by critical sections by using data prefetching and forwarding to minimize the number of misses inside critical sections. In addition, we prefetch and forward data in exclusive mode to reduce the stall time before lock release.

We conclude that a simple prefetching algorithm that we have presented is able to significantly speed up parallel applications at a very low cost. The algorithm prefetches the variables accessed in the critical section. Those variables that are written in the critical section are prefetched in exclusive mode. With this optimization, five Splash applications run 20% faster on average, while one of them runs 52% faster. We also conclude that more complicated, forward-based optimizations are not justified.

## Acknowledgments

We thank Zheng Zhang for all his help during the development of this work and especially for the simulation environment that was provided. We also thank the referees and the graduate students in the I-ACOMA group for their feedback. Pedro Trancoso is supported by a scholarship from Portugal. Josep Torrellas is supported in part by an NSF Young Investigator Award.

## References

[1] J. L. Baer and T. F. Chen. An Effective On-Chip Preloading Scheme to Reduce Data Access Penalty. In *Proceedings of Supercomputing'91*, pages 179–186, November 1991.

[2] S. Goldschmidt. Simulation of Multiprocessors: Accuracy and Performance. Ph.D. Thesis, Stanford University, June 1993.

[3] J. R. Goodman, M. K. Vernon, and P. J. Woest. Efficient Synchronization Primitives for Large-scale Cache-coherent Multiprocessors. In *Proceedings of the 3rd International Conference on Architectural Support for Programming Languages and Operating Systems*, pages 64–73, April 1989.

[4] Alain Kagi, Nagi Aboulenein, Douglas C. Burger, and James R. Goodman. Techniques for Reducing Overheads of Shared-Memory Multiprocessing. In *Proceedings of the 1995 International Conference on Supercomputing*, pages 11–20, July 1995.

[5] Kendall Square Research. *KSR1 Technical Summary*. Waltham, MA, 1992.

[6] D. A. Koufaty, X. Chen, D. K. Poulsen, and J. Torrellas. Data Forwarding in Scalable Shared-Memory Multiprocessors. In *Proceedings of the 1995 International Conference on Supercomputing*, pages 255–264, July 1995.

[7] D. Lenoski, J. Laudon, K. Gharachorloo, W. Weber, A. Gupta, J. Hennessy, M. Horowitz, and M. S. Lam. The Stanford Dash Multiprocessor. *IEEE Computer*, pages 63–79, March 1992.

[8] John M. Mellor-Crummey and Michael L. Scott. Algorithms for Scalable Synchronization on Shared-Memory Multiprocessors. *ACM Transactions on Computer Systems*, 9(1):21–65, February 1991.

[9] Todd Mowry and Anoop Gupta. Tolerating Latency Through Software-Controlled Prefetching in Shared-Memory Multiprocessors. *Journal of Parallel and Distributed Computing*, pages 87–106, 1991.

[10] David K. Poulsen and Pen-Chung Yew. Data Prefetching and Data Forwarding in Shared Memory Multiprocessors. In *Proceedings of the 1994 International Conference on Parallel Processing*, volume II, pages 276–280, August 1994. Also available as CSRD tech report No. 1330.

[11] J. P. Singh, W. Weber, and A. Gupta. SPLASH: Stanford Parallel Applications for Shared-Memory. Technical Report CSL-TR-91-469, Computer Systems Laboratory, Stanford University, April 1991.

[12] Pedro P. M. Trancoso. Performance Optimization Based on Characterizing Synchronization. Master's thesis, University of Illinois at Urbana-Champaign, October 1995.

[13] Zheng Zhang and Josep Torrellas. Speeding up Irregular Applications in Shared-Memory Multiprocessors: Memory Binding and Group Prefetching. In *Proceedings of the 22nd Annual International Symposium on Computer Architecture*, pages 188–199, June 1995.

# SYNCHRONIZATION ELIMINATION IN THE DEPOSIT MODEL

Susan Hinrichs *
Global Internet Software Group
107 S. State St.
Monitcello, IL 61856
shinrich@gi.net

*The deposit message passing model is an effective target for communication code generated by data parallel compilers. This model separates data transfer from control, so the deposit model requires additional control communication to ensure that the memory on the remote node is ready to be overwritten. This control communication is generally provided by barrier synchronization. In some cases, the barrier is redundant and the synchronization can be piggy-backed on previous communication steps. This paper presents a data flow algorithm that determines which control barriers are redundant and can be eliminated.*

## INTRODUCTION

Explicitly parallel programs directly written by human programmers tend to use traditional message passing libraries such as PVM or MPI. These libraries support a rich set of communication functionality, which is necessary for the human programmer. However, communication code generated by the data parallel compiler does not require this support. In our experience with the Fx compiler (which compiles a variation of High Performance Fortran (HPF))[13], the deposit communication model is a more efficient communication target[11].

The deposit message passing model separates the issues of data transfer and program synchronization, so the compiler can find more efficient solutions to each problem separately. In the deposit model, the destination address is passed along with the message, so the receiving message handler can directly store the message. The compiler must also add control messages to ensure that new data is not deposited while data in the target buffer is still in use. The Fx compiler uses barrier synchronization between communication steps to maintain this buffer use sequencing.

In some cases these extra control messages are redundant; the control information can be piggy-backed on messages from previous communication steps. In this paper, we present an algorithm that analyzes the communication patterns in a program to determine when the synchronization information added for the deposit model is redundant.

## Synchronization in parallel programs

Synchronization is needed for programs on parallel systems when two threads (or processes) are operating on the same data location to ensure that the reader is using the proper value. Figure 1(a) shows a writer and reader relationship under the shared memory model. Thread one (T1) writes a location, and thread two (T2) reads that location twice. On the first read, T2 wants the value before the write, and on the second read, T2 wants the value after the write. To ensure that the reading constraints are maintained, a synchronization point is required after the first read and before the write.

The remaining figures show the same situation under the distributed memory model using two different communication models: *traditional* and *deposit* message passing models. Figure 1(b) shows two threads in the traditional message passing model. By buffering messages that arrive too early, this model ties thread synchronization to data transfer. The sending thread does not directly modify memory location on the receiving thread, so no additional synchronization is required.

In the deposit model, the sending thread directly modifies memory used by the receiving thread. After the message is deposited, a semaphore is updated on the remote node to notify the receiver that the new value has appeared. Figure 1(c) shows the exchange in this model. Since T1 directly changes values in T2, synchronization is required to ensure that the last read has passed before the deposit occurs.

This paper addresses synchronization in compiled data parallel programs that use the deposit message passing model for communication. The issues of synchronization analysis have been addressed for other memory models and program models. Working in the shared memory model,

*This research was sponsored in part by the Advanced Research Projects Agency/CSTO monitored by SPAWAR under contract N00039-93-C-0152, and under contract MDA972-90-C-0035.

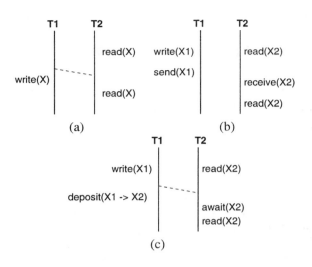

Figure 1: The dashed line shows the required synchronization points between two threads under various communication models: (a) shared memory, (b) buffered message passing, and (c) deposit message passing.

Subhlok addresses the problem of synchronization in Fortran 77 with parallel do and case statements[12]. He developed a data flow algorithm that determines whether the current synchronization points in the program are sufficient to ensure that there are no data race conditions. This algorithm could be used to optimize the number of required synchronization points by iteratively removing synchronization points and re-running the data flow algorithm. By concentrating on the data parallel model, this paper addresses a simpler problem and is able to develop a more efficient synchronization elimination algorithm.

Tseng addresses barrier elimination for parallel programs compiled for a distributed shared memory system using the SUIF compiler[14]. Unlike traditional shared memory compilers, this compiler performs analysis to determine how data and computation should be distributed over the machine. Tseng developed a phase that analyzes the pattern of local and non-local memory accesses to determine when barriers are unnecessary or when barriers can be replaced by cheaper synchronization methods. In the deposit message passing model (unlike the shared memory model), the receiving node knows when data has been updated, so the algorithm described in this paper can be more aggressive about using communication analysis to eliminate barriers.

Gupta and Schonberg also started from the distributed shared memory model and independently developed a data flow algorithm similar to the one presented in this paper[5]. Unlike Tseng, they assumed the existence of flex-

ible memory coherence protocols. Their commuunication primitive is *put*, a finer-grained version of the deposit mechanism.

**Compiler model**

This paper describes work in the context of the Fx compiler, a data parallel compiler that operates on a variant of HPF. Fx can generate code for a variety of distributed memory systems including iWarp, Paragon, and T3D.

The data parallel programming model eases the task of communication analysis for a compiler by providing a global name space. The data parallel compiler translates each data parallel statement into a communication step and a computation step, so the compiler sees the program as a series of alternating communication and computation steps. With the proper analysis tools [2, 9, 15] or user directives[3], a data parallel compiler can discover exactly what communication must take place in each step.

The compiler describes these communication requirements as a sequence of *communication patterns*, sets of node-to-node communications that form system-wide communication steps.[1] These communication patterns are either *regular* or *irregular*. The structure of a regular communication pattern is only dependent on the structure of the program. Many matrix and signal processing programs need only regular communication patterns, and this paper concentrates on such programs.

A shift is a simple example of a regular communication pattern. Assume the nodes have a linear ordering. In a "shift right" pattern, each node sends data to its right neighbor, so node $p$ sends to node $p + 1$. Other examples of regular communication patterns are reductions, transposes, all-to-all communications, scatters, and gathers.

The communication in the successive over relaxation (SOR) solver is one simple example of a communication pattern that can be recognized at compile time. Figure 2 shows data parallel pseudo-code for SOR with the required communication steps added (1a and 2a). Consider one step of the SOR computation corresponding to statements 1a and 1b. In the parallel implementation, both A and B are distributed over a ring of nodes. Each node owns a subregion A and B, and each node shares *overlap* regions with its neighbors[4]. In the overlap region, the node stores duplicated data that is owned by the neighboring node but is needed locally for the next computation step. The top of

To compile programs written in the data parallel model, the compiler must map arrays in the global address space to physical arrays on the target system. Potentially, sub-

---

[1]The communication pattern can be defined over virtual or physical processors. Eventually, the virtual processors are mapped to physical processors, so for the sake of simplicity, this paper considers only the real communication between physical processors.

```
0.     A = initial values
       do i=1,iter_cnt
1a.        overlap_shift(A)
1b.        B(2:n-1) = c1*A(1:n-2) + c2*A(3:n)
2a.        overlap_shift(B)
2b.        A(2:n-1) = c1*B(1:n-2) + c2*B(3:n)
       enddo
```

Figure 2: SOR data parallel pseudo-code.

sections of the global arrays are assigned to arrays on different physical processors, i.e. the physical arrays can be *distributed*. Our compiler uses algorithms based on the data alignment algorithm developed for CM Fortran[9] and the data distribution algorithm developed by Wholey[15] to find this data placement. From this data placement information, the compiler derives communication maps that describe the regular communication steps required in the program[6].

## SYNCHRONIZATION ELIMINATION

The data parallel compiler generates computation organized into global "steps". Within each step, the compiler-generated code is scheduled to access communication buffers correctly. Between steps additional communication may be necessary to ensure that target buffers are ready to be overwritten. Figure 3 shows the logical exchange required between nodes 1 and 2 to guarantee that it is safe for node 1 to deposit data into buffer B on node 2.

Depending on the sequence of communication patterns, this additional control information can be piggy-backed on communication from previous steps. Consider the SOR example shown in Figure 2. In the overlap shift, each node communicates with its two neighboring nodes, e.g. node $P$ exchanges data with nodes $P + 1$ and $P - 1$. Before statement 2a, node $P$ has communicated with its neighbors in statement 1a, so it knows that nodes $P - 1$ and $P + 1$ have

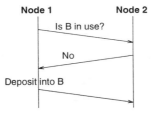

Figure 3: Nodes 1 and 2 must negotiate whether the target buffer is available before node 1 can safely deposit onto node 2.

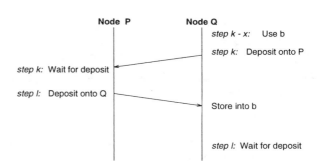

Figure 4: Time-line of an example data exchange between nodes $P$ and $Q$. $Q$ does not use $b$ between steps $k$ and $l$, so $P$ can deposit into $b$ with no additional control messages.

at least started executing statement 1. Node $P$ knows that its local portion of B is up to date and safe to send. Since statement 1b does not access the overlap region of B and $P - 1$ and $P + 1$ have at least reached statement 1a, it is safe for processor $P$ to deposit its new values for B. Therefore, the second overlap shift can be executed without any additional control messages or synchronization. By a similar argument, the first overlap shift does not require additional synchronization either. In both cases, each node can use messages from previous communication steps to know how far the neighboring nodes have progressed in the program.

### Synchronization elimination algorithm

The compiler can determine when additional control messages are unnecessary by running a data flow algorithm over the communication patterns of the program. To define the algorithm, we first formalize the conditions when it is safe to send data under the deposit message passing model.

Figure 4 shows an example data exchange. At step $l$ of the program, assume node $P$ must send data to buffer $b$ on node $Q$. To ensure that $Q$ is no longer using the current data in $b$, node $P$ must know that $Q$ has also reached a step $k$ (such that $k \leq l$) and no longer requires the old data. If $Q$ sent a message to $P$ in step $k$ and does not use buffer $b$ until step $l$, then node $P$ knows that buffer $b$ is no longer being used and can send the new data without any additional negotiation.

In the SOR example, node $P + 1$ sends data to node $P$ at step $k = 1$, and node $P + 1$ does not use the overlap region of buffer $b = $ B again until after step $l = 2$. Therefore, node $P$ knows that it can safely deposit data into buffer $b = $ B at step $l = 2$ without additional synchronization.

These conditions can be defined by the *BufferReady* predicate. The set $BufferReady_l$ encodes when it is safe to piggy-back the sequence information for statement $l$. For each entry $< P, Q, b >$, node $P$ can deposit data into buffer $b$ on node $Q$ with no additional control messages. This set is defined in terms of the following predicates.

$Pred_l$  The set of statements that can be immediate predecessors of statement $l$.

$Used_l(P, b)$  True if node $P$ uses $b$ during statement $l$.

$Sent_l(P, Q)$  True if node $P$ deposits a message onto node $Q$ during statement $l$.

With these predicates, the *BufferReady* set can be recursively defined as follows.

$$BufferReady_l =$$
$$\{< P, Q, b > | \forall k \in Pred_l : \neg Used_k(Q, b) \wedge$$
$$(Sent_k(Q, P) \vee < P, Q, b > \in BufferReady_k)\}$$

This set can be calculated by a forward data flow algorithm. The *gen* set contains all pairs of nodes that communicate in step $l$ combined with all arrays used in the computation. Each communication in step $l$ can potentially carry synchronization information to subsequent steps.

$$gen(l) = \{< P, Q, b > | Sent_l(Q, P)\}$$
$$= \{< P, Q, * > | Sent_l(Q, P)\}$$

The *kill* set contains all pairs nodes and buffers in $Used_l$ combined with all sending nodes. Any array that is used on the receiving node kills any possibility that previous messages can be used to piggy-back state information about that array.

$$kill(l) = \{< P, Q, b > | Used_l(Q, b)\}$$
$$= \{< *, Q, b > | Used_l(Q, b)\}$$

Set intersection is the confluence operator for this problem, so the *in* and *out* sets are calculated from the *gen* and *kill* sets as follows.

$$in(l) = \bigcap_{k \in Pred_l} out(k)$$
$$out(l) = (in(l) \cup gen(l)) - kill(l)$$

Initially, all *in* and *out* sets are the universal set, the set containing all triples. After the reaching the fixed point of the data flow computation, $in(l)$ contains a conservative approximation of $BufferReady_l$.

Instead of working with each pair of nodes separately, the data parallel model lets the compiler work more succinctly with communication patterns. The triples of the *BufferReady* set ($< P, Q, b >$) are replaced with pairs $< m, b >$, where $m$ is a communication map that describes the mapping from all processors $P$ to all processors $Q$ and $b$ is the target buffer. The data flow equations can be changed to operate over communication maps instead of node pairs. The *gen* set includes all maps $m$ that describe communication patterns required in statement $l$.

$$gen(l) = \{< m, b > |$$
$$\forall P, Q : m(Q) = P \to Sent_l(Q, P)\}$$

For a $< Q, b >$ in $Used_l$, the *kill* set includes all maps that include $Q$ in their range.

$$kill(l) = \{< m, b > | \exists P : m(P) = Q \to Used_l(Q, b)\}$$

The same equations can be used to calculate the *in* and *out* sets using the pairs of communication map and buffers. However, set intersection and union becomes slightly more complicated.

Taking the intersection and union of communication maps does not always result in a simple, single communication map. All other communication maps are subsets of the all-to-all communication pattern, $*$, so the union of any map $m$ with $*$ is $*$, and the intersection of $m$ with $*$ is $m$. For other combinations, our algorithm is conservative. For union and intersection, the algorithm creates a compound communication map, which contains a list of simple communication maps to intersect or union.

## Example: SOR

This section shows the computation of the *in* and *out* sets for the SOR example of Figure 2 to illustrate how the data flow algorithm works with communication maps. Table 1 shows the *gen* and *kill* sets computed for each statement. The communication maps in this example are: $+shift(p) = p + 1$, $-shift(p) = p - 1$, and the all-to-all map $*(p) = \{q | 0 \geq q < P\}$.

The universal set for this example is $\{< *, A > < *, B > \}$. For a processor $Q$ that uses a buffer $b$ in a statement, the kill set includes all maps with $Q$ in the map's domain. For simplicity, we make the conservative assumption that $Q$ is in the range of all maps, so all kill sets used by the compiler are of the form $< *, b >$.

Initially, all *in* and *out* sets are the universal set. The fixed point in this example is reached after two iterations. Table 2 shows the *in* and *out* sets for the first two iterations. Once the fixed point has been reached, the *in* sets of each statement contain information that approximates the *BufferReady* predicate. For example, the *in* set of statement 1 shows that it is safe to deposit data into array $A$ on the right

| Stmt | Gen/kill sets |
|------|---------------|
| 0 | $gen = kill = \{\}$ |
| 1 | $gen = \{ < +shift, A > < -shift, A >$ $< +shift, B > < -shift, B >\}$ $kill = \{ < *, A > \}$ |
| 2 | $gen = \{ < +shift, A > < -shift, A >$ $< +shift, B > < -shift, B >\}$ $kill = \{ < *, B > \}$ |

Table 1: *gen* and *kill* sets for the SOR example.

After iteration 1

| Stmt | in/out |
|---|---|
| 0 | $in = \{\ <*, A><*, B>\ \}$ |
| | $out = \{\ <*, A><*, B>\ \}$ |
| 1 | $in = \{\ <*, A><*, B>\ \}$ |
| | $out = \{\ <*, B>\ \}$ |
| 2 | $in = \{\ <*, B>\ \}$ |
| | $out = \{\ <+shift, A><-shift, A>\ \}$ |

After iteration 2

| Stmt | in/out |
|---|---|
| 0 | $in = \{\ <*, A><*, B>\ \}$ |
| | $out = \{\ <*, A><*, B>\ \}$ |
| 1 | $in = \boxed{\{\ <+shift, A><-shift, A>\ \}}$ |
| | $out = \{\ <+shift, B><-shift, B>\ \}$ |
| 2 | $in = \boxed{\{\ <+shift, B><-shift, B>\ \}}$ |
| | $out = \{\ <+shift, A><-shift, A>\ \}$ |

Table 2: *in* and *out* sets for the first two iterations of the data flow algorithm.

and left neighboring nodes without additional synchronization. Similarly, the *in* set of statement 2 shows that it is safe to deposit data into array $B$ on the right and left neighboring nodes. Therefore, the data flow algorithm shows that SOR can piggy-back all sequencing information on previous communication exchanges.

## Example: two dimensional FFT

Programs that have repeating, regular communication patterns are obvious candidates for explicit synchronization elimination. The two dimensional fast Fourier transform (2D FFT) code shown in Figure 5 is one such program. The array A is distributed by columns. The nodes compute FFTs over the columns, transpose A into B, compute FFTs over the columns of B, and transpose B back to A. The transpose operations require all-to-all communication steps.

One might assume that the all-to-all communication

```
do i=1,iter_cnt
0. input(A)
1. fft(A)
2. transpose(A,B)
3. fft(B)
4. transpose(B,A)
5. output(A)
enddo
```

Figure 5: Code for two dimensional fast Fourier transform (2D FFT).

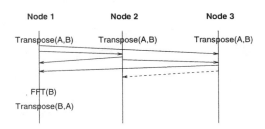

Figure 6: Three nodes computing a 2D FFT. Node 3 is delayed before it finished sending to node 2 as shown by the dashed arrow.

guarantees that all nodes have passed the previous communication step by the time any node reaches the next communication step, but a node may be delayed at the previous communication step after it has exchanged data with some of the other nodes. Figure 6 shows an example of a delayed node. In this example, node 3 is delayed after sending data to node 1. Node 1 receives both messages, computes the FFTs and continues onto the next communication step. Node 2 deposits both of its messages but is stalled waiting for the message from node 3. It is not safe for node 1 to deposit data into A on node 3 until node 3 finishes sending data from A. Since both arrays are used in every communication step, and a node may either be in communication step $l$ or $l + 2$, additional synchronization is necessary to ensure that all nodes are in the same synchronization step.

Table 3 shows the *gen* and *kill* sets for the 2D FFT program. The data flow algorithm takes two iterations to reach a fixed point, and Table 4 shows the *in* and *out* sets for the first two iterations. The *in* sets for the transpose statements are empty, so the all-to-all communication for the transpose statements requires an additional synchronization step.

However, when calculating two independent 2D FFTs in each iteration, no additional synchronization is needed. Alternating transpose operations work on disjoint sets of buffers, so the target buffer of the current all-to-all communication was not used in the previous all-to-all communication.

This data flow algorithm does not consider which subsections of the arrays are read or written during a communica-

| Stmt | Gen set | Kill set |
|---|---|---|
| 0 | $\{\}$ | $\{\ <*, A>\ \}$ |
| 1 | $\{\}$ | $\{\ <*, A>\ \}$ |
| 2 | $\{\ <*, A><*, B>\ \}$ | $\{\ <*, A>\ \}$ |
| 3 | $\{\}$ | $\{\ <*, B>\ \}$ |
| 4 | $\{\ <*, A><*, B>\ \}$ | $\{\ <*, B>\ \}$ |
| 5 | $\{\}$ | $\{\ <*, A>\ \}$ |

Table 3: *gen* and *kill* sets for the 2D FFT example.

| Stmt | After iteration 1 | |
| | in | out |
| --- | --- | --- |
| 0 | $\{< *, A >< *, B >\}$ | $\{< *, B >\}$ |
| 1 | $\{< *, B >\}$ | $\{< *, B >\}$ |
| 2 | $\{< *, B >\}$ | $\{< *, B >\}$ |
| 3 | $\{< *, B >\}$ | $\{\}$ |
| 4 | $\{\}$ | $\{< *, A >\}$ |
| 5 | $\{< *, A >\}$ | $\{\}$ |

| Stmt | After iteration 2 | |
| | in | out |
| --- | --- | --- |
| 0 | $\{\}$ | $\{\}$ |
| 1 | $\{\}$ | $\{\}$ |
| 2 | $\boxed{\{\}}$ | $\{< *, B >\}$ |
| 3 | $\{< *, B >\}$ | $\{\}$ |
| 4 | $\boxed{\{\}}$ | $\{< *, A >\}$ |
| 5 | $\{< *, A >\}$ | $\{\}$ |

Table 4: *in* and *out* sets for the first two iterations of the data flow algorithm over the 2D FFT.

tion step. By increasing the accuracy of the analysis to keep track of array subregions, the need for synchronization can be reduced further. With the more accurate analysis, we can show that the 2D FFT program requires no additional synchronization. See [6] for the details.

## EFFECTS OF ELIMINATION

Data flow synchronization elimination has been implemented in the communication optimization phase of the Fx compiler. This implementation recognizes redundant synchronization in many programs that include repeating communication patterns, including SOR and the pipelined 2D FFT described in the previous section.

While the algorithm can recognize redundant synchronization, it may not always make sense to eliminate the synchronization step. For machines like the Cray T3D with dedicated synchronization hardware, a subset synchronization takes a matter of 5 to 10 cycles, far less than a complete communication step. Removing synchronization on machine like this will not result in a significant reduction in execution time unless the program is inherently asynchronous.

However, for machines like Paragon, synchronization elimination shows more potential for performance improvement. Paragon has no dedicated hardware for synchronization. Instead, it sends control messages over the data network to implement barrier synchronization, so synchronization is relatively expensive compared to the com-

munication step time. We present measurements of the effects of barrier elimination on two applications: an application with a sparse communication pattern (SOR) and an application with a dense communication pattern (pipelined 2D FFT). There programs were measured on a Paragon system running the OSF operating system.

Figure 7(a) shows the average deposit communication time for one iteration of the SOR program. The line labeled **With barrier** shows the communication time including the barrier synchronization. The line labeled **Without barrier** shows the communication time without the barrier synchronization. Finally, the line labeled **64 node barrier** shows the time to execute a barrier synchronization over 64 nodes.

The difference in communication times remains relatively constant for small input sizes, and this difference corresponds to the barrier synchronization time. Table 5 shows

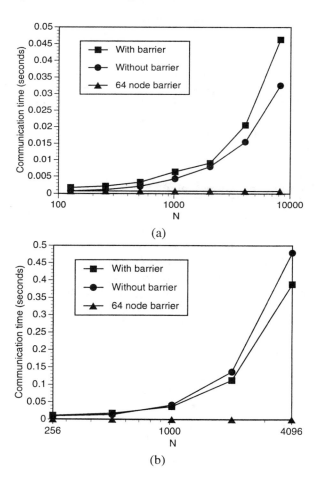

(a)

(b)

Figure 7: Average communication time for one iteration on a 64 node Paragon system for SOR (a) and 2D FFT (b).

the percentage difference in total execution time due to the barrier synchronization elimination. The performance difference for small problems sizes is quite noticeable. As the problem size increases, the relative amount of communication decreases, so the relative benefit in total execution time decreases as the problem size grows.

2D FFT requires an all-to-all communication pattern, where every node sends a potentially unique message to every other node. In the all-to-all communication step, each node sends more messages ($N - 1$ vs 2), so the cost of barrier synchronization is amortized over more messages. Therefore, the performance effects of eliminating synchronization for the 2D FFT are not as clear.

Figure 7(b) shows the average communication time for one iteration of the pipelined 2D FFT program. Again, the line labeled **With barrier** shows the time for the implementation that does not eliminate the synchronization, and the line labeled **Without barrier** shows the time for the implementation that eliminates the synchronization. The total communication time is quite large compared to the synchronization time (shown by the line labeled **64 node barrier** barely visible above the X axis). Merely eliminating the overhead of performing a synchronization should not greatly affect the communication time.

For small problem sizes, eliminating the synchronization improves communication performance. However, for problem sizes greater than $512 \times 512$, removing synchronization actually makes the communication performance worse. Table 5 shows the effect of barrier elimination on total execution time.

For all-to-all communication, synchronization actually performs two functions. In addition to ensuring that no data is deposited before its time, the synchronization acts as a congestion control mechanism, limiting the set of messages that can be in the network at any point in time. Without synchronization, one node can be lucky and insert many mes-

| Problem size | Speed Up | |
|---|---|---|
| | SOR | 2D FFT |
| 128 | 50 % | |
| 256 | 36 % | 6.5 % |
| 512 | 18 % | 7.5 % |
| 1024 | 10 % | -2.1 % |
| 2048 | 1.3 % | -2.6 % |
| 4096 | 1.7 % | -1.9 % |
| 8192 | 1.4 % | |

Table 5: Table of the percent of total program execution speed up due to synchronization elimination for SOR and 2D FFT. The negative percentage is program slow down.

sages for step $i$ while delaying nodes trying to insert messages for step $i - 1$. Eventually, all nodes must wait for the delayed nodes, so by allowing some nodes to go to the next step, total execution time can increase.

Similar performance improvements due to using synchronization for congestion control have been shown in [7] for all-to-all communication on iWarp and T3D. Brewer et al. also report on the benefits of synchronization for congestion control on the CM-5[1]. Stamatopolus and Solworth propose a network architecture that incorporates barrier synchronization for congestion control into regular message passing communication[10]. Their simulations show how varying the frequency of synchronization affects the bandwidth available for the application.

Our measurements indicate the barrier elimination is beneficial for "sparse" communication patterns, but for "dense" communication patterns the benefits of eliminating synchronization are over-shadowed by the costs of losing the synchronization for network congestion.

For other systems without hardware support for barrier synchronization, the tradeoffs may be different. For example, workstation clusters connected by high-speed networks (e.g. ATM switches or FDDI rings) are not likely to have hardware barrier synchronization support, but such systems may still benefit from using the deposit model to avoid buffering. It is not clear how synchronization will control network congestion in networks of workstations. ATM networks will likely provide more bandwidth than the workstations can saturate, so the need for congestion control may not be as pressing.

Some of the benefits of the deposit model can be achieved by using the traditional message passing interface. By posting receives "far enough" in advance, the programmer can guarantee that the receiver is always ready to consume the incoming message directly. In fact, the Paragon User's Guide suggests posting a receive and then exchanging control messages to ensure the data will not be buffered[8]. By using the the traditional message passing interface in this manner, this synchronization elimination analysis can also be used to show where receives can be posted to guarantee that buffering will be unnecessary.

## CONCLUSIONS

We have developed a synchronization elimination algorithm in the data flow framework. For regular communication patterns, the algorithm is very effective for recognizing where explicit synchronization is redundant.

However, our measurements of barrier elimination on Paragon show that estimating the performance effects of barrier synchronization is not straightforward. Eliminating barriers can be beneficial assuming that one of the following conditions hold:

- The communication pattern is not prone to congestion on the target network.

- The barrier synchronization overhead is relatively large compared to the total communication time.

- The application code can benefit from asynchronous execution.

Therefore, as with most optimizations this synchronization elimination algorithm should not be applied blindly. To avoid detrimental side effects, the compiler writer must understand the secondary effects of synchronization on network congestion on the target system.

## ACKNOWLEDGMENTS

Thanks to Jim Stichnoth, Bwolen Yang, Thomas Gross, and the other members of the Fx compiler group. Thanks to Tom Stricker for enlightening conversations about the deposit model.

# References

[1] E. Brewer and B. Kuszmaul. How to Get Good Performance from the CM-5 Data Network. In *International Parallel Processing Symposium*, pages 858–867, Cancun, Mexico, April 1994.

[2] S. Chatterjee, J. R. Gilbert, R. Schreiber, and S.-H. Teng. Automatic Array Alignment in Data-Parallel Programs. In *Proceedings of the Twentieth Annual ACM SIGACT/SIGPLAN Symposium on Principles of Programming Languages*, Charleston, SC, January 1993.

[3] High Performance Fortran Forum. *High Performance Fortran Language Specification Version 1.0.*, May 1993.

[4] M. Gerndt. Updating distributed variables in local computations. *Concurrency: Practice and Experience*, 2(3):171–93, September 1990.

[5] M. Gupta and E. Schonberg. Static Analysis to Reduce Synchronization Costs in Data-Parallel Programs. In *Proceedings of the 23rd Annual ACM SIGACT/SIGPLAN Symposium on Principles of Programming Languages*, St. Petersberg, FL, January 1996.

[6] S. Hinrichs. *Compiler Directed Architecture Dependent Communication Optimizations*. PhD thesis, Carnegie Mellon University, June 1995.

[7] S. Hinrichs, C. Kosak, D. O'Hallaron, T. Stricker, and R. Take. An Architecture for Optimal All-to-All Personalized Communication. Technical Report CMU-CS-94-140, Carnegie Mellon, 1994. Extended version of paper presented at SPAA '94.

[8] Intel Corporation. *Paragon User's Guide*, 1994.

[9] K. Knobe, J. D. Lukas, and G. L. Steele, Jr. Data Optimization: Allocation of Arrays to Reduce Communication on SIMD Machines. *Journal of Parallel and Distributed Computing*, 8:102–118, 1990.

[10] J. Stamatopoulos and J. A. Solworth. Increasing network bandwidth on meshes. In *ACM Symposium on Parallel Algorithms and Architectures*, pages 336–345, Cape May, NJ, June 1994. ACM.

[11] T. M. Stricker, J. Stichnoth, D. R. O'Hallaron, S. Hinrichs, and T. Gross. The Performance Impact of Fast Synchronization in Parallel Computers. In *International Conference on Supercomputing*, pages 1–10, Barcelona, Spain, July 1995.

[12] J. Subhlok. *Analysis of Synchronization in a Parallel Programming Environment*. PhD thesis, Rice University, September 1990.

[13] J. Subhlok, J. M. Stichnoth, D. R. O'Hallaron, and T. Gross. Exploiting Task and Data Parallelism on a Multicomputer. In *Fourth ACM SIGPLAN Symposium on Principles and Practice of Parallel Programming*, pages 13–22, San Diego, CA, May 1993.

[14] C.-W. Tseng. Compiler Optimizations for Eliminating Barrier Synchronization. In *ACM SIGPLAN Symposium on Principles and Practice of Parallel Programming*, 1995.

[15] S. Wholey. *Automatic Data Mapping for Distributed-Memory Parallel Computers*. PhD thesis, Carnegie Mellon University, 1991.

# Prefetching and Caching for Query Scheduling in a Special Class of Distributed Applications*

Aman Sinha  Craig Chase

Parallel and Distributed Systems Laboratory
Electrical and Computer Engineering
University of Texas at Austin, Austin, TX 78712
{sinha,chase}@ece.utexas.edu

## Abstract

*We analyze the scheduling aspects of database queries submitted to an abstract model of a very large distributed system. The essential elements of this model are (a) a finite number of identical processing nodes with limited storage capacity, (b) a finite number of queries to be serviced, (c) a very large read-only data set that is shared by all queries and (d) a fixed inter-node communication latency. This framework models an important class of applications that use distributed processing of very large data sets. Examples of these applications exist in the very large database and multimedia problem domains. To meet the objective of minimizing flow time of queries while exploiting inter-query locality, various heuristics are proposed and evaluated through extensive simulation.*

## 1  INTRODUCTION

In recent years, increasing processor speeds and distributed computing are making feasible query processing over very large databases. The size of the database in some applications can be of the order of terabytes. Such a large data set virtually mandates distributed storage. In a distributed environment, several users could be querying the database in parallel. Further, these users would need to process parts of the data fetched by their queries, thus requiring sufficient cache space in the local disk. To design a cost-effective system, one must accept that most of the database will be on a remote data repository and not resident in the local disk. Yet, to design a high-performance system, one must avoid paying the high cost of network access time if at all possible.

If there is sufficient locality in the accesses to the database, we can have the majority of the data on one or more remote storage servers, but still communicate with the servers infrequently. In this paper we consider how to schedule queries to exploit this locality. To simplify the analysis, we consider only non-mutative, *i.e.*, read-only

database accesses. Second, we assume that each query can be split into parallel subtasks. If the database consists of $M$ data items, then we allow for the query to consist up to $M$ separate subtasks. We assume the flexibility to schedule these subtasks in any order. These two assumptions are made because they allow us the greatest possible flexibility in scheduling the computations so that data accesses will be minimized. We note that, although certainly not all queries meet these restrictions, many types of realistic data processing do meet them. In particular, we are targeting the Nile application, a NSF National Challenge problem in computational science for High Energy Physics research [16]. This project involves distributed computation using read-only distributed data. The data set exceeds 10 Terabytes of experimental results from collisions of sub-atomic particles. A typical query operation involves first scanning the database for relevant records and then engaging in numerically intensive computation with those records. The output of the query is a set of statistics, for example, the number of particle collisions that resulted in the production of a new particle with a specific mass. Hence, the records can be processed in any order. In this paper we choose our objective to be minimization of the *flow time*, *i.e.*, the response time, of a set of dynamically arriving queries. We illustrate the nature of the problem by considering the uniprocessor case. When all data is locally available, for deterministic processing times, the shortest processing time rule (SPT) will produce the minimum response time when release time of all queries are zero. If the release times are non-zero, then a preemptive schedule based on the shortest *remaining* processing time (SRPT) will be optimal. However, as we show in the example in Figure 1, this is not necessarily true when local disk space is limited and locality considerations are ignored. In this example, we assume a local disk capable of holding only one data item (*e.g.*, one record), but a total database size of two data items. The time required to fetch a datum from the server is a fixed 3 time units. Three queries are pro-

---
*This work was supported by NSF grant CCR-9409736

cessed by the system. The following table shows the time each query spends processing each data item:

| Query | $d_1$ | $d_2$ | release time |
|-------|-------|-------|--------------|
| $Q_1$ | 1 | 2 | 0 |
| $Q_2$ | 0 | 4 | 0 |
| $Q_3$ | 1 | 0 | 8 |

Queries $Q_1$ and $Q_2$ are available at time 0. However, $Q_3$ does not arrive at the system until time 8. Figure 1, shows that the SRPT schedule will idle the processor unnecessarily. At time 0, the task with the least processing time is $Q_1$ to process task $d_1$. However, when this task is completed, there are no tasks that require $d_1$, and hence the processor becomes idle for 2 time units while datum $d_2$ is fetched. In the optimal schedule, data item $d_2$ is fetched (and processed) first. For this example, the processor is only idle for 3 time units in the optimal schedule.

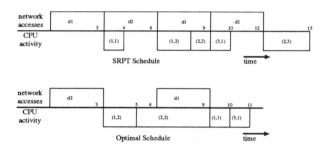

Figure 1: SRPT is not optimal when disk locality must be considered.

The problem of deciding which data should be present in the local "cache" is the principal topic of this paper. In particular, we tackle the applications where processing times are stochastic, with exponential distribution. The corresponding known optimal policy, the shortest expected remaining processing time (SERPT) rule, is used as our base execution policy. We divide the problem into that of global and local scheduling. At each level, we evaluate several heuristics and compare them through extensive simulations, over a wide range of locality and grain sizes. Our experimental results show that although MaxPop (a heuristic based on fetching the most 'popular' data) performs well for some values of locality and grain size, variations of SERPT, implemented at both the global and local levels, consistently produce excellent response times.

## 2 RELATED WORK

The concept of splitting a job into parallel subcomponents has been proposed and analyzed in the literature, in the contexts of minimizing either the flow time or the makespan. In [9], it is proved that the problem of minimizing the schedule length (makespan) of the parallel subtasks

using preemptive scheduling is strongly NP-hard for arbitrary number of processors for a set of independent tasks. In [6], Chang *et. al* consider the problem of minimizing the flow time of a set of jobs on a set of parallel processors, given a job dependent number of tasks. They assume a static list of jobs available at time 0 and do not allow task migration. They analytically prove the conditions under which certain tasks of a job should be processed sequentially instead of in parallel to get optimal results. Empirical results are provided in [13] for the problem of assigning virtual deadlines to parallel subcomponents of a task, in order to meet the global task deadline. For the case of non-preemptive scheduling of a set of parallel independent tasks, Turek *et. al.* [19] provide a shelf packing heuristic and analytically prove that its worst case response time is within a factor of 32 of the optimal. They assume that the number of processors required for each task and corresponding execution times are known. It is not clear how we can adapt the shelf packing algorithm for preemptive dynamic scheduling of tasks. In [1], Abbot and Garcia-Molina consider the problem of scheduling real time transactions, which involve minimizing the makespan. Their scheduling model deals with the problems of concurrency control and I/O scheduling while scheduling the transactions.

In general, considerable work has been done on the problems of preemptive scheduling of jobs, both in the deterministic case and stochastic case, see [14, 3]. One of the earliest works in minimizing response time is reported in [4], where the case of minimizing the weighted flow time for a static list of tasks, on $m \geq 1$ processors is considered. Resource constrained scheduling has long been a subject of active research, see [10, 20]. An excellent survey of complexity results related to various generic scheduling problems appears in [15] and [11].

Most of the research reported above has concentrated on finding good job schedules in cases where data is not shared among the jobs. We consider the applications where there can be varying degrees of inter-query locality. The work reported in this paper highlights the importance of an integrated prefetching and caching strategy, especially when the grain size is small. Equivalent problems relevant to multimedia systems have been analyzed and reported in [7] and [8]. Specifically, the problem of when to fetch a 'hot' video and which video on disk to replace when there is no free space, is conceptually similar to trying to exploit inter-query locality. In [12], a heat-based policy that replaces segments of relatively unpopular videos with segments of currently referenced videos is studied. Theoretical and simulation results of applying integrated prefetching and caching heuristics on several uniprocessor file access traces has been reported in [5].

## 3 MODEL OF THE SYSTEM

We assume a bounded number of queries, $\{ Q_1, Q_2, \ldots, Q_n \}$, are to be processed by a system of $m$ processors, $P = \{p_1, p_2, \ldots, p_m\}$. Queries arrive dynamically at the system, resulting in release times: $\{r_1, r_2, \ldots, r_n\}$. That is, the system has no knowledge of query $Q_i$ until time $r_i$, and cannot process the query or fetch the data for that query before that time. The database consists of $M$ distinct data items denoted as $D = \{d_1, d_2, \ldots, d_M\}$. We assume $M \gg m$. A data item may be a traditional database record, an HTML document, a frame of video data *etc*. To simplify the analysis, we assume all data items are the same size.

We define a *subtask* $\tau_j^k$ as the ordered pair $(Q_j, d_k)$. A *task* $T_i^j$ is considered a component of the aggregate query $Q_i$ and is defined as a tuple of subtasks, $\{\tau_i^k \mid k \leq |D|\}$, all of which have been mapped onto the same processor. Thus, a task $T_2^5$ is the component of query $Q_2$ running on processor $p_5$ and consists of a set of subtasks $\{\tau_2^k \mid k \leq |D|\}$, all of which run on the same processor.

A query is said to be completed only when all its tasks are completed and a task is complete only when all its subtasks have finished processing the relevant data items. We denote as $x(\tau_i^j)$ the *expected processing time* of the subtask.

## 4 SCHEDULING FOR DATA LOCALITY

To characterize the disk cache of a processing node, we define a *slot* as follows: $s_i^j$ = a storage unit $j$ for storing exactly *one* data item on processor $p_i$. Let the set $S_i = s_i^1, s_i^2, \ldots, s_i^l$ denote the disk cache of a processor $p_i$. We introduce a caching constraint, which can be defined as follows: *Caching Constraint*

$$|D| \gg |S_1| + |S_2| + \ldots + |S_m|$$

recall $m = |P|$.

Assume that the space of all data items are statically partitioned among the various processors. Each processor may cache only data in its partition. For simplicity we number the data items as follows: $p_1$ may cache data items $d_1, d_2, \ldots, d_{M/m}$, $p_2$ may access data items $d_{M/m+1}, \ldots, d_{2M/m}$ and so on. Note that we assume homogeneous processing nodes, such that $|S_1| = |S_2| = \ldots = |S_m|$, and processing speeds are the same.

Our goal is to minimize the flow time, the sum of the expected completion times of all the queries. The focus of our research is to achieve this goal while exploiting *data locality* as much as possible. Since all queries are decomposed into parallel subtasks, a *global*, multiprocessor scheduling algorithm would be needed to achieve the above objective. This problem is known to be NP-complete, even when we assume that all data is locally accessible [11]. Given the *caching constraint* introduced in this section, we have developed a set of heuristics to determine what is the best possible flow time we can obtain. The evaluation of these heuristics is done through simulation.

## 5 THE SCHEDULING HEURISTICS

To outline our algorithms, we will use the following notations in addition to those given in Section 3 : for any processor $p_k$ :

$S_k$ = set of all disk slots
$R_k$ = set of all fetch requests
$M_k$ = array of *all* data items assigned to $p_k$
$\omega_i$ = set of waiting subtasks corresponding to data item $d_i$.
$W(x)$ = weight assigned to any arbitrary variable $x$.

We treat scheduling as a two-level problem. A global scheduler determines priorities for each query. A local scheduler attempts to honor these priorities while still ensuring that the processor does not become idle because the necessary data is not available locally.

### 5.1 Global Scheduling

The global scheduler must decide the order in which to process the queries in the system. We evaluated three global policies for deciding the priority ordering of the queries. All of them do the ordering *only* at the time of arrival of a new query. No dynamic load balancing is done. These policies are: (i) **G-SERPT** – In this case, the queries are ordered according to a Global-SERPT policy. We take the remaining time of the longest task of a query as the remaining time of that query. (ii) **L-SERPT** – In this policy, no global ordering of queries is done, allowing the local nodes to process the tasks in a greedy Local-SERPT manner. (iii)**FCFS** – The queries are ordered in a First Come First Serve basis.

### 5.2 Local Scheduling

To simplify the discussion of various scheduling policies, we organize the policies around three independent decisions. These decisions are: (i) **Execution Policy** – At each instant in time, what subtask should be allowed to run? (ii) **Fetch Policy** – If there is more than one subtask that needs data from the disk, which datum should be fetched next? (iii) **Eviction Policy** – When a new datum arrives from the disk, which of the currently resident data items should be removed in order to make room for the new data?

#### 5.2.1 Execution Policy

Only those subtasks whose data are resident in the disk are runnable. Other subtasks must wait at least until the data is fetched over the network. The global scheduling policy has already determined the order of the tasks at the local node. However, note that it does not mandate that a node process the *subtasks* in a given order. We choose to order all the subtasks in the *runnable queue* of a task, using SERPT. Our estimate of processing time is based on probability distribution functions that we assume are known *a priori*. The distribution function provides a "best-case" estimate which is assumed to be an accurate assessment of the processing required *if the necessary data is already resident in disk.* We assume that the scheduler knows the expected value for the processing time of each subtask, but has no other information about the execution time.

Figure 2, illustrates the simulation methodology. The figure shows the procedure used to simulate each processor in the system. Recall that the system consists of $m$ homogeneous processors. Each processor runs the runnable subtask that is closest to the head of the subtask queue. A subtask can be preempted in two situations: (i) When a new query arrives and the global policy mandates that the new query's task receive higher priority. (ii) When it ceases to be runnable because its data has been evicted.

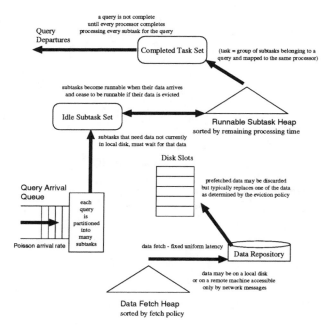

Figure 2: Simulating a single node in the multiprocessor database.

### 5.2.2  Data Fetch Policy

#### Assigning Weights to Data Items

When deciding how to reorder the data request queue or, at the time of a new data arrival, what datum to overwrite (if at all), we assign *weights* to all the data items. For various policies, the assignment is as follows:

- **MaxPop** In this case, the weight of the data item is the *number* of subtasks waiting for it *i.e.,* $W(d_i) = |\omega_i|$

- **MaxEx** The weight of the data item is the *sum* of *expected processing times* of all the subtasks waiting for it *i.e.,* $W(d_i) = \sum_{\tau \in \omega_i} x(\tau)$

- **PSERPT** For each subtask waiting for the data item $i$, compute its *position* from the *head* of the overall subtask queue at the node *i.e.,* $W(d_i) = \min_{\forall \tau \in \omega_i} position(\tau)$

- **SLRU** If $d_i$ is a new arrival, $W(d_i) =$ the arrival time else $W(d_i) =$ last access time

- For **FIFO**, there is no need to assign weights.

The data fetch policy determines which item will next be fetched from the storage server. We assume that data are fetched one at a time and we assume that the data access time is fixed and uniform for all data. As explained in [17], these simplifying assumptions are not completely unrealistic.

Every time a new task arrives at the node, we recompute the weights of the data requests in the request queue. After doing this, we apply the algorithm appropriate to each policy:

- **MaxPop** and **MaxEx** Sort the request queue in *descending* order of data weights.

- **PSERPT** and **SLRU** Sort the request queue in *ascending* order of data weights.

In addition, whenever an in-core data item gets evicted, we add a request for that datum to the request queue, preserving the order of the respective fetch policy. Our fetch policy is aggressive, possibly wasting bandwidth in the aim of ensuring that data is available when it is needed. The actual fetch of a data item is initiated whenever the channel at node $k$ is free and $size(R_k) > 0$. There is no guarantee that the newly fetched data item will be cached into the disk — this depends on the eviction policy, which is the subject of the next subsection. Since the execution time is not known with assurance, our decision to prefetch cannot be perfect. We must either risk wasting bandwidth or risk starving the processor by not prefetching the data. We choose the former evil for this analysis. We note that such aggressive techniques are being contemplated for certain current day applications. In order to meet the response time requirements of the clients connected to the world wide web, [18] proposes a source based anticipatory *presending* of data, as opposed to prefetching. The pre-sent data is marked 'droppable available-bit-rate' traffic (*i.e* a low priority packet) and thus avoids consuming valuable bandwidth during peak transmissions of currently useful data.

### 5.2.3  Eviction Policy

The eviction policy determines which datum will be replaced when a new datum, $d_k$ is fetched from the disk. In order to allow for aggressive speculative prefetching, we permit the scheduler to discard the newly fetched data item if it fails the requirements of the eviction policy. In most instances, such a decision would be a needless waste of disk bandwidth. However, it is possible that during the time that the disk access was in progress new queries arrived. In some pathological cases, the *optimal* response to these new queries may be to discard the just-fetched data and continue to process tasks using the old data. Further, we do not permit the scheduler to overwrite a datum which is currently being used.

Intuitively, the eviction policy must complement the fetch policy. For example, if we are fetching the most popular data items, we should be evicting the least popular. We thus define the eviction policies by the name of their respective fetch policies (except for SLRU). In the following description, $W_{ps}(d_i)$ is used to mean that we calculate the weight of the data item based on the PSERPT policy, as given in Section 5.2.2.

MaxPop and MaxEx

```
choose ((d_min) ∈ S_k | W(d_min) =
        min_∀d_i∈S_k(W(d_i))
if (W(d_new) > W(d_min)), then
   overwrite d_min with d_new
else if (d_min == d_new), then
   if (W_ps(d_new) < W_ps(d_min)), then
      overwrite d_min with d_new
   endif
endif
if d_new is not written, insert
   request for d_new in R_k
```

PSERPT

```
choose ((d_max) ∈ S_k | W(d_max) =
        max_∀d_i∈S_k(W(d_i))
if (W(d_new) < W(d_max)), then
   overwrite d_max with d_new
else insert request for d_new
   in R_k
endif
```

For **FIFO** fetches, the eviction policy is the same as for MaxPop. For **SLRU** the LRU eviction policy is used in conjunction with the PSERPT fetch policy.

# 6  SIMULATION METHODOLOGY

We identify the following three important tunable parameters for the simulation. (i) **Task granularity** – The ratio of the average time to process a runnable subtask to the time required to fetch a datum from disk. (ii) **Locality** – The percentage of the total data set accessed by a single query. (iii) **Load** – The average number of tasks being being processed by a node at any time.

## 6.1  Grain Size

The granularity is an estimate of ratio of computation to communication performed during query processing. If queries are very coarse grained, then the data fetch time is insignificant. Hence, locality will be of little concern in selecting an optimal schedule. We vary the granularity over three orders of magnitude, ranging from data access latency 100 times that of the processing time to data access latency of 1/20th of the processing time. In our simulation, we choose to hold the processing time constant, and vary the data fetch latency, when measuring the effect of granularity.

## 6.2  Locality

Locality is the probability that a data item will be used by more than one query. We do not model locality directly. However, by varying the amount of data accessed by each query, we can control the locality indirectly. In each simulation we select a data access volume for each query. This value is the percentage of the entire database that the query will process. The data items that are accessed are uniformly distributed in the database. If the data access volume is very large, then the locality of data references will naturally be high, since most queries will be processing most of the database. By contrast, if the data access volume is very small, then the probability that any two queries will access the same datum is very small.

## 6.3  System Load

We are interested in the steady state behavior of the system under heavy load. If the load is very light, then virtually any reasonable scheduling algorithm will result in good performance. In our simulations, we control the system load by controlling the interarrival time of the queries. However, an interarrival time that results in "heavy" load with a very large grain size, may result in a relatively light load for fine grained queries. To provide a consistent basis for comparison of the scheduling algorithms, the interarrival time was tuned for each combination of grain size and data locality.

We use the well known Little's result [2] from queuing theory : $N = \lambda * T$, where $N$ is the average number of queries that can be handled by the system, signifying the average load, $\lambda$ is the rate of arrival of queries and $T$ is the average delay of a query in the system. Our simulations process a fixed number of queries, 250, (since we are interested in the response times, we must run all queries to completion). We fix $N$ to be a fraction of the total number of queries and then find $\lambda$, which gives us an approximate estimate of the required interarrival time. Then, we run the experiment iteratively (using the interarrival time from the previous iteration) until the average load per node converges to a 'reasonable' value. In our simulation, we choose this value to be an average load of 1.5-3% of the total number of tasks (roughly 5 active tasks on every processor at steady state). Note that all scheduling algorithms are compared using the same conditions (identical interarrival times and processing times).

Scheduling characteristics are controlled by parameters listed in Table 1.

## 6.4  Processing Times

We assume that a single query will require similar processing of each data item. Different queries, however, may require substantially different processing time. Accordingly, when a query arrives at the system, the simulator selects a mean subtask processing time using a uniformly distributed (pseudo)random number (over the range (0.1,5.0)).

| Parameter | Simulation Range |
|---|---|
| number of queries | fixed at 50 |
| number of CPU's | fixed at 2 |
| data set size | fixed at 100 |
| size of disk cache | fixed at 5 |
| mean subtask proc. time (uniform distribution) | 0.01 to 5.0 |
| data fetch time | 0.05 to 100 |
| locality | 10 to 100 |
| query interarrival time (Poisson distribution) | chosen dynamically |

Table 1: Simulator Parameters

This value is used directly by the global scheduling algorithm to select the task priority for this query. For each subtask, an expected processing time is computed by perturbing the mean processing time by up to 20% using another uniformly distributed random number. This value will be used by the local scheduler when computing SERPT priorities. Finally, the *actual* processing time is calculated by generating an exponentially distributed random number about the mean just computed for that subtask.

Thus, each subtask has an unknown (to the scheduler) processing time, with a known expected value. All of the subtasks for a single query have similar expected processing times (within 20% of a common value). The expected value for query processing time is known to the global scheduler. And query processing time varies over about an order of magnitude.

## 7  EXPERIMENTAL RESULTS

In most of the experiments we ran, it was found that as a local scheduling heuristic, PSERPT outperformed other local heuristics. Thus, while comparing the various global heuristics, it is best to analyze PSERPT's comparative performance under different global policies. This is done in the following subsection.

### 7.1  Comparing Global Heuristics

Figure 3 shows the performance of PSERPT under the three global heuristics: FCFS, L-SERPT and G-SERPT, for locality values of 100 and 50% respectively. From these figures, it is seen that at the global level, for small grain sizes, all three policies perform almost equally well. This can be explained by recognizing that for small grain sizes, the processing time is constrained by the data fetch time. Thus the fetch policy, which is a local policy, will essentially determine the response time. As the grain size increases, L-SERPT performs very poorly. This result indicates that some global coordination is valuable even in homogeneous environments.

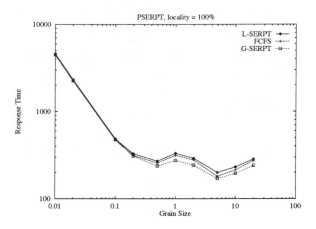

Figure 3: Global Heuristics for locality = 100

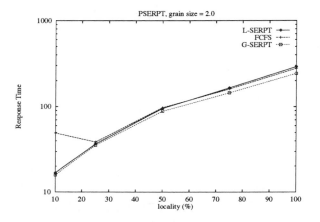

Figure 4: Global Heuristics for Grain Size = 2.0

The simple G-SERPT priority policy provides a noticeable improvement to response time compared to FCFS and L-SERPT. For a locality value of 100%, the improvement is in the range of 4 - 17%, while for a locality value of 75%, the improvement is in the range of 8 - 12%. This trend holds over a large range of locality values, as shown in Figure 4 for a grain size of 2.0 [1]. For this reason, in the following subsection, unless otherwise mentioned, we will focus on the local scheduling heuristics implemented under G-SERPT.

### 7.2  Comparing Local Heuristics

#### 7.2.1  Response Time versus Locality

We conducted several experiments to determine how locality affects the performance of the data fetching heuristics. We measured the response times, keeping grain size

---
[1]For grain size < 1 and for locality values < 100, please see [17]

fixed at 0.25. The results are depicted in Figure 5. PSERPT is found to perform consistently better than most other heuristics, with MaxPop catching up only at very high locality. Note also that the average response time of queries shows a rising trend for lower values of locality and is relatively flat beyond 50%. This is because, at lower values of locality, the chances are higher that a task's in-core dataset does not intersect (or minimally intersects) with another task's dataset. This would force some delay, since a shorter task may not be able to run unless it loads its own fresh set of data. At higher values of locality, a task can be more compute bound, amortizing some of the communication delay, thus reducing the gradient of the response time line.

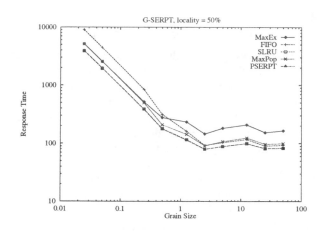

Figure 6: Local Heuristics at Locality = 50

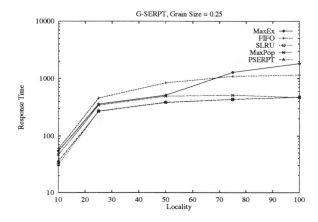

Figure 5: Local Heuristics at Grain Size = 0.25

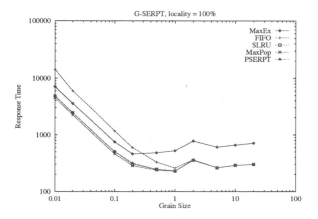

Figure 7: Local Heuristics at Locality = 100

### 7.2.2 Response Time versus Grain Size

In this experiment, we consider the effect of grain size on the heuristics, keeping the locality fixed. We measured the response times for processing times varying from 2 orders of magnitude above to about an order below the fetch time of a data item. This was done keeping the locality fixed at 50% and 100%. The results of this experiment are shown in Figure 6 and Figure 7. An explanation along the same lines of the one in the previous subsection can be offered for the steep falling initial gradient and the flattening thereafter. In effect, there are only two ways to prevent a task from starving: (i) increase the locality (an extreme case: use any data that is available) — this was studied in the previous subsection, or (ii) increase the grain size (negligible fetch time would provide a glut of data and prevent starvation). It is expected that for a given locality, for higher grain sizes, all tasks become more and more compute bound and the query response time is hardly affected by communication delays. This is validated by Figure 6 and Figure 7.

It is interesting to see that while MaxPop was as good as,

if not better than PSERPT at locality = 100, it performed poorly for high grain sizes at locality = 50. Following is a possible explanation for this behavior: at smaller locality, it is more likely that the 'most popular' data item may not have the shortest task in its list of waiting tasks. Further, the chances are higher that the 'least popular' data item does include the shortest task in its list. A pathological case could be when the shortest task has only one remaining subtask but its data item is repeatedly evicted because none of the other tasks need it, preferring instead to fetch some other popular datum.

The important conclusions from this experiment are : (i) MaxEx and FIFO are inadequate over a large range of grain size. (ii) MaxPop's window of 'best performance' is limited to very high locality and low grain sizes. (iii) In terms of consistently good performance, if not the best, over a wide range of both grain sizes and locality, PSERPT is the clear winner.

## 8 CONCLUSION

In this paper, we have studied alternative heuristics for preemptive scheduling of queries accessing a read only data base in a distributed environment. Our objective is minimization of the flow time of the queries. We decompose a query into parallel subtasks in order to allow us the greatest flexibility in scheduling the computations and such that inter query data locality can be exploited. We divide the scheduling problem into global and local scheduling problems and propose and evaluate several heuristics at both levels. Our simulation results establish that variations of the shortest expected remaining time (SERPT) algorithm, implemented at both local and global levels, are very successful in meeting the objective, for a large range of grain size and locality.

## References

[1] Robert Abbot and Hector Garcia-Molina. Scheduling real-time transactions with disk resident data. In *Proceeding of the Fifteenth International Conference on Very Large Data Bases*, pages 385–395, 1989.

[2] Dimitri Bertsekas and Robert Gallager. *Data Networks*. Prentice Hall, 1987.

[3] Jacek Blazewicz. Selected topics in scheduling theory. *Annals of Discrete Mathematics*, 31:1–59, 1987.

[4] J. Bruno, E. G. Coffman, and R. Sethi. Scheduling independent tasks to reduce mean finishing time. *Communications of the ACM*, 17(7), July 1974.

[5] Pei Cao, Edward W. Felten, Anna R. Karlin, and Kai Li. A study of integrated prefetching and caching strategies. In *SIGMETRICS'95*, 1995.

[6] Cheng-Shang Chang, Randolph Nelson, and David D. Yao. Optimal task scheduling on distributed parallel processors. *Performance Evaluation*, 20:207–221, 1994.

[7] A. Dan, D. Sitaram, and P. Shahabuddin. Scheduling policies for an on-demand video server with batching. In *ACM, Multimedia'94*, 1994.

[8] Asit Dan and Dinkar Sitaram. An online video placement policy based on bandwidth to space ratio. In *ACM, SIGMOD'95*, 1995.

[9] Jianzhong Du and Joseph Y-T Leung. Complexity of scheduling parallel task systems. *SIAM Journal of Discrete Math*, 2:473–487, November 1989.

[10] Michael R. Garey and David S. Johnson. Complexity results for multiprocessor scheduling under resource constraints. *SIAM Journal of Computing*, 4(4):397–411, December 1975.

[11] Michael R. Garey and David S. Johnson. *Computers and Intractability - A Guide to the Theory of NP-Completeness*. W. H. Freeman and Company, New York, 1979.

[12] S. Ghandeharizadeh and C. Shahabi. On multimedia repositories, personal computers, and hierarchical storage systems. In *ACM, Multimedia'94*, 1994.

[13] Ben Kao and Hector Garcia Molina. Subtask deadline assignment for complex distributed soft real-time tasks. In *14th International Conference on Distributed Computing Systems*, pages 172–181, 1994.

[14] E.L. Lawler, J.K. Lenstra, and A. H. G. Rinnooy Kan. Recent developments in deterministic and stochastic scheduling: A survey. In *Deterministic and Stochastic Scheduling : Proceedings of the NATO Advanced Study and Research Institute on Theoretical Approaches to Scheduling Problems*, 1982.

[15] Michael Pinedo. *Scheduling: Theory, Algorithms and Systems*. Prentice Hall, Englewood Cliffs, New Jersey, 1995.

[16] A. Ricciardi, M. Ogg, and E. Rothfus. The nile system architecture: Fault-tolerant wide-area access to computing and data resources. In *6th Computing in High Energy Physics*, 1995.

[17] Aman Sinha and Craig Chase. Exploiting data locality for multiprocessor query scheduling. Technical Report TR-PDS-1996-009, Parallel and Distributed Systems Laboratory, University of Texas at Austin, 1996.

[18] Joseph D. Touch. Defining high-speed protocols: Five challenges and an example that survives the challenges. *IEEE Journal on Selected Areas in Communications*, pages 828–835, June 1995.

[19] John Turek, Uwe Schwiegelshohn, Joel L. Wolf, and Philip S. Yu. Scheduling parallel tasks to minimize average response time. In *Proceedings of 5th ACM-SIAM Symposium on Discrete Algorithms*, pages 112–121, 1994.

[20] W. Zhao, K. Ramamritham, and J. A. Stankovic. Preemptive scheduling under time and resource constraints. *IEEE Transactions on Computers*, pages 949–960, August 1987.

# PROGRAM ANALYSIS FOR CACHE COHERENCE: BEYOND PROCEDURAL BOUNDARIES

Lynn Choi
Microprocessor Group
Intel Corporation
Santa Clara, CA 95052
lchoi@mipos2.intel.com

Pen-Chung Yew
Department of Computer Science
University of Minnesota
Minneapolis, MN 55455
yew@cs.umn.edu

Abstract – *The presence of procedures and procedure calls introduces side effects, which complicates the analysis of stale reference detection in compiler-directed cache coherence schemes [4, 6, 8]. Previous compiler algorithms use cache invalidation at procedure boundary [5, 7] or inlining [7] to avoid reference marking interprocedurally. In this paper, we introduce a full interprocedural algorithm, which performs bottom-up and top-down analysis on the procedure call graph. This avoids unnecessary cache misses for subroutine local data and exploits locality across procedure boundaries. The result of execution-driven simulations on Perfect benchmarks demonstrates that, the interprocedural algorithm eliminates up to 36.8% of the cache misses for a compiler-directed scheme compared to an existing invalidation-based algorithm [7].*

## 1   INTRODUCTION

Procedure calls introduce complications in most global program analysis and optimizations due to side effects and potential aliasing caused by parameter passing. Stale access detection [5, 7] is a compile time analysis technique to identify data references that may violate cache coherence in compile-directed coherence schemes [6, 4, 8]. By identifying these potentially stale references at compile time, cache coherence can be maintained by forcing those references to get up-to-date data directly from the main memory, instead of from the cache. In stale reference detection, procedure boundaries force all previous algorithms [5, 7] to use conservative approaches, such as cache invalidation or inlining, to avoid reference marking across procedure calls. However, both approaches have their own problems. Frequent invalidations at procedure call boundaries incur cold-start effects. This leads to a poor cache performance especially for programs that contain many small procedure calls in their critical path of execution. Inlining can achieve the most precise analysis, but it is often prohibitive due to the excessive growth in code size as well as the increase in compile time since the memory requirement and the complexity of the reference marking algorithm is often nonlinear in terms of the procedure size.

In this paper, we develop both intraprocedural and interprocedural compiler algorithms, both of which can perform stale reference detection without relying on either cache invalidation or inlining. The algorithms are based on a combination of interval and def-use chain data-flow analysis performed on a modified program control flow graph which represents both parallel program constructs as well as procedure control flow. To obtain more precise array access information, we compute the array region referenced by each array reference [7]. The interprocedural algorithm performs bottom-up and top-down analysis on the procedure call graph to exploit cache locality across procedure boundaries. First, the bottom-up *side effect analysis* takes into account side effects by summarizing the access information at each call site. Second, the top-down *context analysis* allows the context information of a procedure to be visible by passing the summary access information of its previous activation records. This two-pass analysis avoids redundant computation by performing incremental update of reference marking with a minimal number of computations per procedure. We have implemented both the intraprocedural and interprocedural algorithms on the Polaris parallelizing compiler [11] and demonstrate the performance driven by these algorithms by running execution-driven simulations of two compiler-directed coherence schemes [7, 8] using Perfect benchmarks. The compiler reference marking algorithms developed here are general enough to be applicable to other compiler-directed coherence schemes [4, 6].

### 1.1   Stale reference sequence

We view the execution of a parallel program as a sequence of *epochs*. An epoch is either a parallel loop (*parallel epoch*) or a serial section of the code (*serial epoch*) between parallel loops. In a serial epoch, only a single task is available while in a parallel epoch, multiple tasks are created and can be executed on multiple processors. At each epoch boundary, tasks are scheduled to processors and memory is updated for consistency. Figure 1(a) shows a sample program and the potentially stale data references marked by a compiler. Such references are denoted as Time-Reads in the figure.

In general, the sequence of 1) a write 2) one or more epoch boundaries, and 3) the following read can cause the the last read reference to become a stale data access at runtime. Due to the scheduling boundary in 2), the write in 1) and the read in 3) can be issued by different processors (let's assume that the write is issued by processor $P_i$ and the read is issued by processor $P_j$ where $j \neq i$). However, the read might access the existing cache copy in $P_j$ rather than the new copy created in $P_i$. This memory reference pattern is called a *stale reference sequence*, and the last read reference is called a *potentially stale* data reference [7]. In the example, the read references to X in epochs 3 and 4 can cause stale data accesses at runtime since the variable has been modified in epoch 2. Note that the first read reference to X in epoch 4 is not marked as potentially stale because the region of array X modified in epoch 2 and the region of X accessed in epoch 4 are disjoint.

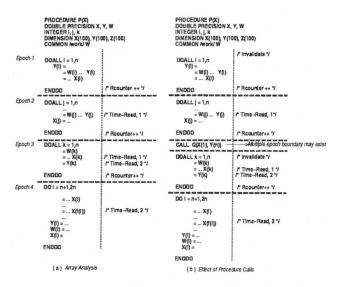

Figure 1: A program example of compiler marking of Time-Reads.

## 1.2   Coherence schemes

**Software Cache-bypass scheme (SC)**   Once all the potentially stale data references are identified by a compiler, cache coherence can be enforced if we guarantee that all such references access up-to-date data from main memory rather than potentially stale cache copies. This can be done by using a by-pass cache operation. This operation bypasses the cache to avoid accessing the potentially stale cached data, and replaces the cached data with the up-to-date copy by directly accessing the main memory.

However, this pure compiler scheme has several limitations. First, the read reference to X(k) in epoch 3 (see Figure 1) will be marked as potentially stale because the variable X was updated in epoch 2. The scheme cannot determine whether the update in epoch 2 and the read in epoch 3 are issued by the same processor or not, due to dynamic runtime scheduling. Second, the read reference to X(f(i)) in epoch 4 cannot be analyzed precisely at compile time due to the unknown index value. To overcome these limitations, we proposed a hardware scheme, called the two-phase invalidation scheme that keeps track of the local cache

states at runtime [8].

**Two-phase invalidation scheme (TPI)**   In this scheme, each epoch is assigned a unique epoch number. The epoch number is stored in an n-bit register in each processor, called *epoch counter* ($R_{counter}$), and is incremented at the end of every epoch by each processor individually. Every word in the cache has an n-bit timetag that records the epoch number when the cache copy is created.

In addition to normal read and write operations, a new memory operation, called Time-Read, is used exclusively for a potentially stale reference marked by the compiler. It is similar to the normal read except that it is augmented with an *offset*. The *offset* indicates the number of epoch boundaries between the current epoch and the epoch in which the data was last updated. At runtime, Time-Read determines whether the cached data is stale or not by comparing the runtime timing information (timetag) of each cache copy with the timing information (offset) provided by the compiler. A Time-Read returns a cache hit if (1) timetag $\geq$ ($R_{counter}$ - offset), which checks whether the cache copy is up-to-date, (2) the address tag matches, and (3) the valid bit is set.

For correct coherence enforcement, the compiler needs to generate appropriate memory and cache management operations. First, the compiler should insert the epoch counter increment operation at the end of each epoch. Second, potentially stale read references need to be identified and issued as Time-Read operations. For such references, the compiler also needs to calculate their offset values.

Let us revisit the program example in Figure 1(a). All the potentially stale data references marked by the compiler should be issued as Time-Reads. The Time-Read operation to Y in epoch 2 will have an offset 1 since the last write occurs in epoch 1 while the Time-Read operations in epoch 3 are assigned an offset 2. Note that, in this scheme, all the potential stale data references (Time-Reads) will be cache hits if the current version of the data item is created by the same processor. For example, the Time-Read to X(k) by $P_i$ in epoch 3 will be a cache hit if the write to X(k) in epoch 2 is also issued by $P_i$, which can be determined by checking condition (1). Also, the second read reference to X in the epoch 4 can be a cache hit if the previous write in epoch 2 is issued by the same processor, or if the memory location is already accessed by the first read reference to X in epoch 4.

**Effect of procedure calls**   Procedure calls complicate the analysis in stale reference detection. To illustrate this, we insert a new procedure CALL statement to the previous program example between the epoch 2 and the epoch 3 as shown in Figure 1(b) Since FORTRAN uses call-by-reference parameter passing mechanism, the parameters X and Y can be modified in the procedure Q. Furthermore, all the global COMMON variables such as variable W in the example can also be modified in the procedure Q. This complicates the analysis in stale reference detection since with an intraprocedural algorithm no access information is available at each call site. In addition, this also causes a problem at the beginning of each procedure since any global COMMON variables and formal parameters could have been previously modified before entering the procedure. To avoid such complications caused by procedure calls, previous algorithms [5, 7] use cache invalidation both at the beginning of a procedure and after each call site. Since the algorithms assume a clean cache at procedure boundaries, their analysis can guarantee the correctness of reference marking. However, note that such invalidations cause unnecessary cache misses for subroutine local variables as well as the global COMMON variables and parameters. Frequent invalidations at procedure boundaries can degrade the cache performance substantially since it limits the scope of locality to be exploited within procedural boundaries. Our simulation results on Perfect benchmarks show that these invalidations increase cache misses dramatically for both the software cache-bypass scheme (SC) and the two-phase invalidation scheme (TPI), resulting in even higher miss rates on some benchmarks than the underlying machine with no cache coherence support. This limitation led us to develop more precise program analysis algorithms which can avoid such invalidations.

In section 2, we first briefly describe our program representation methods: epoch flow graph, array descriptors, and gated single assignment (GSA) [7]. Then, we present an improved intraprocedural stale reference marking algorithm which can detect stale data references in the presence of procedure calls without cache invalidation or inlining. In section 3, we develop a full interprocedural algorithm which performs incremental 2-pass analysis on the procedure call graph to further exploit locality across procedure boundaries. The performance results from our execution-driven simulations follow in section 4. Section 5 concludes the paper.

## 2 INTRAPROCEDURAL ALGORITHM

### 2.1 Data-Flow Framework

We use the following three techniques as a framework for our array data-flow analysis. A more detailed description can be found in [7].

- **Regular Section Analysis** The data-flow information propagated during the flow analysis are implemented as sets of data descriptors D, which consists of three data fields: name(D), subarray(D), and offset(D). The notion of the subarray we use is an extension to the *regular section* used in [3, 9, 13].

- **Gated Single Assignment (GSA) form** To perform effective array flow analysis, symbolic manipulation of expressions is necessary since the computation of array regions often involves the equality and comparison tests between symbolic expressions. For this purpose, we use the gated single assignment (GSA) form [1] to treat arrays

with different access regions as different symbolic variables.

- **Epoch Flow Graph** This is a modified flow graph to represent the epoch boundary information as well as different control flows due to the parallel execution[7]. Figure 2 shows the epoch flow graph for a program example. Bold arcs denote *scheduling edges*, which represent epoch boundaries, while the remaining arcs denote normal control flow edges. A statement which has an incoming scheduling edge is called a *head node*, while a statement which has an outgoing scheduling edge is called a *tail node*. A directed path from each head node to tail node shows the epoch created at runtime.

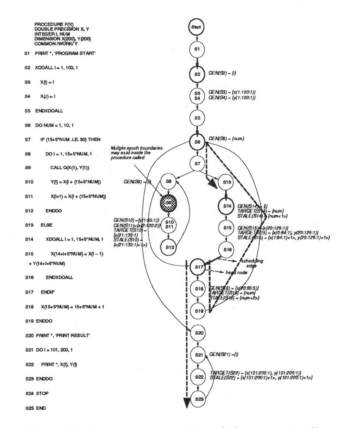

Figure 2: A program example and the corresponding epoch flow graph. The bold-dotted paths show two instances of the epoch where statement S17 can belong at runtime.

**Target reference marking** Not all the potentially stale references lead to a stale data access at runtime. To minimize the number of those potentially stale references marked at compile time, we utilize both temporal and spatial reuse in a program as much as possible.

To consider the temporal reuse in each task, we mark only the first occurrence of upwardly-exposed uses in each epoch. These references are called *target references*. A detailed array data-flow algorithm to find such target references is shown in [7], and for the following discussion, we assume that those target references are already computed.

## 2.2 Stale reference detection

The intraprocedural algorithm for stale reference detection is an improved version of the previous algorithm we developed in [7]. We refine the algorithm to eliminate cache invalidations by considering both side effects and hidden contexts at procedural boundaries.

Each definition of a variable $v$, denoted as $d_{offset}^v$, is associated with an *offset*. Initially, an offset 0 is assigned to each definition, and is incremented when the definition crosses an epoch boundary during flow analysis. The offset represents the number of epoch boundaries crossed. Multiple definitions of a variable with the same offset are considered as a single definition. Therefore, multiple writes in an epoch are considered as a single definition.

**Potentially stale reference** A target reference $u$ of a variable $v$ in statement S1 is *potentially stale* if there is a directed path in the epoch flow graph from a definition $d$ of variable $v$ in statement S2 to S1 including at least one scheduling edge.

When a definition reaches a target reference across at least one scheduling edge, there should exist the stale reference sequence (refer section 1.1), and the target reference to $v$ should be marked as potentially stale and be issued as a Time-Read operation. Since we increment the offset of a definition when we propagate the definition across epoch boundaries, the offset of the definition shows the number of epoch boundaries crossed since the write, and used as an offset for the Time-Read operation.

For each statement S, we define the following sets.

- $GEN(S)_{offset}$ is the set of definitions generated by S. Since all the definitions created in S are assigned the same offset, the offset can be denoted collectively for S as $GEN(S)_{offset}$.

- $IN(S)$ is a set of definitions reaching the beginning of S, $IN(S) = \bigcup_P OUT(P)$ where P is a predecessor of S.

- $OUT(S)$ is a set of definitions reaching the end of S, $OUT(S) = IN(S) \cup GEN(S)_0$.

- $STALE(S)$ is a subset of TARGET(S), where there exists a definition crossing epoch boundaries, whose intersection with the target reference has nonempty subarrays, $STALE(S) = \{$use $u$ of the variable $v$: $u \in$ TARGET(S) and $\exists$ a definition $d$ of the variable $v$ in $IN(S)$ where offset$(d) > 0$ and (subarray$(u) \cap$ subarray$(d)) \neq \phi \}$.

**Procedure call complications** The presence of procedures and procedure calls introduces the following complications to this intraprocedural stale reference detection algorithm.

- **side effect** The execution of a procedure can have a side effect on variables at the point from which the procedure is called. These variables include the actual parameters at the call site as well as the global variables visible to both the calling procedure and called procedure.

- **hidden context** Any of the global variables and formal parameters could have been read or written previously at the beginning of a procedure.

- **aliases** The third issue is the aliasing caused by call-by-reference parameter passing mechanism and EQUIVALENCE statement of FORTRAN.

  1. **static alias** EQUIVALENCE statement causes distinct variables to refer to the same memory location. Since the alias relationship is fixed in any instantiation of the procedure, we call it *static* alias. In our algorithm, all the static aliases are treated as a single variable.

  2. **dynamic alias** The call-by-reference parameter passing mechanism associated with procedure calls in FORTRAN can cause two distinct variables to refer to the same memory location. These aliases make our analysis no longer valid even if we invalidate the cache at procedure boundaries. However, ANSI FORTRAN does not allow programs written with aliases. Therefore, we do not consider the dynamic aliases in the following algorithm. If aliases do occur in a source program, then we use selective inlining if possible, or treat all the aliased variables as a single variable.

The intraprocedural algorithm works as follows. Due to the unknown context information, we assume all the formal parameters and global variables have been previously modified at the beginning of a procedure. This is accomplished by keeping track of the minimum offset from the beginning of a procedure. For a target reference which does not have a reaching definition inside a procedure, we issue a Time-Read with the minimum offset, implying that the referenced data item can be potentially modified before entering the procedure. This is an improvement over previous algorithms [5, 7] which use cache invalidation at the beginning of a procedure since only global and formal variables are affected by the unknown context information. We propagate definitions through the flow graph and increment their offsets when they cross scheduling edges. Note that for procedure CALL statements, we purposely insert all the actual parameters and global variables in its OUT set, implying that those variables can be modified at the call site. Without any information for the procedure called, we have to assume that an entire array can be modified by the procedure. Note that this lack of information also affects the analysis of the subroutine local variables since the offset can be unnecessarily small if the call site has at least one epoch boundary. This small offset can incur unnecessary cache misses at runtime

because the epoch counter will be incremented at run-time by the number of epoch boundaries inside the call site. This will cause the following Time-Reads to miss due to the conservative offset values. For each target reference, whenever there is a reaching definition in IN(S) with an offset greater than 0, the target reference is marked as a Time-Read operation. To refine stale reference marking for an array reference, we take the intersection of subarrays of a reaching definition and the target reference. When there exists a definition whose intersection with the target reference has nonempty subarrays, the target reference is marked as a Time-Read and its offset is determined by taking the minimum of all the offsets of such definitions. Figure 2 shows the result of reference marking for the program example.

## 3  Interprocedural Algorithm

Until now, the algorithm presented assumes program units, i.e. single procedures and, therefore, single flow graphs. The obvious drawback of such an algorithm is that it cannot exploit locality across procedure boundaries for global variables. To further exploit locality, we need to look at an entire program rather than one program unit at a time. To perform the interprocedural analysis, we use the *procedure call graph*, which is the basic data structure for the interprocedural analysis.

**Definition: procedure call graph**  Let a directed multigraph G = (V, E) represent a call graph where V is a set of procedures, and E is a set of directed edges. An edge from node p to node q exists if procedure p can invoke procedure q.

We extend the procedure call graph to contain the following summary information for each procedure.

- Procedure name, code size (number of lines)

- Number/types of formal parameters and global variables

- Number/types of actual parameters for each call site (*call site information*)

- OUT sets of callees at each call site (*summary side effect information*)

- IN sets of callers at the beginning of this procedure (*summary context information*)

- Number of minimum epoch boundaries in a procedure

### 3.1  Side effect analysis

Figure 3 shows the overall structure of interprocedural analysis. It consists of 2 passes on the procedure call graph: bottom-up side effect analysis pass and top-down context analysis pass. The detailed algorithm is presented in Appendix A.

The side effect analysis combines intraprocedural analysis with a bottom-up scan of the procedure call graph to summarize the side effects caused by each call site. The side effects of each call site are summarized by the OUT set of the procedure called. We

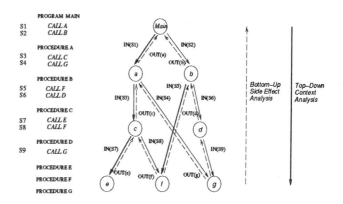

Figure 3: An example of procedure call graph and the overall structure of the two-pass interprocedural analysis.

first start at the bottom of the procedure call graph. We apply the intraprocedural algorithm described in section 2.2 for all the leaf procedures. This can be performed without considering the side effects since those procedures do not include procedure calls. After performing the intraprocedural analysis, we can summarize the side effect information and propagate to the procedures in the next level which have call sites to the current procedure. Note that this requires the translation of the summary information from callee's context to caller's context (see section 3.3).

The summary side effect information should contain the following information for each actual parameter and global variable.

- whether the variable is modified or not

- the number of epoch boundaries from the last write (offset)

- the regions of an array that have been modified (subarray)

Note that all the above information can be represented by OUT set of the procedure called, which is already computed by the intraprocedural analysis. Since a procedure can have multiple return points, the OUT sets at all the return points should be merged. This can be accomplished by taking the conservative union of all the OUT sets and by taking the minimum offset among the OUT sets for each global variable. Since we need the side effect information only for actual parameters and global variables, we eliminate the information for subroutine local variables from the summary information. By using the summary information, we add the translated OUT set from the callee to the OUT set of the CALL statement in a caller.

In addition to the above information, we should compute the minimum number of epoch boundaries crossed for each call site, and add the number to each definition in the OUT set of the corresponding CALL statement. Without this, the offsets for Time-Reads after the procedure call would not reflect the number of epoch boundaries crossed in the call site, which may generate too small offsets to capture the locality across the procedure boundaries.

## 3.2 Context analysis

The side effect analysis summarizes the data-flow information from the descendants of the procedure call graph. However, reference marking using only such analysis is still conservative because we assumed that all the global variables and formal parameters of each procedure have been modified before entering the procedure, due to the unknown context information for the activation records that invoke the current procedure. To remove this conservative assumption, we need to perform the second pass, which is the top-down context analysis.

We start from a main program unit. Since the main program unit does not have any context at the beginning, the previous bottom-up analysis already generates a precise result. But, we need to propagate the context information of the main program unit to all its call sites. Generally, for each call site, we need to propagate the context information of the caller to the callee. The context information in our analysis can be represented by the IN set of CALL statement at each call site. This context propagation allows the IN set at the beginning of a procedure to be replaced by the IN sets of its corresponding callers' CALL statements. Since the context information is necessary only for formal parameters and global variables, we only propagate the summary context information for those variables. As opposed to the side effect analysis, we need to translate the IN set information from the caller's context to the callee's context.

Note that there can be multiple callers to a procedure. So, we need to merge the context information from multiple call sites. This is achieved by taking the union of all the IN sets from the call sites and by taking the minimum offset among multiple callers for each actual parameter and global variable. This is necessary unless we clone the procedure for each call site (duplicate the code for each case), which in the worst case produces the same effect as the inlining.

Using the summary context information, we can refine the conservative reference marking obtained from the previous bottom-up analysis. With the context information, we can compute a more precise (larger) offset for each Time-Read, or can eliminate the Time-Read completely if there has been no previous write to the variable referenced. To do so, we mark all the Time-Reads issued as a result of hidden context (Time-Reads that does not have a reaching definition inside the procedure and all its call sites) during side effect analysis. Note that for context analysis, we only need to update the reference marking results for these references. The other Time-Reads are already precise with the side effect analysis alone.

Using the bottom-up and top-down analyses, we can avoid redundant computation by performing minimal number of computation (twice) per program unit. In addition, our top-down analysis updates the reference marking results only for necessary cases, allowing incremental updates. Note that during the top-down pass, we don't have to propagate the data-flow

information for each procedure again since the summary context information is enough to refine reference marking. We only need to add the offset of each variable in the summary context information at the beginning of a procedure to the Time-Reads for those variables. For the Time-Reads marked which do not have definitions in the summary context, we could eliminate them completely since there have been no previous writes to the variables referenced by them.

In addition, this two-pass analysis allows separate compilation. We don't need to load an entire program in memory for the interprocedural analysis. We only need to load a procedure at a time as well as the procedure call graph with the summary information. This two-pass interprocedural algorithm allows incremental flow analysis without losing any preciseness. We also can limit the scope of the analysis on a level-by-level basis rather than the entire call graph.

## 3.3 Naming translation

To propagate data-flow information interprocedurally, we need to consider the naming translation between callers and callees. In the interprocedural stale reference detection, both the summary side effect information and the summary context information should be translated into the context of the procedure analyzed. There are two cases when a variable can be renamed across procedure boundaries.

- **parameter translation** All the formal parameters of the side effect information should be translated into the corresponding actual parameters during the bottom-up side effect analysis, while all the actual parameters should be translated to their corresponding formal parameters during the top-down context analysis. The translation can be complicated for array variables due to possible reshaping. For example, a variable with one dimension can be mapped to a two-dimensional variable in the procedure called. Maintaining subarray information in such case is difficult since all the subarray information also need to be reshaped.

- **COMMON block translation** A variable in a COMMON block can have different names across procedures sharing the same COMMON block. In addition to possible array reshaping, the translation should consider that a single array variable in a COMMON block declaration can be mapped to several variables (either scalar or array) in the same COMMON block declarations of other procedures.

A simple renaming can be performed both between actual and formal parameters and between COMMON block variables, by looking up the corresponding location in the parameter list or in the COMMON block declaration. However, this renaming can be complicated for array variables due to the potential reshaping and the difference in COMMON block declarations. To take advantage of full array data-flow information, all the subarray information also should be reshaped across procedure boundaries. However, we found that both the array reshaping and the mismatched COMMON block declarations occur rarely (either none or up to 2 cases per benchmark) for the benchmarks tested. Thus, we use a conservative scalar analysis approach when array reshaping is found. For example, if a procedure A with a COMMON block declaration of a single array variable calls a procedure B which maps the same COMMON block to three different variables, then we assume that the COMMON variable in the caller will be modified at the call site if the OUT set of the procedure B includes any of the three COMMON variables. In addition, we treat all the array variables with dimensional reshaping as scalar variables.

## 4  EXPERIMENTATION

We use six programs from the Perfect Club benchmark suite [2] as our target benchmarks. The Perfect benchmarks are first parallelized by the Polaris compiler. In the parallelized codes, the parallelism is expressed in terms of DOALL loops. Then, we mark the Time-Read operations and insert epoch counter operations in the parallelized source codes according to the compiler algorithms in sections 2 and 3 which are implemented on the Polaris compiler. Execution-driven simulations [12] are used to verify the compiler algorithm and to evaluate the performance of compiler-directed coherence schemes. All the simulations assume a 16-processor, distributed shared-memory architecture with each processor containing an on-chip 64-KB direct-mapped cache with 4-word cache lines.

**Compiler algorithms**  We use three different compiler algorithms to generate memory operations for the software cache-bypass scheme (SC) and the two-phase invalidation scheme (TPI).

1. *Invalidation-based intraprocedural algorithm* (**ALG1**) This algorithm performs stale reference detection on a per-procedure basis [7]. To avoid the complications caused by unknown side effects, cache invalidation operations are inserted after each call site and at the beginning of a procedure.

2. *A simple interprocedural algorithm with no cache invalidation* (**ALG2**) Instead of the intraprocedural algorithm in section 2.2, we use a more sophisticated algorithm. By computing the MAY-MOD side effect information for each procedure, we assume that only the variables in MAY-MOD, rather than all the actual parameters and global COMMON variables, are modified at each call site. For hidden context, we assume that all formals and COMMON variables are modified at the beginning of a procedure, as in the intraprocedural algorithm. The algorithm no longer uses cache invalidations.

3. *A full interprocedural program algorithm* (**ALG3**) This algorithm performs the full interprocedural flow analysis by propagating data-flow information across procedures (see section 3.).

### 4.1  Benchmarks and reference statistics

**Static reference statistics**  Table 1 shows the number of potentially stale data references (Time-Reads) marked at compile time using the 3 compiler algorithms. For comparison, we have implemented both array and scalar data-flow analysis versions of each algorithm and show their corresponding results. For both OCEAN and SPEC77, the results of scalar implementations are shown only for algorithms ALG2 and ALG3. The result of the array data-flow algorithms are not available because of its extensive memory usage.

In our compiler implementation, all the variables are treated as shared variables. Therefore, the number of the potentially stale data references are overestimated in Table 1. However, during simulation, we issue normal memory read operations for all private read references.

After considering both side effects and hidden contexts, the simple interprocedural algorithm ALG2 increases the number of potentially stale data references substantially. On average, an additional 8.71% (array) and 20.15% (scalar) of data references are marked as potentially stale compared to ALG1. The full interprocedural algorithm ALG3 eliminates on average 33.8% (array) and 45.1% (scalar) of the potentially stale data references marked by ALG2. For ALG3, the figure also illustrates the number of Time-Reads removed (the difference in the number of Time-Reads between the end of top-down analysis and the end of bottom-up analysis) and the number of offsets incremented by the context analysis. Note that the impact of the more precise array data-flow analysis is greater in ALG2 and ALG3 than in ALG1 since the interprocedural analysis exposes more references to the array analysis for optimizations.

**Dynamic Reference Statistics**  Table 2 shows the dynamic reference counts of Time-Reads generated during our simulations. Note that the percentage of Time-Reads vary significantly depending on the application used, ranging from 1.96% (QCD) to 39.0% (SPEC77). With ALG1, an average of 3.34% of the memory references are marked as Time-Reads. Note that this number is misleading because it represents the reference count on a per-procedure basis, since ALG1 uses invalidations at procedural boundaries. By considering the interprocedural side effects and contexts, ALG2 increases the percentage of Time-Reads to 14.6%. With full interprocedural analysis, ALG3 decreases it to 6.7%. The numbers shown in the parentheses represent the percentage of Time-Reads generated by the corresponding scalar implementation. On average, array data-flow analysis could eliminate 51.7%, 23.5%, and 50.0% of Time-Reads marked by the scalar implementation for ALG1, ALG2, and ALG3 respectively.

### 4.2  Miss Rates

Figure 4 shows how the different compiler algorithms affect the miss rates of both the software cache-bypass scheme (SC) and the hardware scheme (TPI) against the underlying BASE architecture, which uses

Table 1: The static reference counts of Time-Reads generated by different compiler algorithms. The data in parentheses represent the results of a scalar version of each algorithm. For ALG3, the average figure shows the averaged statistics only from 3 benchmarks: FLO52, MDG, and QCD.

| Program | Size (lines) | ALG1 | ALG2 | ALG3 | | |
|---|---|---|---|---|---|---|
| | | | | end of bottom-up | end of top-down | offset incremented |
| FLO52 | 3182 | 5.08% (6.31%) | 16.3% (19.9%) | 11.4% (20.3%) | 8.78% (14.4%) | 1.1% (3.3) |
| MDG | 1523 | 6.76% (10.0%) | 16.2% (22.3%) | 15.0% (23.8%) | 11.2% (16.4%) | 1.2% (2.2) |
| QCD | 3505 | 7.44% (13.5%) | 16.6% (28.8%) | 12.4% (29.3%) | 10.1% (23.2) | 0.4% (1.6%) |
| SPEC77 | 5346 | 4.96% (9.02%) | 9.64% (16.5%) | ** (17.1%) | ** (13.9%) | ** (2.0%) |
| OCEAN | 3101 | 7.71% (8.91%) | 16.6% (18.6%) | ** (18.7%) | ** (13.7%) | ** (3.8%) |
| Avg. | 3122 | 6.39% (9.55%) | 15.1% (29.7%) | 12.7% (24.5%) | 10.0% (18.0%) | 0.9% (2.4%) |

Table 2: Dynamic memory reference statistics for the Perfect Club benchmarks. The data in parentheses show the results of scalar algorithms.

| Program | Size (lines) | % Read | Shared (total refs) | % Time-read | | |
|---|---|---|---|---|---|---|
| | | | | ALG1 | ALG2 | ALG3 |
| SPEC77 | 5346 | 79.3% | 55.3% ($5.0*10^6$) | 3.85% (16.0%) | 23.2% (46.2%) | ** (39.0%) |
| OCEAN | 3101 | 72.6% | 34.9% ($3.2*10^6$) | 0.1% (0.1%) | 4.17% (3.9%) | ** (2.1%) |
| FLO52 | 3182 | 72.9% | 39.4% ($2.8*10^6$) | 10.9% (13.1%) | 16.1% (20.3%) | 12.2% (17.3%) |
| MDG | 1523 | 75.0% | 36.5% ($1.8*10^6$) | 1.71% (1.73%) | 19.5% (**) | 5.94% (5.7%) |
| QCD | 3505 | 78.4% | 18.3% ($1.2*10^6$) | 0.14% (0.57%) | 10.2% (11.0%) | 1.96% (3.0%) |
| Average | 3331 | 75.6% | 36.9% | 3.34% (6.3%) | 14.6% (20.4%) | 6.7% (13.42%) |

remote memory accesses exclusively for all shared memory references.[a] The miss rates are classified into sharing misses and nonsharing misses. A sharing miss occurs when the address tag matches but either the cache copy has been invalidated or the reference is marked as potentially stale. All the other misses account for nonsharing misses as in a uniprocessor system. The sharing misses are further classified into true and false sharing misses. The true sharing misses are necessary misses to avoid cache coherence, while the false sharing misses are the unnecessary misses caused by conservative compiler decisions.

As can be seen in the figure, compared to ALG1, ALG2 can eliminate a significant number of cache misses for both *TPI* and *SC* except SPEC77. This is primarily a result of avoiding cache invalidations at procedure boundaries. The most significant improvement in cache utilization is in benchmarks MDG and QCD. In these benchmarks there are several small procedures in the critical path of execution. The invalidations used by ALG1 not only invalidate shared data but also sweep out private data from the cache unnecessarily. For MDG, ALG2 could eliminate 17.7% and 24.8% of cache misses in *SC* and *TPI* schemes respectively. With full interprocedural analysis (ALG3), an additional 10.8% and 5.5% of cache misses are

eliminated as compared to ALG2. Similar to MDG, ALG2 eliminates 21.9% and 24.0% of unnecessary cache misses of the *SC* and *TPI* schemes in QCD. And, using the full interprocedural algorithm for *SC* scheme eliminates up to 4.0% of additional cache misses in QCD.

A similar but rather modest trend is observed in other benchmarks. In FLO52, ALG2 achieves a modest improvement over ALG1 for both *SC* and *TPI* schemes, eliminating cache misses by 2.6% and 4.1% respectively. Also, using the full interprocedural algorithm for *SC* scheme eliminates 1.9% of additional cache misses. In OCEAN, most of the misses are dominated by non-sharing misses, and both compiler-directed coherence schemes achieve comparable miss rates regardless of the compiler algorithms used.

In SPEC77, an interesting situation is observed. The simple interprocedural analysis (ALG2) substantially increases the cache misses by 20.3% for *SC* scheme as compared to the invalidation-based algorithm (ALG1). In this benchmark, the negative effects of the conservative stale reference marking used in ALG2 are more significant than the gain from avoiding cache invalidations. Note that this is true only for the software cache-bypass scheme. In SPEC77, the procedures are reasonably large, making the impact of the cold start effects of the cache invalidations negligible. However, the conservative marking strategy employed by ALG2 increases the number of potentially stale references substantially (23.2% (ALG2) compared to 3.85% (ALG1) for array analysis, and 46.2% (ALG2) compared to 16.0% (ALG1) for scalar

---

[a] The results of array data-flow analysis are shown for benchmarks FLO52, MDG, and QCD, while the results of scalar versions of algorithms are shown for SPEC77 and OCEAN. This is because SPEC77 and OCEAN require excessive memory using the interprocedural array data-flow algorithm.

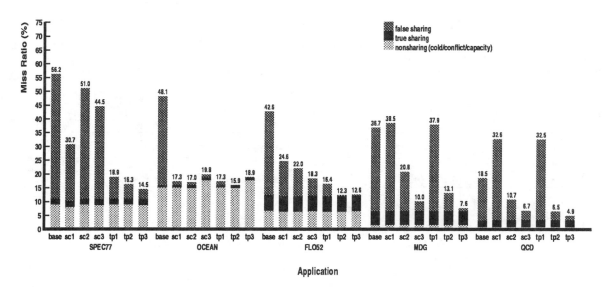

Figure 4: Miss rates using different compiler algorithms for the SC and the TPI scheme compared to an underlying BASE architecture. SC1, SC2, and SC3 represent the software cache-bypass scheme using algorithms ALG1, ALG2 and ALG3 respectively, while TP1, TP2 and TP3 show the two-phase invalidation scheme using ALG1, ALG2 and ALG3 respectively.

analysis; refer to Table 2). This leads to a significant number of unnecessary cache misses for the software cache-bypass scheme. For the *TPI* scheme, the conservative marking can be overcome by keeping track of the runtime cache states. In other words, more Time-Reads marked by ALG2 turn out to be cache hits since *TPI* can determine the staleness of cached data at runtime more precisely using the timetag information.

## 5 CONCLUSION

We proposed improved compiler algorithms for detecting stale data references in the presence of procedures calls. Procedure calls can introduce side effects at a call site and hidden context at the beginning of a procedure, which limit existing compiler-directed cache coherence schemes [3, 6, 4, 8, 10] to exploit locality only within procedure boundaries. Previous algorithms use cache invalidation [5, 7] or selective inlining [7] to solve the problem. However, invalidation at procedure boundaries incur significant performance penalty especially if a program contains many small procedures in its critical path. Inlining allows the most precise analysis but it is often prohibitive due to potential code size expansion as well as the compile time increase.

By considering both side effects and hidden contexts at procedure boundaries, we propose an improved compiler algorithm which avoids cache invalidations at procedure boundaries. We selectively issue Time-Reads only for procedure parameters and global COMMON variables which are shared by multiple procedures. By doing so, the procedure boundary will not affect the access of subroutine local data. We also proposed an interprocedural algorithm which can fully

exploit locality across procedure boundaries. It performs interprocedural analysis according to a bottom-up and a top-down order of the procedure call graph. The bottom-up side effect analysis replaces each call site with summary side effect information from its descendants while the top-down context analysis propagates the context of predecessors to each procedure. This two-pass algorithm eliminates redundant data-flow computation for each program unit by doing minimal number of computation per program unit. In addition, the top-down pass updates the reference marking result of the side effect analysis incrementally, and thus minimize the compilation time.

We have implemented these algorithms on the Polaris parallelizing compiler [11], and demonstrated the performance driven by the new compiler algorithms by running execution-driven simulations of five Perfect benchmarks. The results show that by avoiding cache invalidations, the intraprocedural algorithm eliminates up to 26.0% of the cache misses for a compiler-directed scheme compared to an existing invalidation-based algorithm [7]. With the full interprocedural analysis, up to 10.8% of additional cache misses can be removed.

### Acknowledgments

The research described in this paper was supported in part by the NSF Grant No. MIP 89-20891, MIP 93-07910 and ARPA contract #DABT63-95-C-0097. This work is not necessarily representative of the positions or policies of the Army of the Government. This work was performed while the first author was at the University of Illinois. We thank Hock-Beng Lim at the University of Illinois for his valuable comments.

## REFERENCES

[1] R. Ballance, A. Maccabe, and K. Ottenstein. The Program Dependence Web: a Representation Supporting Control- Data- and Demand-Driven Interpretation of Imperative Languages. *Proceedings of the SIGPLAN '90 Conference on Programming Language Design and Implementation*, pages 257–271, June 1990.

[2] M. Berry and others. The Perfect Club Benchmarks: Effective Performance Evaluation of Supercomputers. *International Journal of Supercomputer Applications*, 3(3):5–40, Fall, 1989.

[3] D. Callahan and K. Kennedy. Analysis of Interprocedural Side Effects in a Parallel Programming Environment. *Journal of Parallel and Distributed Computing*, 5:517–550, 1988.

[4] H. Cheong. Life Span Strategy - A Compiler-Based Approach to Cache Coherence. *Proceedings of the 1992 International Conference on Supercomputing*, July 1992.

[5] H. Cheong and A. Veidenbaum. Stale Data Detection and Coherence Enforcement Using Flow Analysis. *Proceedings of the 1988 International Conference on Parallel Processing*, I, Architecture:138–145, August 1988.

[6] H. Cheong and A. Veidenbaum. A Cache Coherence Scheme with Fast Selective Invalidation. *Proceedings of the 15th Annual International Symposium on Computer Architecture*, June 1988.

[7] L. Choi and P.-C. Yew. Eliminating Stale Data References through Array Data-Flow Analysis. *Proceedings of the 10th IEEE International Parallel Processing Symposium*, pages 4–13, April. 1996.

[8] L. Choi and P.-C. Yew. Compiler and Hardware Support for Cache Coherence in Large-Sca le Multiprocessors: Design Considerations and Performance Study. *Proceedings of the 23rd Annual ACM International Symposium on Computer Architecture*, May 1996.

[9] P. Havlak. Interprocedural Symbolic Analysis. Technical report, Rice University, Dept. of Computer Science, May 1994. Ph.D. Thesis.

[10] A. Louri and H. Sung. A Compiler Directed Cache Coherence Scheme with Fast and Parallel Explicit Invalidation. *Proceedings of the 1992 International Conference on Parallel Processing*, I, Architecture:2–9, August 1992.

[11] D. A. Padua, R. Eigenmann, J. Hoeflinger, P. Peterson, P. Tu, S. Weatherford, and K. Faign. Polaris: A New-Generation Parallelizing Compiler for MPPs. In *CSRD Rept. No. 1306*. Univ. of Illinois at Urbana-Champaign., June, 1993.

[12] D. K. Poulsen and P.-C. Yew. Execution-Driven Tools for Parallel Simulation of Parallel Architectures and Applications. *Proceedings of the Supercomputing 93*, pages 860–869, Nov. 1993.

[13] P. Tu. Automatic Array Privatization and Demand-Driven Symbolic Analysis. Technical report, Univ. of Illinois at Urbana-Champaign, Dept. of Computer Science, 1995. Ph.D. Thesis.

## A Appendix: Interprocedural algorithm

```
Algorithm A.1:   Interprocedural Stale Reference Detection
Input:           Procedure call graph G and TARGET(S)
Output:          STALE(S) for each statement S
Begin
  for bottom-up search of G do /* side effect analysis */
    for each leaf node in the current level of G do
    /* OUT(P) denotes summary side effect for P */
      OUT(P) = φ;
      for each procedure P do
        perform the intraprocedural algorithm in
           Section 2.2 with the following modification;
        for each CALL statement C in P to Q do
          translate OUT(Q) from Q's context
             to P's context;
          add min_offset(Q) to all the definitions in
             OUT(C) which have no side effects in Q;
        end for
        mark Time-Read issued due to hidden context;
        for each return node R in P do
        /* side(R) denotes the side effect of P at R */
          side(R) = OUT(R) - {definitions of the
             local variables of P};
          OUT(P) = OUT(P) ⊕ side(R) where
             choose the minimum offset among the
             definitions for the same variable
             in OUT(P);
        end for
      end for
    end for
    increment the level by 1;
  end for
  for top-down search of G do /* context analysis */
    for each top level node in G do
    /* IN(P) denotes summary context for P */
      IN(P) = φ;
      for each procedure P do /* merge the context */
        for each caller Q do
          translate context(Q,P) from Q's context
             to P's context;
          IN(P) = IN(P) ⊕ context(Q,P) where
             choose the minimum offset among the
             definitions for the same variable
             in IN(P);
        end for
        perform the intraprocedural algorithm in
           Section 2.2 with the following modification;
        for each CALL statement C in P to Q do
        /* context(P,Q) denotes summary context
        from P to Q */
          context(P,Q) = context (P,Q) ⊕ IN(C)
             - {definitions of local variables of P};
        end for
        for each Time-Read R marked
           in the first pass do
          if there is a definition d in IN(P) where
             where (subarray(d) ⊕ subarray(R)) ≠ φ then
             add offset(d) to the offset of Time-Read;
          else if there is no overlapping
             definition d in IN(P) then
                replace the Time-Read with
                   a regular Read;
          endif
        end for
      end for
    end for
    decrement the level by 1;
  end for
End
```

Figure 5: Flow analysis algorithm for stale reference detection. The USE(S) used in the algorithm can be replaced by TARGET(S) after the target reference detection. ⊕ denotes union operation for subarrays.

# A Timestamp-based Selective Invalidation Scheme for Multiprocessor Cache Coherence*

Xin Yuan     Rami Melhem     Rajiv Gupta
Department of Computer Science
University of Pittsburgh
Pittsburgh, PA 15260

*Abstract – Among all software cache coherence strategies, the ones that are based on the concept of timestamps show the greatest potential in terms of cache performance. The early timestamp methods suffer from high hardware overhead. Improvements have been proposed to reduce hardware overhead at the expense of either increasing runtime overhead or sacrificing cache performance. In this paper, we discuss the limitations of the previous timestamp-based methods and propose a new software cache coherence scheme. Our scheme exploits the inter-level locality with significantly less hardware support than the early timestamp methods while introducing only constant runtime overhead for each epoch during the execution of a program. Simulation results show that the proposed scheme achieves higher performance than the previous schemes with comparable hardware overhead.*

## 1 Introduction

Private caches are critical components of high performance multiprocessor systems. The use of private caches reduces network traffic and memory access latency. However, it also introduces the cache coherence problem. A mechanism must be implemented to keep the caches coherent in order for a program to run correctly on a multiprocessor system.

Among the existing software controlled cache coherence schemes, the methods based on the concept of timestamps are more effective in preserving cache lines across task boundaries than other software methods [4, 9]. The early timestamp-based methods, such as the version control method [3] and the timestamp method[10], use an explicit timestamp table to store the current version number for each variable. They also use an additional field in each cache line to store the version number of the cache line. Although the cache performance of these methods approaches that of the hardware schemes, the maintenance of the table and the additional timestamp field introduces hardware and runtime overheads. The later methods, such as TS1 with a 1 bit timestamp [8], the generational algorithm [5] and the two-phase invalidation scheme (TPI) [6], try to reduce these overheads. TS1 avoids most of the hardware overhead by eliminating the timestamp table and reducing the additional timestamp field to one bit for each cache line. However,

explicit invalidation instructions are needed at the end of each level. Hardware support for an efficient cache invalidation mechanism introduces additional hardware overhead in TS1. The generational algorithm eliminates the timestamp table overhead by having all variables share the same timestamp. However, the author does not address implementation issues that greatly affect the algorithm's performance.

TPI seems to be a promising software cache coherence scheme. It requires reasonable hardware and runtime overhead and exploits data locality in most situations. The limitation of this method is that it does not always exploit data locality in the presence of nested looping structures in which serial loops enclose one or more parallel loops. These patterns are often encountered in scientific programs where loop bounds are commonly parameterized.

In this paper, we propose a software cache coherence scheme which combines the advantage of the TS1 and TPI scheme and overcomes their limitations. In addition, the performance of our method can be improved without incurring extra hardware or runtime penalty when better information is available at compile time. The hardware overhead of our scheme is close to that of TPI and TS1 with parallel invalidation mechanism. Simulation results show that the cache hit ratio of our scheme is higher than that of TPI and almost the same as that of TS1. By reducing the runtime overhead, our scheme achieves better performance than TS1. Thus, the overall performance of our method is superior to both TPI and TS1.

The rest of the paper is organized as follows. In section 2 we describe the parallel computation model used in this work. A survey of the previous timestamp-based software cache coherence methods is given in section 3. In section 4 the timestamp-based selective invalidation software cache coherence scheme is presented. In section 5 a detailed comparison between our method and the previous methods is given. Section 6 reports simulation results. Section 7 summarizes the major contributions of this work.

## 2 The Computation Model

A parallel program is composed of a series of **levels**. Each level is either a parallel loop with no internal synchronization (e.g., a DOALL loop) or a serial region (e.g., a DOSER loop) between parallel loops. Serial regions can be nested serial loops or those parts of serials loops that are not in parallel loops. The

---

*This work is supported in part by the NSF awards CCR-9157371 and ASC-9318185 to the University of Pittsburgh. Contact author: xyuan@cs.pitt.edu.

execution of the program is composed of a series of **epochs**. Each epoch consists of one or more tasks which run in parallel. A task is the minimum computation unit that can be scheduled and assigned to a processor for execution at run time. In a serial epoch, a single task is scheduled and executed on a single processor. In a parallel epoch, multiple tasks are created at runtime and executed on multiple processors simultaneously.

```
(1)    DOALL i = 1, n
(2)        u(i) = 0.0
(3)        v(i) = 0.0
(4)    END DOALL
(5)    DOSER i = 1, n
(6)        DOALL j = 1, n
(7)            w(j) = u(j) + v(j)
(8)            x(j) = ...
(9)        END DOALL
(10)       DOSER j= 1, n
(11)           DOALL k = 1, n
(12)               w(k) = w(j) + a
(13)           END DOALL
(14)           a = a* 2.0
(15)       END DOSER
(16)       DOALL j = 1, n
(17)           .. = x(..)
(18)           w(..) = ..
(19)       END DOALL
(20)   END DOSER
```

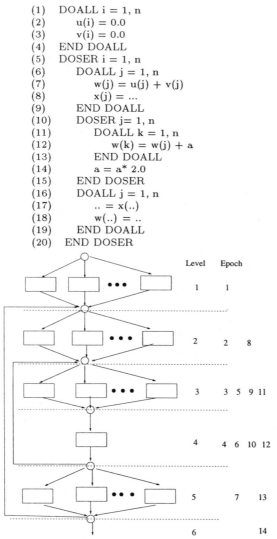

Figure 1: A program and its levels and epochs.

To model dynamic scheduling schemes, we assume that a task may be scheduled on any processor at runtime. We also assume that every processor participates in the execution of every epoch. If there is no useful task to be assigned, the processor will run a task that only performs the coherence operations.

An example parallel program, as well as its levels and epochs during the execution of the program for n = 2, is shown in Fig. 1. This example will also be used in section 4 to describe our cache coherence scheme. The parallel loop in lines (1)-(4) corresponds to Level 1. Level 2 corresponds to lines (6)-(9), level 3 to the

parallel loop in lines (11)- (13), level 4 to line (14) and level 5 to lines (16) - (19). In the execution of the program, the epoch number can be much larger than the level number.

In this paper, we initially assume that a cache line is one word long and that the cache uses a write-through policy. Later we also briefly discuss extensions to handle multi-word cache lines. Data variables are classified into private, shared read-only and shared read-write. Only shared read-write variables can cause cache coherence problems. When we refer to a variable, it is assumed to be a shared read-write variable.

# 3 Timestamp Based Methods
## The Version Control Method

In the version control method [3], the *current version number* (CVN) for each variable is kept in the *variable ID table* in each processor. An entire array is treated as a single variable. For the method to be efficient, the variable ID table must be accessed in parallel with the cache access. Each cache line has an extra field called *birth version number* (BVN). At the time the cache line is created (by either a read or a write), the value of $CVN$ (for read misses) or $CVN+1$ (for writes) is written into the BVN. At the end of each level, the processor increments the CVN for each variable that might have been modified in that level. The compiler is responsible for determining the level boundary and generating code to increase the CVNs. The cache line is valid only if its BVN is bigger than or equal to the corresponding variable's CVN. The version control method is effective in preserving the reuse of cache lines. The major limitation of this method is the hardware and runtime overhead. The timestamp method [10] is not discussed here because it is similar to the version control method.

## The TS1 Method

In TS1, one additional bit, referred to as the *epoch bit*, is required for each cache line. The compiler determines the levels and the variables modified in each level. The epoch bit is reset at the end of each level and is set when the cache line is referenced. At the end of each level, invalidation instructions are issued to invalidate all the variables modified in that level. An invalidation instruction invalidates a specified cache line only if (1) the address tag matches, and (2) the cache line's epoch bit is not set. Once a variable is modified in an epoch, the variable is invalidated in all the processors except the one that modified it. Thus, the cache will always contain valid cache lines.

The performance and overhead of this scheme depends heavily on the mechanism used to invalidate the stale cache lines. Two implementations of the invalidation mechanism are proposed in [8]. The simple and inexpensive invalidation mechanism uses a low level invalidate instruction which could invalidate either a particular line or a particular page. The high level invalidate would then loop over the proper range of pages and lines. Using this simple *serial* scheme, the invalidation overhead is $O(\sum_{i=1}^{n}(s_i))$, where $s_i$ is the size of the $i$th section to be invalidated. A faster, but more complex invalidation method was proposed in [8] and [9]. This *parallel* scheme requires a full associated address tag memory. A bit mask is used to determine which addresses to invalidate. Using this invalidation scheme, the runtime overhead is $O(\sum_{i=1}^{n} log(s_i))$. Besides the invalidation schemes, the runtime overhead of TS1 also depends on the program structure when using precise invalidation. When an epoch contains many discontinuous sections to be invalidated, the overhead for the epoch will be quite large.

In summary, TS1 effectively preserves the reuses of a cache line. Using precise invalidation, this scheme can achieve the best cache hit ratio that any software cache coherence method based on local knowledge can possibly achieve [8]. The limitation is the runtime overhead. The exploitation of higher cache hit ratio by using precise invalidation results in larger runtime overhead. Therefore, it is desirable to develop a mechanism to perform the invalidation more effectively.

### The Generational Algorithm

The goal of the generational algorithm is to improve over the version control method by making all the variables in the program share one common CVN. In the generational method, the shared CVN called *Current generation number* (CGN) is stored in each processor. The CGN is increased at the end of each epoch. When a cache line is updated, the cache line is provided with a *valid generation number* (VGN) indicating when the cache line will become invalid. The system invalidates a cache line implicitly by causing CGN to become larger than the cache line's VGN. The compiler is responsible for determining the VGN for all the memory references. By using a common CVN, the generational algorithm eliminates the variable ID table and the problems associated with it. However, [5] does not address some important issues. For example, it is not clear how the VGNs of the cache lines are updated for the variables modified in a level. If every cache line's VGN is updated individually at the end of each epoch, this method will incur greater runtime overhead than TS1 does. Since the author does not address these important issues, we are unable to determine the efficiency of the method.

### The TPI Scheme

In TPI, the timestamp field associated with the cache line is updated with current epoch number for both read and write instructions. The read instruction is supplied with an additional field to indicate the epoch number of the last write to the variable. The cache copies created after the specified last write epoch are valid. Therefore, the stale cache copies are detected by comparing the timestamp field with the last write epoch number. When the current epoch counter overflows, an explicit invalidation instruction is used to invalidate the cache lines. As shown in [6], the method can preserve most of the localities with reasonable hardware and runtime overhead. Furthermore, interprocedural analysis techniques can be incorporated in this method to preserve the locality across procedure boundaries [7]. The limitation of this method is that it does not always handle nested looping structures shown in Fig. 2 effectively.

The *repeated read pattern* occurs when a shared variable is only read inside a nested loop and is writ-

```
(1) DOALL i = 1, 1000
(2)     x(i) = ...
(3) END DOALL
(4) DOSER i = 1, N
(5)     DOALL j = 1, 1000
(6)         .. = x(j)...
(7)     END DOALL
(8)     ... ! another level
(9) END DOSER
```

(a) Repeated read pattern.

```
(1) DOALL i = 1, 1000
(2)     x(i) = ...
(3) END DOALL
(4) DOSER i = 1, N
(5)     DOALL j = 1, 1000
(6)         ... = x(j)...
(7)         x(j) = ...
(8)     END DOALL
(9)     ... ! another level
(10)END DOSER
```

(b) Write interference pattern.

```
(1) DOSER i = 1, 1000
(2)     DOSER j = 1, N
(3)         DOALL k = 1, 1000
(4)             ...
(5)         END DOALL
(6)     END DOSER
(7)     DOALL j = 1, 1000
(8)         ... = x(j)...
(9)         x(j) = ...
(10)    END DOALL
(11)END DOSER
```

(c) Unknown epoch number pattern.

Figure 2: Examples of reference patterns.

ten in some epochs before the loop. An example is shown in Fig. 2 (a). Consider the read reference of x in line (6). For each distinct iteration of the serial loop, the last write epoch for this reference is different. However, since the read instruction can only carry one timestamp, it cannot preserve all this information even if it can be determined by the compiler. For the program to run correctly, the last write epoch number for the reference is two epochs earlier. As a result, the references to x in line (6) result in cache misses since the cache copies created inside the serial loop are separated by three epochs. Note that in TPI, the DOSER is treated as serial epoch.

The *write interference pattern* occurs when (1) a shared variable is written before a nested loop and is read and written inside the loop, (2) the write to the variable inside the loop takes more epochs to reach the read than the write outside the loop does. Consider the example in Fig. 2 (b). Both the writes to x in line (2) and (7) reach the read of x in line (6). Since the write in line (2) crosses only two epochs to reach the read while the write in line (7) crosses three epochs, the last write epoch number for the read is two epochs earlier. Therefore, except first iteration, the reads in line (6) result in cache misses.

The *unknown epoch number pattern* occurs when the runtime number of epochs inside a nested loop is unknown at compile time. Consider the example in Fig. 2 (c). The epochs between the write in line (9) and the read in line (8) are unknown at compile time due to the value of N being unknown. The compiler must conservatively assume that it takes two epochs for the write in line (9) to reach the read in line (8). Therefore, the last write epoch for the read in line (6) is two epochs earlier. However, in the execution of the program, the level in lines (2) - (6) is usually executed. As a result, the reads in line (8) will cause cache misses.

Some compiler techniques, such as epoch number

adjustment, loop peeling and guard execution, can be used to alleviate some of the problems. However, we believe that the static estimation of the last write epoch number, which is changed dynamically, is the inherent limitation of this method. Therefore, it would be desirable to use a static measurement to decide whether a cache line is valid.

## 4   Timestamp-based Selective Invalidation Scheme

Both TS1 and TPI improve the version control to some extent. Each of the method has its own limitation – the runtime overhead in TS1 and the degradation of performance due to static estimation of dynamic epoch number in TPI. In this paper, we propose a timestamp-based selective invalidation scheme (TBSIS). This scheme combines the ideas of both TS1 and TPI and overcomes their limitations. TBSIS improves over TS1 by having almost the same capability of preserving the cache line reuses and reducing the runtime overhead. TBSIS improves over TPI by having a static measurement, the level number, to decide whether a cache line is valid and avoiding all the problems in TPI when dealing with nested loops. The hardware overhead of TBSIS is close to that of TPI and TS1 with parallel invalidation. Simulation results show that TBSIS exhibits better performance than both TS1 and TPI.

### 4.1   Hardware Support

A timestamp field called *Invalidation Level Number* (ILN) is associated with each cache line. The ILN is composed of two parts, $ILN_m$ and $ILN_r$. The $ILN_m$ is the most significant bit in the ILN and the $ILN_r$ represents the remaining bits. We will denote an ILN as $(ILN_m, ILN_r)$.

A special invalidation instruction must be supported by the cache implementation. We will use $INV\ L$ to represent the instruction, where L is a level number. The invalidation instruction operates on all the cache lines in the cache. The operations of the instruction $INV\ L$ are (1) to invalidate all cache lines whose $ILN_r = L$ and $ILN_m = 0$, (2) to reset the $ILN_m$ fields for all cache lines whose $ILN_r = L$ and $ILN_m = 1$. Other cache lines are unaffected.

The $ILN_m$ bit is used to skip one invalidation. As we will see later, this bit is mainly used to deal with the looping structures. The logic for the instruction is shown in Fig. 3. We assume that the cache implementation can support this instruction in O(1) time. The processor also needs to support the memory reference instructions Read_ILN and Write_ILN. Both instructions are augmented with an extra ILN field. Beside the traditional operations, these instructions also update the ILN fields in the cache lines.

### 4.2   The Scheme

TBSIS is a generalization of TS1 [8]. The main idea is still to explicitly invalidate the stale cache copies if the variable is modified in the current epoch. By using more bits as timestamp for each cache line and augmenting the compiler support, the explicit invalidation in TBSIS can be carried out more efficiently.

In TBSIS, an invalidation instruction $INV\ L$ is issued at the end of each epoch to invalidate all the

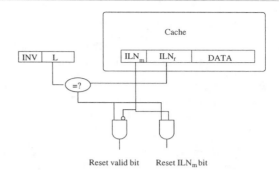

Figure 3: The logic of the invalidation instruction.

cache lines that must be invalidated in that epoch. Here L is the level number corresponding to the epoch. In order for the instruction to invalidate all the stale cache lines, all these lines that are still valid before the instruction should have $ILN_r = L$ and $ILN_m = 0$. The compiler determines the levels of the program, and furthermore, it also determines a proper ILN for each memory reference to ensure that the cache does not contain the stale cache copies.

It is simple to ensure a coherent cache by using the ILN field and the invalidation instruction. For example, the compiler may provide each memory reference with ILN equal to the current level number. TBSIS is then reduced to the simple invalidation scheme [3] which can only exploit the intra-level locality. To exploit maximum locality, the compiler should always try to set ILN to the next write level number.

### 4.3   Software Support

The major task of software support is to determine the next write level number for each memory reference. Due to the branches in programs, there may be several next write levels for a memory reference. The compiler must approximate the next write level and/or introduce extra invalidation instructions at selected points to handle such situations. Two approachs can be used to handles the multiple next write level situation. The conservative approach assigns the ILN conservatively and guarantee the program runs correctly through all paths. The aggressive approach assigns the ILN to be the one that saves the cache lines along the most frequently executed path. This approach needs to introduce extra invalidation instructions along other paths to ensure the correctness of the program. TBSIS adopts the second approach and therefore, the compiler must determine the next write level and find the proper place to introduce the extra invalidation instructions.

For a memory reference, if there is a unique next write level, then that level number will be the ILN for the reference. There may be several possible next write levels due to the branches in the program. If the branch is a forward branch, the nearest level at which the variable is modified is used as the next write level. If there is a backward branch involved, the memory reference is inside a loop. The next write level in the innermost loop is considered as the next write level. In this way, TBSIS always captures the locality inside the loop. Using *epoch flow graph* [6], the next write level information can be obtained in two steps. First, using the algorithm in [1], we determine the looping structures in the flow graph. Then, for each memory reference, the compiler searches forward for all the writes to the same variable that can be reached by the reference in the flow graph. Among the writes, the write that is closest to the current point in the innermost loop is the write of interest.

As for the placement of the extra invalidation instructions, a simple solution is to introduce extra invalidation instructions at the exit of every loop to invalidate all the cache lines whose ILN is equal to any one level inside the loops. The invalidation instruction can be delayed until the first level that modifies the variables that are modified in the loop. The compiler can use similar analysis as in the determination of the next write level for one variable to determine the place for the extra invalidation instruction. In the remainder of this paper, we assume that the simple approach is used.

```
(1)  DOALL i = 1, n          Level   Var   ILN
(2)     u(i) = 0.0            1       u     (0, 6)
(3)     v(i) = 0.0                    v     (0, 6)
(4)  END DOALL
     INV 1

(5)  DO i = 1, n                      u     (0, 6)
(6)     DOALL j = 1, n                v     (0, 6)
(7)        w(j) = u(j) + ....  2      w     (0, 3)
(8)        x(j) = v(j) + x(j)         x     (1, 2)
(9)     END DOALL
        INV 2

(10)    DO j= 1, n
(11)       DOALL k = 1, n             a     (0, 4)
(12)          w(k) = w(j) + a  3      w     (1, 3)
(13)       END DOALL
           INV 3

(14)       a = a* 2.0          4      a     (1, 4)
           INV 4

(15)    END DO
        INV 3, 4        ! extra inv
(16)    DOALL j = 1, n
(17)       .. = x(..)          5      x     (0, 2)
(18)    END DOALL
        INV 5

(19) END DO
     INV 2, 3, 4, 5        ! extra inv
```

Figure 4: An example.

## 4.4  An Example

In this section, we will describe the method through an example. Fig. 4 is the example program in section 2 augmented with the invalidation instructions. The value of ILN is $(0, 6)$ for the write reference to u in line (2), this is because the variable u is not modified after line (2). Since there is no $INV\ 6$ issued in the program, the cache copies will be valid throughout the execution of the program. The value of ILN is $(1, 3)$ for the write reference to w in line (12) since the reference is inside the serial loop and the next write level is the next execution of level 3. Therefore, the cache copies of w will be valid until the end of

Table 1: Cache lines and their ILN.

| Ep. | L | a | u | v | w | x |
|---|---|---|---|---|---|---|
| 1 | 1 | - | (0, 6) | (0, 6) | - | - |
| 2 | 2 | - | (0, 6) | (0, 6) | (0, 3) | (0, 2) |
| 3 | 3 | (0, 4) | (0, 6) | (0, 6) | (0, 3) | (0, 2) |
| 4 | 4 | (0, 4) | (0, 6) | (0, 6) | (0, 3) | (0, 2) |
| 5 | 3 | (0, 4) | (0, 6) | (0, 6) | (0, 3) | (0, 2) |
| 6 | 4 | (0, 4) | (0, 6) | (0, 6) | (0, 3) | (0, 2) |
| 7 | 5 | - | (0, 6) | (0, 6) | - | (0, 2) |
| 8 | 2 | - | (0, 6) | (0, 6) | (0, 3) | (0, 2) |
| 9 | 3 | (0, 4) | (0, 6) | (0, 6) | (0, 3) | (0, 2) |
| 10 | 4 | (0, 4) | (0, 6) | (0, 6) | (0, 3) | (0, 2) |
| 11 | 3 | (0, 4) | (0, 6) | (0, 6) | (0, 3) | (0, 2) |
| 12 | 4 | (0, 4) | (0, 6) | (0, 6) | (0, 3) | (0, 2) |
| 13 | 5 | - | (0, 6) | (0, 6) | - | (0, 2) |

the next iteration and the read reference to w at line (12) will be a cache hit. The next write level for the write reference to x in line (8) is the next execution of level 2. Therefore, the cache copies should survive one $INV\ 2$ instruction at the end of the level 2 and the ILN should be set to $(1, 2)$. Assuming the variable n is equal to 2, Table 1 depicts the ILN of each variable during the execution of the program.

## 4.5  Multi-word Cache Lines

TBSIS can be extended to handle multi-word cache lines. Let us assume that each cache word is associated with an ILN and that arrays are aligned to the cache line boundary. For a cache miss, if the reference is to an array element, then all the ILNs are assigned the ILN value in the instruction. If the reference is to a scalar, only the ILN of the cache word corresponding the scalar is assigned the ILN in the instruction, all other ILNs in the cache line are assigned the current level number. Therefore, those scalar cache lines that are not accessed in the current epoch will be invalidated at the end of the epoch and the cache contains clean data.

TBSIS can also be adapted if a single ILN is associated with an entire cache line. If arrays are aligned to cache line boundaries, then a single ILN per cache line is sufficient to exploit spatial locality. To maintain cache coherence for scalars, a reference to a scalar sets the ILN to be the minimum ILN of all the variables in the corresponding cache line. A frequently accessed shared scalar can be placed in a separate cache line.

## 5  Some Comparisons

TBSIS vs TS1

Compared to TS1 with serial invalidation, TBSIS requires a higher hardware overhead. However, TBSIS has significantly less runtime overhead. In our simulation study, TBSIS has an average of 11.8% speedup on a 16 processor system and 30.9% speedup on a 64 processor system with regard to the total memory reference time against TS1 with serial invalidation. The speedup is gained by reducing the runtime overhead.

TS1 with parallel invalidation and TBSIS have comparable hardware overhead. TBSIS requires fully

```
DOALL m = 1, 1000        Level
   x (m) = ...             i
END DOALL
INV i               if (m is odd) ILN = j
                    else ILN = k
─────────────────────────────────
...
─────────────────────────────────
DOALLl m = 1, 999, 2
   x(m) = ...          j      ILN = l
END DOALL
INV j
─────────────────────────────────
...
─────────────────────────────────
DOALL m = 2, 1000, 2
   x(m) = ...          k      ILN = l
END DOALL
INV k
─────────────────────────────────
...
─────────────────────────────────
DOALL m = 1, 1000
   x(m) = ...          l
END DOALL
INV l
─────────────────────────────────
```

Figure 5: Precise invalidation.

associative ILN memory (6 bits per word) and a regular address tag memory. TS1 requires a fully associative address tag and epoch bit memory (around 20 bits per word) with a bit mask register. TBSIS has a better runtime overhead, especially when exploiting precise invalidation. Consider the example in Fig. 5. To exploit precise invalidation, TS1 requires multiple invalidation instructions to be issued at the end of an epoch. For instance, each processor must issue 499 invalidation instructions in TS1 at the end of level $k$. In TBSIS, precise invalidation is done by assigning proper ILN for memory reference instruction. Regardless of the program structure, only 1 invalidation instruction is needed in TBSIS. However, conditional assignment statements may be needed to assign proper ILNs as shown in Fig. 5. The disadvantage of TBSIS is the potential over–invalidation when the program exits a nested loop. However, the misses caused by the over–invalidation is almost negligible compared to the total number of references since most of the references are inside the nested loop. In our performance study, TBSIS has an average speedup of 1.8% for 16 processor systems and 14.9% for 64 processor systems against TS1 with parallel invalidation.

### TBSIS vs TPI

In comparison to TPI, TBSIS requires a slightly larger overhead. However, TBSIS always exploits data locality inside loops, which accounts for a significant fraction of the data locality in a program, while TPI fails to preserve cache lines in situations where memory references are separated by non-unique number of epochs. Simulation results confirm that our method preserves the reuse of cache lines more effectively. Next, we show how TBSIS handles the patterns for which TPI fails to exploit the locality.

Fig. 6 shows how the repeated read pattern is handled in our method. The read reference to x in line (6) has $ILN = (0, 4)$. Since the instruction $INV\ 4$ is

```
(1)  DOALL i = 1, 1000     Level  var    ILN
(2)     x(i) = ...           1     x    (0, 4)
(3)  END DOALL
     INV 1
──────────────────────────────────────────
(4)  DO i = 1, N
(5)     DOALL j = 1, 1000
(6)        .. = x(j)...      2     x    (0, 4)
(7)     END DOALL
        INV 2
──────────────────────────────────────────
(8)        ...               3
        INV 3
──────────────────────────────────────────
(9)  END DO
```

Figure 6: The repeated read pattern.

not executed until the end of the program, the cache lines created in line (6) will be valid throughout the program under TBSIS. Fig. 7 shows how the write interference pattern is handled. The write reference to x in line (7) has the $ILN = (1, 2)$. Therefore, the cache line created by the statement can survive till the next execution of level 2 and the read references to x in line (6) will result in cache hits. Fig. 8 shows how the unknown epoch number pattern is handled. The write reference to x in line (9) have the ILN = (1, 2), therefore, the cache line created by that statement can survive till the next execution of level 2 and the read references to x in line (8) will result in cache hits no matter how many epochs are executed at level 1.

```
(1)  DOALL i = 1, 1000     Level  var    ILN
(2)     x(i) = ...           1     x    (0, 2)
(3)  END DOALL
     INV 1
──────────────────────────────────────────
(4)  DO i = 1, N
(5)     DOALL j = 1, 1000
(6)        ... = x(j)...     2     x    (1, 2)
(7)        x(j) = ...
(8)     END DOALL
        INV 2
──────────────────────────────────────────
(9)        ...               3
        INV 3
──────────────────────────────────────────
(10) END DO
```

Figure 7: The write interference pattern.

### Counter Overflow and Timestamp Size

Many of the timestamp based methods, such as the version control method and TPI, suffer from the counter overflow problem. Once the timestamp counter is reset, additional actions must be taken to ensure the cache coherence. Our method does not have the counter overflow problem. Using a shorter timestamp only results in the performance penalty for not being able to preserve the cache line for a longer time, while in other methods, using a shorter timestamp results in an additional overhead for dealing with counter overflow. Besides, TBSIS preserves cache lines for $2^{n-1}$ static levels which is usually much larger than the $2^{n-1}$ dynamic epochs. Thus, our method can use a shorter timestamp to provide the same cache performance.

```
(1)   DO i = 1, 1000        Level    var    ILN
(2)       DO j = 1, N
(3)           DOALL k = 1, 1000
(4)               ...                           1
(5)           END DOALL
              INV 1
```

```
(6)       END DO
          INV 1  ! extra INV instruction
(7)       DOALL j = 1, 1000
(8)           ... = x(j)...
(9)           x(j) = ...              2      x      (1, 2)
(10)      END DOALL
          INV 2
```

(11) END DO

Figure 8: The unknown epoch number pattern.

## 6  Performance Study

To compare TBSIS with other schemes, simulations were conducted on three parallel programs for three software cache coherence protocols: TS1, TPI and TBSIS. We study both cache hit ratio and total number of cycles for memory reference, which includes the memory reference cycles and overhead cycles.

The benchmarks are written in CRAFT FORTRAN and are executed on a CRAY-T3D. The simulation is carried out by adding code in the source program that simulates the cache in each processor. For each memory reference that refers to the shared data, a routine is called to simulate the effect of the cache. We assume that no interprocedural analysis is performed by the compiler and thus, all the cache lines are invalidated at the subroutine boundaries.

Table 2: General characteristics.

|  | lp | tscf | ep |
|---|---|---|---|
| total references($\times 10^6$) | 70.8 | 114.4 | 33.6 |
| % of data read | 73.1 | 65. 0 | 62.3 |
| % of data write | 26.9 | 35.0 | 37.7 |
| number of epoch | 5869 | 3041 | 4148 |
| number of level | 11 | 18 | 8 |

The first benchmark program, *lp*, uses Gauss-Siedel iterations to solve Laplace equations on a $64 \times 64$ discretized unit square with Dirichlet boundary conditions. The second program *tscf*, is a program that simulates the evolution of a self-gravitating system using a self consistent field approach. The third program *ep* is the NAS's embarrassingly parallel benchmark [2]. The outermost loop iteration number of the *ep* program is reduced by a factor of 256 to shorten the simulation time. Table 2 shows the general characteristics of the three benchmarks used in our experiment. The epoch number is obtained from the execution of the program on 32 processors. The level numbers are the maximum level number among all subroutines in each program.

The architecture simulated consists of direct-mapped, write through caches. The block size is one word. Only the references to the shared data are simulated. We use 6–bit timestamp for TPI and TBSIS. Table 3 shows the simulation results for different cache sizes using 16 processors. Table 4 shows the result for 64K word cache using different number of processors.

Table 3: Hit ratio for different cache size (16 PEs).

| scheme | prog | 16KW | 32KW | 64KW | 128KW |
|---|---|---|---|---|---|
| TS1 | ep | 74.33 | 81.97 | 85.28 | 93.71 |
|  | lp | 85.64 | 97.86 | 97.86 | 97.86 |
|  | tscf | 70.27 | 70.62 | 70.62 | 70.62 |
| TPI | ep | 73.50 | 74.74 | 75.89 | 83.60 |
|  | lp | 82.82 | 88.94 | 88.95 | 88.95 |
|  | tscf | 70.27 | 70.62 | 70.62 | 70.62 |
| TBSIS | ep | 74.33 | 81.97 | 85.28 | 93.71 |
|  | lp | 85.64 | 97.86 | 97.86 | 97.86 |
|  | tscf | 70.27 | 70.62 | 70.62 | 70.62 |

Table 4: Hit ratio for different PE numbers (64KW cache).

| scheme | prog | 16 PEs | 32 PEs | 64 PEs |
|---|---|---|---|---|
| TS1 | ep | 85.28 | 92.84 | 96.51 |
|  | lp | 97.86 | 95.39 | 90.98 |
|  | tscf | 70.62 | 70.61 | 70.59 |
| TPI | ep | 75.89 | 82.72 | 85.65 |
|  | lp | 88.95 | 86.20 | 82.18 |
|  | tscf | 70.62 | 70.61 | 70.59 |
| TBSIS | ep | 85.28 | 92.84 | 96.51 |
|  | lp | 97.86 | 95.39 | 90.98 |
|  | tscf | 70.62 | 70.61 | 70.59 |

For the *ep* program, 64k word cache size is not large enough to exploit all the data locality in 16 processor systems. Therefore, the hit ratio increases with the number of processors, since the total cache size increases with the number of processors. In a 16 processor system, TS1 and TBSIS have better hit ratio than TPI. TS1 actually has a slightly higher cache hit ratio. But the difference is so small that it doesn't show in the table where values are rounded off. For the *lp* program, 64K word cache size is large enough to exploit all the possible data locality. Therefore, when the number of processors is increased, the hit ratio decreases significantly. TS1 and TBSIS have better hit ratio than TPI. TS1 actually has a slightly higher cache hit ratio when the cache size is large enough. But the difference is so small that it doesn't show in the table. For *tscf* program, the cache hit ratio is almost the same when the number of processors increases. All the three cache coherence methods have exactly the same cache hit ratio. The reason is the extensive usage of subroutine in this program. Without interprocedural analysis, the software cache coherence methods fail to exploit most of inter-level locality.

Table 5: Total memory reference cycles($\times 10^6$).

| prog. | PE | TPI | TS1(ser.) | TS1(par.) | TBSIS |
|---|---|---|---|---|---|
| ep | 16 | 21.88 | 14.55 | 14.70 | 14.19 |
|  | 32 | 8.14 | 4.36 | 4.52 | 4.00 |
|  | 64 | 3.47 | 1.62 | 1.77 | 1.26 |
| lp | 16 | 23.49 | 10.42 | 8.26 | 8.13 |
|  | 32 | 14.12 | 8.49 | 6.33 | 6.20 |
|  | 64 | 8.80 | 7.30 | 5.14 | 5.01 |
| tscf | 16 | 89.09 | 93.17 | 89.29 | 89.10 |
|  | 32 | 44.56 | 48.64 | 44.76 | 44.57 |
|  | 64 | 22.30 | 26.37 | 22.50 | 22.30 |

Table 5 compares the total cycles for memory ref-

Table 6: Runtime overhead percentage.

| prog. | PE | TPI | TS1(ser.) | TS1(par.) | TBSIS |
|-------|-----|-----|-----------|-----------|-------|
| ep    | 16  | 0.0 | 2.6       | 3.6       | 0.1   |
|       | 32  | 0.0 | 8.6       | 11.7      | 0.2   |
|       | 64  | 0.1 | 23.1      | 29.9      | 0.3   |
| lp    | 16  | 0.0 | 22.1      | 1.8       | 0.1   |
|       | 32  | 0.0 | 27.1      | 2.3       | 0.2   |
|       | 64  | 0.1 | 31.5      | 2.9       | 0.2   |
| tscf  | 16  | 0.0 | 4.4       | 0.2       | 0.0   |
|       | 32  | 0.0 | 8.4       | 0.4       | 0.0   |
|       | 64  | 0.0 | 15.5      | 0.9       | 0.0   |

erences. The total cycles consist of memory reference cycles and protocol overhead cycles. We assume that a cache hit takes 1 cycle, a parallel invalidation in TS1 and TBSIS takes 2 cycles, a serial invalidation to invalidate a page of 512 words or a certain cache word in TS1 takes 1 cycle, a cache miss takes 40 cycles. Table 6 shows the runtime overhead percentage of all the protocols. TPI incurs the least runtime overhead. However, it has lower cache hit ratio than both TS1 and TBSIS. Thus the performance of TPI is worse than that of TS1 and TBSIS. The overhead incurred by TS1 with serial invalidation ranges from 2.6% to 22.1% in 16 processor system and 15.5% to 31.5% in 64 processor system. With parallel invalidation scheme, TS1 greatly reduces the runtime overhead. However, we still observe 29.9% overhead in *ep* program with 64 processors. Since TBSIS incurs constant overhead in each epoch and achieves almost the same cache hit ratio as TS1, its performance is better. TBSIS is faster than other methods in the *ep* and *lp* programs. For the *tscf* program, TPI has slightly higher performance than TBSIS. The speedup of TBSIS is shown in Table 7.

Table 7: Percentage speedup of TBSIS.

| prog | PE | TS1(ser.) | TS1(para.) | TPI   |
|------|-----|-----------|------------|-------|
| ep   | 16  | 2.5       | 3.6        | 54.2  |
|      | 32  | 9.2       | 13.1       | 103.8 |
|      | 64  | 28.7      | 41.1       | 176.5 |
| lp   | 16  | 28.2      | 1.7        | 186.4 |
|      | 32  | 36.9      | 2.1        | 127.8 |
|      | 64  | 45.7      | 2.7        | 75.7  |
| tscf | 16  | 4.6       | 0.2        | 0.0   |
|      | 32  | 9.1       | 0.4        | 0.0   |
|      | 64  | 18.3      | 0.9        | 0.0   |

Table 8: Effect of invalidation cycle.

| cycles | TS1(para. inv.) | | TBSIS | |
|--------|----------|---------|----------|---------|
|        | overhead | percent | overhead | percent |
| 2      | 0.147    | 2.3%    | 0.012    | 0.2%    |
| 4      | 0.294    | 4.5%    | 0.024    | 0.4%    |
| 8      | 0.588    | 8.8%    | 0.048    | 0.8%    |
| 16     | 1.176    | 16.0%   | 0.096    | 1.5%    |

Table 8 shows the effect of invalidation cycles on the total performance for both TS1 and TBSIS. We study the case of the *lp* program in 32 processor system. As shown in the table, the performance of TS1 is greatly affected by the efficiency of invalidation scheme while TBSIS sustains a graceful degradation and achieves reasonably good performance with slow invalidation.

## 7 Conclusion

In this paper, we propose a new software cache coherence protocol based on the timestamp concept. Our method combines the ideas in TS1 and TPI and overcomes their limitations. Furthermore, with improved compiler techniques, the performance of our protocol can be further improved without extra hardware and runtime overheads. In our protocol, the timestamp is used for the invalidation of cache lines. By using the timestamp, selective invalidation of O(1) time is possible. This scheme has the characteristic of high cache performance and low hardware and runtime overhead.

## References

[1] Aho, A.V., Sethi, R. and Ullman, J.D. "Compilers: Principles, Techniques and Tools." Addison-Wesley, Reading, Massachusetts, 1986.

[2] Bailey, D. et al. "The NAS Parallel Benchmarks." RNR Technical report, RNR-94-007, March, 1994.

[3] H. Cheong and A. Veidenbaum "Compiler-directed Cache Management for Multiprocessor." *IEEE Computer*, 23(6):39-47, June 1990.

[4] H. Cheong, "Life-span strategy - A Compiler-based Approach to Cache Coherence." In *Proceedings of 1992 International Conference on Supercomputing*, 1992.

[5] T. Chiueh, "A Generational Algorithm to Multiprocessor Cache Coherence." In *Proceedings of the 1993 International Conference on Parallel Processing*, pages I20-I24, 1993.

[6] L. Choi and P. Yew "A Compiler-Directed Cache Coherence Scheme with Improved Intertask Locality." In *Supercomputing'94*, pages 773-782, 1994.

[7] L. Choi and P. Yew "Interprocedural Array Data–Flow Analysis for Cache Coherence." In *8th Intl. Workshop on Languages and Compilers for Parallel Comp.*, pages 6.1-6.15, Aug. 1995.

[8] E.Darnell and K. Kennedy "Cache Coherence Using Local Knowledge." In *Supercomputing'93*, pages 720-729, 1993.

[9] A. Louri and H. Sung. "A Compiler Directed Cache Coherence Scheme With Fast and Parallel Explicit Invalidation." In *Proc. of the 1992 International Conference on Parallel Processing*, pages 2-9, Aug 1992.

[10] S. Min and J. Baer. "Design and Analysis of a Scalable Cache Coherence Scheme Based on Clocks and Timestamps." *IEEE Trans. on Parallel and Dist. Systems*, 3(1):25-44, Jan. 1992.

# Scheduling of Wavefront Parallelism on Scalable Shared-memory Multiprocessors*

Naraig Manjikian and Tarek S. Abdelrahman
Department of Electrical and Computer Engineering
University of Toronto
Toronto, Ontario, Canada M5S 3G4
email: {nmanjiki,tsa}@eecg.toronto.edu

**Abstract**—*Tiling exploits temporal reuse carried by an outer loop of a loop nest to enhance cache locality. Loop skewing is typically required to make tiling legal. This restricts parallelism to wavefronts in the tiled iteration space. For a small number of processors, wavefront parallelism can be efficiently exploited using dynamic self-scheduling with a large tile size. Such a strategy enhances* intratile *locality, but does not necessarily enhance* intertile *locality. We show that dynamic self-scheduling performs poorly on scalable shared-memory multiprocessors where smaller tiles are necessary to provide sufficient parallelism—smaller tiles place greater importance on intertile locality. We propose static scheduling strategies which enhance intertile locality for small tiles. Results of experiments on a Convex SPP1000 multiprocessor demonstrate that our strategies outperform dynamic self-scheduling by a factor of up to 2.3 on 30 processors.*

## 1 Introduction

Scalable shared-memory multiprocessors (SSMMs) have become increasingly viable as platforms for high-performance computing by efficiently supporting coherent shared memory in hardware for large numbers of processors [2]. Examples include the Convex SPP1000 [3], the Stanford FLASH [5], and the University of Toronto NU-MAchine [12]. Although the memory in SSMMs is logically shared by all processors, it is physically distributed to provide scalability, as shown in Figure 1. As a result, memory accesses are non-uniform; access latency for remote memory is considerably higher than for local memory. SSMMs heavily rely on data caching to reduce the effective memory access latency. Consequently, both enhancing locality and exploiting parallelism are instrumental in achieving scaling performance.

A common locality-enhancing technique for loop nests is *tiling*, also known as *blocking* [1]. Tiling is particularly effective in exploiting temporal reuse carried by an outer loop. Iterations from the original loop nest are re-ordered and blocked into units of *tiles*. The data used by

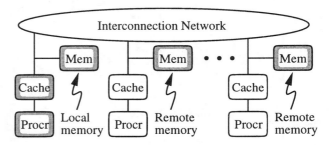

Figure 1: Scalable shared-memory multiprocessor

one tile is loaded once into the cache and retained there for subsequent reuse during the execution of the tile. A loop nest can be legally tiled if it is fully permutable, i.e., if none of its loop-carried dependence vectors have negative elements [13]. Loop skewing [1] is used to eliminate any negative elements and produce a fully-permutable loop nest. However, loop skewing also results in loop-carried dependences in outer loops after tiling. These loop-carried dependences limit the available coarse-grain parallelism to *wavefronts* in the tiled iteration space. Tiles within each wavefront may be executed concurrently, but synchronization between wavefronts is required to satisfy dependences.

In this paper, we consider the problem of *scheduling* the execution of a tiled loop nest to exploit the wavefront parallelism on scalable shared-memory multiprocessors. We demonstrate that the commonly-used strategy of dynamic self-scheduling, while adequate for small-scale multiprocessors, performs poorly on SSMMs. This is because dynamic self-scheduling cannot simultaneously enhance locality and provide sufficient parallelism. We apply two static scheduling strategies in a manner which enhances locality for a large number of processors while still providing sufficient parallelism. We provide analysis and experimental results on a Convex SPP1000 multiprocessor to demonstrate the superiority of our static scheduling strategies.

The remainder of this paper is organized as follows. Section 2 gives background on tiling loop nests and wavefront parallelism. Section 3 presents the two static scheduling strategies and analytically evaluates their benefits. Section 4 provides a comparative experimental evaluation of all three scheduling strategies on the Convex. Section 5 briefly outlines related work. Finally, Section 6 gives concluding remarks.

*This research is supported by grants from NSERC (Canada) and ITRC (Ontario). The use of the Convex SPP1000 was provided by the University of Michigan Center for Parallel Computing.

```
do t=1,T
  do j=2,N−1
    do i=2,N−1
      a[i,j] = (a[i,j]+a[i+1,j]+a[i−1,j]
             +a[i,j+1]+a[i,j−1]) / 5
```

(a)

```
do jj=2,N−1+T,B
  do ii=2,N−1+T,B
    do t=1,T
      do j=max(jj,2+t),min(jj+B−1,N−1+t)
        do i=max(ii,2+t),min(ii+B−1,N−1+t)
          a[i−t,j−t] = (a[i−t,j−t]+a[i+1−t,j−t]+a[i−1−t,j−t]
                     +a[i−t,j+1−t]+a[i−t,j−1−t]) / 5
```

(b)

Figure 2: Tiling the SOR loop nest

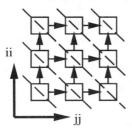

Figure 3: Dependences and wavefronts

## 2 Tiling and Wavefront Parallelism

The SOR loop nest in Figure 2(a) is used to illustrate tiling and the resulting wavefront parallelism. The outer loop carries reuse and the dependences for this loop nest have the distance vectors: $\{(1,0,0), (1,-1,0), (1,0,-1), (0,1,0), (0,0,1)\}$. The loop nest is not fully permutable, and loop skewing must be applied. Both inner loops $i$ and $j$ are skewed by one iteration with respect to loop $t$, resulting in the transformed distance vectors: $\{(1,1,1), (1,0,1), (1,1,0), (0,1,0), (0,0,1)\}$. The loop nest can be then tiled legally by first strip-mining the skewed $i$ and $j$ loops by a factor of $B$, then by permuting the resulting $ii$ and $jj$ loops to the outermost level, as in Figure 2(b). The $ii$ and $jj$ loops carry the same dependences as the $i$ and $j$ loops prior to tiling, hence neither of the outer loops can be executed in parallel. The only available parallelism is along the wavefronts shown in Figure 3; each square represents a $B \times B$ tile of iterations from the original loop nest.

There are two general approaches for exploiting wavefront parallelism. The first is to use additional loop skewing to obtain DOALL loops which reflect the parallelism in each wavefront. For the SOR example, skewing the tiled iteration space shown in Figure 3 yields the iteration space shown in Figure 4. The $ii$ loop iterations may be executed in parallel. The outermost $jj$ loop remains sequential, requiring global synchronization of all processors between successive iterations. Because the number of tiles that can be executed in parallel varies in each wavefront, processors may not be fully utilized between global synchronizations. For example, the middle wavefront in Figure 4 has three

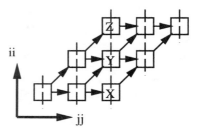

Figure 4: Exploiting parallelism with inner DOALL loops

tiles labelled X, Y, and Z. With two processors executing in parallel, both processors are initially busy executing tiles X and Y. However, one processor must remain idle until the remaining tile Z is executed because of the global synchronization required for the DOALL loop.

The second approach to exploit wavefront parallelism is to treat the two outer loops as DOACROSS loops and execute the independent tiles in each wavefront with dynamic self-scheduling. Processors which become idle obtain the next unassigned tile. Loop-carried dependences are enforced by appropriate synchronization prior to executing the tile to ensure that adjacent tiles in the preceding wavefront have been completed. This approach avoids global synchronization and effectively utilizes idle processors, allowing portions of different wavefronts to proceed concurrently, albeit local synchronization is required between tiles. Consequently, dynamic self-scheduling has been the approach of choice in scheduling wavefront parallelism [13].

### 2.1 Tile Size, Parallelism, and Locality

The tile size has a significant impact on the performance of a tiled loop nest because it determines both the degree of parallelism and the extent to which locality is enhanced. With wavefront parallelism, a smaller tile size increases the number of wavefronts and, more importantly, increases the number of independent tiles in each wavefront. Hence, the degree of parallelism increases with smaller tile sizes, although the frequency of synchronization also increases.

The tile size also dictates the extent of locality enhancement when loop skewing is required for tiling. We classify locality into two types: *intratile* locality and *intertile* locality. Intratile locality is the primary result of applying tiling to capture the temporal reuse carried by the outer loop in the original loop nest; data for each tile is loaded once into the cache, then reused within the same tile. Intertile locality results from exploiting temporal reuse across adjacent tiles. Such reuse arises from the data access patterns created by loop skewing, as illustrated for SOR in Figure 5. The iteration and data spaces of the original SOR loop nest are shown in Figure 5(a). With loop skewing and tiling, each iteration of the original outer loop executed within a tile accesses a slightly different portion of the array, as shown in Figure 5(b). Adjacent tiles in the iteration space access overlapping regions in the data space, as shown

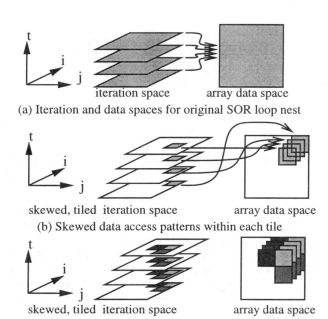

(a) Iteration and data spaces for original SOR loop nest

skewed, tiled iteration space          array data space

(b) Skewed data access patterns within each tile

skewed, tiled iteration space          array data space

(c) Overlapping array regions swept by adjacent tiles

Figure 5: Intertile data reuse for the SOR loop nest

in Figure 5(c). This overlap gives rise to intertile reuse. When adjacent tiles are executed by the same processor, data elements in overlapping regions are retained in the cache, which reduces the number of cache misses incurred to load the data referenced in successive tiles. That is, data in the overlapping regions is loaded only once then reused not only within a tile, but also in adjacent tiles. In this case, intertile locality is enhanced. On the other hand, when adjacent tiles are executed by different processors, cache misses are incurred by each processor to load all the data referenced within each tile, including the data in the overlapping regions. In this case, intertile locality is lost.

The impact of tile size on intratile and intertile locality is illustrated in Figure 6. The shaded regions represent the data accessed by adjacent tiles, as in Figure 5(c). The overlapping regions correspond to the intersection of the data accessed by different tiles. For a given number of iterations in the original outer loop, the amount of data in the overlapping regions is relatively small compared to the total amount of data accessed by the tile when the tile size is large. Consequently, a large tile size enhances intratile locality and diminishes the impact of intertile locality. In contrast, for the same number of iterations and a small tile size, the amount of data in the overlapping regions is a much larger fraction of the total amount of data accessed by the tile. Hence, a small tile size increases the importance of intertile locality.

## 2.2  Self-scheduling and Intertile Locality

Dynamic self-scheduling is adequate for exploiting wavefront parallelism in tiled loop nests for small-scale shared-memory multiprocessors. With a limited number

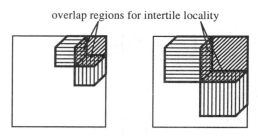

Figure 6: Impact of tile size on locality

of processors, a large tile size generally provides an adequate degree of parallelism. Consequently, intratile locality is enhanced because a large tile size captures most of the reuse from the original loop nest within a single tile, and intertile locality has little impact on performance.

However, dynamic self-scheduling is not appropriate for scalable shared-memory multiprocessors for two reasons. First, a large number of processors requires a relatively smaller tile size to result in sufficient parallelism. A small tile size reduces intratile locality and places greater importance on intertile locality. Dynamic self-scheduling is not likely to enhance intertile locality since tiles are assigned arbitrarily to idle processors. The second reason is that cache misses which result from the reduced intertile locality with small tile sizes are likely to be incurred for remote, rather than local, memory due to the arbitrary assignment of tiles to processors. The performance degradation resulting from these misses may be significant.

## 3  Scheduling for Intertile Locality

In this section, we describe how two common scheduling strategies, namely *static cyclic* and *static block*, can be applied to exploit wavefront parallelism in a manner which enhances intertile locality for the smaller tile sizes which are necessary to provide sufficient parallelism on SSMMs. The static scheduling strategies are then compared with dynamic self-scheduling on the basis of runtime overhead, synchronization requirements, and locality enhancement.

### 3.1  Static Cyclic Scheduling

Static cyclic scheduling assigns rows of horizontally-adjacent tiles to the same processor, as shown in Figure 7. In this manner, temporal intertile reuse along each row of tiles is exploited by one processor to enhance intertile locality. The cyclic mapping of rows of tiles to processors distributes the workload in each wavefront evenly among processors to fully exploit the available parallelism.

Static cyclic scheduling improves over dynamic self-scheduling in three ways. First, cyclic scheduling enhances intertile locality for horizontally-adjacent tiles, whereas dynamic self-scheduling does not necessarily exploit any intertile reuse. Second, synchronization to enforce loop-carried dependences is required only for vertically-adjacent tiles, since horizontally-adjacent tiles are executed in the correct order by the same processor. Third, the scheduling

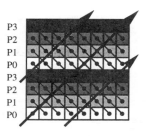

Figure 7: Static cyclic scheduling of tiles

overhead is reduced since the assignment of tiles to processors is determined statically. However, cyclic scheduling still requires synchronization for each tile to enforce dependences, and not all of the intertile reuse is exploited.

## 3.2 Static Block Scheduling

Static block scheduling assigns contiguous blocks of tiles to the same processor, as shown in Figure 8. In this manner, all of the intertile reuse within a block of horizontally- and vertically-adjacent tiles is exploited by one processor to enhance intertile locality. However, the parallelism is not exploited efficiently for the original wavefronts shown in Figure 8(a) because a portion of the processors is left idle for the few initial and few final wavefronts. The block assignment of tiles to processors precludes the use of additional processors even when there is a sufficient number of tiles which can be executed in parallel. Consequently, it takes longer for all processors to become active, and it takes longer for execution to complete.

Block scheduling requires the use of modified wavefronts as shown in Figure 8(b) to provide greater parallelism. This involves rotating wavefronts such that the number of independent tiles in the largest wavefront is exactly equal to the number of processors. This rotation corresponds to the selection of a different *scheduling vector*[1] [4]. The scheduling vector is $(1, 1)$ for the original wavefronts in Figure 8(a). The scheduling vector for the modified wavefronts in Figure 8(b) is given by $(\lfloor (N + T)/(B \cdot P) \rfloor, 1)$, where $N + T$ is the number of iterations (with skewing), $B$ is the tile size, and $P$ is the number of processors. The new scheduling vector preserves the loop-carried dependences, but reduces the time before all processors become active in parallel execution and reduces the completion time.

Static block scheduling improves over both dynamic and cyclic scheduling in two ways. First, block scheduling exploits all intertile reuse, except at block boundaries. Second, synchronization to enforce loop-carried dependences is required only for tiles on block boundaries; no synchronization is required for adjacent interior tiles, since they are executed in the correct order by the same processor. Similar to cyclic scheduling, the scheduling overhead is also reduced since the assignment of tiles to processors is determined statically.

---

[1]A scheduling vector is orthogonal to the wavefronts, and hence defines their orientation in the tiled iteration space.

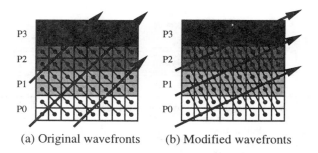

(a) Original wavefronts     (b) Modified wavefronts

Figure 8: Static block scheduling of tiles

## 3.3 Comparison of Scheduling Strategies

The scheduling strategies are compared on the basis of *runtime overhead, synchronization, parallelism*, and *intertile locality enhancement*. The features of each strategy are summarized in Table 1. Dynamic self-scheduling incurs runtime overhead, and requires synchronization for both horizontally- and vertically-adjacent tiles. A synchronization counter is needed for each row of tiles. Static cyclic scheduling requires synchronization only for vertically-adjacent tiles, but counters are still required for each row of tiles. Finally, static block scheduling requires synchronization only for vertically-adjacent tiles on block boundaries. The number of synchronization counters required is therefore equal only to the number of processors.

The impact of the reduced parallelism for block scheduling can be shown by determining the theoretical completion time for each strategy, which is given in Table 1. We define a time step as the theoretical execution time for each tile (i.e., neglecting the impact of synchronization and locality); the completion time is expressed in these units. For simplicity, we assume no variance in the computation per tile. For the example in Figure 8(b), block scheduling takes 22 time steps to execute all tiles. In contrast, dynamic and cyclic scheduling with the same tile size take only 19 time steps. The reduction in parallelism for block scheduling can be mitigated with a smaller tile size that allows the use of a scheduling vector which further reduces the time before all processors become active.

The extent of intertile locality enhancement for each scheduling strategy is shown in Table 1. The importance of enhancing intertile locality can be demonstrated by estimating the total latency for cache hits and misses that occur during the execution of a single tile. Again, we use the SOR loop nest as an example. For a tile size of $B \times B$, and $T$ iterations in the original outer loop of the loop nest being tiled, the total number of data accesses to the cache within each tile is given by $B^2 T$. This number is conservative because register locality reduces the number of cache accesses. Each access to the cache has a latency of $C$ clock cycles. Some fraction of these references miss in the cache and incur the additional cache miss latency $M$. For dynamic self-scheduling, there is no intertile locality, and in the worst case, misses are incurred for all data elements accessed *for the first time* within the tile. The number of such elements is given by $B^2 + (2B - 1)(T - 1)$,

Table 1: Comparison of scheduling strategies for tiling

|  | Dynamic | Cyclic | Block |
|---|---|---|---|
| runtime overhead | yes | no | no |
| synch., #counters | horizontal/vertical *tiles*, $\left\lceil \frac{N+T}{B} \right\rceil$ | vertical *tiles*, $\left\lceil \frac{N+T}{B} \right\rceil$ | vertical *processors*, $P$ |
| completion time | $\left\lceil \frac{N+T}{B} \right\rceil^2 / P + P - 1$ | $\left\lceil \frac{N+T}{B} \right\rceil^2 / P + P - 1$ | $\left( P - 1 + \left\lceil \frac{N+T}{B} \right\rceil \right) \cdot \left\lceil \frac{N+T}{B \cdot P} \right\rceil$ |
| intertile locality | none | horizontal tiles | horizontal/vertical tiles |

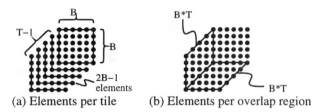

(a) Elements per tile      (b) Elements per overlap region

Figure 9: Number of data elements within a tile

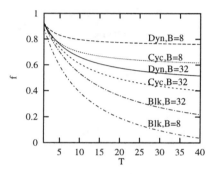

Figure 10: Fraction of miss latency per tile

as shown in Figure 9(a). This number must then be divided by $L$, the cache line size, to arrive at an *estimate* for the number of cache misses. The total latency in clock cycles for memory accesses is then given by multiplying by the cache miss latency $M$. Finally, the total memory access latency, including the cache accesses is given by $B^2TC + (B^2 + (2B-1)(T-1))(M/L)$. To measure the extent of locality enhancement for different values of $B$ and $T$, it is useful to express the fraction $f$ of the total memory access latency per tile that is due to cache misses, which is given by

$$f_{dyn} = \frac{(B^2 + (2B-1)(T-1))(M/L)}{B^2TC + (B^2 + (2B-1)(T-1))(M/L)}.$$

A similar derivation can be made for static cyclic scheduling and static block scheduling. Because there is intertile locality for adjacent tiles, fewer misses are incurred per tile. The reduction in the number of misses is determined by the number of elements in one or both of the overlap regions shown in Figure 9(b). Once again, the fraction of the latency due to misses can be determined. Hence,

$$f_{cyc} = \frac{(B^2 + BT - 2B - T + 1)(M/L)}{B^2TC + (B^2 + BT - 2B - T + 1)(M/L)},$$

and

$$f_{blk} = \frac{(B^2 - 2B + 1)(M/L)}{B^2TC + (B^2 - 2B + 1)(M/L)}.$$

Figure 10 plots the fraction $f$ for different tile sizes $B$ and different values of $T$. The cache line size is $L = 4$ elements, the cache access latency is $C = 1$ clock cycle, and the cache miss latency is $M = 50$ clock cycles. As $T$ increases, $f$ decreases for all three strategies because reuse carried by the original outer loop is captured within

the tile through intratile locality. However, $f$ decreases far more rapidly for block scheduling. This is because block scheduling benefits from enhancing *intertile* locality by reducing the number of cache misses by an amount proportional to the overlap regions in Figure 9(b). Furthermore, for a given value of $T$, $f$ is further reduced with a smaller tile size for block scheduling because intertile locality is more critical when the tile size is small (see Figure 6). In contrast, for a given value of $T$, $f$ *increases* when the tile size is reduced for both dynamic and cyclic scheduling. This is because dynamic and cyclic scheduling do not enhance intertile locality to the same extent for small tile sizes as block scheduling.

In conclusion, all the scheduling strategies considered provide sufficient parallelism with small tile sizes, but small tiles require exploiting intertile reuse for locality. Dynamic scheduling does not exploit any intertile reuse. Cyclic scheduling exploits some intertile reuse while providing the same parallelism for the same tile size. Hence, it is expected to perform better than dynamic scheduling. Block scheduling exploits all intertile reuse, but with slightly less parallelism than either dynamic or cyclic scheduling for the same tile size. However, the benefit of enhancing locality with block scheduling may outweigh the loss of some parallelism and provide the best overall performance. The relative performance of the three strategies for small tile sizes on a large number of processors depends on the tradeoff between parallelism and locality. This tradeoff is explored experimentally in the next section.

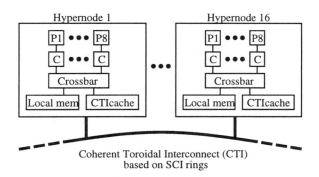

Figure 11: Architecture of the Convex SPP1000

## 4 Experimental Evaluation

We report the results of experiments conducted on a Convex SPP1000 Exemplar multiprocessor [3]. The Convex SPP1000 consists of up to 16 *hypernodes*, each containing 8 processors with a crossbar connection to 512 Mbytes of common memory, as shown in Figure 11. The crossbar provides uniform access to the local memory for processors within a hypernode. Each processor is a Hewlett-Packard PA7100 RISC microprocessor running at 100 MHz with separate 1-Mbyte instruction and data caches. The cache access latency is 1 clock cycle or 10 nsec, and the cache line size is 32 bytes. Hypernodes are connected together with the Coherent Toroidal Interconnect (CTI), a system of rings based on the SCI standard interconnect, clocked at 250 MHz. The CTI permits processors to access memory in any hypernode through coherent global shared memory.

The Convex SPP1000 is a non-uniform memory access (NUMA) multiprocessor. Cache misses to retrieve data from the local hypernode memory incur a latency of 50 cycles, or 500 nsec. However, misses to retrieve data from remote hypernode memory through the CTI incur a latency of 200 cycles, or 2 $\mu$sec. A unique feature of the Convex SPP1000 is the CTIcache, which is a portion of the memory in each hypernode reserved for caching data from other hypernodes in order to reduce the effective memory latency for remote memory accesses. Remote data is retrieved in units of 64 bytes, but supplied to processors in 32-byte cache lines from the CTIcache (i.e., processors do cache remote data). The remote memory access latency is incurred once to load data into the CTIcache, and subsequent accesses by any processor which hit in the CTIcache incur the same access latency as the local memory, i.e., 50 cycles instead of 200 cycles. The Convex SPP1000 provides hardware monitoring for accurate measurement of the number of cache misses and the corresponding latencies to local and remote memory. Our experiments were conducted on a 32-processor Convex SPP1000 consisting of 4 hypernodes. The CTIcache size in each hypernode is 16 Mbytes. Two processors are reserved for system use, leaving 30 processors available for experimentation.

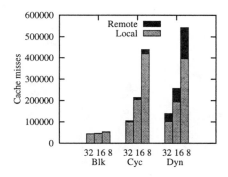

(a) Avg. cache misses for 16 processors

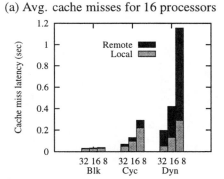

(b) Avg. miss latency for 16 processors

Figure 12: Cache misses for tiled SOR

We first report results obtained from parallel execution of the tiled SOR loop nest. The array size is 1024 × 1024 elements, and each element is an 8-byte floating point value. The number of iterations in the original outer loop is $T = 40$. We use tile sizes of 32 × 32, 16 × 16, and 8 × 8 for each of the three scheduling strategies. Larger tile sizes are not considered because they do not provide sufficient parallelism for a large number of processors. Figure 12 shows the average number of cache misses and corresponding miss latencies per processor on 16 processors (i.e., 2 hypernodes). Both the number of misses and the latencies are broken down into local and remote. Figure 12(a) indicates that block scheduling incurs far fewer misses for a given tile size than dynamic or cyclic scheduling, which agrees with the analytical observations in Section 3. The fraction of misses to remote memory is small for block and cyclic scheduling (4% and 5% respectively for a tile size of 8). This fraction is significantly larger for dynamic self-scheduling (27% for a tile size of 8). Hence, the impact of the remote misses on the total cache miss latency shown in Figure 12(b) is more pronounced for dynamic self-scheduling because of the higher cost of remote misses. As the tile size is reduced, both the number of cache misses and the total miss latencies increase dramatically for both dynamic and cyclic scheduling. In particular, the resulting miss latency for dynamic self-scheduling with a tile size of 8 is *30* times larger than for block scheduling. This clearly

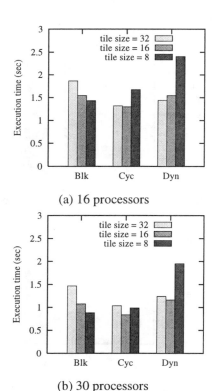

(a) 16 processors

(b) 30 processors

Figure 13: Execution times for tiled SOR

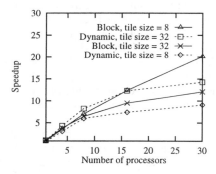

Figure 14: Speedup for tiled SOR

demonstrates the detriment of failing to provide intertile locality when the tile size is small. Block scheduling is much less sensitive to a reduction in the tile size because it exploits all intertile reuse.

The effect of the cache behavior on execution time for the tiled SOR loop is shown in Figure 13 for 16 processors, and also for 30 processors. The results indicate that static scheduling performs better than dynamic scheduling for a large number of processors, but only block scheduling improves consistently when the tile size is reduced to provide greater parallelism. Although the results indicate that cyclic scheduling with an intermediate tile size may

```
do t=1,T
   do j=2,N-1
      do i=2,N-1
         b[i,j] = (a[i+1,j]+a[i-1,j]
                   +a[i,j+1]+a[i,j-1]) / 4
   do j=2,N-1
      do i=2,N-1
         a[i,j] = b[i,j]
```

Figure 15: The Jacobi loop nest sequence

perform better than block scheduling, it may be difficult to predict an optimal tile size for cyclic scheduling which achieves the appropriate balance between sufficient parallelism and sufficient locality. Later results in this section will confirm this observation. Furthermore, block scheduling simplifies the selection of the tile size for a large number of processors. It is sufficient to choose a small tile size for greater parallelism; intertile locality is preserved with block scheduling. Hence, we focus on comparing block scheduling with dynamic scheduling for the largest and smallest tile sizes.

Finally, the parallel speedup of tiled SOR for various numbers of processors over the sequential *untiled* loop nest executed on a single processor is shown in Figure 14. The speedup of block scheduling and dynamic self-scheduling are compared for the largest and smallest tile sizes. When the number of processors is 8 or less, all memory accesses are confined within single hypernode, i.e., there are no remote memory accesses. Dynamic self-scheduling with a large tile size generates sufficient parallelism for the relatively small number of processors, and maximizes intratile locality. The larger tile size and the uniform memory access within a hypernode diminish the impact of intertile locality. Consequently, dynamic self-scheduling with the largest tile size performs the best. However, as the number of processors increases, a large tile size limits the speedup of dynamic self-scheduling due to insufficient parallelism. In addition, memory accesses span hypernodes and become non-uniform, which limits the speedup of dynamic self-scheduling, particularly when a smaller tile size is used to provide greater parallelism. Intertile locality is critical for small tile sizes, and dynamic self-scheduling does not exploit intertile reuse. In contrast, block scheduling with a small tile size provides sufficient parallelism while enhancing intertile locality, improving the speedup by a factor of 1.4 over dynamic self-scheduling at 30 processors.

Our scheduling techniques are applicable to any application which is tiled to exploit reuse carried by an outer loop. We present results for two more applications: the Jacobi loop nest sequence and the LL18 kernel from the Livermore Loops benchmark.

The Jacobi loop nest consists of two loop nests surrounded by an outer loop, as shown in Figure 15. There is reuse between the inner two loop nests in addition to the reuse carried by the outer loop. Tiling requires *fusion* [1] of the inner two loop nests to produce a single loop nest.

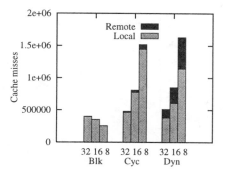

(a) Avg. cache misses for 16 processors

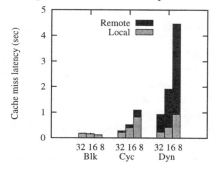

(b) Avg. miss latency for 16 processors

Figure 16: Cache misses for tiled Jacobi

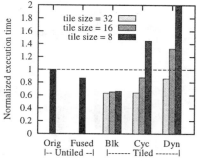

(a) 16 processors

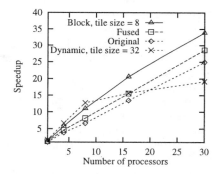

(b) 30 processors

Figure 17: Execution times for tiled Jacobi

Fusion exploits the reuse between the two inner loop nests in addition to enabling tiling. Dependences between the inner two loop nests require the application of *shift-and-peel* [9] to enable legal fusion. Once a single loop nest is obtained with fusion, loop skewing is required just as for the SOR loop nest to obtain a fully-permutable loop nest. The application of shift-and-peel to enable fusion results in dependences which require skewing the inner loops by *two* iterations with respect to the outer loop, rather than one as required for SOR. Once skewed, the loop nest is then tiled to exploit the reuse carried by the outer loop, and any of the three scheduling strategies discussed in the paper can be applied for parallel execution of the tiled loop nest. The final code is not shown due to space limitations, but is similar to the tiled SOR loop nest.

Figure 16 shows the average number of cache misses and corresponding miss latencies per processor for parallel execution of tiled Jacobi with the different scheduling strategies on 16 processors. The array sizes are $2048 \times 2048$ and the number of iterations in the original outer loop is $T = 10$. As before, the number of misses and the latencies are broken down into local and remote. The results are similar to those obtained for SOR. Block scheduling incurs the fewest cache misses as well as having the smallest fraction of remote misses. The cache latency for block scheduling is also the lowest. Dynamic self-scheduling incurs the greatest number of cache misses and a larger fraction of re-

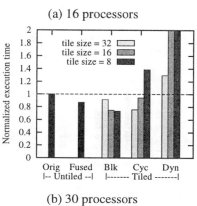

Figure 18: Speedup for Jacobi

mote misses, which results in a dramatic increase in cache miss latency as the tile size is reduced.

Normalized execution times for tiled Jacobi on 16 and 30 processors are shown in Figure 13. All execution times are normalized with respect to time obtained with parallel execution of the *original* code to facilitate comparison. The normalized execution time for fusion of the inner loops without tiling is also shown, since parallel execution of the fused loops is enabled by the shift-and-peel transformation [9]. Once again, the results for tiling are similar to those obtained for SOR. The dramatic increase in execution time for dynamic self-scheduling correlates with the

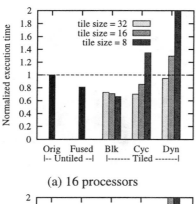

(a) 16 processors

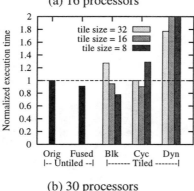

(b) 30 processors

Figure 19: Execution times for tiled LL18

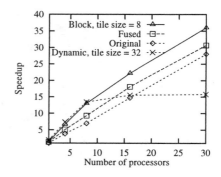

Figure 20: Speedup for LL18

skewing of the inner loops by *three* iterations. The tiled loop nest is scheduled with the different strategies just as for SOR and Jacobi. Normalized execution times for 16 and 30 processors are shown in Figure 19 for array sizes of $1024 \times 1024$ and $T = 10$ iterations in the original outer loop. The results are similar to those obtained for Jacobi. Fusion improves performance by exploiting reuse between the inner loop nests, but tiling with an appropriate scheduling strategy exploits all the reuse for the best performance. Once again, only block scheduling is successful in enhancing locality when the tile is reduced to provide sufficient parallelism for a large number of processors. The speedups for LL18 shown in Figure 20 also agree with the trends observed for Jacobi. Block scheduling improves the speedup at 30 processors by a factor of 2.3 over dynamic self-scheduling.

## 5  Related Work

There exists a large body of work dealing with the scheduling of parallel DOALL loops. Many scheduling strategies have been proposed to strike a balance between load balance and scheduling overhead. Examples include static scheduling [1], self-scheduling [1], guided self-scheduling [11], and factoring [6] to name a few. However, these strategies are not applicable when loops carry dependences, such as in wavefront parallelism.

Markatos and LeBlanc [10] propose Affinity-based Scheduling (AFS), and Li et al. [7] propose Locality-based Dynamic Scheduling (LDS) to schedule parallel DOALL loop iterations for locality as well as load balance. Both techniques address locality by initially assigning each processor a local set of independent iterations from a DOALL loop in a manner which corresponds to a distribution of the data. Load balance is promoted by having processors that become idle retrieve iterations from other processors. Neither AFS nor LDS are applicable for scheduling tiled loop nests with loop-carried dependences.

The scheduling of wavefront parallelism has been addressed by Wolf and Lam [13, 14] to enable parallel

increase in the cache miss latency. Block scheduling with a small tile size performs far better. Fusion exploits reuse between the inner two loops, but tiling goes further to exploit the reuse carried by the outer loop. To ensure that the full benefit of tiling is realized, the tiled loop nest must be scheduled appropriately.

Finally, the parallel speedup of tiled Jacobi for various numbers of processors over the original code executed on a single processor is shown in Figure 18. The speedup for block scheduling and dynamic self-scheduling is compared to the speedup from parallel execution of the original code and the fused version. The speedup for cyclic scheduling is not shown because its performance for small tile sizes is worse than block scheduling. Once again, dynamic self-scheduling with a large tile size is only effective in the absence of remote memory accesses, i.e., when the number of processors is 8 or less. In contrast, block scheduling with a small tile size improves the speedup by a factor of 1.8 over dynamic self-scheduling at 30 processors, and consistently outperforms even the parallel versions of the original and fused code.

The LL18 kernel from the Livermore Loop benchmark consists of *three* loop nests surrounded by an outer loop. A total of nine arrays are used, and there is reuse between the inner loop nests in addition to the reuse carried by the outer loop. Tiling requires fusion with the shift-and-peel transformation to produce a single loop nest, followed by execution of tiled loops. However, they do not distinguish between between intratile and intertile locality, and their experimental results are limited to small-scale multiprocessors with uniform memory access. Hence, they achieve good performance using dynamic self-scheduling with large tile sizes. In contrast, our work demonstrates that large tile sizes are not appropriate for scalable shared-memory multiprocessors with a large number of processors, and that dynamic self-scheduling performs poorly for small tiles because it does not enhance intertile locality.

Li [8] discusses a different notion of intertile reuse in an affinity tiling algorithm aimed at enhancing spatial locality for cache lines at tile boundaries. Unlike the tiling discussed in this paper, affinity tiling does not exploit temporal reuse carried by an outer loop. Reported performance improvements due to affinity tiling are limited; linear loop transformations *prior* to affinity tiling, such as loop interchange, account for most of the reported improvements. In contrast, we show that by exploiting our notion of temporal intertile reuse, we can obtain significant performance improvements.

## 6 Concluding Remarks

In this paper, we have considered scheduling of tiled loop nests to exploit wavefront parallelism on scalable shared-memory multiprocessors. We have distinguished between intratile and intertile locality to evaluate the extent to which locality is enhanced, and we have shown the impact of tile size selection on locality as well as parallelism. We have shown that dynamic self-scheduling of tiles, a common technique for exploiting wavefront parallelism, performs poorly for a large number of processors because it cannot simultaneously enhance intertile locality and provide sufficient parallelism. Failure to enhance locality is particularly detrimental to performance when a large number of processors is used because of the greater cost of accessing remote memory.

We have applied two static scheduling strategies to enhance intertile locality and overcome the shortcomings of dynamic self-scheduling. We have shown analytically that these strategies reduce the number of misses, which in turn reduces the fraction of costly misses to remote memory. Results of experiments conducted on a 30-processor Convex SPP1000 with three representative applications confirm our analysis, demonstrating that static scheduling outperforms dynamic self-scheduling by enhancing intertile locality while providing sufficient parallelism for a large number of processors. Furthermore, the performance of static block scheduling consistently improves with reductions in tile size, unlike static cyclic or dynamic scheduling. Static block scheduling improves the speedup over dynamic self-scheduling at 30 processors by factors of 1.4 for SOR, 1.8 for Jacobi, and 2.3 for LL18.

## References

[1] D. F. Bacon, S. L. Graham, and O. J. Sharp. Compiler transformations for high-performance computing. *ACM Computing Surveys*, 26:345–420, December 1994.

[2] G. Bell. Ultracomputers: A teraflop before its time. *Comm. of the ACM*, 35(8):26–47, August 1992.

[3] Convex Computer Corporation. *Convex Exemplar system overview*. Richardson, TX, USA, 1994.

[4] A. Darte and Y. Robert. Constructive methods for scheduling uniform loop nests. *IEEE Trans. on Parallel and Distributed Systems*, 5(8):814–822, October 1994.

[5] M. Heinrich et al. The Stanford FLASH multiprocessor. In *Proc. 21th Intl. Symp. on Computer Architecture*, pages 302–313, Chicago, IL., April 1994.

[6] S. F. Hummel, E. Schonberg, and L. E. Flynn. Factoring: A method for scheduling parallel loops. *Comm. of the ACM*, 35(8):90–101, August 1992.

[7] H. Li, S. Tandri, M. Stumm, and K. C. Sevcik. Locality and loop scheduling on NUMA multiprocessors. In *Proc. 1993 Intl. Conf. on Parallel Processing*, pages II140–II147, August 1993.

[8] W. Li. Compiler cache optimizations for banded matrix problems. In *Proc. 1995 Intl. Conf. on Supercomputing*, pages 21–30, July 1995.

[9] N. Manjikian and T. Abdelrahman. Fusion of loops for parallelism and locality. In *Proc. 1995 Intl. Conf. on Parallel Processing*, pages II19–II28, August 1995.

[10] E. P. Markatos and T. J. LeBlanc. Using processor affinity in loop scheduling on shared-memory multiprocessors. In *Supercomputing '92*, pages 104–113, November 1992.

[11] C. D. Polychronopoulos and D. J. Kuck. Guided self-scheduling: A practical scheduling scheme for parallel supercomputers. *IEEE Trans. on Computers*, 36(12):1425–1439, December 1987.

[12] Z. Vranesic et al. The NUMAchine multiprocessor. Tech. Rep. CSRI-324, Computer Systems Research Institute, University of Toronto, Canada, April 1995.

[13] M. E. Wolf. *Improving Locality and Parallelism in Nested Loops*. PhD thesis, Department of Computer Science, Stanford University, 1992.

[14] M. E. Wolf and M. S. Lam. A data locality optimizing algorithm. In *Proc. ACM Conf. on Prog. Lang. Design and Impl.*, pages 30–44, Toronto, Canada, 1991.

# AUTOMATIC SELF-ALLOCATING THREADS (ASAT) ON AN SGI CHALLENGE

Charles Severance and Richard Enbody*
Department of Computer Science
Michigan State University
East Lansing, MI 48824-1027
crs@msu.edu, enbody@cps.msu.edu

*Automatic Self Allocating Threads (ASAT) is proposed as a way to balance the number of active threads across a shared-memory multiprocessing system. Our approach is significant in that it is designed for a system running multiple jobs, and it considers the load of all running jobs in its thread allocation. In addition, the overhead of ASAT is sufficiently small so that the run times of all jobs improve when it is in use. In this paper we consider the application of ASAT for improving the scheduling of threads on an SGI Challenge. We demonstrate how the number of threads of an ASAT job adjusts to the overall system load to maintain thread balance and improve system throughput.*

## INTRODUCTION

A multi-threaded runtime environment which supports lightweight threads can be used to support many aspects of parallel processing including: virtual processors, concurrent objects, and compiler run-time environments. However, such a library must depend on the underlying thread mechanism provided by the operating system. Threads working on compute intensive tasks work best when there is one thread performing real work on each processor. Matching the number of running threads to the number of processors can yield both good wall-clock run time and good overall machine utilization. The challenge is to schedule threads to maintain one running thread per processor by dynamically adjusting the number of threads as the load on the machine changes. It is generally not efficient to involve the operating system during a thread switch between lightweight threads. As such, a lightweight thread must operate within the parameters provided by the operating system.

If an application runs on a dedicated system with a known number of available processors, a multithreaded run-time environment can utilize a known number of operating system threads and assume that each operating system thread will have relatively uninterrupted access to CPU resources. However, it is much more common to operate in an environment in which resources are shared by a number of multithreaded applications running on the same multiprocessing system. This work is directed at implementing efficient multi-threaded runtime environments in such a shared environment. This work identifies the situations on a multiprocessing system when the operation of a lightweight thread environment might be negatively impacted by other threads running on the system.

The paper consists of several parts. (1) A proposed mechanism (ASAT) which allows processes to adjust their thread usage to maximize overall system utilization, (2) A characterization of the performance impact of having the improper number of threads on a multiprocessing system, and (3) an experiment using this technique in a multi-threaded compiler run-time environment.

## EXECUTION MODEL

This work focuses on an execution model in which a serial portion of the code is periodically executed between the parallel sections of the code.

In a procedural-language environment such as FORTRAN, a loop similar to the following will generate that pattern:

---
*This work is based on work supported by the National Science Foundation under Grant No MIP-0209402.

```
DO ITIME=1,INFINITY
    ...
    DO PARALLEL IPROB=1,PROBSIZE
        ...
    ENDDO
    ...
ENDDO
```

The parallel portions of the code may be executed by any number of operating system threads. This work focuses on how to insure that the right number of operating system threads are used each time the parallel code is executed.

Our approach does not necessarily apply to all multi-threaded environments. Database or network server environments may want to have significantly more operating system threads than available CPU resources in order to mask latencies due to I/O from the network, disk or other sources.

# 1    PREVIOUS WORK

In [11] the problem of matching the overall system-wide number of threads to the number of processors was studied on an Encore Multimax. They identified a number of the major problems with having too many threads including:

1. Preemption during spin-lock critical section,

2. Preemption of the wrong thread in a producer-consumer relationship,

3. Unnecessary context switch overhead, and

4. Corruption of caches due to context switches (also see [4]).

The general topic of scheduling for parallel loops is one that is well studied. The basic approach of these techniques is to partition the iterations of a parallel loop among a number of executing threads in a parallel process. The goal is to have balanced execution times on the processors while minimizing the overhead for partitioning the iterations. An excellent survey of these techniques is presented in [3].

The implementation of these techniques on most shared-memory parallel processors works with a fixed number of threads determined when the program is initially started. For the purpose of this paper, we call this technique Fixed Thread Scheduling (FTS). The FTS approach is reasonable for many of the existing parallel processing systems as long as each application has dedicated resources. As we point out in this paper, not having a dedicated system can seriously degrade the effectiveness of the FTS approach.

Other dynamic, run-time, thread management techniques which are geared toward compiler detected parallelism include: Automatic Self-Adjusting Processors (ASAP) from Convex [1] and Autotasking on Cray Research [2] computers.

A previous study of the benefits of Automatic Self-Allocating Threads (ASAT) for the Convex Exemplar was done in [6], details on multiple ASAT jobs appears in [7].

# ASAT

The general goal of our Automatic Self-Allocating Threads (ASAT) is to eliminate thread imbalance by detecting thrashing and then dynamically reducing the number of active threads to achieve balanced execution over the long term. In this way, multi-threaded applications will experience thread imbalance only during a small percentage of the execution time of the application. To implement ASAT on a parallel processing system, there are a number of problems which must be solved. The most important are:

1. Detecting if too many active threads exist.

2. Detecting if too few active threads exist.

3. Adjusting the number of threads.

ASAT takes advantage of the basic parallel loop structure shown earlier. Under Fixed Thread Scheduling (FTS) the beginning of the parallel loop activates the same number of threads each time it is executed over the duration of an application. When ASAT is used, the run-time library will activate the appropriate number of threads based on the overall load on the system. The goal is to create the precise number of threads which match the available processors.

A critical concept of ASAT is that a job will examine the availability of system resources with respect to current system load. The process is accurate, efficient and completely decentralized. The thread imbalance detected is for all threads currently on the system, not simply for this job's threads. Whether other jobs are scheduled using ASAT doesn't matter. However, the stability of multiple ASAT jobs is an important question we examine later in the paper.

ASAT uses a timed barrier test to detect thread imbalance on the system. A special barrier routine is inserted to test the system while executing as a single thread. Using the clock, the elapsed time between the first thread entering the barrier and the last thread leaving the barrier is measured. There is a three-orders of magnitude difference between barrier passage times under thread-balanced and thread-imbalanced conditions. That difference is significant enough to make the barrier a good test for load imbalance.

The interval between barrier evaluations can be adjusted. We set the ASAT software to only run the barrier test once every 1 second of elapsed time by default. The ASAT routine could then be called thousands of times per second, but most of the calls would return immediately because the time between ASAT barrier tests had not yet expired.

The number of spawned threads is decreased when the barrier transit time indicates a thread imbalance. ASAT has tunable values which determine the values for what is a "bad" transit time and the number of "bad" transit times necessary to trigger a drop in threads.

To determine whether or not to increase the number of threads, the ASAT barrier test is executed with one additional thread and the barrier transit time is measured. If the barrier transit time indicates that one more thread would execute effectively, the computation is attempted with one more thread. We call it "dipping your toe in the water." If the number of threads we are using has been working smoothly for a while, we test with more threads for a single barrier. If this barrier runs well, we dive in and run the whole application with more threads. Of course, if the increase in threads results in an imbalance, ASAT will drop the thread count at the next spawn opportunity.

## ASAT IN A COMPILER RUN-TIME ENVIRONMENT

The basic goal of ASAT is to allow a multithreaded run-time environment to operate most efficiently in an environment where the overall load on a system changes dynamically.

The first multi-threaded runtime environment which we have investigated is a compiler run-time environment. For this study, ASAT was implemented without modifications to the actual compiler library. Because it is not implemented inside the compiler library, the calls to ASAT must be explicitly added to the application. The two routines are ASAT_INIT and ASAT_ADJUST. ASAT_INIT is called at the beginning of the program before any parallel loops have executed and ASAT_ADJUST is called periodically

outside of a parallel loop. A highly stylized example is as follows:

```
      CALL ASAT_INIT()
      DO ITIME=1,INFINITY
      CALL ASAT_ADJUST()
C$DOACROSS LOCAL(I),SHARE(PARTICLE),SCHED(GSS)
         DO IPART=1,10000
            Work..
         ENDDO
      ENDDO
      END
```

Once ASAT is supported directly by the compiler, its use can be controlled using a directive.

```
C$DOACROSS LOCAL(I),SHARE(PARTICLE),
C$         SCHED(GSS),THREADS(ASAT)

C$DOACROSS LOCAL(I),SHARE(PARTICLE),
C$         SCHED(GSS),THREADS(FTS)
```

It it important to separate the thread management aspects from the chunking and work distribution issues. Work distribution techniques such as Guided Self Scheduling (GSS) depend of the variation of the length of each iteration. Thread management simply controls the number of threads which are used to process the work. Most compiler run-time libraries are designed to check the number of threads at the beginning of each parallel section.

## AN EXISTING MECHANISM

An good example of dynamic thread balancing is the mechanism available on the Convex C-Series (C-240, C-3X00, C4XXX) supercomputers is called Automatic Self Allocating Processing (ASAP) [1]. We use ASAP as a model for comparison.

The ASAP processing in the Convex C-Series systems is made possible because of an architectural feature called "Communication Registers" which are shared by all of the CPUs. These communication registers allow a multi-threaded process to create, delete, or context-switch threads with minimal performance impact. Using this hardware, the compiler can parallize loops without regard for the number of threads which will actually execute in the parallel loop. An idle CPU can dynamically create thread and "join" a parallel computation with a very small overhead.

This hardware support allows users to compile their applications assuming a generalized parallel environment regardless of whether or not there will be

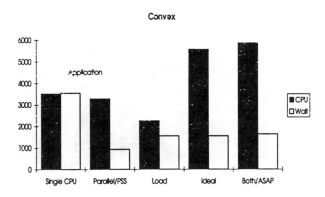

Figure 1: Performance of the Convex on Parallel Jobs

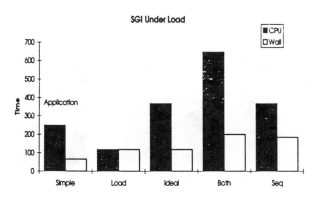

Figure 2: Performance of the SGI Under Load

enough resources at run-time to execute with multiple CPUs. One significant benefit of ASAP is that a long running job that is compiled to run in parallel can "soak-up" idle cycles as load changes. This flexibility allows a parallel/vector computer to be nearly 100 percent utilized over long time periods.

Throughout this section, a simple, very parallel computation will be used as the benchmark application. The kernel for these tests is as follows:

```
C$ DO_PARALLEL
      DO J=1,100000
          // 3Flops, 5 Memory references,
          // no data dependencies
      ENDDO
```

Figure 1 shows the performance of the code with several compiler options and load scenarios. The first pair of bars shows the CPU time (dark) and wall time (white) for the application on a single CPU. The second pair of bars shows the performance of the same application on four CPUs. The third pair of bars is another application which is single-threaded and cannot run in parallel. The fourth pair of bars shows the CPU and wall time for the ideal combination of the two codes assuming perfect load balancing on four CPUs. In this case, the ideal CPU time is the sum of the individual times and the wall time is the maximum of the individual wall times. The last pair of bars shows the actual performance achieved on the Convex C-240 when the jobs are run together. In the actual run using ASAP both the CPU time and the wall time are essentially the same as the ideal times (approximately 1.05 times longer).

## PARALLEL APPLICATIONS AND LOAD ON THE SGI

When multiple jobs are run on a less tightly coupled parallel machine the competing jobs can show dramatic interference with each other. Figure 2 shows what happens when the experiment performed on the Convex (Figure 1) is performed on a loaded and unloaded 4-CPU SGI Challenge system.

As on the Convex, the application code parallelizes automatically without any user modifications. Like the Convex, the load application only runs on a single CPU. However, unlike the Convex, the system performs much worse than ideal when both codes are run simultaneously. The wall time for the combination job is 1.68 times longer than ideal and the CPU time of the combination job is 1.76 times longer than the ideal CPU time. In fact, with the two jobs running simultaneously, the SGI performs worse than if you ran the jobs sequentially (i.e. submitted the jobs to a batch queue).

## COMPILER OPTIONS ON THE SGI

The SGI has several compiler options for load loop scheduling provided as part of its parallel FORTRAN compiler [8] [9]. Similar options are typically available on most parallel FORTRAN compilers. Are these compiler options sufficient to solve the unbalanced threads problem? The scheduling options for a parallel loop on the SGI include:

**Simple** At the beginning of a parallel loop each thread takes a fixed number of iterations of the loop.

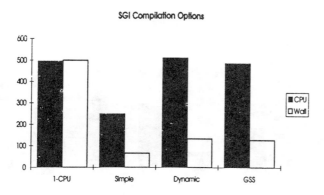

Figure 3: SGI Compiler Options

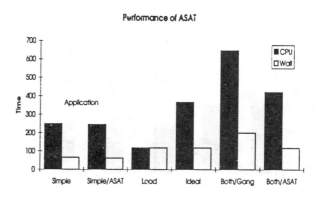

Figure 5: Performance of ASAT on the SGI

**Dynamic** With dynamic scheduling, each thread processes a "chunk" of data and when it has completed processing, a new "chunk" is processed. The "chunk_size" can be varied by the programmer based on the application.

**Guided Self Scheduled** This is essentially a modification of Dynamic scheduling except that large "chunks" are taken during the first few iterations, and the "chunksize" is reduced as the loop nears completion. GSS is designed to even out wide variations in the execution times of the iterations of the parallel loop. GSS is described in [5].

Figure 3 shows parallel performance of the simple application on an unloaded 4-CPU SGI with various compiler options:

The Dynamic and GSS options add overhead to the loops. Unlike the Convex, this overhead is in software and has a greater impact on the performance of the application. These options do not affect the allocation of threads so they only partially solve the the problem of having too many threads in a loaded system.

## PERFORMANCE OF ASAT

In this section we show that adding ASAT to the SGI allows it to run with a balanced number of threads. In addition, we show how competing jobs interact with each other. Figure 4 shows how ASAT generally operates when working on a system with variable load. In this figure, an application using ASAT is executing while other users are using the system. As the load average increases due to other users, the ASAT application releases threads to maintain its balance. Under high load conditions, the ASAT application only has one thread. As the other load de-

creases, the ASAT application adds threads increasing its throughput by using the idle cycles.

The goal for the rest of this section is to compare the application executed with ASAT on the SGI with the execution on the Convex C-240 using ASAP.

The first test is to duplicate the experiment which was performed for Figures 1 and 2 using ASAT to schedule the threads in the application code. Simple scheduling was used along with ASAT.

There are several observations about Figure 5. Running the application with ASAT enabled on an empty system did not change the performance of the program significantly (1-2 percent). The performance of the system with both the application and load running simultaneously is very close to ideal. Wall time for Both/ASAT was the same as ideal because the ASAT application ran to completion using the spare cycles while the load was running. The ASAT job runs at a lower priority than the load job so the load job got 100 percent of the CPU for the duration of its run. CPU time for Both/ASAT was 1.14 times the ideal CPU time. Recall that both the CPU and wall time were 1.05 times ideal for the ASAP on the Convex in Figure 1. Also from Figure 5, the wall time for gang scheduling is 1.68 times longer than ideal and the CPU time for gang scheduling is 1.76 times longer than the ideal CPU time.

To test ASAT under more varied load patterns, two time-oriented tests were performed. The first time-oriented test measured the ASAT response to rapidly changing load patterns. In the rapidly changing load scenario, the varying load conditions consisted of:

1. One job that averaged 5 minutes CPU time and arrived approximately every 15 minutes

2. Three jobs that averaged 1 minute of CPU time and arrived approximately every 4 minutes

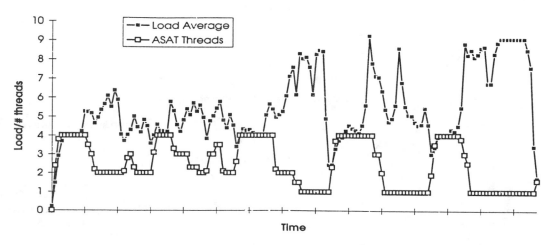

Figure 4: Example operation of ASAT

These load jobs were all sequential and were given higher priority than the ASAT application. The system load for the combination of "load" jobs is shown as the bottom plot in Figure 6.

Gang scheduling and ASAT are compared in Figure 6. In the figure, the combination "load" job finishes 4 minutes (11 percent) earlier when using ASAT scheduling. In addition, because ASAT processes run at lower priority, the time that the random load (simulating other users) completed was only 1 minute (4 percent) later than when the load completed on an empty system. Using gang scheduling, the simulated random load completed 7 minutes (20 percent) later than it would have completed with no load. In essence, the ASAT process "soaked-up" the idle cycles of the system with little or no impact on the rest of the load on the system. Because the ASAT process maintained a balanced number of threads it executed more efficiently and terminated faster than the gang scheduled process which had a significant negative impact on the other jobs.

The second time-oriented test is exactly the same as the previous test except that the applied load is more regular. In 2.5 minute intervals, the load is increased from 1 to 4 and then back down to zero. This applied load is shown in Figure 7 as an inverted "V" representing the increase in threads followed by a decrease. The same ASAT and gang processes were each run together with this new load profile.

Figure 7 again compares gang vs. ASAT—the former is the top line and the latter is the second line. The figure also shows the load by itself (inverted "V") and the number of ASAT threads. As the load is increased over the time of the run, ASAT quickly adjusts the number of threads, maintaining system bal-

ance. When the load goes up, the number of ASAT threads goes down. As resources free up, the number of ASAT threads is increased to take advantage of the idle resources. The dynamic adjustment of threads results in complete and efficient utilization of the resources while providing priority to the short term load on the system.

## CONCLUSION

The ability to dynamically adjust a parallel application to the amount of available resources is an important tool which allows parallel processors to be used more efficiently and applications to complete more quickly.

In this paper, the performance impact of having a system with an unbalanced number of threads was investigated.

ASAT is proposed as a technique which is easily implementable in a run-time library and effectively balances thread use across an entire system. As load increased on the whole system as ASAT job dynamically reduced its threads. When system load decreased the ASAT job dynamically increased its threads to soak up available cycles.

ASAT is examined in the context of a FORTRAN run-time thread management environment. The performance of ASAT is shown to be superior to the existing compiler-provided scheduling mechanisms in SGI Power FORTRAN. ASAT performs nearly as well in diverse load situations as the hardware approach used by Convex ASAP.

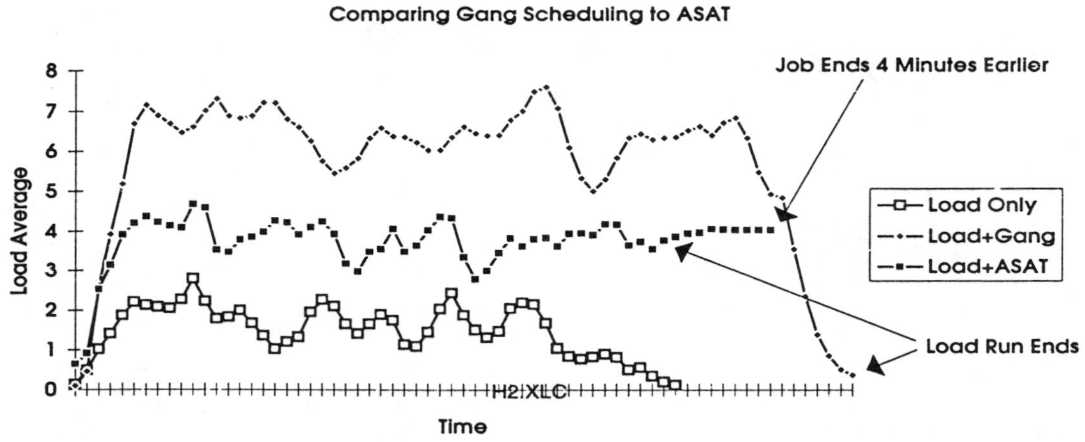

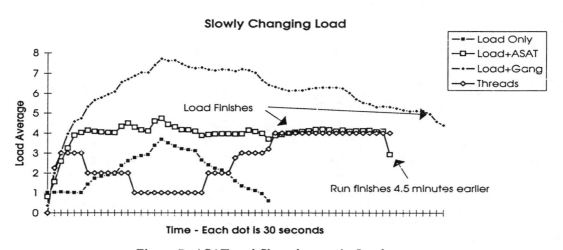

Figure 6: ASAT Response to Rapidly Changing Load

Figure 7: ASAT and Slow changes in Load

## FUTURE WORK

We need to further study how to best implement ASAT using more compiler and operating system modifications. ASAT, as currently implemented, does not make or require any operating system changes. One operating system change we believe would be helpful to ASAT is to assign a lower priority to processes with more active threads. This modification would naturally encourage processes with the largest number of threads to give up their threads and balance overall usage in the long run. Such an approach would also penalize non-ASAT processes which make irresponsible use of system resources.

Another area of work is to do a long-term study of the overall effect of ASAT. This work would allow one to study the average time spent in a parallel section across a wide variety of applications. We hope to have a version of ASAT available via anonymous FTP. Please check the URL http://clunix.msu.edu/~crs/projects/asat for details on the availability of ASAT.

---

Thanks to: David Kuck and Paul Petersen, Kuck and Associates; Jerry McAllister, Michigan State University; Dave McWilliams, National Center for Supercomputing Applications and Lisa Krause, Cray Research.

## References

[1] Convex Computer Corporation, "Convex Architecture Reference Manual (C-Series)", Document DHW-300, April 1992.

[2] Cray Research, *CF77 Compiling System, Volume 4: Parallel Processing Guide.*

[3] J. Liu, V. Saletore, "Self Scheduling on Distributed-Memory Machines," *IEEE Supercomputing'93*, pp. 814-823, 1993.

[4] J. C. Mogul and A. Borg, *The Effect of Context Switches on Cache Performance*, DEC Western Research Laboratory TN-16, Dec., 1990. http://www.research.digital.com/wrl/techreports/abstracts/TN-16.html

[5] C. Polychronopoulos, D. J. Kuck, "Guided Self Scheduling: A Practical Scheduling Scheme for Parallel Supercomputers," *IEEE Transactions on Computers*, Dec. 1987.

[6] Severance C, Enbody R, Wallach S, Funkhouser B, "Automatic Self Allocating Threads (ASAT) on the Convex Exemplar" Proceedings 1995 International Conference on Parallel Processing (ICPPP95), August 1995, pages I-24 - I-31.

[7] Severance C, Enbody R, Peterson P, "Managing the Overall Balance of Operating System Threads on a MultiProcessor using Automatic Self-Allocating Threads (ASAT)," *Journal of Parallel and Distributed Computing* Special Issue on Multithreading on Multiprocessors, to appear.

[8] Silicon Graphics, Inc., "Power FORTRAN Accelerator User's Guide," Document 007-0715-040, 1993.

[9] Silicon Graphics, Inc., "FORTRAN77 Programmer's Guide," Document 007-0711-030, 1993.

[10] Silicon Graphics, Inc., "Symmetric Multiprocessing Systems," Technical Report, 1993.

[11] A. Tucker and A. Gupta , "Process Control and Scheduling Issues for Multiprogrammed Shared-Memory Multiprocessors," *ACM SOSP Conf.*, 1989, p. 159 - 166.

# A Hydro-Dynamic Approach to Heterogeneous Dynamic Load Balancing in a Network of Computers

Chi-Chung Hui    &    Samuel T. Chanson

Department of Computer Science
The Hong Kong University of Science and Technology
Clear Water Bay, Hong Kong
E-mail: {cchui,chanson}@cs.ust.hk

**Abstract**—This paper presents a novel hydro-dynamic approach to solving the dynamic load balancing problem on a network of heterogeneous computers. The computing system consists of a network of processors with different capacities. In the hydro-dynamic approach, each processor is viewed as a liquid cylinder where the cross-sectional area corresponds to the capacity of the processor, the communication links are modeled as liquid channels between the cylinders, and the workload is represented as liquid. An algorithm is proposed to simulate the movement of the liquid such that when the algorithm terminates, the heights of the liquid columns are the same in all the cylinders. In this way, each processor obtains an amount of workload proportional to its capacity. This system is analyzed mathematically, and it is proved that the proposed algorithm converges geometrically.

## 1  INTRODUCTION

In local area networks (LANs) it is possible to improve the overall system throughput by balancing the workload among the workstations. Load balancing techniques can be classified into either *static* or *dynamic*. Static load balancing requires complete information and control of the computing system and the workload, while dynamic load balancing makes little assumption about the system or workload, and the scheduling decision is based on the current state of the system. In LAN environment, the workload characteristics and the workstation utilization are generally not predictable, and the workstations are usually run at different speeds. So it is more practical to employ heterogeneous dynamic load balancing strategies.

The *nearest-neighbor approach* is a dynamic load balancing technique that allows the workstations to communicate and migrate tasks with their immediate neighbors only [13]. Each workstation balances the workload among its neighbors in the hope that after a number of iterations the whole system will approach the balanced state. Since it is not necessary to have a global coordinator, the nearest-neighbor algorithms are inherently local, fault tolerant and scalable. Hence this approach is a natural choice for load balancing in a highly dynamic environment.

In this paper the following *heterogeneous dynamic load balancing problem* is considered: The computing system is modeled as an undirected graph where the nodes represent the workstations and the edges represent the network connections. Each workstation is associated with two real variables, *capacity* and *load*, which reflect its speed in processing workload and the workload currently running on it respectively. The objective is to derive an algorithm to redistribute the workload among the workstations such that each workstation obtains its share of the workload proportional to its capacity. In particular, we model the graph as a *hydro-dynamic* system where the movement of workload is viewed as liquid flow. A *potential energy function* is defined in which the minimum value corresponds to the state of equilibrium. Based on this framework a distributed nearest-neighbor algorithm is proposed which converges geometrically for heterogeneous processors.

The rest of the paper is organized as follow: The related work is presented in Section 2. Section 3 defines the load balancing problem formally. Section 4 describes the hydro-dynamic approach and explains how it is used to solve the problem. The proposed algorithm and its properties are presented in Sections 5 and 6 respectively. The behavior of the algorithm is studied in Section 7, and finally Section 8 concludes the paper.

## 2  RELATED WORK

The major approaches of the nearest-neighbor approach include the *diffusion method*, the *dimension exchange method* and the *gradient based method* [13].

For the *diffusion method*, the processor simultaneously sends workload to its neighbors with lighter workload and receives workload from its neighbors with heavier workload. Under the synchronous assumption, the diffusion method has been proved to converge in polynomial time for any initial workload [2, 3]. If new workload can be generated or existing workload completed during the execution of the algorithm, it has been proved that the variance of the workload is bounded [3, 8]. The convergence of the asynchronous version of the diffusion method has also been proved [1, 11]. For regular network topologies such as mesh, torus and $n$-D hypercube, optimal parameters that maximize the convergence rate have been derived [14].

The processors in the *dimension exchange method* balances the workload with their neighbors one at a time. It has been proved that on a hypercube, the entire system is balanced when all the processors have exchanged the workload with all their neighbors once [3]. This method is generalized to arbitrary by mapping edges into dimensions using edge coloring technique [5]. Optimal parameters have also been derived to maximize the convergence rate on $n$-D mesh, torus and $k$-ary $n$-cubes [12, 15].

The processors in the *gradient based method* maintain gradient maps which describe the workload variations in the computing system. Tasks are migrated toward the processors with the steepest gradient [7, 10].

To handle processors with different speeds, each processor in the *CHARM system* requests workload from its neighbors only when the forecasted finish time of the existing workload falls below a threshold [9]. On the other hand, the jobs under the *microeconomic algorithms* compete the processors using a bidding mechanism [4]. By comparison, the hydro-dynamic framework allows each processor to be assigned a *capacity*. In this way, the amount of workload allocated to each processor can be specified directly. We have proved that the proposed algorithm converges geometrically for all graph topologies and workload configurations. Moreover, the parameters that affect the rate of convergence have been identified. This provides valuable insight into the problem.

## 3 PROBLEM FORMULATION

The computing system is modeled as an undirected graph $G = (N, E)$, where the node set $N = \{n_1, n_2, \ldots, n_{|N|}\}$ represents the set of heterogeneous processors. Each processor may execute multiple processes in a multitasking manner, and is equipped with software/hardware facilities such that non-blocking message delivery is possible. Each node $n_i$ is associated with a *capacity* $c_i > 0$ which specifies the relative amount of workload it can handle. Another attribute *load* $l_i \geq 0$ reflects the amount of workload currently running on $n_i$. It is assumed that $c_i$ and $l_i$ are real numbers, and the workload is infinitely divisible. Since the values of the variables vary with time, the variables are usually expressed as $c_i[t]$ and $l_i[t]$. For simplicity, if a variable is not qualified explicitly it is assumed to be at time $t$. If $c_i = x \cdot c_j$, then $n_i$ and $n_j$ are said to have achieved *fairness* if $l_i = x \cdot l_j$. The edge set $E$ describes the connection pattern among the processors. If there exists a communication link $(n_i, n_j) \in E$, $n_i$ and $n_j$ can communicate and move workload between them. The links are assumed to be FIFO channels with bounded delay times. $G$ is *disturbed* if at least one of the following conditions is satisfied: (i) $N$ is changed, (ii) $c_i$ is changed for some $n_i \in N$, or (iii) the total workload (i.e., $\sum_j l_j$) is changed. To be practical, the algorithm should not assume that $G$ is not disturbed during execution of the algorithm. However, the load balancing algorithm should quickly adapt to perturbations and reach equilibrium if $G$ is not disturbed for a sufficiently long time period. Modifying the edge set $E$ should not affect the convergence of the algorithm as long as $G$ is connected, though it may

affect the rate of convergence. Given any workload configuration, the *heterogeneous dynamic load balancing problem* is to find an algorithm to redistribute the workload among the processors such that if $G$ is not disturbed in some finite time $A$, the workload obtained by each node $n_i$ is fair, that is,

$$l_i[t + A] = \frac{c_i}{\sum_j c_j} \cdot \sum_j l_j \qquad (1)$$

for all $n_i \in N$. When this happens, the system $G$ is said to have achieved *global fairness*. In this paper, we do not explicitly consider task migration during execution. The term *migration* used in this paper means *load index balancing* which does not necessarily result in immediate transfer of tasks. Actual workload migrations may be combined and take place later to reduce the frequency of data transfer.

## 4 HYDRO-DYNAMIC APPROACH

The basic idea of the *hydro-dynamic* approach is shown in Figure 1, where an example system $G_1$ is represented as a system of globally connected liquid cylinders. Each node $n_i \in N$ is associated with a

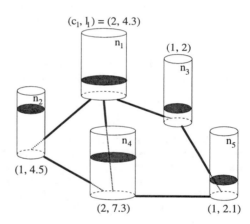

Figure 1: An example system $G_1$ represented by the hydro-dynamic approach.

liquid cylinder; the size of the cross-sectional area corresponds to $c_i$, and the volume of the liquid represents the workload currently allocated to $n_i$ (i.e, $l_i$). There is an infinitely thin liquid channel joining the bottoms of two liquid cylinders if there is an edge between the two corresponding nodes in $G$. Our proposed solution models the flow of liquid among the cylinders. It is intuitive that global fairness is achieved when the heights of the liquid columns are equal. It is also obvious that after global fairness has been achieved there is no liquid flow among the cylinders and therefore the system is stable. In the following subsections we show how this system can be analyzed mathematically.

### 4.1 The Concept of Potential Energy

The core of the analysis is to derive a function of *global potential energy GPE* to measure the level of fairness among the nodes of $G$. Given the node $n_i \in N$, the *height* of $n_i$ is defined as

$$h_i = \frac{l_i}{c_i}.$$

The *mass* of $n_i$ between the height range $(h_j, h_k)$ is denoted by $m_{h_j}^{h_k}(n_i)$ where

$$
\begin{aligned}
m_{h_j}^{h_k}(n_i) &= \int_{h_j}^{h_k} c_i \, dh \\
&= c_i \cdot (h_k - h_j).
\end{aligned}
$$

The *potential energy* of $n_i$ between the height range $(h_j, h_k)$ is defined as

$$
\begin{aligned}
PE_{h_j}^{h_k}(n_i) &= \int_{h_j}^{h_k} PE(n_i, h) \, dh \\
&= c_i \cdot \left[ \frac{h^2}{2} \right]_{h_j}^{h_k} \\
&= c_i \cdot (h_k^2 - h_j^2)/2 \\
&= m_{h_j}^{h_k}(n_i) \cdot (h_k + h_j)/2.
\end{aligned}
$$

The *potential energy* of the liquid column at $n_i$ with a height of $h_i$ is defined as

$$PE(n_i) = PE_0^{h_i}(n_i).$$

Finally, the *global potential energy* of the system is defined as the sum of potential energies of all the nodes, that is,

$$GPE(G) = \sum_{n_i \in N} PE(n_i).$$

### 4.2 GPE and Global Fairness

In this section we prove that $GPE$ is minimized only at the state of global fairness. The following lemma states that for any two liquid segments $\mathcal{L}_a$ and $\mathcal{L}_b$ with the same volume, $\mathcal{L}_a$ has larger potential energy if the bottom of $\mathcal{L}_a$ is equal to or higher than the top of $\mathcal{L}_b$:

**Lemma 1** :  For any two nodes $n_i, n_j \in N$, if $a_2 > a_1 \geq b_2 > b_1$ and $m_{a_1}^{a_2}(n_i) = m_{b_1}^{b_2}(n_j)$, then

$$\Delta PE = PE_{b_1}^{b_2}(n_j) - PE_{a_1}^{a_2}(n_i) \;<\; 0.$$

**Proof**:

$$
\begin{aligned}
\Delta PE &= \frac{m_{b_1}^{b_2}(n_j)}{2} \cdot (b_1 + b_2) - \frac{m_{a_1}^{a_2}(n_i)}{2} \cdot (a_1 + a_2) \\
&= \frac{m_{a_1}^{a_2}(n_i)}{2} \cdot [(b_1 - a_1) + (b_2 - a_2)] \\
&< 0. \quad \square
\end{aligned}
$$

It follows from Lemma 1 that the flow of liquid from a higher position to a lower position reduces the potential energy of the liquid. Given the above lemma, it is easy to prove that the global potential energy of $G$ is minimized when the relative workload allocated to each node is the same (i.e., the system is in the state of global fairness).

**Theorem 1** :    Given $G = (N, E)$, the function $GPE(G)$ is minimized if and only if the state of global fairness is achieved, that is, $h_i = h_{\text{opt}} \quad \forall \; i$ where

$$h_{\text{opt}} = \frac{\sum_j l_j}{\sum_j c_j}.$$

**Proof**:  First we show that the total sum of the workload when $h_i = h_{\text{opt}}$ for all $i$ is equal to $\sum_i l_i$:

$$
\begin{aligned}
\sum_i h_{\text{opt}} \cdot c_i &= h_{\text{opt}} \cdot \sum_i c_i \\
&= \frac{\sum_j l_j}{\sum_j c_j} \cdot \sum_i c_i \\
&= \sum_i l_i.
\end{aligned}
$$

Notice that the heights of all the nodes at equilibrium are the same. Now, the workload $l_i'$ acquired by $n_i$ when $h_i = h_{\text{opt}}$ is given by

$$
\begin{aligned}
l_i' &= h_i \cdot c_i \\
&= h_{\text{opt}} \cdot c_i \\
&= \frac{c_i}{\sum_j c_j} \cdot \sum_j l_j
\end{aligned}
$$

which is equal to that given in equation (1). By definition, the system is in the state of global fairness.

To prove the theorem, we compare the $GPE$ of the globally fair system with those of all the other configurations where the heights of the nodes are not equal. In the latter case, we partition the node set $N$ into three subsets $N_{\text{lower}} = \{n_i| \; h_i < h_{\text{opt}}\}$, $N_{\text{equal}} = \{n_i| \; h_i = h_{\text{opt}}\}$ and $N_{\text{higher}} = \{n_i| \; h_i > h_{\text{opt}}\}$. It is easy to see that $N = N_{\text{lower}} \bigcup N_{\text{equal}} \bigcup N_{\text{higher}}$. As the total workload $\sum_i l_i$ is the same in the two cases, the equality

$$\sum_{n_i \in N_{\text{lower}}} (h_{\text{opt}} - h_i) = \sum_{n_i \in N_{\text{higher}}} (h_i - h_{\text{opt}})$$

holds. This situation is shown graphically in Figure 2. Consider moving the workload above $h_{\text{opt}}$ in $N_{\text{higher}}$

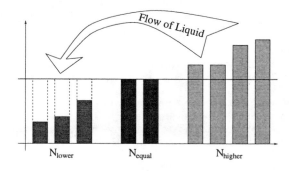

Figure 2: Prove of minimum $GPE$.

to the "holes" in $N_{\text{lower}}$. By Lemma 1, the change in potential energy for every movement must be negative since the workload flows from a position above $h_{\text{opt}}$ to a position below $h_{\text{opt}}$. Hence, it is proved that the $GPE$ of $G$ at the state of global fairness must be strictly smaller than all other configurations. $\square$

# 5  PROPOSED ALGORITHM

The proposed algorithm HeteroLB is shown in Figure 3, in which every node in $G$ executes the same code. Each node $n_i$ initializes its state in steps 1 through 4. The set *info* stores the information of $n_i$ and its neighbors (i.e., $adj(n_i)$). The node also broadcasts its state to its neighbors. The array *togive* stores the values of the workload that $n_i$ is sending to its neighbors. Each node maintains a FIFO message queue which holds the incoming messages. Each message has the format $\langle f, T, c, l, g, h \rangle$ where the message came from $n_f$, $T$ is the type of the message, $c$ and $l$ store the current $c_f$ and $l_f$ of $n_f$ respectively, $g$ contains the migration information, and $h$ represents the height of $n_f$. There are four types of messages:

1. *Disturb message* ("D"): This message is sent by an external process to indicate any disturbance to $n_i$ (e.g., $c_i$ can be reduced when the workstation is reclaimed by its owner). In this case, $c$ and $l$ record the changes in $c_i$ and $l_i$ respectively while $g$ and $h$ are not used.

2. *Give message* ("G"): $n_i$ sends a "G"-message to $n_j$ to indicate that it wants to transfer $g$ units of workload to $n_j$. The height of $n_i$, assuming the movement is successful, is stored in $h$.

3. *Receive message* ("R"): After receiving a "G"-message, a node must respond with a "R"-message to indicate how much workload it has accepted. The amount of accepted workload is stored in $g$.

4. *Broadcast message* ("B"): Notice that for "G"- and "R"-messages, $c$ and $l$ contain the current capacity and workload of $n_f$. This reduces the number of broadcast messages needed to keep *info* up-to-date. However, if the node decides to send its status to its neighbors without waiting for a "G"- or "R"-message, it may send a "B"-message. In this case, $g$ and $h$ are not used.

The main loop of the algorithm starts at step 5, in which the node takes the first message from the queue and processes the message according to its type (steps 6 to 9). It blocks when there is no message in the queue. HeteroLB adopts a two-phase commit protocol in moving the workload. If $n_i$ intends to move some load to its neighbors, it first sends a "G"-message to each candidate (step 13). The workload to be sent is stored in *togive*. The neighbor responds to indicate how much it has accepted by replying with a "R"-message (step 8). The change is finally updated in step 9.

The migration (workload movement) plan $Tr$ is computed by the function ComputeTr in step 10 (see Section 5.1 for details). $Tr$ consists of a set of 2-tuples $(n_j, g_j)$ indicating $n_i$ should transfer $g_j$ units of workload to $n_j$. If $Tr$ is not empty, $n_i$ sends a "G"-message to every neighbor according to the plan (step 13). A mechanism in step 8a makes sure $GPE(G)$ decreases monotonically at every step. This ensures $G$ will not move away from global fairness no matter how the system is disturbed. The hydro-dynamic approach forbids liquid (workload) to flow to a higher position from

**HeteroLB$(n_i)$**

| | |
|---|---|
| $n_i$: | The node where HeteroLB is executed. |
| $adj(n_i)$: | The set of nodes which are adjacent to $n_i$. |

1. For each node $n_j \in adj(n_i)$ do

    (a) Send message $\langle n_i, \text{"B"}, c_i, l_i, 0, 0 \rangle$ to $n_j$.

2. Let *tofinish* = *false*.
3. Let $info = \{\langle n_i, c_i, l_i \rangle\}$.
4. Let $togive(n_j) = 0$ for all $n_j \in adj(n_i)$.
5. Read the first message $\langle f, T, c, l, g, h \rangle$ from the message queue.
6. If $T = $ "D" then

    (a) Let $c_i = c_i + c$.
    (b) Let $l_i = l_i + l$.
    (c) Let $info = info \bigcup \{\langle n_f, c, l \rangle\}$.

7. If $T = $ "B" then

    (a) Let $info = info \bigcup \{\langle n_f, c, l \rangle\}$.

8. If $T = $ "G" then

    (a) Let $R = \max\{0, \min\{h \cdot c_i - l_i, g\}\}$.
    (b) Let $l_i = l_i + R$.
    (c) Let $info = info \bigcup \{\langle n_i, c_i, l_i \rangle, \langle n_f, c, l \rangle\}$.
    (d) Send message $\langle n_i, \text{"R"}, c_i, l_i, R, 0 \rangle$ to $n_f$.

9. If $T = $ "R" then

    (a) Let $l_i = l_i - g$.
    (b) Let $info = info \bigcup \{\langle n_i, c_i, l_i \rangle, \langle n_f, c, l - g \rangle\}$.
    (c) Let $togive(n_f) = 0$.

10. If there exists $togive(n_j) > 0$ for some $n_j \in adj(n_i)$ then

    (a) Let proposed transfer $Tr = \text{ComputeTr}(n_i)$.

11. If $c_i$ and/or $l_i$ changes then

    (a) Let *tofinish* = *false*
    (b) For every node $n_j$ such that $\text{Trigger}(l_i/c_i, l_j/c_j) = true$ do

        i. Send message $\langle n_i, \text{"B"}, c_i, l_i, 0, 0 \rangle$ to $n_j$.

    else if there is no message in the message queue and $|Tr| = 0$ and *tofinish* = *false* then

    (c) Let *tofinish* = *true*
    (d) For every node $n_j \in adj(n_i)$ do

        i. Send message $\langle n_i, \text{"B"}, c_i, l_i, 0, 0 \rangle$ to $n_j$.

12. Let $h_i' = \dfrac{l_i - \sum_{(n_j, g_j) \in Tr} g_j}{c_i}$.

13. For each proposed transfer $(n_j, g_j) \in Tr$ do

    (a) Send message $\langle n_i, \text{"G"}, c_i, l_i, g_j, h_i' \rangle$ to $n_j$.
    (b) Let $togive(n_j) = g_j$.

14. Goto step 5.

Figure 3: Formal description of HeteroLB.

a lower position. Moreover, in step 12, the variable $h$ is set to the lowest possible height which ensures the height of the new workload will not be lower than $h$. This eliminates the fluctuation of workload movement between the adjacent nodes.

**Theorem 2** : Under HeteroLB, the global potential energy of $G$ is a monotonically decreasing function.

**Proof**: Step 8a of HeteroLB ensures all workload is moved from a higher level to a lower level. Therefore, by Lemma 1 $\Delta GPE < 0$ for any workload movement. Moreover, if there is no workload flow, $\Delta GPE = 0$. □

Whenever the state of $n_i$ is changed, it selectively broadcasts its status to those neighbors which have potential for load balancing (steps 11a and 11b). The policy is embedded in the function Trigger which is described in Section 5.2. To make sure that $G$ does not end in a state with outdated neighbor information in the nodes, the nodes also rebroadcast their states one more time before the end of execution (steps 11c and 11d). Hence, the following theorem can be proved:

**Theorem 3** : When $G$ stops balancing the workload after a perturbation, all the nodes block at step 5 with up-to-date neighbor information.

**Proof**: The second part of the if-statement in step 11 forces each node to rebroadcast its state one more time if there is no message in the queue and the migration plan $Tr$ is empty. Therefore, after the remaining "B"-messages are consumed, the nodes must be blocked at step 5, and the neighbor information is up-to-date. □

## 5.1   The Workload Transfer Strategy

The function ComputeTr listed in Figure 4 describes how the nodes in $G$ redistribute the workload. The algorithm can be explained with the help of Figure 5. The neighbors of $n_i$ are modeled by solid columns, which are sorted according to their heights and placed in a container (steps 1 and 2 in ComputeTr). The total cross-sectional area of the container is equal to $c_i + \sum_{n_j \in adj(n_i)} c_j$ (i.e., the variable $C$ in ComputeTr). Each neighbor $n_j \in adj(n_i)$ occupies a cross-sectional area of $c_j$, and an empty space of $c_i$ is reserved for $n_i$. The workload of $n_i$ is modeled as a jar of liquid with volume $l_i$ (i.e., the variable $L$ in ComputeTr), which is poured into the container. The final height of the liquid, which is equal to $H$ in ComputeTr, is computed by the for-loop in step 4. Finally in step 5, $Tr$ is computed by comparing the heights of the liquid columns with $H$. The following theorem proves that the transfer strategy computed by ComputeTr is optimal in the sense that it maximizes the reduction in $GPE(G)$:

**Theorem 4** : The reduction of $GPE(G)$ given by the migration plan computed by ComputeTr is maximal.

**Proof**: The proof is obvious from Lemma 1, since ComputeTr models the situation that the liquid (workload) flows to the lowest possible position. □

**ComputeTr$(n_i)$**

| $n_i$: | The node where HeteroLB is executed. |
|---|---|

1. Let $sorted[0] = \langle i, c_i, l_i, 0 \rangle$.
2. Let $sorted[k \geq 1] = \langle j, c_j, l_j, l_j/c_j \rangle$ where TRIGGER$(l_j/c_j, l_i/c_i) = true$ and $l_j/c_j$ is sorted in increasing of $k$ (Notice that the data comes from $info$).
3. Let $C = 0$, $L = l_i$, and $H = 0$.
4. For $(j = 0; j < |sorted|; j = j + 1)$ do

   (a) Let $k = \max\limits_{h_x = h_j} \{x\}$.

   (b) Let $C = C + \sum_{x=j}^{k} sorted[x].p$.

   (c) If $k = |sorted| - 1$ then
       i. Let $H = H + L/C$.
       ii. Goto step 5.

   (d) Let $maxfill = (sorted[k+1].h - sorted[k].h) \cdot C$.

   (e) Let $tofill = \min\{maxfill, L\}$.

   (f) Let $H = H + tofill/C$.

   (g) Let $L = L - tofill$.

   (h) If $L = 0$ then goto step 5.

   (i) Let $j = k$.

5. $Tr = \bigcup_{x=1}^{k} \{\langle sorted[x].id, (H - sorted[x].h) \cdot sorted[x].p \rangle\}$.

6. return $Tr$.

Figure 4: Formal description of ComputeTr.

## 5.2   Termination Criteria

It is difficult to achieve the state of global fairness exactly. As the differences in workload between the nodes get smaller, the amount of workload exchanged among the nodes decreases. The cost of executing HeteroLB after a number of iterations may outweigh the benefit of further balancing the load. Moreover, it may not be possible to migrate workload if the quantity of transfer is too small since in practice, workload is not infinitely divisible. Therefore, a threshold is defined to stop the nodes from exchanging workload if the difference in workload is less than the threshold value.

The function Trigger$(x, y)$ in HeteroLB and ComputeTr defines the trigger policy for termination of the algorithm and returns true when $x$ is smaller than $y$ by a predefined threshold value. Two schemes have

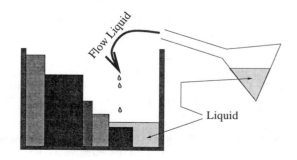

Figure 5: Graphical representation of ComputeTr.

been implemented:

*T1*: $y - x > \delta_1$. The function returns true if $y$ is greater than $x$ by $\delta_1$.

*T2*: $\dfrac{y - x}{\min\{x, y\}} > \dfrac{\delta_2}{100}$. The function returns true if $x$ is less than $y$ by $\delta_2\%$.

The upper bounds of the difference between any pair of nodes are calculated as follows:

**Theorem 5** : For any path $\langle n_{x_1}, n_{x_2}, \cdots, n_{x_p} \rangle$ with length $p-1$, when HeteroLB stops balancing the workload, the differences in heights between $n_{x_1}$ and $n_{x_p}$ are bounded by $\Delta H$ where

$$\Delta H_{T1} = \delta_1 \cdot (p - 1)$$

and

$$\Delta H_{T2} \approx h_{\text{opt}} \cdot \frac{\delta_2}{100} \cdot (p - 1).$$

**Proof**: Notice that for any two adjacent nodes $n_i$ and $n_j$, there is no workload movement between them if and only if both $n_i$ and $n_j$ do not trigger. Under scheme T1, if no node pair is triggered along the path, then

$$
\begin{aligned}
|h_{x_p} - h_{x_1}| &= \left| \sum_{i=1}^{p-1} h_{i+1} - h_i \right| \\
&\leq \sum_{i=1}^{p-1} |h_{i+1} - h_i| \\
&= \delta_1 \cdot (p - 1).
\end{aligned}
$$

Under scheme T2, no trigger implies that

$$
\begin{aligned}
|h_{x_p} - h_{x_1}| &\leq \sum_{i=1}^{p-1} |h_{i+1} - h_i| \\
&\leq \sum_{i=1}^{p-1} \min\{h_{p_{i+1}}, h_{p_i}\} \cdot \frac{\delta_2}{100} \\
&= \sum_{i=1}^{p-1} \frac{\min\{h_{p_{i+1}}, h_{p_i}\}}{p - 1} \cdot \frac{\delta_2}{100} \cdot (p - 1) \\
&\approx h_{\text{opt}} \cdot \frac{\delta_2}{100} \cdot (p - 1). \quad \Box
\end{aligned}
$$

## 5.3 Complexity Analysis

Most of the operations in HeteroLB take $\mathcal{O}(1)$ time. Assuming $d_i = \lceil adj(n_i) \rceil$, the broadcast-related operations (i.e., step 1 and step 11) have time complexities $\mathcal{O}(d_i)$. If *info* and *togive* are implemented as arrays, then step 3 and step 4 have time complexities $\mathcal{O}(d_i)$, and each individual update takes $\mathcal{O}(1)$ time. There are maximally $d_i$ entities each for *togive* and *Tr*, and so steps 10 (excluding ComputeTr), 12 and 13 take $\mathcal{O}(d_i)$ time. For ComputeTr, the sorting step in step 2 has worst case time complexity of $\mathcal{O}(d_i \log d_i)$ if merge sort is used. The for-loop in step 4 only takes $\mathcal{O}(d_i)$ since each entry in *sorted* is referenced only once. The summation statement in step 5 has time complexity $\mathcal{O}(d_i)$ while the remaining statements have time complexities $\mathcal{O}(1)$. So ComputeTr run at $\mathcal{O}(d_i \log d_i)$ time. Therefore, HeteroLB takes $\mathcal{O}(d_i)$ time for initialization and $\mathcal{O}(d_i \log d_i)$ time to process each message (steps 5 to 14).

# 6 CONVERGENCE PROPERTIES

Based on the hydro-dynamic approach, we have proved that HeteroLB converges geometrically to the state of global fairness given sufficient time [6].

**Theorem 6** : When HeteroLB executes on any $G = (N, E)$, the global potential energy of $G$ with respect to time has the following property:

$$GPE[B\tau] < \eta^\tau GPE[0] + (1 - \eta^\tau) GPE_{\min} \quad (2)$$

where

$$\eta = 1 - \frac{1}{2(|N| - 1) \, dia(G)^2} \frac{c_{\min}^2}{c_{\max} \sum_i c_i} \quad (3)$$

for some $B > 0$ and all $\tau \geq 1$. Notice that $B$ is the upper bound of the time required by all the node pairs in $E$ to balance the workload, $c_{\min}$ and $c_{\max}$ are the values of the smallest and largest capacities in $G$, and $dia(G)$ is the diameter of $G$. From Equation (3) it can be seen that $1 > \eta > 0$. This implies that HeteroLB converges geometrically. $\Box$

The crucial observation that led to the proof is that after $G$ has balanced its workload during time period $B$ and if there is no disturbance during this period (i.e., $[t, t + B]$), there is a significant reduction in the $GPE$. First of all, it is proved that after the interaction between any two nodes $n_i$ and $n_j$, the accumulated workload movement of at least one of them is no less than

$$\frac{c_i c_j}{c_i + c_j} |h_i[t] - h_j[t]|.$$

Then, it is shown that if $W$ amount of workload flows into (or out of) $n_i$ then the change in global potential energy, $\Delta GPE$, is given by

$$\Delta GPE < -\frac{W^2}{2c_i(|N| - 1)}.$$

Combining with the fact that the maximum difference in the heights of the node pair has the lower bound

$$\max_{(n_i, n_j) \in E} \{h_i[t] - h_j[t]\} \geq \frac{h_{\max}[t] - h_{\min}[t]}{dia(G)},$$

where $h_{\min}[t]$ and $h_{\max}[t]$ are the minimum and maximum heights of $G$ at time $t$ respectively, it can be proved that the reduction in $GPE$ in period $B$ is greater than a proportion of $(h_{\max}[t] - h_{\min}[t])^2$:

$$GPE[t + B] - GPE[t] < -\alpha(h_{\max}[t] - h_{\min}[t])^2 \quad (4)$$

where

$$\alpha = \frac{1}{8(|N| - 1) \, dia(G)^2} \cdot \frac{c_{\min}^2}{c_{\max}}.$$

This reduction on $GPE$ is significant since the difference between $GPE$ and $GPE_{\min}$ (i.e., the value of $GPE$ at global fairness) is also bounded by a proportion of $(h_{\max}[t] - h_{\min}[t])^2$, that is,

$$GPE[t] - GPE_{\min} \leq \beta(h_{\max}[t] - h_{\min}[t])^2 \quad (5)$$

where

$$\beta = \frac{\sum_i c_i}{4}.$$

The bound in Equation (5) is derived from the workload configuration shown in Figure 6 which has the highest value of $GPE$ (the proof is obvious from Lemma 1). Therefore, by combining equations (4)

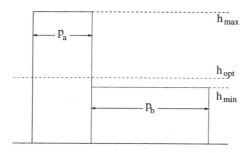

Figure 6: Configuration of $G$ with the highest $GPE$ given $h_{max}$ and $h_{min}$.

and (5) it can be proved that

$$GPE[t + B] < \eta GPE[t] + (1 - \eta) GPE_{min} \quad (6)$$

where $\eta = (1 - \frac{\alpha}{\beta})$, and so Theorem 6 can be proved by induction (see [6] for details).

Bertsekas and Tsitsiklis have proved the convergence property of the diffusion algorithm on a network of processors with the same speed [1]. Their proof relies on the fact that the workload of the lightest loaded processors will eventually increase and converge at the point of equilibrium. Our proof, on the other hand, is based on combining the notions of *capacity* and *load* into the single variable $GPE$. Theorem 6 not only provides a convergence proof for HeteroLB, it also identifies several system parameters that affect the convergence rate of the algorithm. The parameters are embedded in $\eta$ which include: (i) the diameter of the graph, (ii) the capacities of the nodes, and (iii) the number of nodes. It is expected that the larger the values of $dia(G)$ and $|N|$, the slower the convergence rate. On the other hand, if the difference between the values of $c_i$ is small, then $G$ is expected to converge at a faster rate. For a rigorous proof on Theorem 6 and more discussion on these parameters please refer to our technical report [6].

## 7   CASE STUDIES

HeteroLB was evaluated using discrete-event simulations. The smallest divisible time unit is 1 ms. The time to start up HeteroLB in each node is assumed to be $U(0, 5)$ ms, in which $U(x, y)$ returns a uniformly distributed number between $x$ and $y$ inclusively. The time to transfer a message between adjacent nodes is set at $U(10, 30)$ ms. Each node is assumed to spend $U(10, 20)$ ms in processing a message. For the two proposed trigger functions, $\delta_1 = 0.1$ and $\delta_2 = 5$.

### 7.1   Example $G_1$

The result of executing HeteroLB on $G_1$ using the trigger strategy T1 is shown in Figure 7. It

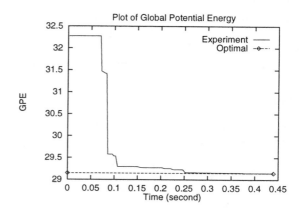

Figure 7: The $GPE$ plot of the example system $G_1$.

can be seen that the $GPE$ curve dropped sharply to a near optimal point very quickly in the period $[0.06s, 0.08s]$. After that, the rate of decrease slowed down ($[0.1s, 0.25s]$), followed by a long tail where the nodes fine tuned the workload to conform to the error requirement ($[0.25s, 0.44s]$). In between these phases, the nodes were exchanging information and calculating the transfer strategies. HeteroLB gives priority to balancing the nodes with the greatest differences in workload which results in geometric convergence.

### 7.2   A Complex System with Disturbance

In order to investigate the behavior of HeteroLB on complex systems with disturbances, another example was studied using the configuration given in Figure 8, where $G_2$ consists of two clusters connected by a path with two nodes. The left cluster has higher capacity

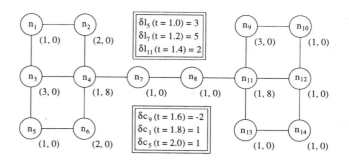

Figure 8: The example system $G_2$.

than the right cluster (10 versus 8). Six disturbance events occurred in the time period $[1s, 2s]$. The first three events added workload to the system, and the remaining events adjusted the capacities of the nodes so that at the end of the period the difference in capacities between the clusters was increased (12 versus 6).

The example was designed to test HeteroLB's ability to transfer workload between the clusters through a single link.

The resultant $GPE$ plot is shown in Figure 9. When

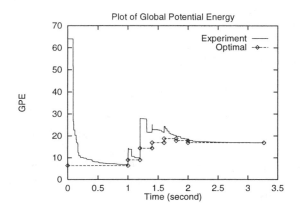

Figure 9: The $GPE$ plot of the example system $G_2$.

disturbances to the system occurred, the optimal $GPE$ and the current $GPE$ of the system changed. However, HeteroLB quickly adapted to the disturbances and the system approached optimal $GPE$ within a fraction of a second after each disturbance.

### 7.3 Discussion

In our example, about 67% of the "G"-messages resulted in workload transfer, and 58% of the proposed workload migration was actually performed. This shows that HeteroLB can minimize network loading by avoiding unnecessary workload fluctuation. Although the "G"- and "R"-messages also include the node information, the "B"-messages still accounted for more than half of all the messages. The message delivery rate depends on the speeds of the nodes and the links and is independent of the network topology and the level of non-fairness. Therefore, it may be possible to improve the message efficiency by decreasing the message rates of the nodes whose loadings are close to those of their neighbors.

## 8 CONCLUSION

We have presented a hydro-dynamic approach to model the dynamic load balancing problem for a network of heterogeneous workstations. An algorithm is proposed which converges geometrically for all configurations. Simulation results show the algorithm adapts very well to workload and system perturbations. This approach is easy to understand and provides a framework applicable to many dynamic systems requiring search for an equilibrium state which is globally optimal in some properties. Our main contribution has been in analyzing this framework mathematically and showing that it converges geometrically.

## References

[1] D. P. Bertsekas and J. N. Tsitsiklis, *Parallel and Distributed Computation: Numerical Methods.* Prentice-Hall, Inc., 1989.

[2] J. E. Boillat, "Load balancing and poisson equation in a graph," *Concurrency: Practice and Experience*, vol. 2, pp. 289–313, December 1990.

[3] G. Cybenko, "Dynamic load balancing for distributed memory multiprocessors," *Jour. of Par. and Distr. Com. (JPDC)*, vol. 7, no. 2, pp. 279–301, 1989.

[4] D. Ferguson, Y. Yemini, and C. Nikolaou, "Microeconomic algorithms for load balancing in distributed computer systems," in *Proc. of 8th Int. Conf. on Distr. Com. Syst. (ICDCS)*, pp. 491–499, 1988.

[5] S. H. Hosseini, B. Litow, M. Malkawi, J. McPherson, and K. Vairavan, "Analysis of a graph coloring based distributed load balancing algorithm," *JPDC*, vol. 10, no. 2, pp. 160–166, 1990.

[6] C.-C. Hui and S. T. Chanson, "Theoretical analysis of the heterogeneous dynamic load balancing problem using a hydro-dynamic approach," Tech. Rep. HKUST-CS96-01, Dep. of Com. Sci., HKUST, 1996.

[7] F. C. H. Lin and R. M. Keller, "The gradient model load balancing method," *IEEE Trans. on Soft. Eng.*, vol. SE-13, no. 1, pp. 32–38, 1987.

[8] X. Qian and Q. Yang, "Load balancing on generalized hypercube and mesh multiprocessors with LAL," in *Proc. ICDCS*, pp. 402–409, 1991.

[9] V. A. Saletore, J. Jacob, and M. Padala, "Parallel computations on the CHARM heterogeneous workstation cluster," in *Proc. of 3th Int. Sym. on High Perf. Distr. Com.*, pp. 203–210, 1994.

[10] W. Shu and L. V. Kalé, "A dynamic scheduling strategy for the Chare-kernel system," in *Proc. Supercomputing'89*, pp. 389–398, 1989.

[11] J. Song, "A partially asynchronous and iterative algorithm for distributed load balancing," *Parallel Computing*, vol. 20, no. 6, pp. 853–868, 1994.

[12] C.-Z. Xu and F. C. M. Lau, "Analysis of the generalized dimension exchange method for dynamic load balancing," *JPDC*, vol. 16, no. 4, pp. 385–393, 1992.

[13] C.-Z. Xu and F. C. M. Lau, "Iterative dynamic load balancing in multicomputers," *Jour. of the Oper. Res. Soc.*, vol. 45, no. 7, pp. 786–796, 1994.

[14] C.-Z. Xu and F. C. M. Lau, "Optimal parameters for load balancing with the diffusion method in mesh networks," *Parallel Processing Letters*, vol. 4, no. 1–2, pp. 139–147, 1994.

[15] C.-Z. Xu and F. C. M. Lau, "The generalized dimension exchange method for load balancing in $k$-ary $n$-cubes and variants," *JPDC*, vol. 24, no. 1, pp. 72–85, 1995.

# A Load-Balancing Algorithm for N-Cubes

Min-You Wu and Wei Shu
Department of Computer Science
State University of New York at Buffalo

## Abstract

*A parallel scheduling algorithm for N-cube networks is presented in this paper. This algorithm can fully balance the load and maximize locality by using global load information. Communication costs are significantly reduced compared to other existing algorithms.*

## 1 Introduction

Parallel scheduling is a promising technique for processor load balancing. In parallel scheduling, all processors are cooperated together to schedule work. Parallel scheduling utilizes global load information and is able to accurately balance the load. It provides high-quality, scalable scheduling. Some parallel scheduling algorithms have been introduced in [4, 3, 11, 15].

Parallel scheduling can be applied to problems with a predictable structure, which are called static problems [1, 18]. It can also be applied to problems with an unpredictable structure, which are called dynamic problems. The load of dynamic problems is usually balanced by dynamic scheduling, which can adjust load distribution based on runtime system load information [5, 6, 14]. However, most dynamic scheduling algorithms, when making a load balancing decision, utilize neither problem characteristics nor global load information. When parallel scheduling is applied at runtime, it becomes an *incremental collective* scheduling. It is applied whenever the load becomes unbalanced. All processors collectively schedule the workload. Such a system has been described in [15].

A category of scheduling sometimes referred to as *prescheduling* is closely related to the idea presented in this paper. Prescheduling schedules workload according to the problem input. Therefore, problems whose load distribution depends on its input and cannot be balanced by static scheduling can be balanced by prescheduling. Applying prescheduling periodically, the load can be balanced at runtime. Fox *et al.* first adapted prescheduling to application problems with geometric structures [7]. Some other works

also deal with this type of problem [4, 2]. The project PARTI automates prescheduling for nonuniform problems [13]. The dimension exchange method (DEM) is applied to application problems without geometric structure [12, 3]. It was conceptually designed for a hypercube system but may be applied to other topologies, such as k-ary n-cubes [19]. It balances load for independent tasks with an equal grain size. The method has been extended by Willebeek-LeMair and Reeves [17] so that the algorithm can run incrementally to correct the unbalanced load due to varied grain sizes. Nicol has proposed a direct mapping algorithm which computes the total number of tasks by using sum-reduction [11]. However, it does not minimize the communication cost, nor eliminate communication conflict. An incremental scheduling for N-body simulation is presented in [8]. The task graph is rescheduled periodically to correct the load imbalance. However, its runtime scheduling has not been parallelized yet.

In this paper, we present a new parallel scheduling algorithm for N-cube systems. This algorithm can fully balance the load and maximize locality. It significantly reduces communication overhead compared to other existing algorithms. This paper is organized as follows. Section 2 reviews the DEM algorithm. In section 3, the optimal scheduling problem is discussed. In section 4, we present the new algorithm and analyze its optimality. Performance is presented in section 5, and section 6 concludes the paper.

## 2 Dimension Exchange Method(DEM)

DEM is a good scheduling algorithm. It has been shown that DEM outperformed other dynamic scheduling algorithms [17]. In DEM, small domains are balanced first and then combined to form larger domains until ultimately the entire system is balanced. The algorithm is described in Figure 1. All node pairs in the first dimension whose addresses differ in only the least significant bit balance the load between themselves. Next, all node pairs in the second dimension balance the load between themselves, and so forth, until each node has balanced its load with each of its neighbors. The number of communication steps of the DEM algorithm is $3d$, where $d$ is the number of dimensions [17].

---

**DEM**

for $k = 0$ $to$ $d - 1$

    node $i$ exchanges with node $j$ the current values of $w_i$ and $w_j$, where $j = i \oplus 2^k$

    if $(w_i - w_j) > 1$, send $\lfloor (w_i - w_j)/2 \rfloor$ tasks to node $j$

    if $(w_j - w_i) > 1$, receive $\lfloor (w_j - w_i)/2 \rfloor$ tasks from node $j$

    update the value of $w_i$

---

Figure 1: The DEM algorithm.

**Example 1:**

The DEM algorithm is illustrated in Figure 2. The load distribution before execution of the DEM algorithm is shown in Figure 2(a). In the first step, nodes exchange load information and balance the load in dimension 0 as shown in Figure 2(b). Then, the load is balanced in dimension 1 as shown in Figure 2(c). After load balancing in dimension 2 (Figure 2(d)), the final result is shown in Figure 2(e). The load is not fully balanced because only integer numbers of tasks can be transmitted between nodes. There are a total of 33 task-hops.

After execution of the DEM algorithm, the load difference $D = \max(w_i) - \min(w_i)$ is bounded by $d$, the dimension of the hypercube [9]. Figure 3 shows an example where $D = 4$ for a 4-dimensional hypercube.

The DEM algorithm is simple and of low complexity. At each load balancing step, only node pairs exchange their load information. No global information is collected. Without global load information, it is impossible for a node to make a correct decision about how many tasks should be sent. Node pairs attempt to average their number of tasks anyway. A node may send excessive tasks to its neighbor. DEM is unable to fully balance the load and to minimize the communication cost.

## 3 The Optimal Scheduling Problem

The scheduling problem can be described as follows. In a parallel system, $N$ computing nodes are connected by a given topology. Each node $i$ has $w_i$

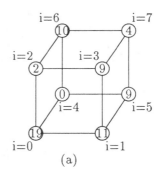

(a)

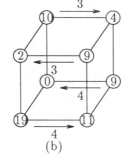

(b)

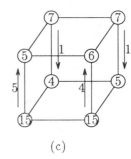

(c)

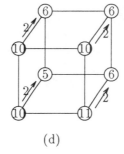

(d)

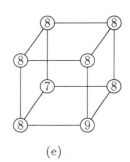

(e)

Figure 2: An example for the DEM algorithm.

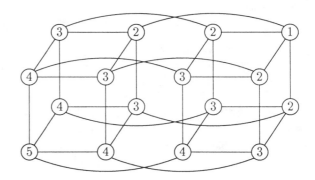

Figure 3: An example which shows that the number of tasks differs by 4 resulting from DEM.

tasks when parallel scheduling is applied. A scheduling algorithm is to redistribute tasks so that the number of tasks in each node is equal. Assume the sum of $w_i$ of all nodes can be evenly divided by $N$. The average number of tasks $w_{avg}$ is calculated by

$$w_{avg} = \frac{\sum_{i=0}^{N-1} w_i}{N}.$$

Each node should have $w_{avg}$ tasks after executing the scheduling algorithm. If $w_i > w_{avg}$, the node must determine where to send the tasks.

For a parallel scheduling algorithm that utilizes global information, the number of communication steps can be of order of $log\,N$, where $N$ is the number of processors. The average time of each communication step depends on the total number of tasks migrated and their traveling distances. The objective function is to minimize the number of *task-hops*:

$$\sum_k e_k,$$

where $e_k$ is the number of tasks transmitted through the edge $k$. In general, this problem can be converted to the minimum-cost maximum-flow problem [10] as follows. Each edge is treated as a bidirectional arc and given a tuple $(capacity, cost)$, where *capacity* is the capacity of the edge and *cost* is the cost of the edge. Set $capacity = \infty$, $cost = 1$, for all edges in the processor network. Then add a source node $s$ with an edge $(s, i)$ to each node $i$ if $w_i > w_{avg}$ and a sink node $t$ with an edge $(j, t)$ from each node $j$ if $w_j < w_{avg}$. Set $capacity_{si} = w_i - w_{avg}$, $cost_{si} = 0$, for all $i$, and $capacity_{jt} = w_{avg} - w_j$, $cost_{jt} = 0$, for all $j$. A minimum cost integral flow yields a solution to the problem. The graph constructed for Figure 2 is given in Figure 4, where $w_{avg} = 8$. The minimum cost algorithm [10] generates a solution as shown in Figure 5.

The complexity of the minimum cost algorithm is $O(N^2 v)$, where $N$ is the number of nodes and $v$ is the desired flow value [10]. The complexity of its corresponding parallel algorithm on $N$ nodes is at least $O(Nv)$. This high complexity is not realistic for run-time scheduling. For certain topology, such as trees, the complexity can be reduced to $O(log\,N)$ on $N$ nodes [16]. For a topology other than trees, we need to find a heuristic algorithm.

## 4    Cube Walking Algorithm

A good heuristic algorithm can be designed by utilizing global load information. Here we present a new

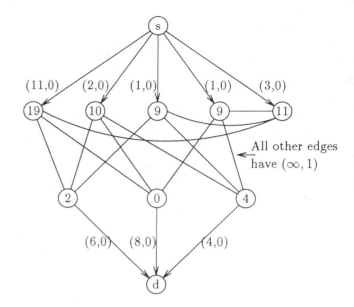

Figure 4: Graph for optimal scheduling problem (Figure 2).

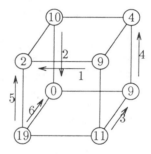

Figure 5: An optimal solution of Figure 2.

parallel scheduling algorithm for the hypercube topology. The algorithm, called *Cube Walking Algorithm* (*CWA*), is shown in Figure 6. Let $w_i^0$ be the number of tasks in node $i$ before the algorithm is applied. The first step collects the system load information by exchanging values of $w_i^k$ to obtain the values of $w_i^{k+1}$. Each node records a $w$ vector, where $w_i^k$ is the total number of tasks in its $k$-dimensional subcube. Here, the $k$-dimensional subcube of node $i$ is defined as all nodes whose numbers have the same $(d-k)$-bit prefix as node $i$. The value of $w_i^d$ in each node is equal to the total number of tasks in the entire cube. In step 2, each node calculates the average number of tasks per node. A quota vector $q$ is calculated in step 3 so that each node knows if its $k$-dimensional subcubes are overloaded or underloaded. The vector $q$ can be computed directly as follows:

$$q_i^k = w_{avg} * 2^k + r_i^k$$

where

$$r_i^k = \begin{cases} 0 & if\ i \wedge (N - 2^k) \geq R \\ 2^k & if\ i \vee (2^k - 1) < R \\ R - i \wedge (N - 2^k) & otherwise \end{cases}$$

where $\wedge$ is the bitwise AND and $\vee$ the bitwise OR. The $\delta$ vector is the difference of $w$ and $q$, which stand for the number of tasks to be sent to or received from other subcubes.

In step 4, task exchanges are conducted among each dimension. We start with the cube of dimension $d - 1$. Recursively, we partition a cube of dimension $k$ into two subcubes of dimension $(k - 1)$. Each node $n(i)$ is paired with the corresponding node $n(i)' = n(i \oplus 2^k)$ in the other subcube. In this particular step, we only exchange tasks between $n(i)$ and $n(i)'$, where $i = 0, 1, ..., N/2 - 1$. And, we send tasks only in one direction — from the overloaded subcube to the other. In this way, an overloaded node does not necessarily commit itself to send tasks out since it may postpone the action. The decision is made globally within the subcube by calculating a $\theta$ vector for every node in the overloaded subcube. The calculation of $\theta$ is a local operation without any communication. The value of $\delta$ of $n'$ can be calculated by $\delta_{i \oplus 2^j}^j = w_i^{j+1} - w_i^j - q_{i \oplus 2^j}^j$. The $\gamma$ vector records the number of tasks reserved for subcubes of lower dimensions. The following lemma shows that at the end of the algorithm, each node has the same number of tasks as its quota.

**Lemma 1:** After execution of CWA, the number of tasks in each node is equal to its quota.

**Proof:** To show after iteration 0 the number of tasks in each node is equal to its quota $q_i^0$, we need to show that after iteration $k$, each $k$-dimensional subcube has $q_i^k$ tasks. Then, the subcube with $\delta_i^k > 0$ needs to send $\delta_i^k$ tasks to the other subcube with $\delta_i^k < 0$. Because tasks are sent in one direction, the number of tasks sent from the overloaded subcube to the underloaded subcube must be equal to $\delta_i^k$. That is, $\sum \theta_i^0 = \delta_i^k = \theta_i^k$. It can be proven by showing that

$$\theta_i^{j+1} = \theta_i^j + \theta_{i \oplus 2^j}^j.$$

There are three cases when assigning the value of $\theta$:
Case 1: when $\delta_i^j < \gamma_i^{j+1}$

$$\theta_i^j = 0$$
$$\theta_{i \oplus 2^j}^j = \theta_{i \oplus 2^j}^{j+1}$$

Hence, $\theta_i^j + \theta_{i \oplus 2^j}^j = \theta_{i \oplus 2^j}^{j+1} = \theta_i^{j+1}$.

---

**Cube Walking Algorithm (CWA)**
Assume the cube dimension is $d$, the number of nodes is $N = 2^d$. Let $\oplus$ denote the bitwise exclusive OR and $\wedge$ the bitwise AND.

1. **Global Information Collection:**
   Perform sum reductions. Each node computes its $w$ vector, $k = 0, ..., d$
   $$w_i^0 = w_i, \quad w_i^k = w_i^{k-1} + w_{i \oplus 2^{k-1}}^{k-1}$$

2. **Average Load Calculation:**
   $$T = w_i^d, \quad w_{avg} = \lfloor T/N \rfloor, \quad R = T \bmod N.$$

3. **Quota Calculation:** Node $i$ computes its vectors $q_i^k$ and $\delta_i^k$, $k = 0, ..., d - 1$
   $$q_i^0 = \begin{cases} w_{avg} + 1 & if\ i < R \\ w_{avg} & otherwise \end{cases}, \quad q_i^k = q_i^{k-1} + q_{i \oplus 2^{k-1}}^{k-1}$$
   $$\delta_i^k = w_i^k - q_i^k$$

4. **Task Exchange:** For $k = d - 1\ to\ 0$ do

   4.1) For node $i$ with $\delta_i^k > 0$, compute the number of tasks to be sent out

   Initialize $\theta_i^k = \delta_i^k$ and $\gamma_i^k = 0$
   For $j = k - 1\ to\ 0$
   $$\theta_i^j = \begin{cases} 0 & if\ \delta_i^j \leq \gamma_i^{j+1} \\ & and\ i \wedge 2^j = 0 \\ \min(\delta_i^j - \gamma_i^{j+1}, \theta_i^{j+1}) & if\ \delta_i^j > \gamma_i^{j+1} \\ & and\ i \wedge 2^j = 0 \\ \theta_i^{j+1} & if\ \delta_{i \oplus 2^j}^j \leq \gamma_i^{j+1} \\ & and\ i \wedge 2^j \neq 0 \\ \max(\delta_i^j, 0) & if\ \delta_{i \oplus 2^j}^j > \gamma_i^{j+1} \\ & and\ i \wedge 2^j \neq 0 \end{cases}$$

   $$\gamma_i^j = \delta_i^j - \theta_i^j$$

   Send $\theta_i^0$ tasks as well as its $\theta$ vector to node $i \oplus 2^k$. Update its own vectors $w_i^j = w_i^j - \theta_i^j$, $\delta_i^j = \delta_i^j - \theta_i^j$, for $j = 0, 1, ..., k - 1$.

   4.2) For node $i$ with $\delta_i^k < 0$, receive tasks as well as the $\theta$ vector from node $i \oplus 2^k$. Update its own vectors $w_i^j = w_i^j + \theta_{i \oplus 2^k}^j$, $\delta_i^j = \delta_i^j + \theta_{i \oplus 2^k}^j$, for $j = 0, 1, ..., k - 1$.

---

Figure 6: The Cube Walking Algorithm.

Case 2: when $\theta_i^{j+1} + \gamma_i^{j+1} \geq \delta_i^j > \gamma_i^{j+1}$,

since $\delta_i^j - \gamma_i^{j+1} \leq \theta_i^{j+1}$,

$\theta_i^j = \min(\delta_i^j - \gamma_i^{j+1}, \theta_i^{j+1}) = \delta_i^j - \gamma_i^{j+1}$

since $\delta_{i \oplus 2^j}^j = \delta_i^{j+1} - \delta_i^j = \gamma_i^{j+1} + \theta_i^{j+1} - \delta_i^j \geq 0$,

$\theta_{i \oplus 2^j}^j = \max(\delta_{i \oplus 2^j}^j, 0) = \delta_{i \oplus 2^j}^j$

Hence,

$\theta_i^j + \theta_{i \oplus 2^j}^j = \delta_i^j - \gamma_i^{j+1} + \delta_{i \oplus 2^j}^j = \delta_i^{j+1} - \gamma_i^{j+1} = \theta_i^{j+1}$.

Case 3: when $\delta_i^j > \theta_i^{j+1} + \gamma_i^{j+1}$,

since $\delta_i^j - \gamma_i^{j+1} > \theta_i^{j+1}$,

$\theta_i^j = \min(\delta_i^j - \gamma_i^{j+1}, \theta_i^{j+1}) = \theta_i^{j+1}$

since $\delta_{i \oplus 2^j}^j = \delta_i^{j+1} - \delta_i^j = \gamma_i^{j+1} + \theta_i^{j+1} - \delta_i^j < 0$,

$\theta_{i \oplus 2^j}^j = \max(\delta_{i \oplus 2^j}^j, 0) = 0$

Hence, $\theta_i^j + \theta_{i \oplus 2^j}^j = \theta_i^{j+1}$. □

In this algorithm, step 1 spends $2d$ communication steps for exchanging load information, where $d$ is the dimension of the cube. Step 4 spends $d$ communication steps for load balancing. Therefore, the total number of communication steps is $3d$.

**Example 2:**

A running example of CWA is shown in Figure 7. At the beginning of scheduling, each node has $w_i^0$ tasks ready to be scheduled. Values of $w_i^k$ are calculated at step 1. The values of $w_{avg}$ and $R$ are as follows:

$$w_{avg} = 8, \ R = 0.$$

Then, each node calculates the values of $q_i^k$ at step 3. Because $R = 0$, every node has the same quota vector:

$$\{8, 16, 32\}.$$

At step 4, when $k = 2$, the subcube $\{0,1,2,3\}$ is the overloaded one. The values of $w_i^k$, $\delta_i^k$, $\theta_i^k$, and $\gamma_i^k$ are as follows:

| Node | d0 | | | | d1 | | | |
|------|-----|------|------|------|-----|------|------|------|
| $i$ | $w_i^0$ | $\delta_i^0$ | $\theta_i^0$ | $\gamma_i^0$ | $w_i^1$ | $\delta_i^1$ | $\theta_i^1$ | $\gamma_i^1$ |
| 0 | 19 | 11 | 6 | 5 | 30 | 14 | 9 | 5 |
| 1 | 11 | 3 | 3 | 0 | 30 | 14 | 9 | 5 |
| 2 | 2 | -6 | 0 | -6 | 11 | -5 | 0 | -5 |
| 3 | 9 | 1 | 0 | 1 | 11 | -5 | 0 | -5 |

| Node | d2 | | | |
|------|-----|------|------|------|
| $i$ | $w_i^2$ | $\delta_i^2$ | $\theta_i^2$ | $\gamma_i^2$ |
| 0 | 41 | 9 | 9 | 0 |
| 1 | 41 | 9 | 9 | 0 |
| 2 | 41 | 9 | 9 | 0 |
| 3 | 41 | 9 | 9 | 0 |

Thus, node 0 sends six tasks to node 4, and node 1 sends three tasks to node 5. Now, the loads between subcubes $\{0, 1, 2, 3\}$ and $\{4, 5, 6, 7\}$ have been balanced. Each subcube has 32 tasks.

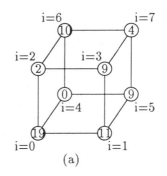

(a)

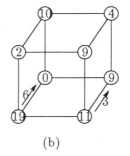

(b)

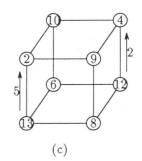

(c)

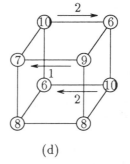

(d)

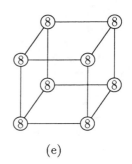

(e)

Figure 7: A running example of CWA.

When $k = 1$, subcubes $\{0,1\}$ and $\{4,5\}$ are overloaded. The values of $w_i^k$, $\delta_i^k$, $\theta_i^k$, and $\gamma_i^k$ are as follows:

| Node | d0 | | | | d1 | | | |
|------|-----|------|------|------|-----|------|------|------|
| $i$ | $w_i^0$ | $\delta_i^0$ | $\theta_i^0$ | $\gamma_i^0$ | $w_i^1$ | $\delta_i^1$ | $\theta_i^1$ | $\gamma_i^1$ |
| 0 | 13 | 5 | 5 | 0 | 21 | 5 | 5 | 0 |
| 1 | 8 | 0 | 0 | 0 | 21 | 5 | 5 | 0 |
| 4 | 6 | -2 | 0 | -2 | 18 | 2 | 2 | 0 |
| 5 | 12 | 4 | 2 | 2 | 18 | 2 | 2 | 0 |

Thus, node 0 sends five tasks to node 2, and node 5 sends two tasks to node 7. The loads between subcubes $\{0, 1\}$, $\{2, 3\}$, $\{4, 5\}$, and $\{6, 7\}$ have been balanced. Each subcube has 16 tasks.

When $k = 0$, nodes 3, 5, and 6 are overloaded. Their values of $w_i^k$, $\delta_i^k$, $\theta_i^k$, and $\gamma_i^k$ are as follows:

| Node | d0 | | | |
|------|-----|-----|-----|-----|
| $i$ | $w_i^0$ | $\delta_i^0$ | $\theta_i^0$ | $\gamma_i^0$ |
| 3 | 9 | 1 | 1 | 0 |
| 5 | 10 | 2 | 2 | 0 |
| 6 | 10 | 2 | 2 | 0 |

Finally, node 3 sends one task to node 2, node 5 sends two tasks to node 4, and node 6 sends two tasks to node 7. This results in a balanced load, each node having eight tasks. The total number of task-hops is 21.

Now, we discuss the scheduling quality, locality, and communication costs of the CWA algorithm. The next theorem shows that this algorithm is able to fully balance the load. If the number of tasks can be equally divided by the number of nodes, each node will have the equal number of tasks; otherwise, the number of tasks in each node differs by one.

**Theorem 2:** The difference in the number of tasks in each node is at most one after execution of CWA.

**Proof:** From Lemma 1, the number of tasks in each node is equal to its quota after execution of CWA. Since the quota is either $w_{avg}$ or $w_{avg} + 1$, the difference in the number of tasks in each node is at most one. □

This algorithm also maximizes locality. *Local tasks* are the tasks that are not migrated to other nodes, and *non-local tasks* are those that are migrated to other nodes. Maximum locality implies the minimum number of non-local tasks. In Lemmas 2 and 3 and Theorem 3, we assume that the number of tasks $T$ is evenly divided by $N$, the number of nodes. When $T$ is not evenly divided by $N$, the algorithms are nearly-optimal. The following lemma gives the minimum number of non-local tasks.

**Lemma 2:** To reach a balanced load, the minimum number of non-local tasks is

$$\sum_i \max(w_{avg} - w_i, 0).$$

**Proof:** Each node where $w_i < w_{avg}$ must receive $(w_{avg} - w_i)$ tasks from other nodes for a balanced load. Therefore, a total of $\sum_i \max(w_{avg} - w_i, 0)$ tasks must be migrated between nodes. □

The next theorem proves that CWA maximizes locality.

**Theorem 3:** The number of non-local tasks in the CWA algorithm is

$$\sum_i \max(w_{avg} - w_i, 0).$$

**Proof:** In CWA, each node sends tasks only when its weight is larger than $w_{avg}$ and no more than

$(w_i - w_{avg})$ tasks are sent out. Thus, in all nodes at least $\sum_i \min(w_i, w_{avg})$ tasks are local. Therefore, the number of non-local tasks is no more than

$$N \times w_{avg} - \sum_i \min(w_i, w_{avg}) = \sum_i (w_{avg} - \min(w_i, w_{avg}))$$

$$= \sum_i \max(w_{avg} - w_i, 0).$$

As stated in Lemma 2, these algorithms minimize the number of non-local tasks and maximize locality. □

CWA is a heuristic algorithm and in general is not able to minimize the communication cost. However, for a system with less than or equal to four nodes, the algorithm minimizes the communication cost.

**Lemma 3:** The CWA algorithm minimizes the communication cost in a system with two or four nodes.

**Proof:** The communication cost in a system is minimized if there is no negative cycle [10]. In a system of two nodes, there is no cycle. In a system of four nodes, only a path consisting of at least three edges can form a negative cycle. With CWA, the longest path has two edges. Therefore, there is no negative cycle. □

The DEM algorithm does not minimize the communication cost for four nodes because there may be a path consisting of three edges.

## 5  Performance Study

CWA is a heuristic algorithm. Its optimality needs to be studied with simulation. For this purpose, we consider a test set of load distributions. In this test set, the load at each processor is randomly selected, with the mean equal to the specified average number of tasks. The number of processors varies from 4 to 256. The average number of tasks (average weight) per processor varies from 2 to 100. The average weight is made to be an integer so that the load can be fully balanced.

First, we compare CWA to DEM. CWA can fully balance the load but DEM cannot in most cases. We run the DEM algorithm on 1,000 test cases. When the number of processors increases, there are less fully-balanced cases. For 32 processors there are a few cases, and for 64 processors, there is no fully-balanced case in this test set.

An important measure of a scheduling algorithm is its locality. The CWA algorithm sends only necessary tasks to other processors so that it maximizes locality. The DEM algorithm results in unnecessary task migration. Here, we study locality of the DEM algorithm. Because DEM is not able to fully balance the load for all cases, only the fully-balanced cases are selected. Each result is the average of the fully-balanced cases in 1,000 test cases. The normalized locality is measured by

$$\frac{T_{DEM} - T_{OPT}}{T_{OPT}},$$

where $T_{DEM}$ is the total number of non-local tasks in the DEM algorithm, and $T_{OPT}$ is the minimum number of non-local tasks. Figure 8 shows the normalized locality on 4, 8, and 16 processors. Because few fully-balanced cases exist on more than 16 processors, they are not reported here.

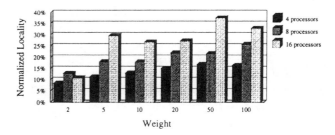

Figure 8: Normalized locality of DEM

Next, we compare the load balancing overhead. DEM is very simple so that the runtime overhead for load balancing decision is small. However, unnecessary task migration leads to a large communication overhead. Compared to the time spent on the load balancing decision, communication time is the dominate factor. CWA, on the other hand, although needing more time to make an accurate load balancing decision, involves less communication overhead. The normalized communication cost is measured by

$$\frac{C_{DEM} - C_{OPT}}{C_{OPT}}$$

and

$$\frac{C_{CWA} - C_{OPT}}{C_{OPT}},$$

where $C_{DEM}$, $C_{CWA}$, and $C_{OPT}$ are the number of task-hops of the DEM, CWA, and optimal algorithms, respectively. Figure 9 compares the normalized communication costs on 4, 8, and 16 processors. Each result is the average of the DEM fully-balanced cases in 1,000 test cases. The number of task-hops of CWA on four processors is the minimum. It can be seen that the communication costs of DEM are much larger than those of CWA. Figure 10 shows the normalized communication costs of CWA on 64 and 256 processors. Each data presented here is the average of 100 different test cases.

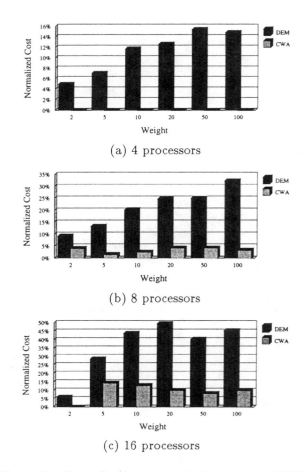

(a) 4 processors

(b) 8 processors

(c) 16 processors

Figure 9: Normalized communication costs of DEM and CWA

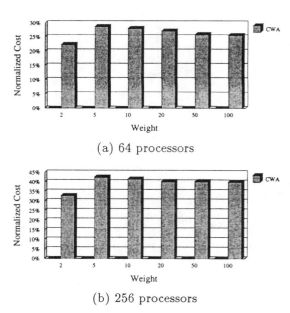

(a) 64 processors

(b) 256 processors

Figure 10: Normalized communication costs of CWA

## 6   Conclusion

In this paper, we described a parallel scheduling algorithm for N-cubes. In this algorithm, all processors cooperate together to collect load information and to exchange workload in parallel. With parallel scheduling, it is possible to obtain a high quality load balancing with a fully-balanced load and maximized locality. Communication costs can be reduced significantly.

## Acknowledgements

The author would like to thank Xin He for his helpful discussion. This research was partially supported by NSF grant CCR-9505300.

## References

[1] I. Ahmad, Y.K. Kwok, and M.Y. Wu. Performance comparison of algorithms for static scheduling of DAGs to multiprocessors. In *Second Australasian Conference on Parallel and Real-time Systems*, September 1995.

[2] M.J. Berger and S. Bokhari. A partitioning strategy for non-uniform problems on multiprocessors. *IEEE Trans. Computers*, C-26:570–580, 1987.

[3] G. Cybenko. Dynamic load balancing for distributed memory multiprocessors. *J. of Parallel Distrib. Comput.*, 7:279–301, 1989.

[4] K. M. Dragon and J. L. Gustafson. A low-cost hypercube load balance algorithm. In *Proc. of the 4th Conf. on Hypercube Concurrent Computers and Applications*, pages 583–590, 1989.

[5] D. L. Eager, E. D. Lazowska, and J. Zahorjan. Adaptive load sharing in homogeneous distributed systems. *IEEE Trans. Software Eng.*, SE-12(5):662–674, May 1986.

[6] D. L. Eager, E. D. Lazowska, and J. Zahorjan. A comparison of receiver-initiated and sender-initiated adaptive load sharing. *Performance Eval.*, 6(1):53–68, March 1986.

[7] G. C. Fox, M. A. Johnson, G. A. Lyzenga, S. W. Otto, J. K. Salmon, and D. W. Walker. *Solving Problems on Concurrent Processors*, volume I. Prentice-Hall, 1988.

[8] A. Gerasoulis, J. Jiao, and T. Yang. Experience with graph scheduling for mapping irregular scientific computation. In *First Workshop on Solving Irregular Problems on Distributed Memory Machines in conjunction with International Parallel Processing Symposium*, pages 1–8, April 1995.

[9] S.H. Hosseini, B. Litow, M. Malkawi, J. McPherson, and K. Vairavan. Analysis of a graph coloring based distributed load balancing algorithm. *Journal of Parallel and Distributed Computing*, 10:160–166, 1990.

[10] E. L. Lawler. *Combinatorial Optimization: Networks and Matroids*. Holt, Rinehart and Winston, 1976.

[11] D.M. Nicol. Communication efficient global load balancing. In *The Scalable High Performance Computing Conference*, pages 292–299, April 1992.

[12] S. Ranka, Y. Won, and S. Sahni. Programming a hypercube multicomputer. *IEEE Software*, pages 69–77, September 1988.

[13] J. Saltz, R. Mirchandaney, R. Smith, D. Nicol, and K. Crowley. The PARTY parallel runtime system. In *Proceedings of the SIAM Conference on Parallel Processing for Scientific Computing.* SIAM, 1987.

[14] Niranjan G. Shivaratri, Phillip Krieger, and Mukesh Singhal. Load distributing for locally distributed systems. *IEEE Computer*, 25(12):33–44, December 1992.

[15] W. Shu and M. Y. Wu. Runtime Incremental Parallel Scheduling (RIPS) for large-scale parallel computers. In *Proceedings of the 5th Symposium on the Frontiers of Massively Parallel Computation*, pages 456–463, February 1995.

[16] W. Shu and M.Y. Wu. Runtime parallel scheduling for distributed memory computers. In *Int'l Conf. on Parallel Processing*, pages II. 143–150, August 1995.

[17] Marc Willebeek-LeMair and Anthony P. Reeves. Strategies for dynamic load balancing on highly parallel computers. *IEEE Trans. Parallel and Distributed System*, 9(4):979–993, September 1993.

[18] M. Y. Wu. On parallelization of static scheduling algorithms. Technical Report 95-49A, Dept. of Computer Science, State University of New York at Buffalo, October 1995.

[19] C. Z. Xu and F. C. M. Lau. The generalized dimension exchange method for load balancing in k-ary n-cubes and variants. *Journal of Parallel and Distributed Computing*, 24(1):72–85, January 1995.

# EFFICIENT RELIABLE MULTICAST ON MYRINET*

Kees Verstoep          Koen Langendoen          Henri Bal

Dept. of Mathematics and Computer Science

Vrije Universiteit

Amsterdam, The Netherlands

Abstract - - *This paper describes a reliable multicast algorithm on top of reliable point-to-point communication. The algorithm uses a flow control method based on a credit scheme to prevent message loss caused by overflow of software buffers. The multicast algorithm has been implemented by extending the Illinois Fast Messages software for Myrinet, which supports reliable point-to-point communication but no multicast. To obtain low latency and high throughput, forwarding of messages is handled entirely by the network adapter boards without involving the hosts. Measurements on an 8-node Myrinet system show that the implementation achieves high performance.*

## 1  INTRODUCTION

Multicast is an important communication primitive for parallel programming. It is useful both for the application programmer and for the implementation of parallel languages. Several programming systems (e.g., SR [1], MPI [11]) provide multicasting to the programmer. Languages like Orca, HPF, and Jade use multicasting in their implementation (runtime system) [3, 5, 13]. In particular, multicast is much more suitable than unicast (i.e., point-to-point) communication for implementing replicated global information [14].

Although the designers of software systems have recognized the importance of multicast, modern network technology often does not support it in hardware. For example, Myrinet (a high-speed network intended for parallel computing on clusters of workstations) only provides unicast communication along point-to-point links [4].

Efficiently implementing *reliable* multicast communication in software is a difficult problem, even if the point-to-point links are reliable. One issue, studied in many papers (e.g., [6, 10]) is how to forward a message to all destinations. Another critical issue, studied in this paper, is how to manage software buffer space at all destinations, in order to prevent overflow of this scarce resource. Buffer management also is a problem for unicast communication. Many programming systems do not solve the problem, and thus provide unreliable unicast communication (even though

the hardware links are reliable). Recently, the Fast Messages (FM) software from the University of Illinois has addressed the problem for unicast communication, using a simple but effective flow control mechanism [12].

Flow control for multicast communication, however, is much more difficult than for unicast communication, because each message is sent to many destinations, instead of just one. Buffer space must thus be available at all receiving hosts, and at all hosts involved in forwarding the message. One solution is to implement an unreliable multicast primitive (which may drop fragments if it runs out of buffer space), and implement a reliable protocol at a higher level, using retransmissions whenever messages are lost. We implemented such a scheme on Myrinet (using FM), but our experiences showed that this results in a significant overhead. The one-way latency for FM unicast messages on Myrinet is 25 $\mu$s, so even starting a timer is already costly in comparison to this low latency.

In this paper we present an efficient algorithm for reliable multicast on Myrinet. The algorithm uses a multicast flow control scheme to prevent software buffers from overflowing, so reliable multicast delivery can be guaranteed with minimal overhead. In particular, the multicast algorithm does not use timers and acknowledgements to implement reliability. The flow control based algorithm has been implemented on an 8-node Myrinet configuration. Both actual measurements and simulations are used to determine its performance and scalability.

The paper is structured as follows. The basic design of the reliable multicast protocol is presented in Section 2. The actual implementation including many details is then described in Section 3. The performance of the reliable multicast algorithm is studied in Section 4. Section 5 discusses the scalability of the flow control mechanism and the applicability to other network technologies, and finally draws some conclusions.

## 2  DESIGN

The two major issues in designing a reliable multicast algorithm for usage on top of a reliable point-to-point interconnection network like Myrinet are to find the optimal span-

---

*This research is supported in part by a PIONIER grant from the Netherlands Organization for Scientific Research (N.W.O.).

ning tree and to guarantee reliable message delivery at the software level. These two issues are discussed below.

## 2.1 Spanning tree multicast

Multicast can be implemented in software by forwarding messages over point-to-point links along a spanning tree. Often the underlying hardware topology of a point-to-point network (e.g., a mesh structure) limits the potential shape of the spanning tree that can be used for broadcasting, since communication between neighbors is much cheaper than communication between arbitrary nodes. In the case of Myrinet, however, the network interconnect consists of multi-ported crossbar switches, which can be easily connected in a hierarchical manner to produce one large (virtual) crossbar switch interconnecting all nodes used for parallel processing. Due to the usage of wormhole routing, the switching latency is very low (less than 1 $\mu$s per switch). Communication performance is thus independent of which nodes want to exchange messages. Consequently, we have complete freedom in choosing an appropriate spanning tree for our multicast protocol.

Figure 1 shows four of the many possible spanning trees for multicasting a message to a group of 8 nodes. The performance of a particular tree is mainly determined by its shape, which directly influences average latency and throughput. Another factor is the ratio of the time needed to put the message on the network (send latency) to the time needed to get the message from the network into local memory (receive latency). Assuming that the send latency is of the same order as the receive latency, which is the case for Myrinet, the expected performance of the various forwarding methods can be characterized as follows:

- Binomial trees [6] have the lowest latency, but throughput drops for larger groups. The reason is that the rate at which nodes can forward messages decreases due to the increasing number of replicas that have to be sent.

- Binary trees have slightly higher latency than binomial trees, but throughput should remain quite high for large groups (because of the constant maximum binary fan-out).

- Serial communication sustains highest throughput, since it effectively pipelines messages, but latency increases linearly with the number of nodes.

- Iterative unicast is quite fast for small groups since it avoids the forwarding overhead altogether. Latency increases linearly with the group size, but the increase is less than for serial communication, because sending is cheaper than forwarding. The throughput of iterative unicast, however, is very bad for large groups, because of the high fan-out.

Which spanning tree is *optimal* depends on what is considered more important: average latency or maximum throughput. Since for many parallel applications a low average latency is vital, but throughput is also important, we use binary trees in our multicast implementation. In Section 4 we will give measurements for the four kinds of trees on top of a Myrinet network.

## 2.2 Reliability

Given a suitable spanning tree, the remaining design issue is how to ensure reliable message delivery to all destinations. The general approach of setting timers and sending acknowledgement messages to achieve reliability is too costly given that Myrinet, like many other point-to-point networks, already provides reliable communication across individual links. Instead of treating the network as unreliable, our multicast protocol explicitly builds on top of reliable point-to-point communication to ensure reliable delivery of multicast messages. Note that we do not address the issue of fault tolerance and assume that network and node failures do not occur.

Given reliable point-to-point communication, the only source of message loss is buffer overflow; when messages arrive too fast at a certain node, the multicast protocol cannot keep up, so receive buffers fill up, which eventually leads to message loss. A suitable flow-control mechanism can be exploited to prevent buffer overflow by adjusting the transmission rate of nodes sending multicasts so that hosts do not become overloaded with messages. If the usage of flow control can guarantee that no buffers will ever overflow then the multicast is automatically reliable.

In general we can distinguish two types of flow control: reactive and preventive. With reactive flow control, the system detects a congested state and then throttles the senders explicitly by sending control messages. Reactive flow control is also known as *congestion control* and is employed in many existing network protocols (e.g., TCP/IP [7]). With preventive flow control, also known as *congestion avoidance*, the system avoids congestion from occurring in the first place by conservatively limiting the outgoing message rate. Examples of a preventive flow-control policy are sliding window and credit-based protocols (e.g., FLIP [9]), which fragment a message into fixed-sized fragments and limit the number of outstanding (unacknowledged) fragments at the sending node.

The problem with reactive flow-control policies is that with current gigabit/sec networks, many message fragments may have been transmitted already before the sending node gets the first indication of congestion. Hence, very large buffers are needed to avoid dropping fragments. This makes reactive flow-control impractical for our reliable multicast protocol on Myrinet, which has small mem-

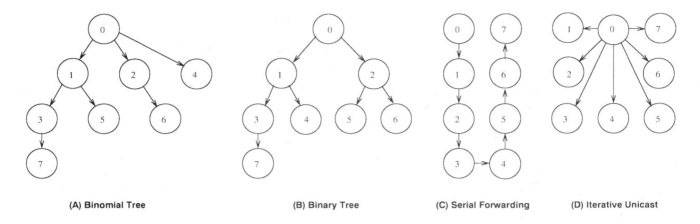

Figure 1: Alternative spanning trees for multicast to a group of 8 nodes.

ories on the network adapter boards. Consequently, we have designed a preventive flow-control multicast protocol.

Flow control for multicast is difficult because of the many nodes involved in handling one message. Also, if each multicast source is using a private spanning tree, then an individual node can receive messages from any node in the system. This unbounded (logical) connectivity makes it impossible to use a pair-wise preventive flow-control protocol, because the available buffer space on one node has to be divided among all potential senders. Limiting the fan-in is one possibility, but this limits the shape of the spanning trees. We have chosen to use a centralized scheme where flow is controlled through *credits*.

In our credit-based flow control scheme, a multicast source has to obtain credits before it may start sending multicast fragments into the network. A single credit gives a source the right to multicast one fragment to all destinations. A credit represents buffer space for one fragment at the destinations. The total number of credits in the system is limited to the maximum number of fragments that can be stored at a node, which ensures that no buffer will ever overflow.

An important issue is how to distribute the credits among all source nodes. Flow control schemes for point-to-point communication often give each node an equal share of the credits for other hosts. For multicast, this approach is undesirable, because each node may get only very few credits, even if only a small number of nodes wants to multicast data. In our algorithm, we therefore distribute the credits dynamically, based on demand. The credits are managed by a central node, which services credit requests and records the number of outstanding credits. To improve performance, each node maintains a credit cache so the

costs of requesting credits are amortized over multiple multicast messages; also, credits can be acquired outside the critical path, which reduces latency.

Another issue is how to recycle credits. If a node has finished processing an incoming multicast fragment, its free buffer space is increased. To determine the total number of credits currently available in the system, the amount of free buffer space on all nodes needs to be known. This information can be obtained in various ways. Our algorithm uses a token protocol. Occasionally a token is rotated among all hosts to find out how many multicasts have been processed so credits can be recycled. This approach might become a bottleneck for systems with many processors, in which case a combining tree could be used to gather credits. In any case, the token processing does not take place on the critical path of a multicast message, but occurs in the background.

Details about the preventive flow-control mechanism based on credits are given in the next section. Measurements show that the flow control mechanism adds hardly any cost to the sending of a multicast message (see Section 4).

## 3 MULTICAST ON MYRINET

In this section we first explain how unicast messages are transferred with Fast Messages over Myrinet. More details can be found in a recent paper by Pakin et al. [12]. Next we give an overview of our implementation of the multicast forwarding protocol that we added to FM (henceforth referred to as FM/MC). Finally we discuss in some detail the additional flow control algorithms we designed and implemented to make our multicast protocol reliable.

## 3.1 Message transfer in FM

In Fast Messages, the application is linked to a communication library in user space that takes complete control over the Myrinet network interface. The operating system kernel takes care only of mapping the device into the application's address space, and allocating an uncached memory region for DMA access from the network interface. Standard kernel interfaces (e.g., UNIX sockets) typically add too much overhead to make them suitable for low-latency message transfer. In the current implementation, it is not possible to share the network interface among different applications. The network interface contains a special-purpose processor (LanAI) that is responsible for interfacing the host with the network. This board also contains 128 Kbyte SRAM memory (host adapter memory). The original control program running on the LanAI (named LCP) was completely rewritten for FM to achieve extremely low roundtrip latencies [12].

Figure 2 shows how FM transfers a message over the Myrinet network. The FM library on the sending host fragments a message in small, fixed size fragments, transfers them to a send queue in host adapter memory, and increments a send counter. As soon as the LCP discovers that the host has deposited one or more fragments in the send queue, it will send them over the network to the destination indicated in the fragment header.

Before a fragment reaches its destination, it generally passes through one or more crossbar switches, but these add very little to the latency (less than 1 $\mu$s each). If the destination channel is busy (e.g., an other host is sending a fragment to it at the same time) the hardware flow control mechanism of Myrinet will temporarily block the outgoing fragment.

The arrival of the fragment at the destination network adapter is signaled to the LCP by means of a bit in a status word which the LCP frequently polls during its send/receive loop. The LCP then DMAs the fragment from the packet interface to the on-board receive queue. This fragment is next transferred to the host DMA region by means of an LCP-initiated DMA over the SBus. Note that DMA is used to clear the (small) receive queue as fast as possible without the need to synchronize with the host.

The availability of new fragments is indicated to the application by means of an update of a fragment-received counter on the LanAI. This counter has to be polled frequently by the application, or its runtime system. When the polling primitive from the FM library finds that new fragments have arrived, they are reassembled into a new message which is allocated in regular (cached) memory. When the message is complete, an upcall is performed to allow the application to process the message.

## 3.2 Adding Multicast to FM

We implemented Multicast in FM/MC by means of a spanning tree forwarding procedure that is completely handled by the software running on the LanAI processor of the network interface. The host processors are not involved in the forwarding of fragments, resulting in a low latency for the multicast. The application first has to explicitly tell the FM/MC library about the structure of the multicast group it wants to use by specifying the members. (A *broadcast* group consisting of all hosts is constructed by default.) The FM/MC library on each node updates the group membership table on its network adapter. A handle is returned that can be used for subsequent multicasts to the group.

The actual transmission of multicast messages is implemented as follows. The FM/MC library handles the multicast message as a sequence of fragments. For each fragment, the data is copied to the send queue and the send counter is incremented, similar to what is done for unicast. The LCP will notice that the next outgoing fragment is a multicast fragment, causing it to forward replicas of this fragment to the nodes adjacent to the root of the tree for the multicast group specified. The network adapters receiving the multicast fragment will, after having initiated a DMA transfer to the local host's DMA area, immediately forward it on to other members, if necessary. Binary spanning trees are used for their balance between latency and throughput (see Section 2).

## 3.3 Flow Control in FM

Before we describe our flow control protocol for multicast messages in FM/MC, we briefly discuss the unicast flow control scheme used in Fast Messages (version 1.1). As explained in the previous section, buffering of messages and message fragments happens at the following places:

- The fragment send queue in source host adapter memory.

- The fragment receive queue in destination host adapter memory.

- The destination host DMA receive buffer in main memory.

Fast Messages uses a credit scheme to prevent buffer overflow at the destination host DMA receive buffer [12]. Every host gets an equal share of the credits of all other hosts. Each credit represents an entry in the host DMA area. The credit scheme is completely implemented by the FM library. If the application does not read messages quickly enough, other hosts sending to it will run out of credits, and block until a credit update comes in.

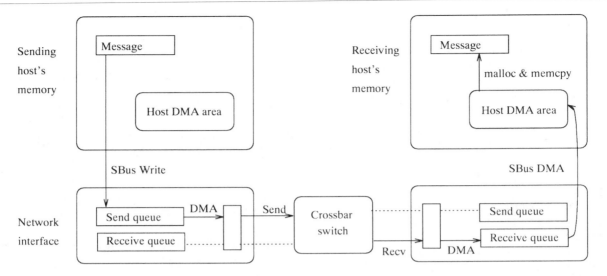

Figure 2: FM message flow path.

The fragment receive queue will never overflow since incoming fragments can be transferred to the host DMA area without any intermediate processing. This DMA area always has enough space left because of the credit scheme just mentioned. If the LCP is busy sending fragments, the hardware flow control in the Myrinet network will prevent new fragments arriving at the host for this short amount of time. Fragments are never dropped.

Finally, the fragment send queue on the host adapter is simply flow controlled by means of *back pressure*. The FM library's send primitive busy-waits until it can add a new fragment to the send queue. Note that in principle the memory for the reassembled messages also is a resource that ought to be flow controlled. However, the implicit assumption is that enough virtual memory is available for this not to be a problem in practice.

### 3.4 Multicast Flow Control

Our flow control method for multicast is based on a similar idea (a credit scheme) as for FM unicast. As described earlier, the Myrinet host adapter has a fixed FIFO receive queue for incoming fragments. Incoming fragments are always DMA-ed to the host, but multicast fragments may require additional forwarding. To avoid deadlock in the network, which could arise if multiple hosts are forwarding fragments to each other at the same time, the LCPs must keep reading fragments from the packet interface during the actual forwarding.

Since the arrival rate of new fragments may exceed the rate at which multicast fragments can be forwarded, it is possible that the receive queue becomes completely filled at some point. If this happens, no more fragments can be received until receive buffers are freed. Currently, hardware flow control will take care of blocking the next incoming fragment temporarily, but this fragment has to be read within a certain time or the network interface will get an automatic hardware reset (which happens to prevent one board from blocking a part of the entire network).

A second problem is caused by the host receive queue. To receive incoming fragments, the kernel reserves a static 512 Kbyte buffer in which the LCP deposits fragments using DMA. The FM unicast credit scheme ensures that this buffer will never overflow, even if the user program never polls. But without introducing some kind of additional flow control, this is not the case for multicast fragments.

For both problems mentioned above (overflow in the LCP receive queue and in the host receive queue) we will present a solution in the remainder of this section.

Overflow in the LCP receive queue. It would appear that overflow of the LCP receive queue can only be prevented by using a flow control method that takes its size into account. However, the rather small amount of host adapter memory (128 Kbyte, which is used to store the LCP and send/receive queues) would make this too restrictive. Instead, overflow of the LCP queue can be resolved by extending its *effective* length to the size of the host receive queue. Assuming that an additional flow control method ensures that no more fragments will be sent to a host than fit in its DMA area, the latter can be used as temporary storage (similar to *swap space*) for multicast fragments that still have to be forwarded. So, if the on-board LCP queue fills up, we swap part of it to host memory.

We implement this idea as follows. We split the receive queue into two parts:

- The *current* queue which contains the oldest fragments received. Some of these may still have to be forwarded to other members.

- The *overflow* queue which acts as temporary storage for newer fragments that have not yet been examined.

Typically, the overflow queue will not have overflowed when we are finished forwarding the fragments from the current queue. In this case we can just reverse the roles of the current and overflow queues, and proceed without any extra DMA overhead.

The interesting case is when the overflow queue is completely filled while we are still forwarding multicast fragments from the current queue. In that case the overflow queue is completely DMA-ed to the host (which is guaranteed to have room), and is simply *reused* for newly arriving fragments. After a while the LCP will be finished with the current queue, and notice that it overflowed the other queue. However, the original contents of the overflow queue can just be retrieved (*swapped back*) from the host buffer, by performing a DMA in the opposite direction. The situation after the overflow queue has overflowed once is shown in Figure 3-a. The situation after all fragments from the "current" queue have been forwarded is shown in Figure 3-b.

We conclude that lack of buffer resources in the LCP presents no problem provided that another proper flow control method guarantees that the host receive queue never overflows.

Overflow in the host receive queue. We begin by noting that the credit scheme described for unicast messages (see Section 3) could be generalized to multicast fragments. In this scheme the sender of a multicast fragment consumes (unicast) credits for all destinations. There are a number of problems with this solution, however:

- The sender has to check that it has a send credit for *each separate* destination of a multicast fragment. This does not scale.

- If there are many (say hundreds) of hosts, and each gets an equal share of the credits, each host only gets few credits, even if there are only a few members interested in sending multicasts concurrently. Note that the same problem exists for unicast, only it does not occur when using a small number of hosts.

- Once a number of fragments has been received and processed at the destinations, *all* these destinations will want to inform the sender about it. If they all simply unicast a credit update to the sender, this would cause a great deal of processing overhead at the network interface and the host itself. This does not scale either.

Therefore we have enhanced the simple-minded multicast credit scheme in a number of ways to make it practical:

- We let every host keep *separate* credit counters for multicasts and unicasts. The total number of credits (each representing an entry in a host's DMA receive buffer) is split in two parts: one for incoming unicasts, the other for incoming multicasts.

- It is not necessary to give each host an equal number of send credits at all times. Instead, each node keeps a small cache of multicast credits. The number of credits residing at a particular node is only increased temporarily when large messages are multicast, or when small multicasts cause it to run below some level. The credits are requested from a central *credit manager* that does multicast credit accounting.

- To avoid congestion and overhead for credit acknowledgements at the sending host, credits are recycled in the background by the credit manager. This retrieval mechanism is completely implemented on the LCPs, without any additional overhead at the hosts.

To elaborate on the last two topics, what is done in FM/MC is the following. During initialization, the LCP on a predetermined node is assigned the job of maintaining the global multicast credit pool. If a node needs more credits, the FM/MC library automatically issues a credit request to this central credit LCP. This LCP directly replies with a number of credits (depending on the number requested and the current credit pool status). Therefore, multicast credit requests do not introduce any additional processing overhead on the credit host. They are handled entirely by the host adapter.

As soon as the number of credits in the credit pool drops below a certain level, the credit LCP needs to get information from all hosts on the network, in order to determine if any credits can be returned to the credit pool. For this purpose a special *credit gathering token* is rotated among all hosts on the network. The token contains an array of counters, each entry recording how many fragments the corresponding host processed since the last token rotation. Since the FM/MC library increments a special counter in LCP memory after processing a multicast fragment from the DMA area, each LCP can add this information before forwarding the token to the next member, without interrupting the host. Furthermore, each LCP must take into account that some of the multicasts it initiated might only be directed to a multicast group containing a proper subset of all the hosts. The other hosts will never receive these fragments, hence, never return the corresponding credit. To avoid losing these credits, the sending host increments the credit counters of the non-member hosts in the rotating token.

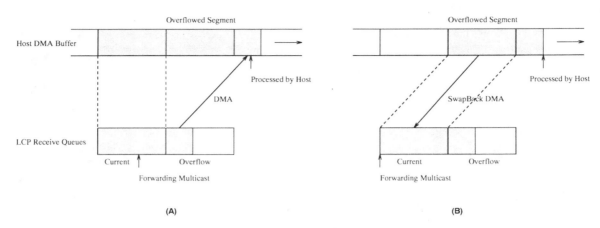

Figure 3: LCP Receive queue overflow handling.

## 4 PERFORMANCE

With respect to the retrieval of additional multicast credits it should be noted that our main application area (the Orca runtime system [2]) uses *totally-ordered* multicast [8]. On Myrinet, we implement the total ordering by letting one of the LCPs hand out sequence numbers. By letting the credit administration be handled by the same LCP, we are able to save the extra roundtrip for multicast credits in practice. Since the size of the message to be multicast is known in advance in the Orca runtime system, the request for the corresponding number of credits can simply be piggybacked on the request for a new sequence number.

## 4 PERFORMANCE

In this section we present the results of the performance measurements performed with our FM/MC multicast implementation. The measurements were done on a configuration of 8 Tsunami MicroSparcs running at 50 MHz, which are connected by a Myrinet network (LanAI version 2.3) and a single 8-port switch.

When comparing our results with the FM performance reported by Pakin et al. [12], it must be taken into account that the hosts they used are faster in several respects. Their configuration consisted of a SPARCstation 20 with a 50 MHz SuperSparc processor (without secondary cache) and a SPARCstation 10 with a 55 MHz RT100 HyperSparc.

To quantify these hardware differences we repeated the latency and throughput tests reported in [12] on our system. With the unmodified FM 1.1 code we achieved a minimal round-trip latency of 58 $\mu$s for 16-byte messages (compared to 50 $\mu$s reported for FM 1.0) and a maximum throughput of 13.3 Mbyte/sec for messages of 128 bytes (16.2 Mbyte/sec reported). We conclude that our different hardware causes a reduction in performance of almost 20%. Also, it must be noted that for messages larger than the fragment size, the fragments have to be reassembled at the receiving host. On our system this reduces the practical throughput to 8.6 Mbyte/sec for messages of 16Kbyte.

Given this base version of FM, we subsequently made a number of changes to the LCP and FM library software, each of which added to the baseline latency of 58 $\mu$s. Calls to a mutex library to achieve thread safety added 7 $\mu$s. Multicast related changes to the LCP resulted in an additional 5 $\mu$s overhead. Finally, to increase the throughput for large messages, we doubled the FM fragment size to 256 bytes. The roundtrip unicast time for 16 byte messages this time increased with another 12 $\mu$s (i.e., 58+7+5+12=82 $\mu$s in total). This can be explained by the doubling of the host DMA and network latency. Using 256-byte fragments we are now able to achieve a sustained throughput of 10.1 Mbyte/sec for 16 Kbyte messages. The maximum throughput is currently bounded by the rate at which the destination is able to copy fragments out of the DMA area.

We investigated the behavior of the various multicast forwarding methods discussed in Section 2. The maximum throughputs obtained are shown in Figure 4. The average roundtrip latencies shown in Figure 5 are measured by a program that repeatedly multicasts a 32-byte message and waits for a single 16-byte reply; this reply comes from a different destination each time to obtain the *average* latency. Also we have measured that the maximum rate at which our 8 node system can reliably multicast messages is 35,000 messages per second.

It is hard to estimate the effectiveness of the various forwarding methods for large groups (e.g., 64 nodes) based on the actual results for only 8 nodes. Therefore we developed a simulation program that models the reliable multicast protocol of FM/MC. The various parameters for the model (e.g., DMA and network send/receive latency) were obtained from timings of the actual implementation. The results for throughput and latency are shown in Fig-

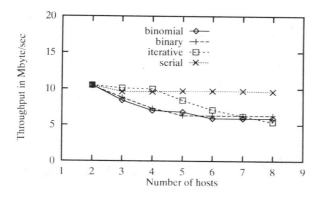

Figure 4: Measured throughput for different multicast forwarding methods.

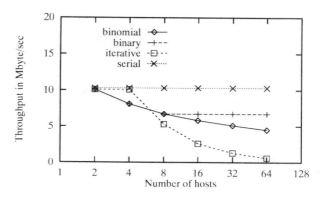

Figure 6: Simulated throughput for different multicast forwarding methods.

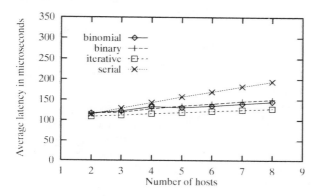

Figure 5: Measured roundtrip latency for different multicast forwarding methods (with 16-byte reply).

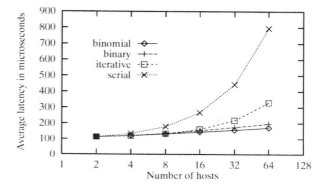

Figure 7: Simulated average latency for different multicast forwarding methods.

ure 6 and Figure 7 respectively. We conclude that for FM/MC on Myrinet the binary forwarding method provides a good tradeoff between low latency and high bandwidth for groups of eight or more members. All remaining performance tests described in this section were done using binary forwarding.

Figure 8 compares the unicast and multicast latency for increasing request sizes. In this test, after sending the request, the sending host always waits for a single 16-byte reply. In the case of multicast, we always use 8 hosts and measure the average roundtrip latency. The roundtrip latencies reported include about 10 $\mu$s overhead from the send/receive loop of our (rather general) latency/throughput measuring program. The fast 16-byte reply itself takes 41 $\mu$s. Figure 9 compares the unicast and multicast throughput for increasing request sizes.

Furthermore, we performed a number of tests in which there were multiple senders. We were especially concerned about the following issues:

- Does the network adapter distributing the credits become a bottleneck under heavy load?

- How does the distributed multicast credit protocol perform when multiple multicast groups are used?

- What is the *fairness* of the multicast implementation when there are multiple senders in a single group?

First we investigated whether the node running the credit manager was going to be a bottleneck. To test this, we let our test program create four disjoint multicast groups, each with 2 members. All groups contained a single sender that was trying to push as much data through the network (using multicast) as possible. For 32Kbyte messages, we achieved a sustained throughput of exactly four times the point-to-point throughput (i.e., 41.2 Mbyte/sec in total).

To make sure that the LCP acting as credit manager was also able to handle a higher rate of credit requests, we repeated the test with a message size of only 248 bytes (the maximum message size that fits in one fragment). As in the previous case, the throughput was almost 4 times the maximum point-to-point throughput measured for this message size (3 times 6.8 Mbyte/sec, and only a minor decrease to 6.3 Mbyte/sec at the multicast group containing the credit

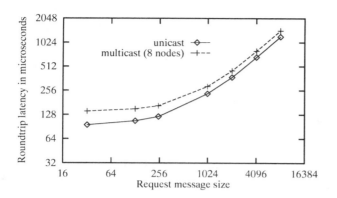

Figure 8: Measured roundtrip latency for unicast and multicast (with 16-byte reply).

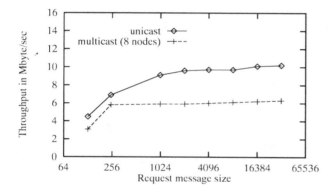

Figure 9: Measured throughput for unicast and multicast.

manager). We conclude that the current credit cache size of 5 to 15 credits reduces the credit request rate sufficiently in situations where the member processes of the application repeatly issue small requests.

For the third issue, fairness, the results were less favorable in the original implementation. It turned out that the latency and throughput for multiple senders was dependent on the way in which their multicast trees overlapped. A node that was only sending and receiving multicast messages had a notable advantage over a node that also had to forward messages from other nodes. This happened because the implementation favored the forwarding of fragments over the transmission of fragments from the local member's send queue.

By changing the LCP to interleave forwarding and sending, we managed to improve the fairness significantly. In the case of 8 nodes with two senders, the throughput of the disfavored sender is currently about 40% of bandwidth of the other sender. In the worst case it used to get only 15%. In cases where everyone is sending, or where the senders are placed symmetrically (e.g., on nodes 0 and 4, in the 8 node case) the senders get a completely fair share of the multicast bandwidth. For all-to-all communication

on 8 nodes, the throughput per sender is 1.1 Mbyte/sec, so 8.8 Mbyte/sec in total. To improve the fairness further we might try to let the LCP maintain an estimate of the current set of sending nodes, and derive an appropriate multicast forwarding/sending ratio from that. However, it is debatable whether a slight unfairness warrants this increase in LCP code complexity, especially since this also might hurt the performance of the cases in which there is no multicast tree overlap.

## 5 DISCUSSION AND CONCLUSIONS

We have described a reliable multicast algorithm for Myrinet. The most important new idea in the algorithm is a flow control method based on a credit scheme, which effectively solves the buffer management problem for multicast. We have also described an efficient implementation of the algorithm (based on the Illinois Fast Messages software) and we have shown, through performance measurements and simulations, that the multicast implementation achieves high performance.

The multicast primitive will be useful for parallel programming on top of networks of workstations. Many programming systems either provide multicast to the programmer or use it in their implementation. For our research, we have implemented the Orca parallel language [3] on top of the multicast primitive. Orca is a language based on shared objects. The objects are automatically replicated in the local memories, and multicasting is used to update all copies. The performance of Orca thus depends heavily on the efficiency of multicasting. By making the low-level multicast reliable, we were able to avoid higher-level, expensive protocols (based on timers and retransmissions).

The Orca system needs totally-ordered multicasting. As described briefly in Section 3, we implemented this on Myrinet by using a sequencer. The overhead of getting a sequence number is about 75 $\mu$s, so we are able to do a totally-ordered multicast on Myrinet in less than 200 $\mu$s (for short messages). The maximum rate at which the sequencer node can handle totally-ordered multicasts is 20,000 messages per second; another ordering protocol is needed to approach the unordered multicast performance of 35,000 messages per second. The speed of the network interface has a significant impact on the overall performance of the multicast protocol. We anticipate that the new LANai 4.1, which is a much faster processor, will improve both latency and throughput considerably.

Our implementation uses two properties of Myrinet: the reliability of the physical point-to-point links and the programmability of the host adapter boards. For other network technologies (e.g., ATM or FastEthernet), links are not reliable. For such networks, our credit-based flow control method could be used to avoid excessive congestion, but not to make multicast totally reliable. Higher-level protocols are needed to obtain reliability. The ability to program the Myrinet host adapter board allowed us to implement the forwarding and flow control without involving the main CPU, resulting in a high performance.

The most important conclusion from our work is that it is feasible to make multicasting on a network like Myrinet reliable. Reliability is implemented at a low level, without using acknowledgement messages or timers. The key idea in our reliable multicast algorithm is a credit-based flow control scheme for congestion avoidance. Without such a scheme, the host receive queues could overflow, resulting in unreliable communication. We also described solutions to several implementation problems, such as how to manage the small host adapter memory, and how to distribute and recycle credits.

We presented performance measurements on an 8-node Myrinet system. Our algorithm obtains a good latency and high throughput on this system, both of which are important for parallel programming. In addition, we have implemented a simulator with which the scalability of the algorithm can be predicted. Since the intended usage is parallel programming on networks of workstations, the algorithm should scale to at least dozens of processors. The main scalability problem we expect concerns the token protocol, which is used for updating credits. If a large number of processors wants to send many messages simultaneously, the token protocol might become a performance bottleneck (although systems like Orca generally avoid such communication behavior [2]). The usage of a combining tree for gathering credit information would be an interesting alternative in such cases.

## ACKNOWLEDGEMENTS

We thank Raoul Bhoedjang, Rutger Hofman, Ceriel Jacobs, and Tim Rühl for their discussion about the reliable multicast protocol during our weekly meetings. We thank Andrew Chien and Scott Pakin for making the FM software available to us. Finally, we thank Raoul Bhoedjang, Leendert van Doorn, Ceriel Jacobs, Mario Lauria, Tim Rühl, Greg Sharp and Andy Tanenbaum for reading and commenting on draft versions of this paper.

## REFERENCES

[1] G.R. Andrews and R.A. Olsson. *The SR Programming Language: Concurrency in Practice.* The Benjamin/Cummings Publishing Company, Redwood City, CA, 1993.

[2] H.E. Bal and M.F. Kaashoek. Object Distribution in Orca using Compile-Time and Run-Time Techniques. In *Conference on Object-Oriented*

*Programming Systems, Languages and Applications,* pages 162–177, Washington D.C., September 1993.

[3] H.E. Bal, M.F. Kaashoek, and A.S. Tanenbaum. Orca: A Language for Parallel Programming of Distributed Systems. *IEEE Transactions on Software Engineering,* 18(3):190–205, March 1992.

[4] N.J. Boden, D. Cohen, R.E. Felderman, A.E. Kulawik, C.L. Seitz, J.N. Seizovic, and W. Su. Myrinet: A Gigabit-per-second Local Area Network. *IEEE Micro,* 15(1):29–36, February 1995.

[5] M. Gupta, S. Midkiff, E. Schonberg, V. Seshadri, D. Shields, K.-Y. Wang, W.-M. Ching, and T. Ngo. An HPF Compiler for the IBM SP2. In *Supercomputing '95,* San Diego, CA, December 1995.

[6] C.-T. Ho and S.L. Johnsson. Distributed Routing Algorithms for Broadcasting and Personalized Communication in Hypercubes. In *Proc. 1986 Int. Conf. Parallel Processing,* pages 640–648, Washington, D.C., August 1986.

[7] V. Jacobson. Congestion Avoidance and Control. *ACM Computer Communication Review; Proceedings of the SIGCOMM '88 Symposium,* 18(4):314–329, August 1988.

[8] M.F. Kaashoek. *Group Communication in Distributed Computer Systems.* PhD thesis, Vrije Universiteit, Amsterdam, December 1992.

[9] M.F. Kaashoek, R. van Renesse, H. van Staveren, and A.S. Tanenbaum. FLIP: an Internet Protocol for Supporting Distributed Systems. *ACM Transactions on Computer Systems,* 11(1):73–106, January 1993.

[10] P.K. McKinley, H. Xu, A.-H. Esfahanian, and L.M. Ni. Unicast-Based Multicast Communication in Wormhole-Routed Networks. *IEEE Transactions on Parallel and Distributed Systems,* 5(12):1252–1265, December 1994.

[11] Message Passing Interface Forum. *MPI: A Message-Passing Interface Standard,* final report v1.0 edition, April 1994.

[12] S. Pakin, M. Lauria, and A. Chien. High Performance Messaging on Workstations: Illinois Fast Messages (FM) for Myrinet. In *Supercomputing '95,* San Diego, CA, December 1995.

[13] M.C. Rinard. Communication Optimizations for Parallel Computing Using Data Access Information. In *Supercomputing '95,* San Diego, CA, December 1995.

[14] A.S. Tanenbaum, M.F. Kaashoek, and H.E. Bal. Parallel Programming using Shared Objects and Broadcasting. *IEEE Computer,* 25(8):10–19, August 1992.

# A FLEXIBLE PROCESSOR ALLOCATION STRATEGY
# FOR MESH CONNECTED PARALLEL SYSTEMS

Vipul Gupta and Arun Jayendran
Dept. of Computer Science
State University of New York
Binghamton, NY 13902
{*vgupta, jayen*}*@cs.binghamton.edu*

Abstract — *Large mesh connected parallel systems allow multiple applications to run simultaneously on distinct, non-overlapping sub-meshes. This improves overall efficiency, since few (if any) individual applications can effectively use all of the available processors. The sub-mesh allocation strategy forms a crucial component in such systems and affects many performance criteria including system throughput, processor utilization, and application turnaround time. In this paper, we propose a new sub-mesh allocation strategy called flexfold. When a request for an $a \times b$ sub-mesh arrives, flexfold first searches for $a \times b$ and $b \times a$ sub-meshes, as expected. If appropriate, it may additionally search for $\frac{a}{2} \times 2b$, $2a \times \frac{b}{2}$, $2b \times \frac{a}{2}$, and $\frac{b}{2} \times 2a$ sub-meshes. At the expense of sometimes increasing their execution time, flexfold accommodates incoming applications earlier than other strategies. Simulation results indicate that a simple test suffices to determine when this trade-off is beneficial and flexfold achieves better overall performance compared to other algorithms. Flexfold is completely transparent to the application programmer and does not require additional architectural support beyond what already exists.*

**Index Terms:** Processor allocation, sub-mesh allocation, resource management, mesh architectures, space sharing.

## 1   INTRODUCTION

Due to their scalability and simplicity, two dimensional meshes have emerged as a popular interconnection topology for large parallel machines. Based on this topology, many prototypes and commercial systems have been built or are under construction. These include the ILLIAC IV, Goodyear Aerospace MPP [3], the Tera Computer System [1], the Touchstone Delta [9], the Intel Paragon [10], and the Stanford DASH and FLASH multiprocessors [11; 12].

Since few applications can effectively utilize all the processors in a large system, most systems allow *space sharing*, *i.e.* multiple applications (tasks) may execute simultaneously on different, non-overlapping sub-meshes. Space sharing improves system utilization and throughput, *i.e.* the rate at which tasks are completed. Upon arrival, each task specifies the sub-mesh size it requires and a processor allocation algorithm tries to find a free sub-mesh that is large enough to accommodate it. Once allocated, a task runs to completion before freeing up its processors. By convention, a sub-mesh consisting of $a$ columns and $b$ rows is said to be of size $a \times b$.

The processor allocation algorithm attempts to optimize a number of criteria including minimizing job turnaround time and mesh fragmentation, maximizing system utilization, and maintaining fairness. Several processor allocation algorithms have previously been proposed and are reviewed in Section 2. Earlier algorithms do not allow a job to run unless a sub-mesh large enough to accommodate the requested shape is found to be free. Newer algorithms allow some flexibility in this respect, *e.g.* if the incoming task requests a sub-mesh of size $a \times b$, the algorithm may allocate a $b \times a$ sub-mesh, if the requested size is unavailable. Most mesh connected parallel systems provide a level of translation between the *virtual node numbers* in a programmer's view to the *physical node numbers* used by the architecture [6]. Consequently, this 90 degree rotation performed by the allocation algorithm is transparent to the programmer, *i.e.* the programmer need not rewrite his or her program to run on the rotated sub-mesh. Since the translation mechanism uses a table lookup, even the more complex manipulations used by *flexfold* can be easily accommodated.

In this paper, we propose a new sub-mesh allocation strategy called *flexfold*. When an incoming task requests a sub-mesh of size $a \times b$, *flexfold* not only considers $a \times b$ and $b \times a$ sub-meshes, but also $\frac{a}{2} \times 2b$, $2a \times \frac{b}{2}$, $2b \times \frac{a}{2}$, and $\frac{b}{2} \times 2a$.[1] Using any of the last four

---

[1]This assumes that both $a$ and $b$ are even; otherwise,

shapes may cause an increase in the running time of the application. This could occur due to two factors:

(i) processes that would have been allocated to neighboring processors may now be allocated to processors that are farther apart, and

(ii) some communication paths may now share network links thereby increasing congestion.

Using simulations, we show that even when this increase in running time is accounted for, significant overall gains can be achieved by using the *flexfold* strategy. Flexfold gets its name from the fact that it is more flexible than previously proposed strategies and some of its manipulations resemble folding a mesh.

The rest of the paper is organized as follows. Section 2 is a brief overview of previously proposed allocation algorithms. Section 3 describes the motivation behind *flexfold* and its general outline. Section 4 presents simulation results comparing flexfold to other allocation algorithms. Section 5 contains conclusions and potential extensions to this work.

## 2  RELATED WORK

### Two Dimensional Buddy Strategy

The two dimensional buddy (2DB) algorithm, proposed by Li and Cheng [14], is a generalization of the one dimensional buddy system used in memory management. It can only allocate square sub-meshes in which each length is restricted to be some power of two. As such, this strategy is not applicable to rectangular mesh systems and can cause a significant amount of internal fragmentation (*i.e.* a task may be allocated more processors than it needs). The expected internal fragmentation for 2DB is 42%, when the side lengths for incoming requests are drawn from a uniform distribution [14].

### Frame Sliding Strategy

The Frame Sliding strategy (FS), proposed by Chuang and Tzeng [5], is applicable to meshes with arbitrary sizes and shapes and eliminates internal fragmentation by allocating the exact sub-mesh size requested by a task. A *frame* is a sub-mesh of the requested size and is identified by its lower left corner (also referred to as the frame base). A *frame* is *available* if and only if all the processors in that frame are *free*. The algorithm starts searching for the frame starting at the first idle processor in the lower left corner. It then slides over the width and height of the mesh in strides equal to the width and height of the incoming request.

some of these options will not be considered.

Simulation results presented by Chuang and Tzeng [5] indicate that the FS strategy performs better than the 2DB strategy. It results in greater system utilization and shorter response times.[2] The disadvantage of the FS strategy is that, due to its use of fixed strides, it may fail to find a free sub-mesh for an incoming task even if such a sub-mesh is available. It may also introduce unnecessary external fragmentation.

### First Fit and Best Fit Strategies

The First-Fit (FF) and Best-fit (BF) strategies, proposed by Zhu [16], are also applicable to mesh systems of arbitrary sizes and avoid internal fragmentation. These strategies check for all frames of the requested size without checking all processors in the system. Two binary arrays are used to speed up the search process. The first array, called a *busy* array, is used to store the allocation state of a mesh (a 0/1 indicates that the corresponding processor is free/busy). The second array, called a *coverage* array, is computed from the first with respect to an incoming task. An element in the coverage array is 1 iff the corresponding processor cannot serve as the base of an available frame for the incoming request. The coverage array can be computed in time proportional to the number of processors in the architecture. The processor allocation problem then reduces to finding a zero in the coverage array. The BF strategy searches for the smallest zero region in the coverage array in an effort to reduce external fragmentation. It has been shown that the simpler first-fit strategy offers about the same performance, in terms of response time and utilization [16]. However, neither strategy looks for a free sub-mesh of size $b \times a$ even if a sub-mesh of size $a \times b$ is unavailable.

### Adaptive Scan Strategy

The Adaptive Scan (AS) strategy, proposed by Ding and Bhuyan [8], also eliminates internal fragmentation and is applicable to mesh systems of arbitrary sizes. It improves upon the FS strategy by using a stride of 1 in the vertical direction and an adaptive stride in the horizontal direction. The search for a frame starts at the lower left corner of the mesh system and proceeds in a row by row fashion. If no free frame is found, the request is rotated by 90 degrees and the same algorithm is repeated, *i.e.* if a sub-mesh of size $a \times b$ is not available, the algorithm tries to find a sub-mesh of size $b \times a$. The FS algorithm is *recognition complete* — it always finds an available frame if one exists.

---

[2] *Response time* is defined as the delay between the submission of a task and its termination.

## 3 FLEXFOLD ALGORITHM

Motivation

Consider the scenario depicted in Figure 1. It shows a mesh of size $7 \times 8$ being shared by three tasks. These tasks occupy non-overlapping sub-meshes of size $3 \times 5$, $4 \times 3$ and $3 \times 3$ with their lower left corners at processors (1, 8), (1, 3) and (5, 4), respectively. If a new task arrives and requests a $1 \times 8$ sub-mesh, none of the allocation strategies discussed in Section 2 would be able to accommodate it immediately.[3] On the other hand, the *flexfold* strategy would recognize that a $1 \times 8$ sub-mesh can be folded to fit in a $2 \times 4$ sub-mesh (see Figure 2(a)) and a sub-mesh of that size is currently available, *e.g.* with a lower left corner at processor (4, 8). In this example, flexfold is able to accommodate a task sooner than other algorithms.

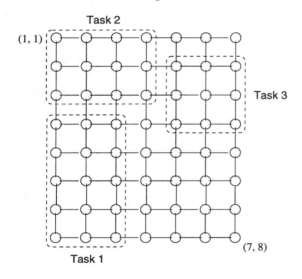

Figure 1: An example illustrating the behavior of the *flexfold* processor allocation strategy.

As already mentioned, parallel systems invariably provide a level of translation between the *virtual* node numbers referred to by a programmer and the *physical* node numbers used by an architecture. Consequently, all shape manipulations performed by *flexfold* are transparent to the application programmer.

Folding a $1 \times 8$ sub-mesh into a $2 \times 4$ sub-mesh (as shown in Figure 2(a)) does not increase the previous distance between communicating processes (it might actually bring them closer!) and has no adverse effect on the application running time. Unfortunately, this isn't always true. Figure 2(b) illustrates how a sub-mesh request of size $2 \times 8$ can be accommodated

---

[3]This in spite of the fact that there are 20 processors available and the new request only needs 8.

in Figure 1 by folding it into a $4 \times 4$ request. Nodes 1 and 2 that were adjacent in the original sub-mesh are two hops apart in the folded sub-mesh. Similarly, the edge between nodes 2 and 3 is now shared by the communication path between two pairs of nodes 1-2 and 3-4. These effects could increase the task execution time. Flexfold is motivated by the idea that if the decrease in *waiting time* is large enough to compensate for the increase in *execution time*, the user will experience an overall decrease in task *response time*.

Effect of folding on task execution time

In order to analyze the effect of sub-mesh folding on task execution time, it helps to view such folding as a *graph embedding* of one sub-mesh into another [13]. An embedding $\mathcal{E}$ of a graph $G(V, E)$ into another graph $G'(V', E')$ maps each vertex in $v \in V$ to a vertex $\mathcal{E}(v) \in V'$. As a consequence of the embedding, some of the edges in $G$ may be transformed into multi-edge paths in $G'$. The *dilation* of an embedding refers to the distance between two nodes $\mathcal{E}(u)$ and $\mathcal{E}(v)$ in $V'$ such that $u$ and $v$ are adjacent in $G$. The maximum number of edges in $G$ whose equivalent paths share a common edge in $G'$ is termed *congestion*. Based on this terminology, the embedding shown in Figure 2(b) has a dilation of 2 and a congestion of 2.

Next, we show that shape manipulations attempted by *flexfold* will never result in a dilation greater than two nor congestion greater than two. It should be obvious that embedding an $a \times b$ sub-mesh into an $a \times b$ or $b \times a$ sub-mesh results in a dilation and congestion of 1. Without loss of generality, consider the embedding of an $m \times 2n$ sub-mesh into a $2m \times n$ sub-mesh. Suppose that the left corner is numbered (1, 1) and the lower right corner is $(m, 2n)$. If node $(i, j)$ is mapped to node $(i', j')$ where

$$i' = \begin{cases} 2i & \text{if } \lfloor j/2 \rfloor \text{ is odd} \\ 2i - 1 & \text{otherwise} \end{cases}$$
$$j' = \lceil j/2 \rceil$$

then it can be easily seen that the *dilation* and *congestion* are 2. This embedding is illustrated in Figure 2(b) for $m = 2$ and $n = 4$. Note that node pairs that are vertically adjacent in the $m \times 2n$ sub-mesh are still adjacent in the $2m \times n$ sub-mesh (represented by thick edges). Only the horizontally adjacent nodes have their separation increased to two.[4]

Manipulations performed by flexfold can only affect the communication time (rather than the computation time) of a task. Consider the communication between

---

[4]Effectively, each column has been folded in a zig-zag fashion to take up twice the width but half of its previous height.

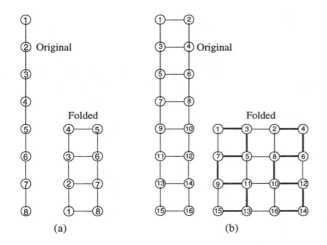

Figure 2: Possible consequences of folding a mesh. In (a), there is no change in the adjacency of different nodes. This is not true for case (b) and the communication time of the application will increase due to folding.

an arbitrary pair of nodes $p$ and $q$ in a task. After folding, the distance between these nodes will increase by a factor of at most two (the average increase will be less). Furthermore, due to congestion, messages might take up to twice as long to traverse each network link. This reasoning leads us to conclude that the communication time may increase by a factor of at most four.

It turns out that this naive estimate is quite misleading, and the actual increase can be expected to be much smaller. The time to transfer a message from one process to another process running on a different processor consists of two main components. The *network propagation* time is the time spent by a message within the network including delays incurred at the routers. The *end-node processing* refers to the time a message spends within the source and destination nodes. It includes the software overhead of copying between user and system buffers, buffer management, and related processing (*e.g.* attaching a routing header at the source and stripping it off at the destination). The end-node processing time is usually much larger than the network propagation time. For example, message transfer on Intel's Delta multicomputer requires 67 microseconds, of which less than 1 microsecond is spent in the network [15]. Since sub-mesh folding does not affect *end-node processing* time, its overall effect on task execution time is quite small, *e.g.* on the Delta, even for an application that spends 90% of its time in communication, the maximum increase will be $\approx 4\%$.

### Flexfold Outline

When an incoming task requests a sub-mesh of size $a \times b$, *flexfold* looks for free sub-meshes in the sequence $a \times b$, $b \times a$, $\frac{a}{2} \times 2b$, $2a \times \frac{b}{2}$, $2b \times \frac{a}{2}$ and $\frac{b}{2} \times 2a$ till either a free sub-mesh is found or all choices are exhausted. If an allocation can be made, our algorithm returns the size and position of the free sub-mesh and a factor $\alpha \in \{1, 4\}$ by which the *network propagation time* will increase. The algorithm carefully avoids unnecessary searches, *e.g.* if the number of free processors is less than $a \cdot b$, it immediately signals an allocation failure. Similarly, if $a$ and $b$ are equal, at most only three options ($a \times a$, $2a \times \frac{a}{2}$ and $\frac{a}{2} \times 2a$) are ever tried.

The flexfold algorithm does not always avail of the opportunity to accommodate a new task if doing so may increase its execution time. It uses a simple test to decide whether the increase in execution time will be compensated by a concomitant decrease in waiting time. It compares the expected increase in execution time with the time left for the earliest finishing job and chooses to wait if the former is larger. This can be explained using the scenario shown in Figure 1. Assume that Tasks 1 through 3 are scheduled to finish in that order when a new task, Task 4, arrives and requests a $2 \times 8$ sub-mesh. We assume that for each incoming Task $i$, $t_i$ denotes its estimated execution time and $f_i$ (referred to as the *communication fraction*) indicates the fraction of $t_i$ that will be affected due to folding. Note that architectural characteristics (*e.g.* ratio of network propagation time to end-node processing time) will impose an upper bound on $f_i$. Flexfold will decide in favor of allocating a $4 \times 4$ sub-mesh to Task 4 (instead of waiting for a $2 \times 8$ to become available) only if Task 1 will not finish within the next $4f_4t_4$ time units. This is a *conservative check* since a $2 \times 8$ (or $8 \times 2$) sub-mesh cannot be allocated for Task 4 in Figure 1 even when Task 1 finishes.

Our algorithm performs up to six times the number of sub-mesh searches performed by other algorithms. Instead of manipulating bit matrices (as done in [16]), we use a compact rectangular representation of busy sub-meshes and *symbolically pre-computed* rectangle differences for our searches (as described in [4]). This results in a very fast algorithm with a complexity of $\mathcal{O}(m^2)$ where $m$ is the number of already allocated sub-meshes. In comparison, the bit-map approach has a complexity proportional to the size of the architecture. This represents significant savings in time and memory, especially for architectures containing hundreds of nodes. Even for large architectures (4,000 nodes), the time to search for a free sub-mesh is in the order of milliseconds compared to the running time of parallel applications which is typically several seconds.

Thus the time spent by flexfold in extra searches represents a negligible overhead.

## 4 PERFORMANCE RESULTS

We have developed an event-driven simulator to compare the performance of different sub-mesh allocation algorithms. The simulator consists of roughly 2800 lines of C code and is designed to be versatile. It models many different task parameters, system characteristics and performance metrics.

<u>Simulation Model</u>

In our simulation model, new tasks arrive in the system as determined by the *task inter-arrival time* and are characterized by the following parameters:

*Requested Size:* The sub-mesh size requested by the task.

*Requested Residency:* The time for which an application will run if it is allocated a sub-mesh of the requested size.

*Communication Fraction:* The fraction of the running time that will be affected by a re-shaping of the requested sub-mesh.

All three parameters, as also the *task inter-arrival time*, can be chosen from a number of distributions including uniform, exponential, normal, fixed and vector.[5]

Tasks waiting to be allocated are held in a queue and the task at the head is the first one to be allocated. For the simulations reported here, we keep this queue ordered by arrival time which results in first-come-first-served scheduling. Due to its attractive fairness characteristics, FCFS scheduling is also used in [5; 8; 14; 16]. Our simulator is quite general, however, and can use the following alternative criteria for ordering the wait queue:

*Request size*: results in smallest-job-first scheduling,

*Requested residency*: results in quickest-job-first scheduling,

*Product of requested size and residency*: results in the job, that places the least demand on system resources, to be scheduled earliest.

Whenever a task leaves, or the head of the wait queue changes, the system attempts to accommodate

---

[5]The vector distribution generates values in consecutive, non-overlapping intervals with specified probabilities. Zhu [16] refers to this distribution as *uniform distribution in intervals*.

the first request in the wait queue. Depending on the allocation strategy, the simulator searches for different sized free sub-meshes (as described below). In all cases, a task is allocated a single contiguous rectangular region. This prevents the communication generated within distinct tasks from interfering with each other.

We model the following eight allocation strategies:

*Best-Fit (BF)* Only searches for the requested sub-mesh size. It chooses the tightest fit amongst multiple choices of free sub-mesh regions.

*First-Fit (FF)* Only searches for the requested sub-mesh size. It picks the first one amongst multiple choices of free sub-mesh regions.

*Adaptive Scan with Best Fit (ASBF)* Searches for the requested sub-mesh size and its 90 degree rotation. It chooses the tightest fit amongst multiple choices of free sub-mesh regions.

*Adaptive Scan with First Fit (ASFF)* Searches for the requested sub-mesh size and its 90 degree rotation. It picks the first one amongst multiple choices of free sub-mesh regions.

*Flexfold with Best Fit (FlexBF)* Searches for the requested sub-mesh, its 90 degree rotation and up to four other possibilities (see Section 3). It uses the conservative check, described previously, to decide if any of the last four possibilities should be attempted. It chooses the tightest fit amongst multiple choices of free sub-mesh regions.

*Flexfold with Best Fit without the Conservative Check (FlexBFnoCC)* Same as above but without the conservative check.

*Flexfold with First Fit (FlexFF)* Same as FlexBF but picks the first one (not necessarily the tightest fit) amongst multiple choices of free sub-mesh regions.

*Flexfold with First Fit and without the Conservative Check (FlexFFnoCC)* Same as above but without the conservative check.

We do not model the 2DB and FS algorithms since they are known to have worse performance: 2DB is applicable only to square meshes and suffers from internal fragmentation; FS may fail to recognize a free sub-mesh even when one is available.

We define the *system load* as

$$\text{System Load} = \frac{\text{Avg. residency} \times \text{Avg. request size}}{\text{Architecture size} \times \text{Avg. inter-arrival time}}$$

and choose simulation parameters in a manner that ensures this load never exceeds 1; or else, the system will be unstable. From a user's perspective, the *task turnaround time* (a.k.a. *response time*), is the most important performance index. We use plots of *turnaround time* against *system load* to compare different allocation strategies. For brevity, we refer to these plots as TL-plots. We obtained a number of plots by varying different simulation parameters and the representative trends are presented below. These results have confidence intervals of 5% or less at the 95% confidence level.

## Results

Figure 3 shows TL-plots comparing different allocation strategies when the system load is varied by changing the task inter-arrival time. It assumes an architecture size of 32 × 32, exponentially distributed *requested residencies* with a mean of 50 time units, and *request sizes* based on uniformly distributed side lengths (between 2 and 20). The value of the *communication fraction* is assumed to be fixed at 0.1, *i.e.* the network propagation time constitutes 10% of the application running time. The effect of changing this value is studied later.

AS, and finally BF/FF. With flexfold, the system remains stable for a 10% higher load than AS and 20% higher load than BF/FF. For a given load, the average turnaround time with flexfold is lower than that with the AS and BF/FF strategies. This advantage becomes more prominent as the system load increases. For example, at a load of 0.39, the turnaround time for these strategies is 65, 75, and 110 and respectively. When the system load increases to 0.49, the turnaround time is 100 for flexfold and 150 for AS (representing a 33% saving). The BF/FF strategies result in an unstable (saturated) system at this load.

Figure 4 shows TL-plots for similar parameters as those used for Figure 3. However, this time the inter-arrival time is exponential with a mean of 60 and system load is varied by changing the requested residency instead. The general nature of these plots is very similar to those in the previous figure. Once again, various flavors of the flexfold algorithm (FlexFF, FlexBF, FlexFFnoCC, FlexBFnoCC) outperform variations of Adaptive Scan and Best-Fit/First-Fit algorithms. The system stays stable for higher loads with flexfold than with other allocation strategies. Furthermore, at any given load, flexfold results in the smallest turnaround values.

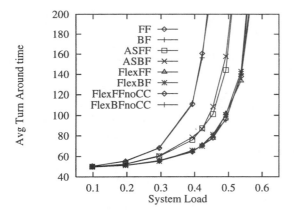

Figure 3: Variation of Turnaround time v/s System load (varying inter-arrival time, communication fraction = 0.1).

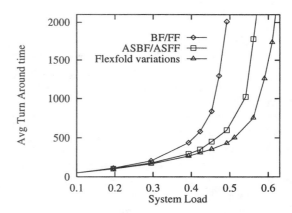

Figure 4: Variation of Turnaround time v/s System load (varying residencies, communication fraction = 0.1).

According to these plots, other things being the same, choosing the first-fit or the best-fit variation does not have any perceptible effect on performance. We found this to be true for other simulations as well and this observation is in agreement with those of other researchers [2; 16]. To avoid clutter in subsequent plots, we show only one of these plots for each allocation strategy. Figure 3 clearly indicates that the flexfold algorithm (with or without the conservative check) has the best performance, followed by

Plots shown in Figures 5(a) through 5(d) depict the effect of *communication fraction* on different variations of the flexfold strategy. Recall that none of the other allocation strategies are dependent on this parameter. Nevertheless, we include their TL-plots for ease of comparison. Except for the *communication fraction* which takes different values from the set {0.0, 0.2, 0.4, 0.8}, these figures share the same simulation parameters.

Flexfold (with the conservative check) still outper-

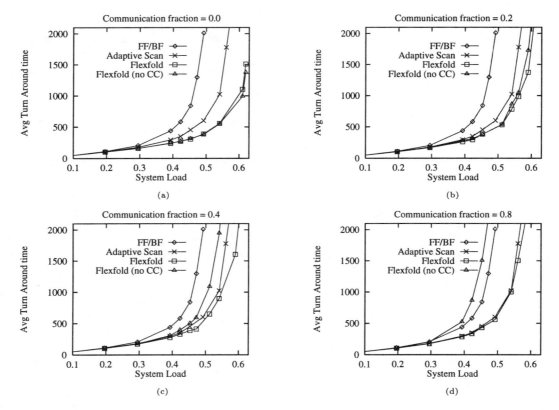

Figure 5: The effect of changing *communication fraction* on different flavors of the Flexfold algorithm.

forms FF/BF and Adaptive Scan. However, as the value of *communication fraction* increases, its performance starts approaching that of Adaptive Scan. This isn't surprising because at high values of *communication fraction*, we expect flexfold to reject most shape manipulations that might increase the application run time. In these situations, flexfold will restrict itself to searching for the requested sub-mesh or its 90 degree rotation. Figure 5 also underscores the importance of the *conservative check* employed by flexfold. Without it, the performance of flexfold may fall below that of Adaptive Scan (see Figure 5(c)) or even FF/BF (see Figure 5(d)). In the absence of this check, flexfold is over-aggressive in its attempt to accommodate a task as early as possible and frequently chooses costly shape manipulations.

Space restrictions do not allow us to present all of our simulations but the main results may be summarized as follows. The actual performance of *flexfold* (with the conservative check) depends on the value of the *communication fraction* but is never worse than that of previously proposed allocation algorithms. The software overhead of message passing in current multiprocessor systems restricts this value to be in the

order of 1-2%.[6] In this range (and up to values as high as 10%), *flexfold* performs significantly better (30%-40% lower turnaround times) than other algorithms. So even as the software overhead of message passing decreases in newer architectures, *flexfold* should continue being an attractive alternative to other allocation schemes for several years.

## 5 CONCLUSIONS

In this paper, we have proposed a new algorithm called *flexfold* for sub-mesh allocation in mesh-connected multicomputers. Flexfold is applicable to mesh systems of any size and shape, avoids internal fragmentation, and is transparent to the application programmer. It offers greater flexibility than previously proposed algorithms and is capable of allocating requests when other strategies can not. At the expense of possibly increasing the running time of the application, *flexfold* reduces the application waiting time. To the best of our knowledge, *flexfold* is the first allocation algorithm that attempts to exploit this trade-off. Using

---

[6]For the Delta architecture, even if an application spends all of its time in communication, the *communication fraction* value will be at most 1/67 (see Section 3) or 1.5%.

simulations, we have shown that a simple test suffices to determine when this trade-off is beneficial and *flexfold* achieves better overall performance compared to other allocation strategies.

It should be pointed out that the *conservative check* mentioned in Section 3 requires a prior estimate of the application's running time. However, due to the high software overhead in contemporary message passing environments, flexfold can deliver performance gains even with this check turned off.

This paper has dealt only with 2-dimensional meshes, but the basic idea behind *flexfold* is just as applicable to three dimensions. The Cray T3D and Cray T3E [6; 7] are examples of parallel architectures with three dimensional topologies. The number of allocation choices available to *flexfold* in a 3-dimensional architecture will be more and we expect it to offer even greater performance benefits. Our simulations, so far, have not explored the effect of scheduling strategy on *flexfold* nor have we tried experimenting with even greater allocation flexibility, *e.g.* using a $4a \times \frac{b}{4}$ sub-mesh. Incorporating this level of flexibility in the allocation strategy may not be worthwhile since $\alpha$ (described in Section 3) may be as large as 16 and the increase in network propagation time due to folding may overshadow any decrease in waiting time even for small values of *communication fraction*. It would be more interesting to study how the choice of a scheduling strategy affects *flexfold*'s performance. We intend to explore these issues in the near future. It is heartening to note that even with simple FCFS scheduling, flexfold maintains stability at fairly high system loads (around 0.6). In comparison, other algorithms become unstable at loads of around 0.55 even when augmented with more sophisticated scheduling strategies, *e.g. scan scheduling* [2].

## REFERENCES

[1] R. Alverson et al. "The Tera Computer System", In *Int'l Conf. on Supercomputing*, pp. 1-6, 1990.

[2] D. Babbar, P. Krueger. "A Performance Comparison of Processor Allocation and Job Scheduling Algorithms for Mesh-Connected Multiprocessors", In *IEEE Symposium on Parallel and Distributed Processing*, pp. 46-53, 1994.

[3] K. E. Batcher. "Bit-Serial Parallel Processing Systems", In *IEEE Trans. Computers*, C-31, 5 pp. 377-384, May 1982.

[4] S. Bhattacharya and W. T. Tsai. "Lookahead Processor Allocation in Mesh-Connected Massively Parallel Multicomputer", In *8th Int'l Parallel Processing Symposium*, pp. 868-875, Apr. 1994.

[5] P. Chuang and N. Tzeng. "Allocating Precise Submeshes in Mesh Connected Systems", In *IEEE Trans. on Parallel and Distributed Systems*, Vol. **5**, No 2, Feb 1994.

[6] Cray Research Inc. "Cray T3D System Architecture Overview", *Tech. Report*, Sep 1993. On Cray's Web page at http://www.cray.com.

[7] Cray Research, Inc. "The Cray T3E Scalable Parallel Processing System", At http://www.cray.com/PUBLIC/product-info/T3E/CRAY_T3E.html.

[8] J. Ding and L. N. Bhuyan. "An Adaptive Submesh Allocation Strategy for Two-Dimensional Mesh Connected Systems", *Int'l Conference on Parallel Processing*, Vol. II, pp. 193-200, 1993.

[9] Intel Corporation. "A Touchstone DELTA System Description", 1991.

[10] Intel Corporation. "Paragon XP/S Product Overview", 1991.

[11] D. Lenoski *et al.* "The Stanford DASH Multiprocessor", *IEEE Computer*, Vol. **25**, pp. 63-79, Mar. 1992.

[12] J. Heinlein *et al.* "Integration of Message Passing and Shared Memory in the Stanford FLASH Multiprocessor", In *6th Int'l Conf. on Architectural Support for Prog. Lang. and Operating Systems*, pp. 38-50, Oct. 1994.

[13] J. W. Hong, K. Melhorn and A. L. Rosenberg. "Cost Trade-offs in Graph Embeddings, with Applications", *Journal of the ACM*, Vol. **30**, No. 4, pp. 709-728, Oct. 1983.

[14] K. Li and K. H. Cheng. "A Two-Dimensional Buddy System for Dynamic Resource Allocation in a Partitionable Mesh Connected System", In *Journal of Parallel and Distributed Computing*, pp. 79-83, May 1991.

[15] R. J. Littlefield. "Characterizing and Tuning Communications Performance for Real Applications", In *Proc. of the First Intel DELTA Applications Workshop*, pp. 179-190, Feb. 1992.

[16] Y. Zhu. "Efficient Processor Allocation Strategies for Mesh-Connected Parallel Computers", *Journal of Parallel and Distributed Computing*, **16**, pp. 328-337, 1992.

# Task Spreading and Shrinking on a Network of Workstations with Various Edge Classes

J. C. Jacob
School of Electrical Engineering
Cornell University
Ithaca, NY 14853

S.-Y. Lee
Department of Electrical Engineering
Auburn University
Auburn, AL 36849

## Abstract

*In this paper we describe how our computational model can be used for the problems of processor allocation and task mapping on a network of workstations. The intended applications for this model include the dynamic mapping problems of* shrinking *or* spreading *an existing mapping when the available pool of workstations changes during execution of the problem. The concept of* problem edge class *and other features of our model are developed to realistically and efficiently support task partitioning and merging for static and dynamic mapping. Algorithms for shrinking and spreading are presented and execution times on a network of workstations are used to illustrate the utility of our model.*

## 1 Introduction

In a distributed computing environment such as a *network of workstations (NOW)*, the communication overhead incurred for passing messages between processors can be much larger than in a tightly coupled multiprocessor. Therefore, it is especially important to accurately and realistically consider the communication behavior of a problem when deciding how to distribute it across a NOW. The load at each workstation may change dynamically throughout the execution of a program. Furthermore, a NOW is usually a nondedicated system so it is reasonable to expect that the number of workstations available for execution of a problem may change *during execution*. It may be necessary to *spread* or *shrink* the problem onto a new subset of the workstations on the network.

Recently the parallel processing community has focused considerable attention on distributed computing on a NOW. An example of work done in this area is Baratloo, et al. [1], who developed a software system for distributed computing that assigns threads of computation to available workstations. However, their system simply uses all available workstations and does not consider the optimal number of workstations that should be used for a given problem.

Numerous task mapping and load balancing schemes, e.g. [2, 3, 4, 5], require that each task reside *completely* at a PE, and do not support partitioning and/or merging of tasks, i.e. the initial partitioning of the problem is maintained. Other task mapping approaches that allow partitioning and/or merging of tasks, e.g. [6, 7], are based on a model that is too simplistic to accurately reflect the behavior of a real problem. The actual computation and communication behavior of a problem being partitioned actually depends on the *class* of problem, which has been largely ignored in the literature.

There are some fundamental justifications for supporting problem partitioning and merging during mapping onto a NOW. In the dynamic case, the number of workstations available to a problem may change *during execution*, so some mechanism is required to partition the load at the existing workstations so that some computation can be migrated to a new workstation (in the case where the number of available workstations increases) or distributed across the available workstations (in the case where the number of available workstations decreases). In addition, the load imbalance at some time may not be so extreme as to require migrating whole tasks from heavily loaded workstations to lightly loaded workstations. For static mapping, it may not be possible to achieve a satisfactory load balance with the original problem partitioning. Partitioning a problem too finely could result in intolerably high mapping overhead.

Our ultimate goal is to develop an efficient (static and dynamic) task mapping scheme which considers the characteristics of a given problem and system, adapts its procedures accordingly, and also determines the optimal numbers of PE's or workstations to be used for execution of the problem. As a first step in this effort, we formulated a task mapping model that is accurate, flexible, and practical [8]. In this paper, this model is applied to the problems of *shrinking* and *spreading* on a NOW. The shrinking (spreading) problem involves modification of a mapping due to the removal (addition) of workstations *during execution*. Experimental results indicate that both the number of workstations actually used and the resulting execution times are heavily dependent on the class of problem under these conditions.

## 2  Computational Model

In this section the computational model supporting partitioning and merging of tasks during mapping is reviewed [8]. A classification system for problem edges is developed in order to accurately model the variation in computation and communication overhead due to problem repartitioning.

### 2.1  Basic Formulation

A standard formulation of the task mapping problem requires mapping a *problem graph* onto a *system graph*. The quality of a particular mapping is evaluated with an *objective function*, which measures the overall execution time for the problem. The problem graph is composed of a set, $V_p$, of nodes, $v_{pi}$, representing tasks, and a set, $E_p$, of directed edges, $e_{pij}$, representing communication between tasks $v_{pi}$ and $v_{pj}$. Each problem node, $v_{pi}$, is associated with a node weight, $\Phi_i$, giving the size of the computation. To enable quantification of the communication penalty for partitioning a task, we also associate an *intra-task coefficient* (defined in Section 2.2), $\alpha_i$, with each problem node, $v_{pi}$. A problem edge representing communication between tasks $v_{pi}$ and $v_{pj}$ is associated with an edge weight, $W_{ij}$, giving the size of the message. Similarly, the system graph is composed of a set, $V_s$, of nodes, $v_{si}$, representing workstations, and a set, $E_s$, of undirected edges, $e_{sij}$, representing communication links between workstations $v_{si}$ and $v_{sj}$. In a NOW the workstations are typically connected in a local area network (LAN) on a bus so that the cost of communicating between any pair of workstations is identical and only one pair of workstations may communicate at a time. In larger networks, multiple LANs may be connected through one or more gateway machines. The communication cost incurred for sending a message between two workstations increases as the number of gateways between them increases.

In our model, the execution time for a problem is estimated using the following objective function:

$$OF = \max_{\forall v_{si} \in V_s} (COMP_{v_{si}} + COMM_{v_{si}}) \quad (1)$$

$$COMP_{v_{si}} = \sum_{v_{pi} \in \Theta} COMP_{v_{pi}} \quad (2)$$

$$COMM_{v_{si}} = \sum_{v_{pi} \in \Theta} COMM_{v_{pi}}, \quad (3)$$

where $COMP_{v_{pi}}$ and $COMM_{v_{pi}}$ denote the size of computation and communication, respectively, for task $v_{pi}$, $COMP_{v_{si}}$ and $COMM_{v_{si}}$ denote the size of computation and communication, respectively, for workstation $v_{si}$, and $\Theta \subseteq V_p$ is the set of tasks assigned to workstation $v_{si} \in V_s$.

### 2.2  Partial Task Migration

*Partial Task Migration* refers to the process of partitioning a task assigned to a workstation, migrating one of the components to another (destination) workstation, and possibly merging the migrated task with another task assigned to the destination workstation. The extent to which a task can be partitioned depends on the granularity of the problem. We will use the term *unit operation* to denote the smallest component that can be partitioned from a task. The *intra-task coefficient* refers to the net sum of the intra-task communication between all pairs of unit operations that comprise a task. As described below, partial migration of tasks may positively and negatively affect both the computation and communication components of the objective function value for a mapping.

#### 2.2.1  Partitioning and Merging of Tasks

We now examine the effect of task partitioning and merging on the problem graph. Since merging is simply an inverse operation of partitioning, we will restrict our discussion to task partitioning for this paper, due to space limitations.

Figure 1(a) shows a section of the original problem graph consisting of a problem edge with weight $W_{SD}$, representing communication from a source task S to a destination task D. Our model supports partitioning of a task into any number of subtasks. The example in Figure 1(b) illustrates the case where the source task S is partitioned into two subtasks s1 and s2, and the destination task D into two subtasks d1 and d2. The $\mu$ notation denotes the percentage of the original task that is contained in the subtask.

This task partitioning causes the computational characteristics of the problem graph to be modified as follows. Let the computational intensities (node weights) of tasks S and D in Figure 1 be denoted by $\Phi_S$ and $\Phi_D$, respectively. Also, the computational intensities of subtasks s1, s2, d1, and d2 are represented by $\phi_{s1}$, $\phi_{s2}$, $\phi_{d1}$, and $\phi_{d2}$, respectively. We assume that $\phi_{s1} = \mu_{s1}\Phi_S + \epsilon_{s1}$, $\phi_{s2} = \mu_{s2}\Phi_S + \epsilon_{s2}$, $\phi_{d1} = \mu_{d1}\Phi_D + \epsilon_{d1}$, and $\phi_{d2} = \mu_{d2}\Phi_D + \epsilon_{d2}$, where $\epsilon_{s1}$, $\epsilon_{s2}$, $\epsilon_{d1}$, and $\epsilon_{d2}$ represent the computational penalties due to task partitioning. These penalties include such things as each partition of a task requiring some "static computation", e.g. initialization, setup

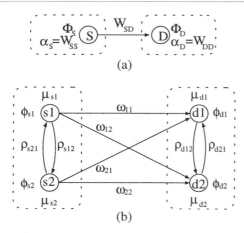

(b)

Figure 1: Problem graph modification under task partitioning. (a) Original problem edge and nodes before partitioning. (b) Problem edges and nodes after partitioning of both tasks S and D.

for loops, etc. Also, if a task is partitioned, some additional computation may be needed to combine the results.

Next, we discuss the effect of task partitioning on the communication characteristics of the problem graph. Again, refer to Figure 1. In this example, while there is just one original communication edge before partitioning, there can be up to eight new communication edges after partitioning. The edges that are actually created depends on the task; the situation shown in the figure is the worst case, where all eight edges are created. The original communication edge between tasks S and D with weight $W_{SD}$ is replaced by four new edges with weights $\omega_{11}$, $\omega_{12}$, $\omega_{21}$, and $\omega_{22}$. Additional communication overhead may result from the intra-task communication (quantified by the intra-task coefficient), which is converted into inter-task communication after partitioning. In the figure, the intra-task coefficients of tasks S and D are shown to be $\alpha_S$ and $\alpha_D$, respectively. Note that $\alpha_S$ and $\alpha_D$ are equivalent to $W_{SS}$ and $W_{DD}$, respectively, since the edge weight $W_{ij}$ represents communication from task $i$ to task $j$.

We now describe how to determine the values of the edge weights resulting from partitioning tasks ($\omega_{11}$, $\omega_{12}$, $\omega_{21}$, $\omega_{22}$, $\rho_{s12}$, $\rho_{s21}$, $\rho_{d12}$, and $\rho_{d21}$). It should be noted that, in terms of determination of edge weight, there is no difference between the edges with weights $\omega_{11}$, $\omega_{12}$, $\omega_{21}$, and $\omega_{22}$ and the edges with weights $\rho_{s12}$, $\rho_{s21}$, $\rho_{d12}$, and $\rho_{d21}$ except that the former four arise from the original inter-task communication and the latter four from the original intra-task communication. Thus, the values of all of the edge weights can

be determined in the same way. Consider an edge with weight, $\lambda_{xy}$, representing communication from a subtask, $x$, to a subtask, $y$. Also, assume that $x$ is $100\mu_x$ percent of the original task $X$ and $y$ is $100\mu_y$ percent of the original task $Y$. $X$ and $Y$ may be the same or different tasks. Clearly, the edge weight $\lambda_{xy}$ depends on the original communication edge $W_{XY}$, which may represent intra-task or inter-task communication.

### 2.2.2 Problem Edge Classes

The actual value of $\lambda_{xy}$ depends on the type of problem under consideration. Specifically, in terms of how $\lambda_{xy}$ is related to $W_{XY}$, we may classify a problem edge into one of the following six classes:

**Class C:** Edge weight is a constant, independent of $\mu_x$ and $\mu_y$.

**Class S:** Edge weight is proportional to $\mu_x$.

**Class D:** Edge weight is proportional to $\mu_y$.

**Class SD*:** Edge weight is proportional to the product of $\mu_x$ and $\mu_y$.

**Class SD+:** Edge weight is proportional to the sum of $\mu_x$ and $\mu_y$.

**Class Z:** Edge weight is zero.

An example of a Class C edge is the case where the source task computes some constant number of results (e.g. image statistics like mean, variance, etc.) which are forwarded to the destination task. An example of a Class S edge is the case where the source task applies a threshold to each of the pixels in an image and forwards the result to the destination task. An example of a Class D edge is the case where the source task computes a histogram of an image which is forwarded to the destination task for further processing. The Class SD* and Class SD+ edges are hybrid classifications for which the edge weight depends on the size of both the source and destination. For Class Z edges, communication is ignored. This unrealistic case is included for comparison with those mapping schemes in the literature that consider only computational load balance during mapping.

Using this classification, the edge weight $\lambda_{xy}$ can be determined as follows:

$$\lambda_{xy} = \begin{cases} W_{XY} & \text{if class} = \text{C} \\ W_{XY}\mu_x & \text{if class} = \text{S} \\ W_{XY}\mu_y & \text{if class} = \text{D} \\ W_{XY}\mu_x\mu_y & \text{if class} = \text{SD*} \\ \frac{W_{XY}}{2}(\mu_x + \mu_y) & \text{if class} = \text{SD+} \\ 0 & \text{if class} = \text{Z} \end{cases} \quad (4)$$

In Section 4 we present experimental results which demonstrate that the number of workstations that should be allocated to a problem, as well as the mapping of partitionable tasks onto those workstations is heavily dependent on problem edge class. This is because there is a significant variation with problem edge class in the communication penalty for partitioning. This is clearly demonstrated by the fact that, for the task partitioning shown in Figure 1, the sum of $\omega_{11}$, $\omega_{12}$, $\omega_{21}$, $\omega_{22}$, is $4W_{SD}$ for Class C, $2W_{SD}$ for Classes S, D, and SD+, $W_{SD}$ for Class SD*, and 0 for Class Z.

## 3 Task Mapping Strategy

The ultimate goal of this study is to develop an efficient task mapping method using the model described in Section 2. The task partitioning and mapping strategy described in this section is applicable to both the static and dynamic mapping problems. Specifically, this strategy is used in Section 4 to illustrate the importance of problem edge class for the dynamic problems of *spreading* and *shrinking* commonly encountered in non-dedicated systems. Spreading (shrinking) involves dynamically modifying a mapping due to the addition (removal) of workstations from the set available to a problem during execution as described in Section 3.2.

### 3.1 Static Mapping

We perform the task mapping in two stages: (*i*) simple initial mapping, and (*ii*) iterative refinement.

#### 3.1.1 Initial Mapping

The initial mapping strategy is to map communicating tasks as close together in the system as possible. No task partitioning or merging is done at this stage.

For each problem node, $v_i$, a communication intensity, $c_i$, is computed as the sum of the sizes of all messages for which node $v_i$ is the source or destination. The initial mapping then proceeds as described in Figure 2.

#### 3.1.2 Iterative Refinement

The refinement algorithm is an iterative greedy optimization as outlined in Figure 3. Note that two moves are attempted in each iteration of the algorithm to make it less likely for the greedy optimization procedure to get stuck in a poor quality local minimum. Each move transfers part of a randomly selected task from the maximum cost workstation to another randomly selected workstation and the size of the subtask being transferred is selected to best balance the computational load. The problem edge class and Equation (4) can be used to determine the new edge weights after task partitioning.

```
Let vm be the task for which the communication
 intensity is maximum.
Map vm to the most lightly loaded workstation.
Let F = {vm}.
While there are tasks not yet mapped do:
   Let vm be the task, neighboring those tasks
   in the set F, with maximum communication
   intensity.
   Map vm to the most lightly loaded workstation
   that results in the lowest maximum nominal
   distance between all pairs of communicating
   tasks that have already been mapped.
   Add vm to the set F.
End While
```

Figure 2: Algorithm: initial mapping stage.

```
Let Na = 0 (Number of moves attempted so far)
Let Nf = 0 (Num. of consecutive failed attempts)
Let OF1 = Cost of initial mapping
While Na < 1500 and Nf < 80
   Attempt a move
   Attempt a move
   Na = Na + 2
   OF2 = New objective function value
   if OF2 ≤ OF1 then
      The moves are accepted.
      Nf = 0
   else  The moves are rejected.
      Nf = Nf + 2
   endif
EndWhile
```

Figure 3: Algorithm: Iterative Refinement

### 3.2 Dynamic Mapping

As mentioned previously, this approach is also applicable to the dynamic mapping problems of spreading and shrinking.

#### 3.2.1 Spreading

When new workstations become available during execution of a problem, it is reasonable to propagate some of the computational load to the new workstations as long as doing so will decrease the total execution time for the problem. The decision to spread to a new workstation should depend on (*i*) the time until completion of the problem, (*ii*) the relative size of communication and computation intensities, (*iii*) the problem edge class, and (*iv*) the cost for modifying the mapping and redistributing the load.

For this paper, the spreading problem is solved by

Table 1: Single problem node graph allowed to spread from 2 PE's onto up to $N_m$ PE's.

| %C | Cl | $N_m = 4$ N | $N_m = 4$ t(s) | $N_m = 6$ N | $N_m = 6$ t(s) | $N_m = 8$ N | $N_m = 8$ t(s) |
|---|---|---|---|---|---|---|---|
| 5% | C | 2.0 | 4.86 | 2.0 | 4.86 | 2.0 | 4.89 |
| 5% | D | 4.0 | 2.64 | 4.6 | 3.50 | 4.2 | 2.62 |
| 5% | S | 4.0 | 3.07 | 4.8 | 2.36 | 4.6 | 2.75 |
| 5% | SD* | 4.0 | 2.54 | 6.0 | 2.32 | 8.0 | 1.71 |
| 5% | SD+ | 4.0 | 2.97 | 4.4 | 2.60 | 4.8 | 2.51 |
| 5% | Z | 4.0 | 2.45 | 6.0 | 1.65 | 8.0 | 1.27 |
| 10% | C | 2.0 | 4.86 | 2.0 | 4.87 | 2.0 | 4.89 |
| 10% | D | 3.0 | 3.66 | 3.0 | 3.90 | 3.0 | 4.14 |
| 10% | S | 3.0 | 3.65 | 3.0 | 3.66 | 3.0 | 3.68 |
| 10% | SD* | 4.0 | 2.81 | 6.0 | 2.15 | 7.6 | 1.80 |
| 10% | SD+ | 3.0 | 3.66 | 3.0 | 3.67 | 3.0 | 3.72 |
| 10% | Z | 4.0 | 2.45 | 6.0 | 1.66 | 8.0 | 1.28 |
| 20% | C | 1.0 | 9.67 | 1.0 | 9.69 | 1.0 | 11.55 |
| 20% | D | 2.0 | 4.84 | 2.0 | 4.84 | 2.0 | 4.89 |
| 20% | S | 2.0 | 4.87 | 2.0 | 4.86 | 2.0 | 4.88 |
| 20% | SD* | 4.0 | 3.43 | 5.8 | 2.35 | 6.2 | 2.29 |
| 20% | SD+ | 2.0 | 4.87 | 2.0 | 4.88 | 2.0 | 4.88 |
| 20% | Z | 4.0 | 2.44 | 6.0 | 1.66 | 8.0 | 1.27 |

Table 3: 16 node irregular problem graph allowed to spread from 2 PE's onto up to $N_m$ PE's.

| %C | Cl | $N_m = 4$ N | $N_m = 4$ t(s) | $N_m = 6$ N | $N_m = 6$ t(s) | $N_m = 8$ N | $N_m = 8$ t(s) |
|---|---|---|---|---|---|---|---|
| 5% | C | 4.0 | 2.92 | 6.0 | 2.66 | 7.8 | 2.56 |
| 5% | D | 4.0 | 2.98 | 6.0 | 2.36 | 8.0 | 2.23 |
| 5% | S | 4.0 | 2.70 | 6.0 | 2.02 | 8.0 | 1.65 |
| 5% | SD* | 4.0 | 2.74 | 6.0 | 1.94 | 8.0 | 1.62 |
| 5% | SD+ | 4.0 | 3.28 | 6.0 | 3.04 | 8.0 | 2.07 |
| 5% | Z | 4.0 | 2.50 | 6.0 | 1.76 | 8.0 | 1.30 |
| 10% | C | 4.0 | 3.68 | 5.8 | 3.32 | 7.0 | 3.76 |
| 10% | D | 4.0 | 3.44 | 6.0 | 2.92 | 8.0 | 2.96 |
| 10% | S | 4.0 | 2.94 | 6.0 | 2.20 | 8.0 | 2.07 |
| 10% | SD* | 4.0 | 3.38 | 6.0 | 3.24 | 8.0 | 2.17 |
| 10% | SD+ | 4.0 | 3.19 | 6.0 | 2.72 | 7.2 | 2.74 |
| 10% | Z | 4.0 | 2.54 | 6.0 | 2.14 | 8.0 | 1.79 |
| 20% | C | 4.0 | 4.83 | 5.6 | 4.42 | 7.0 | 4.38 |
| 20% | D | 4.0 | 4.43 | 5.6 | 4.39 | 7.6 | 4.60 |
| 20% | S | 4.0 | 3.14 | 6.0 | 2.79 | 7.6 | 2.53 |
| 20% | SD* | 4.0 | 3.45 | 6.0 | 2.54 | 8.0 | 2.16 |
| 20% | SD+ | 4.0 | 3.59 | 6.0 | 3.66 | 6.8 | 3.95 |
| 20% | Z | 4.0 | 2.75 | 6.0 | 1.92 | 8.0 | 1.39 |

Table 2: $2 \times 2$ mesh problem graph allowed to spread from 2 PE's onto up to $N_m$ PE's.

| %C | Cl | $N_m = 4$ N | $N_m = 4$ t(s) | $N_m = 6$ N | $N_m = 6$ t(s) | $N_m = 8$ N | $N_m = 8$ t(s) |
|---|---|---|---|---|---|---|---|
| 5% | C | 4.0 | 3.52 | 5.6 | 3.05 | 6.0 | 2.88 |
| 5% | D | 4.0 | 3.19 | 6.0 | 2.33 | 7.0 | 2.38 |
| 5% | S | 4.0 | 3.12 | 6.0 | 2.25 | 7.0 | 2.30 |
| 5% | SD* | 4.0 | 2.79 | 6.0 | 2.14 | 8.0 | 1.71 |
| 5% | SD+ | 4.0 | 3.20 | 6.0 | 2.31 | 7.8 | 2.35 |
| 5% | Z | 4.0 | 2.43 | 6.0 | 1.65 | 8.0 | 1.26 |
| 10% | C | 4.0 | 3.81 | 4.6 | 4.08 | 5.2 | 4.01 |
| 10% | D | 4.0 | 3.75 | 5.8 | 3.25 | 5.6 | 3.53 |
| 10% | S | 3.8 | 3.59 | 5.4 | 3.16 | 5.8 | 3.12 |
| 10% | SD* | 4.0 | 3.04 | 5.8 | 2.56 | 7.6 | 2.03 |
| 10% | SD+ | 4.0 | 3.60 | 5.6 | 3.13 | 6.0 | 3.25 |
| 10% | Z | 4.0 | 2.44 | 6.0 | 1.66 | 8.0 | 1.27 |
| 20% | C | 2.8 | 5.64 | 3.8 | 5.65 | 2.6 | 5.84 |
| 20% | D | 3.6 | 4.78 | 4.8 | 4.16 | 5.0 | 4.25 |
| 20% | S | 4.0 | 4.04 | 4.2 | 4.13 | 4.6 | 4.44 |
| 20% | SD* | 4.0 | 3.83 | 5.6 | 3.11 | 7.2 | 2.86 |
| 20% | SD+ | 3.8 | 4.39 | 4.0 | 4.61 | 4.0 | 4.79 |
| 20% | Z | 4.0 | 2.44 | 6.0 | 1.67 | 8.0 | 1.27 |

Table 4: Single problem node graph allowed to shrink from 8 PE's onto up to $N_m$ PE's.

| %C | Cl | $N_m = 2$ N | $N_m = 2$ t(s) | $N_m = 4$ N | $N_m = 4$ t(s) | $N_m = 6$ N | $N_m = 6$ t(s) |
|---|---|---|---|---|---|---|---|
| 5% | C | 2.0 | 4.84 | 2.6 | 4.86 | 3.0 | 4.85 |
| 5% | D | 2.0 | 5.04 | 4.0 | 3.05 | 4.2 | 2.85 |
| 5% | S | 2.0 | 4.86 | 4.0 | 3.00 | 4.2 | 3.20 |
| 5% | SD* | 2.0 | 4.92 | 4.0 | 2.56 | 6.0 | 1.98 |
| 5% | SD+ | 2.0 | 4.91 | 4.0 | 3.02 | 4.6 | 2.73 |
| 5% | Z | 2.0 | 4.83 | 4.0 | 2.44 | 6.0 | 1.66 |
| 10% | C | 2.0 | 4.85 | 2.0 | 4.87 | 2.0 | 4.89 |
| 10% | D | 2.0 | 5.33 | 3.0 | 4.12 | 3.0 | 3.89 |
| 10% | S | 2.0 | 4.86 | 3.0 | 3.65 | 3.0 | 3.66 |
| 10% | SD* | 2.0 | 4.89 | 4.0 | 2.76 | 6.0 | 2.13 |
| 10% | SD+ | 2.0 | 4.83 | 3.0 | 3.65 | 3.0 | 3.65 |
| 10% | Z | 2.0 | 4.86 | 4.0 | 2.45 | 6.0 | 1.66 |
| 20% | C | 1.0 | 9.68 | 1.0 | 9.67 | 1.0 | 9.69 |
| 20% | D | 2.0 | 4.99 | 2.0 | 4.86 | 2.0 | 4.89 |
| 20% | S | 2.0 | 4.84 | 2.0 | 4.87 | 2.0 | 4.89 |
| 20% | SD* | 2.0 | 5.11 | 4.0 | 3.19 | 5.8 | 2.24 |
| 20% | SD+ | 2.0 | 4.83 | 2.0 | 4.85 | 2.0 | 4.88 |
| 20% | Z | 2.0 | 4.86 | 4.0 | 2.45 | 6.0 | 1.66 |

running the optimization procedure described in Figure 3 on the existing mapping.

### 3.2.2 Shrinking

In a real system it is also sometimes necessary to shrink a mapping onto fewer workstations than were available when the mapping was initially computed. This may be due to failure of one or more of the workstations, network interruptions, or simply the need to dedicate some of the processing power in the system to another process having higher priority. Also, a problem may be near execution so that the communication overhead dominates the remaining computation.

For this paper, this situation is handled by first randomly assigning each task residing at a workstation that is no longer available to one that is still available. Once the load is transferred to the available workstations the optimization described in Figure 3 is used to partition tasks and perform task propagation to improve the mapping quality.

## 4 Experimental Results

In this section, experimental results are presented to illustrate the importance of problem edge class for the dynamic mapping problems of spreading and shrinking. A network of twelve Sun Sparc 1+ workstations running under PVM is used to emulate the execution of the problems on a NOW. Emulation and simulation results are provided for a few problem graphs exhibiting different communication and computation characteristics. The problem graphs represented are a single partitionable problem node with intra-task communication, a $2 \times 2$ mesh topology, and a 16 node irregular graph. The computational intensities of the nodes in the graphs are such that the most heavily communicating node has 90% of the total computation and the other nodes have equal portions of the remaining computation.

Tables 1, 2, and 3 show the average number of workstations actually used and the execution time on the NOW when the mapping is allowed to spread from 2 workstations onto up to $N_m$ workstations for $N_m = 4$, 6 and 8. The first column shows the relative percentage of communication to computation for the graph and the second column shows the problem edge class. The remaining columns show the average number of workstations actually used ($N \leq N_m$) and the execution times. Tables 4 and 5 show similar results for the case where shrinking is done from 8 workstations down to $N_m$ workstations for $N_m = 2$, 4, and 6.

For the spreading problem, it is clear from the data in Tables 1, 2, and 3 that the processor allocation and execution time is heavily dependent on the prob-

Table 5: $2 \times 2$ mesh problem graph allowed to shrink from 8 PE's onto up to $N_m$ PE's.

| %C | Cl | $N_m = 2$ | | $N_m = 4$ | | $N_m = 6$ | |
|---|---|---|---|---|---|---|---|
| | | N | t(s) | N | t(s) | N | t(s) |
| 5% | C | 2.0 | 5.22 | 4.0 | 3.58 | 5.8 | 2.77 |
| 5% | D | 2.0 | 5.10 | 4.0 | 3.08 | 6.0 | 2.45 |
| 5% | S | 2.0 | 5.20 | 4.0 | 2.98 | 6.0 | 2.40 |
| 5% | SD* | 2.0 | 5.09 | 4.0 | 2.77 | 6.0 | 2.30 |
| 5% | SD+ | 2.0 | 5.15 | 4.0 | 3.03 | 5.8 | 2.60 |
| 5% | Z | 2.0 | 4.86 | 4.0 | 2.45 | 6.0 | 1.66 |
| 10% | C | 2.0 | 5.43 | 4.0 | 4.09 | 5.0 | 4.06 |
| 10% | D | 2.0 | 5.60 | 4.0 | 3.84 | 5.8 | 2.96 |
| 10% | S | 2.0 | 5.48 | 4.0 | 3.72 | 5.6 | 2.74 |
| 10% | SD* | 2.0 | 5.22 | 4.0 | 3.25 | 6.0 | 2.54 |
| 10% | SD+ | 2.0 | 5.57 | 4.0 | 3.70 | 5.6 | 3.11 |
| 10% | Z | 2.0 | 4.85 | 4.0 | 2.44 | 6.0 | 1.66 |
| 20% | C | 2.0 | 6.05 | 4.0 | 5.51 | 5.0 | 5.54 |
| 20% | D | 2.0 | 5.72 | 4.0 | 4.34 | 5.0 | 4.06 |
| 20% | S | 2.0 | 5.78 | 4.0 | 4.12 | 4.6 | 4.09 |
| 20% | SD* | 2.0 | 5.94 | 4.0 | 3.57 | 5.8 | 3.38 |
| 20% | SD+ | 2.0 | 6.16 | 4.0 | 4.47 | 4.8 | 4.27 |
| 20% | Z | 2.0 | 4.87 | 4.0 | 2.44 | 6.0 | 1.67 |

lem edge class. As expected, more communication overhead generated due to task partitioning results in fewer workstations used (fewest for Class C and highest for Class SD*) and higher execution times (highest for Class C and lowest for Class SD*). The variation in average number of workstations used and execution time with problem edge class tends to increase as the relative percentage of communication to computation increases. This variation is much less pronounced for the larger 16 node problem graph in Table 3. This is because less task partitioning is required due to the larger number of tasks.

The same variation in execution times with edge class is seen in the shrinking problem data compiled in Tables 4 and 5. Again, the Class C execution times are highest and the Class SD* times are lowest (except for Class Z). For the single problem node graph in Table 4, the variation in processor allocation seen for spreading is also present. However, the variation is less pronounced for the $2 \times 2$ mesh problem in Table 5. Since the only conceptual difference between spreading from 2 to 4 workstations and shrinking from 8 to 4 workstations is the initial mapping, the smaller variation due to problem edge class in this case is most likely due to the small number of workstations on the network. For example, the SD* problems are restricted to a smaller number of workstations than could be used beneficially if available. Also, for smaller values of $N_m$

Table 6: Single problem node graph allowed to spread from 2 workstations onto up to $N_m$ workstations.

| %C | $Cl_a$ | $N_m = 8$ | | | | | | $N_m = 12$ | | | | | |
|----|--------|---|---|---|---|---|---|---|---|---|---|---|---|
| | | N | Time (s) for Real Class | | | | | N | Time (s) for Real Class | | | | |
| | | | C | D | S | SD* | SD+ | | C | D | S | SD* | SD+ |
| 5% | C | 2.0 | **7.02** | 6.02 | 6.02 | 5.52 | 6.02 | 2.0 | **7.02** | 6.02 | 6.02 | 5.52 | 6.02 |
| 5% | D | 4.2 | 15.44 | **5.04** | **5.25** | 3.24 | **5.13** | 5.0 | 21.38 | **5.39** | 5.52 | 2.99 | 5.39 |
| 5% | S | 4.6 | 18.41 | 5.21 | 5.28 | 3.17 | 5.21 | 5.0 | 21.39 | 5.39 | **5.48** | 2.90 | 5.39 |
| 5% | SD* | 8.0 | 57.28 | 8.28 | 8.28 | **2.17** | 8.28 | 10.0 | 91.23 | 10.24 | 10.24 | **2.15** | 10.24 |
| 5% | SD+ | 4.8 | 19.90 | 5.30 | 5.39 | 2.97 | 5.30 | 5.0 | 21.38 | 5.39 | 5.48 | 2.83 | **5.39** |
| 10% | C | 2.0 | **9.02** | 7.02 | 7.02 | 6.02 | 7.02 | 2.0 | **9.02** | 7.02 | 7.02 | 6.02 | 7.02 |
| 10% | D | 3.0 | 14.54 | **6.54** | 6.87 | 5.04 | 6.54 | 3.0 | 14.54 | **6.54** | 6.92 | 5.20 | 6.54 |
| 10% | S | 3.0 | 14.54 | 6.54 | **6.78** | 4.72 | 6.54 | 2.6 | 12.33 | 6.73 | **6.87** | 5.24 | 6.73 |
| 10% | SD* | 7.6 | 102.06 | 14.46 | 14.46 | **3.00** | 14.46 | 9.2 | 152.45 | 17.66 | 17.66 | **3.04** | 17.66 |
| 10% | SD+ | 3.0 | 14.54 | 6.54 | 6.78 | 4.72 | **6.54** | 3.0 | 14.54 | 6.54 | 6.87 | 5.04 | **6.54** |
| 20% | C | 1.0 | **10.00** | 10.00 | 10.00 | 10.00 | 10.00 | 1.0 | **10.00** | 10.00 | 10.00 | 10.00 | 10.00 |
| 20% | D | 2.0 | 13.01 | **9.02** | 9.02 | 7.02 | 9.02 | 2.0 | 13.01 | **9.02** | 9.02 | 7.02 | 9.02 |
| 20% | S | 2.0 | 13.01 | 9.02 | **9.02** | 7.02 | 9.02 | 2.0 | 13.01 | 9.02 | **9.02** | 7.02 | 9.02 |
| 20% | SD* | 6.2 | 132.54 | 22.15 | 22.15 | **4.67** | 22.15 | 6.4 | 140.55 | 22.96 | 22.96 | **4.66** | 22.96 |
| 20% | SD+ | 2.0 | 13.01 | 9.02 | 9.02 | 7.02 | **9.02** | 2.0 | 13.01 | 9.02 | 9.02 | 7.02 | **9.02** |

it is less likely for the mapping to be shrunk onto fewer than $N_m$ workstations because each additional workstation that is not used adds an increasingly larger computational load to the other workstations.

Next, simulation results are shown for the case where a problem edge class is assumed during mapping for problems having various real edge classes. The assumed edge class may be the same as or different from the real edge class. The same single node problem graph used for Tables 1 and 4 is used for this experiment. Table 6 shows these results for the case where the mapping is allowed to spread from 2 workstations onto up to $N_m$ workstations for $N_m$ = 8 and 12. The first column shows the relative percentage of communication to computation for the graph. The second column shows the problem edge class that is assumed during mapping. The remaining columns show the average number of workstations actually used ($N \leq N_m$) and the execution times when the real problem edge class is as specified. Note that the average number of workstations used for the problem depends on the edge class that is assumed during mapping. Similar results for the case where shrinking is done are shown in Table 7. In these cases, the number of workstations available to the mapping is shrunk from 12 workstations down to $N_m$ workstations for $N_m$ = 4, and 8. As before, the data in the tables show that the average number of workstations used for the problem is heavily dependent on the edge class that is assumed during mapping. Class SD* is

allocated the most workstations, Class C is allocated the fewest, and the other classes lie in between these two extremes. For each real edge class, compare the execution times for the five assumed classes in each section of the table (sections are separated by a horizontal line). In each case, the minimum execution time out of the five assumed classes is shown in boldface in the tables. In the vast majority of cases, the execution time for the real edge class is lowest when the assumed edge class is correct. The few deviant cases are due to the suboptimal nature of the optimization algorithm. In each of the deviant cases, the communication percentage is 5%. For more communication intensive problems, errors in modeling the communication behavior of a problem after partitioning and merging are more costly, as supported by the data in the tables. Another observation is that the severity of the performance penalty (increase in execution time) due to assuming an incorrect edge class is in direct proportion to the difference in communication behavior between the assumed class and the real class.

## 5 Conclusion

In this paper, we addressed the static and dynamic mapping problem, emphasizing the dynamic problems of spreading or shrinking a mapping during execution if the number of available workstations changes. An iterative optimization algorithm for static and dynamic mapping was used to solve the mapping problem under conditions of spreading and shrinking. Since the algorithm is based on our previously proposed com-

Table 7: Single problem node graph allowed to shrink from 12 workstations onto up to $N_m$ workstations.

| | | $N_m = 4$ | | | | | | $N_m = 8$ | | | | |
| | | N | Time (s) for Real Class | | | | | N | Time (s) for Real Class | | | | |
| %C | $Cl_a$ | | C | D | S | SD* | SD+ | | C | D | S | SD* | SD+ |
|---|---|---|---|---|---|---|---|---|---|---|---|---|---|
| 5% | C | 2.4 | **7.63** | 5.82 | 6.02 | 5.42 | 5.92 | 2.8 | **8.24** | 5.62 | 6.02 | 5.32 | 5.82 |
| 5% | D | 3.8 | 12.77 | **4.86** | 5.12 | 3.85 | **4.95** | 4.4 | 16.74 | **5.13** | 5.46 | 3.48 | 5.27 |
| 5% | S | 4.0 | 14.06 | 5.06 | **5.12** | 3.31 | 5.08 | 4.6 | 18.46 | 5.26 | **5.30** | 3.19 | **5.26** |
| 5% | SD* | 4.0 | 14.31 | 5.31 | 5.31 | **3.17** | 5.31 | 8.0 | 57.26 | 8.26 | 8.26 | **2.17** | 8.26 |
| 5% | SD+ | 4.0 | 13.74 | 4.92 | 5.22 | 3.52 | 5.04 | 4.8 | 19.93 | 5.33 | 5.39 | 3.04 | 5.33 |
| 10% | C | 2.0 | **9.02** | 7.02 | 7.02 | 6.02 | 7.02 | 2.0 | **9.02** | 7.02 | 7.02 | 6.02 | 7.02 |
| 10% | D | 3.0 | 14.54 | **6.54** | 6.83 | 4.88 | 6.54 | 3.0 | 14.54 | **6.54** | 6.87 | 5.04 | 6.54 |
| 10% | S | 3.0 | 14.54 | 6.54 | **6.78** | 4.72 | 6.54 | 3.0 | 14.54 | 6.54 | **6.78** | 4.72 | 6.54 |
| 10% | SD* | 4.0 | 26.16 | 8.16 | 8.16 | **3.76** | 8.16 | 7.0 | 85.22 | 13.22 | 13.22 | **2.91** | 13.22 |
| 10% | SD+ | 3.0 | 14.54 | 6.54 | 6.78 | 4.72 | **6.54** | 3.0 | 14.54 | 6.54 | 6.78 | 4.72 | **6.54** |
| 20% | C | 1.0 | **10.00** | 10.00 | 10.00 | 10.00 | 10.00 | 1.0 | **10.00** | 10.00 | 10.00 | 10.00 | 10.00 |
| 20% | D | 2.0 | 13.01 | **9.02** | 9.02 | 7.02 | 9.02 | 2.0 | 13.01 | **9.02** | 9.02 | 7.02 | 9.02 |
| 20% | S | 2.0 | 13.01 | 9.02 | **9.02** | 7.02 | 9.02 | 2.0 | 13.01 | 9.02 | **9.02** | 7.02 | 9.02 |
| 20% | SD* | 4.0 | 49.86 | 13.86 | 13.88 | **5.07** | 13.86 | 6.0 | 121.20 | 21.20 | 21.20 | **4.48** | 21.20 |
| 20% | SD+ | 2.0 | 13.01 | 9.02 | 9.02 | 7.02 | **9.02** | 2.0 | 13.01 | 9.02 | 9.02 | 7.02 | **9.02** |

putational model for task partitioning and merging, it is applicable to cases where (*i*) the number of workstations available to a problem is subject to change during execution, (*ii*) the computational intensities of the problem nodes is greatly unbalanced, and (*iii*) the number of problem nodes is less than the number of available workstations. In particular, the problem edge class attribute included in the model dictates the communication characteristics of a problem after tasks are partitioned. Experimental results indicate that the number of workstations allocated to a problem and the resultant execution times should be heavily dependent on the problem edge class and relative communication intensiveness of the problem. Simulation results indicate that the minimum execution time is achieved when the edge class assumed during mapping matches the real edge class of the problem.

## References

[1] A. Baratloo, P. Dasgupta, and Z.M. Kedem. Calypso: A novel software system for fault-tolerant parallel processing on distributed platforms. In *Proceedings of the Fourth IEEE International Symposium on High Performance Distributed Computing*, pages 122–129, August 1995.

[2] V.M. Lo. Heuristic algorithms for task assignment in distributed systems. *IEEE Trans. on Computers*, 37(11):1384–1397, November 1988.

[3] J. Yang, L. Bic, and A. Nicolau. A mapping strategy for mimd computers. In *Proc. of the Intl. Conf. on Parallel Processing, Vol. I*, pages 102–109, 1991.

[4] B.-R. Tsai and K.G. Shin. Communication-oriented assignment of task modules in hypercube multicomputers. In *Proc. of the 12th Intl. Conf on Distributed Computing Systems*, pages 38–45, 1992.

[5] L. Schwiebert and D.N. Jayasimha. Mapping parallel computations to multiprocessor architectures considering the effects of communication. Technical report, The Ohio State University, Computer and Information Science Research Center, May 1992.

[6] G. Cybenko. Dynamic load balancing for distributed memory multiprocessors. *Journal of Parallel and Distributed Computing*, 7:279–301, 1989.

[7] T. Yang and A. Gerasoulis. A fast static scheduling algorithm for dags on an unbounded number of processors. In *Proc. of Supercomputing*, pages 633–642, November 1991.

[8] J.C. Jacob and S.-Y. Lee. A new task mapping model supporting partitioning and merging of tasks. In *Proceedings of the ISCA International Conference on Parallel and Distributed Computing and Systems*, pages 216–221, October 1993.

# LOAD BALANCING FOR PARALLEL LOOPS IN WORKSTATION CLUSTERS*

Tae-Hyung Kim and James M. Purtilo

Computer Science Department
University of Maryland
College Park, Maryland 20742
{thkim,purtilo}@cs.umd.edu

**Abstract:** *Load imbalance is a serious impediment to achieving good performance in parallel processing. Global load balancing schemes cannot adequately manage to balance parallel tasks generated from a single application. Dynamic loop scheduling methods are known to be useful in balancing parallel loops on shared-memory multiprocessor machines. However, their centralized nature causes a bottleneck even for the relatively small number of processors in workstation clusters because of order-of-magnitude differences in communications overheads. Moreover, improvements of basic loop scheduling methods have not dealt effectively with irregularly distributed workloads in parallel loops, which commonly occur in applications for workstation clusters. In this paper, we present a new decentralized balancing method for parallel loops on workstation clusters.*

## 1  INTRODUCTION

In a distributed parallel program, tasks are generated and distributed to multiple processors to be processed simultaneously. Load imbalance is a serious impediment to achieving good performance as it leaves some processors idle, when they could be working to make progress. While global load balancing should still be an issue in the whole operating system's concern, our focus is on balancing parallel tasks within an application. Since minimizing the execution time of an application is more important than average response time, each processor needs to keep making progress rather than merely to have a balanced load. Although the latter state may finally lead to the former, this is not a primary goal to shorten the finish time. From a program's viewpoint, loops are the largest source of task parallelism in a parallel application. A loop is called a *parallel loop* (DOALL-loop) if there are no data dependences among all iterations. The question of how to allocate an iteration to a particular processor for minimizing the total execution time is known as a loop scheduling problem [19, 12, 15, 20, 5].

If there are $I$ uniformly distributed iterations, and $P$ identical processors, load can be balanced simply by assigning $I/P$ iterations to each processor. Since both factors may not be known in advance or may vary substantially, such a static method is often difficult or inefficient. *Self-scheduling* (SS) [19] is the simplest dynamic solution. It assigns a new iteration to a processor only when the processor becomes available. However, this method requires tremendous synchronization overhead; to be practical, hardware support to fast barrier synchronization primitives is desirable. *Uniform-sized chunking* (CSS) reduces such synchronization overhead by sending $K$ iterations instead of one [12]. In this method, the overhead is amortized to $1/K$, but the possibility of load imbalance increases when K is increased. In *guided self-scheduling* (GSS), the fixed chunk function ($K$) is replaced with a non-linearly decreasing chunk function in order to reduce the overhead at the beginning of a loop by allocating larger chunks, and also to reduce the chance of load imbalancing at the end of the loop by allocating smaller chunks [15]. *Trapezoid self-scheduling* (TSS) uses a linearly decreasing chunk function, which helps to reduce scheduling overhead while still maintaining a reasonable balance [20].

Recently, networks of workstations have emerged as viable candidates for running parallel applications. To our knowledge, the first work on parallel loop scheduling in a network of heterogeneous workstations was done by Cierniak *et al.* [5]. They considered three aspects of heterogeneity — loop, processor, and network — and developed algorithms for generating optimal and sub-optimal schedules of loops. Two major limitations are that it is static and that the loop heterogeneity model is linear. In this paper, we present a dynamic load balancing method for parallel loops of more general patterns, since many non-scientific applications such as the DNA sequence search problem [4] or the Mandelbrot set computation [8], which are good candidate applications for workstation clusters, often do not carry conventional regular loop patterns. The unpredictable patterns can even be detrimental to those improvements [12, 15, 20], although the pure SS scheme is orthogonal to the loop patterns.

---

*This research has been supported by Office of Naval Research under contract No. N000149410320.

## 1.1 Programming Environment

Networks of workstations have by nature easy-to-change configurations; programs must be adapted accordingly whenever the hardware configuration is changed. Without having to manually rewrite module programs, diverse performance-related configurations can be incorporated with the aid of an automatic adaptation tool. Our work, called CORD (Configuration-level Optimization of RPC-based Distributed programs) [10], is a framework for automatically generating all necessary executables from RPC-based distributed programs according to a configuration-level description intended for high performance. Programs written to the RPC paradigm become reusable even after changes in executing platform, which is significantly necessary for workstation clusters, because decisions that affect the performance are isolated from the module programming level. Under our framework, performance-oriented decisions are annotated with the interconnections in configuration programs. Normally, RPC does not consider the case of multiple servers for the same function — except for some variations like PARPC [14] and MultiRPC [16]. Server replication is an important configuration for high performance. This paper presents a load balancing method that is employed in generating automatically configured source programs by the CORD when the configuration program specifies server replication possibly to deal with parallel loops.

## 1.2 Motivation

Under a heterogeneous network of workstations, a simple policy like equally distributing workloads to multiple processors may lead to a parallelization anomaly. That is, the execution time of the given workload may take longer even if the number of workstations is increased. Suppose there are $n$ processors $\{P_1, \ldots, P_n\}$, and $T$ identical tasks. Let $\tau_i$ be the number of tasks per unit time that the processor $i$ can process. In equal distribution, each processor has $T/n$ numbers of tasks. The execution time of the program is determined by the critical processor that has the smallest $\tau_i$ value; let's say it is $\tau_{min}$. Then the execution time is $\frac{T/n}{\tau_{min}} = \frac{T}{n\tau_{min}}$. Now, let's add a new processor of $\tau_{new}$ to the cluster for the application. Each processor will have $T/(n+1)$. Therefore, if $\tau_{new} < \frac{n}{n+1}\tau_{min}$, the execution time of $(n+1)$-processors cluster is $\frac{T}{(n+1)\tau_{new}}$, which is longer than that of $n$ processors!

One may want to circumvent this problem by allocating tasks according to the known computing power of each processor [9, 3]. However, their methods were static, thus of limited usefulness. Dynamic loop scheduling methods can deal with more general cases, but the centralized nature of the methods — the central processor that generates sub-tasks has to manage all other processors — may cause a bottleneck in a network of many workstations. For example, if there are 100 servers, and if a master needs $10^{-2}$ second to prepare and send a task, the master would create a bottleneck unless the average time for each server to finish a task is greater than one second. In our ex-

perimentation with the Mandelbrot set computation on $[0.5, -1.8]$ to $[1.2, -1.2]$ using a $400 \times 400$ pixel window, the program reached its saturation point at 25 workstations under the *self-scheduling* scheme. To avoid such a situation, sub-tasks should be sufficiently large grained compared to communication overheads, but it is not likely considering relatively high communication costs in workstation clusters. Since there are many "embarrassingly parallel" applications, a decentralized load balancing scheme is called for. We present such a method that can reduce the overheads by means of establishing proper migration topology based on the known computing powers of the processors involved.

## 1.3 Our Approach

Parallel tasks ("objects") and their working platforms ("bases") are two ingredients in parallel processing. Nonetheless, only the "objects" part has been the focus of load balancing. There has been nothing wrong in this because the "bases" part has been mostly fixed. Meanwhile, workstation clusters have become viable platforms for parallel processing. As mentioned before, the conventional global load balancing and dynamic loop scheduling methods become problematic when they are employed to applications on workstation clusters. One of the key issues in dynamic load balancing is how to reduce the accompanying overheads. The main idea of our approach is balancing the "bases" to facilitate balancing the "objects;" i.e. we construct a special migration topology based on relative processor speeds in order to reduce migration overheads. Basically our method adopts demand-driven migrations the same way that dynamic loop scheduling methods do. Well-constructed topology reduces unnecessary migrations. The theme of this paper is how to construct such a topology that aims to do demand-driven migrations in a decentralized way for efficient load balancing.

## 1.4 Outline

Sec. 2 delineates models of parallel loops that need to be balanced and of workstation clusters that process those parallel tasks. Sec. 3 formally describes the cluster model and presents how to construct such a cluster and its corresponding task migration network based on the model. Sec. 4.1 provides preliminary characteristics that explain task migration behaviors under our method. Sec. 4.2 is devoted to the complexity issues incurred by migration using the results in Sec. 4.1. Sec. 4.3 addresses initial load distributions. In Sec. 5, we show experimental results using our implementation of the balancing scheme for an irregular and unpredictable loop.

## 2 LOOP AND WORKSTATION CLUSTER MODELS

In this section, we classify four typical parallel loop patterns that affect performance of load balancing schemes based on workload distribution in an iteration space. Next, we discuss our workstation cluster model to deal with those diverse patterns, especially if the workstations involved are heterogeneous.

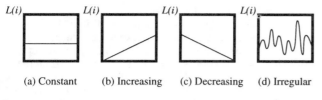

Figure 1: Four typical parallel loops.

## 2.1 Loop Model

Fig. 1 shows four typical parallel loops where $L(i)$ represents the execution time of the $i$-th iteration. The workload may be uniformly distributed over an iteration space as shown in Fig. 1 (a). It may also be non-uniform but *linearly* distributed as in Figs. 1 (b) and (c); this kind of distribution is often contained in scientific programs. Finally, as in Fig. 1 (d), the workload may be quite irregular. Many non-scientific applications carry parallel loops of this type. The first three cases have been specially considered by conventional loop scheduling methods [15, 20, 5] in order to improve on the basic self-scheduling method.

Particularly for irregular loops, we can distinguish between the two cases: predictable vs. unpredictable. For example, the parallel tasks in the DNA sequence search problem and the Mandelbrot set computation are all irregular, but the tasks in the first problem are predictable [4] unlike those in the second one.

## 2.2 Workstation Cluster Model for Load Balancing

Fig. 2 shows two representative topologies in the workstation cluster model for parallel loops. Fig. 2 (a) represents the topology of traditional loop scheduling methods [19, 12, 15, 20], in which load migration is not performed. Instead, the main processor (shaded circle) prepares a set of tasks and allocates them to each server whenever the server demands them. Since the scheduling process is dedicated to the main processor, its chance of creating a bottleneck rises as the number of servers present on the network increases. Fig. 2 (b) illustrates the topology of our workstation cluster model. The main processor distributes workloads to all servers initially. Load balancing is attempted by task migration via pre-determined paths, deeming load state polling or exchange overhead unnecessary, unlike in global dynamic load balancing schemes. The migration is performed in a decentralized fashion between only the two processors involved. The workstation cluster model for load balancing is characterized by the following parameters:

- $N$: the number of workstations, $\{W_1, \ldots, W_N\}$.

- $\tau_i$: the throughput of $W_i$, which is defined by the number of unit tasks per unit time.

- $\gamma_{ij}$: the amount of load to migrate from $i$ to $j$.

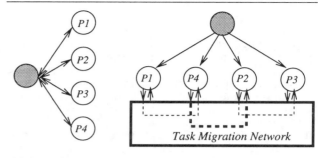

(a) Loop Scheduling    (b) Our Approach

Figure 2: Topologies in workstation cluster model for load balancing.

## 3 LOAD BALANCING METHOD

Two important components of dynamic load balancing schemes are *transfer policy* and *location policy* [7, 11]. The transfer policy determines whether a task should be processed locally or remotely by transferring it at a particular load state. The location policy determines which process initiates the migration and its source or destination. These are for global load balancing from the OS's viewpoints. Multidimensional load vectors determine the load state of a processor. In our system, we aim to balance parallel loops in an application. A simple 'demand' message is enough to initiate load migration rather than load state exchange [11] or random polling of candidate processors [7] because the only load vector is the number of sub-tasks in a processor. The transfer policy then becomes simple: if a processor receives a request message for transfer from a processor that is running out of sub-tasks to work on, it migrates some of its sub-tasks to that processor.

Likewise, the location policy is now modified by the problem of establishing proper task migration paths. Workstation clusters have virtually no restrictions on topology for migration. It may be assumed that any two point-to-point communication overheads are equal, but identifying the optimal sender and receiver pair is essential. Considering all possible candidates for sender (or receiver) to migrate the excess load causes high overhead, but it is avoidable. The key is how to identify the busy and the idle processors in the middle of computations. Since the relative processing speeds of workstations in a cluster are known in advance, the possible senders and receivers of migrations are not unknown — momentary overload by other activities is the reason for uncertainty.

In this section, we present how to construct such a task migration network as shown in Fig. 2 (b). Once the network is constructed, load balancing is pursued through task migration on it. For example, each pair connected in a dotted line in Fig. 2 (b) $(P_i \rightarrow P_j)$ is a basic unit of migration; whenever the faster processor $(P_j)$ depletes its workload, it demands that its pre-determined partner $P_i$ share some of $P_i$'s workload, and $P_i$ migrates $\gamma_{ij}$ of its current workload to

```
/* P_i:  sender */
for (i = 0; i < taskcnt; i++) {
    if (pvm_nrecv( P_j, MoreTaskReq )) {
        /* a request arrived */
        n = (taskcnt-i+1) * Ratio_ij;
        /* Migrate to P_j */
        if (n) {
            pvm_initsend( PvmDataDefault );
            pvm_pkint( &n, 1, 1 );
            pvm_pkint( &TaskQ[i], n, 1 );
            pvm_send( P_j, TaskMigrating );
            i += n;
            continue;
        }
    }
    /* loop body on TaskQ[i] */
}

/* P_j:  receiver */
LOOP:
    for (i = 0; i < taskcnt; i++) {
        /* loop body on TaskQ[i] */
    }
    /* Check the partner processor P_i */
    pvm_initsend( PvmDataDefault );
    pvm_pkint( &more, 1, 1 );
    pvm_send( P_i, MoreTaskReq );
    /* Wait until killed by parent */
    while(1)
        if (pvm_nrecv( P_i, TaskMigrating )) {
            /* migrated tasks arrived */
            pvm_upkint( &taskcnt, 1, 1 );
            pvm_upkint( TaskQ, taskcnt, 1 );
            goto LOOP;
        }
```

Figure 3: Programs generated for a migration path.

$P_j$. Fig. 3 shows the generated source codes for such a connection. First, we will formally define the cluster model in Sec. 2.2. Then, we will describe how to construct such a cluster and its corresponding migration network based on the model.

A cluster is a bipartite form of $(w_s, w_f)$, in which $w_s$ is slower than $w_f$: i.e. $\tau_s < \tau_f$. Throughout the paper, we use the notation $(\tau_s, \tau_f)$ interchangeably with the notation $(w_s, w_f)$ when we focus on throughputs. An entire workstation cluster is defined as follows:

**Definition 3.1** The *cluster tree (CT)* of $N$ workstations $\{W_1, \ldots, W_N\}$ is a binary tree $CT = (V, E_{left} \cup E_{right})$, where

- The vertices $V$ represent *clusters*. A distinguished vertex 'root' represents an entire cluster, and the right sub-cluster is faster than (or equal to) the left sub-cluster.

- $E_{left}$ is a set of edges to the left sub-trees. $E_{right}$ is a set of edges to the right sub-trees.

- For $c, v, w \in V$, if $(c, v) \in E_{left}$ and $(c, w) \in E_{right}$, a load migration path exists from $v$ to $w$. When $v$ and $w$ are not terminal nodes, the path

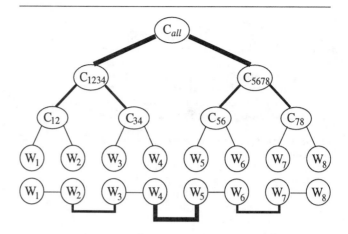

Figure 4: A cluster tree and its corresponding task migration paths.

is established from the fastest node in cluster $v$, which is the rightmost terminal in the subtree of $v$, to the slowest node in cluster $w$, which is the leftmost terminal in the subtree of $w$.

Terminal nodes are individual workstations. Each terminal $v$ is associated with its throughput $\tau_v$. Throughput of non-terminal node $C = (v, w)$ is defined by $(\tau_v + \tau_w)$, which is explained by Theorem 4.3. □

**Definition 3.2** In a cluster $C_1 = (\tau_1, \tau_2)$, the *balance ratio* $B_{C_1}$ is defined by $\frac{(\tau_2 - \tau_1)}{(\tau_2 + \tau_1)}$. A cluster $C_1 = (\tau_1, \tau_2)$ is said to be *more balanced* than another cluster $C_2 = (\tau_3, \tau_4)$, if the *balance ratio* of $C_1$ is less than that of $C_2$, i.e. $\frac{(\tau_2 - \tau_1)}{(\tau_2 + \tau_1)} < \frac{(\tau_4 - \tau_3)}{(\tau_4 + \tau_3)}$. □

**Definition 3.3** A cluster $C_1 = (\tau_1, \tau_2)$ is *faster* than another cluster $C_2 = (\tau_3, \tau_4)$ if $\tau_{C_1}$ is greater than $\tau_{C_2}$, or if $\tau_{C_1}$ is equal to $\tau_{C_2}$ and $C_1$ is *more balanced* than $C_2$. □

In the extreme case that $\tau_1$ is equal to $\tau_2$, the *balance ratio* is zero; thus load is perfectly balanced. Likewise, in the other extreme in which $\tau_2$ is much greater than $\tau_1$, the ratio is asymptotically 1. The *balance ratio* in a cluster can be related to the amount of load migration. When the components in a cluster are equally loaded initially, if the cluster is perfectly balanced, then no intra-cluster migration is necessary. In other words, the more balanced a cluster is, the less migration is needed.

The process of constructing a cluster tree from a set of workstations is done in recursive "bitonic" fashion. First, workstations in the set $\{w_1, \ldots, w_n\}$ become terminal nodes in the tree. They are sorted in ascending order by their throughputs. Let the sorted set be $\{w'_1, \ldots, w'_n\}$. The fastest one $(w'_n)$ is coupled with the slowest one $(w'_1)$, the second fastest one $(w'_{n-1})$ is coupled with the second slowest one $(w'_2)$, and so forth. The couples come to have parents in the tree, i.e. $\{c_1 = (w'_1, w'_n), \ldots, c_{n/2} = (w'_{n/2}, w'_{n/2+1})\}$, which are likewise sorted by their throughputs. Again, they are coupled in bitonic fashion. This process continues until it reaches a single cluster. Notice that the cluster of the two identical components still needs an intra-cluster migration because an equal distribution is not always possible. Once such a tree is constructed, the task migration topology is determined as follows:

**Algorithm 3.1** *Task migration network from CT*
**Begin**
> **For** all clusters (non-terminal nodes) $c$ in $CT$
> > **For** two children $v$ and $w$ such that
> > $(c, v) \in E_{left}$ and $(c, w) \in E_{right}$
> > > **if** ($v, w$ are terminals)
> > > **then** *CONNECT* $v$ *TO* $w$
> > > **else** *CONNECT* RightmostTerminal($v$)
> > > *TO* LeftmostTerminal($w$)

**End**

Fig. 4 shows the relationship between the cluster tree and the migration topology. For example, the rightmost terminal of $C_{1234}$ is $W_4$, and the leftmost terminal of $C_{5678}$ is $W_5$, so the link for the root cluster $C_{all}$ is constructed between $W_4$ and $W_5$. The thicker links denote higher level links; they will be used only if the load cannot be balanced through the lower links.

## 4   ANALYSIS OF MIGRATION BEHAVIORS

There are two important concerns in devising a load balancing scheme [7]. First, the overhead should not negate the benefits of an improved load distribution. Next, the potential migration instability[a], in which processors spend too much time transferring tasks, should be avoided. Our method is orthogonal to the stability issue because a demand is issued only when the processor is idle. In this section, we present an analytic result on the overheads incurred by our method. We start with an example case to explain our method qualitatively.

**Example 4.1** Suppose there are four processors $P1, P2, P3$ and $P4$ that have $N$ identical tasks initially and we know their relative throughputs, which are $\tau, 2\tau, 3\tau$ and $4\tau$. When a load state of a potential sender $P1$ is probed by other processors, migration to $P2$ or $P3$ would be wasteful because its resulting resolution of $P1$'s overloaded state may be merely temporal. Since $P4$ is the fastest, the then-migrated load may have to be migrated again to $P4$, while a single migration directly to $P4$ would have been more efficient. Thus we can say the $P1$ has the greatest affinity to $P4$ among all possible receiver candidates.   □

The above example suggests that the slowest processor should be connected to the fastest processor,

and the second slowest one is to the second fastest one, and so on, in bitonic fashion. The resulting pairs would tend to be *more balanced* in terms of the combined throughputs. We will elaborate on the effects of this kind of bitonic pairing in Sec. 4.1. This method calls for load migration to be done in as much bulk as possible. One ten-byte sized load migration is cheaper than ten one-byte sized load migrations. This is particularly important in workstation clusters where the communication overheads are still high.

**Example 4.2** Let us consider the topology of $P1 \rightarrow P4$ and $P2 \rightarrow P3$ as shown in Fig. 2 (b). Throughputs are the same as in Example 4.1. In this case the combined throughputs of the two sub-clusters turn out to be equal. That is, no further load migration is necessary through the link between the two clusters $(P1, P4)$ and $(P2, P3)$!   □

However, now that cluster $(P2, P3)$ is *more balanced* than cluster $(P1, P4)$, the resulting decrease in the intra-cluster migration makes cluster $(P2, P3)$ process more tasks. That is why this cluster is defined as the faster one in Def. 3.3. In general, such an ideal case may not be common in real situations; throughputs may fluctuate in the middle of computing and initial distributions are not always equal. For the case that the load is not balanced in the first cluster for some reason, we continue to balance the load through inter-cluster migrations. In the following analysis, we use $\gamma_{ij} = 1/2$, for all $i, j$, which guarantees uni-directional migration is enough for load balancing (notice $P_j$ is faster), although more aggressive choice like $\gamma_{ij} = \tau_i/\tau_j$ may reduce overheads.

### 4.1   Preliminaries

To examine migration overhead, we need a communication time model. The conventional approach to modeling communication time for transferring a message of $m$ bytes is a simple linear function, i.e. $T_{comm} = \alpha + \beta m$, where $\alpha$ is startup time and $\beta$ is transfer time per byte [2]. The empirical values for $\alpha$ and $\beta$ under the PVM system [18] at LAN-based clustered workstations are 4.527 *msec*, 0.0024 *msec* and 1.661 *msec*, 0.00157 *msec* for datagram and stream transmission cases, respectively, which imply $\alpha \gg \beta$ [17].

In Theorems 4.1 and 4.2, we compute the total number of migrated tasks ($\beta$'s multiplier) and the frequencies of migrations ($\alpha$'s multiplier) in a cluster. Furthermore, we also illustrate an important characteristics of our method, which is that balance ratio gets improved as clustering happens at higher levels.

**Theorem 4.1** In a cluster $C = (v, w)$ where $v$ and $w$ are terminal nodes in $CT$, and they have initially loaded $N$ identical tasks respectively, the total number of tasks to be migrated from $v$ to $w$ ($M_{v \rightarrow w}$) to meet the finish times at both processors is $\frac{\tau_w - \tau_v}{\tau_w + \tau_v} N$, i.e. the balance ratio of $C$ times $N$.

*Proof.* Let us determine the general terms of the number of tasks to be migrated from $v$ to $w$ at the time $w$ becomes idle. Since $w$ is faster than $v$, $w$'s first

---

[a]For example, in a two-processor system where both are overloaded, they may continuously migrate each part of loads to the other processor, which does not improve the situation at all.

incidence of task depletion occurs after $\frac{N}{\tau_w}$; thus the number of tasks in the first migration is half of what remains in $v$ at that time, which is $\frac{1}{2}(N - \frac{N}{\tau_w} \cdot \tau_v) = \frac{N}{2}(1 - \frac{\tau_v}{\tau_w})$. Notice that $\tau_v/\tau_w$ is less than 1. $T_w$, the total number of tasks that are eventually processed by $w$, is a summation of the following series:

$$T_w = N + \frac{N}{2}(1 - \frac{\tau_v}{\tau_w}) + \frac{N}{4}(1 - \frac{\tau_v}{\tau_w})^2 + \cdots$$
$$= N \lim_{k \to \infty} \frac{1 - (\frac{1}{2}(1 - \frac{\tau_v}{\tau_w}))^{k+1}}{1 - \frac{1}{2}(1 - \frac{\tau_v}{\tau_w})} = \frac{2N\tau_w}{\tau_v + \tau_w}$$

Therefore, $M_{v \to w} = T_w - N$, which yields $\frac{\tau_w - \tau_v}{\tau_w + \tau_v} N$. □

**Theorem 4.2** In a cluster $C = (v, w)$ where $v$ and $w$ are terminal nodes in $CT$, and they have initially loaded $N$ identical tasks respectively, the frequency of migration from $v$ to $w$ to meet the finish times at both processors is $\log_{\frac{1}{2}(1 - \frac{\tau_v}{\tau_w})} \frac{1}{N}$.

*Proof.* The general term in the series is $\frac{N}{2^k}(1 - \frac{\tau_v}{\tau_w})^k$. Thus, $k = \log_{\frac{1}{2}(1 - \frac{\tau_v}{\tau_w})} \frac{1}{N}$. □

**Theorem 4.3** In a cluster $C = (v, w)$ where $v, w$ are arbitrary nodes in $CT$, and they have initially loaded $N$ identical tasks, the combined throughput of cluster $C$ is $\tau_v + \tau_w$, assuming no migration overhead.

*Proof.* Suppose $v$ and $w$ are terminal nodes in $CT$. In Theorem 4.1, the total number of tasks processed by $v$ and $w$ is given by $\frac{2N\tau_v}{\tau_v + \tau_w}$ and $\frac{2N\tau_w}{\tau_v + \tau_w}$, respectively, and the finish time is $\frac{N}{(\tau_v + \tau_w)/2}$ at either processor. As cluster $C$ have loaded $2N$ tasks in total, this may be interpreted to mean that the *de facto* throughputs of the cluster is $\tau_v + \tau_w$. Now let us assume this holds for two clusters $C_1 = (\tau_1, \tau_2)$ and $C_2 = (\tau_3, \tau_4)$; i.e. $\tau_{C_1}$ and $\tau_{C_2}$ are $\tau_1 + \tau_2$ and $\tau_3 + \tau_4$, respectively. For a cluster $C = (C_1, C_2)$ (we can assume $C_1$ is slower without loss of generality), we can calculate the number of tasks processed by $C_2$ as follows:

$$T_{C_2} = N \sum_{i=0}^{\infty} \frac{1}{2^i}(1 - \frac{\tau_{C_1}}{\tau_{C_2}})^i = N \cdot \frac{2\tau_{C_2}}{\tau_{C_1} + \tau_{C_2}}$$
$$= N \cdot \frac{\tau_{C_2}}{(\tau_{C_1} + \tau_{C_2})/2}$$

By induction, this completes our proof. □

Theorem 4.3 implies that the sum of the two throughputs in a cluster may represent the combined throughput of the cluster so that we can cluster recursively in bitonic fashion. The real combined throughput can be yielded by subtracting the throughput loss incurred by migration overheads (see Sec. 4.2) from that amount.

**Theorem 4.4** If there are two clusters $C_1 = (\tau_1, \tau_4)$ and $C_2 = (\tau_2, \tau_3)$, and $C_1$ is slower than $C_2$, then another cluster $C = (C_1, C_2)$ is always *more balanced* than the *less balanced* cluster between $C_1$ and $C_2$.

*Proof.* Consider the case when $B_{C_1}$ is greater than $B_{C_2}$ (i.e. $C_1$ is *less balanced* than $C_2$). Due to the property of bitonic coupling, $\tau_1 \leq \tau_2 \leq \tau_3 \leq \tau_4$ must hold. Let us write $\tau_2 = a\tau_1$, $\tau_3 = ab\tau_1$ and $\tau_4 = abc\tau_1$, where $a, b, c \geq 1$. By Theorem 4.3, $B_C$ is yielded by $\frac{\tau_2 + \tau_3 - \tau_1 - \tau_4}{\tau_1 + \tau_2 + \tau_3 + \tau_4}$. That is, $B_{C_1} = \frac{abc - 1}{abc + 1}$ and $B_C = \frac{a + ab - (abc + 1)}{abc + ab + a + 1}$. Since $(abc + ab + a + 1) \cdot (abc - 1) - (a + ab - (abc + 1)) \cdot (abc + 1) = 2abc(abc + 1) - 2a(b + 1) \geq 0$, $B_C$ is less than or equal to $B_{C_1}$. But if $2abc(abc+1) - 2a(b+1) = 0$, all $a$, $b$, $c$ must be 1, which implies $\tau_1 = \tau_2 = \tau_3 = \tau_4$ that contradicts the given assumption ($\tau_{C_1} < \tau_{C_2}$ or $B_{C_1} > B_{C_2}$). Hence $B_C$ is strictly less than $B_{C_1}$. Likewise, when $B_{C_1}$ is less than $B_{C_2}$ (i.e. $C_2$ is *less balanced* than $C_1$), we also can show that $B_C$ is less than $B_{C_2}$ — now $\tau_2 \leq \tau_1 \leq \tau_4 \leq \tau_3$ holds. Finally, consider the case when $B_{C_1}$ is equal to $B_{C_2}$. Again, due to the property of bitonic coupling, this condition implies $\tau_1 = \tau_2 = \tau_3 = \tau_4$, which is a contradiction. This completes the proof. □

Theorem 4.4 contains an important subtlety. It implies the amount of inter-cluster migration is always less than that of intra-cluster migration in a critical sub-cluster. Since migrations through a higher-level link may need multi-hop communications, they result in higher overheads. Theorem 4.4 assures that the amount of migrations of such higher overheads get smaller. Consequently, the complexity of migration overheads is bounded.

### 4.2 Complexities of Migration Overhead

Consider the topologies in Fig. 2 (a) and (b) extended to $p$ processors and the total number of tasks are $pN$. Self-scheduling requires $pN(\alpha + \beta)$, where $N$ is the total number of tasks between a master and its servers. Putting aside the fact that the master can easily create a bottleneck in that topology, we investigate the complexity of our method and compare it with that of self-scheduling.

The worst case happens when the fastest processor (the rightmost one in a cluster tree) is far faster than the remaining ones: i.e. $\tau_3 \gg \tau_1, \tau_4, \tau_2$ in Fig 2 (b). Let us calculate the overhead for a one-hop migration in this scenario. For example, in a link between $P2$ and $P3$, the total number of tasks to migrate is, by Theorem 4.1, $\frac{\tau_3 - \tau_2}{\tau_3 + \tau_2} N$. As $\tau_3 \gg \tau_2$, the number becomes $N$. In other words, all of the task in a slower processor must be migrated to the infinitely faster one. Likewise, by Theorem 4.2, the frequency of migrations is given by $\log_{\frac{1}{2}} \frac{1}{N} = \log_2 N$. Thus, the one-hop overhead $(OH_1)$ is $\alpha \log_2 N + \beta N$. Since the farthermost tasks need $p - 1$ hops, we obtain the worst case complexity of migration overhead as follows:

$$OH_{worst} = \sum_{k=1}^{p-1} k \cdot OH_1 = \frac{1}{2}p(p-1)(\alpha \log_2 N + \beta N)$$

Recalling the facts that $\alpha \gg \beta$ and $N \gg p$, $OH_{worst}$ can hardly be worse than $pN(\alpha + \beta)$. Now let us consider an average case where each processor contains the average number of tasks $(N)$ at any moment during computation.[b] Consider a lowest-level cluster $(v, w)$; i.e. $v$ and $w$ are terminal nodes in $CT$. By Theorem 4.2 and 4.1, the one-hop migration overhead is obtained as follows:

$$OH_1 = \frac{1}{1 - \log_2 \frac{\tau_v}{\tau_w}} \log_2 N \cdot \alpha + \frac{\tau_w - \tau_v}{\tau_w + \tau_v} N \cdot \beta$$

By Theorem 4.4, the balance ratio of a higher-level cluster is always less than the maximum of those of the two sub-clusters. That is, the maximum balance ratio among all clusters $(v, w)$ at the lowest level is the maximum balance ratio of all clusters in an entire cluster tree. Let it be $B_{max}$. Then, no $(p-1)$ links in the topology can migrate more than $B_{max} \cdot N$ tasks. Therefore, the average case complexity of migration overhead is a lower bound of the following formula, where $r_{max}$ is the maximum of $\frac{\tau_v}{\tau_w}$ for all clusters $(v, w)$ at the lowest level in $CT$:

$$OH_{average} = \sum_{k=1}^{p-1} OH_1 = \frac{p-1}{1 - \log_2 r_{max}} \log_2 N \cdot \alpha + B_{max}(p-1)N\beta$$

Notice that $0 < r_{max} < 1$ and $0 < B_{max} < 1$. $OH_{average}$ is always better than $pN(\alpha + \beta)$. Furthermore, since $\alpha \gg \beta$ and $N \gg p$, it is significantly better in general.

**Example 4.3** Let us consider Fig. 2 (b) again. Each processor initially has $N$ identical sub-tasks. Throughputs are the same as in Example 4.1: i.e. $\tau, 2\tau, 3\tau, 4\tau$ for $P1, P2, P3$ and $P4$, respectively. For brevity, suppose all processors have constant throughputs, and we assume no migration overhead for the time being. Then the following table shows each snapshot of load distribution under our load balancing method in case we chose $\gamma_{14} = \frac{4}{5}$ and $\gamma_{23} = \frac{3}{5}$ particularly.

Table 1: Snapshots during load migrations.

| | P1 | P4 | P2 | P3 |
|---|---|---|---|---|
| *Initial Load* | $N$ | $N$ | $N$ | $N$ |
| *After $N/4\tau$* | $\frac{3N}{4}$ | $0$ | $\frac{N}{2}$ | $\frac{N}{4}$ |
| *After Migration* | $\frac{3N}{20}$ | $\frac{3N}{5}$ | $\frac{N}{2}$ | $\frac{N}{4}$ |
| *After $N/12\tau$* | $\frac{N}{15}$ | $\frac{4N}{15}$ | $\frac{N}{3}$ | $0$ |
| *After Migration* | $\frac{N}{15}$ | $\frac{4N}{15}$ | $\frac{2N}{15}$ | $\frac{3N}{15}$ |
| *After $N/15\tau$* | $0$ | $0$ | $0$ | $0$ |

The table shows that total execution time is $\frac{N}{4\tau} + \frac{N}{12\tau} + \frac{N}{15\tau} = \frac{2N}{5\tau}$; in other words, the average throughput of this 4-processor cluster with $4N$ sub-tasks is

---

$10\tau$. However, the real behavior deviates from this ideal behavior because of migration overheads. We calculate the overhead for two different choices of $\gamma$: when $\gamma$ is taken proportionally based on throughput (**Case 1**) and when all $\gamma = \frac{1}{2}$ (**Case 2**).

**Case 1:** As shown in Table 1, migrations occur twice of amount $3N/5$ and $3N/15$, respectively. Thus, the overhead is yielded by $\alpha + \frac{3}{5}N\beta + \alpha + \frac{3}{15}N\beta = 2\alpha + \frac{4}{5}N\beta$.

**Case 2:** By Theorem 4.1, the number of tasks to migrate for $P1 \to P4$ and $P2 \to P3$ links is calculated as follows:

$$M_{14} = \frac{4\tau - \tau}{4\tau + \tau}N = \frac{3}{5}N, \quad M_{23} = \frac{3\tau - 2\tau}{3\tau + 2\tau}N = \frac{1}{5}N$$

Similarly, by Theorem 4.2, the number of migrations that occur for the two links is as follows:

$$k_{14} = \log_{\frac{1}{2}(1-\frac{1}{4})} \frac{1}{N}, \quad k_{23} = \log_{\frac{1}{2}(1-\frac{2}{3})} \frac{1}{N}$$

Thus, the overhead is yielded by

$$\begin{aligned} OH &= \alpha(k_{14} + k_{23}) + \beta(M_{14} + M_{23}) \\ &= \alpha(\log_{\frac{3}{8}} \frac{1}{N} + \log_{\frac{1}{6}} \frac{1}{N}) + \frac{4}{5}N\beta \\ &\approx 3.63 \log N\alpha + \frac{4}{5}N\beta \end{aligned}$$

In either case, the overhead is much less than that of *self-scheduling*, which is $4N(\alpha + \beta)$. □

### 4.3 Initial Load Distribution

While any initially distributed load should be balanced through a dynamic load balancing method, the resulting overhead is associated. We discuss now the initial load distribution issue that can lower overhead, compared with the equal distribution that was assumed for analysis in the previous sections.

When loops are predictable, the cases are either when we know the amount of the required computation exactly, as in Fig. 1 (a), (b), (c) and sometimes (d), or when we can determine just the orderings, like in the DNA sequence search problem [4]. For the former case, as $L(i)$ is known in advance, if we distribute proportionately according to each processor's throughput, we can reduce the likelihood of migration. In other words, the processor $P_i$ with $\tau_i$ will get $\tau_i \sum_i L(i) / \sum_k \tau_k$. Dynamic adjustments to this approximation are made by our load balancing method. In a lowest-level cluster $(v, w)$ in $CT$, we allocate $\lfloor \tau_i \sum_i L(i) / \sum_k \tau_k \rfloor$ to $v$, and $\lceil \tau_i \sum_i L(i) / \sum_k \tau_k \rceil$ to $w$. Since $v$ is slower than $w$, uni-directional migration is enough. If we cannot guarantee the faster processor finishes earlier, the migration paths must be bi-directional as in the following cases.

For the latter case, we cannot initialize in the above way as the value of $L(i)$ is unknown. The *LPT* (Largest Processing Time first) algorithm [1] is for this class of loop models. The tasks are sorted in descending order based on execution time $L(i)$. Each proces-

---

[b]Obviously this is a harsher condition than what a real average case needs to be, since the number of remaining tasks gets decreased as time goes by. Therefore, our obtained complexity is an upper-bound of the average complexity.

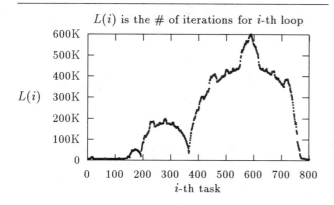

Figure 5: The load distribution pattern of a loop in the Mandelbrot set computation.

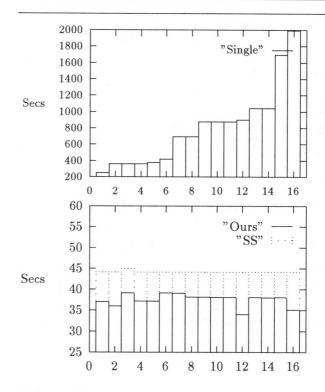

Figure 6: Elapse times: Mandelbrot set computation on [0.5,-1.8] to [1.2,-1.2]

sor should process the largest task first. Otherwise, an unfortunate processor may happen to take a large task (say, about 100 times larger than the small ones) as a last one at the near end of all computations, which results in a load imbalance — other processors are idle because few tasks left to migrate at this moment.

When tasks are not "orderable" and quite irregular like in the Mandelbrot set computation problem, we can neither quantify the loads to proportionately distribute to processors of diverse throughputs nor sort in decreasing order and apply the $LPT$ algorithm. No general heuristics can be used — random distribution does not need to be worse.

## 5 EXPERIMENTS

To demonstrate the performance of our method, we conducted our experiment on a 16-workstation cluster using PVM message passing systems. The example program was Mandelbrot set computation on $[0.5, -1.8]$ to $[1.2, -1.2]$ using a $800 \times 800$ pixel window. This program contains unpredictably irregular loops as shown in Fig. 5, which cannot be analyzable as in Sec. 4. The $x$-value indicates the $x$-th row in an outer loop. The $y$-value is the number of inner iterations $(L(x))$ to compute the corresponding $x$-th row. The total number of sub-tasks are 800, and the result size of a sub-task is 800 in integers: one integer per pixel.

We have initially distributed those tasks in a round-robin style. A variety of heterogeneous workstations have been used as shown in Fig. 6 (a) which shows the elapse time for each of 16 workstations[c] to compute the given Mandelbrot set; the range is from 250 seconds to 2000 seconds. The results by the 16-workstation cluster are given by Fig. 6 (b). The dotted boxes represent the finish times of each workstation under the pure self-scheduling method, which substantiate the expected good load balance. The result by

our method is seemingly imbalanced but the actual finish time is much improved. Perfect balance may be good but the evaluation should be based on how much its overheads negate its resulting benefits.

Table 2: Migration units: sizes and frequencies

| taskcnt | 1 | 2 | 3 | 4 | 5 | 6 | 7 | 10 | 11 | 12 | 17 | 19 | 20 | 30 |
|---------|---|---|---|---|---|---|---|----|----|----|----|----|----|----|
| freq | 13 | 6 | 3 | 3 | 3 | 1 | 4 | 1 | 1 | 1 | 1 | 1 | 1 | 1 |

Table 2 summarizes the size of each migration and its frequency that are counted in our experimentation. For example, the single-task migration occurred 13 times, and the 30-tasks migration occurred once, etc, during the entire task migration attempts. In the table, we can compute the total occurrences of migrations by summing all frequencies up, that is 40. If we calculate this figure from our formula on $OH_{average}$, that is $\frac{p-1}{1-\log_2 r_{max}} \log_2 N$, where $p = 16$, $N = 800/16 = 50$, $r_{max} = 692/693 \approx 1$. This formula gives $15 \log_2 50 \approx 84.7$. Considering this formula is obtained as an upper bound, the experimental value is said to conform to the theoretically obtained value. Although the theoretical model does not exactly match with our experimental environments, the model gives us a reasonable implication about the mi-

---

[c]1 SPARCstation 20, 3 SPARCstation 5's, 2 SPARCstation 10's, 2 DECstation 5000/25's, 4 SPARCstation IPX's, 2 DECstation 23/100's, 2 SPARCstation IPC's are used.

gration behaviors in general cases.

## 6  CONCLUSION

We have presented a new decentralized load balancing method for parallel tasks in heterogeneous workstation clusters to deal with various patterns of parallel loops. We discussed why the conventional global dynamic load balancing methods are not adequate to our application area. Loop scheduling schemes that have been useful under shared-memory multiprocessor machines cause a bottleneck in workstation clusters because the communication overheads are so high. To our knowledge, migration topology for load balancing is considered for the first time. The topology has not been considered important heretofore because sometimes it is given in a hard-wired form [13] or it is meaningless where distributed load patterns cannot be assumed to be known in advance [7, 11]. More interesting topologies can be studied in the future. We have shown analytically that the overhead of our method is lower than that of the self-scheduling scheme when an "predictability" condition is given. We have also provided some experimental data for cases when the loop pattern is unpredictably irregular.

## REFERENCES

[1] K. P. Belkhale and P. Banerjee. An approximate algorithm for the partitionable independent task scheduling problem. In *Proceedings of '90 International Conference on Parallel Processing*, August 1990.

[2] L. Bomans and D. Roose. Benchmarking the iPSC/2 hypercube multiprocessor. *Concurrency: Practice and Experience*, Vol. 1(1):3–18, September 1989.

[3] Clemens H. Cap and Volker Strumpen. Efficient parallel computing in distributed workstation environments. *Parallel Computing*, Vol. 19:1221–1234, 1993.

[4] N. Carriero and D. Gelernter. How to write parallel programs: A guide to the perplexed. *ACM Computing Surveys*, Vol. 21(6):322–356, September 1989.

[5] M. Cierniak, W. Li, and M. J. Zaki. Loop scheduling for heterogeneity. In *Proceedings of the 4th International Symposium on High-Performance Distributed Computing*, August 1995.

[6] F. DeRemer and H. Kron. Programming-in-the-large versus programming-in-the-small. *IEEE Transactions on Software Engineering*, Vol. 2(2), June 1976.

[7] Derek L. Eager, Edward D. Lazowska, and John Zahorjan. Adaptive load sharing in homogeneous distributed systems. *IEEE Transactions on Software Engineering*, Vol. 12(5):662–675, May 1986.

[8] J. D. Foley, A. van. Dam, S. K. Feiner, J. F. Hughes, and R. L. Phillips. *Introduction to Computer Graphics*. Addison-Wesley Publishing Company, 1993.

[9] A. S. Grimshaw, J. B. Weissman, E. A. West, and Jr. E. C. Loyot. Metasystems: An approach combining parallel processing and heterogeneous distributed computing systems. *Journal of Parallel and Distributed Computing*, Vol. 21:257–270, 1994.

[10] T.-H. Kim and J. M. Purtilo. Configuration-level optimization of RPC-based distributed programs. In *Proceedings of the 15th International Conference on Distributed Computing Systems*, May 1995.

[11] Philip Krueger and Niranjan G. Shivaratri. Adaptive location policies for global scheduling. *IEEE Transactions on Software Engineering*, Vol. 20(6):432–444, June 1994.

[12] C. P. Kruskal and A. Weiss. Allocating independent subtasks on parallel processors. *IEEE Transactions on Software Engineering*, Vol. 11(10):1001–1016, October 1985.

[13] Frank C. H. Lin and Robert M. Keller. The gradient model load balancing method. *IEEE Transactions on Software Engineering*, Vol. 13(1):32–38, January 1987.

[14] Bruce Martin, Charles Bergan, and Brian Russ. PARPC: A system for parallel remote procedure calls. In *Proceedings of the International Conferences on Parallel Processing*, pages 449–452, 1987.

[15] C. D. Polychronopoulos and D. J. Kuck. Guided self-scheduling: A practical scheduling scheme for parallel supercomputers. *IEEE Transactions on Computer*, Vol. C-36(12):1425–1439, December 1987.

[16] M. Satyanarayanan and E. H. Siegel. MultiRPC: A parallel remote procedure call mechanism. Technical Report CMU-CS-86-139, Carnegie-Mellon University, 1986.

[17] B. K. Schmidt and V. S. Sunderam. Empirical analysis of overheads in cluster environments. *Concurrency: Practice and Experience*, Vol. 6(1):1–32, February 1994.

[18] V. S. Sunderam. PVM: A framework for parallel distributed computing. *Concurrency: Practice and Experience*, Vol. 2(4):315–339, December 1990.

[19] P. Tang and P. C. Yew. Processor self-scheduling for multiple nested parallel loops. In *Proceedings of '86 International Conference on Parallel Processing*, pages 528–535, August 1986.

[20] T. H. Tzen and L. M. Ni. Dynamic loop scheduling for shared-memory multiprocessors. In *Proceedings of '91 International Conference on Parallel Processing*, pages II:247–250, August 1991.

# Performance Analysis of Task Migration in a Portable Parallel Environment*

**Balkrishna Ramkumar**    **Gopal Chillariga**

Department of Electrical and Computer Engineering

University of Iowa Iowa City, IA 52242

ramkumar@eng.uiowa.edu

**Abstract:** *The performance of a preemptive task migration algorithm implemented in a portable parallel programming environment is reported. The experiments were conducted using the* ELMO *system which extends languages like C with migratable parallel tasks. Preemptive task migration support has been provided for checkpointing of tasks during debugging and replay in the Intrepid [35] environment, as well as for transparent checkpointing and recovery support for dynamic reconfiguration upon failure. However, its implementation is general, and can be used transparently by the system for other purposes like load redistribution and adaptive scheduling on workstation networks. The performance of task migration on a variety of application programs on the nCUBE/2 is reported.*

**Key words and phrases:** task migration, parallel programming, task parallelism, concurrent objects.

## 1  Introduction

Task migration is defined as the ability to move tasks from one processor to another during the course of program execution. We define preemptive task migration as the ability to interrupt a task which has partially executed on one processor, migrate it to another processor, and then resume its execution from the point of interruption. We use the term migration to mean preemptive migration in this paper.

Task migration is rapidly becoming a important and necessary tool in parallel and distributed systems. Among systems with unpredictable loads like networks of workstations, it may be necessary to move tasks from heavily loaded to lightly loaded processors dynamically to optimize resource utilization. Such systems are becoming increasingly popular, (e.g. the NOW project [2]), and are likely to be more so as MPPs continue to fail. Task migration support can be effectively used to provide fault tolerance via periodic checkpointing and dynamic reconfiguration of the system upon failure. A checkpoint can be simply viewed as the migration of a task to stable storage. Recovery then corresponds to restoring the checkpointed state of tasks that were active on the failed processor. Finally, for parallel debugging, if repeatibility is desired it is necessary to save the state of a run and replay the execution. This requires "migration" of tasks to and from secondary storage.

---

*This research is supported in part by the National Science Foundation grant CCR-9308108.

The Intrepid project [35] at the University of Iowa has been investigating language, compiler and runtime support necessary for debugging portable task-parallel programs. As part of this effort, the project also aims to support *portable checkpointing*, where it is possible to checkpoint the state of a task running on one procesor and recover the checkpointed state on a different processor in a heterogeneous environment. Intrepid has been designed to support features commonly found in portable systems proposed to date. As part of this effort, an efficient task migration algorithm was proposed [17] and implemented to support checkpointing of program state during debugging, but was general enough to serve other purposes like load redistribution and adaptability to local process loads on workstation networks. Intrepid serves the ELMO compiler which extends languages like C, Fortran and C++ with migratable parallel tasks. Several application programs have been implemented using the ELMO extensions to C and are used evaluate task migration performance in this paper.

The remainder of this paper is organized as follows. In Section 2 we present related work in the area of task and object migration. We then briefly describe the ELMO extensions to C and the runtime support provided by Intrepid in Section 3. Section 4 outlines the task migration algorithm implemented in the Intrepid runtime system, while Section 5 evaluates the algorithm on the nCUBE/2 hypercube using a range of benchmark programs.

## 2  Related Work

A substantial amount of work has been done in the area of process migration in distributed operating systems such as Sprite [15], DEMOS/MP [33], Charlotte [3], V [12], Mach [30] and MOSIX [5]. Nuttall [31] provides an excellent survey of distributed operating systems that support task migration. This research has shown that process migration can be used to distribute the load and improve the overall performance of the system. However, it also exposes the high cost of migration and the need for it to be used sparingly.

Distributed operating systems pose several problems that limit their widespread use. Such systems require exclusive control of all the resources in a distributed system. Most of them cannot support heterogeneity of architectures. Programming environments, on the other hand, are more versatile. They can port more easily across different hardware platforms and can even exist on heterogeneous systems. They can coexist with other applications and share system resources. However, programming environments do not usually offer transparent task migration. Typically, if migration is supported, the user is responsible for using task migration in the program as desired.

Systems like PVM [22] and Express [18] do not support migration. However, the DOME environment [6] supports object migration in "SPMD C++" running on top of PVM. Sloop [29], an object-oriented system for programming a network of distributed machines, permits the user to request object migration. However, the system may override the programmer in certain situations. Amber [11] is an object-oriented system for parallel programming on a network of multiprocessors that also supports task migration. It supports *mobility* primitives which are derived from similar primitives in the Emerald system [26]. However, the user must use them to implement an application-specific load balancing algorithm if needed.

The Piranha system [9, 23] is designed to provide adaptive parallelism for Linda [8]. Piranha allows workstations to dynamically join or withdraw from a computation as it proceeds. Workstation loads due to other applications are considered. However, the tasks are still heavy-weight and cannot be frequently migrated. Moreover, the tasks must be specified in a manner that permits them to be preempted at any time and *re-started* at a later time without adversely affecting the overall computation.

Condor [7] also attempts to utilize idle machines, periodically checkpointing the processes and restarting them on other systems when migration is required. However, it limits migration to single independent processes.

MOSIX [5] is a distributed operating system that is well-known for using migration in load balancing. Migration has also been proposed in a general model for dynamic load balancing [41]. However, no implementations on real machines are discussed or presented. Load balancing using migration has also been proposed for Time Warp [24] and evaluated on a multiprocessor simulator.

Several concurrent object-oriented systems have been proposed to date that do not support task migration. We briefly list below those that can benefit from the approach presented in this paper. Compositional C++ or CC++ [10] supports task parallelism in a C++ context and also provides synchronization primitives for thread-based programming. IC-C++ [13] aims to support fine-grain concurrency in C++ and is designed for massively parallel machines for expressing highly concurrent programs. Concurrent C++ [20, 21] also supports processes that communicate with blocking or nonblocking transactions. Jade [39] is a task-based programming system that has been designed for portability as an extension of the C programming language. It has been implemented on shared and distributed memory and on heterogeneous workstation clusters.

Charm [37], Charm++ [27], Mentat [4, 25], and ProperCAD II [32] are coarse-grained message-driven systems that support portable programming on MIMD systems. Charm extends the C programming language with concurrent objects. Charm++, Mentat, and ProperCAD II extend C++ with parallel class types. These systems do not currently support migration.

# 3  ELMO

The ELMO system comprises a compiler that supports simple task-parallel extensions to languages like C, Fortran, and C++. It is supported by the Intrepid runtime system that provides dynamic load balancing, scheduling, task migration, communication and other system services to ELMO programs. Currently, the implementation of ELMO-C has been completed; ELMO-C++ and ELMO-Fortran are under development. The ELMO system supports both SPMD and task-parallel programming and supports portable parallel programming on a variety of target architectures, including shared memory systems, message passing systems and networks of workstations.

## 3.1  The Language

ELMO programs are expressed as a collection of *task* definitions. Instances of these tasks are typically small-grained and are created dynamically at run time. Task instances may reside on any processor; in general, this may change from run to run without affecting correctness of the program. For SPMD programming on $N$ processors, $N$ instances of a single task are created and one placed on each processor. These tasks then cooperate to solve the desired problem. Tasks in ELMO communicate with each other using conventional nonblocking sends, and blocking or nonblocking receives. The task-parallel model distinguishes ELMO from systems like PVM [22], Express [18], DOME [6], Linda [8], Piranha [23], pC++ [28] and Split-C [14], which only support heavyweight SPMD processes in their programming models. The ELMO task model is similar to the concurrent object-oriented model [1, 13], but distinguishes itself through its support for blocking communication primitives and SPMD programming.

On each processor, the ELMO runtime system uses message-driven scheduling of tasks to maximize processor utilization. Whenever messages arrive from the network they are enqueued in a *task block* which stores the task's current execution state. A task is ready to be scheduled for execution if it has one or more messages enqueued in its task block, unless it is currently blocked on a specific message which has not yet arrived. When a task is scheduled for execution, it processes a single message in its message queue (or blocks on an receive) and relinquishes the processor. Like ELMO, Charm [37] also uses message-driven scheduling, but Charm tasks are purely nonblocking to minimize state saving during a context switch.

All ELMO tasks and messages are derived from a base type called a *portable structure* [34]. The portable structure in ELMO is a simple object extension of an aggregate type like a C *struct*, for which marshalling and unmarshalling operations must be provided by the programmer if the aggregate data is noncontiguous. We believe this does not impose an unreasonable demand on programmers, since such functions need to be provided in all message-passing systems when such data needs to be moved across processor boundaries. Moreover, in most systems, the programmer is also responsible for invoking these operations correctly whenever they are required. In ELMO, the marshalling functions are used by the runtime system only when required for migration purposes.

With the aid of compiler support, this restricted inheritance permits support for task migration in ELMO (see Section 4) to be as efficient as message transmission. The use of a portable structure to facilitate efficient transparent task migration distinguishes ELMO from systems supporting migration like Sloop [29], Amber [11], DOME [6], Piranha [23] and Condor [7].

Another important feature of the ELMO compiler is its ability to generates code to compute *closures* of task states whenever a task is blocked on a receive primitive. Closures are essential for portable checkpointing, since they eliminate all pointers in a task's state and marshall the state in contiguous memory. The closure can then be used to restore or migrate the state of the task on another processor's memory. This feature is supported transparently through code generated by the ELMO compiler [38] and is used at run time to efficiently save and restore state for task migration. The closure computation saves only in-scope variables and is effective even when a task is blocked on a receive arbitrarily deep inside a recursive function call.

The ELMO-C compiler translates ELMO-C programs into SPMD C programs, which are then compiled using the C compiler on the respective parallel machine and linked to the ELMO runtime system developed for that machine. This approach was previously used in the Charm [37] compiler. The runtime system has also been written in ELMO-C, thereby making it possible to checkpoint and save the runtime system state using exactly the same mechanism as applicable to application programs. The runtime system is also equally amenable to the extensive debugging support provided to ELMO by the Intrepid debugging environment [35].

### 3.2 The Runtime System

Instances of an ELMO task can be dynamically created at run-time using a *create_task*() system primitive, which creates a message requesting the run-time system to create an instance of a named task. The task may not be created immediately, however an ID for the task instance is returned by the *create_task*() primitive, and may be used to communicate with the task. An attempt to invoke one of its methods will transparently block until the task instance is actually created. Once an instance of a task is created, it is considered *active*, although it may not be *executing* at a given moment.

Tasks may invoke methods in other tasks or send messages to explicit blocking "receives" in the body of these methods. The ELMO compiler transparently distinguishes between method invocations on the same processor and remote invocations. Note that due to task migration, invocations of a given method by a task may sometimes be local and sometimes remote. This can only be determined at the time of the invocation at runtime. The term entry point identifies a legal destination for a message. These messages are delivered to their respective destinations when picked by Intrepid's run-time scheduler. Delivery of a message to an entry point implies executing the corresponding body of code until completion of the method, or until a blocking communication primitive is encountered. At this point, another message is scheduled by the run-time system.

Each processor in the system can only process one message at a time, such that no more than one task can be executing on a given processor. Concurrency is exploited by executing a different task on each processor in parallel. Also, since a task is only active on one processor at any given time, multiple messages for the same task cannot be processed concurrently.

A task can explicitly terminate its existence using the *exit_task*() primitive, at which time it is considered inactive, and can no longer be considered for execution.

## 4  Task Migration

The task migration algorithm implemented in ELMO is described in [17]. We describe it briefly below.

In order to migrate an instance of a task, it is necessary to suspend the execution of the task on one processor, and then continue it on another. Every instance of a task has its own unique identifier (ID) which is used to send messages to it. Such an ID can be used to send messages to a task even after it has migrated. Messages sent to a processor that are destined for a task that has already been migrated from that processor will be forwarded to that processor.

A migrating task is assigned a new ID by the processor to which it migrates. Thus a migrating task may have multiple logical IDs assigned to it during the course of its existence. Messages may be sent to such a task using any one of its multiple IDs.

A task which has migrated will have used more than one ID during the course of its existence. When such a task terminates, its current ID is now obsolete, as are all of its previous IDs which are now forwarding addresses. Issues relating to name resolution and forwarding addresses have been studied in detail in [19]. The primary contribution of this work is the effective use of message-driven execution in minimizing the effective latencies of task migration, even when it performed very frequently.

## 5  Performance

The cost of migration limits the frequency with which a task can be migrated without sacrificing performance. In this section, we evaluate the cost of migration in the Intrepid runtime system.

As mentioned earlier, one of the important uses of task migration is checkpointing for fault tolerance. Checkpointing introduces overheads during fault-free execution, which may be quite significant depending on the checkpointing frequency and the volume of data to be checkpointed. Unlike checkpointing of a heavy UNIX-style process which needs to be performed as one potentially costly operation, the granularity of task checkpointing is small and can be performed independently of other tasks on the same processor. This also permits checkpointing of multiple tasks on a processor to be scheduled more effectively so as to hide their effective overhead during failure-free execution.

The objectives of the experiments reported below are (*a*) to determine the frequency with which it is possible to migrate small-grained tasks without significantly affecting the overall performance, and (*b*) study the effect of varying the amount of information to be checkpointed on performance. We note that, in our programming model, tasks are typically small and are not typically "data-heavy". In all the experiments reported, it was necessary to inflate the amount of data per task for all but the smallest data size.

Experimental results are presented for four benchmark programs. In each case, the experiments were designed to determine the realistic cost of task migration. The benchmarks are fine-tuned programs which achieve high processor utilization with excellent speedups without the use of migration. Tasks in these benchmark program were artificially migrated in a controlled manner to study the effect of migration on these programs. Since these applications were fine-tuned to perform well without migration, any observed degradation in performance will be the direct consequence of migration.

## 5.1 The Benchmarks

Four parallel benchmark programs were used to evaluate migration on the nCUBE/2 hypercube. They are a traveling salesman problem (*TSP*), a grid-based computation (*grid*), a primes computation program (*primes*) and a parallel test pattern generator for sequential circuits (*testgen*) [36]. We describe them briefly below.

The *TSP* program uses a parallel branch-and-bound algorithm to find the best solution to a 7-city traveling salesman problem. Each node in the branch-and-bound tree was represented by a concurrent task. The program was modified to force every node in the branch-and-bound tree to migrate to another processor before it begins processing. The amount of data and frequency of migrations were varied to study their effect on program performance. The small problem instance was deliberately chosen to study the effect of frequent migrations on short running programs. Due to the speculative nature of parallel search in this program, the number of tasks created from run to run varied between 80-300 leading to a wide range of execution times.

In this experiment, an 85 x 85 grid of nodes was statically created and distributed among the available processors. A total of 7225 tasks were created, one per grid point, but were placed randomly on the available nCUBE processors. 50% of the nodes in the grid were designed perform twice the computation as the other 50%. A load imbalance was deliberately created by assigning the "light" tasks on the first (#num_processors/2) processors, and the "heavy" tasks on the remaining (#num_processors/2) processors. All tasks were eligible for migration. This benchmark was designed to study the effect of random migration of tasks at varying frequencies on performance.

The *primes* program computes the number of prime numbers less than a given bound. This program creates a binary tree of tasks using a simple divide-and-conquer algorithm that partitions the interval recursively. The computation is evenly divided among the leaves of the tree. The inner nodes of the tree are then used to collect the final result at the root. The internal nodes of the divide and conquer tree are migrated to observe its effect on performance. The program was also used to compare the effect of marshaling and unmarshaling migrated task data on performance, and the effect of migration on speedup as the number of processors were increased.

*Testgen* is a parallel test pattern generator for sequential circuits [36]. The program created one task for each fault in its fault list. These tasks were load balanced on the available processors. The program was modified to make each task execute one time slice on a processor, and then migrate itself to the next processor in a round-robin manner. The frequency of migrations were increased in a controlled manner to determine its effect on execution time.

## 5.2 Analysis

In an earlier paper [17], we reported the raw cost of moving a task with no data to be 800 $\mu s$. This reflects the time nec-

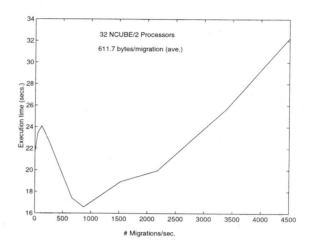

Figure 1: The effect of migration on the performance of the *grid* benchmark on 32 processors on the nCUBE/2 hypercube. The nodes in the computation were initially statically distributed so as to exhibit load imbalance. Random task migration, even at the rate of almost 1000 migrations/second, is shown in this example to improve the execution time by effectively redistributing the load.

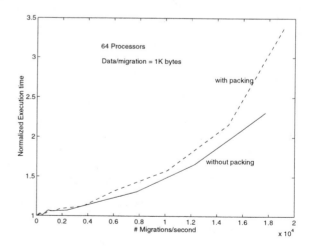

Figure 2: Effect of marshaling on the overhead of migration on the **primes** application on 64 nCUBE/2 processors.

Table 1: The effect of migration on the performance of the *TSP* benchmark. A small problem instance was chosen to study the effect of migration on programs with short execution times.

| # Pes | # Migrations | Data/migration (bytes) | Exec. time (sec.) |
|-------|--------------|------------------------|-------------------|
| 2 | 0 | n/a | 0.29 |
| 2 | 925 | 215.7 | 1.86 |
| 2 | 760 | 10211.7 | 2.66 |
| 4 | 0 | n/a | 0.14 |
| 4 | 1422 | 215.7 | 1.16 |
| 4 | 1540 | 10211.7 | 1.54 |
| 16 | 0 | n/a | 0.17 |
| 16 | 1845 | 215.7 | 0.59 |
| 16 | 1315 | 10211.7 | 0.96 |
| 32 | 0 | n/a | 0.30 |
| 32 | 1125 | 215.7 | 0.58 |
| 32 | 1809 | 10211.7 | 0.66 |
| 64 | 0 | n/a | 0.50 |
| 64 | 1287 | 215.7 | 0.37 |
| 64 | 1737 | 10211.7 | 0.85 |

(a) Effect of migration on execution time.

| # Pes | Migrations/. (sec.pe) | Data/migration (bytes) | Exec. time (sec.) |
|-------|-----------------------|------------------------|-------------------|
| 64 | 104.25 | 215.7 | 0.53 |
| 64 | 94.47 | 611.7 | 0.51 |
| 64 | 42.25 | 4211.7 | 0.58 |
| 64 | 21.08 | 10211.7 | 0.60 |
| 64 | 16.11 | 20211.7 | 0.71 |
| 64 | 11.60 | 40211.7 | 1.18 |

(b) Increasing the amount of data per migration with approximately fixed execution time.

Table 2: The effect on execution time when objects were forced to migrate repeatedly for the *Testgen* program on the nCUBE/2. The data/migration column includes the messages that needed to be forwarded due to migration. Three ISCAS 89 circuits were randomly selected as input.

| PEs | Migrations/ (seconds.pe) | Data/ migration | Execution time (secs.) |
|-----|--------------------------|-----------------|------------------------|
| 4 | 0 | n/a | 15.83 |
| | 51.5 | 8080 bytes | 18.69 |
| | 504.3 | 8080 bytes | 19.01 |
| 16 | 0 | n/a | 6.38 |
| | 34.3 | 8078 bytes | 7.02 |
| | 330.6 | 8078 bytes | 7.25 |
| 32 | 0 | n/a | 5.03 |
| | 21.4 | 8075 bytes | 5.61 |
| | 207.0 | 8075 bytes | 5.79 |
| 64 | 0 | n/a | 4.70 |
| | 12.3 | 8070 bytes | 4.89 |
| | 120.3 | 8070 bytes | 4.98 |

2(a) ISCAS 89 Circuit s208 (216 tasks)

| PEs | Migrations/ (seconds.pe) | Data/ migration | Execution time (secs.) |
|-----|--------------------------|-----------------|------------------------|
| 4 | 0 | n/a | 79.94 |
| | 26.9 | 4080 bytes | 81.86 |
| | 246.3 | 4080 bytes | 82.01 |
| 16 | 0 | n/a | 30.15 |
| | 18.8 | 4078 bytes | 29.22 |
| | 172.4 | 4078 bytes | 29.30 |
| 32 | 0 | n/a | 20.63 |
| | 13.9 | 4075 bytes | 19.79 |
| | 127.5 | 4075 bytes | 19.80 |
| 64 | 0 | n/a | 16.63 |
| | 8.9 | 4070 bytes | 15.52 |
| | 81.4 | 4070 bytes | 15.51 |

2(b) ISCAS 89 Circuit s820 (851 tasks)

| PEs | Migrations/ (seconds/pe) | Data/ migration | Execution time (secs.) |
|-----|--------------------------|-----------------|------------------------|
| 4 | 0 | n/a | 182.30 |
| | 22.1 | 2080 bytes | 186.60 |
| | 202.2 | 2080 bytes | 187.32 |
| 16 | 0 | n/a | 65.30 |
| | 16.1 | 2078 bytes | 64.52 |
| | 146.8 | 2078 bytes | 64.52 |
| 32 | 0 | n/a | 44.44 |
| | 12.4 | 2075 bytes | 41.66 |
| | 111.0 | 2075 bytes | 42.67 |
| 64 | 0 | n/a | 31.46 |
| | 8.9 | 2070 bytes | 28.95 |
| | 80.4 | 2070 bytes | 29.45 |

2(c) ISCAS 89 Circuit s1494 (1507 tasks)

essary to uninstatiate a chare at a source processor, transfer it to a new destination processor, and then reinstantiate it. This increases slightly depending on the amount of data to be migrated, assuming no marshaling is necessary. Marshaling introduces an additional overhead that depends on the nature of the data (see below). The absolute time required to forward a message with no data was measured to be 210 $\mu s$. However, much of these costs can be amortized significantly by overlapping computation and communication.

Two experiments are reported with the *TSP* benchmark (see Table 1). In the first experiment, the number of processors was varied from 2 to 64. Two different data sizes per migration were tried. The effect of migration on execution time is reported in Table 1(a). Due to the speculative nature of the parallel search, wide variations in execution time were observed, making a controlled comparision with the "no migration" case difficult. However, the absolute

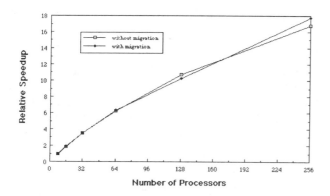

Figure 3: Relative speedups for **primes**, with and without migration. In the migration case, approximately 585 migrations/second were performed with 1024 bytes/migration. Speedups are relative to the execution time for 8 processors.

---

overhead of over 1000 migrations, even for a small program, is small, and clearly reduces (as one might expect) with increase in the number of processors.

In the second experiment with the *tsp* benchmark, the execution time was kept approximately fixed on 64 processors and the frequency of migration and the data per migration were varied (see Table 1). As expected, the data shows that a very high frequency of migration could be sustained when the data per migration is relatively small. However, it was noteworthy that even for a problem with a short running time, the time penalty incurred for over 10 migrations/second per processor with 10-40K bytes of data per migration was quite small, and within experimental error.

In Figure 1, the effect of random migration of tasks at varying frequencies on execution time is reported. The experiment was conducted on 32 processors of a nCUBE/2 hypercube. Initially, 7225 tasks arranged in a 85 x 85 grid were distributed uniformly across 32 processors, using a static distribution. Recall that load imbalance was deliberately introduced in the initial distribution. The data in Figure 1 suggests that even random migration can improve performance significantly under these circumstances. This clearly suggests that intelligent use of our task migration algorithm as part of a load balancing tool can yield significant improvements in program performance.

For the *primes* benchmark, the number of primes in the range 2-100,000,000 was sought. All tasks were eligible for migration. In addition, for each task, two cases were tried. In the first case, the task state was artificially inflated to 1K bytes of contiguous data (i.e., the data did not need marshaling before migration). In the second case, the task state was 1K bytes of data arranged as a linked list of integers, which needed to be marshaled before migration. The data in Figure 2 shows that while the marshaling overhead clearly degrades performance, upto 4000 migrations/second could be performed before a perceptible difference was evident between the two. Moreover, the overhead, even at this migration frequency, was quite small.

The second experiment with *primes* consists of comparing the execution of *primes* with no migration *vs* migration at a constant frequency of approximately 585 migrations/second with 1K bytes/migration, as the number of processors is varied. Figure 3 shows that the execution time of the two versions is statistically indistinguishable. The speedups plotted are relative to the execution time on 8 processors.

Results for the *Testgen* program on the nCUBE/2 hypercube are presented in Table 2. Three randomly selected ISCAS 89 benchmark circuits were used as input and the number of processors, as well as the frequency of migration was varied. The data per migration was artificially inflated to approximately 2K bytes, 4K bytes and 8K bytes for the three benchmarks. The data suggests that over 80 migrations/second with 8K bytes per migration could be sustained on each processor without a statistically significant degradation of performance.

In all cases, the destination processor for migration was selected arbitrarily. Locality effects were not exploited for any of the above experiments. The data presented for the range of applications strongly suggests that a large number of small lightweight parallel tasks coupled with a message-driven computation model is very effective in controlling the cost of task migration. The actual cost of moving a task from one processor to another is largely amortized by scheduling other tasks when data transmission is in progress. We note that computation and communication can be overlapped in other ways besides message-driven scheduling, e.g. multithreading or hidden synchronous communication and software latency hiding [40].

Besides the use of message-driven scheduling, ELMO's lightweight task model makes tasks highly amenable to closure computations. Their small granularity also makes them easier to schedule for latency hiding than large-grain processes. Moreover, ELMO tasks may be migrated to different instruction-set architectures in a heterogeneous processor environment more easily than threads or a UNIX-style processes.

Thus, in the presence of sufficient parallel activity, the cost of initiating a migration (including the cost of marshaling the data when necessary), and the cost of reinstantiating a task at the destination (including the cost of unmarshaling the data when necessary) are the only costs that affect the execution time. This is typically a small fraction of the total cost of migration, and more importantly, this can be frequently offset by other improvements due to migration, e.g. better load distribution.

## 6  Conclusions and Future Work

We have successfully implemented efficient task migration in a system that extends existing sequential languages with simple task/object parallelism. The ELMO system supports small-grained light-weight tasks and supports features typical of concurrent object-oriented systems proposed to date. Performance data on a series of controlled experiments on realistic benchmark programs have been reported. The results clearly demonstrate that it is possible to efficiently support task migration in such systems without significantly affecting the performance of the application. In our implementation, the key to realizing this efficiency was the use of lightweight tasks and message-driven scheduling. This permitted effective amortization of migration overheads by overlapping useful computation with communication.

The results also demonstrate that it is possible to migrate tasks at a high frequency (over 50 migrations/second per processor for moderately sized tasks in most cases) without suffering statistically significant performance losses. The data sizes for which these results are valid have been shown to be as high as 10K bytes per task for certain applications. The efficient latency hiding afforded by the message-driven scheduling was instrumental in achieving this performance. This, however, relies on the availability of sufficient parallel activity to permit the computation-communication overlap. Programs that do not exhibit sufficient parallelism will exhibit a higher overhead than other programs, and consequently will be expected to tolerate a lower frequency of migration.

The deviation found in measured performance with and without migration (see [16] for empirical evidence) was found to be significantly lower the deviations observed in the measurement of the execution times on the nCUBE/2.

We propose to further validate these results on different architectures including the IBM SP/2, the Intel Paragon, an SGI Power Array, and a network of workstations. New load balancing algorithms using task migration to improve performance on message passing machines, and especially networks of workstations are already under development. Other work includes the development of a scheme for supporting the fault tolerance on MIMD architectures by using our migration scheme to support checkpointing of tasks. This will also be used in the development of replay support for interactive debugging of concurrent object-oriented programs.

## Acknowledgements

We would like to thank Sandia National laboratories for access to the nCUBE/2. Our thanks are also due to Raymond Richards and Rohit Natarajan for their help in collecting the data presented in this paper.

## Bibliography

[1] Agha, G.A. *Actors: A Model of Concurrent Computation in Distributed Systems*. MIT press, 1986.

[2] Anderson T.E., Culler D.E., Patterson D.A. A Case for NOW (Network of Workstations). *IEEE Micro, Special Issue*, March 1995.

[3] Artsy Y., Finkel R. Designing a Process Migration Facility: The Charlotte Experience. *IEEE Computer*, 22 no. 9:47–56, September 1989.

[4] Grimshaw A.S. *Mentat: An Object-Oriented Macro Dataflow System*. PhD thesis, Dept. of Computer Science, University of Illinois, Urbana-Champaign, June 1988.

[5] Barak A., Guday S., Wheeler R.G. The MOSIX Distributed Operating System: Load Balancing for UNIX. *Lecture Notes in Computer Science, Springer Verlag*, no 672, 1993.

[6] Beguelin A., Seligman E., Starkey M. DOME: Distributed Object Migration Environment. Technical Report CMU-CS-94-153, Carnegie-Mellon University, May 1994.

[7] Bricker, A., Litzkow, M. and Livny, M. Condor Technical Summary. Technical Report TR-1069, Dept. of Computer Science, University of Wisconsin-Madison, 1992.

[8] Carriero, N., Gelernter, D. How to Write Parallel Programs: A Guide to the Perplexed. *ACM Computing Surveys*, 21 no. 2:323–357, September 1989.

[9] Carriero N., Gelernter D., Kaminsky D., Westbrook J. Adaptive Parallelism with Piranha. Technical report, Department of Computer Science, Yale University, 1992.

[10] Chandy K.M., Kesselman C. Compositional C++: Compositional Parallel Programming. In *Proceedings the 5th Workshop on Compilers and Languages for Parallel Computing*, pages 79–93, 1992.

[11] Chase J.S., Amador F.G., Lazowska E.D., Levy H.M., Littlefield R.J. The Amber System: Parallel Programming on a Network of Multiprocessors. In *Twelvth ACM Symposium on Operating System Principles*, December 1989.

[12] Cheriton, D.R. The V Distributed System. *Communications of the ACM*, 31:314–333, March 1988.

[13] Chien A.A., Karamcheti V., Plevyak J. The Concert System – Compiler and Runtime Support for Efficient Fine-Grained Concurrent Object-Oriented Programs. Technical Report UIUCDCS-R-93-1815, Department of Computer Science, University of Illinois, Urbana, IL,, June 1993.

[14] Culler D.E., Dusseau A., Goldstein S.C., Krishnamurthy A., Lumetta S., vonEicken T., Yelick K. Parallel programming in split-c. In *Proceedings of Supercomputing*, November 1993.

[15] Douglis, F., Ousterhout, J. Process migration in the Sprite Operating System. In *Proceedings of the Seventh Int'l Conf. on Distributed Computing Systems*, 1987.

[16] Doulas, N. Task Migration for Message-Driven Parallel Execution on Distributed Memory Architectures. Master's thesis, Dept. of Electrical and Computer Engineering, University of Iowa, Iowa City, August 1994.

[17] Doulas, N., Ramkumar B. Efficient Task Migration for Message-Driven Parallel Execution on Non-shared Memory Architectures. In *International Conference on Parallel Processing*, August 1994.

[18] Flower, J., Kolawa, A., Bharadwaj S. The Express Way to Distributed Processing. In *Supercomputing Review*, pages 54–55, May 1991.

[19] Fowler R. J. *Decentralized Object Finding Using Forwarding Addresses.* PhD thesis, Dept. of Computer Science, University of Washington, Seattle, December 1985. Tech. Report 95-12-1.

[20] Gehani N.H., Roome W.D. Concurrent C++: Concurrent Programming with Class(es). *Software: Practice and Experience*, pages 1157–1177, December 1988.

[21] Gehani N.H., Roome W.D. Implementing Concurrent C. *Software: Practice and Experience*, pages 266–285, March 1992.

[22] Geist A., Beguelin A., Dongarra J., Jiang W., Manchek R., Sundaram V. *PVM: Parallel Virtual Machine A Users' Guide and Tutorial for Networked Parallel Computing* . MIT Press, 1994. (Also see http://www.epm.ornl.gov/pvm).

[23] Gelernter D., Kaminsky D. Supercomputing out of Recycled Garbage: Preliminary Experience with Piranha. In *Sixth ACM International Conference on Supercomputing*, July 1992.

[24] Glazer D.W., Tropper C. On Process Migration and Load Balancing in Time Warp. *IEEE Transactions on Parallel and Distributed Systems*, 4 no. 3:318–327, March 1993.

[25] Grimshaw A.S., Weissman J.B., Strayer W.T. Portable Run-time Support for Dynamic Object-oriented Parallel Processing. Technical Report CS-93-40, University of Virginia, 1993.

[26] Jul E. *et al.* Fine-Grained Mobility in the Emerald System. *ACM Transactions on Computer Systems*, February 1988.

[27] Kale L.V., Krishnan S. Charm++: A Portable Concurrent Object-Oriented System Based on C++. In *Proceedings of OOPSLA*, March 1993.

[28] Lee J.K., Gannon D. Object-oriented Parallel Programming Experiments and Results. In *Proceedings of Supercomputing, 1991*, pages 273–282, November 1991.

[29] Lucco S.E. Parallel Programming in a Virtual Object Space. In *Proceedings of the ACM Conference on Object-oriented Programming Systems, Languages and Applications*, October 1987.

[30] Milojicic D.S., Giese P., Zint W. Experiences with Load Distribution on Top of the Mach Microkernel. In *Symposium on Experiences with Distributed and Multiprocessor Systems*, September 1993.

[31] Nuttall M. A Brief Survey of Systems Providing Process or Object Migration Facilities. *ACM Operating System Review*, 28:4, October 1994.

[32] Parkes S.,Chandy J.A., Banerjee P. A Library-Based Approach to Portable, Parallel, Object-oriented Programming: Interface, Implementation and Application. In *Proceedings of Supercomputing*, 1994.

[33] Powell, M.L., Miller, B.P. Process Migration in DEMOS/MP. *ACM Operating System Review*, 17:5, 1990.

[34] Ramkumar B. *Portable Structures:* A Distributed Data Type for Efficient Portable Parallel Programming. Technical report, University of Iowa, Department of Electrical and Computer Engineering, December 1994.

[35] Ramkumar B. INTREPID: An Environment for Debugging Concurrent Object-Oriented Programs. In *International Conference on High-Performance Computing*, December 1995.

[36] Ramkumar, B., Banerjee P. Portable Parallel Test Generation for Sequential Circuits. In *Proceedings of the International Conference on Computer-Aided Design*, pages 220–223, November 1992.

[37] Ramkumar B., Sinha A.B., Kale L.V., Saletore V.A. The CHARM Parallel Programming Language and System. *IEEE Transactions on Parallel and Distributed Systems*, 1994. (submitted, revised 1996.) Also, technical report, Department of Computer Science, University of Illinois.

[38] Richards, R.J., Ramkumar B. Blocking Entry Points in Message-Driven Parallel Systems. In *International Conference on Parallel Processing*, August 1995.

[39] Rinard M.C., Scales D.J., Lam M.S. Jade: A high-level, machine-independent language for parallel programming. *IEEE Computer*, 26 no. 6, June 1993.

[40] Strumpen V. *The Network Machine.* PhD thesis, Swiss Federal Institute of Technology (ETH), 1995. Diss. ETH No. 11227.

[41] Willebeek-LeMair M.H., Reeves A.P. Strategies for Dynamic Load Balancing on Highly Parallel Computers. *IEEE Transactions on Parallel and Distributed Systems*, 4 no. 9:979–993, September 1993.

# DYNAMIC TASK SCHEDULING AND ALLOCATION FOR 3D TORUS MULTICOMPUTER SYSTEMS *

Hee Yong Youn, Hyunseung Choo, Seong-Moo Yoo, and Behrooz Shirazi
Department of Computer Science and Engineering
The University of Texas at Arlington
Arlington, Texas 76019-0015
youn@cse.uta.edu

**Abstract** – *Multicomputer systems achieve high performance by utilizing a number of computing nodes. Multidimensional meshes have become popular as multicomputer architectures due to their simplicity and efficiency. In this paper we propose an efficient processor allocation scheme for 3D torus based on first-fit approach. The scheme minimizes the allocation time by effectively manipulating the 3D information as 2D information using CST(Coverage Status Table). Comprehensive computer simulation reveals that the allocation time of the proposed scheme is always smaller than the earlier scheme based on best-fit approach, while allowing comparable processor utilization. The difference gets more significant as the input load increases. To investigate the performance of the proposed scheme with different scheduling environment, non-FCFS scheduling policy along with the typical FCFS policy is also studied.*

## 1 Introduction

As real-life applications get more complicated and diverse, computer systems are required to be much more powerful than before. Parallel computing [1] is an efficient approach for achieving this goal, which was expedited due to the drastically reduced hardware cost. Each node in a parallel computer system consists of a processor, local memory, and other supporting devices, while communication between them occurs through message-passing or shared memory. The overall performance of a parallel system is determined mostly by how efficiently the jobs are distributed and processed in parallel.

There are many ways for interconnecting the nodes in multicomputers where messages are passed [2]. Until late 1980's, hypercube architecture had been most popular as represented by nCUBE [3] and Caltech Cosmic [4]. However, mainly the poor scalability disallowed hypercube to remain as a major architecture of parallel systems especially with massively parallel processing applications. Since early 1990's, two-dimensional (2D) mesh has become popular due to

its simplicity and efficiency as represented by Intel Paragon [5] and Intel/DARPA Touchstone Delta [6]. The node degree of 2D mesh is fixed unlike hypercube architecture. Due to the wormhole routing technique [7], the communication delay between two nodes in multicomputers is not proportional to the node distance. Recently, with the significant reduction in communication delay, fine grain multicomputer based on three-dimensional (3D) mesh such as Caltech Mosaic [2] and MIT J-Machine [2] has emerged as a new candidate for multicomputer systems.

Task in a parallel computer system is the scheduling unit which consists of one or more processes. Each task requests a certain number of processors for some duration to be executed in parallel. Tasks submitted to a multicomputer system are first placed in a waiting queue. The host processor then selects a task to be processed from the waiting queue according to the scheduling policy. It also finds the free processors for allocating them to the selected task. Therefore scheduling and processor allocation are strongly related, and they significantly affect the overall system performance.

Even though a number of scheduling and allocation schemes for 2D meshes have been proposed in the literature [8-12], not many schemes have been proposed for 3D torus. In the allocation scheme [13] for Cray T3D, the dimension of each allocated submesh must be a power of 2, which causes *internal fragmentation* if the requested size is not power of 2. Qiao and Ni [14] proposed an allocation scheme for 3D torus using free list which allows complete submesh recognition without internal fragmentation. It is based on best-fit approach, which usually requires much larger search time than first-fit approach.

In this paper we propose an efficient processor allocation scheme for 3D torus based on first-fit approach. The scheme minimizes the allocation time for an incoming task by effectively manipulating the 3D information on torus as 2D information using CST(Coverage Status Table). A similar approach was employed in the 2D mesh allocation scheme proposed by Yoo and Youn [9], where the 2D information was mapped into one-dimension array. Comprehensive computer simulation reveals that the allocation

*This work was supported in part by Texas State Government Grant AMP-94.

Table I. The range in each dimension of eight possible 3D submeshes in 3D torus.

| Case | Relative Position | $R_x$ | $R_y$ | $R_z$ |
|------|-------------------|-------|-------|-------|
| 1 | $x \leq x',\ y \leq y',\ z \leq z'$ | $[x, x']$ | $[y, y']$ | $[z, z']$ |
| 2 | $x \leq x',\ y \leq y',\ z > z'$ | $[x, x']$ | $[y, y']$ | $[z, H], [1, z']$ |
| 3 | $x \leq x',\ y > y',\ z \leq z'$ | $[x, x']$ | $[y, W], [1, y']$ | $[z, z']$ |
| 4 | $x \leq x',\ y > y',\ z > z'$ | $[x, x']$ | $[y, W], [1, y']$ | $[z, H], [1, z']$ |
| 5 | $x > x',\ y \leq y',\ z \leq z'$ | $[x, L], [1, x']$ | $[y, y']$ | $[z, z']$ |
| 6 | $x > x',\ y \leq y',\ z > z'$ | $[x, L], [1, x']$ | $[y, y']$ | $[z, H], [1, z']$ |
| 7 | $x > x',\ y > y',\ z \leq z'$ | $[x, L], [1, x']$ | $[y, W], [1, y']$ | $[z, z']$ |
| 8 | $x > x',\ y > y',\ z > z'$ | $[x, L], [1, x']$ | $[y, W], [1, y']$ | $[z, H], [1, z']$ |

Table II. The length, width, and height of eight possible 3D submeshes.

| Case | $l$ | $w$ | $h$ |
|------|-----|-----|-----|
| 1 | $x' - x + 1$ | $y' - y + 1$ | $z' - z + 1$ |
| 2 | $x' - x + 1$ | $y' - y + 1$ | $z' - z + 1 + H$ |
| 3 | $x' - x + 1$ | $y' - y + 1 + W$ | $z' - z + 1$ |
| 4 | $x' - x + 1$ | $y' - y + 1 + W$ | $z' - z + 1 + H$ |
| 5 | $x' - x + 1 + L$ | $y' - y + 1$ | $z' - z + 1$ |
| 6 | $x' - x + 1 + L$ | $y' - y + 1$ | $z' - z + 1 + H$ |
| 7 | $x' - x + 1 + L$ | $y' - y + 1 + W$ | $z' - z + 1$ |
| 8 | $x' - x + 1 + L$ | $y' - y + 1 + W$ | $z' - z + 1 + H$ |

time of the proposed scheme is always smaller than that of the earlier scheme based on best-fit approach [14]. The difference gets bigger as the input load increases, and it is as small as about $\frac{1}{3}$ for high load. To investigate the performance of the proposed scheme in different scheduling environment, we also consider non-FCFS scheduling policy along with the typical FCFS policy.

The rest of the paper is organized as follows. In Section 2, definitions and notation are introduced which will be used throughout the paper. The existing processor allocation scheme is also briefly reviewed. Section 3 proposes our processor allocation scheme for 3D Torus. In Section 4, the proposed scheme is evaluated by computer simulation, and compared with the existing scheme. Finally, we conclude the paper in Section 5.

## 2 Preliminaries

### 2.1 Definitions and Notation

Here, to be consistent with earlier schemes, we employ the same definitions and notation as [14] unless it is difficult. A three-dimensional(3D) torus, $3DT(L, W, H)$, is an $L \times W \times H$ cubic grid of $LWH$ number of nodes where $L$, $W$, and $H$ represent the length, width, and height of the torus, respectively. 3D torus is a variation of 3D mesh with wraparound connections. Torus is a symmetric topology, and the extra ring connections added to the mesh reduce the maximum shortest distance between any two nodes to one-half of that of 3D mesh. Each node in torus is represented by a coordinate $(x, y, z)$ ($1 \leq x \leq L$, $1 \leq y \leq W$, $1 \leq z \leq H$), and each edge corresponds to a direct communication link. Let us assume that the length, width, and height indices increase from

left to right, front to rear, and bottom to top beginning from 1.

**Definition 1:** The *identity* of a submesh $S(l, w, h)$ with length $l$, width $w$, height $h$ in $3DT(L, W, H)$ consists of two 3D coordinates $((x, y, z), (x', y', z'))$, where $(x, y, z)$ and $(x', y', z')$ are called as the *base* and *end* of $S$, respectively.

When no wraparound links are used for $S((x, y, z), (x', y', z'))$, i.e. $x \leq x'$, $y \leq y'$ and $z \leq z'$, the left-front-bottom node is the *base* and the right-rear-top node is the *end* of $S$ as shown in Figure 1(a). On the other hand, if wraparound links are used for $x$-dimension, $y$-dimension, and/or $z$-dimension, i.e. $x > x'$, $y > y'$, and/or $z > z'$, the relative positions of base and end of $S$ is one of the 7 possible cases shown in Figure 1(b)-(h). The position of a submesh is determined by the given identity of the submesh. The eight relative possible positions between *base* and *end* of a 3D submesh in a 3D torus are summarized in Table I. Here $[x, x']$ denotes the range of $x$-coordinates($R_x$) of the submesh. Table II lists the length, width, and height of the submesh of each case. Even though a submesh can be represented by its original identity, it is difficult to assume and manipulate a submesh consisting of several smaller partitioned cubes. For the extreme case of Figure 1(h), the logical cube consists of eight submeshes resided at the eight corners of 3D torus, which are connected by the wraparound links. Here the logically adjacent nodes do not have contiguous indices, and thus manipulating the array for allocation is cumbersome. Hence we employ the concept of *virtual space* to include the extended logical indices, which allow contiguous indices. In the later part of this section, we present how the virtual 3D coordinates are translated to physical coordinates by using a mapping function. Next we define the identity of a virtual submesh in the virtual space.

**Definition 2:** The identity of a virtual submesh

of a submesh $S((x, y, z), (x', y', z'))$, $S_v$, is a pair of 3D coordinates $((x, y, z), (x'_v, y'_v, z'_v))$, where $(x, y, z)$ $(1 \leq x \leq L, 1 \leq y \leq W, 1 \leq z \leq H)$ and $(x'_v, y'_v, z'_v)$ $(1 \leq x'_v \leq (2L - 1), 1 \leq y'_v \leq (2W - 1), 1 \leq z'_v \leq (2H - 1))$ are the *base* and *end* of the virtual submesh $S_v$, respectively. Here, $x'_v$ is $(x' + L)$ if $x > x'$, otherwise $x'$. Similarly, $y'_v$ is $(y' + W)$ if $y > y'$, otherwise $y'$. $z'_v$ is $(z' + H)$ if $z > z'$, otherwise $z'$.

**Definition 3:** The *size* of a submesh $S(l, w, h)$ is defined as the number of nodes in the submesh, i.e. $l \times w \times h$.

**Definition 4:** A *busy submesh*, $B$, is a submesh in which all the nodes are currently allocated to a task and thus busy. A virtual busy submesh is obtained by Definition 2. The busy list, *B-list*, is a list which contains all the identities of busy submeshes.

**Example 1:** In Figure 2, three busy submeshes exist in $3DT(4, 4, 4)$, i.e. $B_1(1, 3, 1) = ((1, 2, 1), (1, 4, 1))$, $B_2(2, 2, 1) = ((3, 3, 3), (4, 4, 3))$, and $B_3(1, 3, 2) = ((3, 2, 4), (3, 4, 1))$. Thus *B-list* contains $B_1$, $B_2$, and $B_3$. Note that $B_{1v} = B_1$ and $B_{2v} = B_2$, while $B_{3v}(1, 3, 2) = ((3, 2, 4), (3, 4, 5)) \neq B_3$. □

**Definition 5:** The *virtual coverage submesh* for an incoming task $T(l, w, h)$ with respect to a virtual busy submesh $B_{iv}$, $VC_{B_{iv}, T} = ((x_{vc}, y_{vc}, z_{vc}), (x'_{vc}, y'_{vc}, z'_{vc}))$, is a virtual submesh which covers a virtual busy submesh, where $x_{vc} = x - l + 1$, $y_{vc} = y - w + 1$, $z_{vc} = z - l + 1$, and $(x'_{vc}, y'_{vc}, z'_{vc}) = (x'_v, y'_v, z'_v)$.

Recall that $1 \leq x \leq L$ and $1 \leq l \leq L$. Therefore the minimum value of $x_{vc}$ is obtained when $x = 1$ and $l = L$, and it is $1 - L + 1 = 2 - L$. On the other hand, the maximum value is obtained when $x = L$ and $l = 1$, and it is $L - 1 + 1 = L$. Therefore $(2 - L) \leq x_{vc} \leq L$. Similarly $(2 - W) \leq y_{vc} \leq W$ and $(2 - H) \leq z_{vc} \leq H$. In the virtual space, thus, the ranges of a virtual submesh $S((a, b, c), (d, e, f))$ are $(2 - L) \leq a \leq L$, $(2 - W) \leq b \leq W$, $(2 - H) \leq c \leq H$, $1 \leq d \leq (2L - 1)$, $1 \leq e \leq (2W - 1)$, and $1 \leq f \leq (2H - 1)$, respectively. The virtual coverage list, *VC-list*, is a list which contains all identities of virtual coverage submeshes generated for the incoming task $T$.

**Example 2:** In Figure 3, with $T(2, 2, 2)$, the virtual coverage submeshes due to virtual busy submeshes $B_{1v}$, $B_{2v}$, and $B_{3v}$ are $VC_{B_{1v}, T} = ((0, 1, 0), (1, 4, 1))$, $VC_{B_{2v}, T} = ((2, 2, 2), (4, 4, 3))$, and $VC_{B_{3v}, T} = ((2, 1, 3), (3, 4, 5))$, respectively. □

Notice here that, in Figure 3, there actually exist 10 planes in $z$-dimension. The four planes ($z = -2, -1, 6, 7$) are omitted since no submesh exist in those planes.

**Definition 6: Coordinate Mapping.** A physical 3D coordinate of a node is obtained from a virtual 3D coordinate by coordinate mapping. Given a virtual 3D coordinate $(x_v, y_v, z_v)$, the corresponding physical 3D coordinate $(x, y, z)$ due to the mapping function $\Psi(x_v, y_v, z_v)$ is

$$x = \begin{cases} x_v & 1 \leq x_v \leq L \\ x_v + L & x_v < 1 \\ x_v - L & x_v > L, \end{cases}$$

$$y = \begin{cases} y_v & 1 \leq y_v \leq W \\ y_v + W & y_v < 1 \\ y_v - W & y_v > W, \end{cases}$$

and

$$z = \begin{cases} z_v & 1 \leq z_v \leq H \\ z_v + H & z_v < 1 \\ z_v - H & z_v > H. \end{cases}$$

**Definition 7:** A coverage submesh of a busy submesh $B = ((x, y, z), (x', y', z'))$ for $T(l, w, h)$, denoted as $C_{B,T} = ((x_c, y_c, z_c), (x'_c, y'_c, z'_c)) = (\Psi(x_{vc}, y_{vc}, z_{vc}), \Psi(x'_{vc}, y'_{vc}, z'_{vc}))$, is defined as a submesh consisting of nodes mapped from the nodes of the virtual coverage submesh $VC_{B,T}$. None of the nodes in the coverage submesh can serve as the base of a free submesh for accommodating $T$ because of the busy submesh.

**Example 3:** In Figure 2 and 3, with $T(2, 2, 2)$, coverage submeshes for $B_1$, $B_2$, and $B_3$ are obtained from virtual coverage submeshes using the mapping function $\Psi$. That is $C_{B_1, T} = (\Psi(0, 1, 0), \Psi(1, 4, 1)) = ((4, 1, 4), (1, 4, 1))$, $C_{B_2, T} = (\Psi(2, 2, 2), \Psi(4, 4, 3)) = ((2, 2, 2), (4, 4, 3))$, and $C_{B_3, T} = (\Psi(2, 1, 3), \Psi(3, 4, 5)) = ((2, 1, 3), (3, 4, 1))$. □

As a summary, we obtain a coverage submesh from a busy submesh as follows: busy submesh $\rightarrow$ virtual busy submesh $\rightarrow$ virtual coverage submesh $\rightarrow$ coverage submesh.

## 2.2 Previous Scheme

Qiao and Ni [14] proposed a 3D free list scheme with lookahead scheduling based on FCFS discipline. A *free submesh* is a 3D submesh in which none of the processors have been allocated to any task currently. A *maximal free submesh* is a free submesh which cannot be expanded in any dimension. A *free list* is a list of all the maximal free submeshes. Given a new incoming task $T$, this scheme first computes all the maximal free submeshes and then makes a free list accordingly. With the free list generated, several heuristics are implemented to choose a free submesh to be allocated to $T$. Submeshes in the free list may be overlapped. By allowing the overlapping, it is possible to completely recognize the existing free submeshes. The basic idea is to search the free list for finding the *best* free submesh which is able to accommodate $T$, where the best submesh is the one which fits closest to $T$ in terms of size. It searches the entire list from the head to the tail to identify the best candidate. It is not necessary to recalculate the free list when a task is allocated in this scheme. With each allocation, however, the free list is updated by adjusting the maximal free submeshes. Whenever a deallocation occurs, the entire free list is recalculated completely.

Assume that there are $n$ busy submeshes and $m$ maximal free submeshes in the free list. Then the time complexity of the allocation scheme is $O(nm)$ where $m = O(n^3)$ and $n = O(LWH)$. It is $O(n^4) = O(L^4 W^4 H^4)$ in the worst case even though it will be much better in the average case. The time complexity of deallocation is also $O(n^4)$.

## 3 Proposed Allocation Scheme

For the processor allocation of an incoming task in a multicomputer system, dispatcher first searches for a free submesh which is big enough to host the task. In the *first-fit* approach, the firstly found free submesh is allocated. *Best-fit* approach tries to select presumably the best one among all candidate free submeshes. Since earlier studies [15,16] revealed that best-fit approach does not necessarily outperform first-fit approach, we employ the first-fit strategy for quick allocation. To minimize the allocation time, in our design, we utilize a new data structure called *coverage status table*(CST), which is constructed when the coverage submeshes are determined. Using CST, the base of a free submesh for the incoming task can be easily found if it exists without individually checking the nodes in the 3D torus system.

### 3.1 Coverage Status Table(CST)

Let a *segment* be a consecutive nodes in an $x$-dimensional row of the 3D torus system. If a segment starts from the first node in a row and all the nodes in the segment belong to any coverage submesh, then it is called *covered segment from 1*. Similarly, if a segment ends at the last node and it belongs to any coverage submesh, it is called *coverage segment from $L$*. A segment which covers an entire row and all the nodes belong to some coverage submeshes is called *complete coverage segment*.

CST$(W,H)$ is a two-dimensional array whose entry holds the $x$-coordinate of the rightmost node of the 'covered segment from 1' and that of the leftmost node of the 'covered segment from $L$' of each $x$-dimensional row. CST stores the information on each row (there are $W \times H$ rows in 3D torus) after VC-list is constructed.

Refer to Figure 4 where three coverage submeshes exist. Assume that we illuminate the 3D torus from the right to left direction. Then, as shown in Figure 2 and 4, the projected image of each coverage submesh appears as a shaded area in the 2D plane. CST is a two dimensional array, $W \times H$, and the entries of CST$(W,H)$ corresponding to the shaded area are determined according to the residence range of $x$-coordinates of covered segments as mentioned above.

Recall that each coverage submesh is obtained from the corresponding virtual coverage submesh and the coordinate mapping function $\Psi$. Given a virtual coverage submesh $S((a,b,c),(d,e,f))$ where $(2-L) \le a \le L, (2-W) \le b \le W, (2-H) \le c \le H, 1 \le d \le (2L-1), 1 \le e \le (2W-1)$, and $1 \le f \le (2H-1)$, there exist 16 possible configurations of the projected image of $S$ in CST. According to the residence range in $y$-dimension of $S$ with respect to $W$ of CST, there exist four cases. They are Y-1) $e-b+1 \ge W$, Y-2) $1 \le b$ and $e \le W$, Y-3) $e-b+1 < W$ and $e > W$, and

Y-4) $e-b+1 < W$ and $b < 1$. There also exist four cases according to that in $z$-dimension such as Z-1) $f-c+1 \ge H$, Z-2) $1 \le c$ and $f \le H$, Z-3) $f-c+1 < H$ and $f > H$, and Z-4) $f-c+1 < H$ and $c < 1$. Therefore, total 16 combinations are possible as shown in Figure 5. A coverage submesh is computed from the virtual coverage submesh by the coordinate mapping function $\Psi$, and the shaded area for the coverage submesh represented by $x$ and $y$-coordinate of CST are determined from $y$ and $z$-coordinate of the coverage submesh, respectively.

**Example 4:** In Figure 2 and 3, $VC_{B_1,T} = ((0,1,0),(1,4,1))$ corresponds to Case Y-1 and Z-4. Thus $R_y = [1,4]$ and $R_z = [1,1]$ and $[4,4]$. These are obtained from $C_{B_1,T} = ((4,\underline{1},\underline{4}),(1,\underline{4},\underline{1}))$. $VC_{B_2,T} = ((2,2,2),(4,4,3))$ corresponds to Case Y-2 and Z-2. Hence $R_y$ and $R_z$ are $[2,4]$ and $[2,3]$, respectively. For $VC_{B_3,T} = ((2,1,3),(3,4,5))$, Case Y-1 and Z-3 apply. Thus $R_y = [1,4]$ and $R_z = [1,1]$ and $[3,4]$, which are obtained from $C_{B_3,T} = ((2,\underline{1},\underline{3}),(3,\underline{4},\underline{1}))$. □

Let us discuss about how to update the values of CST for a given *VC-list*. Initially, CST$[j,k]$.from1 $= 0$ and CST$[j,k]$.fromL $= L+1$ for all $j$ and $k$ $(1 \le j,k \le L)$. As mentioned earlier, the values of CST are determined by the residence ranges of $x$-coordinates of coverage submeshes. Let us assume that the shaded area of a virtual coverage submesh $S$ has been already determined. There exist four cases with respect to the residence ranges of $S$ in $x$-dimension such as X-1) $d-a+1 \ge L$, X-2) $1 \le a$ and $d \le L$, X-3) $d-a+1 < L$ and $d > L$, and X-4) $d-a+1 < L$ and $a < 1$. In Case X-1, CST$[j,k]$.from1 $= L$. This is because all the nodes in this range are mapped to the nodes between 1 to $L$ in a coverage submesh by the coordinate mapping function $\Psi$ and become the complete coverage segment.

In Case X-2, if $a \le$ CST$[j,k]$.from1 $+1 \le d$, then CST$[j,k]$.from1 $= d$. This is because if the current value of CST$[j,k]$.from1 is not the rightmost covered node starting from 1 and also the nodes between $a$ and $d$ belong to the same coverage submesh, $d$ becomes the rightmost covered node starting from 1. In Case X-3, if $(d-L) >$ CST$[j,k]$.from1, CST$[j,k]$.from1 $= (d-L)$, and also if $a <$ CST$[j,k]$.fromL, then CST$[j,k]$.fromL $= a$. This is the case that the wraparound connections are used and thus the virtual coverage submesh intersects with CST and the length of the virtual coverage submesh is less than $L$. There exist two residence ranges along the $x$-dimension of the coverage submesh as $[1, d-L]$ and $[a,L]$ which are obtained by the coordinate mapping function $\Psi$. If $d-L \le a$, CST$[j,k]$.from1 $= d-L$ and CST$[j,k]$.fromL $= a$.

In Case X-4, if $d >$ CST$[j,k]$.from1, then CST$[j,k]$.from1 $= d$ and also if $(a+L) <$ CST$[j,k]$.fromL then CST$[j,k]$.fromL $= (a+L)$. This is also the wraparound case but the length of the virtual coverage submesh is smaller than $L$. Two residence ranges along the $x$-dimension of the coverage submesh are $[1, d]$ and $[a+L, L]$ due to the coordinate mapping. Again if $d \le a+L$, CST$[j,k]$.from1 $= d$ and CST$[j,k]$.fromL $= a+L$.

**Example 5:** Assume that CST has already been initialized. In Figure 2 and 3 of $3DT(4,4,4)$, $VC_{B_1,T}$ corresponds to Case X-4. $d(=1) >$ CST$[j,k]$.from1$(=0)$, and therefore CST$[j,k]$.from1 $= 1$. Since $a + L(=4) <$ CST$[j,k]$.fromL$(=5)$, CST$[j,k]$.fromL $= 4$ for all $(j,k)(1 \leq j \leq 4$ and $k = 1,4)$. $VC_{B_2,T}$ corresponds to Case X-2. $a(=2)$ and $d(=4)$ are both greater than CST$[j,k]$.from1 $+ 1(=1)$ for all $(j,k)(2 \leq j \leq 4, 2 \leq k \leq 3)$. Therefore, CST is not changed. $VC_{B_3,T}$ also corresponds to Case X-2. $a(=2) \leq$ CST$[j,k]$.from1 $+ 1 \leq d(=3)$ for all $(j,k)(2 \leq j \leq 4, k = 1,3,4)$. Here CST$[j,k]$.from1 is 1 for all $(j,k)$ $(1 \leq j \leq 4, k = 1,4)$ and 0 for all $(j,k)(1 \leq j \leq 4, k = 3)$. Thus CST$[j,k]$.from1 $= 3$ for all $(j,k)(1 \leq j \leq 4, k = 1,4)$. $\square$

For each incoming task $T(l,w,h)$ and $n$ busy submeshes $B_i(1 \leq i \leq n)$, the pseudo-code for building CST is presented below. Initially, $VC\text{-}list$ is set to $nil$, and CST$[j,k]$.from1 $= 0$ and CST$[j,k]$.fromL $= L+1$ for all $j,k(1 \leq j \leq W, 1 \leq k \leq H)$.

**Input:** Busy submeshes $B_i$ $(1 \leq i \leq n)$, and a new incoming task $T$;
**Output:** Coverage Status Table CST$[j,k]$ for $1 \leq j \leq W$ and $1 \leq k \leq H$;
**Procedure BUILD-CST**

**For** each $B_i = ((x,y,z),(x',y',z'))$ **do**
    Compute $VC_{B_i,T} = ((x_{vc}, y_{vc}, z_{vc}),(x'_{vc}, y'_{vc}, z'_{vc}))$.
    Insert $VC_{B_i,T}$ into the $VC\text{-}list$
       by the increasing order of $x_{vc}$.
    /* If $x'_{vc} > L$, $x_{vc}$ is assumed to 1 when
       $VC_{B_i,T}$ is inserted since the submesh
       has the wraparound connection. */
**For** $i = 1$ to $n$ **do**
/* beginning from the head of the $VC\text{-}list$ */
    Calculate $C_{B_i,T}$ from $VC_{B_i,T}$
       by the coordinate mapping function $\Psi$.
    Obtain $R_y$ and $R_z$ of $C_{B_i,T}$.
    /* The residence ranges in $y$ and $z$-dimension
       will be used as $x$-ranges and $y$-ranges
       of CST, respectively. */
    Obtain $R_x$ of $C_{B_i,T}$ and update the CST$(W,H)$
       accordingly.

Here initialization of CST takes $O(WH)$, computing and inserting $VC_{B_i,T}$ to VC-list take $O(n \log n)$, and updating CST takes $O(nWH)$. As $WH$ dominates $\log n$ for reasonable size tasks in 3D torus, $O(nWH)$ is the time complexity of the procedure BUILD-CST.

## 3.2 Processor Allocation and Deallocation

In this subsection, submesh allocation scheme is presented based on the procedure BUILD-CST. We find the free submesh for any incoming task in the 3D torus by using the information provided by CST. Once CST is given as the result of BUILT-CST, we check each element of CST containing two fields, $from1$ and $fromL$, until we find an element which satisfies $from1 + 1 < fromL$. This has the effect of checking each row only once. For $T(l,w,h)$, the first free

submesh large enough to hold $T$ is allocated to $T$ in 3D torus as described in the following procedure. Initially, the $base\_found$ flag is set to FALSE.

The orientation of incoming task $T$ may affect the allocatability as well as allocation time. Since 3D torus is symmetric, we allow the rotation of the task from $T(l,w,h)$ to any of $T'(l,h,w)$, $T''(w,l,h)$, $T'(w,h,l)$, $T'(h,l,w)$, or $T'(h,w,l)$, if $T$ cannot be allocated by the original orientation.

**Procedure PROCESSOR-ALLOCATION**

**Step 1.** If (the number of free processors $< L \cdot W \cdot H$)
    go to **Step 6**.
**Step 2.** Determine the orientation of $T$.
    There are up to 6 different orientations.
**Step 3.** Based on current B-list and $T$,
    run the procedure BUILD-CST.
**Step 4.** For $k = 1$ to $H$ **do**
    For $j = 1$ to $W$ **do**
       if (CST[j,k].from1$+1 <$ CST[j,k].fromL)
          $x =$ CST$[j,k]$.from1$+1$;
          $y = j; z = k$;
          $base\_found=$ TRUE; go to **Step 5**.
**Step 5.** If ($base\_found =$ TRUE)
    Allocate the free submesh whose base is
    $(x,y,z)$ to $T$ of the current orientation.
    Add $T$ to $B\text{-}list$. **Stop**.
    Otherwise, if all possible orientations have
       been checked, go to **Step 6**.
       else go to **Step 2**.
**Step 6.** Wait until a deallocation occurs.

The task dispatcher checks the number of available processors in Step 1. In Step 2, the procedure first starts with the original orientation of $T$. Later its orientation is changed if the current orientation does not allow the allocation. If $l$, $w$, and $h$ are all different, there are 6 different orientations. If two of them are same, there are 3 different orientations. If $l = w = h$, only one orientation exists. At Step 3, CST is built by calling the procedure BUILD-CST. At Step 4, CST is scanned from CST$[1,1]$ to CST$[W,H]$. While scanning CST, if the condition becomes true, then a base of $T$ is determined and $base\_found$ is set to TRUE. Also $T$ is put into the $B\text{-}list$ in Step 5. If the allocation fails, another orientation is checked until all of them are checked. If the allocation is not possible, it is held until a deallocation occurs. Clearly Step 1 and 2 take only $\Theta(1)$, respectively. Step 4 takes $\Theta(WH)$ because of the two for-loops. The main body of the for-loops is executed at most $WH$ times. Step 5 takes $\Theta(n)$ when $base\_found =$ TRUE, otherwise $\Theta(1)$. Step 3 for running the procedure BUILD-CST and constructing CST take $O(nWH)$, and thus dominates the procedure PROCESSOR-ALLOCATION. The procedure for deallocating a submesh $S$ is very simple as deleting $S$ from $B\text{-}list$.

## 4 Performance Evaluation

The time complexities of allocation and deallocation of the proposed scheme and [14] are compared in Table III.

Table III. Time and space complexity comparison.

|              | Our scheme    | [14]              |
|--------------|---------------|-------------------|
| Allocation   | $O(LW^2H^2)$  | $O(L^4W^4H^4)$    |
| Deallocation | $O(LWH)$      | $O(L^4W^4H^4)$    |
| Memory       | $O(LWH)$      | $O(L^3W^3H^3)$    |

The proposed scheme for 3D torus is next evaluated by computer simulation and compared with [14]. The simulation is event-driven with the events being the allocation and deallocation of tasks. Simulations are conducted for the 3D Tori ranging from $16 \times 16 \times 16$ to $64 \times 64 \times 64$. Since the simulation results for different sizes follow a similar trend, we here report the simulation results for only the $16 \times 16 \times 16$ torus. All the simulations use 90% confidence level with an error range of $\pm 5\%$. The simulator was developed in C language running on a Sun 4/490. The simulation results are collected from five independent runs. When the input load is relatively high, the system can be saturated and the job waiting queue grows boundlessly. This results in an infinite mean response time. We thus consider only the system loads which guarantee a stable system.

The simulation model is as follows. Initially the entire mesh is free, and 5,000 tasks are generated and processed. Task service time and inter-arrival time are assumed to have exponential distribution. The time unit is assumed to be large enough such that the time needed for the submesh allocation is negligible as other did [14]. The length $l$, width $w$, and height $h$ of incoming tasks are assumed to follow one of the three distributions – uniform, decreasing, and increasing – to study the performance of the scheme for various distributions of the size of the tasks. For the uniform distribution, the lengths of incoming tasks are uniformly distributed between 1 and the side length of the torus $L$. For the decreasing distribution, the range $[1, L]$ is divided into four intervals, $[1, L/8]$, $[L/8 + 1, L/4]$, $[L/4 + 1, L/2]$, and $[L/2 + 1, L]$. Also the probabilities that a side length falls into the range $[1, L/8]$ is 0.4, $[L/8 + 1, L/4]$ is 0.2, $[L/4 + 1, L/2]$ is 0.2, and finally $[L/2 + 1, L]$ is 0.2. The distribution of $l$, $w$, and $h$ within each interval is still uniform. For example, the probability that a side length falls into the range $[s_1, s_2]$ of $3DT(16, 16, 16)$, denoted as $P_{[s_1, s_2]}$, is as follows; $P_{[1,2]} = 0.4$, $P_{[3,4]} = 0.2$, $P_{[5,8]} = 0.2$, and $P_{[9,16]} = 0.2$. Essentially, the decreasing distribution on $l$, $w$, and $h$ represents a system where the tasks requesting small size submeshes are prevalent. For the increasing distribution, the distributions are opposite to the decreasing distribution. For $3DT(16, 16, 16)$, again, $P_{[1,8]} = 0.2$, $P_{[9,12]} = 0.2$, $P_{[13,14]} = 0.2$, and $P_{[15,16]} = 0.4$. For this distribution, the system will have greater chances of receiving the tasks requesting relatively large submeshes. The lengths, widths, and heights of tasks are generated independently based on one of the three distributions. The simulation results of the three distributions are quite similar, and thus we report the simulation results for only the uniform distribution.

In order to study the performance of the schemes under different load, we define the *load* as $\frac{n \times MSVT}{N \times MIAT}$. Here $n$ is the average size of the requested submesh in terms of the number of processors, and $N$ is the total number of processors in the 3D torus system. Also MSVT is the mean task service time and MIAT is the mean task inter-arrival time, respectively. In the simulation, we fix MSVT to be 10 time units and adjust MIAT according to the desired load. Clearly, the system will become unstable with too small MIAT values. The performance measures collected are *processor utilization* which is the percentage of a processor being utilized per unit time over the completion time (the time taken to finish all the 5,000 tasks), and the *average task allocation time* which is the time a task at the head of the waiting queue takes to be allocated.

The task dispatcher is assumed to follow the First-Come-First-Serve (FCFS) discipline, i.e., the dispatcher always tries to find a free submesh for the first task in the queue. If it fails to find a free submesh, the dispatcher simply waits for a submesh to be deallocated.

Figure 6 plots the average allocation time of our scheme and [14] for uniformly distributed side lengths. Observe that our scheme takes consistently smaller allocation time than the other scheme regardless of the input load. The difference gets much more significant as the input load increases. Our scheme thus can be said to be more effective for high load condition. Figure 7 compares the utilization of the two schemes under different workload from 0.1 to 0.9. Under the input load of up to 0.5, our scheme shows a little better performance, while slightly worse under the load above 0.5. However, the difference is very small, and it confirms that the best-fit approach does not significantly increase the utilization.

We also investigate the performance of the proposed scheme with the different scheduling policy called ScanAll. Here if the first task in the queue is not allocatable, the queue is scanned if there exists any allocatable task behind it unlike the FCFS policy. Then allocate it before the first one. To avoid the starvation, however, if the task at the head has spent a preset time period, then the scanning is halted until it is allocated. Figure 8 and 9 plot the utilization and average allocation time of the proposed scheme under two different scheduling policies, FCFS and ScanAll. Observe that the utilization under ScanAll is slightly better than that under FCFS as expected. However, the average allocation time is worse.

## 5   Conclusion

In this paper we have proposed a fast first-fit processor allocation scheme for 3D torus multicomputer systems, which has complete recognition capability. Comprehensive computer simulation reveals that the average allocation time of the proposed scheme is much smaller than that of the earlier scheme based on best-fit approach [14] for practical ranges of input load. This was achieved by the efficient search mechanism for finding a free submesh using the two-dimensional coverage status table.

Most of the existing allocation schemes for higher dimensional mesh or torus parallel computers employ the FCFS scheduling policy due to its simplicity and fairness property even though it may unnecessarily block the subsequent tasks. We have also studied the effect of a different scheduling policy which may avoid the potential performance loss due to blocking. More studies are underway to identify the relationship between different scheduling policies and the task allocation scheme in terms of average waiting time, utilization, and throughput for various input load and operational conditions.

**Acknowledgement:** The authors thank to Drs. Wenjian Qiao and Lionel Ni for providing us with their simulator for 3D torus.

# References

[1] M. J. Quinn, Parallel Computing Theory and Practice, McGraw-Hill, New York, 1994.

[2] K. Hwang, Advanced Computer Architecture: Parallelism, Scalability, Programmability, McGraw-Hill, New York, 1993.

[3] NCUBE Corp., NCUBE/ten: An Overview, Beaverton, OR, Nov. 1985.

[4] C. L. Seitz, "The cosmic cube," Commun. ACM, vol. 28, no. 1, pp. 22-23, January 1985.

[5] "Paragon XP/S Product Overview," Intel Corporation, 1991.

[6] "A Touchstone DELTA System Description," Intel Corporation, 1991.

[7] L. M. Ni and P. K. McKinley, "A survey of wormhole routing techniques in direct networks," IEEE Computer, pp. 62-76, February 1993.

[8] D.D. Sharma and D.K. Pradhan, "A fast and efficient strategy for submesh allocation in mesh-connected parallel computers," Symp. on Parallel and Distributed Processing, pp. 682-689, Dec. 1993.

[9] S.M. Yoo and H.Y. Youn, "An efficient task allocation scheme for two-dimensional mesh connected systems," Int'l Conf. on Dist. Comp. Systems, pp. 501-508, May 1995.

[10] J. Ding and L.N. Bhuyan, "An adaptive submesh allocation strategy for two-dimensional mesh connected systems," Int'l Conf. on Parallel Processing, pp. II-193-200, Aug. 1993.

[11] P.J. Chuang and N.F. Tzeng, "An efficient submesh allocation strategy for mesh computer systems," Proc. Int'l Conf. on Dist. Comp. Systems, pp. 256-263, Aug. 1991.

[12] T. Lin, W-K. Huang, F. Lombardi, and L.N. Bhuyan, "A submesh allocation scheme for mesh-connected multiprocessor systems," Int'l Conf. on Parallel Processing, pp. II-159-163, Aug. 1995.

[13] R. E. Kessler and J. L. Schwarzmeier, "CRAY T3D: A new dimension for Cray research," in Proc. COMPCON, pp. 176-182, Feb. 1993.

[14] W. Qiao and L. M. Ni, "Efficient processor allocation for 3D tori," IEEE Int'l Parallel Processing Symp., pp. 466-471, April 1995.

[15] Y. Zhu, "Efficient processor allocation strategies for mesh-connected parallel computers," Journal of Parallel and Distributed Computing, vol. 16, pp. 328-337, Dec. 1992.

[16] D. Babbar and P. Krueger, "A performance comparison of processor allocation and job scheduling algorithms for mesh-connected multiprocessors," Symp. on Parallel and Distributed Processing, pp. 46-53, Oct. 1994.

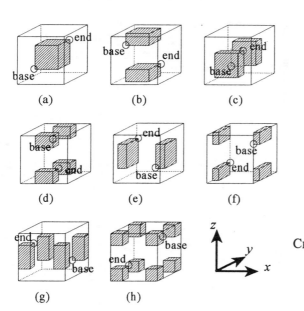

Figure 1. The eight possible 3D submeshes in 3D torus.

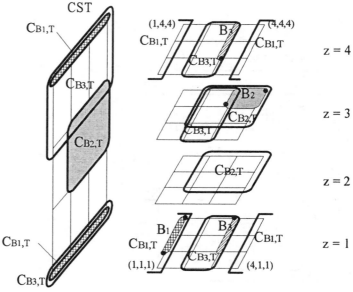

Figure 2. Examples of busy, coverage submeshes, and projected images on CST.

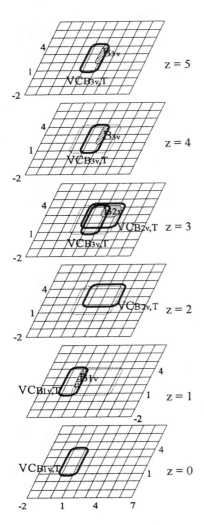

Figure 3. Examples of virtual busy and coverage submeshes.

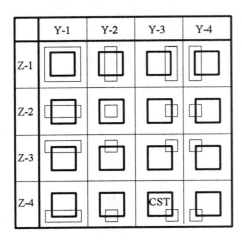

Figure 5. 16 configurations of CST and the projected image of a virtual coverage submesh.

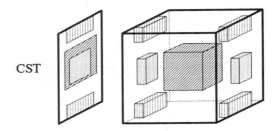

CST

Figure 4. Projected images of three coverage submeshes on CST.

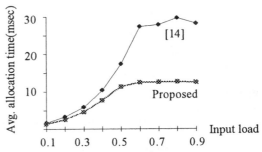

Figure 6. Average allocation time comparison.

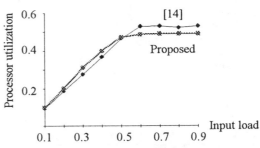

Figure 7. Processor utilization comparison.

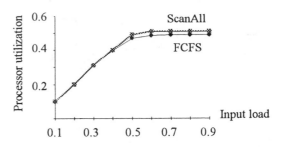

Figure 8. Processor utilizations with different scheduling.

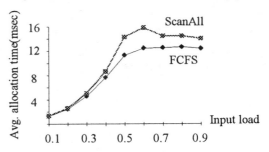

Figure 9. Avg. allocation times with different scheduling.

# A NOVEL ALGORITHM FOR BUDDY-SUBCUBE COMPACTION IN HYPERCUBES

Hsing-Lung Chen

Department of Electronic Engineering
National Taiwan Institute of Technology
Taipei, Taiwan, R. O. C.

Shu-Hua Hu

Department of Electronic Engineering
Jin-Wen College of Business and Technology
Hsin-Tien, Taipei, Taiwan, R.O.C.

*Abstract -- Earlier buddy-subcube compaction dealt with compacting free buddy-subcubes with the same dimension concurrently. All migration paths are pairwise disjoint and contain no links of active subcubes, so that task migration can be performed without suspending the execution of other jobs. This paper considers quick buddy-subcube compaction in that not only do free subcubes with two adjacent dimensions be compacted concurrently, but two disjoint paths are established between every pair of source-target nodes. This approach could lead to a considerable saving in compaction time for hypercubes which support circuit switching or wormhole routing.*

## 1. Introduction

When a job enters the hypercube system, it is assigned to one subcube of an appropriate size (if it exists), referred to as subcube allocation. The occupied subcube is released on termination of the job, called subcube deallocation. After repeated subcube allocation and deallocation, the hypercube system tends to become fragmented, in which no available subcube is large enough to accommodate an incoming job even if there are a sufficient number of free nodes in the system. The process of subcube compaction relocates active tasks by migrating them to respective target subcubes so as to create a large enough free subcube for the incoming job.

A partial compaction scheme described in [1] is designed to work with the buddy allocation strategy, and it requires $O(2^d)$ migration steps to compact and free a $d$-subcube, one job (which is assigned to a node) migration at each step. Kim *et al.* [2] presented a partial compaction scheme working with the buddy allocation strategy, which takes at most $d$ migration steps to free up a $d$-subcube. In each migration step, their scheme finds an appropriate set of source-target pairs and establishes totally disjoint paths between nodes in source subcubes and their corresponding nodes in the corresponding target subcubes such that the selected jobs can always be migrated in parallel.

During task migration, all necessary information has to be transferred to the target subcube. The amount of information transferred from each participating node is dependent on the size of the program and the size of its associated data set. It is often quite large, possibly involving hundreds of $K$-bytes or more. Transmitting such a large amount of information over an established path could take a long time. A hypercube system of the second generation supports either circuit-switching (such as Intel's *i*PSC/2 [3] and *i*PSC860) or wormhole routing (such as NCUBE's *n*-Cube/2 [4]) for efficient message transmission. The experiments described in [5, 6] have shown that the communication time under circuit switching or wormhole routing is distance-insensitive, if no conflicts occur. Hence, it is desirable to transmit messages through two disjoint paths between every pair of corresponding nodes concurrently, reducing the size of a message transmitted over a path. Ignoring the overhead caused by splitting a large message into smaller ones and assemblying them at the receiving node, the transmission time can be cut down by one half.

Chen [7] proposed a fast subcube compaction scheme realized by establishing two disjoint paths between every pair of corresponding nodes in a hypercube system with the buddy allocation strategy under circuit switching or wormhole routing. None of the disjoint paths contains any link of active subcubes, called *block links*. As a result, migration takes place in an online manner where all active jobs proceed without suspension, as links of their occupied subcubes are not used by any migration paths. To implement this fast subcube compaction, every node is assumed to have a dedicated router permitting *all-port* communication [8], so that multiple messages can be transmitted simultaneously from a node over different paths. With such a router, computation and communication at the node can be overlapped.

Tseng [9] presented another fast subcube compaction scheme realized by compacting free subcubes with two adjacent dimensions concurrently. Since it can process free subcubes with at most two dimensions in each step, it takes at most $\lceil d/2 \rceil$ migration steps to free up a $d$-subcube, thus reducing the compaction time. Note that it dealt with the establishment of a single path from each participating node for transmitting migrated information.

In this paper, we investigate quick subcube compaction in that not only do free subcubes with two adjacent dimensions be compacted concurrently, but two disjoint paths are established between every pair of source-target nodes. This approach not only reduces the size of a message over a path but cuts down the number of migration steps, thus leading to a considerable saving in compaction time for hypercubes which support circuit switching or wormhole routing.

## 2. Preliminaries

Let $H_n$ denote an $n$-dimensional hypercube, which consists of $2^n$ nodes, each labeled by an $n$-bit string, $b_{n-1}b_{n-2} \cdots b_1b_0$, where bit $b_i$ corresponds to dimension $i$. A link joins two nodes whose labels differ in exactly one bit position. All links are bidirectional and full duplex, i.e., two messages can be transmitted simultaneously in the opposite directions of any link. A link is assumed to have *dimension number $i$* if it connects two nodes whose addresses differ only in the $i^{th}$ bit position (where the least significant bit is bit 0). Every path between an arbitrary pair of nodes can be specified uniquely by an ordered sequence of links, and the length of a path is the number of its constituent links. The *relative address* of two nodes $\alpha$ and $\beta$ is the *bit-wise Exclusive-OR* of their addresses, $\alpha \oplus \beta$. A $k$-dimensional subcube in $H_n$ is represented by a string of $n$ symbols over the set $\{0, 1, *\}$, where $*$ is a *don't care* symbol, such that there are exactly $k$ $*$'s in the string. A 2-dimensional subcube involving nodes 0001, 0011, 0101, and 0111 in $H_4$, for example, is addressed by $0**1$.

The *buddy* system can only recognize the $d$-subcubes, $0 \leq d \leq n$, of the form $x_{n-1}x_{n-2} \cdots x_d * \cdots *$, where $x_i$, $i \geq d$, is 0 or 1; such subcubes are referred to as *buddy subcubes*. For a buddy $d$-subcube $T_i^d = x_{n-1}\underline{x_{n-2}} \cdots x_d * \cdots *$, the subcube $\overline{T_i^d} = x_{n-1}x_{n-2} \cdots x_{d+1}\overline{x_d} * \cdots *$, which differs from $T_i^d$ in exactly bit $d$, is called the *complement* of $T_i^d$. The subcube $T_i^{d+1} = x_{n-1}x_{n-2} \cdots x_{d+2}x_{d+1} * \cdots *$, which contains $T_i^d$, is called the *container* of $T_i^d$. The subcube $T_i^{d+2} = x_{n-1}x_{n-2} \cdots x_{d+3}x_{d+2} * \cdots *$, is also called the *container* of $T_i^d$.

Since every node in a buddy source $k$-subcube follows the same sequence in traversing links to reach the corresponding node in the target $k$-subcube, the *migration path* for this source-target pair is defined as consisting of those $2^k$ paths, one for each source node, and it is represented by this sequence of links traversed. Let $S \xrightarrow{\alpha} T$ denote that the migration path from $S$ to $T$ passes through a sequence of links, $\alpha$. For the sake of easy explanation, we view every buddy $k$-subcube as a supernode and $2^k$ links between a pair of adjacent $k$-subcubes as a superlink.

Ho and Johnsson [10] proposed an algorithm represented by spanning binomial trees (SBT) for distributing and broadcasting. The spanning binomial tree rooted at node 0 of an $n$-cube contains the edges that connect a node $i$ with the subset of its neighbors having addresses obtained by complementing any bit of leading zeroes of the binary encoding of $i$. In this paper, we modified it a little bit: replacing "leading zeroes" by "trailing zeroes" in the definition of SBT. Similarly, the modified spanning binomial tree rooted at node $2^n-1$ of an $n$-cube contains the edges that connect a node $i$ with the subset of its neighbors having addresses obtained by complementing any bit of trailing ones of the binary encoding of $i$. Without confusion, we refer this modified SBT as SBT in this paper. Two SBT's rooted at nodes 0 and $2^n-1$ of an $n$-cube are referred as the upper SBT and the lower SBT, respectively. Let $H_6$ be viewed as a 4-dimensional hypercube with each node being a supernode, which represents a 2-subcube with dimensions 0 and 1. Each superlink in this $H_6$ denotes $2^2$ links between a pair of adjacent 2-subcubes. Fig. 1 shows two SBT's in $H_6$ rooted at nodes $0000**$ and $1111**$, referred as the upper SBT and the lower SBT, respectively. Note that we ignore $*$ bits when we consider "trailing zeroes" or "trailing ones". The SBT in $H_6$ can be partitioned into two smaller SBT's, each of which resides in one $H_5$, by removing a superlink 5. This partition can be applied recursively.

It is obvious that links traversed up the SBT from an arbitrary node are in ascending order. For example, the path from node $1011**$ to the root $0000**$ in the upper SBT is $(2, 3, 5)$, whose links are in ascending order. In the following, we use $x_i$ to represent the bit $i$ of node $x$. For an arbitrary source-target pair $(s, d)$, the path in the upper SBT can be identified by the following procedure.

**Procedure** USBT_Path$(s, d)$
{   PATH := empty string;
   Let $i$ be the bit number of the first 1 in $s \oplus d$
     starting with the most significant bit rightwards;
   Appending every $j$, $s_j = 1$ and $j \leq i$, on PATH
     in ascending order;    /* travel up the SBT */
   Appending every $j$, $d_j = 1$ and $j \leq i$, on PATH
     in descending order;    /* travel down the SBT */
   Return PATH;
}

In Fig. 1, for example, the path from node $1011**$ to node $1110**$ first travels up the upper SBT through links 2 and 3 to reach node $1000**$, and then travels down the upper SBT through links 4 and 3 to reach the target. Similarly, the path from $s$ to $d$ in the lower SBT can be identified by the following procedure.

**Procedure** LSBT_Path$(s, d)$
{   PATH := empty string;
   Let $i$ be the bit number of the first 1 in $s \oplus d$
     starting with the most significant bit rightwards;
   Appending every $j$, $s_j = 0$ and $j \leq i$, on PATH
     in ascending order;    /* travel up the SBT */
   Appending every $j$, $d_j = 0$ and $j \leq i$, on PATH

in descending order;    /* travel down the SBT */
Return PATH;
}

The upper SBT and lower SBT posses the following two properties which establish the foundation of this paper.

**Property 1:** Assume that neither source subcubes nor target subcubes are contained in any active buddy subcubes. The migration path in the SBT between each pair of source-target pairs contains no block links.

**Property 2:** The upper SBT and the lower SBT of an $n$-cube have no common links except the links with the lowest number.

## 3. Speedy Subcube Compaction

Suppose that the hypercube has at least $2^d$ free processors, an algorithm that takes at most $\lceil d/2 \rceil$ migration steps to compact up a free $d$-subcube has been introduced in [9]. In each migration step, given even number, say $2m$, of free $b$-subcubes and $l$ free $(b+1)$-subcubes ($l+m$ must be even), they are compacted in parallel into $(l+m)/2$ $(b+2)$-subcubes. By compacting free 0-subcubes and 1-subcubes, some free 2-subcubes are generated, which are merged with other given free subcubes into bigger free subcubes if possible. Then compacting free 2-subcubes and 3-subcubes is taken to obtain free 4-subcubes, which are also merged with other given free subcubes into bigger subcubes if possible. By repeating above migration steps in increasing dimension order, a free $d$-subcube is finally obtained.

Now, we consider one migration step that given free $b$-subcubes and free $(b+1)$-subcubes are concurrently compacted into $(b+2)$-subcubes. Note that all the $(b+2)$-subcubes are the basic nodes in the SBT. We consider only these $(b+2)$-subcubes which contain free $b$-subcubes and $(b+1)$-subcubes to be compacted. There are four cases for the considered $(b+2)$-subcubes: 1 active $b$-subcube, 2 active $b$-subcubes, 1 active $(b+1)$-subcube, and 1 active $b$-subcube and 1 active $(b+1)$-subcube, inside the $(b+2)$-subcube. Let $K^b = \{T_1^b, T_2^b, ..., T_{2j}^b\}$ be a set of active $b$-subcubes in the considered $(b+2)$-subcubes and $K^{b+1} = \{T_1^{b+1}, T_2^{b+1}, ..., T_k^{b+1}\}$ a set of active $(b+1)$-subcubes in the considered $(b+2)$-subcubes, where $j+k$ must be even. By migrating tasks in $T_r^b$ to $\overline{T_s^b}$, $T_r^b$ and $\overline{T_s^b}$ together become a free $(b+1)$-subcube. If $\overline{T_s^{b+1}}$ is free, $T_s^b$ and $\overline{T_s^b}$ together can be regarded as an active $(b+1)$-subcube; otherwise, $\overline{T_s^{b+1}}$ needs not to be considered further since there is no free subcube in $T_s^{b+2}$. Followed by migrating tasks in $T_u^{b+1}$ to $\overline{T_v^{b+1}}$, $T_u^{b+1}$ and $\overline{T_u^{b+1}}$ together become a free $(b+2)$-subcube. The key procedures for each migration step are to find these source-target pairs such that there are two migration

paths for each source-target pair and all the migration paths are pairwise link-disjoint and contain no block links. In order to achieve this goal, we employ two SBT's. Let all the migration paths for $b$-dimensional source-target pairs travel the upper SBT and the others travel the lower SBT. In the following, the procedure in the first stage is to find $b$-dimensional source-target pairs, and some special $(b+1)$-dimensional source-target pairs which are used to avoid link-conflict. After the first stage is done, all the resulting active subcubes are $(b+1)$-subcubes and then $(b+1)$-dimensional source-target pairs are searched in the second stage.

### 3.1. The first stage

It is apparent that we don't need to consider $K^{b+1}$ in the first stage. However, from Property 2, the lower SBT and the upper SBT have common links $b+2$. Hence, $K^b$ and $K^{b+1}$ together must be considered in the first stage to avoid using the same links $b+2$ by any two migration paths. The procedure Match1($G$, $Type$, $Src$, $Dest$, $i$, $Pairs$) for finding $b$-dimensional source-target pairs applies the divide-and-conquer technique below. Initially, $G = K^b \cup K^{b+1}$ and $i = n-1$ and $Type = $''null''. The resulting $(b+1)$-dimensional and $b$-dimensional source-target pairs will be returned in the $Pairs$. $M^{b+1}$ is used to store the resulting active $(b+1)$-subcubes for the second stage. The resulting free $(b+2)$-subcubes are put in $F^{b+2}$ for the next migration step.

Let $|G|$ denote the size of $G$ in terms of $b$-subcubes. There are three cases for $Type$: ''null'', ''in'' and ''out'', which represent nothing moving in or out the SBT, tasks of one active $b$-subcube moving in the SBT, and tasks of one active $b$-subcube moving out the SBT, respectively. If $Type = $''null''( or ''in'' or ''out''), $|G|$ must be even (or odd) so that it guarantees $b$-dimensional source-target pairs can be found.

**Procedure** Match1($G$, $Type$, $Src$, $Dest$, $i$, $Pairs$)
**if** ($|G|=0$) **then** {$Pairs := \varnothing$; **return**; }
**elseif** ($i = b+1$) **then**
  **switch**($Type$) {
  **Case** ''null'':
    **if** (there exists a $T_v^{b+1} \in G$) **then** {
      Move $T_v^{b+1}$ into $M^{b+1}$;
      $Pairs := \varnothing$;  }
    **else** {  /* assume $G = \{T_r^b, T_s^b\}$ */
      $Pairs := \{(T_s^b, \overline{T_r^b})\}$;
      Move $T_r^{b+1}$ into $M^{b+1}$;  }
    **return**;
  **Case** ''in'' :
    there exists a $T_r^b \in G$ ;
    $Dest := \overline{T_r^b}$;
    **if** ($|G|=1$) **then**
      Move $T_r^{b+1}$ into $M^{b+1}$;
    $Pairs := \varnothing$;

```
    return;
  Case "out" :
    there exists a T_r^b ∈ G ;
    Src := T_r^b;
    if (|G|=1) then
      Move T_r^{b+2} into F^{b+2};
    else {       /* assume a T_s^{b+1} ∈ G */
      Move T_s^{b+1} into M^{b+1};  }
    Pairs := ∅;
    return;
  }
else {
  Partition G into G^{(0)} and G^{(1)} according to the value
  of i^{th} bit of each element in G;
  if (i = b+2) then
    switch(Type) {
    Case "null":
      if (|G^{(0)}|=3) then {
        Match1(G^{(0)}, "in", Src_0, Dest_0, i−1, Pairs_0);
        Match1(G^{(1)}, "out", Src_1, Dest_1, i−1, Pairs_1);
        Pairs := Pairs_0 ∪ Pairs_1 ∪ {(Src_1, Dest_0)};
        return;  }
      else break;
    Case "in" :
      if (|G^{(0)}|=2) then {
        there exists a T_t^b ∈ G^{(1)} ;
        Dest := \overline{T_t^b};
        if (there exists a T_v^{b+1} ∈ G^{(0)}) then
          Pairs := {(T_t^{b+1}, \overline{T_v^{b+1}})};
        else {  /* assume G^{(0)}={T_r^b, T_s^b}  */
          Pairs := {(T_s^b, \overline{T_r^b}), (T_t^{b+1}, T_s^{b+1})};  }
        if (there exists a T_u^{b+1} ∈ G^{(1)}) then
          Move T_u^{b+1} into M^{b+1};
        else Move T_t^{b+2} into F^{b+2};
        return;  }
      else break;
    Case "out" :
      if (|G^{(0)}|=2) then {
        there exists a T_t^b ∈ G^{(1)} ;
        Src := T_t^b;
        if (there exists a T_v^{b+1} ∈ G^{(0)}) then
          Pairs := {(T_v^{b+1}, T_t^{b+1})};
          Move T_t^{b+2} into F^{b+2};  }
        else {  /* assume G^{(0)}={T_r^b, T_s^b}  */
          Pairs := {(T_s^b, \overline{T_r^b}), (T_r^{b+1}, T_t^{b+1})};
          Move T_r^{b+2} into F^{b+2};  }
        if (|G^{(1)}|=1) then
          Move T_t^{b+1} into M^{b+1};
        return;  }
      else break;
  }
  switch(Type) {
  Case "null":
    if (|G^{(0)}| is odd) then {
      Match1(G^{(0)}, "out", Src_0, Dest_0, i−1, Pairs_0);
      Match1(G^{(1)}, "in", Src_1, Dest_1, i−1, Pairs_1);
      Pairs := Pairs_0 ∪ Pairs_1 ∪ {(Src_0, Dest_1)};  }
    else {
      Match1(G^{(0)}, "null", Src_0, Dest_0, i−1, Pairs_0);
      Match1(G^{(1)}, "null", Src_1, Dest_1, i−1, Pairs_1);
      Pairs := Pairs_0 ∪ Pairs_1;  }
    return;
  Case "in" :
    if (|G^{(0)}| is odd) then {
      Match1(G^{(0)}, "in", Src_0, Dest_0, i−1, Pairs_0);
      Match1(G^{(1)}, "null", Src_1, Dest_1, i−1, Pairs_1);
      Dest := Dest_0;  }
    else {
      Match1(G^{(0)}, "null", Src_0, Dest_0, i−1, Pairs_0);
      Match1(G^{(1)}, "in", Src_1, Dest_1, i−1, Pairs_1);
      Dest := Dest_1;  }
    Pairs := Pairs_0 ∪ Pairs_1;
    return;
  Case "out" :
    if (|G^{(0)}| is odd) then {
      Match1(G^{(0)}, "out", Src_0, Dest_0, i−1, Pairs_0);
      Match1(G^{(1)}, "null", Src_1, Dest_1, i−1, Pairs_1);
      Src := Src_0;  }
    else {
      Match1(G^{(0)}, "null", Src_0, Dest_0, i−1, Pairs_0);
      Match1(G^{(1)}, "out", Src_1, Dest_1, i−1, Pairs_1);
      Src := Src_1;  }
    Pairs := Pairs_0 ∪ Pairs_1;
    return;
  }
}
```

All the elements in $G$ are subcubes of a common $i$-subcube, which can represented by an SBT, say $S$. Conceptually, $S$ is divided into $S_0$ and $S_1$ according to the value of bit $i$ of $S$. Let $G^{(0)}$ and $G^{(1)}$ be the sets of all the elements in $G$ which are contained in $S_0$ and $S_1$, respectively. In order to apply the procedure recursively, $S_0$ and $S_1$ must preserves the property that the size of net active subcubes are even in terms of $b$-subcubes.

At first, we consider the case of $Type =$ "null". If $|G^{(0)}|$ is odd, $Type$'s of $S_0$ and $S_1$ must be set to "out" and "in", respectively. This setting can be regarded as if tasks in an active $b$-subcube of $S_0$ must be moved to $S_1$ through the link $i$ of $S$, as shown in Fig. 2(a). The source-target pair of this move will be found in the following recursive calls. There is no move for $|G^{(0)}|$ being even; i.e., $Type$'s of $S_0$ and $S_1$ are set to "null", as shown in Fig. 2(b).

Secondly, we consider the case of $Type =$ "in". Either $|G^{(0)}|$ or $|G^{(1)}|$ must be odd, but not both. If $|G^{(1)}|$ is odd, $Type$'s of $S_0$ and $S_1$ must be set to "null" and "in", respectively. This setting can be regarded as if tasks in an active $b$-subcube outside of $S$ are moved to $S_1$ bypass $S_0$ through link $i$ of $S$, as shown in Fig. 2(c). For $|G^{(0)}|$ being odd, the move enters $S_0$ directly; i.e., $Type$'s of $S_0$ and $S_1$ must be set to "$in$" and "$null$", respectively, as shown in Fig. 2(d).

Finally, the case of $Type =$ "$out$" is considered. Either $|G^{(0)}|$ or $|G^{(1)}|$ must be odd, but not both. If $|G^{(1)}|$ is odd, $Type$'s of $S_0$ and $S_1$ must be set to "$null$" and "$out$", respectively. This setting can be regarded as if tasks in an active $b$-subcube of $S$ are moved outwards bypass $S_0$ through link $i$ of $S$, as shown in Fig. 2(e). For $|G^{(0)}|$ being odd, the move goes outwards from $S_0$ directly, as shown in Fig. 2(f); i.e., $Type$'s of $S_0$ and $S_1$ must be set to "$out$" and "$null$", respectively.

Recall that the upper SBT and the lower SBT have common links $b+2$. Usually, the termination condition of the recursive calls Match1 is "$i = b+1$". In order to avoid reusing the links $b+2$ in the second stage, six cases for "$i = b+2$", as shown in Fig. 3, need special cares. Those special cares guarantee that when a super-link $b+2$ is used in the first stage, the resulting $S_0$ either is totally free or contains no free subcubes; i.e., this superlink $b+2$ will not be reused in the second stage since current $S_0$ is a leaf node of the lower SBT. For example, if $|G^{(0)}| = 3$ and $|G^{(1)}| = 3$, then tasks in one active $b$-subcube of $S_1$ are moved to $S_0$ and $S_0$ contains no free subcubes consequently.

We then consider the termination cases, as shown in Fig. 4. For the case of $|G| = 1$ or 3, there must exists a $T_r^b$ and the source (or target) of the move can be set to $T_r^b$ (or $\overline{T_r^b}$) if the value of $Type$ is "$out$" (or "$in$"). The resulting $(b+2)$-subcube, after the move is done, could contain one free $(b+2)$-subcube, one free $(b+1)$-subcube, or no free subcube. The free $(b+2)$-subcube $T_r^{b+2}$ usually is stored into $F^{b+2}$ for the next migration step. The complement of the free $(b+1)$-subcube is put in $M^{b+1}$ for the second stage. If $|G| = 2$ and there exists an active $(b+1)$-subcube $T_r^{b+1}$, $T_r^{b+1}$ is simply put in $M^{b+1}$ for the second stage. For the remaining case of $|G| = 2$, there exists two active $b$-subcubes, say $T_r^b$ and $T_s^b$, and some actions are taken to rearrange two active $b$-subcubes into one active $(b+1)$-subcube: the source-target pair $(T_s^b, \overline{T_r^b})$ is obtained and $T_r^{b+1}$ is put in $M^{b+1}$ for the second stage.

We illustrate this procedure by presenting an example. Suppose that there are six free 0-subcubes and three free 1-subcubes to be compacted in $H_6$, say $F^0 = \{001001, 001011, 001101, 010110, 011101, 111011\}$ and $F^1 = \{00111*, 01111*, 11100*\}$. We can get the corresponding active 0-subcubes and active 1-subcubes to be considered, say $K^0 = \{001000, 001010, 001100, 010111, 011100, 111010\}$ and $K^1 = \{01010*\}$. Initially, $G = K^0 \cup K^1$ and $Type =$ "$null$". Set $G$ is partitioned into two sets $G^{(0)} = \{001000, 001010, 001100, 010111, 011100, 01010*\}$ and $G^{(1)} = \{111010\}$ along

dimension 5. Because it belongs to the case in Fig. 2(a), there must be one move from $G^{(0)}$ to $G^{(1)}$ and the source and the target of this move can be found by applying the procedure Match1 on $G^{(0)}$ and $G^{(1)}$ with $Type =$ "$out$" and $Type =$ "$in$", respectively. For $G^{(1)} = \{111010\}$, after applying the procedure Match1 three times as shown in Fig. 2(c) and 2(d), we reach the termination case in Fig. 4(b). In this case, the target of the move is set to be the complement of 111010, i.e., $Dest := 111011$, and 111010 and 111011 together can be regarded as an active 1-subcube 11101* which is put into $M^i$ for the second stage. The remaining of the example can be treated by the procedure Match1. At the end of the first stage, we get four source-target pairs (001000, 001011), (001100, 111011), (010111, 011101) and (00101*, 00110*).

### 3.2. The Second Stage

Since the special cares are considered in the first stage, it ensures that the links $b+2$ used in the $b$-dimensional task migrations are not reused by the $(b+1)$-dimensional task migrations. Hence, the second stage becomes quite simple and is similar to the first stage without the special cares. The procedure Match2($G$, $Type$, $Src$, $Dest$, $i$, $Pairs$) for finding $(b+1)$-dimensional source-target pairs also applies the divide-and-conquer technique, referred to [11]. Initially, $G = M^{b+1}$ and $i = n-1$ and $Type =$ "$null$". The resulting $(b+1)$-dimensional source-target pairs will be returned in the $Pairs$.

Recall that the migration paths in the second stage will use the lower SBT. All the elements in $G$ are $(b+1)$-subcubes of a common $i$-subcube, which can represented by an SBT, say $S$. Conceptually, $S$ is divided into $S_0$ and $S_1$ according to the value of bit $i$ of $S$. Let $G^{(0)}$ and $G^{(1)}$ be the sets of all the elements in $G$ which are contained in $S_0$ and $S_1$, respectively. In order to apply the procedure recursively, $S_0$ and $S_1$ must preserves the property that the size of net active subcubes are even in terms of $(b+1)$-subcubes. The processing of partitions is similar to that of the first stage, as shown in Fig. 5.

For the termination cases shown in Fig. 6, there must exists a $T_r^{b+1}$ and the source (or target) of the move can be set to $T_r^{b+1}$ (or $\overline{T_r^{b+1}}$) if the value of $Type$ is "$out$" (or "$in$"). The resulting $(b+2)$ subcubes, after the move is done, could be one free $(b+2)$-subcube or one active $(b+2)$-subcube. The free $(b+2)$-subcube $T_r^{b+2}$ should be put in $F^{b+2}$ for the next migration step.

Consider the example in Section 3.1 again. Recall that $M^1 = \{11101*, 00110*, 01010*, 01110*\}$ is derived from the first stage. Initially, $G = M^1$ and $Type =$ "$null$". Set $G$ is partitioned into two sets $G^{(0)} = \{00110*, 01010*, 01110*\}$ and $G^{(1)} =$

{11101*} along dimension 5. Because it belongs to the case in Fig. 5(a), there must be one move from $G^{(0)}$ to $G^{(1)}$ and the source and the target of this move can be found by applying the procedure Match2 on $G^{(0)}$ and $G^{(1)}$ with *Type* = "*out*" and *Type* = "*in*", respectively. For $G^{(1)}$ = {11101*}, after applying the procedure Match2 three times as shown in Fig. 5(d) and 5(c), we reach the termination case in Fig. 6(b). In this case, the target of the move is set to be the complement of 11101*, i.e., *Dest* := 11100*. The remaining of the example can be treated by the procedure Match2. At the end of the second stage, we obtain two source-target pairs (00110*, 11100*) and (01010*, 01111*).

### 3.3. The Migration Paths

Thus far, we get $b$-dimensional source-target pairs and $(b+1)$-dimensional source-target pairs. Let $S$ and $D$ denote the source and the target, respectively, of a source-target pair. The partial path in the SBT for these source-target pairs can be determined by the procedures USBT_Path or LSBT_Path. In order to get two link-disjoint paths for each source-target pair, we need to take care of the remaining partial paths inside $(b+2)$-subcubes by adding links $b$ or $b+1$ at the head or the tail of its corresponding partial path USBT_Path or LSBT_Path. At first, we consider $b$-dimensional source-target pairs.

Case 1: $S_b = D_b$ and $S_{b+1} = D_{b+1}$
       Path 1 := USBT_Path($S$, $D$)
       Path 2 := b, USBT_Path($S$, $D$), b

Case 2: $S_b \neq D_b$ and $S_{b+1} = D_{b+1}$
       Path 1 := USBT_Path($S$, $D$), b
       Path 2 := b, USBT_Path($S$, $D$)

Case 3: $S_b = D_b$ and $S_{b+1} \neq D_{b+1}$
       Path 1 := USBT_Path($S$, $D$), b+1
       Path 2 := b, USBT_Path($S$, $D$), b+1, b

Case 4: $S_b \neq D_b$ and $S_{b+1} \neq D_{b+1}$
       Path 1 := USBT_Path($S$, $D$), b+1, b
       Path 2 := b, USBT_Path($S$, $D$), b+1

Consider the example again. For the source-target pair (001100, 111011), its corresponding USBT_Path is (2, 3, 5, 4, 3). Because it belongs to Case 4, one path is derived by concatenating two partial paths (2, 3, 5, 4, 3) and (1, 0), and another path is obtained by concatenating three partial paths (0), (2, 3, 5, 4, 3) and (1), as shown in Fig. 7.

$K_1$: 001100 $\xrightarrow{\ 2,\ 3,\ 5,\ 4,\ 3,\ 1,\ 0\ }$ 111011
$K_2$: 001100 $\xrightarrow{\ 0,\ 2,\ 3,\ 5,\ 4,\ 3,\ 1\ }$ 111011

On the other hand, considering the source-target pair (010111, 011101), its corresponding USBT_Path is (2, 3, 2). Because it belongs to Case 3, one path is

derived by concatenating two partial paths (2, 3, 2) and (1), and another path is obtained by concatenating three partial paths (0), (2, 3, 2) and (1, 0), as shown in Fig. 7.

$L_1$: 010111 $\xrightarrow{\ 2,\ 3,\ 2,\ 1\ }$ 011101
$L_2$: 010111 $\xrightarrow{\ 0,\ 2,\ 3,\ 2,\ 1,\ 0\ }$ 011101

**Lemma 1:** Two migration paths for each $b$-dimensional source-target pair are link-disjoint.

We then consider $(b+1)$-dimensional source-target pairs.

Case 1: $S_{b+1} = D_{b+1}$
       Path 1 := LSBT_Path($S$, $D$)
       Path 2 := b+1, LSBT_Path($S$, $D$), b+1

Case 2: $S_{b+1} \neq D_{b+1}$
       Path 1 := LSBT_Path($S$, $D$), b+1
       Path 2 := b+1, LSBT_Path($S$, $D$)

Consider the example again. For the source-target pair (01010*, 01111*), its corresponding LSBT_Path is (3). Because it belongs to Case 2, one path is derived by concatenating two partial paths (3) and (1), and another path is obtained by concatenating two partial paths (1) and (3), as shown in Fig. 7.

$M_1$: 01010* $\xrightarrow{\ 3,\ 1\ }$ 01111*
$M_2$: 01010* $\xrightarrow{\ 1,\ 3\ }$ 01111*

**Lemma 2:** Two migration paths for each $(b+1)$-dimensional source-target pair are link-disjoint.

**Theorem 1:** All the migration paths for each migration step are pairwise link-disjoint and contain no block links.

*Proof:* please refer to [11].     ☐

Not all source-target pairs are each corresponding to one task migration. The target of a source-target pair may be the source of another source-target pair, thus necessary to combine these two pairs. In Fig. 3(c), an active $(b+1)$-subcube is moving into a free $(b+2)$-subcube, say $(T_r^{b+1}, T_s^{b+1})$. This resulting active $(b+1)$-subcube may be the source of another source-target pair, say $(T_s^{b+1}, T_t^{b+1})$. Since paths of both pairs are in the lower SBT, both pairs can be combined into source-target pair $(T_r^{b+1}, T_t^{b+1})$. Consider the example again. (00101*, 00110*) and (00110*, 11100*) can be combined into (00101*, 11100*).

We then consider that an active $b$-subcube $T_r^b$ is moving into the complement of another active $b$-subcube, $\overline{T_s^b}$, and the resulting $(b+1)$-subcube may be the source of another source-target pair, $(T_s^{b+1}, T_t^{b+1})$. It is obvious that there are actually two $b$-dimensional task migrations. Conceptually, $(T_s^{b+1}, T_t^{b+1})$ is split into $(T_s^b, T_t^b)$ and $(\overline{T_s^b}, \overline{T_t^b})$, where bit $b$ of $T_t^b$ is equal to bit $b$ of $T_s^b$. Thus, we can obtain two task migrations: (a) $(T_s^b, T_t^b)$, and (b) $(T_r^b, \overline{T_s^b})$ and $(\overline{T_s^b}, \overline{T_t^b})$. Consider the example again. Because $001011$ is a subcube of $00101*$, $(001000, 001011)$ and $(00101*, 11100*)$ can be transformed into two task migrations: (a) $(001010, 111000)$, and (b) $(001000, 001011)$ and $(001011, 111001)$. Thus, we get two migration paths for each task migration as shown in Fig. 7.

$$I_1: 001000 \xrightarrow{1,0} 001011 \xrightarrow{2,4,5,2,1} 111001$$
$$I_2: 001000 \xrightarrow{0,1} 001011 \xrightarrow{1,2,4,5,2} 111001$$
$$J_1: 001010 \xrightarrow{2,4,5,2,1} 111000$$
$$J_2: 001010 \xrightarrow{1,2,4,5,2} 111000$$

Note that two adjacent links 1 in path $I_2$ should be removed. In Fig. 7, all the maximal buddy subcubes except the $(b+2)$-subcubes participating the migration are enclosed by dashed lines. All the migration paths are given in the figure, and they indeed are totally disjoint and contain no block links.

## 4. Conclusions

We have proposed a buddy-subcube compaction scheme in that not only do free subcubes with two adjacent dimensions be compacted concurrently, but two disjoint paths are established between every pair of source-target nodes. The motivation of our compaction scheme stems from two facts. One fact is that a limited number of free subcubes can be compacted concurrently in each migration step so that all migration paths are pairwise disjoint and contain no block links. Another fact is the amount of information to be transferred is often large and the migration duration for such a hypercube is dictated mainly by network latency, which is proportional to the message size.

With applying two SBT's, our method becomes quite simple. All migration paths selected are pairwise disjoint and contain no block links. In general, it appears that there are no more than two disjoint paths between every pair of corresponding nodes. For the migration steps which compact exactly two free subcubes, finding more than two disjoint paths between every pair of corresponding nodes is worth further investigating.

## References

[1] C.-H. Huang and J.-Y. Juang, "A Partial Compacting Scheme for Processor Allocation in Hypercube Multiprocessors," *Proc. 1990 International Conference on Parallel Processing*, vol. I, Aug. 1990, pp. 211-217.

[2] Y. M. Kim, T.-H. Lai and Y.-C. Tseng, "Compacting Free Buddy Subcubes in a Hypercube," *Proc. 1992 International Conference on Parallel Processing*, vol. III, Aug. 1992, pp. 355-358.

[3] R. Arlauskas, "iPSC/2 System: A Second Generation Hypercube," *Proc. 3rd Conf. Hypercube Concurrent Computers and Applications*, vol. I, Jan. 1988, pp. 38-42.

[4] NCUBE Corporation, "n-Cube 2 Processor Manual," NCUBE Corporation, 1990.

[5] O. Frieder *et al.*, "Experimentation with Hypercube Database Engines," *IEEE Micro*, pp. 42-56, Feb. 1992.

[6] L. M. Ni and P. K. McKinley, "A Survey of Wormhole Routing Techniques in Direct Networks," *IEEE Computer*, vol. 26, pp. 62-76, Feb. 1993.

[7] H.-L. Chen, "Fast Subcube Compaction in Hypercubes with the Buddy Allocation Strategy," *Journal of Information Science and Engineering*, vol. 11, no. 3, pp. 453-463, Sept. 1995.

[8] P. K. McKinley and C. Trefftz, "Efficient Broadcast in All-port Wormhole-Routing Hypercubes," *Proc. 1993 International Conference on Parallel Processing*, vol. II, Aug. 1993, pp. 288-291.

[9] Y.-C. Tseng, "Strategies for Processor Allocation and Inter-Processor Communication in Multicomputer Networks," Ph.D. dissertation, Dept. of Computer and Information Science, The Ohio State University, 1994.

[10] C.-T. Ho and S. L. Johnsson, "Distributed Routing Algorithms for Broadcasting and Personalized Communication in Hypercubes," *Proc. 1986 International Conference on Parallel Processing*, Aug. 1986, pp. 640-648.

[11] H.-L. Chen and S.-H. Hu, "Quick Buddy-Subcube Compaction in Hypercubes," Tech. Rep. *NTIT-ET-TR96003*, Department of Electronic Engineering, National Taiwan Institute of Technology, Taipei, Taiwan, 1996.

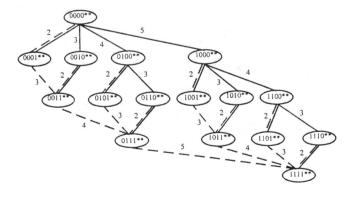

Fig. 1. Two SBT's in an $H_6$, where $H_6$ is viewed as an $H_4$ with each node being a buddy 2-subcube.

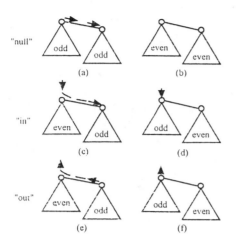

Fig. 2. General partition rules for the procedure Match1.

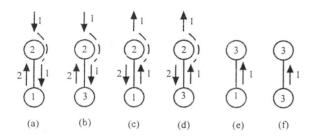

Fig. 3. Special termination cases for the procedure Match1.

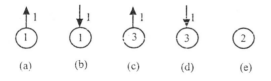

Fig. 4. Termination cases for the procedure Match1.

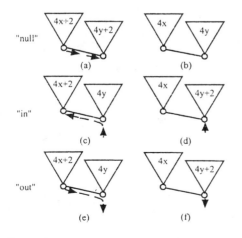

Fig. 5. General partition rules for the procedure Match2.

Fig. 6. Termination cases for the procedure Match2.

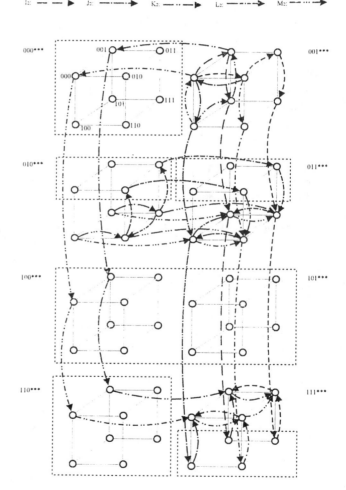

Fig. 7. A 6-dimensional hypercube, $H_6$, where two disjoint paths between every migration pair are shown.

# MpPVM : A Software System
## for
# Non-Dedicated Heterogeneous Computing

Kasidit Chanchio        Xian-He Sun

Department of Computer Science
Louisiana State University
Baton Rouge, LA 70803-4020

## Abstract

*This paper presents the design and preliminary implementation of MpPVM, a software system that supports process migration for PVM application programs in a non-dedicated heterogeneous computing environment. New concepts of migration point as well as migration point analysis and necessary data analysis are introduced. A preliminary implementation of MpPVM and its experimental results are also presented, showing the correctness and promising performance of our process migration mechanism in the scalable non-dedicated heterogeneous computing environment.*

## 1   Introduction

The construction of national high-speed communication networks, or the so-called "information highway", marks the beginning of a new era of computing in which communication plays a major role. Until recently, computing resources on networks remained separate units. Now, while the World Wide Web and electrical mail are changing the way people do business, heterogeneous networks of computers are becoming commonplace in high-performance computing. Several commercial and non-commercial software systems, such as PVM software, the *P4* system, *Express*, and MPI [1, 2, 3], have been developed to support distributed computing.

In a non-dedicated environment, computers are privately owned. Individual owners do not want to see their systems being saturated by others when they need them. This means the privately owned machines may only be used for parallel processing on an "availability" basis. The uncertainty of the "availability" of an individual machine makes the performance of each individual machine non-deterministic. In addition, a non-dedicated network of computers is more likely to be heterogeneous than is a dedicated system. "Availability" and "heterogeneity" are new issues which do not arise in tightly coupled parallel systems. Competition for computing resources does not lead to guaranteed high performance. "Stealing" of computing cycles, instead of competing for computing cycles, is a more reasonable way to achieve parallel processing in a non-dedicated parallel and distributed environment [4]. The process migration mechanism is proposed as a solution to simultaneously utilizing idle machines and maintaining high capabilities for local computations. The simple idea underlying this mechanism is that when the imbalanced workload of a distributed system occurs, parallel processes residing on overloaded machines are migrated to other available machines.

The MpPVM (Migration-point based PVM) software system proposed in this study is designed to support process migration in a non-dedicated, heterogeneous computing environment. Along with the components of MpPVM and the migration mechanism, we present novel ideas of *migration point* and *necessary data analysis*. Finally, experimental results are presented to verify the applicability of the design and to demonstrate the performance gain of process migration. The results have shown the feasibility and high potential of process migration in a non-dedicated heterogeneous environment.

## 2   Related Works

There are several software systems available to support parallel processing in a distributed environment [1]. Among these, PVM [1] and MPI [3] are the most popular software environments. The migration approach proposed in MpPVM can be applied to any existing message passing software. We chose to implement the migration mechanism on PVM instead of MPI because of many reasons. First, PVM's structure and implementation are well–defined. On the other hand, MPI has many different implementations such as LAM [5], MPICH, and UNIFY. Second, some MPI implementations are built on top of PVM, such as MPICH/PVM. Finally, the nature of MPI processes is relatively static compared to those of PVM. Processes in MpPVM can be dynamically created, terminated, or migrated from one machine to another. Therefore, it is more natural to incorporate our ideas into PVM than MPI.

## 2.1 Transparency and Heterogeneity

Unlike MPVM and ULP [6] developed at Oregon Institute of Science & Technology, migration in Mp-PVM will be performed at *Migration Points (Mp's)* only. These *Mp's* will be inserted automatically by the precompiler. Users can also specify their migration points. In the latter case, the precompiler will adjust the arrangement of its Mp's to fit the user's needs and the needs of the underlying computing environment.

Process migration is transparent to users of Mp-PVM. The precompiler will modify the PVM source code to support the migration mechanism. All necessary definitions and operations are put to the input file by the precompiler and require no work from the user. With the use of this precompiler, most of PVM's applications are able to run on MpPVM as well. Note that MpPVM also allows users to customize the automatically generated migration operations in their application programs to improve the performance of their parallel computations. With the awareness of process migrations during parallel executions, the users can help the precompiler select the migration points which are most suitable to the structure of their applications.

MpPVM supports process migration in a heterogeneous computing environment. The precompiler will add migration definitions to its input source program. When a migration event occurs, a process will perform migration operations at a high level by executing a set of programming language statements. Therefore, a process can migrate from one machine to another without any restriction regarding the machines' architectures.

In MPVM and ULP, although the migrations can be operated at any point within an application program, they do not support migration in a heterogeneous environment. In their designs, the migrations

are performed at low level by transferring data, stack, and heap segments of the execution code to another machine. Thus, source and target machines for migration events must be binary compatible.

## 2.2 Migration Point and Checkpoint

In DOME [7] and Condor [8] developed at CMU and Wisconsin, Madison, respectively, checkpointing can be used for both fault-tolerance and process migration purposes. DOME uses its high-level checkpointing scheme mostly for fault-tolerance purposes. However, because the checkpointed processes can be restarted at other machines in a heterogeneous environment, DOME's checkpointing scheme can be used for process migration as well. In Condor, checkpointing is used mostly for process migration. During the migration, Condor will create a checkpoint file before terminating an original process. This checkpoint file will be used when the process is restarted at a new machine.

Checkpoint involves the access of file system and disk. It is a good scheme for fault-tolerance but is not the best way to support process migration in a non-dedicated network of computers. Migration and checkpointing schemes should be designed separately for best performance. In MpPVM, necessary data is transferred directly from migrating machine to migrated machine through network communication. The compiler-assisted and user-directed concepts will be applied to migration points instead of checkpoints.

## 3  Overview of MpPVM

MpPVM has three main components. They are:

- *MCL* (MpPVM's precompiler), the precompiler that translates PVM source code into MpPVM source code by dividing its input program into several subsequences of instructions and inserting migration points to separate those subsequences from each other. MCL will perform *migration point analysis* and *necessary data analysis* to determine the locations of migration points in the source program and to evaluate the minimum set of variables to be transferred at each migration point, respectively. Finally, MCL will insert migration operations including global definitions and macros to the source program to produce its output.

- *Mpd* (MpPVM's daemon), the modified version of *pvmd*, which handles reliable point-to-point, indirect message passing mechanism in the migration environment. It also provides a protocol to support signaling among the scheduler, the migrating process, and the new process on an idle machine.

- *Mlibpvm* (MpPVM's library), the modified version of *libpvm*, which provides programming language subroutines for the application programs and for the scheduler (the resource manager).

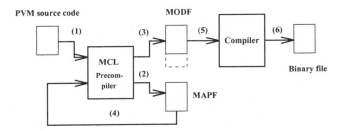

Figure 1: Basic steps in developing application programs for MpPVM.

To develop software on MpPVM, users must feed an application program written in C or FORTRAN to the precompiler (see Figure 1). The precompiler will give two output files, a map file (MAPF) and a modified file (MODF). The map file (MAPF) will show locations of every migration point. If the users are not satisfied, they may change this map file and then input it to the precompiler again. The modified file (MODF) is the original PVM source file that was modified by the precompiler (MCL) to support process migration. MCL will analyze a structure of the program and then insert necessary definitions and macros at every migration point (Mp). After getting the acceptable MAPF and MODF, the MODF will be sent to the compiler for creation of the MpPVM executable file.

Before running the applications, Mpd and the scheduler must be running in a parallel computing environment. Like *pvmd*, Mpd is a daemon process that runs on every computer. The cooperation of every Mpd in the system can be viewed as a logical computing unit called a *virtual machine*. On the other hand, the scheduler is a process (or processes) that monitors and controls work loads of the environment. At run–time, the applications will request services from the virtual machine and the scheduler. The virtual machine provides indirect message passing services for the applications; while, the scheduler handles requests such as process creation, termination, and other process operations that affect the work loads and configuration of the system.

When load imbalance occurs, process migration may be employed to solve the problem. In migrating a process, the scheduler will determine the migrating process and choose one of the idle or lightly loaded machines to be the destination of the migration. Then, the scheduler will signal the destination machine to load the *equivalent* MpPVM executable file, the binary files that were generated from the same MODF file as that of the migrating process, into its system. In heterogeneous environment, these equivalent execution files have the same functionalities and execution behaviors since they are generated from the same source code. This loading operation is called *process initialization*. According to the definitions and operations generated in the MODF, the loaded process will wait for the connection from the migrating process. Usually, the initialization is performed when the scheduler wants to migrate a process. In our model, the process can also be initialized at any time before the migration is needed. This situation is called *pre–initialization*. Since the destinations of process migration are the idle or lightly–loaded machines, pre-initialization will not effect anybody in the system. The strategies to manage pre–initialization depend mostly on the design of the scheduler. Although the implementation detail of the scheduler is not a focus of this study, pre-initialization is recommended as an option to reduce migration overhead.

After the initialization, the scheduler will send information of the initialized process to the migrating process. The migrating process will make a direct TCP connection to the initialized process and start transferring its data. When finished, the migrating process will terminate. The execution will be resumed at the new process on the destination machine.

## 4 MCL

In this section, we describe the functionalities of MCL including the migration point analysis and data analysis. We also introduce the global variables and macros generated in the MODF file.

### 4.1 Migration Points Analysis

MCL adopts a new approach for migration point analysis which is different from any existing software environment. MCL views each programming language statement as an *instruction*. The instructions are classified into three types: control instruction, plain instruction, and library instruction. Control instruction consists of branching, loop, and subroutine instructions. Branching instructions are the conditional statements such as the IF–THEN–ELSE or CASE statements in FORTRAN. Loop instructions are those that create repetitive executions such as *while()* and *for()* loops in C, and *do··· continue loops* in FORTRAN. A subroutine instruction is a subroutine calling statement in a programming language. Plain instructions are the instructions or operations that come with the programming language such as +, -, *, /, etc. Finally, library instructions are subroutines or operations defined in a standard library, such as functions and subroutines in *stdlib* or *libpvm*, etc.

For simplicity, in our analysis model for automatic migration-point insertion, we assume that every control, plain, and library instruction associates a fixed number of CPU cycles for its execution. Arithmetic (+,-,*,/, etc.), logical (.AND., .OR., etc), relational (.EQ., .LE., .GE., etc.) operations and other instructions that do not depend on run-time information are examples of these type of instructions. Five rules are specified in [9] for automatic insertion of migration points which are based on the maximum cumulative Execution Cost (EC) between any two migration points.

## 4.2 Data Analysis

The goal of data analysis is to minimize the data transfer time during process migration. MpPVM does this by conducting *necessary data analysis*. MCL finds a set of variables that have been initialized before the migration point and a set of variables that will be referred to by other instructions after the migration point. In Figure 2, a migration point (Mp) and its data analysis are given. In this example the sets would be {a, b, x} and {x, b, c, y}, respectively. The intersection of these two sets, {x, b}, gives us the minimal set of data needed to be migrated at Mp.

The idea behind the data analysis methodology is that the valid set of variables to be migrated should be those that have already been initialized before the migration point and will be used by other instructions after the migration is finished. Algorithms are given in [9] for conducting data analysis under different circumstances.

## 4.3 Migration Macros and Variables.

After defining migration points and their data, MCL will insert special global variables and macros to create its output (the MODF file). These global

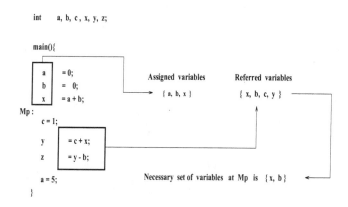

Figure 2: A simple example of necessary data analysis.

variables and macros are reserved by MCL and must be different than those defined by a user. These variables and macros are built for two major purposes: to migrate a process from the original machine, and to resume the execution of the process at the destination machine.

The global variables include a Control Stack (CS), a Data Stack (DS), an Execution Flag (EF), and other variables such as those for inter–process communications at the top of the file. The *control stack (CS)* is used to keep track of function calls before the migration; whereas, *data stack (DS)* is used to store the necessary local and global data. The Execution Flag is a variable that stores a signal sent from the scheduler.

After inserting variables to the MODF file, MCL will insert migration macros at various locations over a source program. During a process migration, these macros will collect CS and DS stacks, transfer data across machines, and restore data to the appropriate variables in the target process. These macros are WAIT_MACRO, JMP_MACRO, MR_MACRO, and STK_MACRO. The pseudo codes of the macros can be found in [9].

## 5 Mpd, Mlibpvm, and Scheduler

Mpd is a modified version of pvmd. It has been modified to support process migration by adding protocols to support data communications and signaling among the scheduler, a migrating process, and a new process in the idle machine as well as creating the migration process table (MPT) and message forwarding mechanism to handle point-to-point communication in the migration environment.

Mlibpvm is a modified version of libpvm. It is a programming language library containing subroutines for schedulers and application programs. The *Scheduler Interface* is a collection of subroutines to monitor and control work loads of the computing environment. These subroutines are used only by the scheduler. The *Application (or User) Interface* contains PVM subroutines that are modified to support efficient distributed computing in the migration environment. These subroutines are used mostly for application programs.

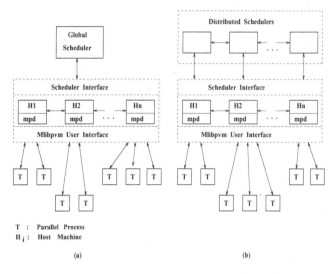

T  : Parallel Process
H$_i$ :  Host Machine

(a)                                        (b)

Figure 3: The overall structure of MpPVM virtual machine environment. (a) and (b) show two environments where global and local schedulers are used to control load balancing of the system.

In a migration environment, the scheduler is required to have functions to control the dynamic workload of the system. For the sake of brevity, the design and implementation of the scheduler are not discussed in this paper. Its structure could be either global or distributed as shown in Figure 3. In any case, we assume the scheduler has the following functionalities:

- The scheduler must classify parallel processes running under its supervision into two types: static and dynamic. The static process resides on one machine until its termination; whereas, the dynamic process can migrate from one machine to another.

- The scheduler must exhaustively seek the idle or lightly loaded machines in the heterogeneous environment and make them ready for utilization by the application processes.

- At the migration event, the scheduler must initialize the process at the new machine before notifying the migrating process to make a connection and transfer its data to the new process. If the parallel process is already pre-initialized, the scheduler will send the identification of pre-initialized process to the migrating one. In this case, we can substantially reduce the migration overhead.

- To maintain reliable data communication, in migrating a process, the scheduler must *inform* every Mpd of processes in the same processing group as the migrating process to update contents of its migration process table (MPT).

In an Mpd, a daemon for each host in the virtual machine, a data structure called *Migration Process Table (MPT)* is implemented. This table, containing a list of original task id's along with the corresponding current host id, is used mainly to support data communication in a migration environment. Every time a process sends messages to another process, the Mpd will scan through its MPT table to find out the current machine of the target process. If it cannot find anything, Mpd will assume that the target process has never been migrated to other machines before. Then, the original PVM strategies of searching for a target machine will be employed.

There are three possible communicating situations that may occur in this model during a migration. They are:

- If the message arrives at the current Mpd of the migrating process before the migration and has not yet been read by a pvm_recv() function call, the Mpd will store these messages in its buffer.

- If the message reaches the current Mpd of the migrating process during the migration, it will also be stored in the buffer. Once the migration is complete, the Mpd will flush this data to the destination machine.

- After migration, if the Mpd of the process that wants to send message to the migrated process has got the broadcasted migration information from the scheduler and has updated its MPT, the message will be sent directly to the Mpd of the new machine. Otherwise, the message will be sent to the Mpd of the last host and then forwarded to a new machine. Therefore, the faster we update the MPT of every Mpd in the same processing group, the less we have to forward the messages.

Before its termination, each parallel process will send a termination signal to the scheduler. The scheduler will collect these termination signals until every process in the same processing group is terminated. Then, it will broadcast signals to every Mpd of that processing group to delete informations of the terminated process from their MPT.

## 6 Preliminary Implementation and Experimental Results

A few prototypes and experimental programs have been developed to test the correctness and applicability of the design of MpPVM. Routines for transferring data and process states have also been developed. *pvmd* and *libpvm* of PVM were modified to support the experimental MpPVM protocol.

In pvmd, we have implemented the MPT table and modified PVM point-to-point message passing mechanism to cooperate with the MPT. The Task-Pvmd and Pvmd-Pvmd protocols are also modified to support signaling among the migrating process, the new process, and the scheduler. In libpvm, a few subroutines for transferring data during process migration are implemented. These data must be encoded into the XDR format before being transferred across machines in a heterogeneous environment. The subroutines which are used by the scheduler, such as those to initialize and to migrate the parallel process, are also added to the libpvm library.

Based on the implemented prototype, we have conducted experiments to verify the feasibility and applicability of the migration point and necessary data analysis in the MpPVM design. A parallel matrix multiplication program with Master-Slave communication topology developed in [7] was chosen for our experiments. Both the PVM and MpPVM versions of this program are implemented. These two versions are different in that the MpPVM one contains a number of migration points at various locations in the program. Both experiments are performed on the same LAN environment consisting of four SUN Sparc IPC and fourteen DEC 5000/120 workstations.

The purpose of our first experiment is to verify the heterogeneous process migration of MpPVM and to examine the performance degradation of the PVM version when parallel tasks have to compete with local jobs for computing cycles. We assume the new process at a destination of a process migration is pre-initialized. Since the process initialization involves many factors such as disk accesses and NFS that might cause substantial amount of overhead, the availability of pre-initialization benefit a faster process migration. However, this assumption requires the scheduler

to have efficient resource allocation policy in a migration environment.

In this experiment we run four parallel processes on two SUN and two DEC workstations. One of the two DEC workstations was the test site that had continued requests from the machine owner (or other local users). When the workload on the test site increased, MpPVM migrated its process from the test site to one of the unused SUN workstations on the network. In the competing situation, we simulate the increasing workload of local computation by gradually adding light-weighted processes, i.e. programs with few floating-point operations and small data size, to share more time slices from the CPU.

From Figure 4 we can see that MpPVM achieved a superior performance over PVM especially when the owner's jobs request more CPU time. In 4(a), a 3x400 and a 400x3 matrix are multiplied for ten times. With competing with local jobs, both parallel processing versions have an increased execution time with the requests from the owner. However, the execution time increase of MpPVM is about a half of that of PVM when the machine owner actively uses the test site. This is because in this implementation only one migration-point is used and is located at the half-way point of the total required computation. In 4(b), we still use the same configuration as 4(a) except that we increase the order of the matrices to 3x1600 and 1600x3 respectively. As a result, the parallel processing performance becomes more sensitive to the owner requests than in 4(a). In this test we have developed two MpPVM programs which will migrate from the overloaded machine after 10 percent and 50 percent of their executions, respectively. The performance of migration at 10 percent is better than that at 50 percent since the process spends less time competing with the owner computations. In general, the more migration points in a parallel program, the less the duration of competing with local computation will be and, therefore, the better performance is achieved.

In the second set of experiments, the goal is to investigate the effects of process migrations when both the problem and ensemble size scale up. Since we want to detect the degradation caused from process migrations only, the tests are conducted in a dedicated environment[1].

We scale the problem size of the MpPVM matrix multiplication program with the number of processors on 4, 6, 8, 10, and 12 workstations by following the memory-bounded scale-up principle [10],

---

[1] The tests were conducted at midnight on Friday's when no one else was on the system.

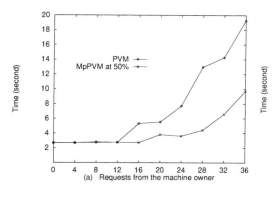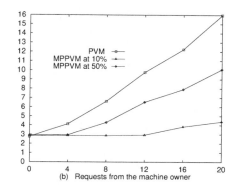

Figure 4: Comparisons of execution time between PVM and MpPVM matrix multiplication programs

respectively[2]. At each ensemble size, at most 3 and 5 slave processes are migrated when the program runs on 4 and 6 workstations respectively; whereas, 6 slave processes are migrated when the program uses a greater number of workstations. New processes of process migration are pre-initialized, and overlapping of process migrations are prevented in this experiment. The experimental results are depicted in Figure 5.

In Figure 5(a), each curve represents a relationship between execution time and the scaled problem size, indicated by the number of workstations, at a specific number of process migrations ($m$). At $m = 0$, there is no process migration. Likewise, the curves at $m = 1$ to $m = 6$ give the results with one to six process migrations, respectively. We can see that these curves increase approximately in parallel. For example, the curve of $m = 6$ (migrate six times) grows in parallel with the curve of $m = 0$ (no migration). Since the difference of execution time of $m = 6$ and $m = 0$ is the migration cost, we can conclude that the migration costs caused by six process migrations at the scaled problem size on 8, 10, and 12 workstations are approximately the same. Therefore, the migration cost is a constant and does not increase with the ensemble size in our experiments. The execution time increase is mainly due to the increase of computation and communication, not due to the migration cost, which is especially true when the ensemble size is large.

Figure 5(b) further confirms that the migration cost does not increase with problem and ensemble size. In this figure, different curves depict the relation between the execution time and the number of process migrations at a specific ensemble size. We can see that the increase of execution time with the number of pro-

cess migrations is consistently small compared with the computing and communication time. For example, at 12 workstations ($p = 12$), with six migrations, the total migration delay is less than 10% of the total execution time. In addition, the increasing rates of the execution time at every ensemble size ($p$) are approximately the same.

The experimental results show that the proposed process migration mechanism is implementable and practical in a distributed heterogeneous environment. Process migrations are prevented from being overlapped with each other or with computation and communication in our experiments. Process migration cost may be reduced with these overlapping. On the other hand, however, while the experimental results are very encouraging, the results are preliminary and based on certain assumptions. In our experiments, we assume the destination processes in a process migration are pre-initialized. Thus, at a migration event, the migrating process can transfer its data promptly to the destination process. Migration cost will be increased if the new process is initialized during process migration.

Efficient process migration needs the cooperation of many components such as the scheduler, the virtual machine (MpPVM), and the application processes. Since MpPVM is just one of the components with certain functionalities to support process migration, certain assumptions and limitations are unavoidable in current examination of the applicability and feasibility of its design. The measured migration cost is only true for our application on our environment. It may vary with the computation/communication ratio of the application and hardware parameters of the underlying distributed platform, though we believe it represents the trend of general applications. Further experiments are planed for other parallel applications with different computing and communication structures.

---

[2]For the matrix multiplication $A \times B$, the order of matrix A is 3x1600, 3x2400, 3x3200, 3x4000, and 3x4800 for ensemble size 4, 6, 8, 10, 12 respectively. The order of matrix B is symmetric to the order of matrix A.

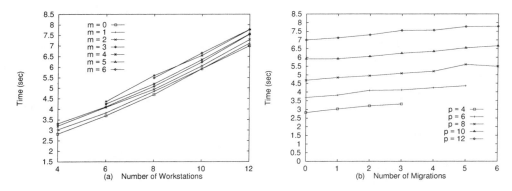

Figure 5: Comparisons of execution times of MpPVM matrix multiplication programs when the problem size scales up.

## 7 Conclusion and Future Works

We have introduced high-level process migration mechanisms and methodologys to reduce migration overhead in a heterogeneous computing environment. In addition, we have also proposed modifications of pvmd and pvmlib of PVM to maintain reliable data communications among processes in a migration environment. Our implementation and experimental results have shown the applicability and potential of the proposed MpPVM software system. Experimental results indicate MpPVM is scalable in the sense that the migration costs becomes less notable when the problem and ensemble increase. Since the implementation of MpPVM is still preliminary, the Mpd and Mlibpvm need to be improved to maintain high reliability and efficiency on various parallel applications. The MCL software and its supporting tools are also under development.

## Acknowledgment

The authors are grateful to A. Beguelin of Carnegie Mellon University for his help on understanding the implementation of PVM and on recommending related works in process migration in a distributed environment.

## References

[1] A. Geist et al., *PVM: Parallel Virtual Machine – A Users' Guide and Tutorial for Networked Parallel Computing.* MIT Press, 1994.

[2] A. Beguelin et al., "Recent enhancements to PVM," *The international Journal of Supercomputer Applications*, vol. 9, pp. 108–127, 1995.

[3] W. Gropp et al., *Using MPI: Portable Parallel Programming with the Message Passing Interface.* MIT Press, 1994.

[4] S. Leutenegger and X.-H. Sun, "Distributed computing feasibility in a non-dedicated homogeneous distributed system," in *Proceedings of Supercomputing'93*, pp. 143–152, 1993.

[5] G. Burns et al., "Lam: An open cluster environment for MPI." Available at ftp:://tbag.osc.edu/pub/lam/lam-papers.tar.Z.

[6] J. Casas et al., "Adaptive load migration systems for PVM," in *Proceedings of Supercomputing'94*, pp. 390–399, 1994.

[7] J. N. C. Arabe et al., "Dome: Parallel programming in a multi-user environment," Tech. Rep. CMU-CS-95-137, Carnegie Mellon University, School of Computer Science, Apr. 1995.

[8] M. J. Litzkow et al., "Condor–a hunter of idle workstations," in *Proceeding of the 8th IEEE International Conference on Distributed Computing Systems*, pp. 104–111, June 1988.

[9] K. Chanchio and X.-H. Sun, "Mppvm: The migration–points based PVM," Tech. Rep., Lousiana State University, Dept. of Computer Science, 1995.

[10] X.-H. Sun and L. Ni, "Scalable Problems and Memory-Bound Speedup," *The Journal of Parallel and Distributed Computing*, vol. 19, pp. 27–37, 1993.

# SIMULATING MESSAGE-DRIVEN PROGRAMS *

Attila Gürsoy
Department of Computer Science
University of Illinois, Urbana IL
email: gursoy@cs.uiuc.edu

Laxmikant V. Kalé
Department of Computer Science
University of Illinois, Urbana IL 61801
email: kale@cs.uiuc.edu

*Abstract – Simulation studies are quite useful for performance prediction on new architectures and for systematic analysis of performance perturbations caused by variations in the machine parameters, such as communication latencies. Trace-driven simulation is necessary to avoid large computational costs over multiple simulation runs. However, trace-driven simulation of nondeterministic programs has turned out to be almost impossible. Simulation of message-driven programs is particularly challenging in this context because they are inherently nondeterministic. Yet message-driven execution is a very effective technique for enhancing performance, particularly in the presence of large or unpredictable communication latencies. We present a methodology for simulating message-driven programs. The information that is necessary to carry out such simulations is identified, and a method for extracting such information from program executions is described.*

## 1 INTRODUCTION

An accurate performance prediction of parallel computations plays an important role in designing parallel algorithms and evaluating machines. Many computational complexity models have been derived for parallel algorithms. Although these analytical approaches are very useful to determine the fundamental performance limits of parallel algorithms, they are often inadequate to analyze the parallel computations and the interactions between computations and parallel architectures. Particularly, the load imbalance, scheduling, synchronization, and the dynamic properties of the parallel computations make the analytical approaches difficult, if not impossible, for this purpose.

Simulation techniques offer a more realistic analysis in this regard, and they have been used extensively to predict the performance of parallel programs on specific computers. There are various simulation techniques that are suitable for different purposes depending on the accuracy of the prediction desired and the complexity of the simulator itself. For example, one can emulate the user code instruction by instruction in the simulated environment. Although this method provides very accurate results, the simulator itself is very costly in terms of both the development and the computation (for instance, emulating every instruction of a parallel code on a 1000 processors would be very time-consuming). Another approach which makes simulations more affordable is to use an abstract model of the computation instead of emulating a specific computation. The model may contain some statistical properties such as average number of messages sent, average computation size etc. As no user computation is executed during the simulation, the simulation time (and the computation power required) is small. However, this approach too may not capture adequate details of the computation and is not useful to predict the performance of a specific program.

Trace-driven simulation is another approach which combines the advantages of both. Its complexity is in between the above two, and yet it is powerful enough to capture the details of the computation. A trace is a time ordered sequence of significant events that happened during the execution of a program. The traces are collected from an actual execution of the program, and it is fed to the simulator. The simulator, then, executes these traces on a model of the new system. Trace-driven simulation has been successfully used in studies of uniprocessor systems such as memory designs, cache performance etc [11]. In such studies, the order of events in the system to be simulated (such as the sequence of addresses accessed) was assumed to be deterministic. Therefore, the changes in the simulated environment affected only the length of the time interval between the events, not the actual sequence of events.

The trace-driven simulation has been extended to study parallel computations also [4, 9, 5]. However, application of the trace-driven simulation to parallel systems poses a problem. The behavior of a parallel computation may change under a new environment which invalidates the traces. Some of the trace-driven simulations of parallel computations were limited to programs written in traditional message-passing style (i.e., single process per processor and *blocking* message receives that ask a specific message with a given tag and source processor). In these cases, the behavior of the programs remains the same despite the changes in the environment [9]. In general, message-passing programs may contain nonblocking message passing primitives which introduce nondeterminism. With nonblocking receives, the behavior of the program may

*This research was supported in part by the National Science Foundation grants CCR-91-06608 and ASC-93-18159.

depend on the arrival order of messages. For example, the program may check for a particular message, if the message is not there, the program may choose a different action. In a simpler context, the problem posed by this sort of non-determinism was addressed in some trace-driven simulation studies [8]. These studies used a hybrid method combining trace-driven simulations and real execution of user code to study the performance of shared memory systems. This approach is difficult and expensive since it requires execution of a part of user code during simulation. The execution-driven simulation [3] or hybrid simulation of message passing programs whose behavior depends on message arrival order would be more difficult and impractical.

Message-driven execution, explained in Section 2, is based on the ability to run computations in different orders. Therefore, the simulation of message-driven computations inherently involves dealing with this difficulty. In a message-driven computation, the messages may arrive in a different order due to numerous reasons in the new simulated environment. The execution trace of the program becomes invalid at that point because the rest of the computation is different from the traces. In order to achieve accurate simulation, it is necessary to reconstruct remaining sequence of computation steps. This is impossible, in general, without rerunning or interpreting the program instruction by instruction. In some special cases, using the knowledge about the algorithm/computation model, the sequence of computations can be reconstructed.

In this paper, we will describe a method to simulate message-driven programs written in the Dagger language [7]. The Dagger language, in addition to helping the expression of message-driven programs, also turns out to expose sufficient parts of dependence structure of each parallel object so as to render accurate trace-driven simulations feasible. Our approach depends on extracting some semantic information from the Dagger programs satisfying certain conditions (which will be described later), and using this information together with the execution traces to conduct the simulation. The technique is not limited to the Dagger language. It can be extended to other parallel programming languages such as CC++ [1], OCCAM with some modification.

The rest of the paper is organized as follows: Section 2 describes the message-driven execution and the Dagger coordination language. Section 3 discusses the simulation of Dagger programs. The abstract machine model that is used by the simulator is explained in Section 4. The design of the trace-driven simulator is discussed in Section 5. Some examples of illustrating the usage of the simulator are presented in Section 6, and the conclusion in Section 7.

## 2 MESSAGE-DRIVEN EXECUTION AND DAGGER

The traditional method of programming distributed memory parallel computers involves a traditional message-passing style of programming. This style involves one process per processor. The processes may send messages to each other and issue blocking system calls to receive a specific message. They may also invoke global operations such as reductions and scans which act as barriers, i.e. all processors must invoke these operations in identical sequence and each processor must wait until all processors have arrived at each barrier. Despite its simplicity, this style of parallel programming often leads to severe performance impediments, because it requires the programmers to commit to a particular sequence in which the messages must be processed. Although, one may use nonblocking communication primitives to overlap communication and computation in traditional message-passing style, its usage is limited to a single module: it is difficult to overlap communication latencies across multiple modules [6] without loosing modularity.

In message-driven execution, there are typically many processes per processor. A process does not block the processor it is running on while trying to receive a message. Instead, processes are scheduled for execution depending on the availability of the messages for them. Processes typically provide code in the form of entry functions or continuations and a way of associating them with specific incoming messages. With this information, the runtime system can invoke the appropriate code in the appropriate process to handle a particular incoming message. Therefore, Message-driven execution provides the ability to overlap computation and communication, and tolerates communication latencies. It helps latency tolerance in two ways: First, when one process is waiting for data from a remote process, another ready process may be scheduled for execution. Secondly, even a single process may wait for multiple data items simultaneously, and continue execution whenever any of the expected items arrive. Message-driven style also supports the use of parallel libraries without loss of efficiency. In traditional message-passing programs, the program has to yield control completely to the parallel library. Thus, the idle times in the library computation cannot be utilized effectively. Message-driven execution on the other hand, allows the control to switch between multiple concurrent library computations. Details of performance benefits of message-driven execution can be found in [6].

Charm [10] is one of the first systems to embody message-driven execution in a portable parallel programming system running on stock multicomputers. A Charm program/computation consists of potentially small-grained processes or objects, called chares. A chare consists of local data, entry-point functions, and private and public functions. Public functions can be called by any object on the same processor. Entry functions are invoked asynchronously by an object on any processor. Invoking an entry function in a remote object can also be thought of as sending a message to it.

Despite its performance benefits, the expression of programs in a pure message-driven language, such as Charm, is difficult due to the split-phase style that it requires and the nondeterministic arrival of messages. Consider a concurrent object (listed in Figure 1) which performs the following calculations. The object executes C0 when it is created (assume entry e0 is invoked by the creation message). Then, it can perform either C1 or C2 in any order whenever their corresponding entry is invoked due to message arrival. After both C1 and C2 have been completed, then it performs C3. Since e1 or e2 can be invoked in any order, each entry must keep track of whether the other one is already done, so that the later one invokes C3. To achieve this, a counter is used as shown in the code. The counter is set to 2 at the beginning (number of subcomputations before C3). Whenever the counter reaches zero, then C3 is called. In more complex computations, the expression of such cases becomes quite difficult (in addition to being difficult to simulate as we will show later). In order to simplify the expression of message-driven programs, a new notation, Dagger [7], was developed to express dependences between subcomputations and messages within a single object on top of Charm language.

```
chare G {
    int count;

    entry e0 :  {    C0(); count=2;}
    entry e1 :  {    C1();
                     if(--count==0) C3()};
    entry e2 :  {    C2();
                     if(--count==0) C3();}
}
```

Figure 1: The Charm code for chare G

A Dagger program includes *dag-chares* as a special form of concurrent objects in addition to regular chares. The dag-chare for the previous Charm code is listed in Figure 2. The message receiving points are specified by entry declarations. The subcomputations within a dag-chare are called *when-blocks*. The when-block when e0 is executed when a message has been received at the entry e0. The execution of a when-block is completed without interruption. The when-block code may contain some sequential computation as well as some specific Dagger statements for synchronization such as Expect, and Ready. The instruction Expect($e_i$) tells the Dagger that the message for the entry $e_i$ can be made available to the dependent when-blocks. In other words, reception of message is not sufficient to trigger a subcomputation, it must be expected also. Ready is equivalent to sending a message to an entry-point within the same dag-chare and issuing an Expect for this message. Since the message is local to the dag-chare, it can be implemented more efficiently than actually sending the message. The efficient implementation is achieved by conditional variables — a special synchronization variable that is local to the dag-chare. In addition to simplifying

```
dag chare G {

    local-variable-declarations

    entry e0 :   (message MSG *m0);
    entry e1 :   (message MSG *m1);
    entry e2 :   (message MSG *m2);

    CONDVAR c1;
    CONDVAR c2;

    when e0:{C0();expect(e1);expect(e2);}
    when e1:{C1();ready(c1);}
    when e2:{C2();ready(c2);}
    when c1,c2:  {C3();}
}
```

Figure 2: The Dagger code for dag-chare G

the expression of message-driven programs, it turns out that Dagger also provides necessary information to simulate message-driven programs by allowing us to trace additional events as discussed in the next section.

## 3 SIMULATION OF DAGGER PROGRAMS

An accurate trace-driven simulation of message-driven programs is not possible without a complex dependence analysis of various paths through the each entry-point. Traces from one instance of execution may not cover all the possible execution paths which may depend on message arrival order.

We will explain why simulation is not possible without the dependence information for the program given in Figure 1. Traces from an instance of execution of the program consist of the duration of execution of each entry-point (and relative timings of any message sent during it). Assume that an instance of the chare G is created when a message for the entry e0 is received. Then, G awaits two messages concurrently, one for e1 and one for e2. In a particular execution, assume that the message for e1 arrives first. This causes the execution of C1. Then, when the message for e2 arrives, C2 is executed followed by C3. However, if the messages arrived in the reverse order, the code at e2 would only execute C2 leaving the execution of C3 to the other entry-point. If traces are obtained with the former sequence with A time units for the execution of e1, and B time units for e2, and during simulation the machine conditions lead to the latter sequence, it is not possible to reconstruct the times of e2 and e1 from A and B.

If the individual times for computations C1, C2 and C3 were recorded, one would be able to reconstruct the timings in presence of the new sequence. It may seem simple then to record these times. However, note that C1, C2 and C3 need not be function calls as shown here. The if statements as well as the computation blocks might be deeply buried inside complex control structures. Therefore, in general, it is not easy to retrieve the timings of the individual blocks. Furthermore, the connection between the value of counter becoming zero and arrival of messages may not be easy for the compiler to deduce.

In order to accurately simulate a message-driven program via trace-driven simulation, the simulator needs to reconstruct the execution sequence under the new runtime conditions. Dagger facilitates this reconstruction by

- tracing the execution at the level of basic blocks rather than only messages, and

- providing information about dependences among messages and computations.

Dagger statically captures the dependences, and its runtime is able to trace the beginning and end of each individual when-block. The dependencies among the blocks and messages forms a partial ordering. The actual execution sequence in a given run will depend upon message arrival sequence, but must be consistent with the partial order. The simulator knows the message arrival order from its runtime environment and the dependence structure from the Dagger translator, and thus, can mimic the Dagger runtime to reconstruct the new sequence correctly without re-executing the user code.

For the example in Figure 2, let's assume that message arrival order in the real execution is (e0,e1,e2) and the order of subcomputations is (C0,C1,C2,C3). During simulation in a new environment, assume that messages arrive in the order (e2,e0,e1). When a message has been received at e2, the subcomputation C2 cannot be executed because C0 is not completed yet. Later, when the message for e0 arrives, we can execute C0. Now the subcomputation C2 is ready for execution. However, in the execution trace, the next one is the subcomputation C1. In the partial order, C1 and C2 are incomparable, that is, they can be executed in any order. So we can execute C2. When e1 receives a message, then we can execute C1 and then C3. So the simulator executes the blocks in the order (C0,C2,C1,C3) without violating the partial order.

For the above reconstruction to be valid, an additional condition, which is quite natural, must be satisfied. To see the need for this condition, consider the same example again. If the code inside the block C1 contains sections whose execution time and data values depend on variables set in C2, the execution under the new arrival order will not match the traces (i.e., block C1 may take more or less time or even may send out different number of messages). Such uncaptured dependences constitute a bad programming style and occur very rarely in parallel programs. The condition required for accurate simulations can be stated concisely as follows:

> A variable *used* in a when-block W must not be modified by any other when-block that is incomparable[a] to W in the partial order defined by the DAG (dependency graph).

The Dagger compiler extracts the dependency information from the user program to be used by the simulator. The compiler also inserts the necessary code to produce the traces during execution. The traces from an execution are gathered and combined with the static dependency information. Since we know the basic blocks and their dependencies, we do not need to trace every instruction that is executed during the run. Only a small number of events have to be traced, and only a small amount of data needs to be stored for each event. This reduces the computational cost of the simulations significantly. The events to be traced that are sufficient for the simulation are:

1. beginning of a when-block

2. send message

3. broadcast message

4. expect and ready,

5. initialization of condition variables, and

6. end of a when-block.

## 4 ABSTRACT PARALLEL MACHINE MODEL

In this section, we will define a model for the parallel machine to be simulated. Despite the large diversities among the parallel machines, they have a common property: to access remote data takes longer than to access local data. The machine model emphasizes this property. In this model, a parallel machine is a collection of processing elements (PE) interconnected by a communication network. A processing element consists of a processor, a local memory, and possibly a communication processor. The communication processor interfaces the processor to the network. It can access to the local memory and interact with the network without blocking the processor, therefore it releases the processor from most of the communication related tasks. The network provides communication among PEs. In reality, there exist various communication network structures with different topologies and communication protocols. From the point of view of our simulator, the network provides data transfer with a latency that may depend on the network load in an arbitrary fashion, and it has a finite capacity.

Communication between two processors involves a number of steps. Each step requires a distinct time

---

[a]Two blocks are incomparable if neither is a successor or predecessor of the other

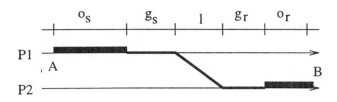

Figure 3: Sending A Message

interval which must be charged to appropriate component of the system. We will explain these steps by an example which is depicted in Figure 3. Processor $P_1$ starts sending a message to $P_2$ at time $A$. $P_1$ spends $o_s$ time units for the send operation. Then, the communication processor interacts with the network and spends $g_s$ time units. After $l$ time units, the message arrives at the destination node. The communication processor on the destination node receives the message. The message becomes available to the processor after $g_r$ time units, and to the user program after an additional $o_r$ time units. The total delay that the message experiences, or the time between the user program issues a send operation and the message becomes available to the user program at the destination processor is the sum of these delays:

$$o_s + g_s + l + g_r + o_r$$

The sending processor is blocked only during the $o_s$ time units (similarly the receiving processor is blocked $o_r$ time units), and duration of the other parts of the delay, the processor is free to perform computation. Similarly, the communication processor is blocked by $g_s$ (or $g_r$) time units. (This limits the amount of and the number of messages a processor can inject and receive from the network per unit time.) Therefore, the $g_s + l + g_r$ part of the remote information access delay, can be potentially overlapped with useful computation.

Each of these parameters has a fixed part and a variable part that depends on the size of messages. As in many studies, we have chosen to model each of these parameters as

$$\alpha + \beta n$$

where $\alpha$ is the startup cost, $\beta$ is the time per data item and $n$ is the number of data items in the message. The time spent in the network, $l$, in our model is also affected by the finite capacity of the network. The capacity limitations are similar to those described by [2]. The finite capacity of the network is modeled by blocking the sender communication processor if the volume of messages traveling in the network is above a threshold. The communication processor has a finite buffer to hold messages deposited by the processor also. If it runs out of buffer space, then the processor is blocked. This model subsumes the LogP model presented in [2].

## 5 SIMULATOR

The simulator consists of three major components: the preprocessor, the parallel machine simulator, and the trace interpreter. The traces may be obtained from a run on a parallel machine or on a uniprocessor emulating a parallel machine.

A simulation session starts with the preprocessing of the execution traces. The output of this stage then is interpreted by the the trace interpreter on the simulated parallel machine model.

### Preprocessor

The Charm/Dagger programming system allows multiple module compilation, i.e., independently compiled Dagger programs can be linked at run time. The Dagger translator produces a separate dependence information for each module. Therefore, dependence information from individual modules and the runtime trace information are reconciled and a single consistent dependence graph and trace information are produced. The preprocessor also converts all timing information to relative times. The traces from Dagger programs contain absolute times. For example, a when-block trace with absolute times might look like this:

```
when-block instance A started at time t1,
sent message B at t2,
when-block instance A ends at t3
```

The simulator uses relative timings:

```
when-block instance A elapsed time t3-t1,
sent message B at t2-t1,
when-block instance A ends
```

After the preprocessing, a when-block record in the trace information forms one entity. The simulator reads a when-block record at a time and processes it. The instances of when-blocks are identified by a quadruple <p,b,i,r> where p is the processor number, b is the static identification of the when-block, i is the instance of the dag-chare to which the when-block belongs, and r is the reference number. A program may contain many instances of a particular chare (and dag-chare), and a particular instance is identified by this dynamic component, i. The reference number is a feature in the Dagger language that has not been discussed in this paper. Within the context of the simulator, it is sufficient to assume that a when-block is completely identified with this quadruple.

### Parallel Machine Simulator

The simulator uses an event-list based approach to simulate the machine model. An event contains the event-time, event-type, and other information depending on the event type. The events are kept in a heap. There is one entry for each processor and communication processor in the heap. Each entry contains a sorted list of events that are to happen on that processor or communication processor. The time stamp of the heap entry is that of the earliest time event in its list. The simulator removes the next event from the heap and processes it until the heap becomes empty. The communication processor events handle network level the message transfers. They contain the necessary information about the communication including message destination, length, priority etc. Processor events are either user events (a when-block execution) or system events such as send or receive a message.

Interpreting the Traces

Interpreting the traces requires modeling of the Dagger runtime. The simulator has to schedule when-blocks based on the arrival order of messages without violating the dependencies in the same way the Dagger does. The simulator models the Dagger by maintaining three major queues: a scheduling queue, a when-block-wait-queue, and a when-block-ready-queue. All the incoming messages are buffered in the scheduling-queue. The management of this queue is FIFO by default. It may use other queuing strategies. The simulator supports LIFO (stack), prioritized FIFO, and prioritized LIFO strategies. The prioritized message scheduling can be used in certain applications to decrease the execution time. By adding this feature to the simulator, it is possible to experiment with such applications also. The wait-queue is a list of when-block instances waiting for some messages or completion of other when-blocks. This queue is necessary because a when-block may depend on multiple messages or when-blocks. When all the dependences of a when-block are satisfied, it is moved from the wait-queue to the ready-queue.

The processor continuously fetches the messages from its incoming message queue (where the communication processor puts the messages received from the network) and puts into the scheduling queue. If the incoming message queue is empty, the next message from the scheduling queue is retrieved and the simulator emulates the Dagger runtime to process the message. It checks the dependency graph to determine if any when-block instance depends on this message. If so, then it checks the wait-queue to see if the when-block instance has already been created, otherwise it creates the when-block instance and puts it in the wait-queue. If the arrival of the message causes additional when-block instances to become eligible for execution, those when-blocks are put in the ready-queue for execution. If there are more than one when-block instances in the ready-queue, the first when-block instance from the ready-queue is interpreted by default (however, this queue can be managed differently similar to the scheduling queue). The trace record of the when-block instance is then is read from the trace files and the events that are recorded in the when-block trace are executed in the same sequence. Note that the trace contains only the events that denote sending of messages, synchronization, and the elapsed time between these events. The local time of the processor is incremented by the appropriate delay of each action including blockings due to network load. At the end of the execution of the when-block, the dependence

graph is inspected again to see if any other when-block instance is waiting for the completion of the currently executing when-block. The cost of management of when-block-queues and cost of moving messages between various queues are also reflected in the simulation time by user supplied various cost parameters.

## 6 SOME SIMULATION RESULTS

We will present some of simulation studies taken from a larger study [6] to illustrate the impact of a single machine parameter on the performance. The broader study demonstrated that message-driven execution often leads to better performance compared to the traditional message-passing style. In this paper, we only present some of the data from that study to illustrate the utility of the simulation framework.

These studies are intended to analyze and project the trends in a somewhat qualitative manner. For full-fledged performance prediction (e.g., performance of a new, yet to be available, machine), such trend analysis is not adequate. Repeated calibration and validation studies with accurate machine parameters are necessary. This is a topic for future research.

The example code that is used in this simulation study is abstracted and modified from a real application — a communication module in a parallelized version of a molecular dynamics simulation code. Each processor has an array of size $n$ elements. The computation consists of many iterations. Every iteration involves computation of all the elements in each processor locally and then the global sum of each element across all processors, i.e., each processor gets the sum of the first elements, the sum of the second elements etc. The computation of each element and its global sum is independent of other elements with the iteration.

In the traditional message-passing implementation, each processor first computes all the elements of its array, then calls a single global reduction operation (of size $n$) which is a blocking library call usually provided by the message-passing library. The message-driven version, on the other hand, exploits the the fact that global sum of the elements can be done concurrently. Each processor divides its array into $k$ partitions. Then, the global sum of elements in a partition is computed with a non-blocking reduction operation. Thus, it pipelines the global sum operation of $k$ partitions of size $\frac{n}{k}$ each. The traditional message-passing version could divide the arrays into $k$ partitions but it would experience performance loss due to the blocking nature of the reduction operation it invokes.

We gathered traces from both traditional message-passing (which will be referred as traditional-spmd) and message-driven programs on 64 processors, and conducted simulations by changing various machine parameters. Figure 4, illustrates the impact on performance of the two programs as we increased the network latency. The time is reported in terms of simulation time units. In these examples, one simulation time unit corresponds 100 nanoseconds. The graph

(a) plots the completion time versus the network latency. That is, $o_s$, $g_r$, $o_r$, and $g_r$ is kept fixed, but the network latency, $\alpha_{net}$, (i.e., $\alpha$ in $l = \alpha + \beta n$) is varied. For $k = 1$, the elapsed time of traditional-spmd and message-driven programs are the same, and as $\alpha_{net}$ is increased, the elapsed time for both programs increases slightly since the communication takes place in one reduction operation only. For pipelined cases (i.e, $k > 1$), the performance of the traditional-spmd program shown by dotted lines deteriorates rapidly with increasing communication latency, whereas the performance of the message-driven program does not deteriorate indicating that it is tolerating the latency. Also notice that, the message-driven performance for $k = 8$ and $k = 64$ is better than the case $k = 1$ (note that the problem size per processor, $n$, is fixed). However, the $k = 64$ case is worse than the one for $k = 8$. This is due to the overhead per message incurred by the message-driven execution. For $k = 64$, the total overhead exceeds the performance benefits achieved for $k = 8$.

To illustrate some other features of the simulator, the second plot in Figure 4 shows the result obtained by varying the the network latency in a random fashion. Randomized variation can be found in ethernet connected workstations for instance. In this experiment, additional random delays (exponentially distributed) were introduced to the network latency. The message-driven program appears to tolerate the unpredictability of communication latencies better than traditional-spmd program as indicated by the slope of the curves.

Figure 5 illustrates how a communication processor differentially impacts the performance of the two programs. The horizontal axis shows the fraction of message passing overhead taken over by the communication processor. Again it was seen that, the message-driven program can exploit the presence of a communication processor better than the traditional-spmd program. As the communication processor handles more of the message delays, the total elapsed time of the two programs decreases. However, the elapsed time for the message-driven program is less than the traditional one, and the rate of decrease in elapsed time is better also. It should be noted that multi-threaded programming style will yield similar performance benefits as message-driven execution.

## 7 SUMMARY

We presented a technique to conduct trace-driven simulation of message-driven programs. The message-driven execution has performance advantages by providing the ability to overlap the latency with computation. However, the simulation of such programs poses problems. The difficulties in carrying out simulation of such programs has been identified. For a specific class of programs using the expressions of the Dagger language, it has been shown that the compile time information and execution traces are enough to achieve accurate simulation of message-driven programs even the runtime conditions changes. The design of the sim-

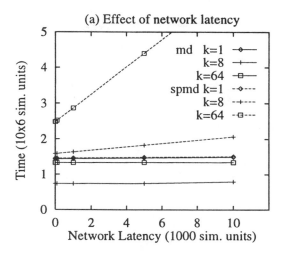

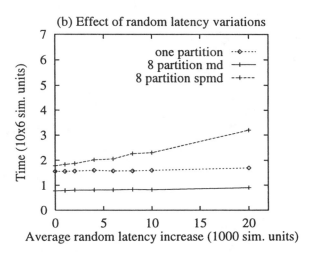

Figure 4: Impact of latency on message-driven and traditional message-passing programs (64 processors)

ulator has been presented, and some preliminary performance studies conducted using the simulator were discussed. Results of a larger study conducted using this simulator are presented in [6]. Although the simulator is limited to the programs written in Dagger language, the technique can be applied to programs written in other languages with parallel constructs (such as `parbegin parend`) provided that the programs satisfy the condition described in Section 3 and the compiler produces dependence graph for subcomputations.

## 8 ACKNOWLEDGEMENTS

The authors would like to thank to Sandia National Laboratories for providing access to the nCUBE/2 and Intel Paragon computers.

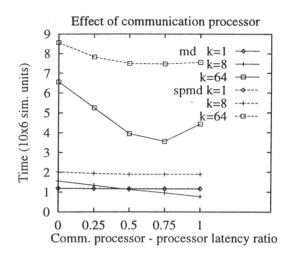

Figure 5: Impact of communication processor on message-driven and traditional message-passing programs

# References

[1] Chandy, K.M. and Kesselman, C., "CC++: A Declarative Concurrent Object-oriented Programming Notation", Editors Agha, G. et al., *Research Directions in Concurrent Object-Oriented Programming*, MIT Press, 1993, pp281-313.

[2] D.E. Culler et al, "LogP: Towards a Realistic Model of Parallel Computation", *Proceedings of the Fourth ACM SIGPLAN Symposium on Principles & Practice of Parallel Programming*, May 1993, pp1-12.

[3] H. Davis, S. Goldschmidt, and J. Hennesy, "Multiprocessor Simulation and Tracing using Tango", *Proceedings of the International Conference on Parallel Processing*, Vol II, Aug 1991, pp99-107.

[4] M. Dubois, F.A. Briggs, I. Patil, M. Balakrishnan, "Trace-Driven Simulation of Parallel and Distributed Algorithms in Multiprocessors", *Proceedings of the International Conference on Parallel Processing*, Aug 1986, pp909-915.

[5] C. Eric Wu, et al, "The Design of A Timing Simulator for Distributed Applications", *Proceedings of 1992 International Conference on Parallel and Distributed Systems, Taiwan* Dec 1992, pp50-57.

[6] A. Gursoy, "Simplified expression of message-driven programs and its impact on performance", Ph.D. thesis, University of Illinois at Urbana-Champaign, May 1994.

[7] A. Gursoy, L.V. Kale, "Dagger: combining the benefits of synchronous and asynchronous communication styles", *Proceedings of the International Parallel Processing Symposium*, Cancun, Mexico, Apr 1994, pp590-596.

[8] M.A. Holliday, C.S. Ellis, "Accuracy of Memory Reference Traces of Parallel Computations in Trace-Driven Simulation", *IEEE Trans. TPDS*, Vol.3, No.1, Jan 1992, pp97-109.

[9] J.M. Hsu, P. Banerjee, "Performance Measurement and Trace Driven Simulation of Parallel CAD and Numeric Applications on a Hypercube Multicomputer", *IEEE Trans. TPDS*, Vol.3, No.4, Jul 1992, pp398-412.

[10] L.V. Kale, "The Chare Kernel parallel programming language and system", *Proceedings of the International Conference on Parallel Processing*, Vol II, Aug 1990, pp17-25.

[11] A. Smith, "Cache Memories", ACM Comput. Surveys, Vol.14, No.3, Sep 1992, pp473-530.

# TABLE OF CONTENTS
# FULL PROCEEDINGS

(R): Regular Papers
(C): Concise Papers

**Session 9C. Systems Issues**
Chair: Bal Ramkumar

# Notes

# IEEE COMPUTER SOCIETY
## 50 YEARS OF SERVICE • 1946-1996

**http://www.computer.org**

## Press Activities Board

## IEEE Computer Society Press Publications

The world-renowned Computer Society Press publishes, promotes, and distributes a wide variety of authoritative computer science and engineering texts. These books are available in two formats: 100 percent original material by authors preeminent in their field who focus on relevant topics and cutting-edge research, and reprint collections consisting of carefully selected groups of previously published papers with accompanying original introductory and explanatory text.

**Submission of proposals:** For guidelines and information on CS Press books, send e-mail to csbooks@computer.org or write to the Acquisitions Editor, IEEE Computer Society Press, P.O. Box 3014, 10662 Los Vaqueros Circle, Los Alamitos, CA 90720-1314. Telephone +1 714-821-8380. FAX +1 714-761-1784.

## IEEE Computer Society Press Proceedings

The Computer Society Press also produces and actively promotes the proceedings of more than 130 acclaimed international conferences each year in multimedia formats that include hard and softcover books, CD-ROMs, videos, and on-line publications.

For information on CS Press proceedings, send e-mail to csbooks@computer.org or write to Proceedings, IEEE Computer Society Press, P.O. Box 3014, 10662 Los Vaqueros Circle, Los Alamitos, CA 90720-1314. Telephone +1 714-821-8380. FAX +1 714-761-1784.

**Additional information regarding the Computer Society, conferences and proceedings, CD-ROMs, videos, and books can also be accessed from our web site at www.computer.org.**

3/21/96